CW01649695

SCI-FI ART

A GRAPHIC HISTORY

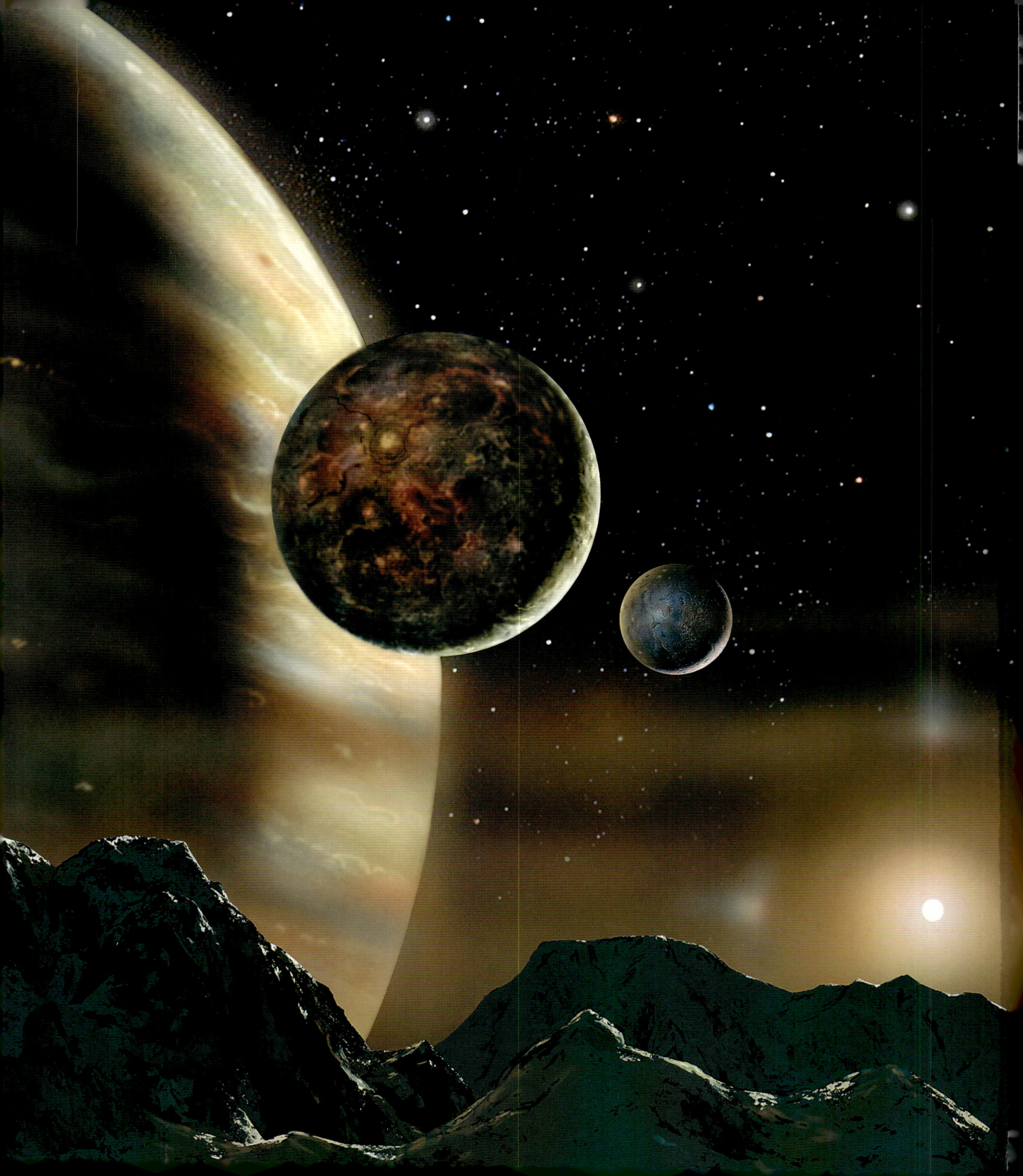

SCI-FI ART

A GRAPHIC HISTORY

STEVE HOLLAND

WITH

ALEX SUMMERSBY / STEVE WHITE / TOBY WEIDMANN

ADRIAN FAULKNER / TIM MURRAY

COLLINS DESIGN

An Imprint of HarperCollins*Publishers*

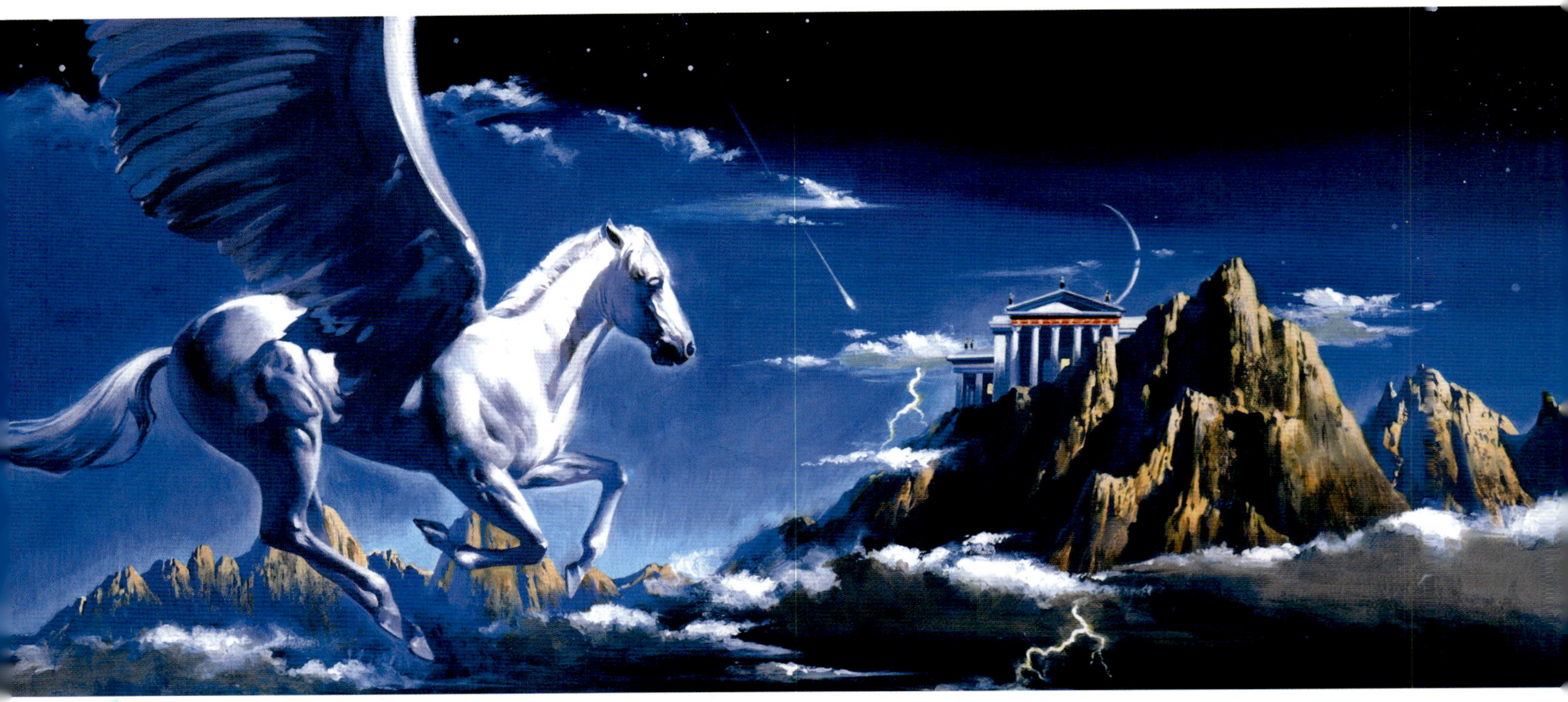

SCI-FI ART: A GRAPHIC HISTORY

Copyright © 2009 by The Ilex Press Limited

All rights reserved. No part of this book may be used or reproduced in any manner whatsoever without written permission except in the case of brief quotations embodied in critical articles and reviews. For information, address Collins Design, 10 East 53rd Street, New York, NY 10022.

HarperCollins books may be purchased for educational, business, or sales promotional use. For information, please write: Special Markets Department, HarperCollins*Publishers*, 10 East 53rd Street, New York, NY 10022.

First published in the United States and Canada in 2009
by Collins Design
An Imprint of HarperCollins*Publishers*
10 East 53rd Street
New York, NY 10022
Tel: (212) 207-7000
Fax: (212) 207-7654
collinsdesign@harpercollins.com
www.harpercollins.com

Distributed throughout the United States and Canada by
HarperCollins*Publishers*
10 East 53rd Street
New York, NY 10022
Fax: (212) 207-7654

This book was conceived, designed, and produced by
ILEX, Cambridge, England

Library of Congress Control Number: 2008937225

ISBN: 978-0-06-168489-0

Printed in China
First Printing, 2009

CONTENTS

FOREWORD

Ah, the old ones are the best! How strangely moving are all these old covers that once seemed to foretell exciting futures where the galaxy teemed with bad-tempered aliens and such things as mortgages were unknown. How excellent it is to have them preserved, jostling together in one grand volume.

Curiously, a good percentage of these covers show no human beings. A good percentage show astronomical scenes. To take one instance, look again at David Hardy's artwork for *Nature* on page 131. What grandeur, what desolation! So often grandeur and desolation combined are features of both story and artwork, and have been since Mary Shelley set *Frankenstein* among the cold magnificence of the Alps.

Those unfortunates who cannot read SF complain that SF lacks characters; yet so often a vital character is the environment. Man faces alien nature. The environment is as strong a matter of characterization as you could wish for.

My personal taste is against funny aliens. The writing and production of SF is important business. By the same token, I feel that SF should stay clear of the comics. That it is a serious matter—or maybe a satiric matter—which concerns the future, the planet on which we so far live, and the enigma of human consciousness itself. In other words, less pretentiously maybe, humanity. The enigma of human life. As aspects in this collection indicate.

On my shelves are two earlier volumes whose intentions are similar to this book. Firstly, there is Anthony Frewin's *One Hundred Years of Science Fiction Illustration* (1974), strong on earlier work. My large size *Science Fiction Art* was published in 1975. Clearly it is time for another collection, with illustrations available from a wider number of sources. You should not—indeed, you cannot—forget editor Harry Harrison's *Great Balls of Fire* (1977), which concentrates on illustrations concerning the problems of near-naked space women, while looking further afield than usual by including covers from such brilliant French publications as *Métal Hurlant*.

Three illustrations among many which particularly strike me are the poster for *Star Trek: The Motion Picture* on page 151; the cover by Jack Gaughan, shown in the middle of three covers at the bottom of page 49... (Why? Because it indicates that strange psychologies, as well as strange technologies, form a part of SF). But my favorite of all covers comes from the classic period of John W. Campbell's editorship of *Astounding*: Hubert Rogers' painting for Laurence O'Donnell's *Fury*, on page 35. The color is intense but subdued and the mood both triumphal and melancholy. (Earth has been destroyed, but humanity lives on in the deeps of a Jurassic Venus). This fine story contains the classic line, "Anything less than six inches long was classified as a bug."

Campbell tried to teach us all a little science. He also taught me something about writing. Like, for instance, if you have written a short story and cannot think of a title for it, then it is probably a lousy story. And he thought that for a novel a one-word title was best. This may no longer be the fashion; but it stuck with me from *Non-Stop*, *Hothouse*, and *Greybeard*, to my latest, *HARM*. Thanks, John—another good idea...

Strange how all these forays into space do not reveal Heaven. Heaven must have been one enormous fiction, long prevailing! In Britain, the CofE (Church of England) worries about homosexuality among the clergy, while in the US, you worry about creationism. It could be claimed that while the States took eagerly to engineering, the UK took eagerly to Darwinism. In practice, these differences are slight, but there are artists not represented here who were drawn to a fairly Darwinian SF, such as Brian Lewis and in particular the earlier Bruce Pennington. In the US there is a fine abstract artist influenced by SF, by name Philip Morsberger. But after all there is not room for everyone, even in a weighty tome such as this.

To conclude, I have put forward a problem as difficult to formulate as it is to resolve. As the years go by and readers and viewers become more sophisticated, we find greater acceptance of SF/fantasy than previously was the case. Recent example: the notice given to Julie Phillips' biography *James Tiptree, Jr.: The Double Life of Alice B. Sheldon*.

Traditional covers were designed as generic signifiers—a lure to the SF reader. Here's an example: *Non-Stop* has gone through about 20 paperback reprints and translations. It concerns people trapped inside a starship for so long they believe the ship to be the world. The story has a metaphoric quality. Every one of those paperbacks has carried a picture of

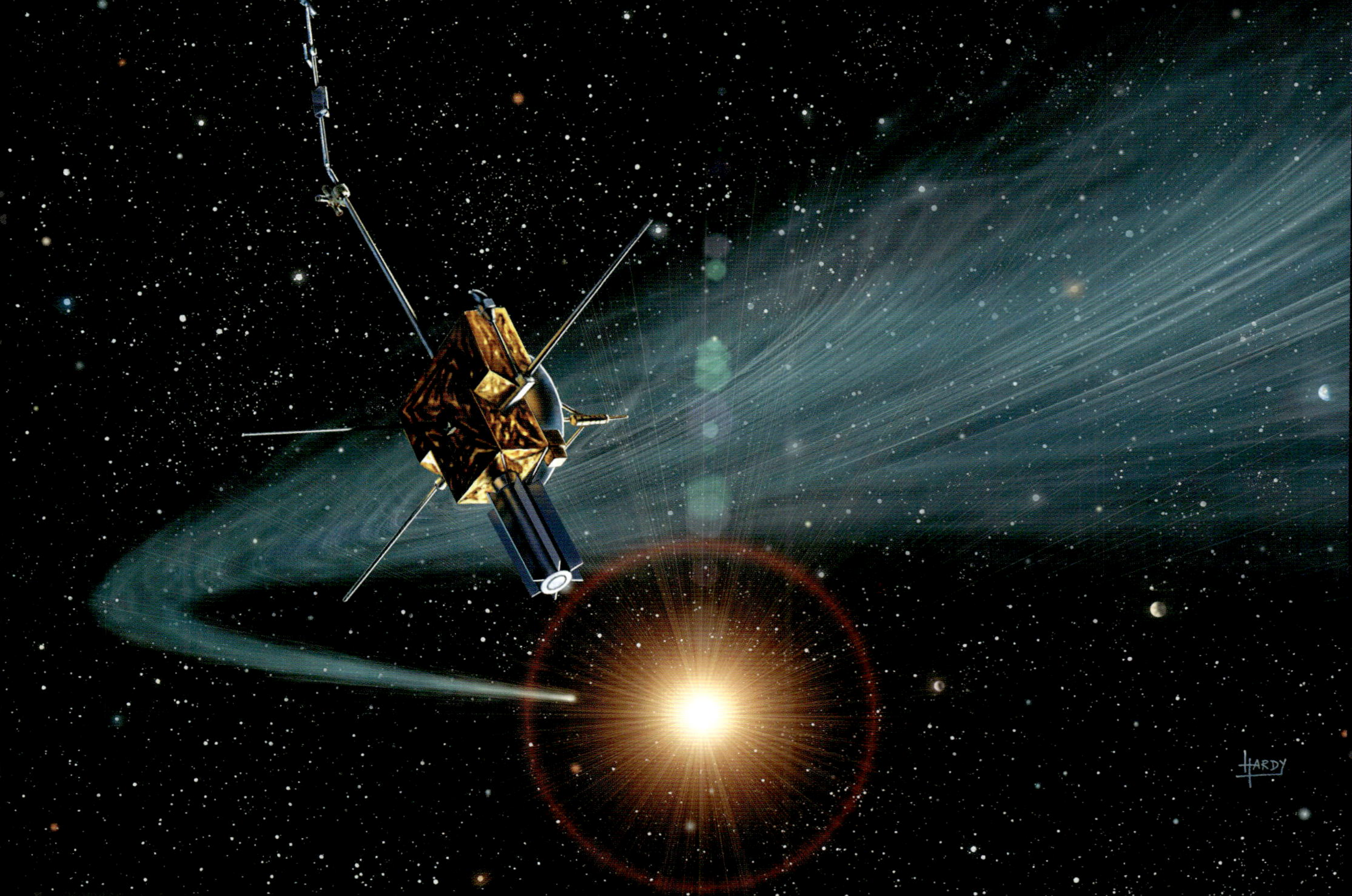

a spaceship on the cover. This gives away the problem the survivors have of recognizing they are trapped in a ship. Thus the various publishers trade away a vital part of the story for a tired old generic signifier.

Only in a Polish translation out in 2008 does the cover take us inside the ship—where all of the action takes place—depicting a dramatic moment in the novel. You may think the publisher does not know his own business. I believe he actually read the book.

All these space machines and armored spacesuits serve as a danger signal to the non-SF reader, telling him to stay away. Flipping through these pages at random, I could believe that Stephen Hickman's cover for David Drake's *The Far Side of the Stars* is unlikely to attract the non-SF reader (whether it attracts an SF reader is another question).

Such covers are indicators of a closed society, unlikely to attract the non-SF reader. Many of us think this is no bad thing and are proud of our isolation. But the generic signifier may also influence the writer, urging him to conform to a perceived standardization. And standardization is the enemy of invention.

Gaughan's cover for *F&SF*, already mentioned, carries both beauty and mystery. SF readers are savvy enough to recognize their favorite literature, while outsiders may also be lured in and—we trust—converted. Hollywood seems to have grasped the notion. That brilliant Dickian movie, *The Truman Show* (1998), did not advertise the fact that it was striking SF. They knew the word would get around.

We want more readers and viewers, don't we?

Have pity on those poor devils who are missing so much and so much!

—Brian Aldiss O.B.E.

▲ **David A. Hardy, untitled/ Ulysses' encounter with the comet Hyakutake.**

INTRODUCTION
THE VIEW FROM THE MIND'S EYE

Let's begin with a question or three. Where did you first hear of *2001*? Or *Star Wars*? Or *Blade Runner*? Chances are you first became aware of these movies when you saw a poster advertising them. And, just to satisfy our curiosity, were you ever first attracted to a book—be it by Brian Aldiss, or Roger Zelazny, or Isaac Asimov—or video game thanks to an eye-popping image on the cover?

A poster or cover conjures up an image in the mind's eye, and the mind expands upon that image; a Pan-Am space shuttle exiting the vast hub and wheel of a space station hanging gracefully above the curve of the Earth was an image that promised *2001: A Space Odyssey* would be a truly majestic experience. Coded in the image is the idea that, unlike other movies where rockets begin on Earth and head toward the stars, the space station is already there, and regular shuttle flights are as ordinary as air flights. In 1968 before man had set foot on the Moon, Robert McCall's poster inferred that, by 2001, space flight would be commonplace, and the odyssey of the title must be a journey of some other kind.

In the hands of a master draughtsman, like book cover artists Michael Whelan or Jim Burns, or movie poster artist Drew Struzan, an image has a life beyond the printed artifact, be it a dust jacket or one-sheet. You just need to look carefully and use your imagination.

In comic books, expanding upon what is set down on the page is implicit in how comics work—the reader fills in the missing narrative in the spaces between the panels. A skilled storyteller like Alex Raymond, or Frank Hampson, or Katsuhiro Otomo can control the amount of information the reader needs to bring along.

Technology has changed how we interact with the images we see. It's not much more than a century since we only had the printed page; now, computers and video game systems take the notion that the reader also brings something to an image a triple-jump further by immersing the player in the game.

But even as technology moves forward and the way readers interface with images changes, it is still the task of the science fiction artist and designer to stay one jump ahead of what we, the reader and viewer, imagine for ourselves. For no matter how much the technology advances, what we see still begins in the mind's eye of an artist.

Science fiction is a notoriously hard concept to pin down, although most people recognize it when they see it. One definition could be: fiction that features concepts or subjects or objects that science says might be possible—as opposed to, say, fantasy, which could be said to feature concepts or subjects or objects that science says are probably impossible.

But like any glib rule of thumb, there will be things that don't quite fit. So dreaming up a faster-than-light drive to get you to the planet where you want the action to take place doesn't necessarily turn your science fiction book into a fantasy; nor does creating an army of Uruk-hai super-Orcs by genetic manipulation make a fantasy book science fiction.

To deal with such a slippery term, there have been countless sub-genres of science fiction over the years. Space opera, new wave, cyberpunk, steampunk, slipstream, transrealist, new wave fabulist… call it what you like, it all involves a degree of speculation.

Science fiction art is even more difficult to define unless the obvious tropes of science fiction are included. But it's more than "the thing that illustrates science fiction;" it's about turning the mind's eye on the world and letting it take you places that you think can barely be imagined. Thankfully, there are

▶ **Robert McCall, poster for *2001: A Space Odyssey*.**

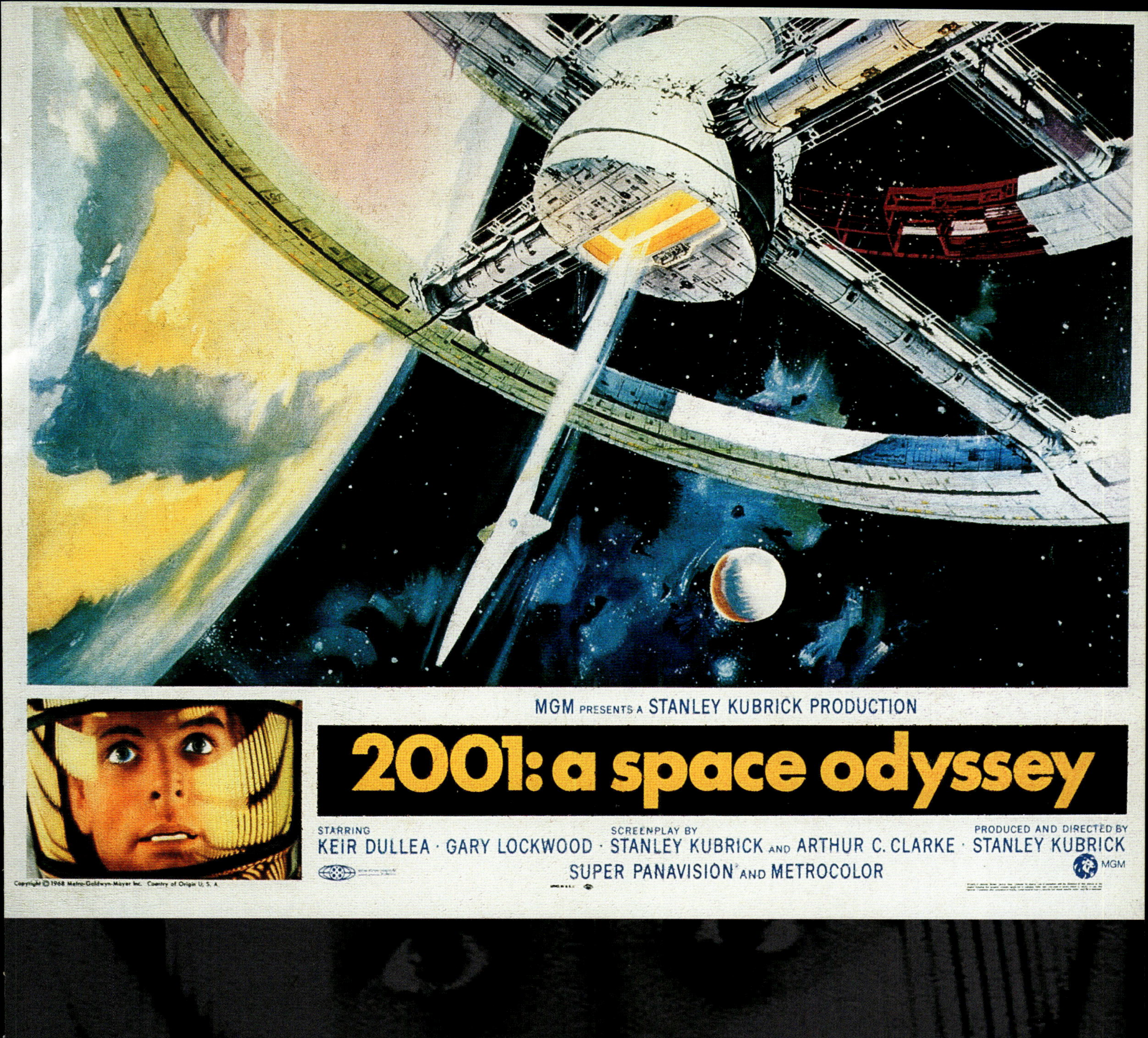
MGM PRESENTS A STANLEY KUBRICK PRODUCTION
2001: a space odyssey
STARRING
KEIR DULLEA · GARY LOCKWOOD
SCREENPLAY BY
STANLEY KUBRICK AND ARTHUR C. CLARKE
PRODUCED AND DIRECTED BY
STANLEY KUBRICK
SUPER PANAVISION AND METROCOLOR
MGM
Copyright © 1968 Metro-Goldwyn-Mayer Inc. Country of Origin U. S. A.

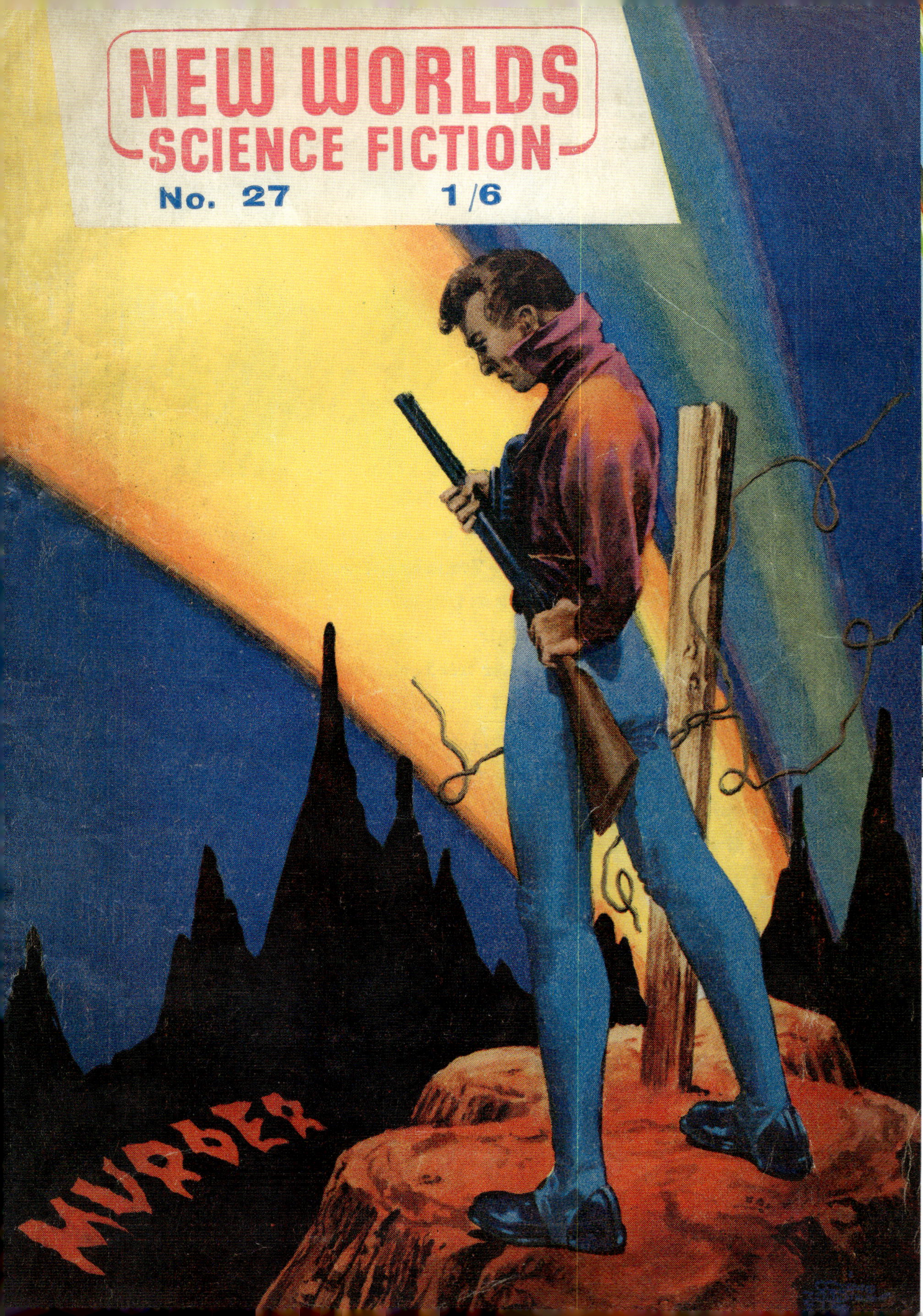

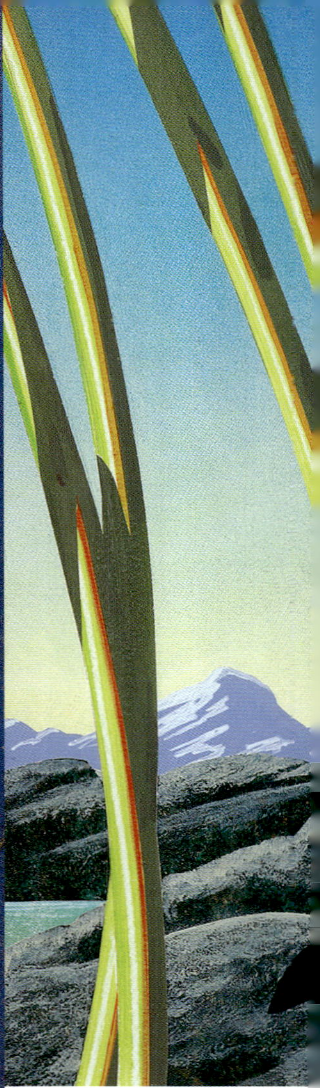

▲
Roger Dean, *Chronoquest.*

◄
Gerard Quinn, cover for *New Worlds* magazine.

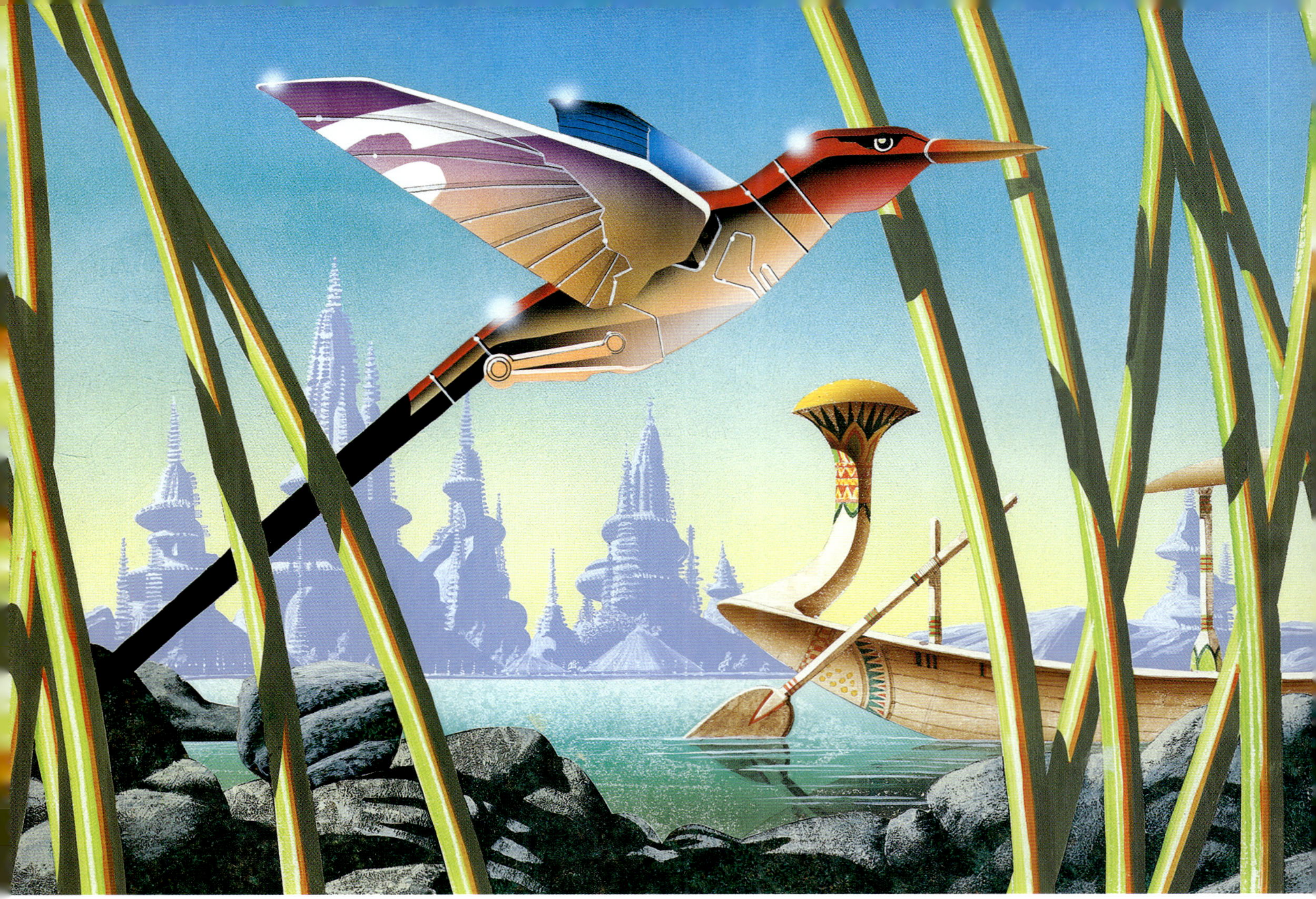

dreamers out there who can imagine the most exotic dreams of all; who see not only this world, but what this world could be, and can turn that spark of an idea in their mind's eye into reality, whether it's in the shape of a toy, or an image on paper, digital canvas, or celluloid.

These dreamers have drawn from the well of science fiction (and it is a very deep well) to bring us—the readers, the viewers, the players—some of the most startling, imaginative, visionary art ever conceived and created.

Years before a tiny two-foot wide metal ball called Sputnik-1 took mankind's first step into space, Chesley Bonestell was able to offer vivid portraits of the planets in our solar system, giving readers of *Life* and *Collier's* a glimpse of what it might be like to look up from one of Saturn's moons and see the vast, colorful planet filling the heavens. "In our visually-oriented society, pictures go where words cannot," says Vincent Di Fate in his mammoth and influential compendium of SF illustration, *Infinite Worlds*. "Even those who wince at the prospect of reading an SF story know the popular icons of the genre (e.g., spaceships, robots, ray-guns, etc.)... The movies, TV shows, and video games so popular with today's consumers begin with the written word but require the skills and sensibilities of the illustrator to transform those words into compelling images. The illustrator is often the critical link between the visionary and the mass audience."

Science fiction art and design has played an important role in the perception of science fiction among the wider world of non-SF fans, for both good and bad. In the world of *Blade Runner*, nobody questions the visual futurism of the movie (the crowded, neon lit streets, outsized floating advertising,

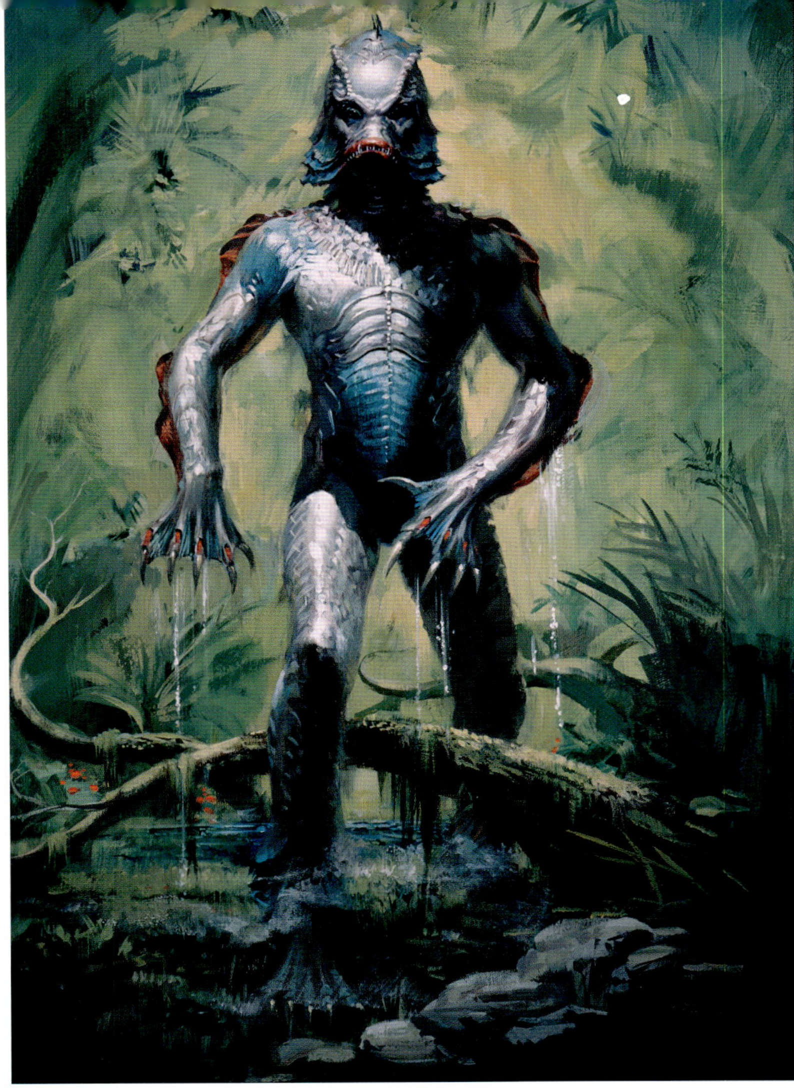

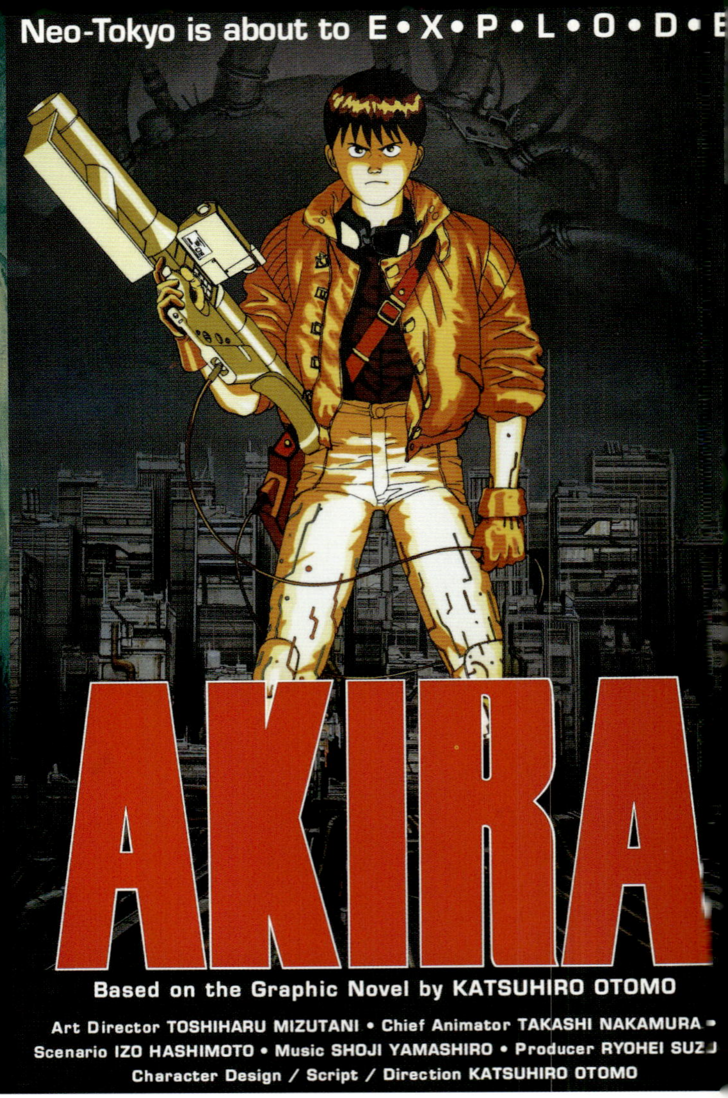

etc.) or the functionality of the flying cars, leaving the viewer free to concentrate on the important questions the movie raises about what it means to be human.

At the other end of the scale, science fiction has been dismissed as nothing more than "that crazy *Buck Rogers* stuff," referring to the popular comic strip that ran for over 50 years in hundreds of newspapers. While *Buck Rogers* is used as a term of derision by critics, at what point does it become fine art? Roy Lichtenstein's painting *Emeralds*—an oversized version of a 1961 *Buck Rogers* panel by George Tuska—sold in 1999 for $1.6 million, so the answer could be as simple as "two feet wide or more."

Where science fiction art was once limited to paintings and illustrations, we now see it in the designs of action figures (even if some are science fiction in disguise) and video games. Advances in CGI have resulted in fully realized environments in the latest releases of *Final Fantasy* and *Halo*. To the digitally adept, fan fiction has given way to machinima—animation using code from video games. We re-imagine ourselves as avatars in role-playing, chatrooms, and the virtual world games.

Sci-Fi Art: A Graphic History is a celebration of the work of the dreamers who have produced covers, concept art, and designs for things that may not exist but could exist, and those who have translated the dreams of others into visual reality. Art—fine or otherwise—should stimulate the imagination and, over the following pages, you'll find a world of possibilities, of dreams, dark and light, and things that might have been, and might still be.

Welcome to the view from the mind's eye.

—Steve Holland

◀▲
Vincent Di Fate, untitled.

▲
Katsuhiro Otomo, movie poster for *Akira*.

▶
Oliver Frey, cover of *Zzap!64*.

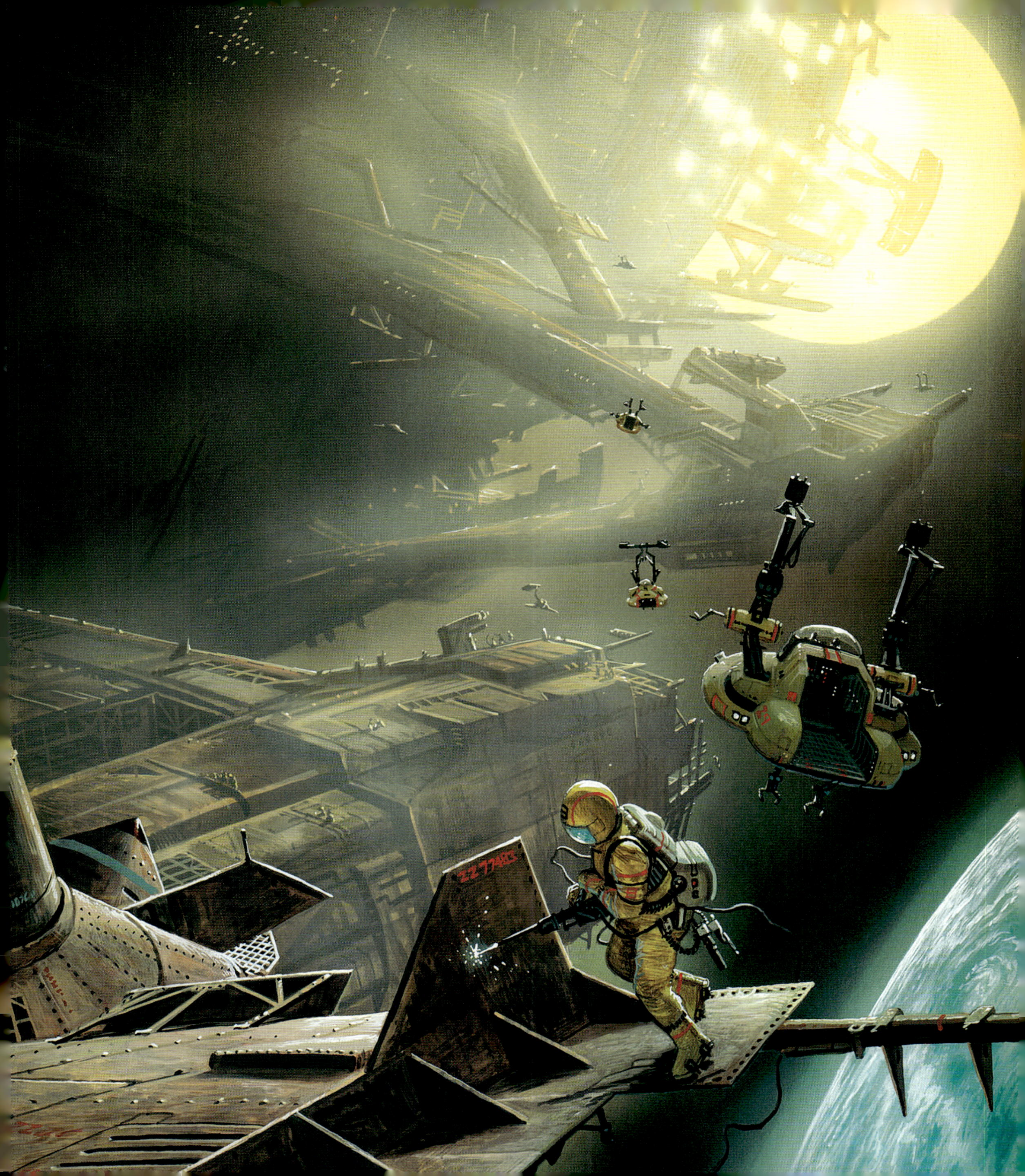

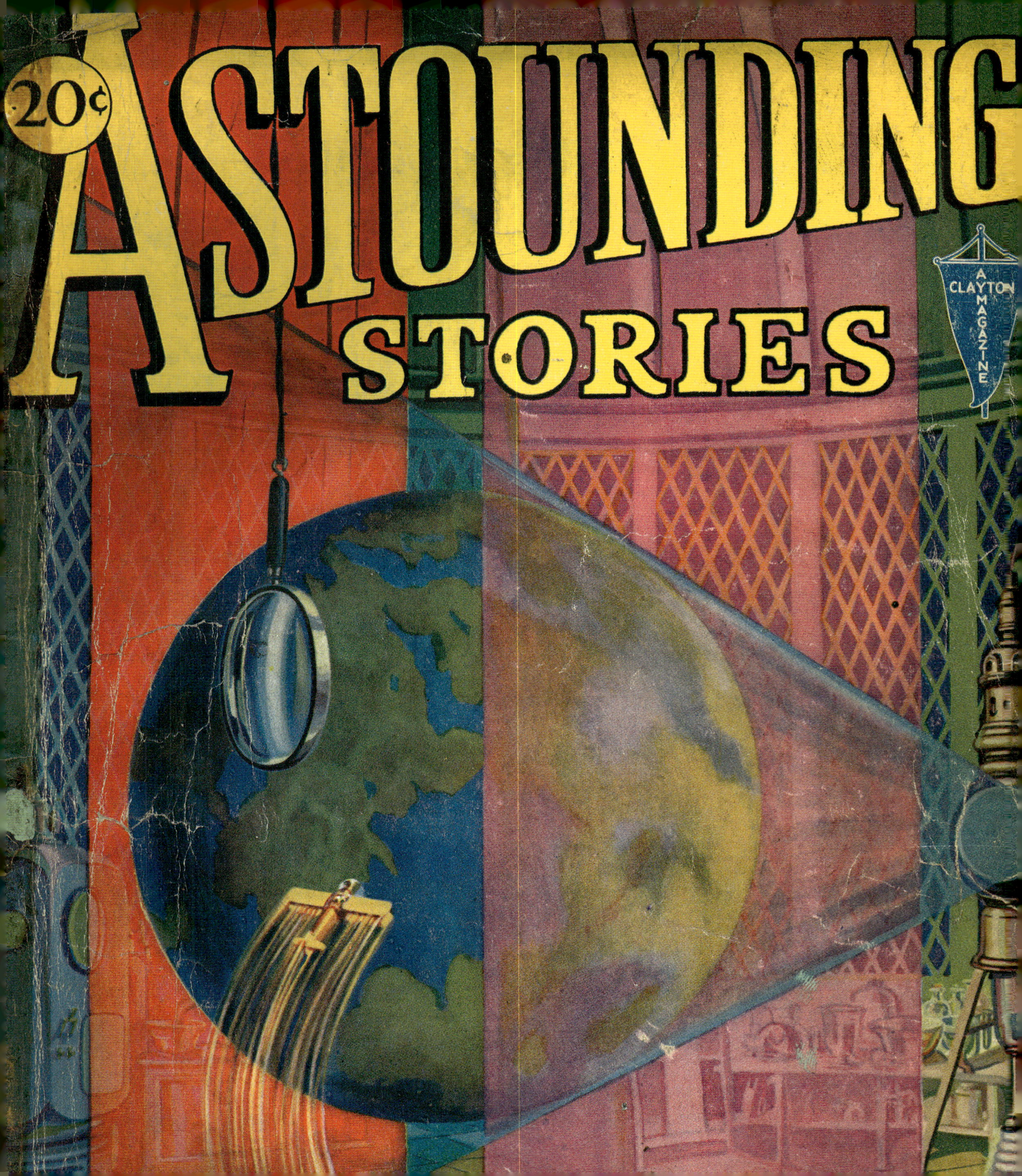
20¢
ASTOUNDING
STORIES
A CLAYTON MAGAZINE

1 FOUNDATIONS OF SF ART

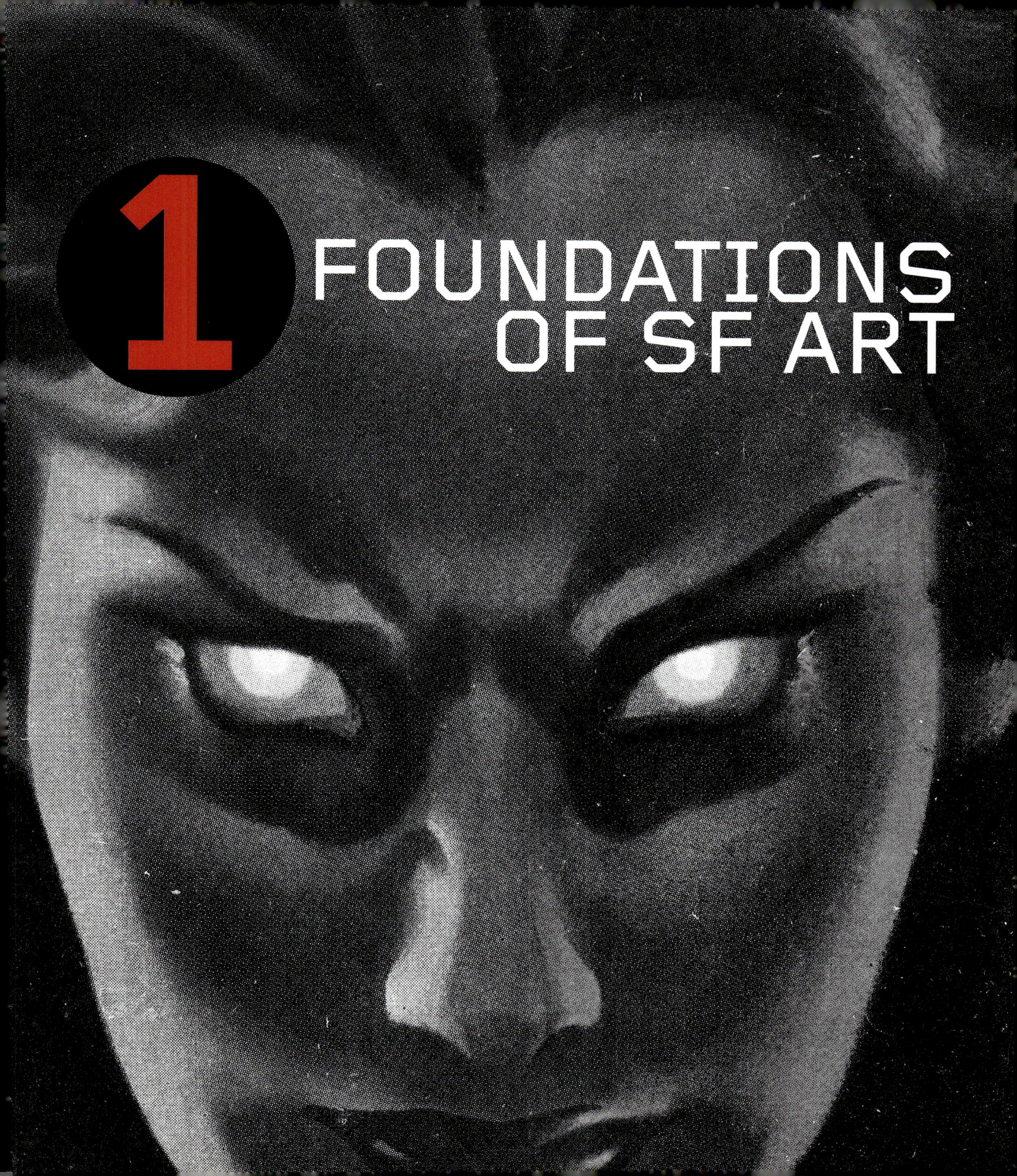

19TH CENTURY SCIENCE FICTION ILLUSTRATORS

Images of the fantastic have been one of man's fascinations from the moment that primitive peoples began scratching on cave walls. While those first daubs of color may have represented life as it was lived—stick figures hunting for food would summarize cave painting for most—representations of things that could only be imagined were not far behind. Pictures of gods and monsters were probably mankind's first foray into the realms of fantasy.

By the 19th century, these twin fascinations had evolved into a wider world of imagination. SF author Brian Aldiss has argued that science fiction has its roots in Gothic horror, specifically in Mary Shelley's *Frankenstein* (1818), and that science fiction illustration and the Gothic are "inseparably intertwined." Gothic encompasses the grotesque squatting demon of Henri Fuseli's *The Nightmare* (1781) and the biblical paintings of John Martin (1789-1854). Martin's grand halls and buildings —*Satan Presiding at the Infernal Council* (1824), *Pandemonium* (c.1825), *Fallen Angels in Hell* (c.1841)—could almost be set designs for *Star Wars.*

Where *Frankenstein* owed its origins to Darwin and electricity, the advances in flight inspired François-Louis Bruel's *Histoire De L'Aéronautique* (1909). Gathering together prints dating back to 1830 representing manned flight, it depicted vast lighter-than-air machines bombarding both each other and the battlefields below. Fred T. Jane (later famous for *Jane's Fighting Ships*) was the author and illustrator of *Blake of the "Rattlesnake,"* or *The Man Who Saved England* (1895), about a near-future war, as well as illustrations for the similarly-themed *The Angel of the Revolution* by George Griffith, and *Hartmann the Anarchist* by E. Douglas Fawcett (both 1893).

J. J. Grandville is often cited as the first science fiction illustrator, his *Un Autre Monde* (1844) populated by alien creatures, hybrids, and steam-powered objects that should be inanimate. France was also home to Jules Verne, whose novels ignited the imaginations of illustrators Edouard Riou, Alphonse de Neuville, and Léon Benett, and who was, in turn, inspired to stretch his imagination even further by the illustrations of Albert Robida.

The illustrated magazines that sprang up in the late 19th century in Britain in the wake of *The Strand* brought with them stories inspired by the scientific advances of the Victorian age, and illustrations to match. Warwick Goble (1862-1943) provided the dramatic illustrations to H. G. Wells' *The War of the Worlds* when it appeared in *Pearson's Magazine* (1897), and his association with *Pearson's* and science fiction continued (*The Raid of Le Vengeur* by George Griffiths, 1901; *The Four Days Night* by Fred M. White, 1903) for some years. *Pearson's* was a ready market for stories of lost worlds and future wars and employed Ernest Prater (*The Lost Continent* by C. J. Cutcliffe Hyne, 1899), Stanley L. Wood (*Stories of Other Worlds* by George Griffiths, 1900), and others who matched illustrations to imaginative texts.

▶ **Warwick Goble's seminal depictions of H. G. Wells' Martian invaders are a world away from the fairy tale illustrations he was later to become famous for.**

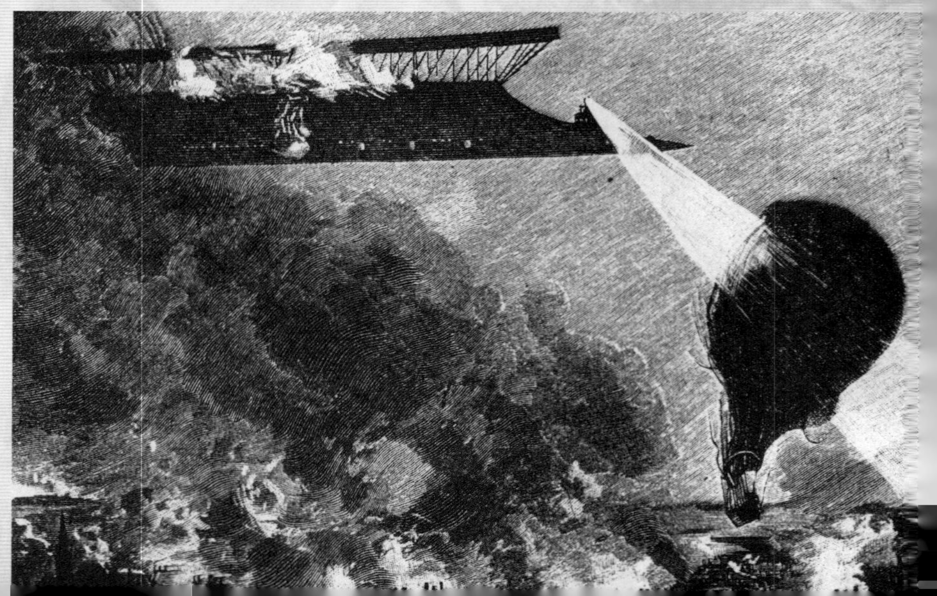

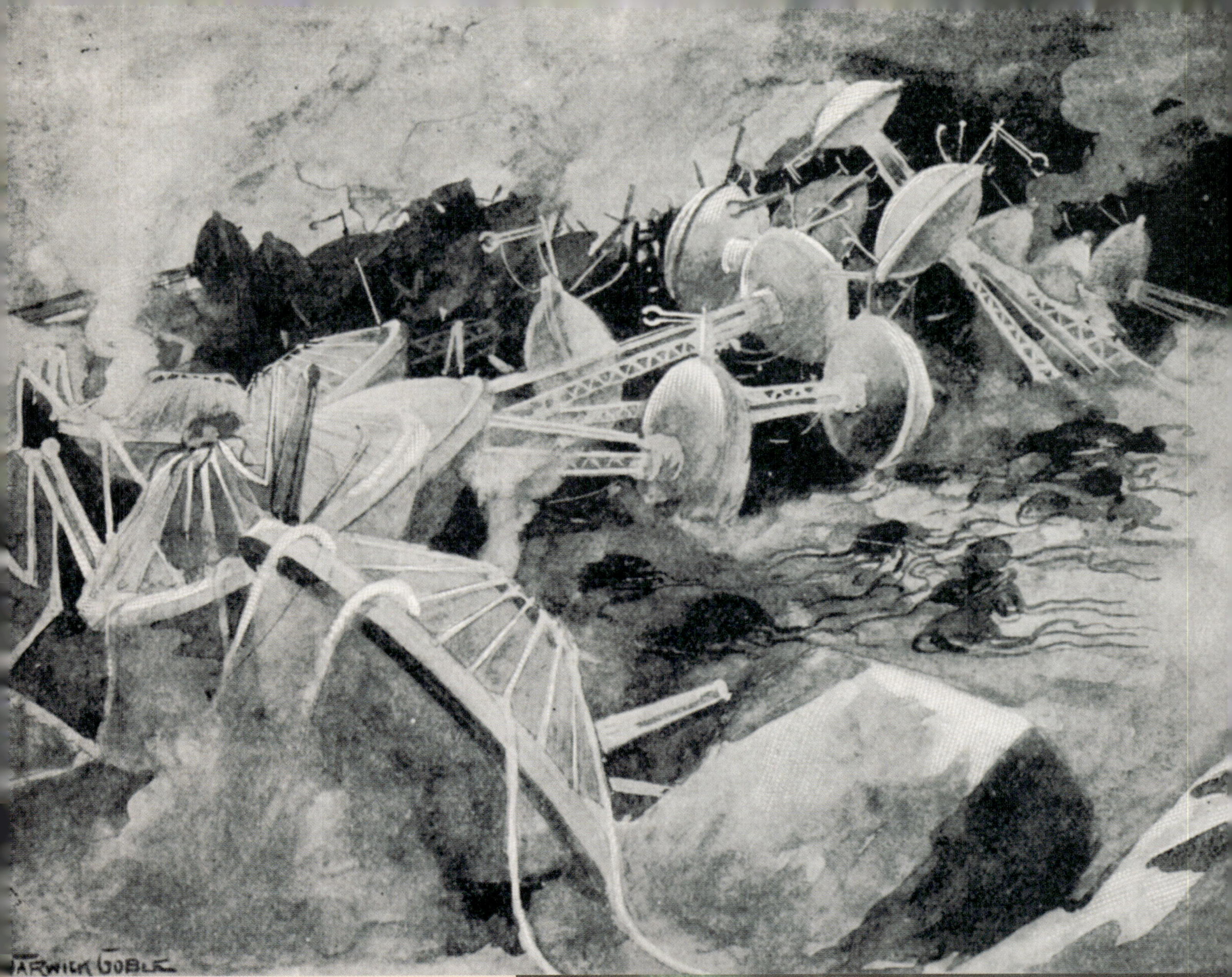

◀
E. Douglas Fawcett's *Hartmann the Anarchist* attacks London in his flying machine, the "Attila." Artist Frederick Thomas Jane (1865-1916) lived to see his terrifying portrayal of aerial bombardment become reality.

▶
Images such as *Satan Presiding at the Infernal Council* earned their artist the nickname "mad John Martin." His vast hall, dominated by the central throne, could be a film set designed by Ken Adams for Stanley Kubrick's *Dr. Strangelove*.

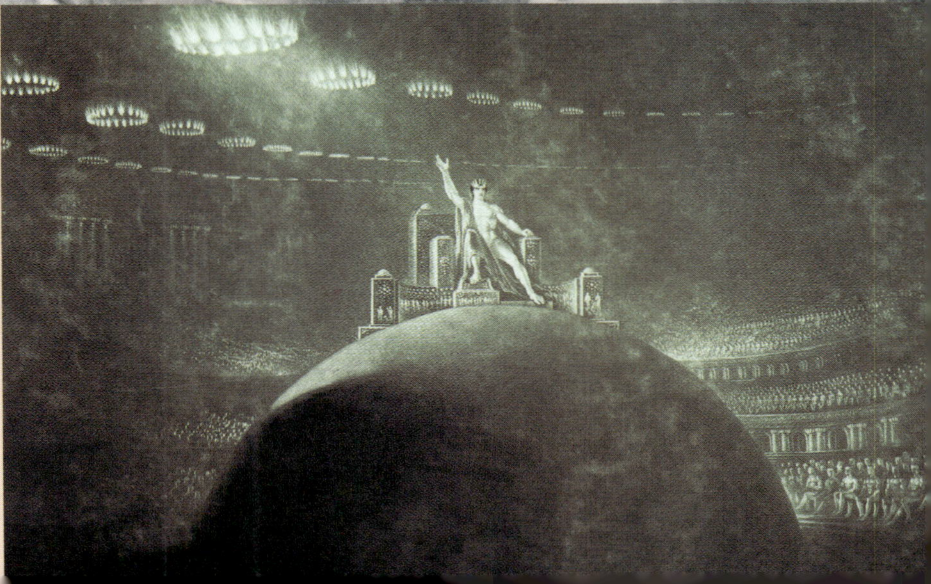

J. J. GRANDVILLE

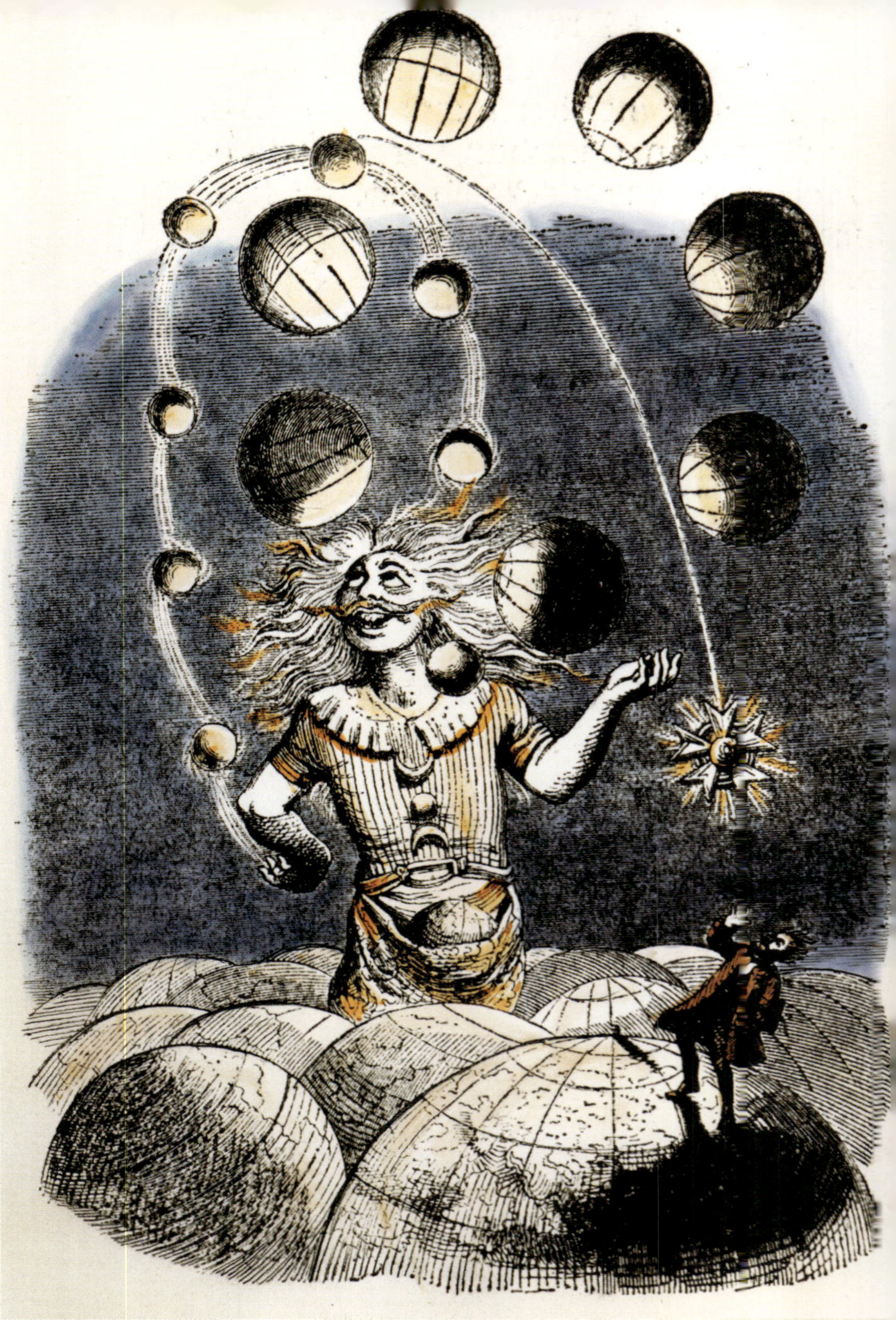

▲
God may not play dice with the universe, as Einstein claimed in 1926, but he does juggle worlds, according to Grandville in *Un Autre Monde*. The image was later used by the group Queen on their 1991 album *Innuendo*.

The religious images of Hieronymus Bosch (c.1450-1516) were precursors to the surrealist paintings of Max Ernst (*Murdering Airplane*, 1920) and Salvador Dalí (*Shirley Temple*, 1939). But paintings like the triptych *The Garden of Earthly Delights* (c.1510), with its depictions of a bizarre earthly paradise filled with giant birds and fruit (not to mention the horrific bird-headed demon that awaits sinners in hell), and the part-bird flying machines and part-fish boats that populate *The Temptation of St Anthony* (c.1500) were also an influence on the more expressionistic science fiction and fantasy art and illustration throughout the 19th and 20th centuries.

J. J. Grandville populated his book *Les Metarmorphoses du Jour* (1829) with similar chimeras of animals, birds, and fish with human bodies. Grandville's transformed creatures—also visible in his illustrations for Jean de la Fontaine's *Fables* (1818) and *Scènes de la Vie Privée et Publique des Animaux* (1842), written by Honoré de Balzac—influenced Randolph Caldecott's anthropomorphized animal artwork and, in turn, Beatrix Potter and others. His work was also much appreciated by surrealists André Breton and Georges Bataille.

Grandville—born Jean Ignace Isidore Gérard (1803-1847)—had earned himself an early reputation for his social satires, although it was as a caricaturist that his fame grew. Grandville worked extensively for *La Caricature* (much despised by the French government), *Monthly Association,* and the newspaper *Le Charivari;* one of his regular targets was the Comte d'Argout, the government's censor. When press censorship was introduced in 1835, Grandville concentrated on book illustration.

Grandville continued to poke fun at contemporary society, but it is with *Un Autre Monde* ("Another World," 1844) that his reputation as a science fiction artist rests. Subtitled "Transformations, visions, incarnations, ascensions, locomotions, explorations, pérégrinations, excursions, stations, cosmogonies, fantasmagories, rêveries, folâtreries, facéties, lubies, métamorphoses, zoomorphoses, lithomorphoses, métempsycoses, apothéoses et autres choses," he explored the widest expression of social and scientific

▶
A literal stag party for animals in human guise from *Les Metarmorphoses du Jour*. Grandville's chimeras—including foxes eloping with chickens, gossiping birds, and military rabbits—were an influence on children's fantasy art, especially that where anthropomorphized animals abound.

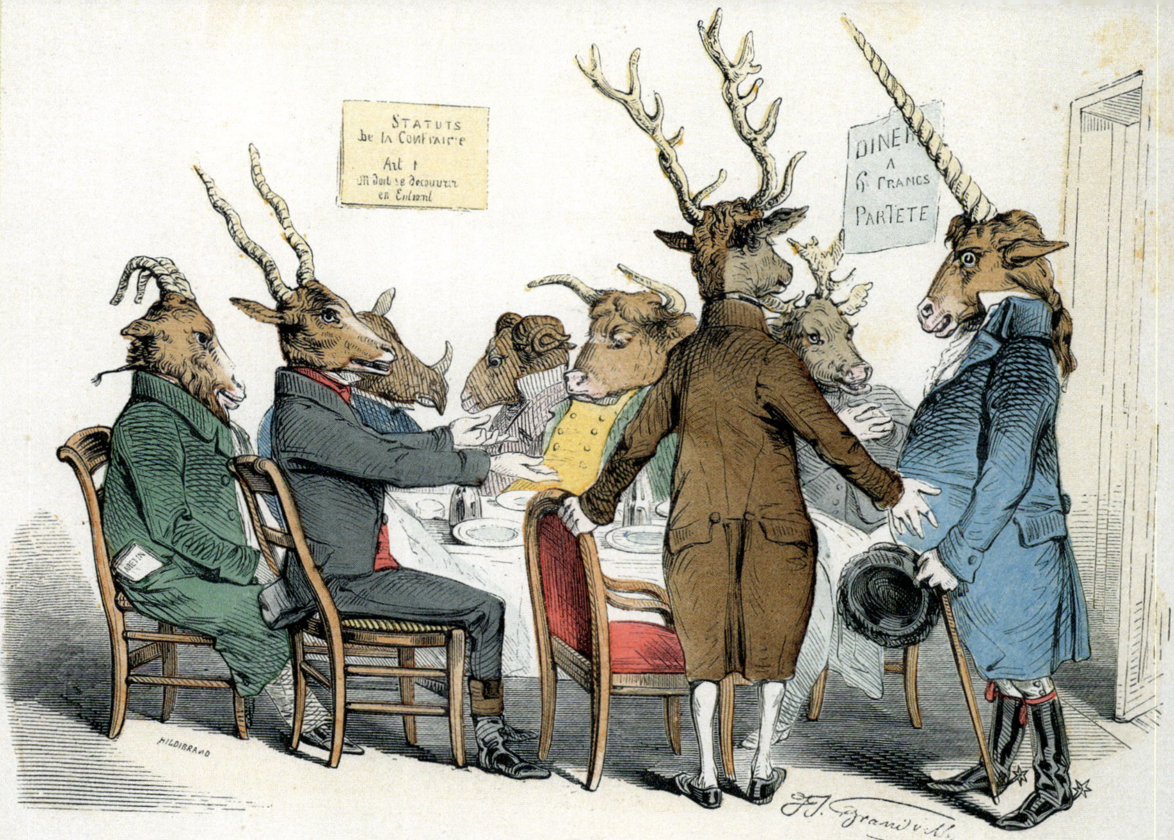

VII.

Repas de corps.

advances, filling every page with everyday objects juxtaposed with dream images, bizarre fusions of animals with plants and objects, planet-spanning bridges, and everyday items in odd, sometimes threatening situations. Grandville had a colleague from *Le Charivari*, Taxile Delord, write text, which was woven around the illustrations.

Grandville returned to the realms of imagination in two later books: *Les Fleurs Animées* ("Animated Flowers," 1847) and *Les Étoiles* ("The Stars," 1849), with text by Joseph Méry, the latter of which was published posthumously.

However imaginative it was, Grandville's influence was not quite as great on science fiction as it was on children's illustration. His importance is, as the author Anthony Frewin has said, that "his work represents the culmination of many disparate elements of 19th century fantasy and reverie, and his vision is the culmination of a pre-technological approach to the universe, that his themes and concerns… are ones that he would share with the writers and artists of SF one hundred years later."

▶
A whimsical image from *Un Autre Monde*. The steam-powered orchestra appears to be playing for no one but themselves, and one wonders if the hand reaching in from the bottom left is turning off their power supply.

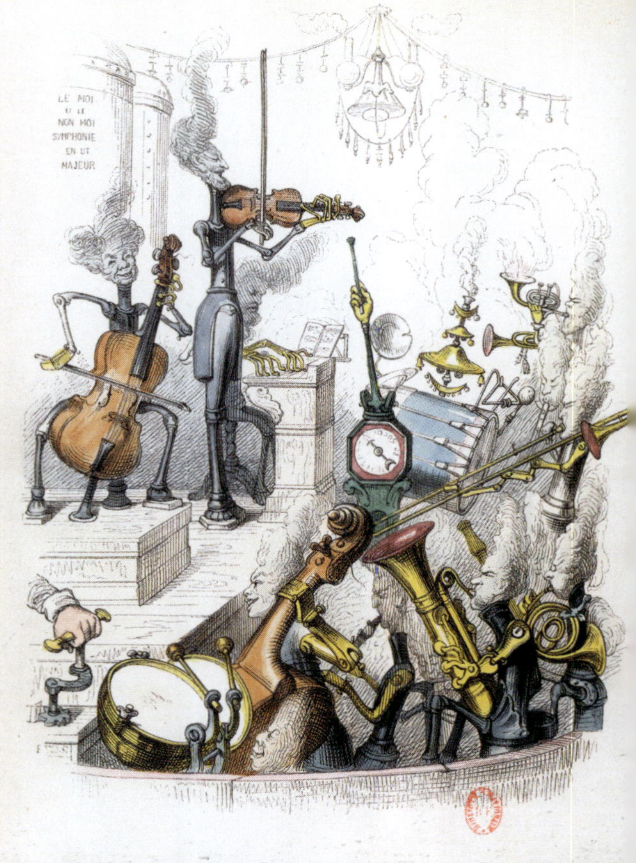

CONCERT A LA VAPEUR.

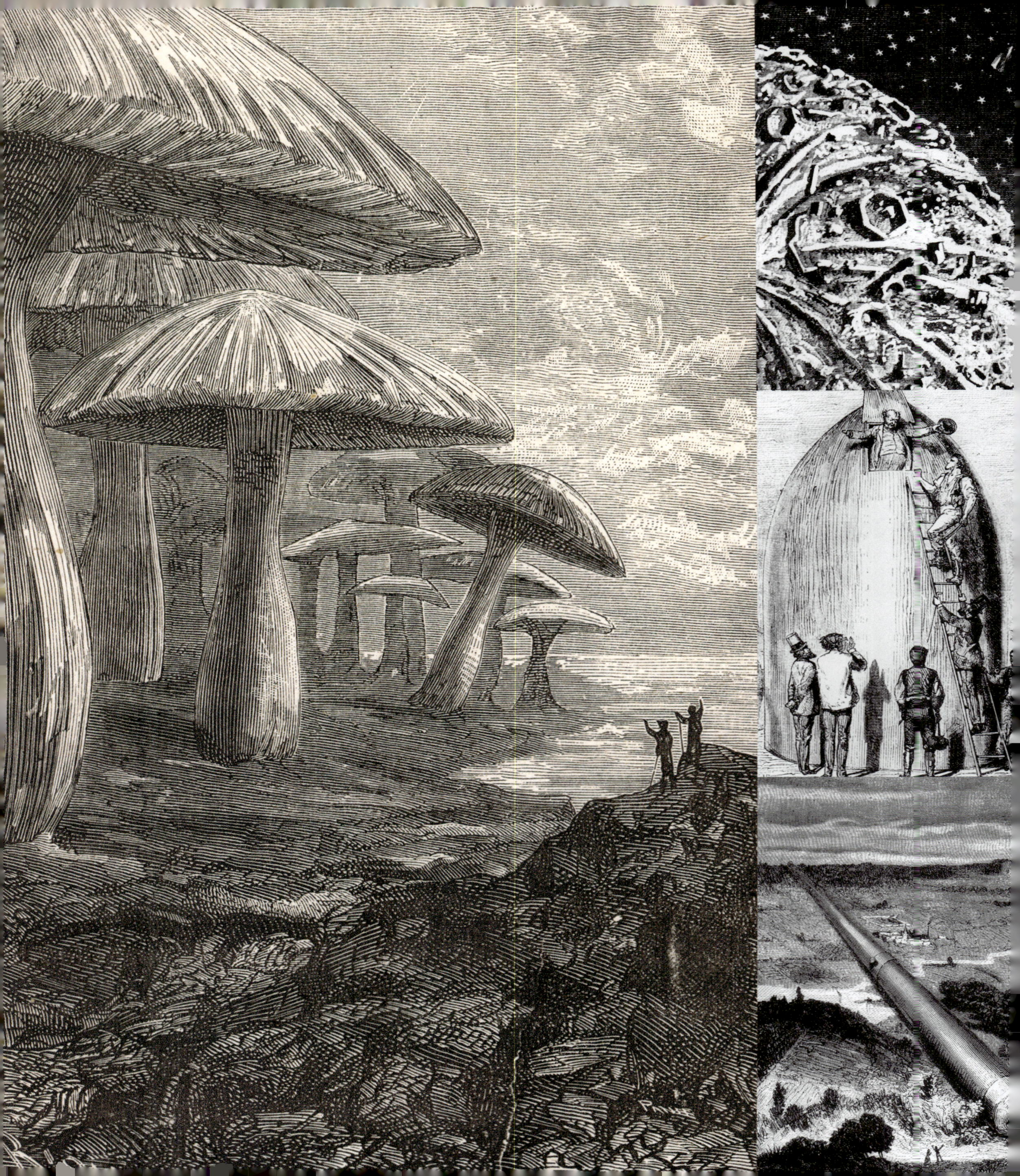

JULES VERNE & HIS ILLUSTRATORS

◀
Between 1834-37—over 30 years before Verne wrote *Around the Moon*—our nearest celestial neighbor had been thoroughly studied by German astronomers Wilhelm Beer and Johann Heinrich Mädler, who concluded that "der Mond" had no seas or appreciable atmosphere. Émile-Antoine Bayard's craggy, desolate moonscape was based on then current knowledge, predating the space art of Chesley Bonestell.

◀
Verne accurately predicted that launching a mission into space would be most easily achieved from the equator, and had his bullet-shaped projectile and three-man crew, depicted here by Henri de Montaut, blast off from Florida and land in the Pacific Ocean on its return, as did the Apollo missions a century later.

◀
Henri de Montaut's iconic rendition of the mighty cannon, the Columbiad, created by The Gun-Club of Baltimore for the journey *From the Earth to the Moon*. Although Verne's method of firing his heroes into space couldn't have worked, some of his calculations were surprisingly close to the reality of space travel.

Creator of the first successful line of *roman scientifique*, Jules Verne's wildly imaginative novels remain among the most famous in the world. Often called "the father of science fiction," Verne (1828-1905) was in his mid-thirties when the first of his *Voyages Extraordinaires* was published, and it is true to say that, although he continued to write until his death, the success of his early novels overshadowed the remainder of his output.

Sent to Paris to study as an attorney, Verne was instead inspired by contact with Parisian literary circles to write. Plays, poems, and short stories poured from his pen, but it was some years before he conceived of writing novels. These would be modeled on the writings of Sir Walter Scott, James Fenimore Cooper, and Edgar Allan Poe—whose works were translated in France as *Histoires Extraordinaires*—and would mix science with action and adventure.

Married and with a son, Verne would spend long days in the quiet reading rooms of the Bibliotèque Nationale, researching scientific texts and gathering information that would inform his later novels. His first "extraordinary voyage" was published in 1863, *Cinq Semaines en Ballon* ("Five Weeks in a Balloon"), about three intrepid Englishmen floating over the largely (at that time) unexplored Africa. Inspired by his friendship with Félix Tournachon (a photographer and balloonist known widely as Nadar), and scientifically informed via Nadar's contacts among the engineering and scientific community, the novel was published by Pierre-Jules Hetzel, who had made a number of suggestions how it could be improved narratively. Hetzel was to become an important partner in Verne's career, publishing all of his novels as serials in the *Magasin d'Education et de Récréation* and in bound volumes.

Voyage au Centre de la Terre ("Voyage to the Center of the Earth," 1864) continued the theme of exploration, this time a subterranean adventure through which Verne was able to discuss cryptography, history, geology, and evolution as his heroes encountered geysers, prehistoric men, mushroom forests, and other marvels, leading one reviewer to describe it as a "compound of wild imagination and sound science." The same description could be given to *De la Terre à la Lune* ("From the Earth to the Moon," 1865), which—at that time—was the first science fiction novel to have a plausible scientific method of launching a spaceship to the Moon, rather than have it towed by geese (*The Man in the Moon* by Francis Godwin, 1638) or simply floating there in a box (*A Voyage to the Moon* by Cyrano de Bergerac, 1650).

In *Vingt Mille Lieues Sous les Mers* ("Twenty Thousand Leagues Under the Sea," 1870), Verne introduced the brooding Captain Nemo and his submarine Nautilus, later to reappear in *L'Ile Mystérieuse* ("Mysterious Island," 1875). Verne had his biggest commercial success soon after with *Le Tour du Monde en Quatre-Vingts Jours* ("Around the World in Eighty Days," 1873), which took its hero Phileas Fogg on a circumnavigation of the globe, punctuated by various adventures along the way.

Later novels like *Robur-le-Conquérant* ("Robur the Conqueror," 1886) and its sequel *Maître du Monde* ("Master of the World," 1904) continued to show Verne's imagination, as Robur uses his vast "clipper of the clouds," the Albatross, to, at first, conquer the air, and then the world. But they also began to show a pessimistic concern with issues other than flights of wild fancy: environment, social change, politics, finance, industrialization, and militarism.

◀◀
One of Edouard Riou's luminous images from *Voyage au Centre de la Terre*: on the shoreline of the subterranean sea, the travelers discover a mushroom patch the size of a forest.

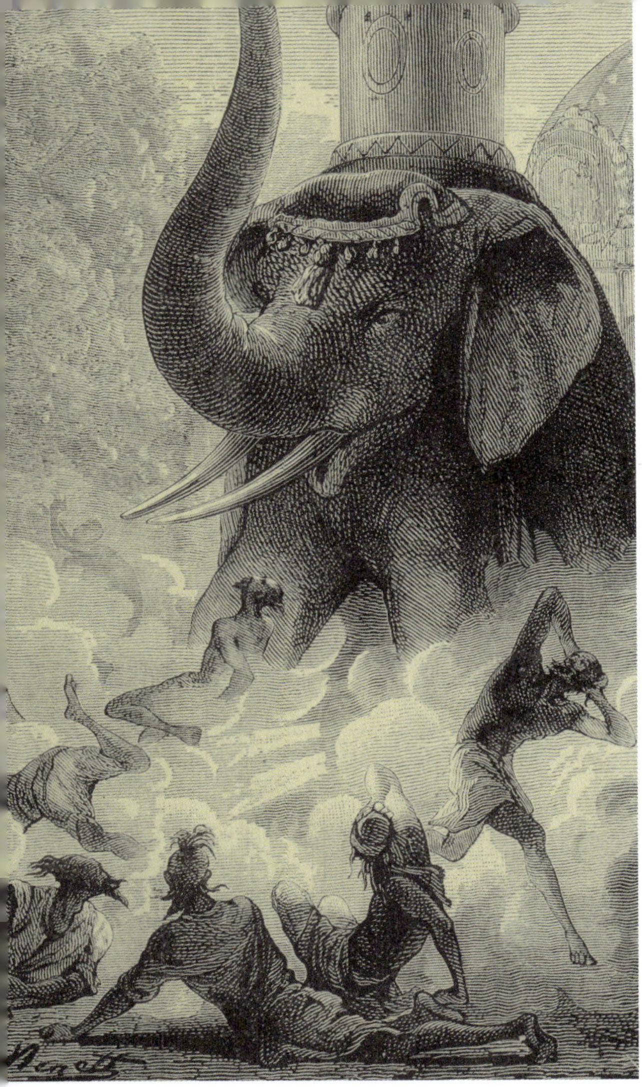

Edouard Riou (1833-1900) was Verne's most prominent illustrator. A former landscape and portrait painter, he illustrated many of his early novels (*Five Weeks in a Balloon, Voyage to the Center of the Earth, The Voyages and Adventures of Captain Hatteras, The Children of Captain Grant,* and the opening chapters of *Twenty Thousand Leagues Under the Sea*).

Henri de Montaut (c.1840-c.1905), after assisting Riou with illustrations for *Five Weeks in a Balloon* and *Voyages and Adventures of Captain Hatteras,* became the sole illustrator of *From the Earth to the Moon,* producing some iconic images of Verne's first voyage into space.

Alphonse de Neuville (1835-1885) was a painter (often of military subjects) who illustrated the bulk of *Twenty Thousand Leagues Under the Sea* but quit working for Hetzel after producing a small number of illustrations for the famous *Around the World in Eighty Days.* This work was completed by Léon Benett (1839-1917), a widely-traveled artist who would illustrate almost half of Verne's novels.

Other artists included Jules Férat (*L'Île Mystérieuse*), Emile-Antoine Bayard (*Autour de la Lune*), and Paul-Dominique Philippoteaux (*Hector Servadac,* translated as *Off on a Comet*). George Roux illustrated many of the later novels, including *Sans dessus dessous* and *Maître du Monde,* sequels to *From the Earth to the Moon* and *Robur the Conqueror.*

Verne's work had a worldwide audience in translation by the 1870s and, although not always well translated, the accompanying illustrations often survived intact. Riou's luminescent drawings were well received, although only a handful had any real action (the best being *Les Enfants du Capitaine Grant*). Léon Benett's finest works were probably *La Maison à Vapeur* (1880), about a trip to India in a wheeled house pulled by a steam-driven mechanical elephant, and *Robur-le-Conquérant,* with its magnificent Albatross flying machine.

Verne's influence on science fiction was immeasurable and his sales immense, making the work of his illustrators the most widely viewed science fictional art of the Victorian age. It could not fail to have an influence, especially when artists were called upon to illustrate outlandish tales in British magazines in the 1890s.

Verne worked closely with his illustrators and, as in his novels, the illustrations were not always there simply to entertain: there was, as with the texts, a degree of education involved. The illustrations also helped anchor the more outlandish ideas (of giant submarines, sky ships, and rocket capsules, for example) in the minds of the audience. The books were heavily illustrated, and hectic correspondence between the author, artists, and publisher tried to ensure that every illustration was precisely how Verne imagined a scene. That did not stop the odd mismatch between art and text, however, or even the occasional correction—Alphonse de Neuville drawing a squid with ten tentacles, for example, rather than the (incorrect) eight described by Verne in *Twenty Thousand Leagues Under the Sea.* Verne himself posed for the character of Professor Aronnax in *Leagues.*

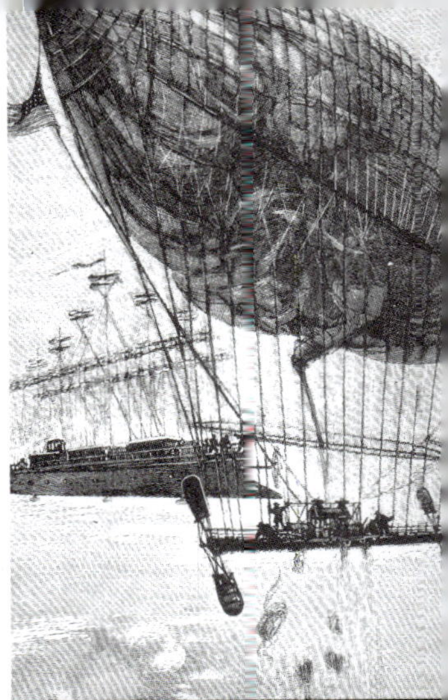

◀
The steam-powered elephant-shaped engine is a science-fictional McGuffin in Verne's *La Maison à Vapeur* ("The Steam House"), which was in essence a travelogue of India. It did, however, inspire some of Léon Benett's most delightful illustrations.

▶
The thirst for scientific knowledge drives the plot of *Twenty Thousand Leagues Under the Sea* and Verne's interest in marine biology perhaps inspired illustrator Alphonse de Neuville to base the character of Professor Aronnax on Verne himself.

▲
The lighter-than-air dirigible Go-Ahead is attacked by the heavier-than-air "clipper of the clouds," the Albatross, as Robur proves his mastery of flight. In turn, Léon Benett proves his mastery of action and dramatic perspective in *Robur-le-Conquerant.*

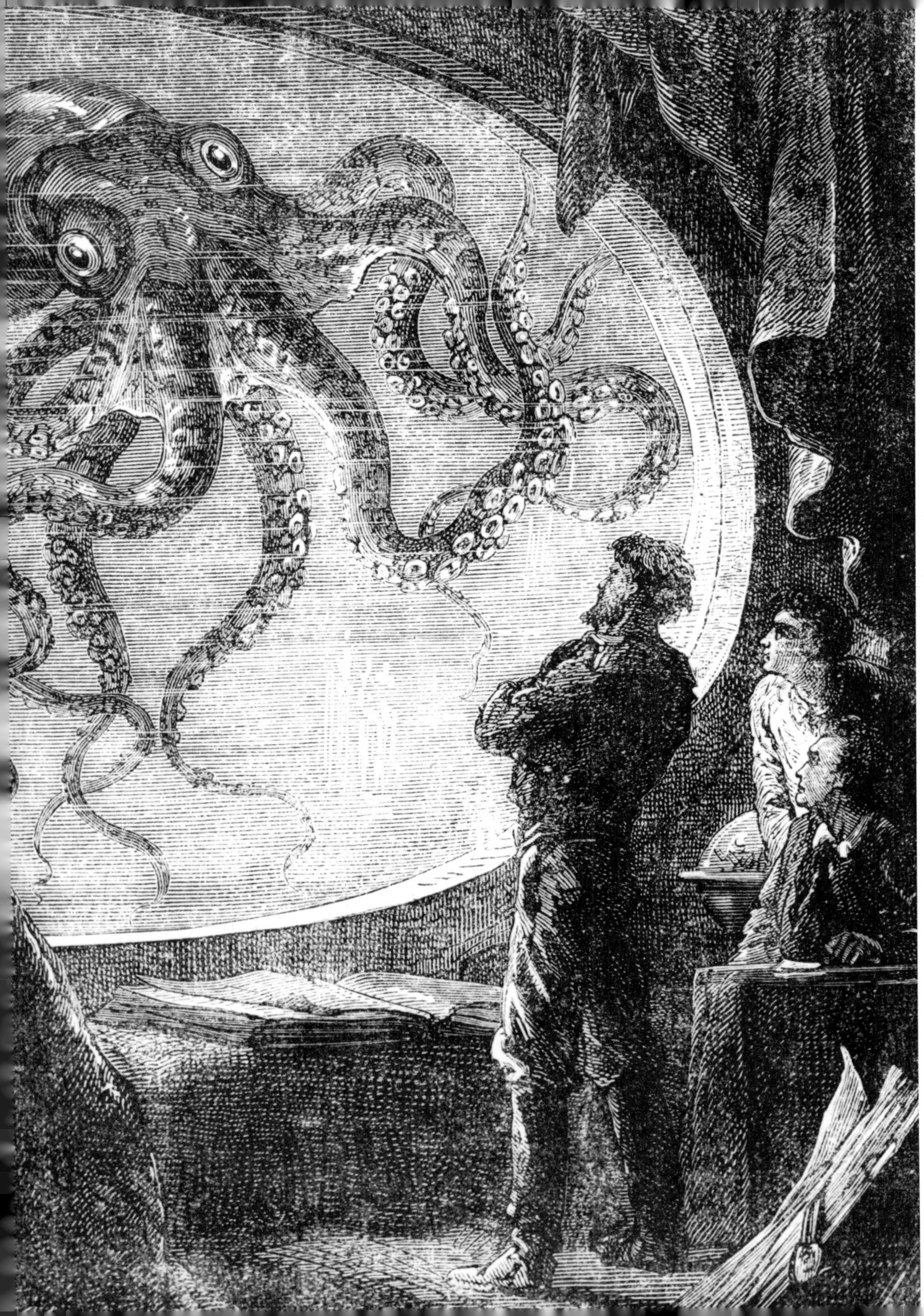

ALBERT ROBIDA

Albert Robida (1848–1926) lived to see some of the advances of the 20th century he had predicted years earlier would become reality. Perhaps not in the fanciful way he had predicted, but a reality nonetheless. Expert and historian I. F. Clarke ranked Robida's predictions of future war devices alongside those of H. G. Wells. Robida "tried to imagine what might happen if the aeroplane, the submarine, even dynamite and Röntgen rays were developed for use in warfare."

Robida was already an illustrator firmly established in French periodicals. Born in Compiègne in northern France, he had trained to become a notary, but was more interested in art and design. He began drawing for *Le Journal Amusant* in 1866 and contributed to *Paris-Caprice, La Vie Elegante, Paris-Comique,* and elsewhere. In the 1870s and 1880s he produced a number of successful books inspired by travels around Europe.

His links with Jules Verne were firmly established with his novel *Voyages Très Extraordinaires de Saturnin Farandoul* ("The Very Extraordinary Voyages of Saturnin Farandoul," 1879), in which the hero (aged four) is shipwrecked and raised by orangutans before escaping his island home on the trunk of a coconut tree. These are just the beginning of a wildly fanciful adventure that eventually brings Farandoul into contact with Maltese pirates and Verne's Captain Nemo. Pastiching Verne's love of imparting knowledge along the way, Farandoul also meets Phileas Fogg in South America and Hector Servadoc on a comet, before going to (future) war with Australia.

In 1880, Robida became associated with *La Caricature* and serialized a number of novels that contained a great many remarkable predictions for the mid-20th century. Robida's three major volumes—*Le Vingtième Siècle* ("The Twentieth Century," 1883), *La Guerre au Vingtième Siècle* ("The War of the Twentieth Century," 1887), and *Le Vingtième Siècle: La Vie Electrique* ("The Twentieth Century: The Electric Life," 1890)—dealt with the future humorously and optimistically, showing a world in which every middle-class Frenchman would own his own airship. Unlike Verne, who based all his scientific advances on current knowledge, Robida made a number of leaps of imagination that, in places, proved highly accurate. Among the advances Robida dreamed of for his whimsical drawings are radio, wide-screen televisions with multiple channels and 24-hour global news networks, video phones through which you can do your shopping, fast food outlets, test tube babies, genetic engineering, bullet trains, and transcontinental air travel. But, beyond technology, he also predicted changes in society (the emancipation of women) and in fashion (mini-skirts, figure-hugging jeans); the rise of the military; chemical and biological warfare; and the environmental damage wrought by mass industrialization.

Robida's other science fiction works show just as much imagination. *L'Horloge des Siècles* ("The Clock of the Centuries," 1902) related how a cosmic catastrophe causes time to run backwards, while *La Guerre Infernal* ("The Infernal War," 1908) and *L'Ingénieur Von Satanas* ("The Engineer Von Satanas," 1919) were both future war stories. His final book, *Un Chalet dans les Airs* ("A Castle in the Air," 1925) was another future fantasy.

▶
Robida imagined a civilization existing on Mars in the article "À la Surface de Mars" in the *Journal des Voyages* in 1901, although their clothing and telescope—with its intricate, Byzantine design—seem to indicate that Robida thought they still had some catching up to do with their technologically advanced neighbors.

▶▶
***Un Quartier Embrouille* imagines the future of Paris' red-light district, as this neighborhood of questionable business takes to the air in Robida's *Le Vingtième Siècle*.**

▶
In the 20th century, fish would no longer survive in rivers, and disease-carrying bacteria would poison the air. An all-too-accurate prediction from Robida's 1890 *La Vie Electrique*, in which he foresaw the continued rise of the industrialization that had begun to impact on society 50 years earlier.

▶▶
Robida's imaginative depiction of the military of the future appeared in the 1908 serial *La Guerre Infernal*. Here we see the Japanese navy and air force. In the same series, he also depicted aircraft and airships over London, predating the WWII Battle of Britain by over 30 years.

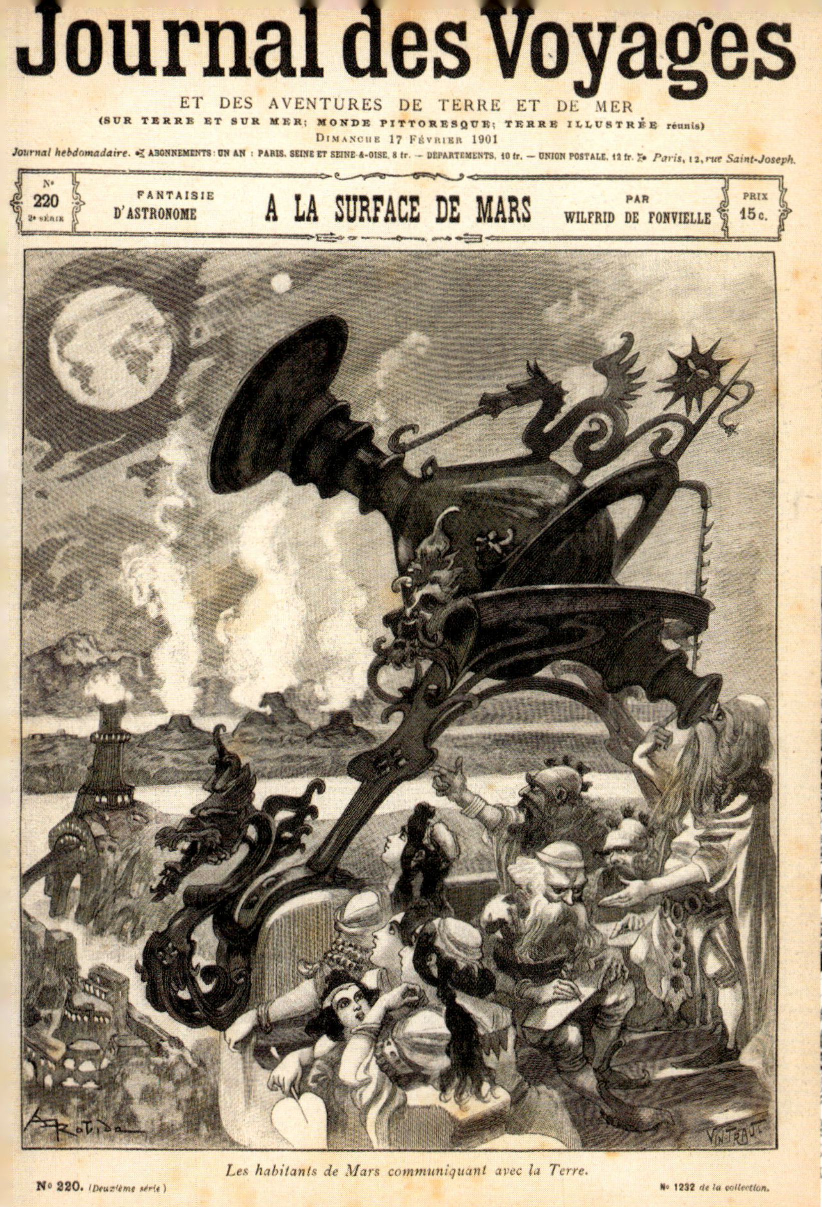
Journal des Voyages

ET DES AVENTURES DE TERRE ET DE MER

(SUR TERRE ET SUR MER; MONDE PITTORESQUE; TERRE ILLUSTRÉE réunis)

DIMANCHE 17 FÉVRIER 1901

Journal hebdomadaire. — ABONNEMENTS: UN AN : PARIS, SEINE ET SEINE-&-OISE, 8 fr. — DÉPARTEMENTS, 10 fr. — UNION POSTALE, 12 fr. — Paris, 12, rue Saint-Joseph.

N° 220 2e SÉRIE — FANTAISIE D'ASTRONOME — A LA SURFACE DE MARS — PAR WILFRID DE FONVIELLE — PRIX 15c.

Les habitants de Mars communiquant avec la Terre.

N° 220. (Deuxième série) — N° 1232 de la collection.

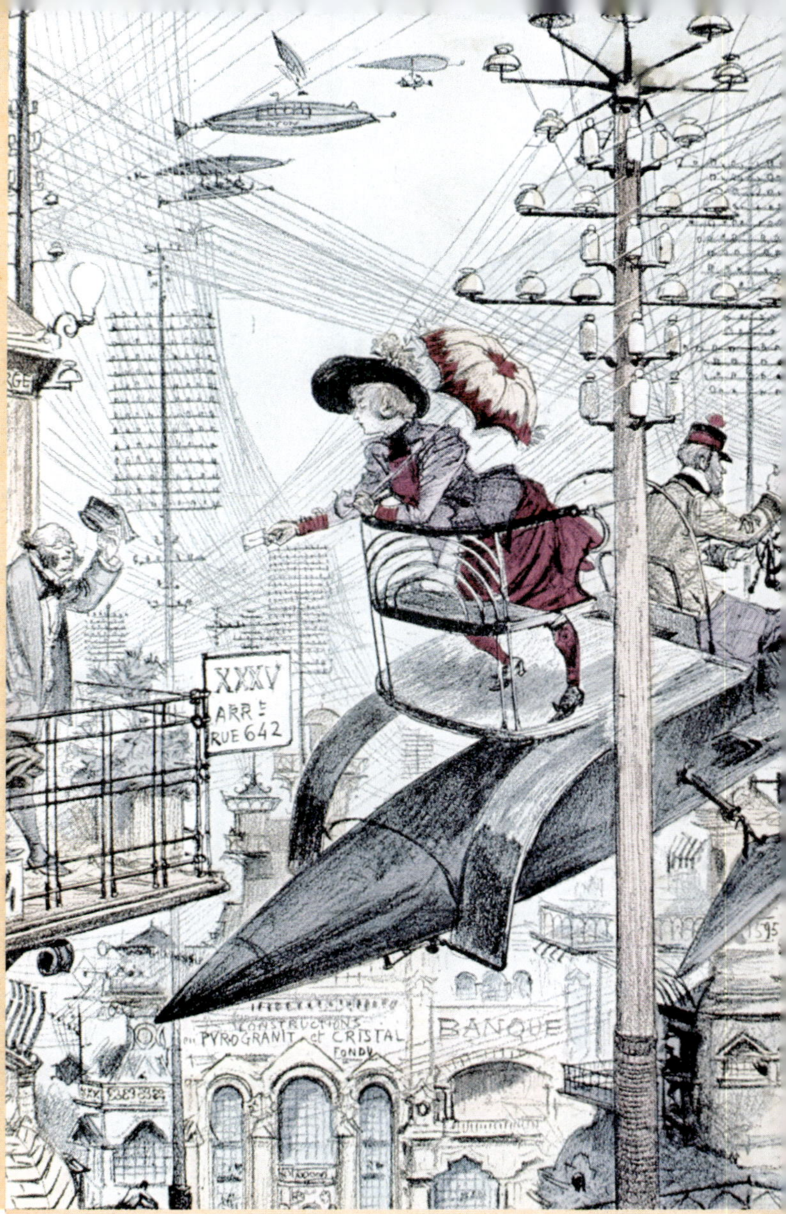

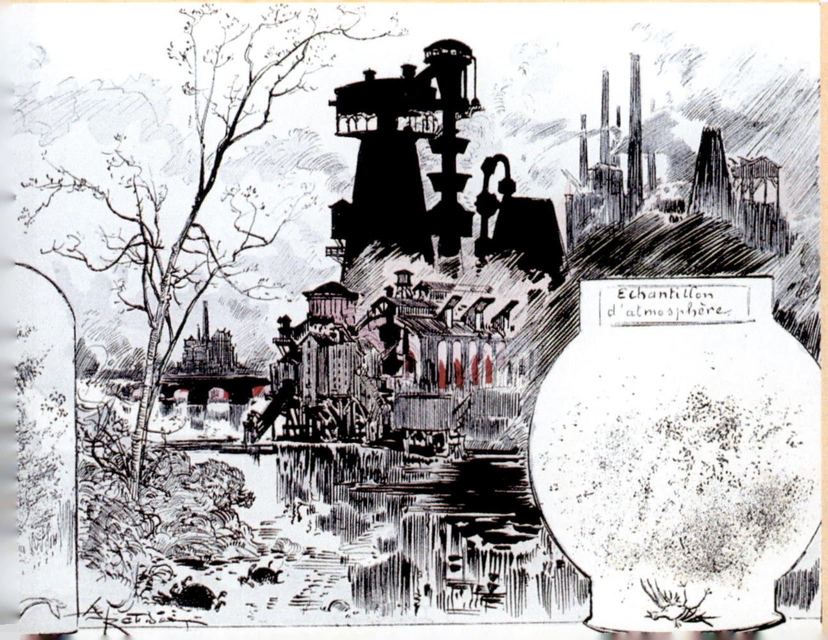

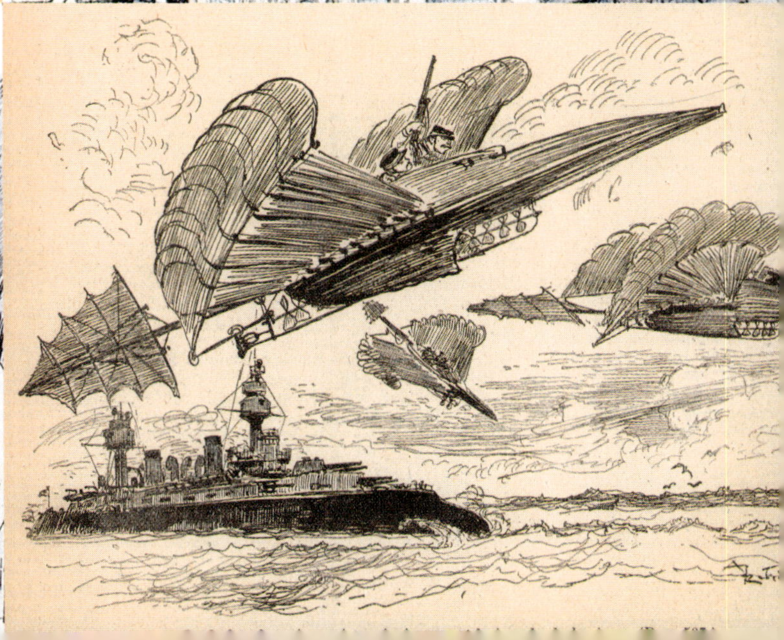

SCIENCE AND WONDER:
THE PULPS OF THE 1920S & 1930S

When the first science fiction magazine, *Amazing Stories*, appeared on newsstands in 1926, it was far from the first American magazine to feature science fiction.

Edgar Allan Poe can rightly be called the father of the science fiction short story with tales like *MS. Found in a Bottle* (1833) and *The Unparalleled Adventures of One Hans Pfaal* (1835). American magazines such as *Harper's* and *Atlantic Monthly* carried early SF stories by Fitz-James O'Brien and Edward Everett Hale and, in June 1890, *Overland Monthly* published a special "Twentieth Century Number" looking forward to the next two centuries.

The popularity of "dime novels" with younger audiences helped establish a whole new literary field, the Edisonade. Named after Thomas Alva Edison, the Edisonade featured boy inventors of wonderful new modes of transport or weapons. *The Steam Man of the Prairies* (1868) by Edward S. Ellis introduced the genre, but Frank Reade, created by Harry Cohen (writing as Harry Enton for *The Boys of New York* in 1876), was to become the Edisonade's most famous hero. After starring in a few serials, his adventures were taken over by new author Luis Senarens, who switched his attentions to Frank Reade Jr., and, as "Noname," wrote increasingly inventive, Verne-ian yarns of steam men, lost worlds, and flying machines.

Pulp magazines (named after the wood-pulp paper they were printed on) began to appear in the 1890s. Their importance was not just in establishing a format, but in establishing science fiction as a genre—not to mention helping create a group of authors who would be associated with science fiction for years to come. Early pulps like *The Argosy* and *All-Story* carried the works of William Wallace Cook, Garrett P. Serviss, and George Allan England. Edgar Rice Burroughs made his debut with *Under the Moons of Mars* in *All-Story* in 1912, followed shortly after by the first appearance of *Tarzan of the Apes*, which shot him to fame. Abraham Merritt's *The Moon Pool* was another *All-Story* success in 1918. New pulps specializing in the strange and mysterious, *The Thrill Book* and *Weird Tales*, soon began to appear.

It was an immigrant with a fascination for developments in science that took science fiction to the next level. Hugo Gernsback was born in Luxembourg in 1884, arriving in America in 1904. He immediately established The Electro Importing Company, shipping in scientific equipment from Europe, and contributed an article on a new portable radio to *Scientific American*. In 1908 he launched *Modern Electrics*, in which he serialized his novel *Ralph 124C41+* (1911). Gernsback sold his stake in the magazine and launched *The Electric Experimenter* in 1913 (re-titled *Science and Invention* in 1920), in which fiction would regularly appear, including reprints of H. G. Wells; the August 1923 issue was a "Scientific Fiction Number."

Through *Science and Invention*, Gernsback also discovered two artists who were to take science fiction by storm: Frank R. Paul and Howard Brown. For Gernsback, it was the testing ground for his next innovation: *Amazing Stories*.

▶ ***Argosy All-Story Weekly*** **resulted from the merger of two early pulp magazines. While *The Fire People* didn't really live up to the hype—definitely more improbable than interesting—the anonymous cover artist focused on the action of Ray Cummings' Mercurian-invasion serial to create a standout cover.**

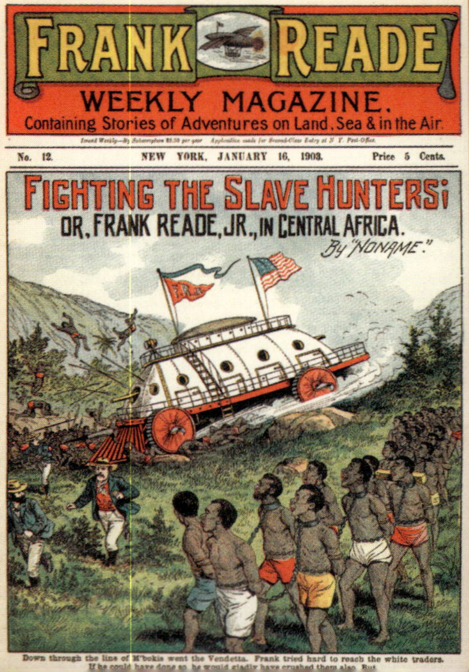

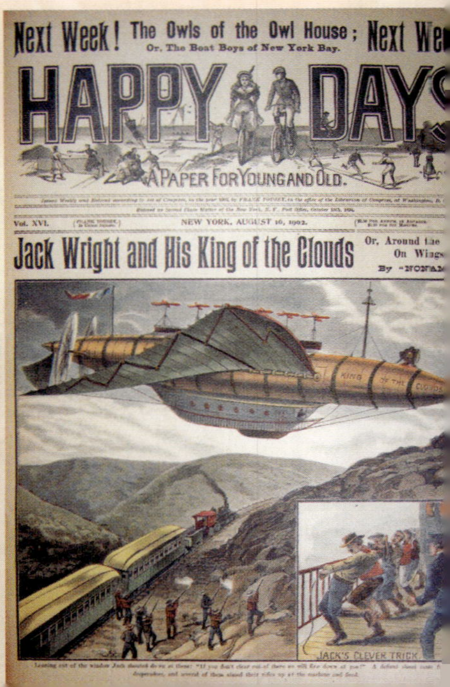

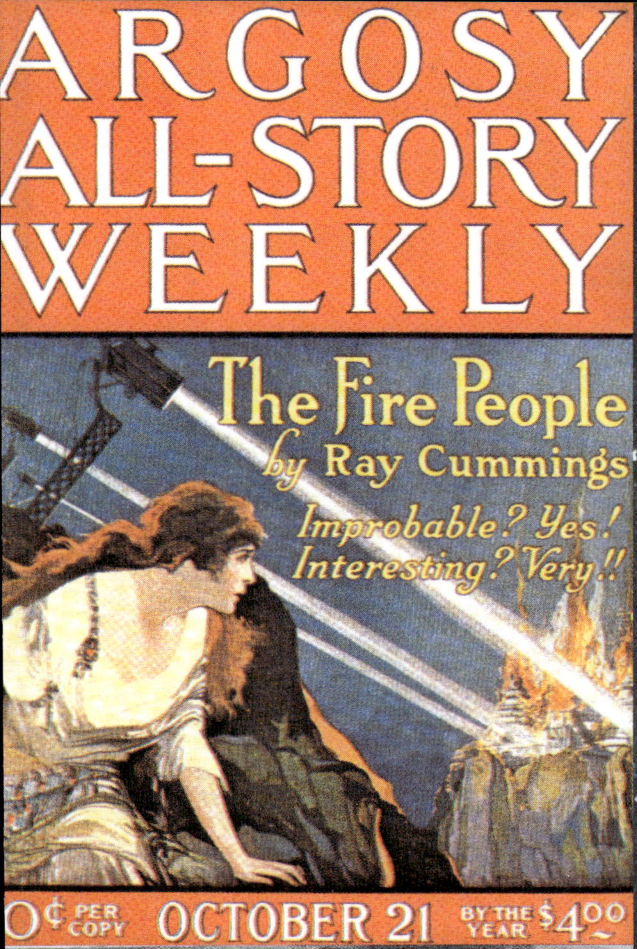

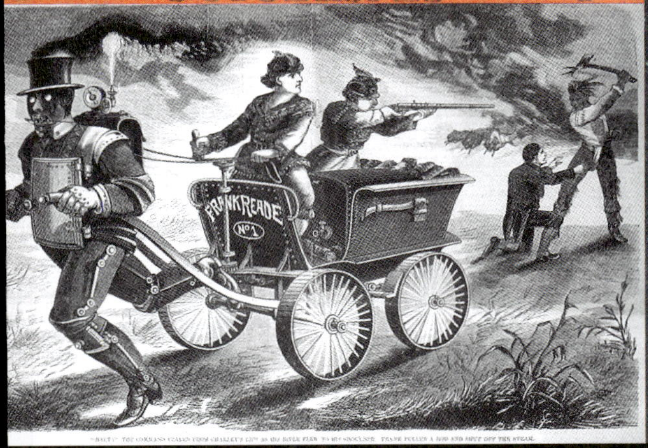

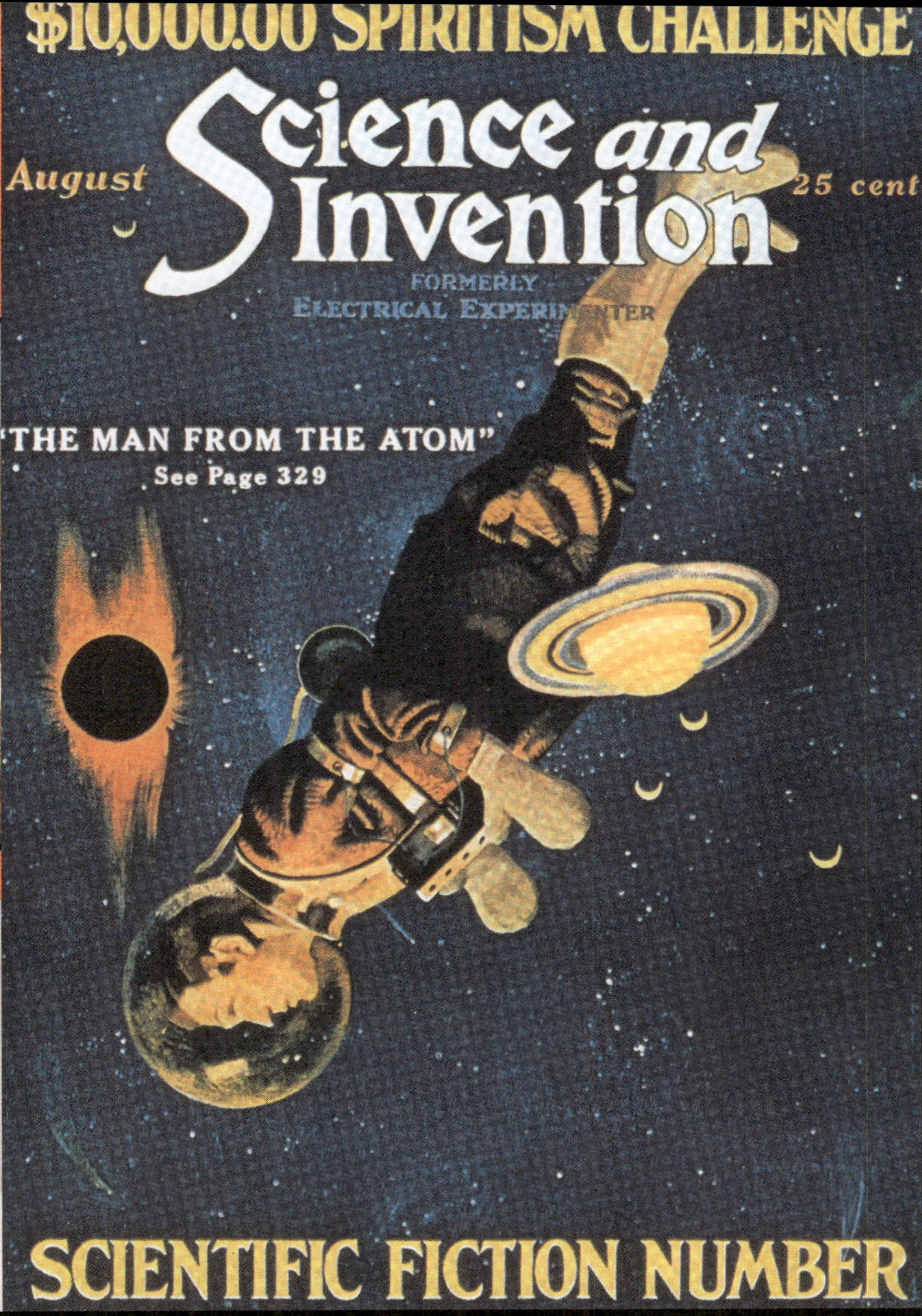

▲ The original "Steam Man," created by Edward S. Ellis, appeared in *Irwin's American Novels* no. 45 in 1865; later, Harold Cohen (writing as Harry Enton) lifted the concept wholesale for the boys' paper *Boys of New York* (1876) when he created the character Frank Reade.

◄ These adventures proved so popular that new adventures featuring Frank—and the very similar Jack Wright—appeared weekly, written by Luis Senarens under the pseudonym "Noname." Flying machines, tanks, submarines, and vehicles that combined all three appeared regularly.

▲ This surprisingly muted cover, by Howard V. Browne, adorned the "Scientific Fiction Number" of Hugo Gernsback's *Science and Invention* for August 1923—the precursor of his famed SF magazine, *Amazing Stories*.

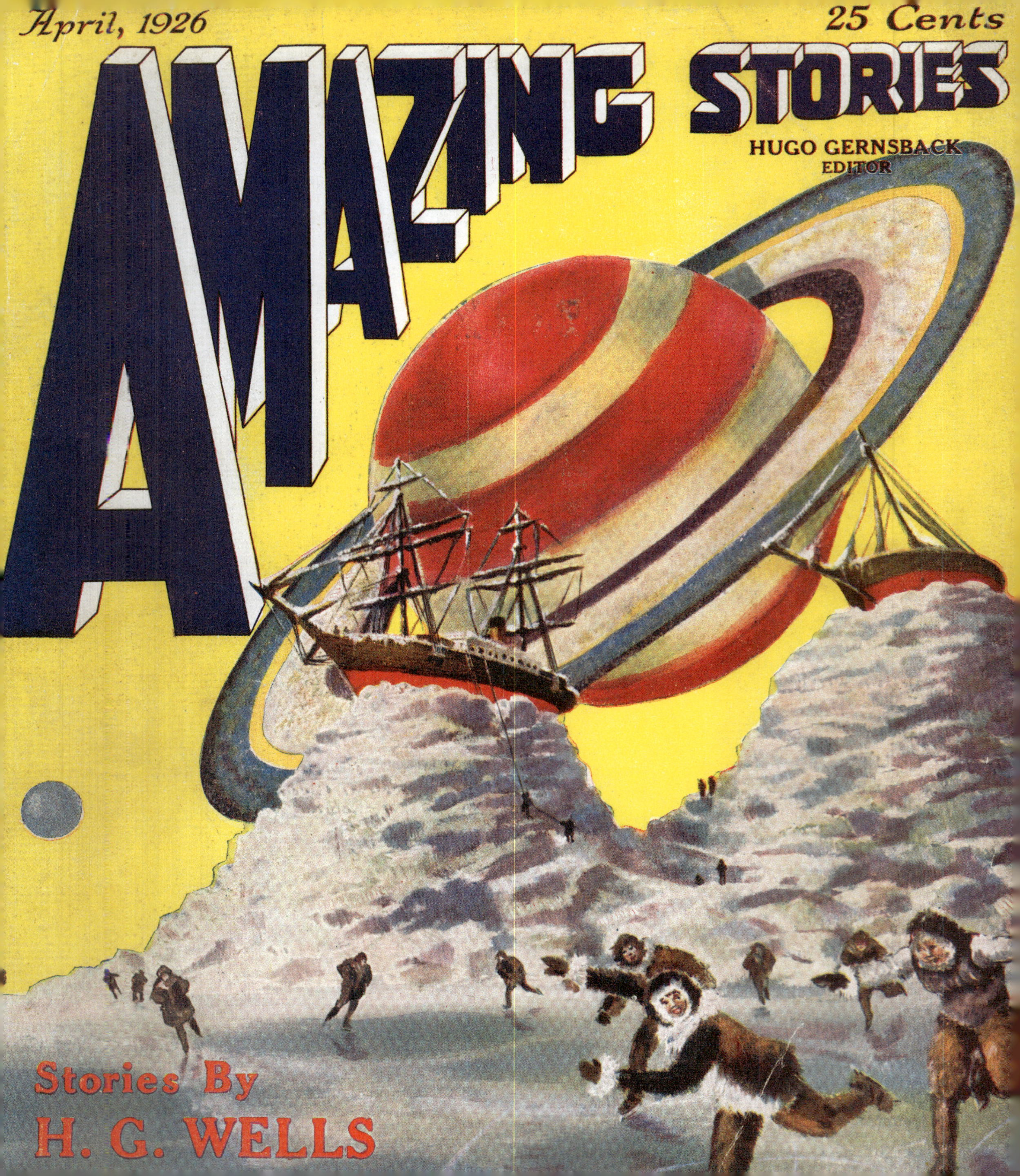
April, 1926
25 Cents
AMAZING STORIES
HUGO GERNSBACK
EDITOR
Stories By
H. G. WELLS

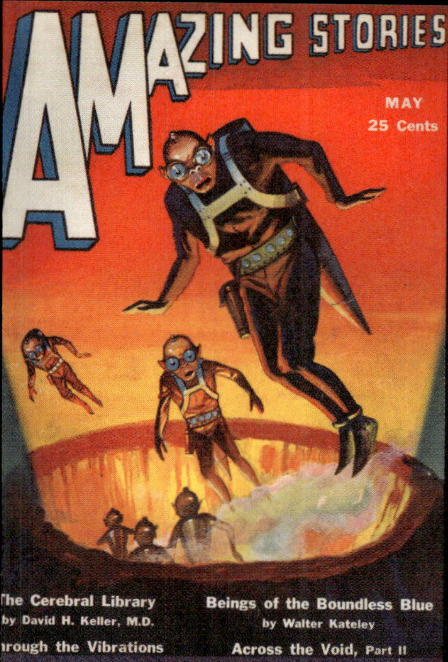

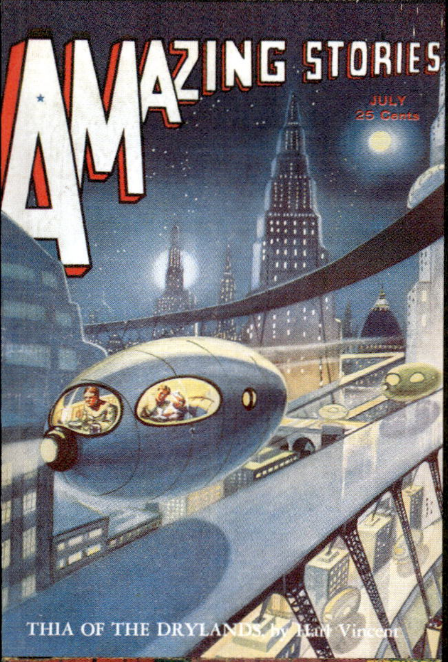

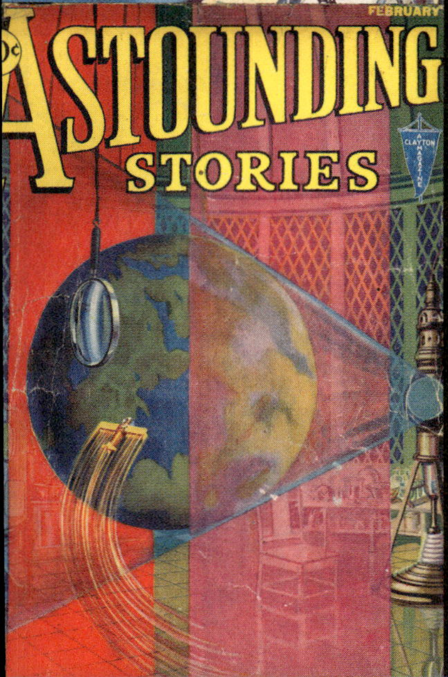

The first issue of *Amazing Stories* was dated April 1926 and Gernsback explained his definition of "scientifiction" as "the Jules Verne, H. G. Wells, and Edgar Allan Poe type of story—a charming romance intermingled with scientific fact and prophetic vision." Verne, Wells, and Poe were well represented in that first issue and *Amazing* soon attained a monthly circulation of over 100,000.

Over the next few years Gernsback discovered numerous writers, some now forgotten—Miles J. Breuer, David H. Keller, Harl Vincent, Stanton A. Coblenz—and was able to publish Burroughs' *The Master Mind of Mars* (*Amazing Stories Annual*, 1927) and many memorable stories of early super-science. None exemplify the "space opera" better than *The Skylark of Space* by E. E. Smith—a sprawling tale of good against evil with the universe as a backdrop. Edmond Hamilton's *Crashing Suns* and *The Sun-Stealers* in *Weird Tales* were on a similarly galactic scale. Financial reporter Philip Francis Nowlan published *Armageddon 2419 A.D.* in *Amazing*, where it was spotted by John F. Dille, president of National Newspaper Syndicate. Dille saw potential in a comic strip version of Nowlan's story and lead character, Anthony Rogers, was dubbed "Buck" Rogers in the strip that launched in 1929.

The emergence of "that Buck Rogers stuff," as it is still known to this day, overshadowed the more imaginative fiction that was appearing. The presentation of science fiction, via the covers that appeared on *Amazing* and, subsequently, on *Science Wonder Stories*, which Gernsback launched in 1929, did not help. Gernsback's main cover artist, Frank R. Paul, emphasized technology over human characters, a criticism that has dogged science fiction ever since.

Leo Morey (1899-1965) became *Amazing*'s main artist from 1929. Born Leopoldo Pena Morey in Peru, Morey had studied at Louisiana State University and worked as an engineer before taking up commercial art. Self-taught, his work lacked Paul's inventiveness when it came to futuristic cityscapes, and his early covers were quite lurid. By the mid-1930s, Morey was using a more muted color palette and his covers had improved dramatically in both content and design.

In 1930, *Astounding Stories* was launched by Clayton Magazines; the new market attracted most of the bigger names of the time because pay rates were better, but the editor demanded formulaic action stories and, as a consequence, the fiction was less experimental. *Astounding*'s artist was Hans Waldemar Wessolowski (a.k.a. "Wesso," 1894-1961), born in Graudenz, Poland. After training at the Berlin Royal Academy, he emigrated to America in 1913 and worked as an artist in advertising. After producing a handful of covers for *Amazing* he switched to *Astounding* and between 1930-1933, his action-packed but poorly executed covers matched the fiction content. Humans defended themselves from aliens/robots/ape-men with guns, flame-throwers, cudgels, or their fists. Only one or two showed any real sophistication and in these instances the covers could be most attractive and effective.

◀◀
The very first issue of *Amazing Stories* showed ice-skaters enjoying a frolic on one of the moons of Saturn, which hangs looming in the background. The illustration, by Frank R. Paul, was based on an episode from Jules Verne's *Off on a Comet; or, Hector Servadac*, which was serialized in the magazine's first two issues.

◀▲ ▲▲
Leo Morey's illustrations showed a wide diversity. The image for the May 1931 *Amazing* is one that defines science fiction for many: the bug-eyed creature. Morey was in futuristic mode for the July 1932 issue, the sleek transporters and towering cityscape usually the domain of Frank R. Paul.

◀
A rather muted (despite the garish colors) cover from Hans Wesso. Usually associated with multi-tentacled alien creatures, Wesso was also capable of producing rather more abstract images, as for the February 1932 issue of *Astounding Stories*.

FRANK R. PAUL

Frank R. Paul (1884–1963) was the main cover artist for Hugo Gernsback's *Amazing Stories*—the first devoted SF magazine—right from its debut issue in April 1926. Trained in architecture and technical drawing, Paul brought solidity, credibility, and a remarkably garish color palette to SF.

As science fiction author Frederick Pohl later observed, "Frank R. Paul loved machines, and loved to draw them. Hugo Gernsback discovered this about him early on, and as exciting drawings of strange machinery were what Hugo liked to publish in his magazines, Paul was Gernsback's principal artist for a couple of decades. He was probably the first human being ever to make a living drawing pictures of spaceships."

Gernsback, himself an immigrant from Luxembourg, discovered the Austrian-born Paul working for an American provincial newspaper in 1914, and hired him for his technical hobbyist magazine *Electrical Experimenter*. When Gernsback launched *Amazing Stories*, Paul painted all the magazine's covers for its first three years and produced a large proportion of the interior illustrations. When Gernsback lost control of *Amazing* in 1929 and founded *Science Wonder Stories*, Paul went with him. They were to work together for some 40 years.

Paul's artwork displayed the strengths and the weaknesses of his architectural training. Buildings and machinery were impeccably rendered, while (with some noteworthy exceptions) human figures were awkward and naively drawn. This didn't matter, however, because most of the time they were only set-dressing. It was the technology that counted: in Paul's own words, it was "science fiction, with the accent on the science."

For the first two decades of the existence of modern SF, Paul defined the look of the future. The technology he depicted was firmly grounded in the familiar, with gears and valves, rivets and touches of rococo ornamentation, making it all the more credible. His artwork was so detailed, so three-dimensional, so wonderfully complex, that it was utterly convincing.

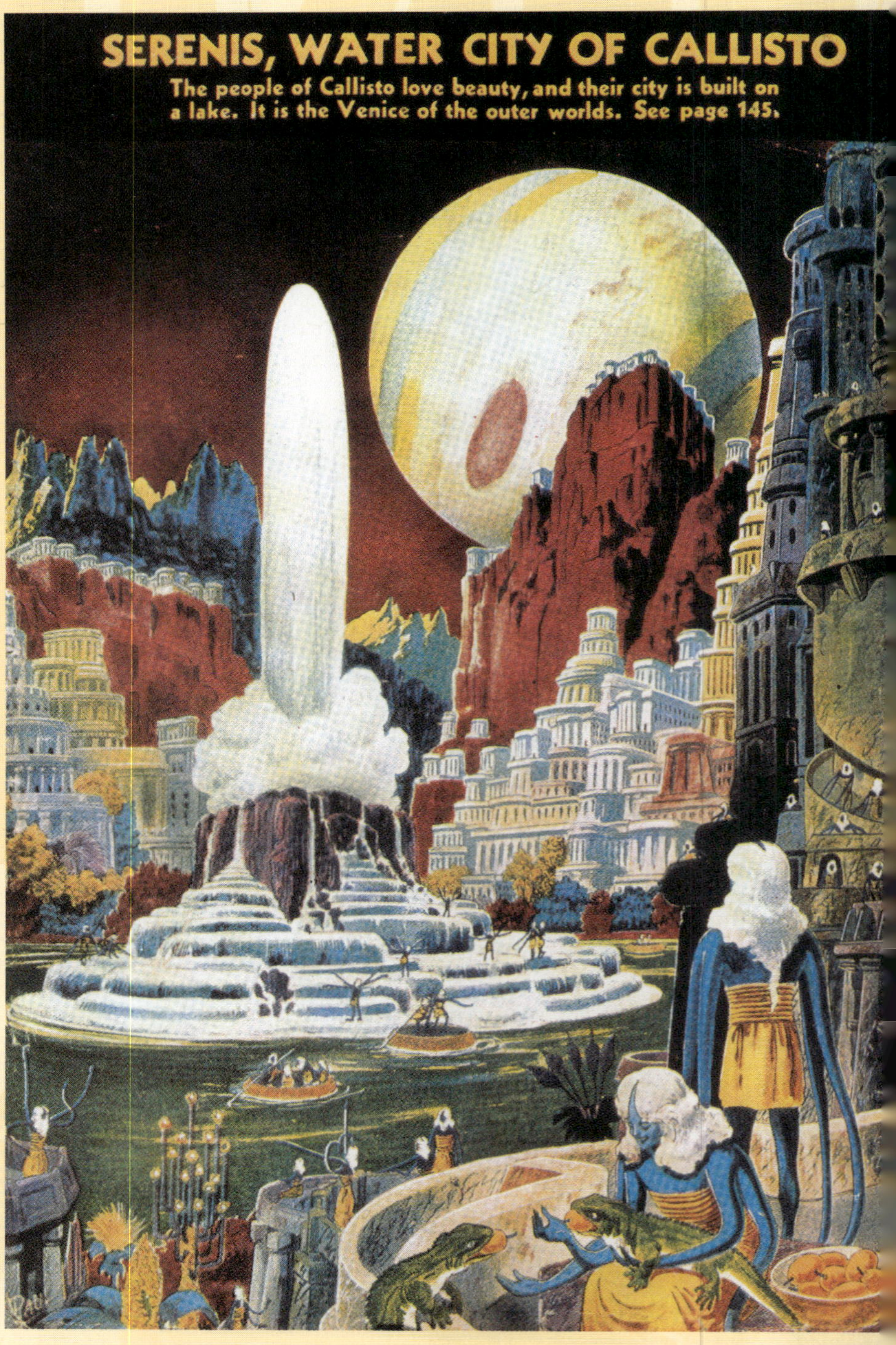

Under Paul's hand, the future was also brighter—literally. That said, those trademark eye-popping, flat colors reportedly weren't entirely Paul's choice; they were actually necessary because, to cut costs, Gernsback seemingly used a three-color printing process rather than the normal four-color. But Paul's gaudy covers certainly caught the eye, and the readers and fans loved them. In 1939, at the first World Science Fiction Convention, the guest of honor was not one of the pioneer authors of the genre, nor its father Hugo Gernsback—it was Frank R. Paul

◀
Serenis, the water city of Callisto, was one of a series of imaginative back cover illustrations produced by Paul for *Amazing Stories* that showed off his ability to create alien architecture.

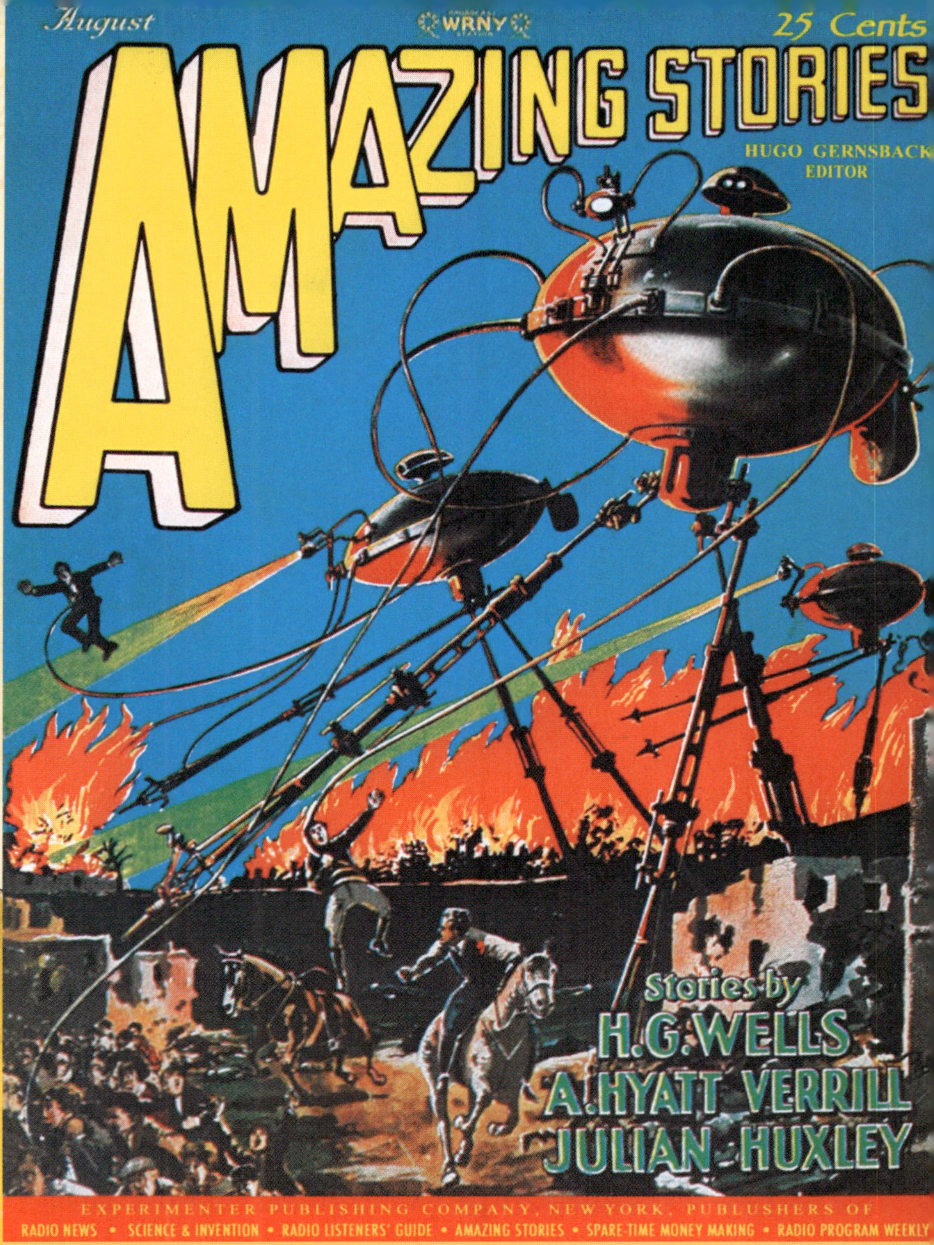

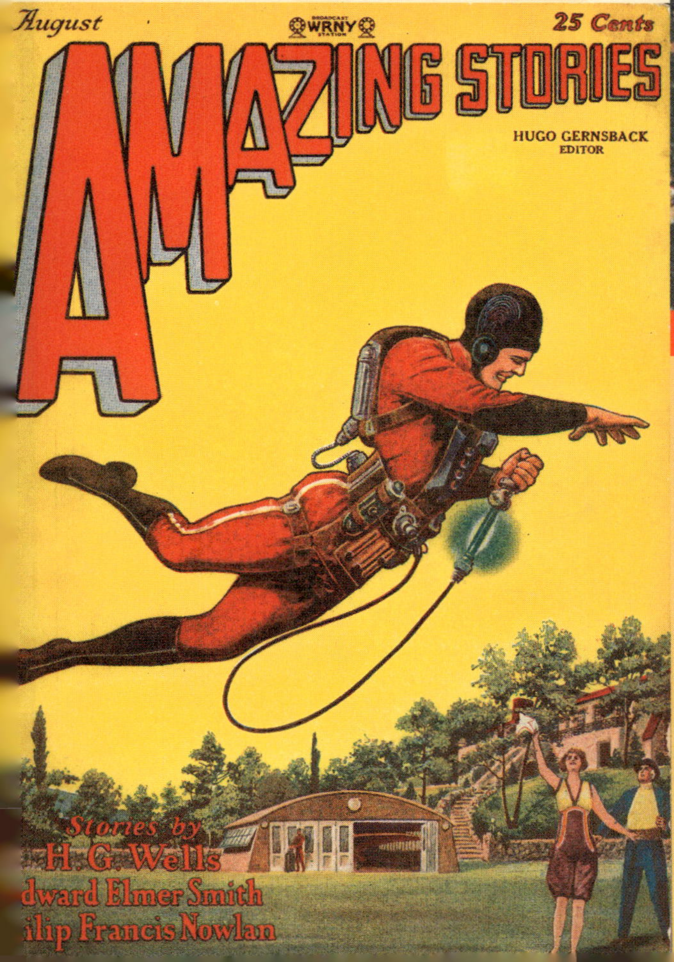

◀
***Amazing*'s "Buck Rogers" cover actually isn't Buck at all. Although the issue does include Philip Francis Nowlan's novella *Armageddon 2419 A.D.*, the first appearance of pilot Anthony Rogers (he earned the nickname "Buck" only in the comic strip), the story illustrated is an episode of E. E. "Doc" Smith's *The Skylark of Space*.**

▲
One of Paul's most deservedly famous covers, illustrating H. G. Wells' *War of the Worlds*. Paul declared to the 1939 WorldCon audience: "I have always tried to interpret what the author had in mind, but you'll admit I have never tried to scare you with the purely grotesque."

INTO THE GOLDEN AGE:
THE PULPS OF THE 1930s & 1940s

It is true to say that early science fiction magazines did not have a particularly good reputation for quality. As the 1930s progressed, however, new editors strove to raise the bar. David Lasser and Charles Hornig at *Wonder Stories* and F. Orlin Tremaine at *Astounding Stories* sought new, original ideas to energize the genre. *Astounding* published *The Legion of Space* by Jack Williamson, *The Skylark of Valeron* by E. E. Smith, and *The Mightiest Machine* by John W. Campbell in quick succession—wide-screen space opera at its best—alongside "thought variant" stories, in which common SF themes (time travel, other dimensions, alien invasion, micro- and macro-universes) were given a new twist.

Artists responded to this with some grandiose artwork, although the improvements were often on the inside rather than on the covers. William Elliott Dold Jr. (1889–1967) had been a prolific illustrator of Western and adventure pulps in the 1920s, and his science fiction illustrations proved he was a capable figure drawer. But his strength was in design: Dold's Art Deco influences showed in the vast, intricate spaceships he drew. They dwarf the people around them and were sorely missed when Dold fell ill in 1935 and all but disappeared from magazines, only briefly re-emerging in 1938–1941.

Charles E. Schneeman (1912–1972) was another talent whose artwork captured the mood of space opera. Best remembered for illustrating *The Legion of Time* by Jack Williamson (1938) and *Gray Lensman* by E. E. Smith (1939), he rarely painted covers, but provided *Astounding* with two classics—realistic renditions of planets that pre-dated the work of Chesley Bonestell. Schneeman worked with Isaac Asimov on an unpublished comic strip (*Star Empire*) in 1944 but was rarely seen in SF magazines after the war.

While *Astounding* went from strength to strength, Hugo Gernsback had been forced to sell *Wonder Stories* in 1935. New editor Leo Margulies aimed the re-launched *Thrilling Wonder Stories* at a younger audience, and, with the arrival of John W. Campbell as editor of *Astounding* in 1937, the two magazines diverged further. *Thrilling Wonder* was home to Otto Binder and Ray Cummings, with covers emphasizing alien monsters with bug eyes.

Things improved with the arrival of Howard Vachel Brown (1878–1945). Brown had worked alongside Frank R. Paul on *Science and Invention* in the 1920s, but came to the fore on *Astounding* in 1933 and *Thrilling Wonder* in 1936. Brown's covers were a great improvement over those of Hans "Wesso" Wessolowski; using a muted palette, Brown let his imagination roam over spaceships, scientific equipment, humans, and aliens, along the way producing what SF author Lester Del Rey called "one of the best paintings of aliens of all time." Already in his fifties when he started, Brown invigorated *Thrilling Wonder Stories* with some of its best covers and also contributed to a later launch, *Startling Stories*; his departure from SF in 1940 was a big loss to the genre.

► ▼
Two examples of Howard V. Browne's colorful and energetic covers for *Astounding Stories* from 1934. The larger illustrates a story of early spaceflight by Frank K. Kelly, but it was Murray Leinster's *Sidewise in Time* that would be considered a classic.

◄ ▼
Hans Wesso provides a classic, glowing cover for the opening episode of *Galactic Patrol* by Edward E. "Doc" Smith, which introduced the world to Kimball Kinnison, the Gray Lensman and interstellar policeman.

◄◄ ▼
John Russell Fearn's *Dark Eternity* inspired this cover by Howard V. Browne. The tiny gathering of people along the lower border of the picture gives you some idea of the scale of the machine.

◄◄◄ ▼
Charles Schneeman introduced *Astounding*'s new logo with a playful cover based on L. Sprague de Camp's equally playful story *The Merman*.

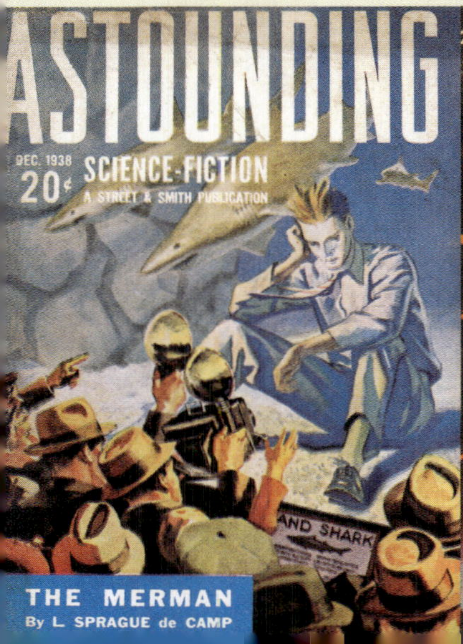

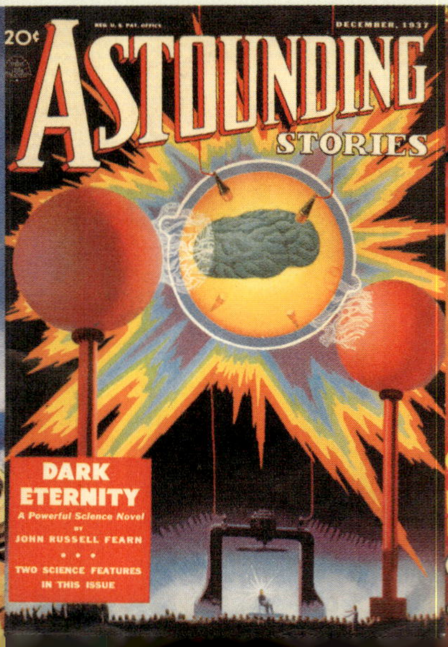

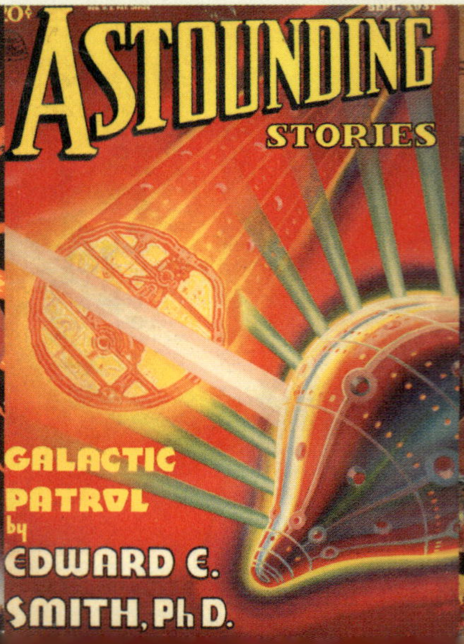

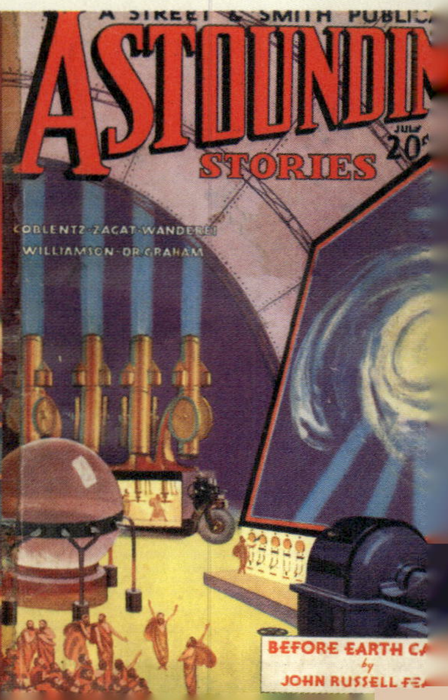

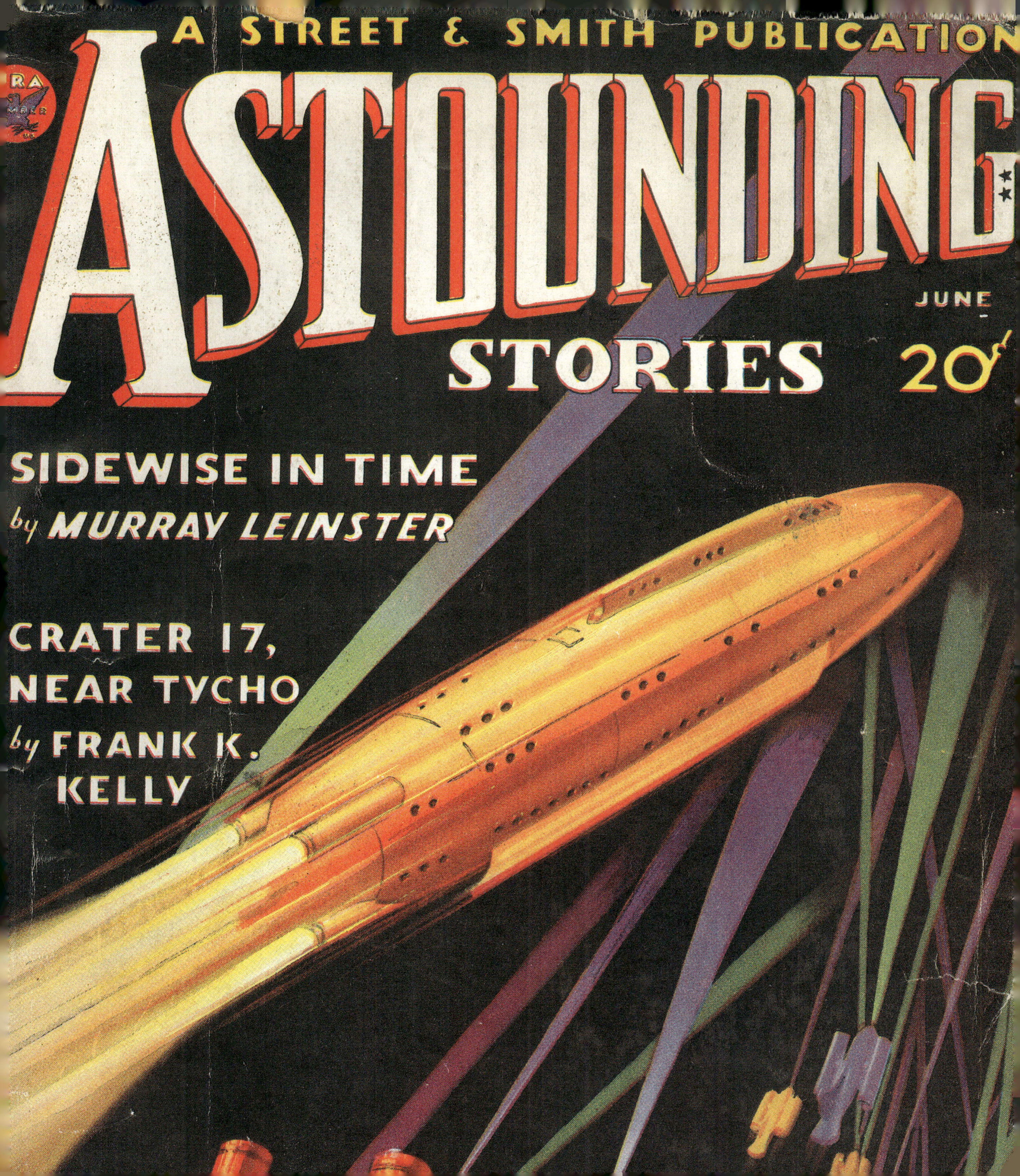
A STREET & SMITH PUBLICATION
ASTOUNDING
STORIES
JUNE
20¢
SIDEWISE IN TIME
by MURRAY LEINSTER
CRATER 17,
NEAR TYCHO
by FRANK K.
KELLY

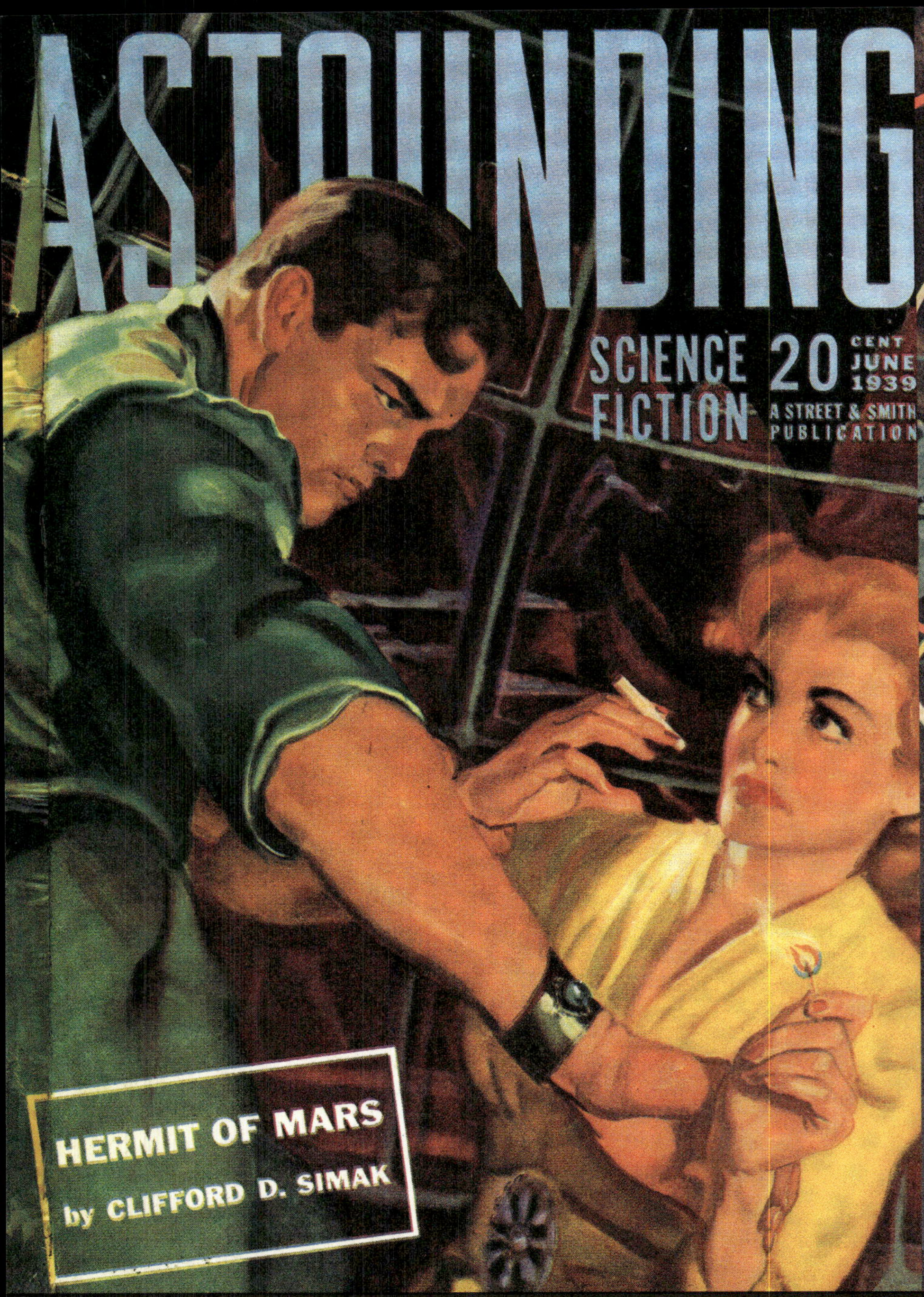

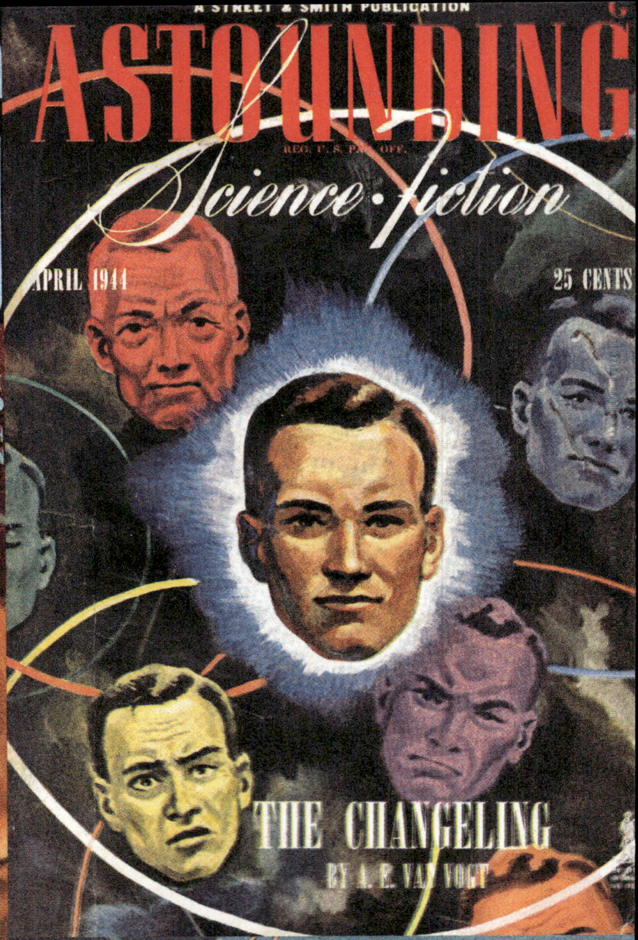

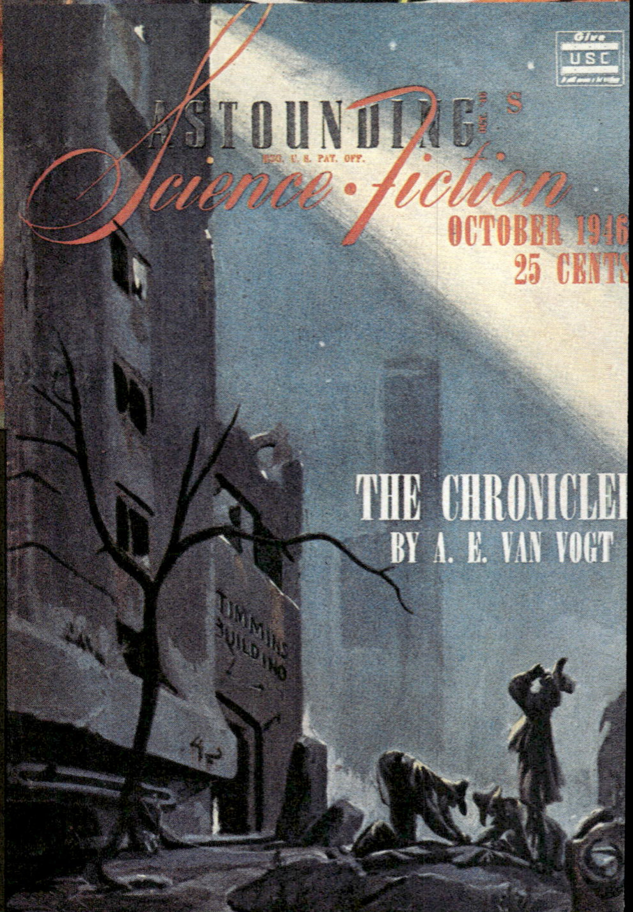

▲
Graves Gladney (1907-1976) was one of the artists drafted in to help Hubert Rogers fill the schedule on *Astounding* and *Unknown* in 1939. Gladney was better known as a major cover artist for hero pulps, as hinted at by the muscular hero and cigarette-smoking heroine.

►
Same author, same artist, but these two covers couldn't be more different. Overshadowed by Hubert Rogers, whose position as chief cover artist for *Astounding* he took while Rogers served during the war, William Timmins deserves a second and third look. Laid end-to-end, the 50 covers he produced between 1942 and 1947 show an astonishing diversity and growing confidence.

As Brown departed, *Astounding Stories* found a replacement in (Reginald) Hubert Rogers (1898-1982), a Canadian from Prince Edward Island who had trained in Nova Scotia and New York. In 1925, after a period working in Boston, he relocated to New York and began working for pulp magazines. Rogers' work was even more muted than Brown's, and often relied on symbolism to make a statement about the relationship between science, technology, and humans. Rogers had one advantage over his predecessors: he was an excellent figure painter and could encapsulate the essence of stories that were, in *Astounding* at least, becoming more concerned with how mankind would face the future.

This was the beginning of the golden age of science fiction, as new writers arrived and old writers responded to the changes John Campbell was making in *Astounding*. In a two-year period (1938-1940) Campbell introduced Lester Del Rey, L. Ron Hubbard, A. E. Van Vogt, Robert A. Heinlein, Theodore Sturgeon, and Leigh Brackett, as well as publishing the best work of writers who had debuted elsewhere, including Jack Williamson, Arthur J. Burks, Don A. Stuart (Campbell himself), Isaac Asimov, and E. E. Smith.

Rogers left in 1942 to join the Canadian War Department, leaving *Astounding*'s covers in the hands of William Timmins, a capable artist already established in pulps elsewhere. Timmins produced some fine covers, deceptively simple at first glance, continuing the trend for expressive rather than gaudy images. Five years later, Rogers returned, and Timmins spent a few years drawing black and white illustrations before departing the field.

During Rogers' five-year absence, SF had matured considerably, and Rogers' covers were the perfect fit. His failure to produce imaginative designs for spaceships (they tended to look like torpedoes) was less of a problem when stories emphasized the impact of technology on people rather than the technology itself.

Paul Orban (1896-1974) was equally at home with both people and technology, although, with only a few covers to his name, his work has tended to be forgotten. Following Rogers' departure in the early 1950s, Henry Richard Van Dongen (1920-) became a regular, his covers often dominated by a single vast face or figure, continuing the trend for symbolism established by Rogers. Although Van Dongen disappeared from *Astounding* in 1961, he was to make a triumphant return to SF as a paperback cover artist in the 1970s and 1980s, working for DAW Books and Ballantine.

Astounding could also boast covers by the dean of realistic space art, Chesley Bonestell (1888-1986), including a scarce example of Bonestell drawing a symbolic image (a hand reaching for Jupiter). Although an infrequent contributor (and often only in reprint), Bonestell was to have a major influence on space illustration for decades.

▼
Hubert Rogers was intimately associated with *Astounding Science Fiction*, producing 58 covers between February 1939 and April 1952. Rogers was an artist whose work improved with the years. Perhaps his five years enforced absence due to the Second World War gave him a different perspective, but his post-War work, exemplified by this cover for *Fury* by Lawrence O'Donnell (Henry Kuttner), was among the best science fiction has to offer.

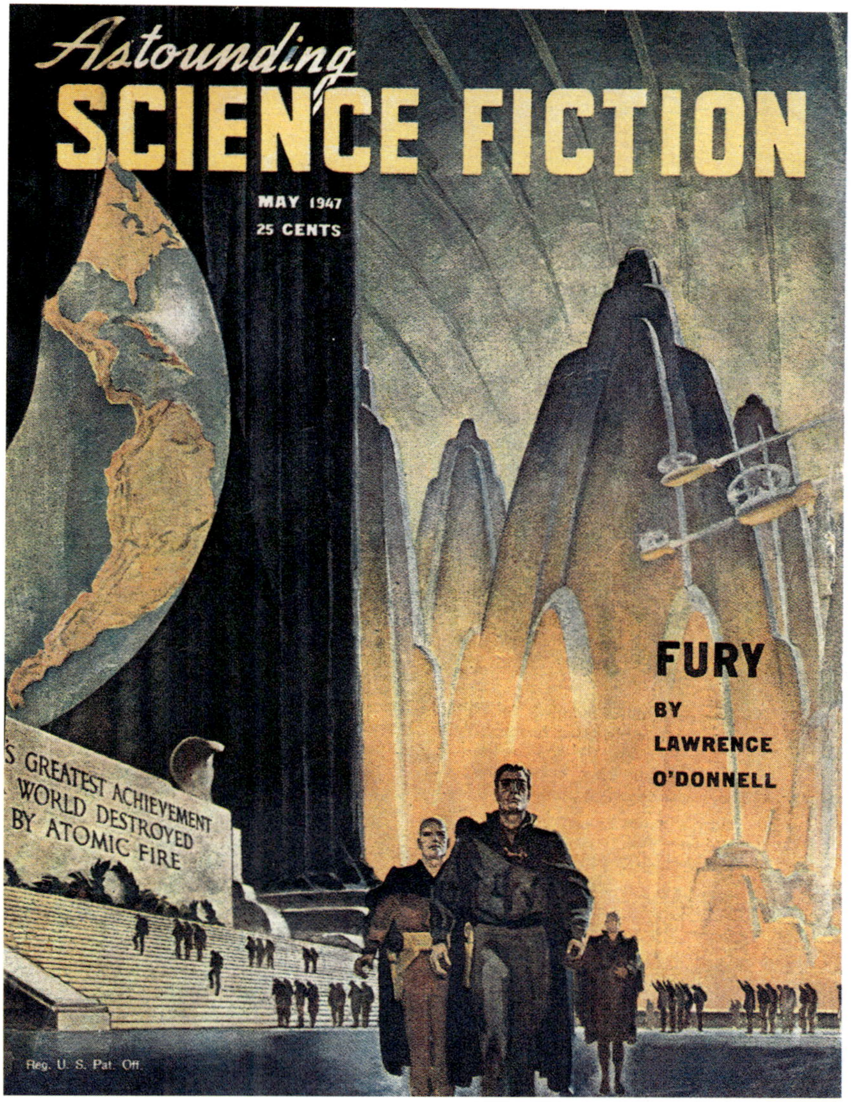

Of course, *Astounding Stories* was just one magazine. But the maturing of science fiction in general in the 1940s—a decade that had seen rockets and atomic bombs become a reality—had trickled down to other magazines. The real juvenilia took a sideways step into the thriving world of comic books, which had begun in the late 1930s and exploded during the war.

The 1930s had also seen the growth of the "hero pulps," featuring bizarre crime fighters and air aces, but often given a science fictional twist. *The Shadow* (launched in 1931), *Doc Savage* (1933), *The Spider* (1933), *Dusty Ayres and his Battle Birds* (1934), and *Terence X. O'Leary's War Birds* (1935) could always be counted on for the creation of some monstrous weapon or SF McGuffin to get a plot moving, and the best of the covers—usually those of George Rozen (1895-1973) and Walter M(artin) Baumhofer (1904-1987)—were eye-catching to say the least.

Not that science fiction was any less colorful. You only had to look as far as *Amazing Stories* and *Fantastic Adventures*, with their vibrant covers by Robert Gibson Jones and Harold W. McCauley (1913-1983), or *Thrilling Wonder* and *Startling Stories*, where Earle K. Bergey (1901-1952) put pin-up models in bug-eyed alien peril for most of the decade. For many critics (who perhaps wondered how these half-dressed girls in their brass brassieres or torn dresses could survive in space or on alien planets), Bergey exemplifies a style of SF cover that almost became synonymous with the genre.

What cannot be denied is that Bergey did this kind of thing very well, and there was often more to his covers than first met the eye. Harry L. Parkhurst (1878-1950) and Allen Anderson (1908-1995), on the other hand, were veterans of the "spicy" pulps, and their covers for *Planet Stories* were more exploitational. Alexander Leydenfrost (1888-1961), another of *Planet Stories*' women-in-alien-peril cover artists, went on to greater things as an illustrator for *Esquire* and *Life*.

Perhaps the finest of all the artists to tackle the female form was Virgil Finlay (1914-1971). Although more a fantasy and horror artist, Finlay's contributions to science fiction magazines were extraordinary. Instantly recognizable through his use of stippling and bubbles (often a requirement to cover up otherwise naked female forms), John Gustafson and Peter Nicholls, editors of *The Encyclopedia of Science Fiction*, declared him "possibly the greatest craftsman in the history of SF illustration," and stated that "[Finlay] revolutionized its quality."

Finlay was a victim of the collapse of the pulp magazines in the early- to mid-1950s, as the population turned from cheap magazines to the cinema and television for their entertainment. The pulps were replaced by the digest-sized magazines and paperbacks that had began to flourish after the war, which often eschewed interior illustrations. Thus the golden age of science fiction could also be said to have been the golden age of science fiction magazine illustration.

◄ ►
Virgil Finlay was one of the greatest artists to work in science fiction and horror magazines. His exquisite black and white artwork was instantly recognizable, not only because of his use of stipple but his superb draftsmanship, as in his illustration for Leigh Brackett's *The Big Jump* (background, *Space Stories*, February 1953). His covers were varied and imaginative and, in the case of the May 1957 *Fantastic Universe*, somewhat surreal.

► ►
Earle K. Bergey's rocket-crushing octopus gets a shot right between the eyes in this 1944 issue of *Thrilling Wonder Stories*, although teenage readers were more likely to be attracted by the girl with model looks and no visible pantyline.

► ► ►
Harold W. McCauley was one of the finest artists at Ziff-Davis, able to turn out the expected in a delightful way. (And what, in 1939, said "science fiction" more than a mad scientist in a laboratory cloning good-looking girls?) Yet he was capable of much more, as the accompanying moody 1948 cover shows.

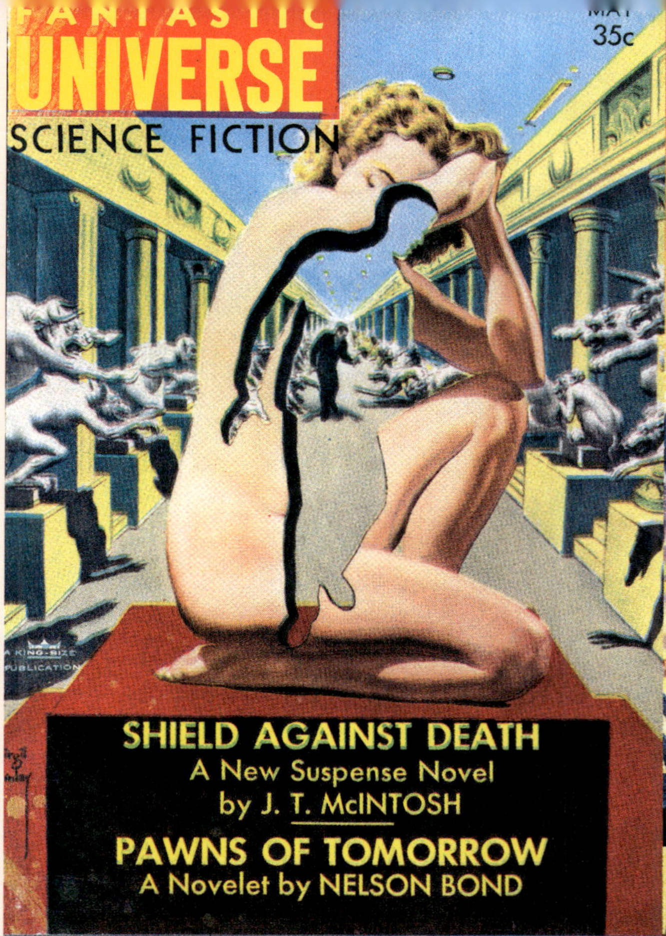
FANTASTIC
UNIVERSE
SCIENCE FICTION
MAY
35c
SHIELD AGAINST DEATH
A New Suspense Novel
by J. T. McINTOSH
PAWNS OF TOMORROW
A Novelet by NELSON BOND

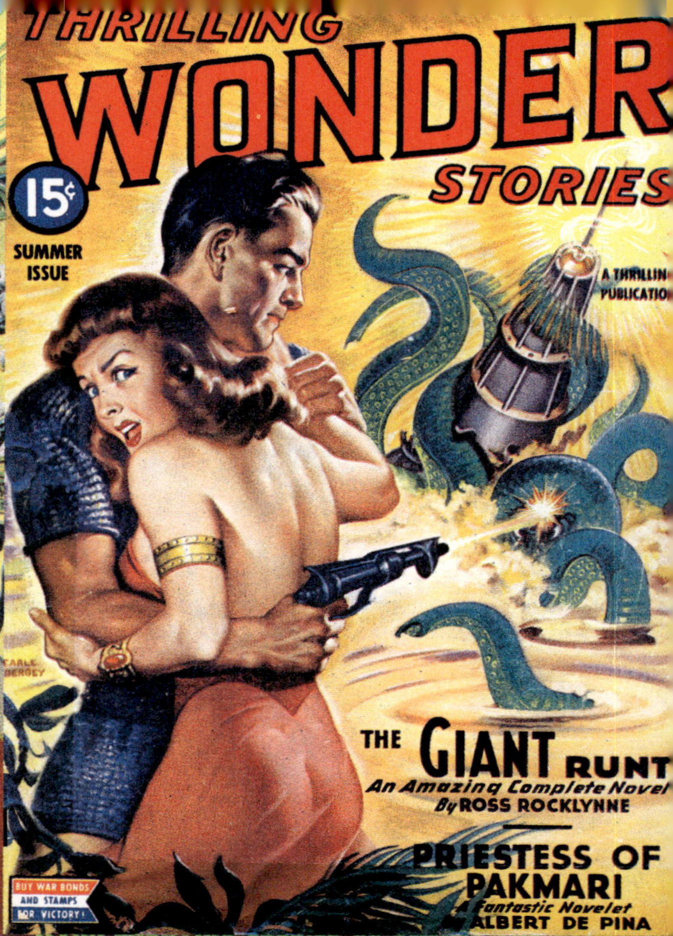
THRILLING
WONDER
STORIES
15¢
SUMMER ISSUE
THE GIANT RUNT
An Amazing Complete Novel
By ROSS ROCKLYNNE
PRIESTESS OF PAKMARI
A Fantastic Novelet
ALBERT DE PINA
BUY WAR BONDS AND STAMPS FOR VICTORY!

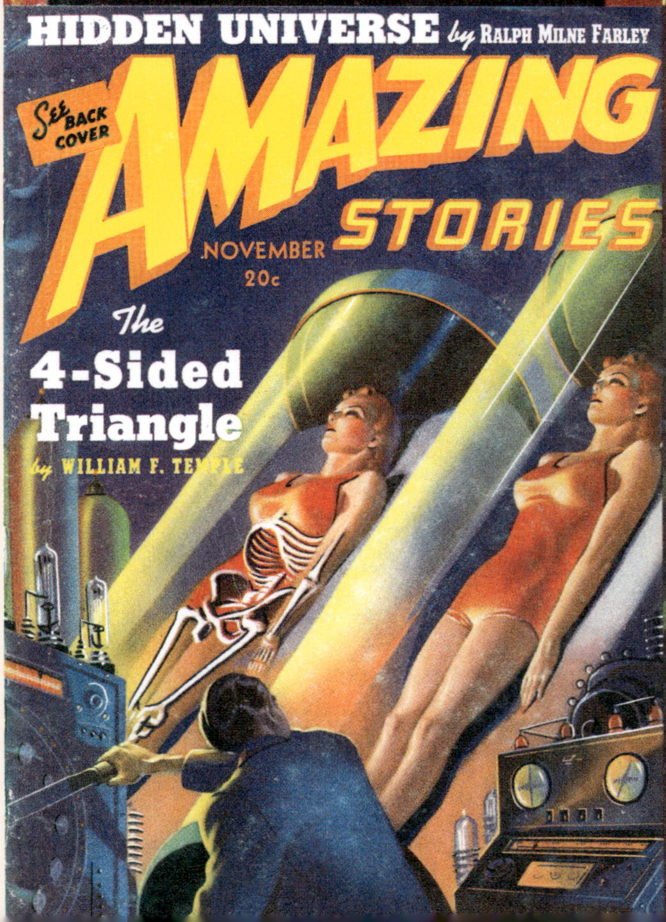
HIDDEN UNIVERSE by RALPH MILNE FARLEY
See BACK COVER
AMAZING
STORIES
NOVEMBER
20c
The
4-Sided
Triangle
by WILLIAM F. TEMPLE

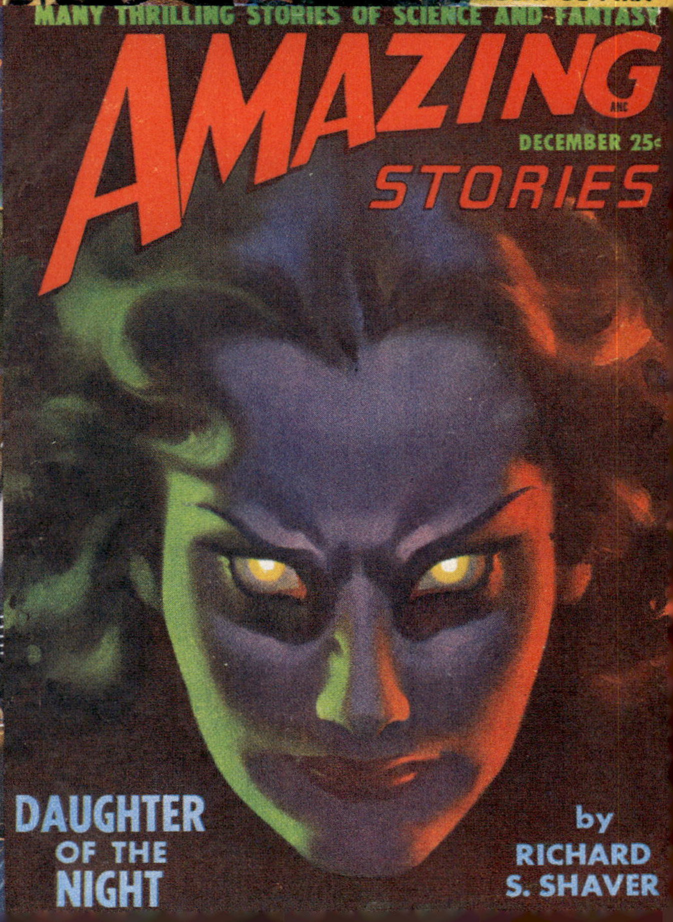
MANY THRILLING STORIES OF SCIENCE AND FANTASY
AMAZING
DECEMBER 25¢
STORIES
DAUGHTER
OF THE
NIGHT
by
RICHARD
S. SHAVER

THE BRITISH REVOLUTION

Where American SF fans have had a steady, if fluctuating, supply of magazines to feed their fascination for the past 80 years, Britain has had neither the variety nor the frequency. While story papers such as *Pearson's* had championed science fiction—primarily future war epics—in the Edwardian period, the genre had fallen out of favor after the Great War, with only sporadic appearances. *Passing Show* was one of the few magazines to feature SF to any great extent in the 1930s.

Instead, fans had to direct their attention to juvenile papers where, for instance, Captain Justice battled robots and megalomaniacs bent on world domination in the pages of *Modern Boy* and *The Boys' Friend Library*. Britain's first dedicated SF magazine was also aimed at boys: *Scoops* was published in 1934, its fiction dominated by more robots and megalomaniacs. It lasted a scant 20 issues.

A fan-base had begun to grow thanks to imported pulps, and it was the energetic SF enthusiast Walter Gillings who persuaded a publisher, World's Work, to issue a science fiction title alongside their "Master Thriller" series of pulps, which had successfully introduced a number of weird and horror issues. *Tales of Wonder* appeared in 1937, a mixture of new and reprint stories, illustrated colorfully by John Nicolson and W. J. Roberts.

The initial success prompted George Newnes to issue *Fantasy*, which lasted only three issues. Gillings returned to the fray in 1946 with a magazine also called *Fantasy*, which again folded after three issues. Far more successful was *New Worlds*, launched by editor Ted Carnell, which *almost* folded, but was rescued by fans. It was to prove the most successful of all British magazines and lasted in one format or another until 1997.

As the post-war paper shortage came to an end in 1950, a new, mostly juvenile, boost came to SF through the comic *Eagle* and its front-page hero, Dan Dare. More juvenilia could be found in the pages of *Futuristic Science Stories*, *Tales of the Spaceways*, and other interchangeable paperback magazines published by John Spencer, with their colorful—although naïve—covers by Gerald Facey (1919-1999) and Norman Light (1920-2000). Vargo Statten led a boom in paperbacks for a few years with richly inventive covers by Ron Turner (1922-1998), the best of the artists working in SF, and himself a comic strip artist (*Rick Random—Space Detective*, *Space Ace*).

Not that the 1950s were wholly juvenile: *New Worlds* developed the talents of Gerard Quinn (1927-), Terry Mahoney (1917-2008), and Brian Lewis (1929-1978), while *Authentic Science Fiction* featured the artwork of John Richards, later the art director of Corgi Books. With the addition of *Science-Fantasy* in 1950 and *Nebula* in 1952, Britain had, for the first time, a group of magazines that were treating science fiction seriously and where artistic talent could also be nurtured.

▶ **Brian Lewis (*New Worlds*) and John Richards (*Authentic*) brought a new sophistication to British SF magazines that reflected the quality of the stories inside.**

▶ **Colorful images of space battles dominated many paperbacks in the early 1950s. Publishers with little taste for quality over quantity brought the same attitude to cover art. Gerald Facey's naïve, juvenile images (*Worlds of Fantasy*) were published alongside the action-packed work of Norman Light (*Tales of Tomorrow*) and the genuinely imaginative art of Ron Turner (*Wonders of the Spaceways*).**

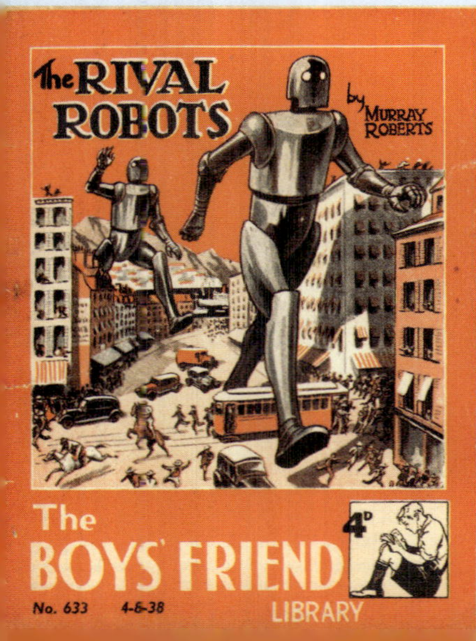

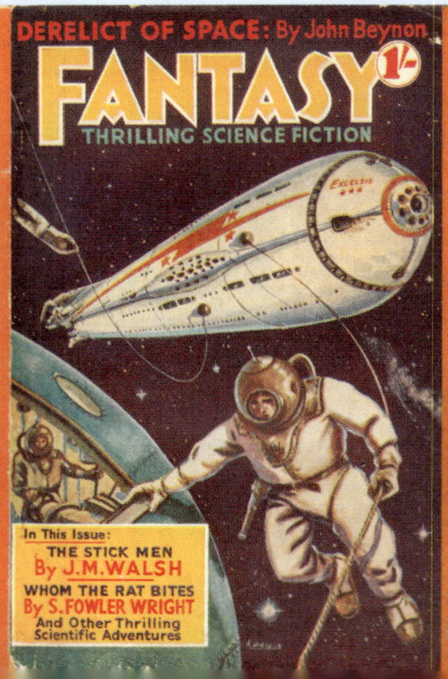

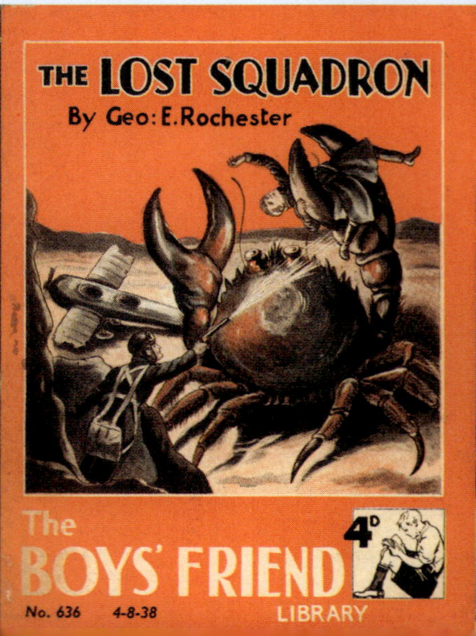

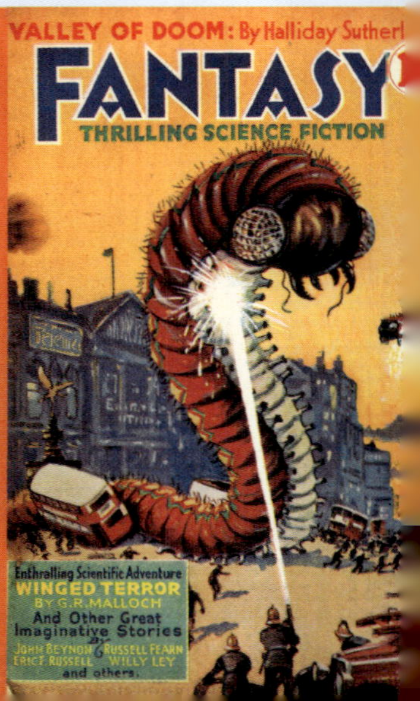

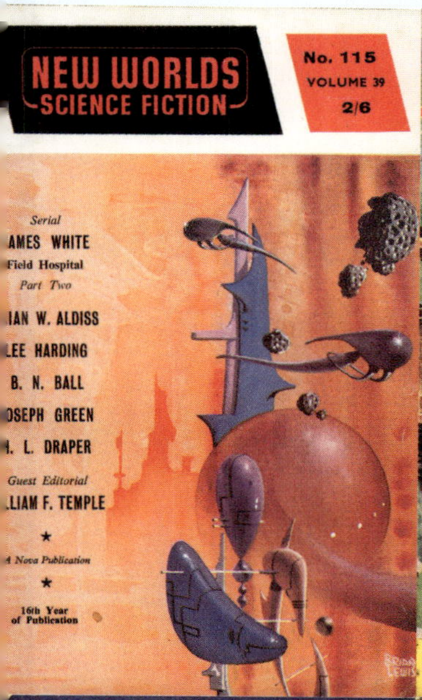

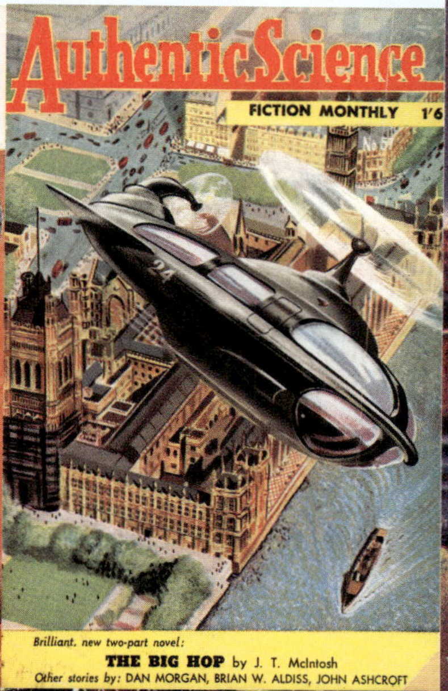

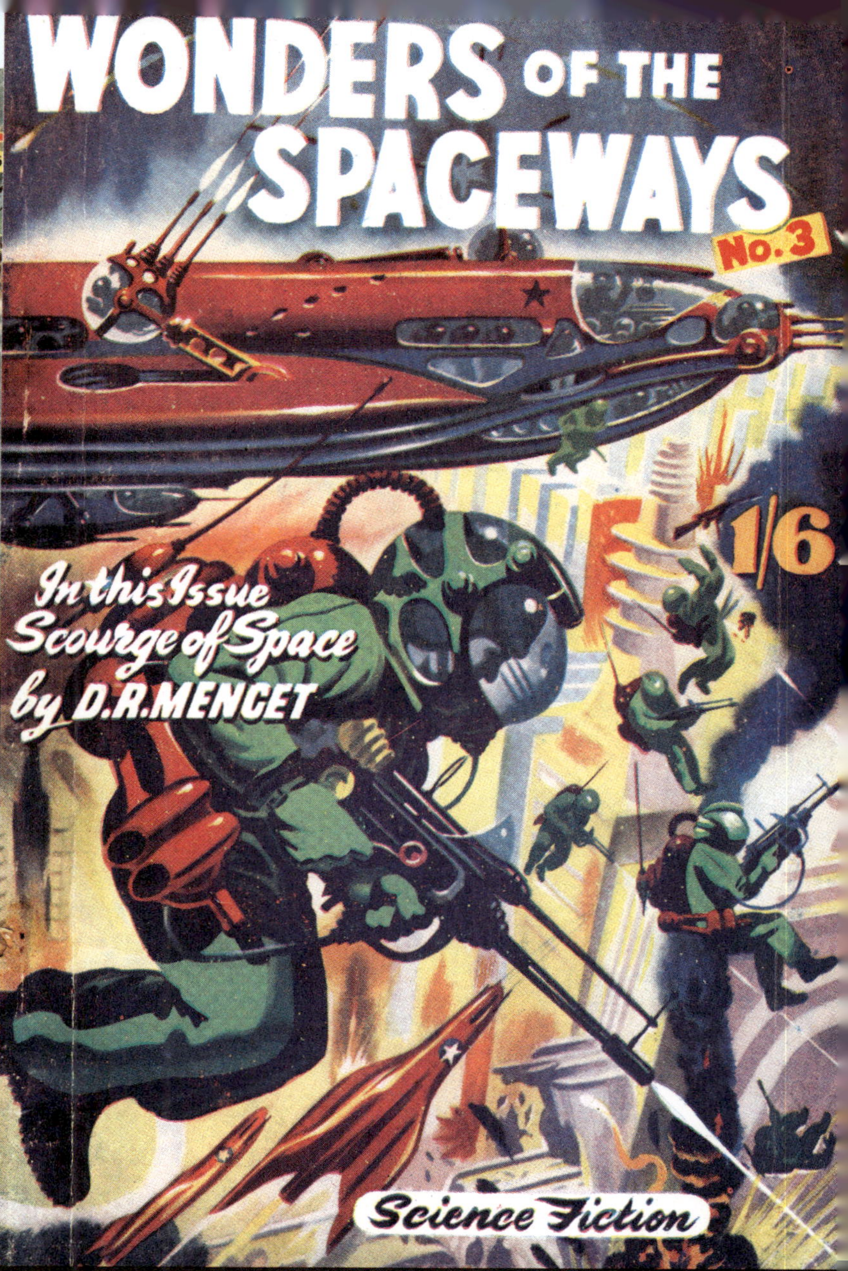

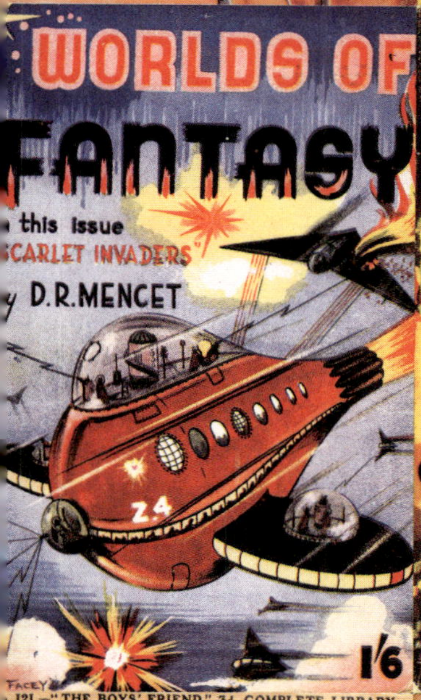

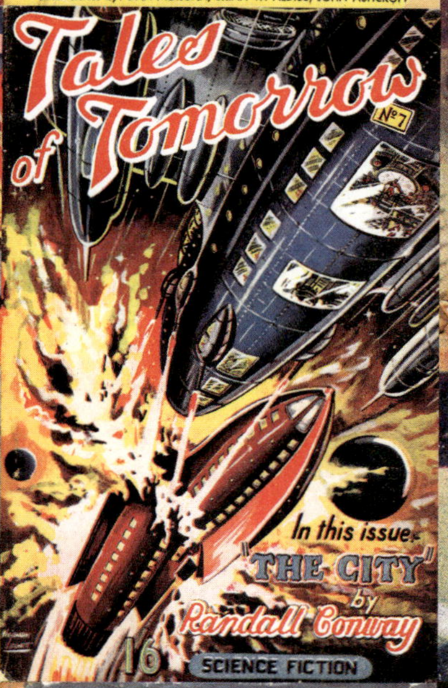

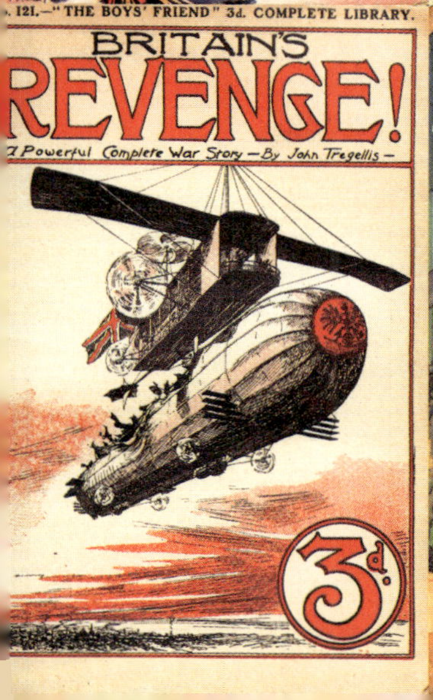

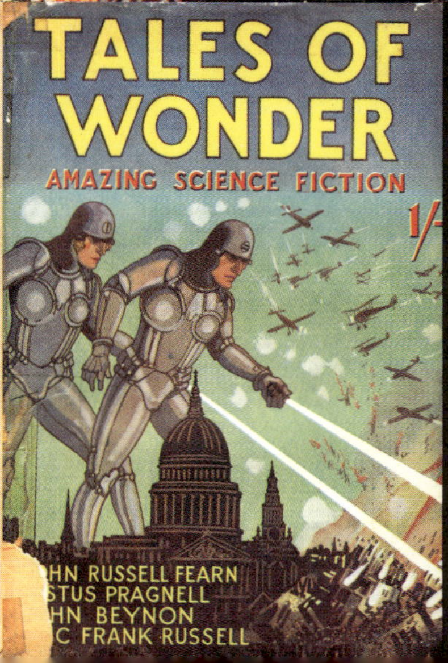

◄ *The Boys' Friend Library* reflected the main themes of juvenile SF: future war (*Britain's Revenge*, 1910), giant monsters (*The Lost Squadron*, 1938), and technology gone bad (*The Rival Robots*, 1938). The same themes dominated early British pulps, albeit treated a little more seriously, as can be seen in the covers for *Tales of Wonder* (issue #1, John Nicolson) and *Fantasy* (#2 and #3, Serge Drigin).

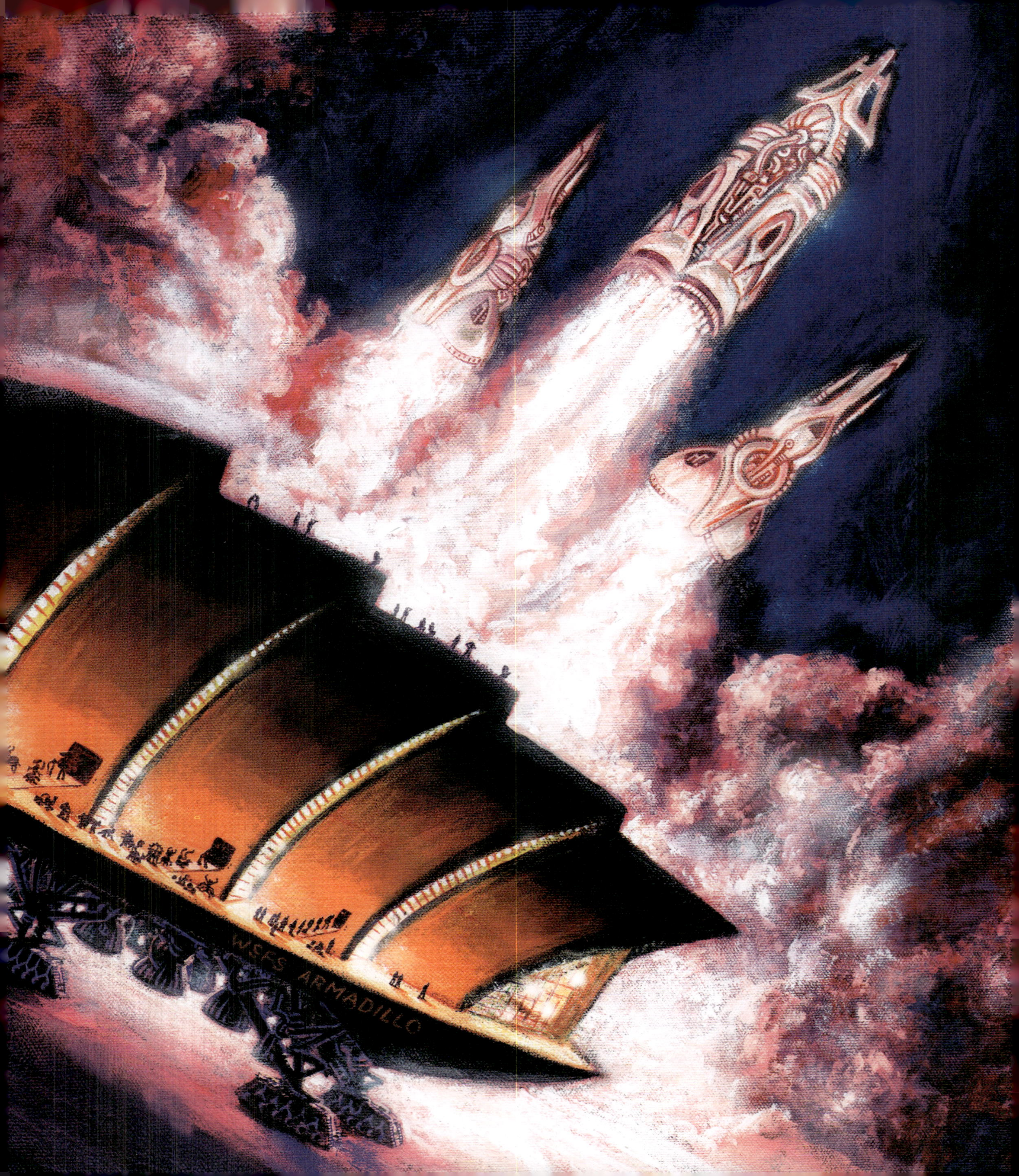
WSFS ARMADILLO

2 BOOK COVERS & MAGAZINES

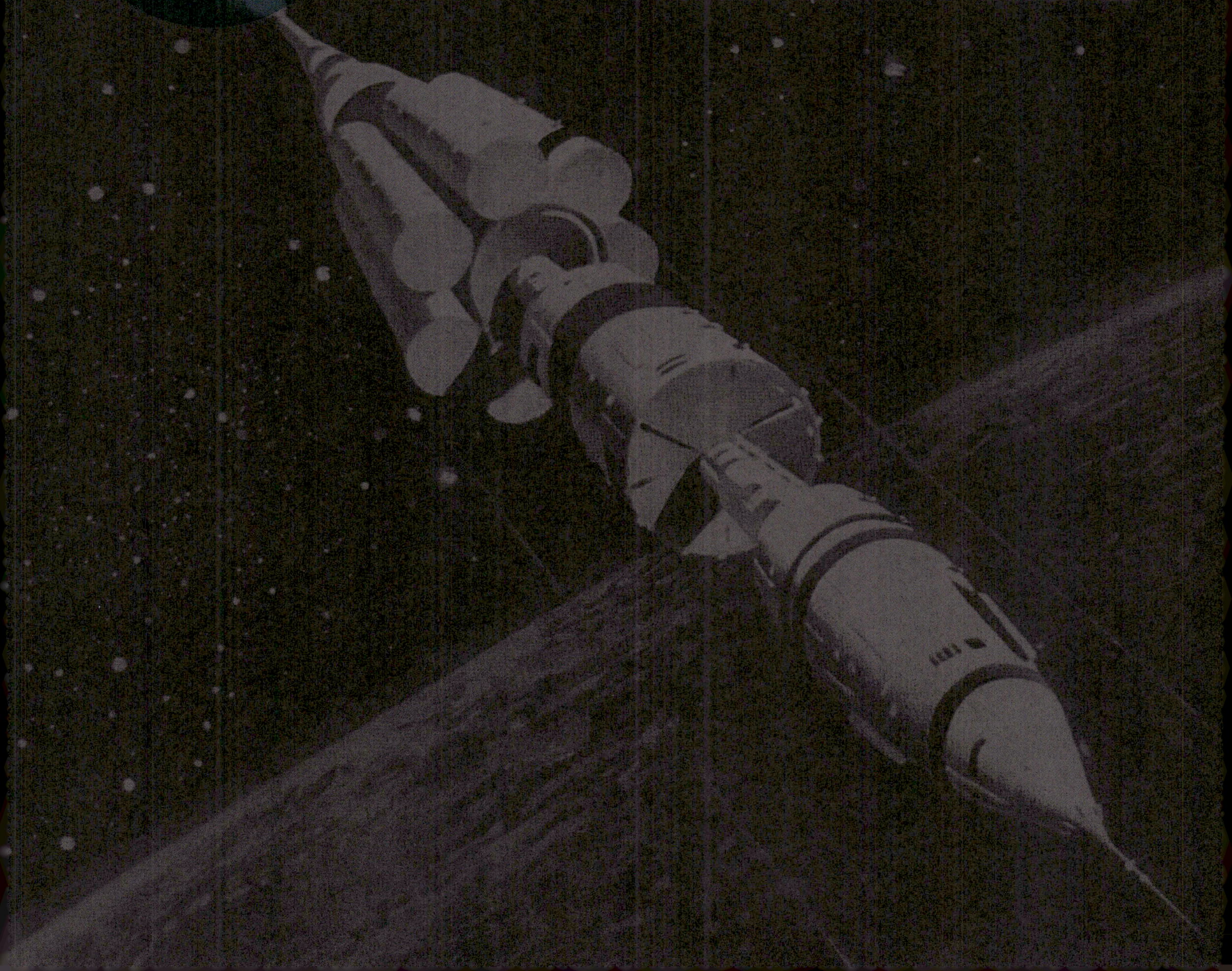

THE NEW AGE OF SF ILLUSTRATIONS

The rise in popularity of paperbacks and digest-sized (named after *Reader's Digest*) magazines on the newsstands marked a new era for science fiction. Titles like *Thrilling Wonder Stories*, *Startling Stories*, and *Planet Stories* were able to cling on until 1955. *Astounding* had shrunk to digest size in 1943; *Amazing* followed in 1953.

Among the late arrivals in the dying days of the pulps were *Other Worlds* and *Imagination*, which benefited from some delightful artwork by Hannes Bok (Wayne Woodward, 1914–1964), an occasional although steady contributor to SF pulps in the 1940s, notably *Weird Tales*. The influence of Maxfield Parrish can be seen in the intricate, angular design of his black and white work and vibrantly colored covers.

Bok was one of the mainstays of the specialist publishing houses that were beginning to spring up, most notably Arkham House (founded in 1939), Fantasy Press (1946), Shasta Publishers (1947), and Gnome Press (1948). Often fan-backed, they reissued the best of SF in hardcover, bringing classics-to-be by E. E. Smith, Jack Williamson, A. E. Van Vogt, Robert Heinlein, Eric Frank Russell, L. Sprague de Camp, Isaac Asimov, and Henry Kuttner to a new audience, with A. J. Donnell, Ric Binkley, and Edd Cartier (1914–) among the suppliers of early jackets and chapter heading illustrations. Cartier was already well established as an adventure artist, with more than 800 illustrations for *The Shadow* alone, but came to the fore as a humorous fantasy artist in *Unknown Worlds* in the 1940s, his illustrations at once whimsical and menacing. "Cartier's outlandish full-color illustrations for the 1951 Gnome Press edition of *Travelers of Space* were especially influential during the great SF movie boom of the 1950s," remarked artist Vincent Di Fate.

Alex Schomburg (1905-1998) debuted in *Thrilling Wonder* in the 1930s, and his last SF cover appeared in 1993. His dozens of magazine covers in the 1950s and 1960s featured some of the best SF hardware of the era, his airbrushed spaceships predating the vogue for such things by many years.

The first two major digest SF magazines were *The Magazine of Fantasy & Science Fiction* (1949) and *Galaxy* (1952). The former was notably more sedate in its approach than earlier magazines. Early covers were an odd mix of surrealistic images by George Salter (c.1897-1967) and realistic space scenes by Chesley Bonestell; space won out over the next few years with covers by George Gibbons, Jack Coggins (1911-2006), Fred Kirberger, and Nicholas Solovioff (1927-1994), ably backing up Ed Emshwiller, the magazine's most prolific artist. *F&SF* (as it was usually abbreviated to) introduced an innovative series of wraparound covers in 1952.

Galaxy shared many of the same artists; Mel Hunter (1927-2004) debuted in *Galaxy* but was equally at home on *F&SF* and paperbacks. Hunter is probably best known for a series of bittersweet images of a lonely robot in usually desolate landscapes that featured on *F&SF* for many years. *Galaxy* could also boast the magazine cover debuts of Ed Emshwiller, Jack Coggins (1911-2006), John Pederson Jr., and EC Comics star Wallace "Wally" Wood (1927-1981).

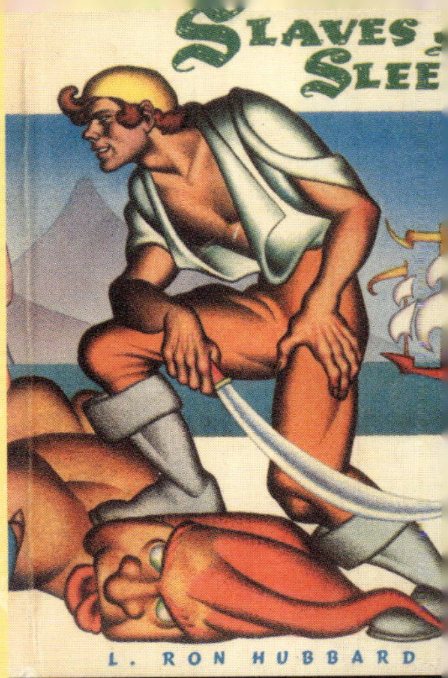

▶ ▲
Hannes Bok—born Wayne Woodward—was uncompromising in his work: the colors were vibrant, the girls elfin and beautiful, and the results were some of the finest fantastic imagery to be found in the 1950s.

▶▶ ▶▼
The early years of *The Magazine of Fantasy & Science Fiction* were enlivened by the colorful surrealism of George Salter and the realistic space images of Chesley Bonestell.

▶
Sympathetic robots were already around—Lester del Rey's *Helen O'Loy* and Eric Frank Russell's *Jay Score* spring to mind—but Mel Hunter was able to encapsulate the sub-genre in a series of covers for *F&SF*. Whether he was reading catalogs, watering a rose, visiting an art exhibition, or watching a slowly setting planet, there was something inherently sad and lonely about the actions of Hunter's spindly robot.

▶▶
Edd Cartier produced only a handful of color illustrations for SF magazines and books, but their strength—often coupled with humor—have made them his best known work. This dark, brooding cover from *Unknown* (April 1940) harkens back to his work on *The Shadow*.

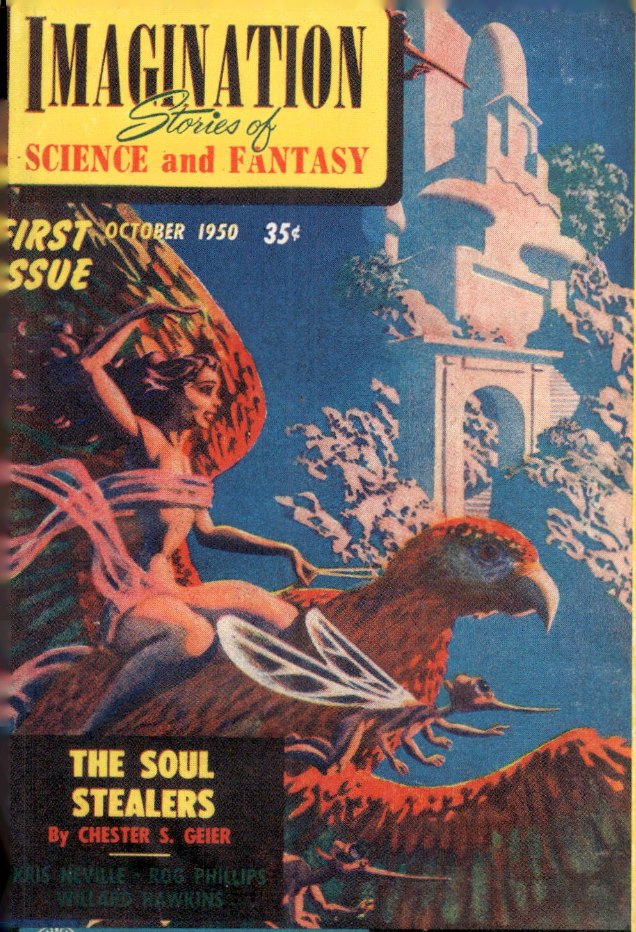
IMAGINATION
Stories of
SCIENCE and FANTASY
FIRST ISSUE
OCTOBER 1950
35¢
THE SOUL STEALERS
By CHESTER S. GEIER

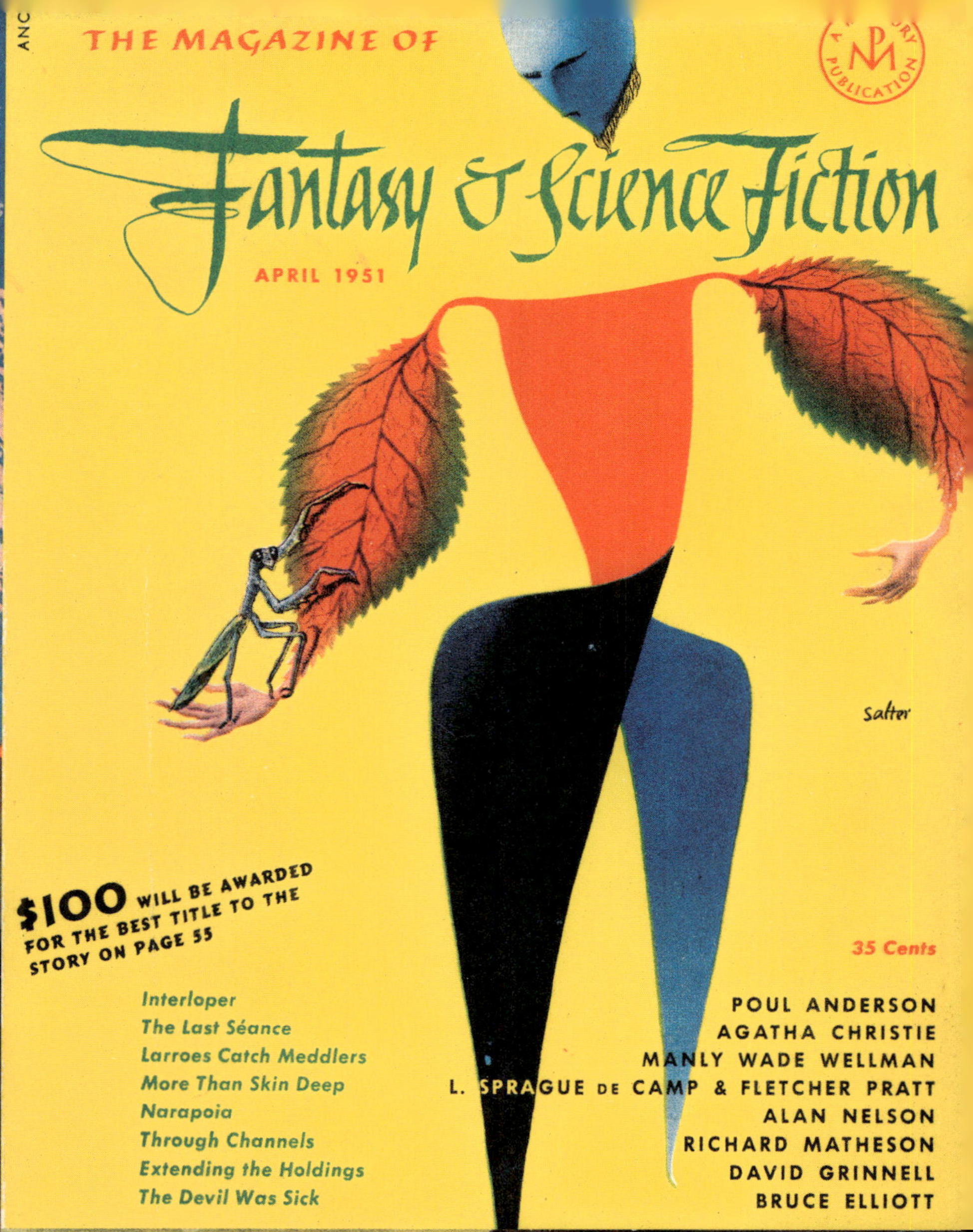
THE MAGAZINE OF
Fantasy & Science Fiction
APRIL 1951
Salter
$100 WILL BE AWARDED FOR THE BEST TITLE TO THE STORY ON PAGE 55
35 Cents
Interloper
The Last Séance
Larroes Catch Meddlers
More Than Skin Deep
Narapoia
Through Channels
Extending the Holdings
The Devil Was Sick
POUL ANDERSON
AGATHA CHRISTIE
MANLY WADE WELLMAN
L. SPRAGUE DE CAMP & FLETCHER PRATT
ALAN NELSON
RICHARD MATHESON
DAVID GRINNELL
BRUCE ELLIOTT

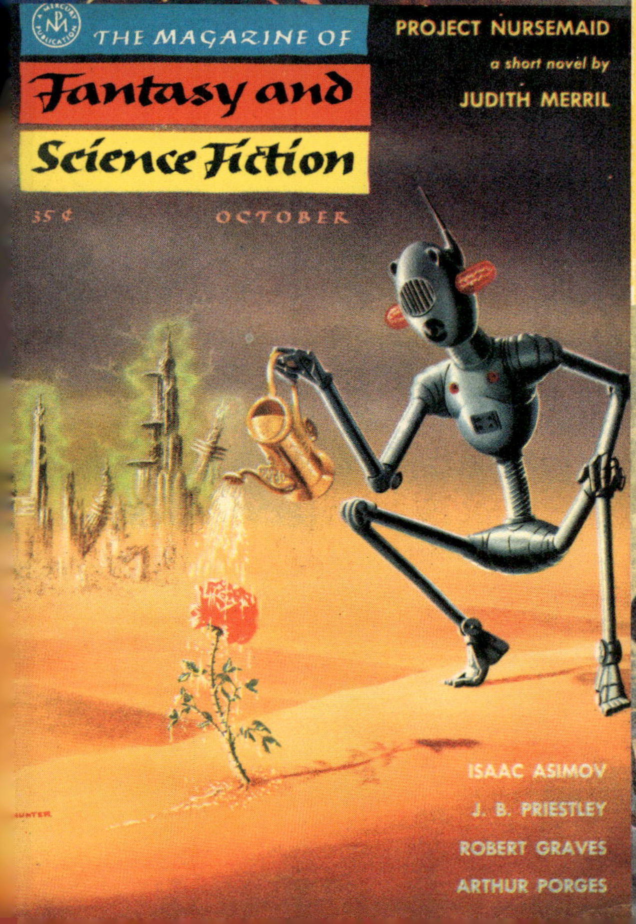
THE MAGAZINE OF
Fantasy and
Science Fiction
35¢
OCTOBER
PROJECT NURSEMAID
a short novel by
JUDITH MERRIL
ISAAC ASIMOV
J. B. PRIESTLEY
ROBERT GRAVES
ARTHUR PORGES

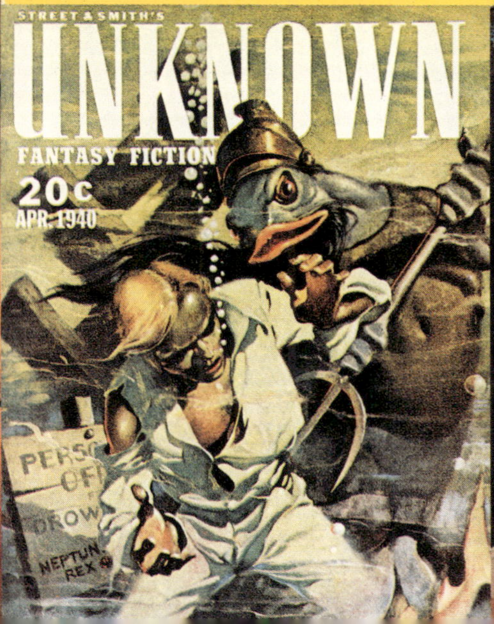
STREET & SMITH'S
UNKNOWN
FANTASY FICTION
20c
APR. 1940

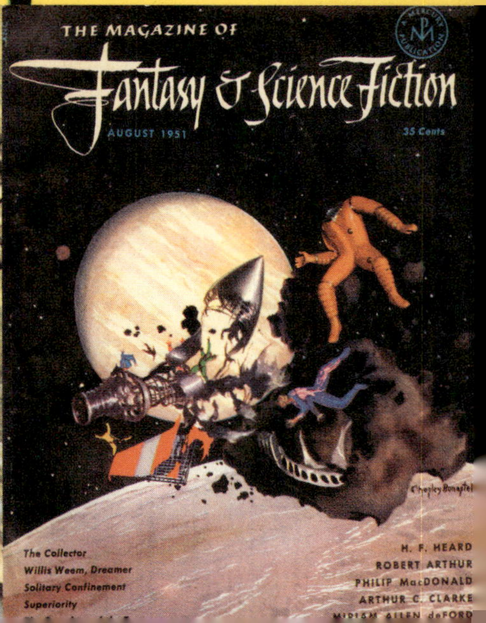
THE MAGAZINE OF
Fantasy & Science Fiction
AUGUST 1951
35 Cents
The Collector
Willis Weem, Dreamer
Solitary Confinement
Superiority
H. F. HEARD
ROBERT ARTHUR
PHILIP MacDONALD
ARTHUR C. CLARKE

FRANK KELLY FREAS

From the appearance of his first cover (*Weird Tales*, November 1950), Frank Kelly Freas enriched the covers of hundreds of magazines and books, producing some of science fiction's most iconic images along the way. His first cover for *Astounding Science Fiction*, illustrating a story about the limits of artificial intelligence, was of a pleading, childlike robot, stripped of all mechanical clutter, holding out the dead body of a man in his palm. Another cover (*Astounding*, March 1954) was of an outstretched plain on which discarded toys (a building block, a cowboy gun, a baseball) drew the eye towards a spaceship on the horizon and a distant star in the dark skies above it. Freas' ability to condense even the biggest themes into a single, stunning, often humorous image was recognized from the start by fans, who rewarded him with 11 Hugo Awards and three Chesley Awards, among many other lifetime accolades.

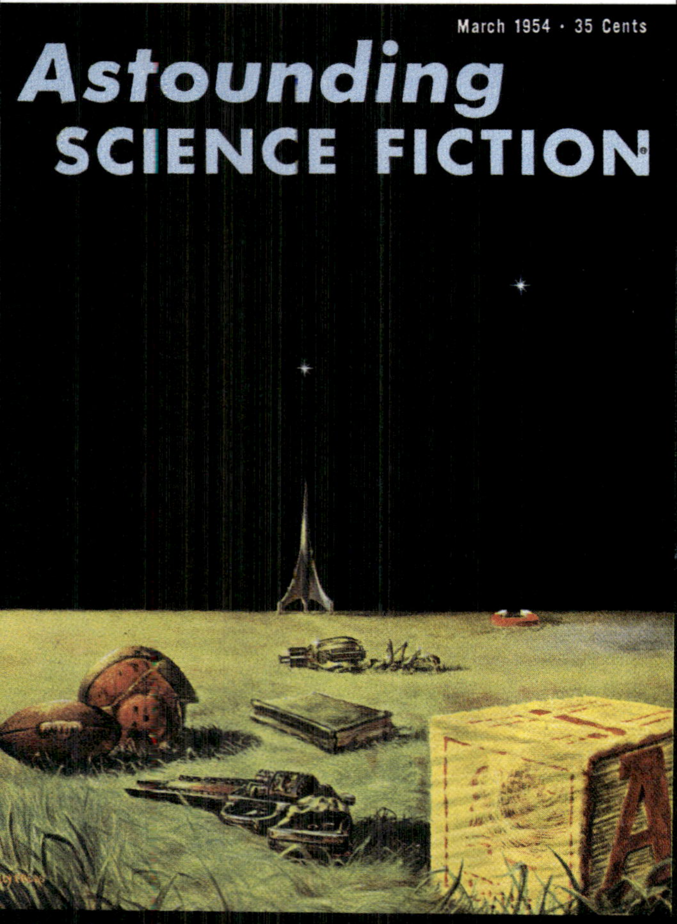

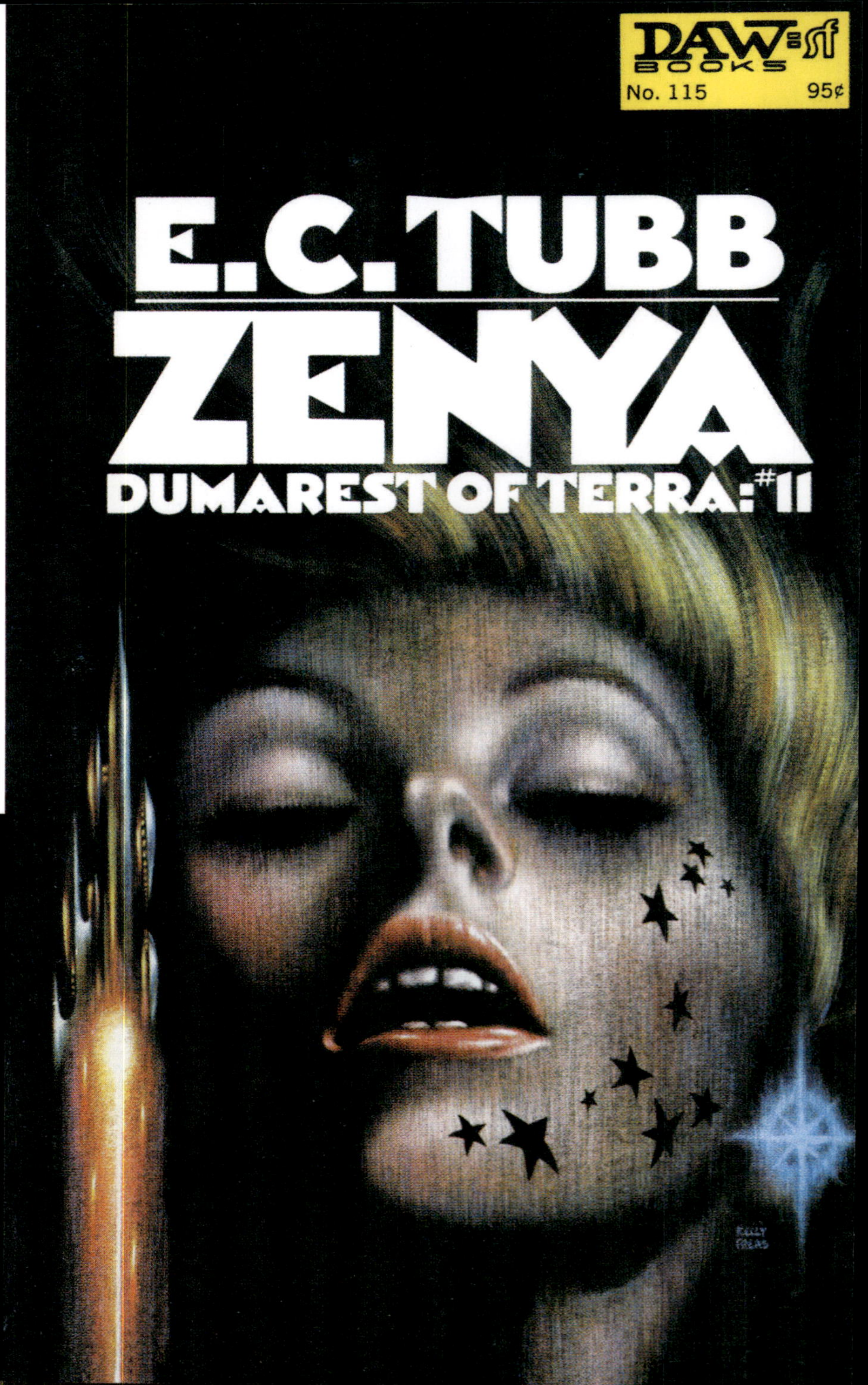

▲ Trying to capture the sense of both reality and illusion, Freas noted that this was one of his most satisfying cover illustrations. E. C. Tubb's *Dumarest* novels—about the hero's search for his lost home world—were each named after a woman who was symbolic of his quest.

▶
An iconic image by Freas for Tom Godwin's debut story, *The Gulf Between*. A quarter of a century after its first appearance, Freas' robot was used as the album cover for Queen's *News of the World*, with the band in the place of the body.

◀◀▼
Freas eschewed the "rockets and ray guns" stereotype, preferring an image that was representational of the heart of the story. As he would later say: "One of the things I brought to science fiction art was people. Not always well-painted, but still real, understandable, believable *people*, whether they were rock-jawed, bristle-headed Terran topkicks or blue-furred aliens with three eyes and a prehensile tail. The approach was never well-received by the gizmo-and-gadget set, who simply could not understand that what made Asimov, Heinlein, Clarke, Anderson, et al, *great*, was *not* their cosmological expertise or their technical ingenuity, but their ability to communicate with intensity, sensitivity and sympathetic understanding the reaction of human beings to technological, cosmological, or even xenobiological (I *love* that word) pressures."

▶
Freas in a more playful mood was always a delight. *The Magazine of Fantasy and Science Fiction* occasionally published a special issue dedicated to an author. The issue dedicated to Harlan Ellison contained his award winning *Jeffty is Five*, but Freas chose to illustrate the humorous *Working with the Little People*, in action helping Harlan write his latest tale.

Nicknamed "the dean of science fiction art," Freas (1922-2005), the son of two photographers, was born in New York but spent much of his childhood in Canada. After toying with medicine or engineering as a career he settled on art, graduating in 1951 from the Art Institute of Pittsburgh.

At the suggestion of a fellow student, he submitted one classroom assignment, a picture of Pan dancing in the moonlight, to the editor of *Weird Tales*, his first professional sale. This was quickly followed by sales to *Astounding*, *Planet Stories*, *Fantastic Universe*, *The Magazine of Fantasy & Science Fiction*, and others. His work illustrated the best talents of the day, including Isaac Asimov, Arthur C. Clarke, Clifford Simak, Poul Anderson, John Brunner, and many more. Some of his most famous images were created for Algis Budrys' *Who?* (Lancer, 1968), E. C. Tubb's *Zenya* (DAW, 1974), and Robert Heinlein's *The Green Hills of Earth* (Caedmon Records, 1977). His versatility can be seen on the 111 covers he produced for *Astounding SF/Analog* and 57 covers for the Laser Books SF line published by Harlequin Enterprises between 1975 and 1977.

Beyond SF, Freas' sense of humor was best seen in his four years as cover artist for *Mad Magazine* (1958-62), depicting the impish, gap-toothed Alfred E. Neuman. He was also a NASA artist, designing the Skylab 1 shoulder patch and producing posters for the Agency, the first to be hung in the Smithsonian Institution. He was elected a Fellow of the International Association of Astronomical Artists in 2000. A Freas painting of a werewolf can be seen in the movie *Harry Potter and the Prisoner of Azkaban* (2003).

Some of his best work was collected in the volumes *Frank Kelly Freas: The Art of Science Fiction* (1977), and *Frank Kelly Freas: As He Sees It* (2000)).

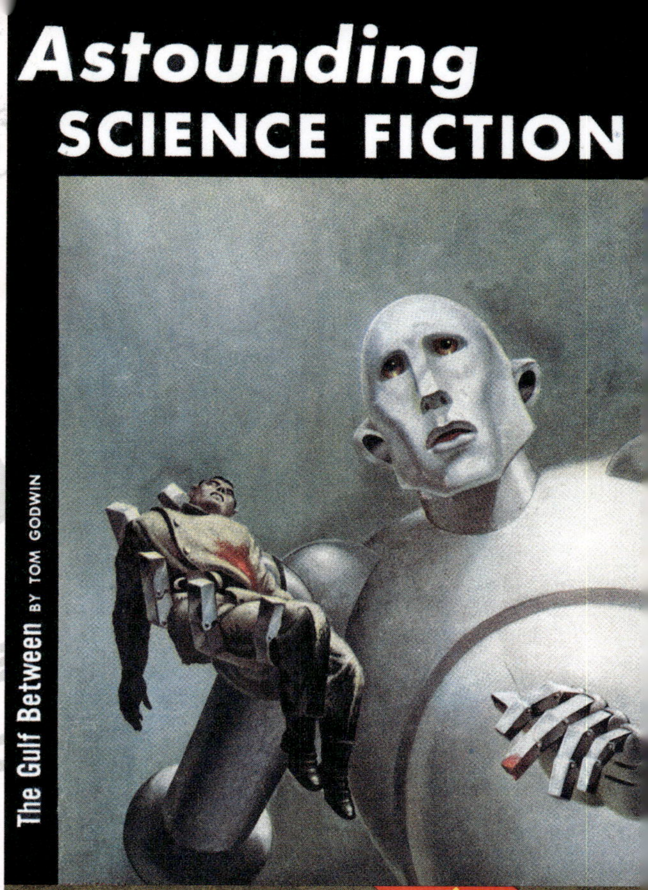

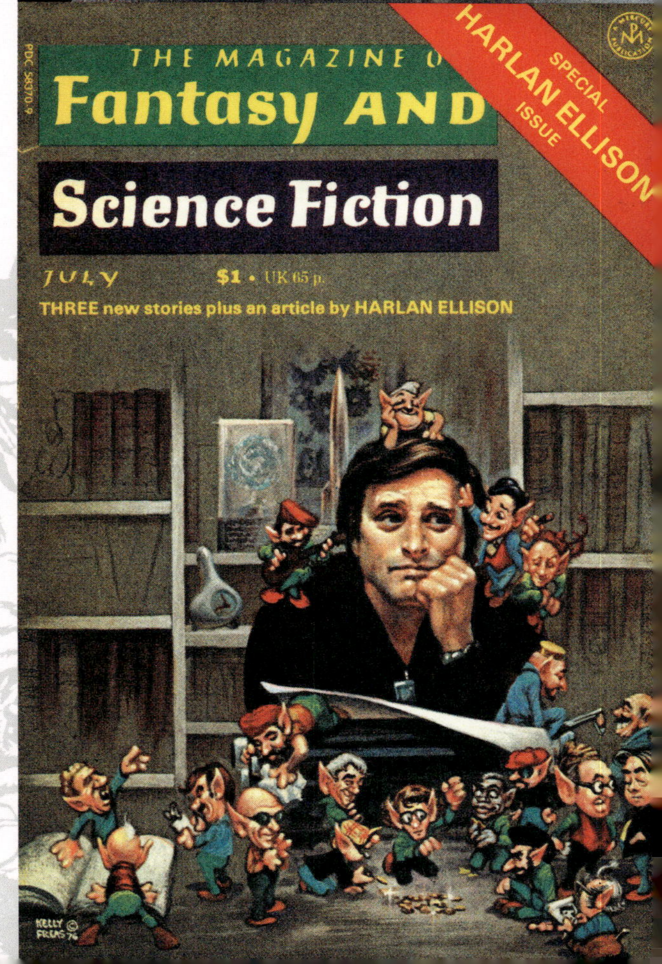

EVOLUTION TO REVOLUTION

The rise of paperbacks began to gather steam in the late 1930s, following the successful launch of Penguin Books in the UK in 1936. Pocket Books, Avon Books, Popular Library, and Dell Books became the first successful mass-market paperback publishers to spring up shortly before America joined the Second World War. As wartime paper shortages began to ease, they were joined by Bantam Books, New American Library/Signet, Pyramid Books, Gold Medal, Permabooks, Ballantine, and Ace, so that, by 1952, most of the pre-war pulp magazines had been swept from the newsstands.

Initially, the paperback companies had no dedicated artists for science fiction, although former pulp artist Earle Bergey did some covers for Pocket Books and Popular Library, and Virgil Finlay painted covers for Pyramid. Dell published their first title, a reprint of *The First Men in the Moon* by H. G. Wells, as part of their famous "map book" series with a cover by Earl Sherwan; Dell regulars Gerald Gregg and Robert Stanley took on science fiction as they would a crime or historical novel; *Esquire* pin-up artist Mike Ludlow (1921–) was drafted in for de Camp's *Rogue Queen*; and London-born Griffith Foxley (1912-1964) provided the cover for their first paperback original, *Madball* by Fredric Brown. However, it wasn't until the arrival in 1954 of Richard Powers that SF paperbacks found their first star.

Although Avon could boast publishing the first all-new anthology (Don Wollheim's *The Girl With the Hungry Eyes*, 1949, with a cover by Ann Cantor) and a dedicated line of novels (the very brief Avon Fantasy Novels series), they could boast no regular artist. Everett Kinstler (1926–) and Art Sussman (1927-2008) provided occasional covers until Richard Powers became their main artist from 1956.

Other artists associated with early SF paperbacks included Herman E. Bischoff, Charles Binger, Mitchell Hooks (1923–), Barye Phillips (1905-1968), Robert Schulz (1928-1978), Robert V. Engle (c.1923-1989), Victor Kalin (1919-1991), and Stan Meltzoff (1917-2006).

For the most part these artists were not solely associated with science fiction. Only a handful produced SF regularly; Art Sussman, for instance, worked for Avon, Permabooks, Pyramid, and Dell, and

Paul Lehr (1930-1998) worked for Bantam, Crest, Gold Medal, and Dell, becoming one of the main SF artists for Signet around 1959-1960, where he produced covers for novels by Robert A. Heinlein, Arthur C. Clarke, and Brian Aldiss. Artist Bob Eggleton described his work as "the true embodiment of SF 'art' and not just 'illustration' as his incomparable work allowed the viewer to return for multiple times and walk away having been told a new story each instance."

▼
During the 1960s, Paul Lehr took over for Richard Powers as the foremost science fiction paperback cover artist in the US. The cover for Robert A. Heinlein's *Door Into Summer* (Signet, 1959) is a fine example of his early, naturalistic style. In later years he developed a looser, less figurative and more colorful approach to covers.

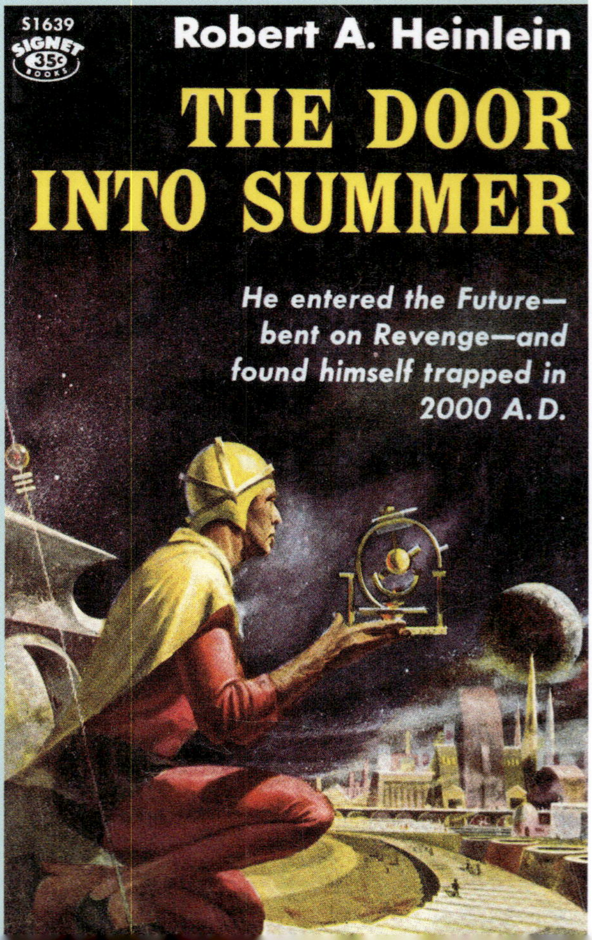

▶
Charles Binger's 1955 cover for *Takeoff*—a near-future thriller about the building of the first Moon rocket by C. M. Kornbluth—could almost be mistaken for a conventional wartime adventure, probably a deliberate choice by a publisher uncertain whether science fiction would sell.

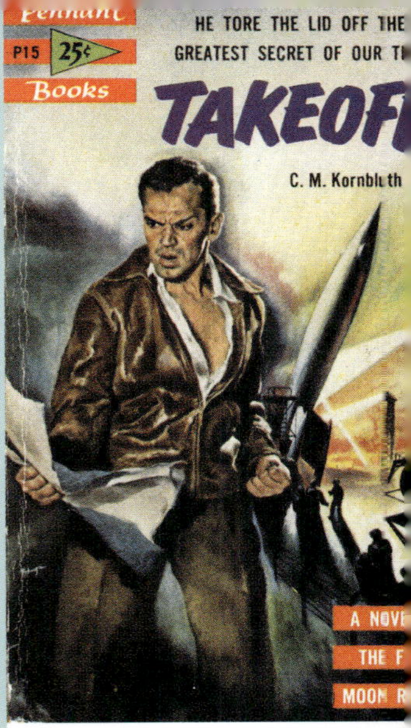

▶
The striking cover for Dell's paperback edition of L. Sprague de Camp's *Rogue Queen* (1952) is by Mike Ludlow, who famously drew the three-page centerfold pin-ups for *Esquire* in the 1950s and was a well-respected female figure artist with illustrations appearing in *The Saturday Evening Post*, *Good Housekeeping*, *Collier's*, and other major magazines.

▶
As well as being one of the first established mass market paperback publishers in America, Avon Books also produced the first dedicated line of science fiction paperbacks: Avon Fantasy Novels. It lasted only two numbers in 1950, but the first featured a fabulous, if anonymous, cover for Ray Cummings' *The Princess of the Atom*.

▶▶
Stanley Meltzoff was a near-legendary paperback cover artist working for Signet, Gold Medal, and others in the 1950s. Although his output of SF covers was small, his influence was extensive, either directly—both Paul Lehr and John Schoenherr studied under him at the Pratt Institute—or simply from the impact his work had, as with Gold Medal's 1954 paperback original edition of *I Am Legend*.

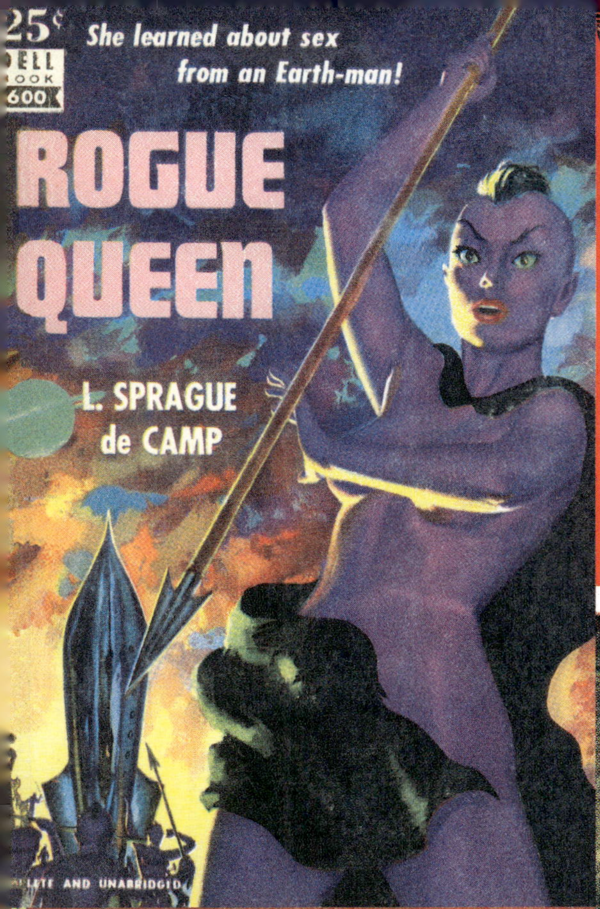
25¢
She learned about sex from an Earth-man!
ROGUE QUEEN
L. SPRAGUE de CAMP

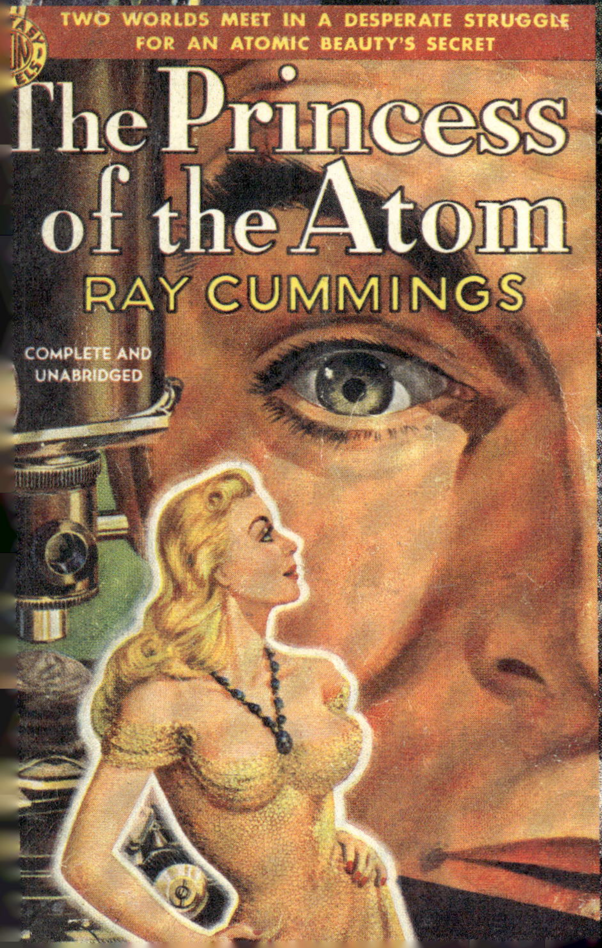
TWO WORLDS MEET IN A DESPERATE STRUGGLE FOR AN ATOMIC BEAUTY'S SECRET
The Princess of the Atom
RAY CUMMINGS
COMPLETE AND UNABRIDGED

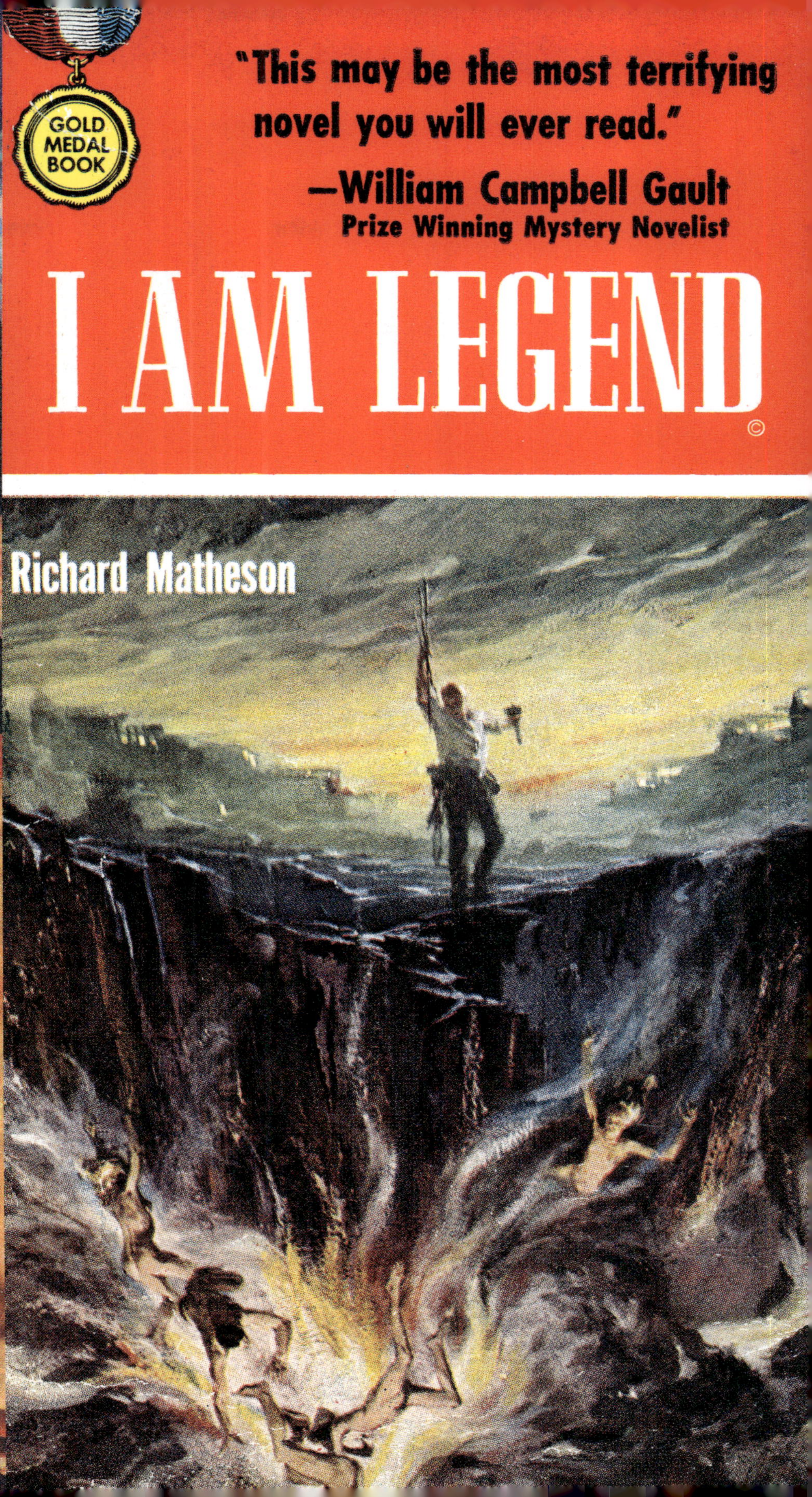
GOLD MEDAL BOOK
"This may be the most terrifying novel you will ever read."
—William Campbell Gault
Prize Winning Mystery Novelist
I AM LEGEND
©
Richard Matheson

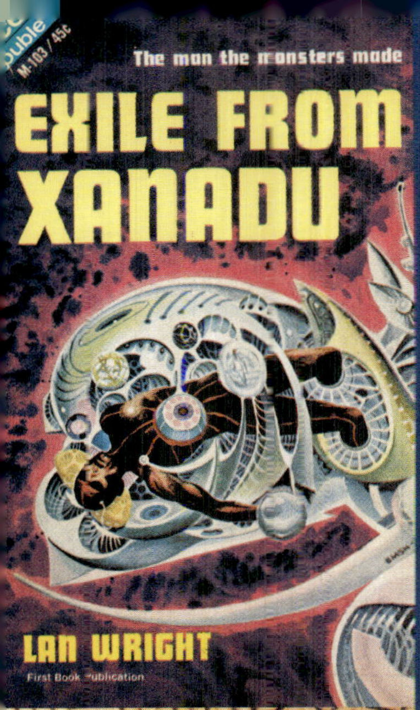
The man the monsters made
EXILE FROM XANADU
LAN WRIGHT
First Book Publication

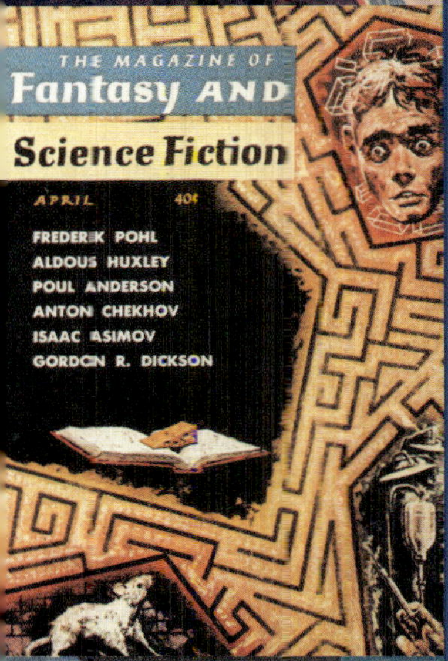
THE MAGAZINE OF
Fantasy AND
Science Fiction
APRIL
40¢
FREDERIK POHL
ALDOUS HUXLEY
POUL ANDERSON
ANTON CHEKHOV
ISAAC ASIMOV
GORDON R. DICKSON

SAMUEL R. DELANY
THE EINSTEIN INTERSECTION
"Delany is bringing new and vigorous life to science fiction."
— ANALOG

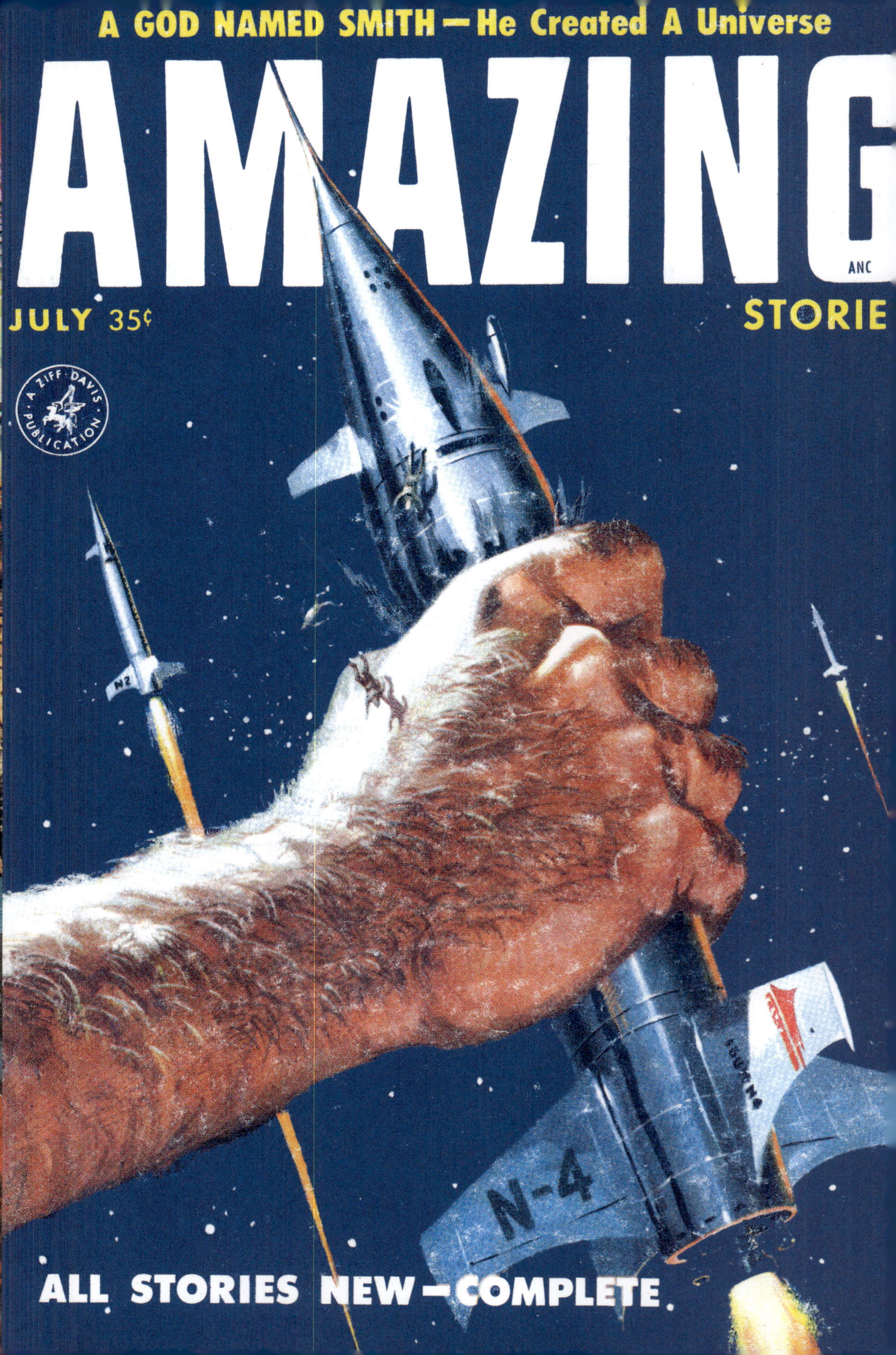
A GOD NAMED SMITH—He Created A Universe
AMAZING
JULY 35¢
A ZIFF-DAVIS PUBLICATION
N2
N-4
ALL STORIES NEW—COMPLETE

◀
Ed Valigursky was comfortable with both figurative and gadget paintings for SF magazines and paperbacks. He could also turn out the occasional—often startling—representational image, like this cover for *Amazing Stories* (July 1957).

◀◀
Ed Emsh often mixed the real and the surreal. The machinery may be overly complex and abstract but it is drawn meticulously, giving it a realism that menaces the also realistically drawn human figure trapped inside.

◀◀
For *The Magazine of Fantasy and Science Fiction* (April 1959), Emsh took a number of elements—a rat, a book, cheese, a syringe—to create a cover based on Daniel Keyes' famous, award-winning *Flowers for Algernon*. The maze allows the rat to reach the drugs and the cheese, but Daniel has no visible way of reaching anything.

One of the most popular innovations of paperbacks was the Ace Double, two novels packaged back-to-back. Ace Books was launched in 1952 by former pulp publisher A. A. Wyn and was responsible for publishing more SF than any other paperback firm in the 1950s and 1960s. The dos-a-dos format also meant two covers, but it was some time before Ace established a regular team of artists. Early titles could boast work by Paul Orban and Ed Valigursky (1926-), the latter responsible for many covers for *Amazing* and *Fantastic* in the 1950s before he switched almost exclusively to paperbacks. Best known for his spaceships and technical hardware, Valigursky was later art editor of *If* magazine and went on to produce covers for *Popular Science* and *Popular Mechanics*.

The artist most associated with Ace Books was "Emsh," the abbreviated signature of Edmund Alexander Emshwiller (1925-1990). After studying at the University of Michigan, he enrolled at the École Nationale Supérieux des Beaux-Arts, Paris, for a year before returning to New York to paint abstract expressionist art and take classes at the Art Students League. After the appearance of his first SF cover, for *Galaxy* (June 1951), he went on to dominate that magazine, producing 33 covers in 1951-1956; he was the main cover artist for *F&SF* in 1958-1964 (49 covers); and, from 1956, produced hundreds of paperback covers for Ace.

Emsh was adept at dramatic realism and surrealistic images, and often juxtaposed realistic figures with abstract elements. It was a potent mixture that earned Emshwiller a strong following and, when fans created the Hugo Award in 1953, he was joint winner (with Hannes Bok) of the very first award for Professional Artist. He won four more Hugos in 1960-1965. In the late 1950s he had begun experimenting with film and by the mid-1960s had for the most part abandoned illustration.

In 1962, another artist had begun to appear on Ace Doubles who was to replace the departing Emsh. Jack Gaughan (1930-1985) hailed from Ohio and made his first sales while still studying at Dayton Art Institute. A fan of Hannes Bok, he befriended the artist and learned much from Bok's instruction. After working for various studios he turned freelance and established himself as a regular with *Galaxy*, its companion, *If*, and *F&SF*; for a while he was art director for *Galaxy* and *If*.

His superb sense of design and mastery of mixed media meant Gaughan produced an astonishingly diverse range of covers and illustrations over the years, often against tight deadlines. Despite this pressure, Gaughan was notably generous with his artwork and uniquely won Hugo Awards for best professional and fan artist in the same year (1967); he went on to win the Professional Artist category in 1968 and 1969. Gaughan was also a fine calligrapher and often produced hand-lettered title pages and maps, including Ace Books' pirated editions of Tolkien's *Lord of the Rings* trilogy. The Jack Gaughan Award for Best Emerging Artist was established in 1986 by the New England Science Fiction Association.

◀◀
The Nebula Award-winning *Einstein Intersection* by Samuel R. Delany (Ace, 1967) is set in a far future in which aliens try to understand and assimilate humanity from the cultural artifacts mankind has left behind. Jack Gaughan's cover is suitably mythic.

▶
This selection of covers shows the diversity of Jack Gaughan's work—some drawing on standard SF tropes, others spinning off into abstraction.

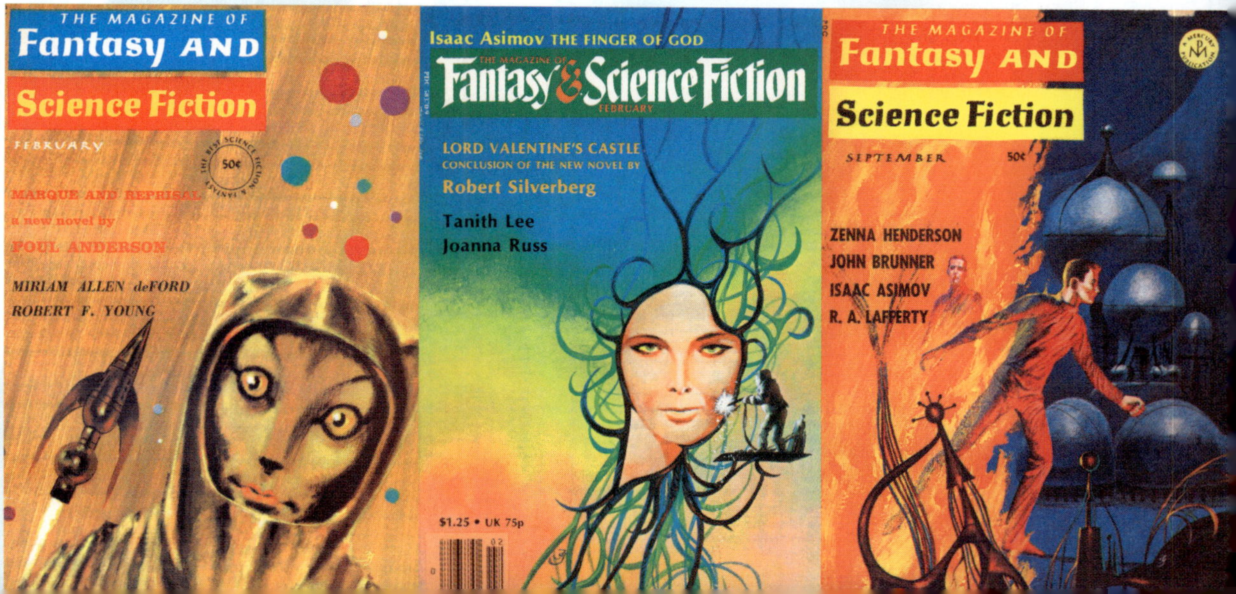

RICHARD POWERS

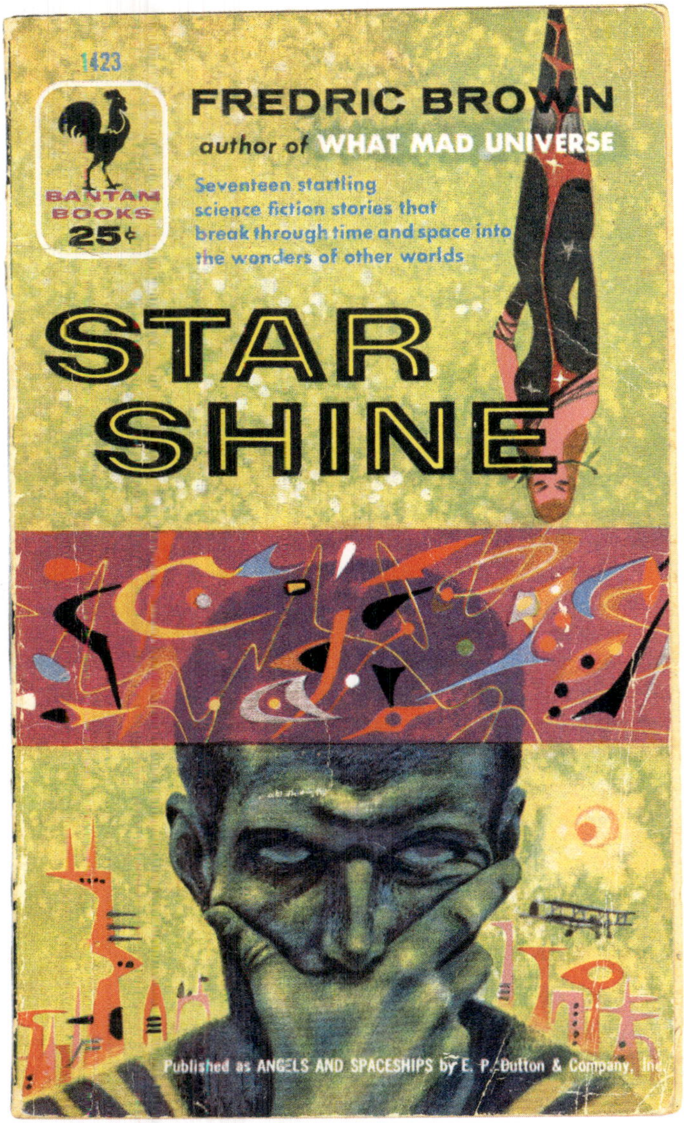

Richard Powers is something of an enigma in SF art. For the most part, the demands of publishers were for their artists to create images that were recognizably science fiction and represented a science fictional idea or theme, be it an alien creature, a robot, a spaceship, a futuristic city, or something more specific to the story illustrated. This was certainly the attitude of the pulp magazine publishers and the bulk of the paperback publishers. But it was not true of all publishers and artists and certainly wasn't true of Richard Powers.

Powers was a surrealist artist who worked in abstract images that were not necessarily representative of the books his covers adorned. What they represented was a feeling or an emotion.

Ian Ballantine recognized this and Powers became the main provider of SF covers for Ballantine Books from 1953. Berkley, Fawcett, Permabooks, and Dell also used Powers' paintings in the early 1950s, and he would provide covers for most major publishers during the 1960s and 1970s. It was, however, with covers for Ballantine's editions of Arthur C. Clarke, Theodore Sturgeon, Robert A. Heinlein, James Blish, and the *Star Science Fiction* series edited by Frederik Pohl that he established himself. Some of his best work can be found in the collection *The Art of Richard Powers* by Jane Frank (2001).

Born in Chicago in 1921, Richard Michael Powers attended art classes at Mizen Academy, Chicago Art Institute, and the University of Illinois. He made his first professional sales after the war, including his first book for children, *Double-Decker*.

Surrealism was an extension of Powers' personal philosophy, as it was uncompromisingly the vision of the artist, and Powers, an arch liberal, despised commercialism and compromise. Science fiction gave Powers the freedom to express himself. His dislike of the commercial success of pop art led him to create the fictional LAZ/org, under which name he signed some of his covers.

In 1960, Ervine Metzl, one of America's finest poster artists, profiled Powers' career and stated that his commercial work "stands head and shoulders above the utilitarian commercial requirements that bought it. It belongs in the realm of fine art." His representational work began to lose favor in the 1970s as, by then, realism was demanded (many publishers switched to photographic covers); Powers often had realistic figures and objects underlying the dreamscapes he created, but his work was uncompromising and his appearances on book covers became fewer and fewer in the 1980s and 1990s. His reputation as an abstract painter remained intact, however, and he was able to travel, paint, and exhibit his more personal work throughout his career, which came to a sudden end when he died of a stroke during a trip to Spain in 1996.

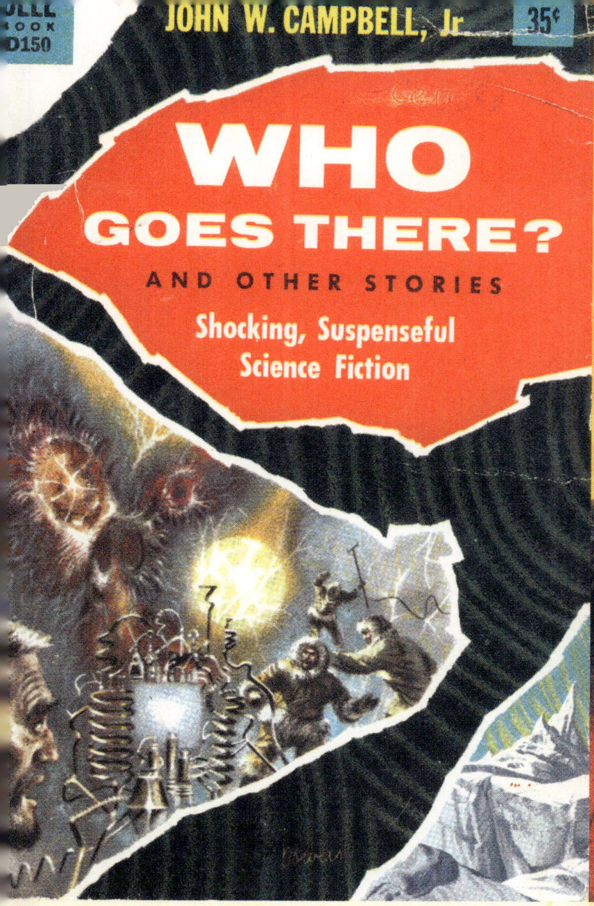

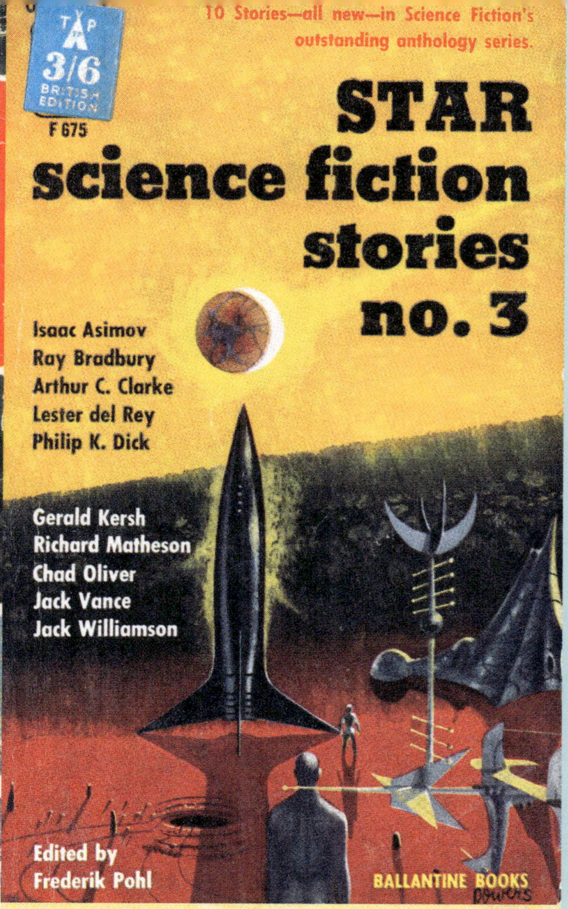

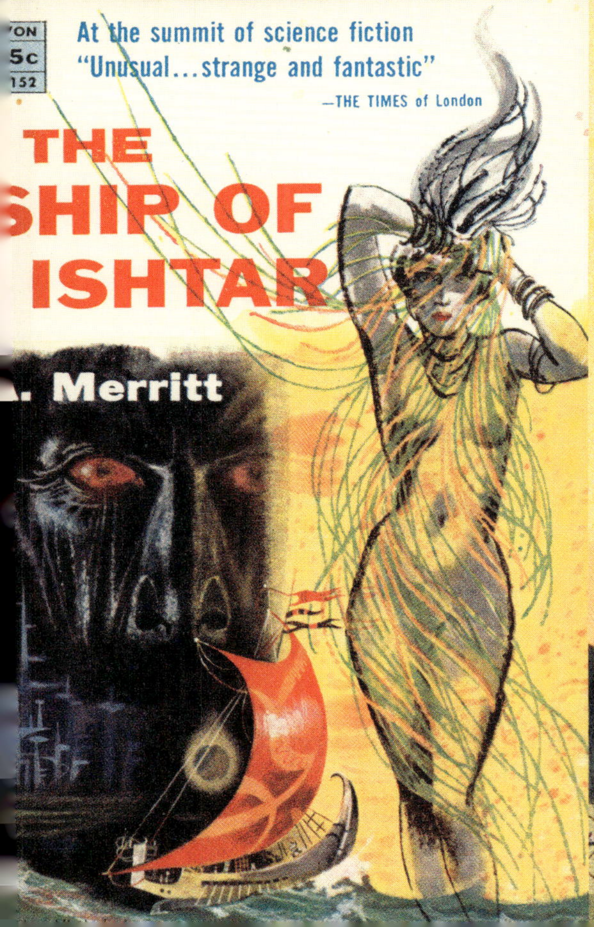

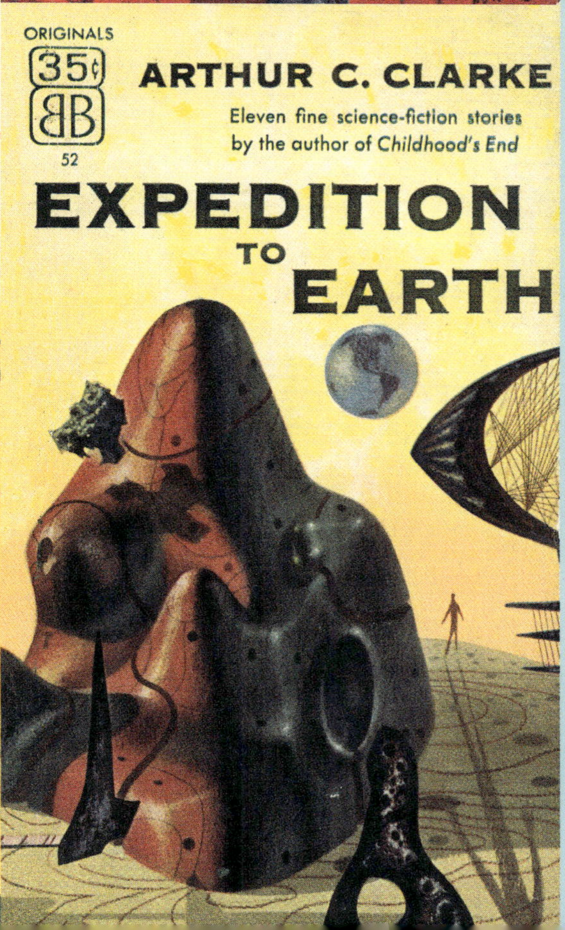

◄◄

A more illustrative cover by Powers for *Who Goes There? and Other Stories* by John W. Campbell (Dell, 1955). The lead story—about an encounter between isolated scientists in the Antarctic and a malevolent and seemingly unstoppable alien—was filmed twice: as *The Thing from Another World* (1951), and *John Carpenter's The Thing* (1982).

◄

Powers summarizes various concepts of science fiction in one image—alien architecture is incidental to the three main elements: a man looking towards a rocket aimed at a planet clearly not Earth. Frederik Pohl's *Star Science Fiction Stories* was the first regular SF anthology series, this third volume published by Ballantine in 1955.

◄◄◄

Some of Powers' covers contain little stories of their own: is the skyward-glancing man having confused thoughts about the girl hanging upside-down above him? Fredric Brown's *Star Shine* (Bantam, 1956) was originally published as *Angels and Spaceships*... so could the girl represent an angel?

◄◄

As more SF novels crowded the shelves in the 1950s, Powers' illustrations became more representative of the books they graced without losing any of their evocative and expressive strength, as seen here on *The Ship of Ishtar* by Abraham Merritt (Avon, 1956).

◄

Surreal shapes dominate a planet's surface, with Earth a small globe in the background. There is something truly alien about Powers' cover for Arthur C. Clarke's *Expedition to Earth* (Ballantine, 1953).

The 1960s saw many new artists debut in magazines. Cele Goldsmith, editor of *Amazing* and *Fantastic*, encouraged female artists Jacquelyn R. Blair and Paula McLane to contribute both interior and cover art, although Lloyd Birmingham (1924–) was probably Goldsmith's most notable discovery. *Galaxy* and its companion *If* added Doug Chaffee, Richard McKenna, and Paul Wenzel to its roster of artists, while Gray Morrow and George Schelling worked for all four magazines.

The artist who dominated *Analog* (as *Astounding SF* became in 1960) was John Schoenherr, of whom Vincent Di Fate has said, "Once in a while an artist comes along with so much innate ability that he instantly gains the respect of his peers and becomes known as an 'artist's artist'... Schoenherr possesses just such a talent and, to put a finer point on the matter, he is one of the best compositionalists who ever worked in the field of commercial art."

John Carl Schoenherr (1935–) was born in New York and studied under Will Barnett and Frank Reilly at the Arts Students League, and under Richard Bové and Stanley Meltzoff at the Pratt Institute, where he graduated as a Bachelor of Fine Arts in 1956. His first SF illustration appeared in *Amazing* in 1957 and he was a regular cover artist for Pyramid and Ace Books in the early 1960s. But it was his work for *Analog* that really brought him to the attention of fans.

Schoenherr's first *Analog* cover was for the June 1960 issue and he was to produce 50 more covers over the next nine years. Although capable of providing realistic space scenes and planetscapes—which featured in a number of his early paintings—Schoenherr showed far more imagination with the creation of alien creatures. These were not the bug-eyed monsters of yesteryear but often beasts of burden and intelligent alien races. That he could create credible aliens is perhaps no surprise; Schoenherr was known to the wider world as the illustrator of dozens of children's books, often featuring animals, and a popular wildlife artist, exhibiting at the New York Zoological Society in 1968 and publishing *The Art of Painting Wild Animals* (1974).

The mixture of alien creatures and planetscapes were brought together in Schoenherr's illustrations

▶▼▼
Dune was one of *Analog*'s most successful serials and Schoenherr was on hand to illustrate both the 1963 *Dune World* and, as seen here, the 1965 sequel, *Prophet of Dune*. He set the bar for illustrators who would follow, but few have matched his vision of the sandworms of Arrakis. Schoenherr also illustrated the dust jacket to the first hardcover edition.

◀◀▼
Schoenherr, in more abstract mood, illustrates *The Weather Man* by Theodore Thomas for *Analog*, June 1962.

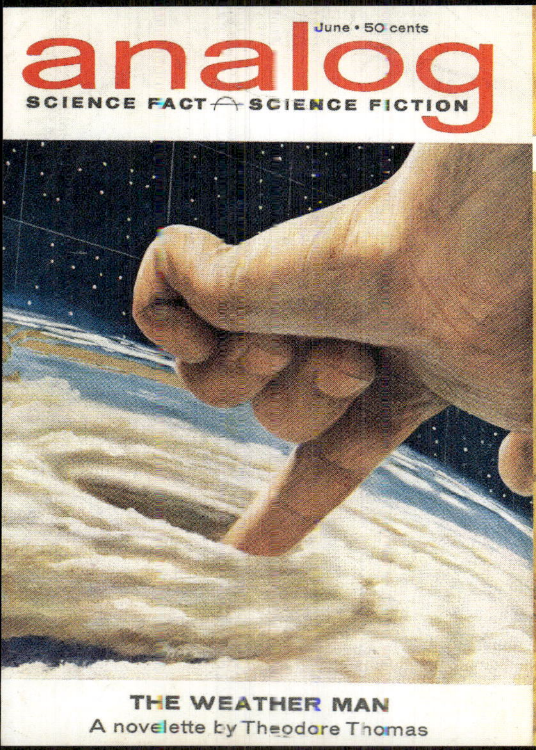

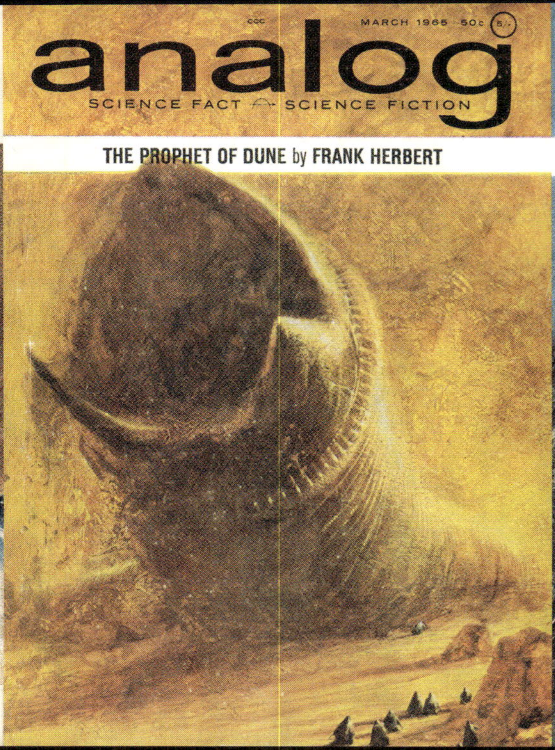

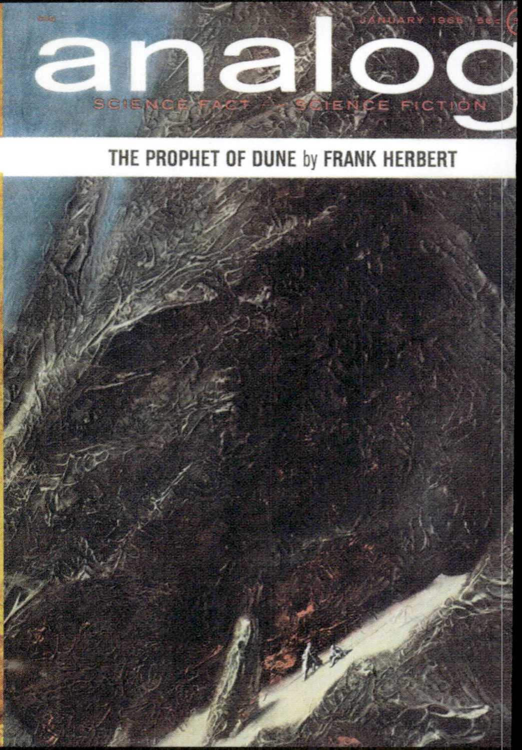

for Frank Herbert's *Dune*, serialized in *Analog* in 1963 and 1965 as *Dune World* and *The Prophet of Dune*. Schoenherr won the Hugo Award in 1965. He would later return to *Dune* when he produced a series of new illustrations for *The Illustrated Dune* (1978), which showed how Schoenherr's style had changed: his early drawings were often produced very precisely in scratchboard; the later dry brush illustrations are looser and more diffuse but have lost none of his command of composition.

After a brief departure, Schoenherr returned to *Analog* in the 1970s for a further two-dozen covers, after which he left illustration behind in order to concentrate on painting wildlife.

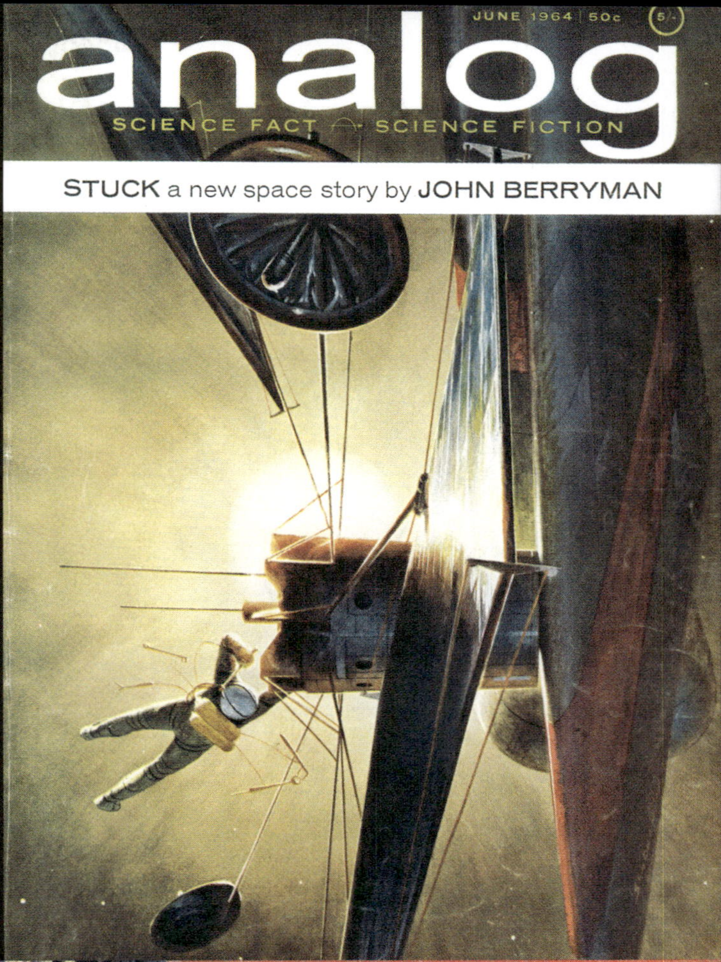

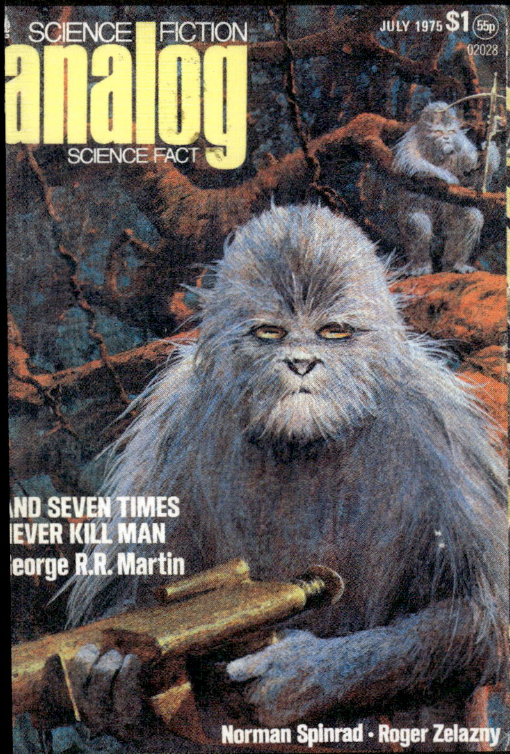

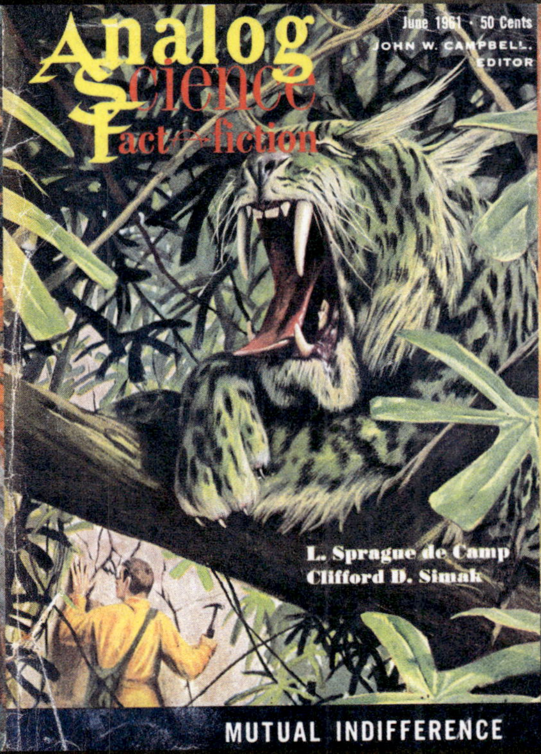

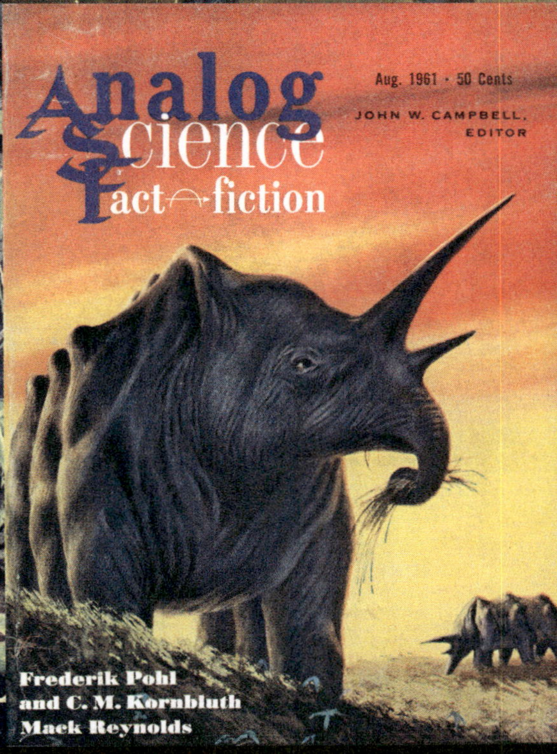

▼ ▶▼ ▶▶▼
The diversity of Schoenherr's alien entities was wide, from giant cats to giant herd creatures. The cover for the July 1975 edition of *Analog* depicted George R. R. Martin's Hugo-nominated story about alien genocide, *And Seven Times Never Kill a Man*.

▶
Although known for his alien creatures, Schoenherr was more than capable of producing hardware paintings, too.

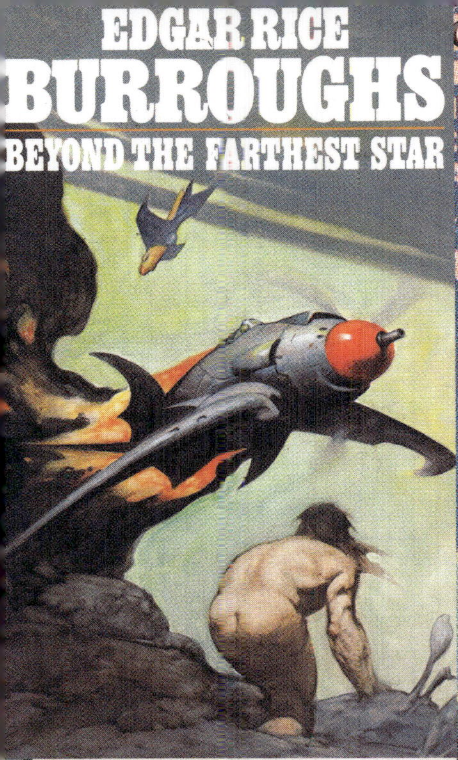

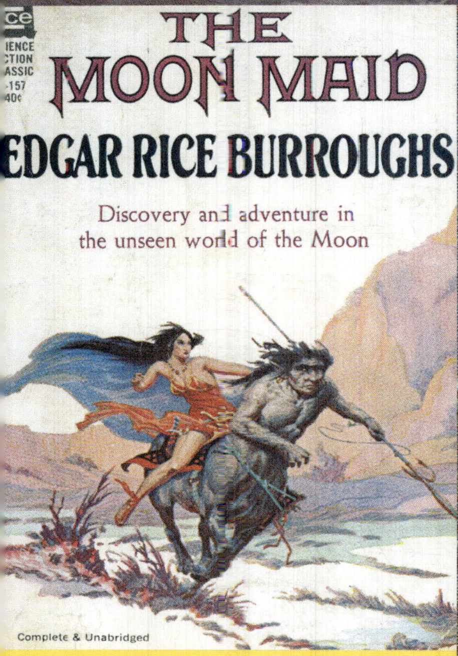

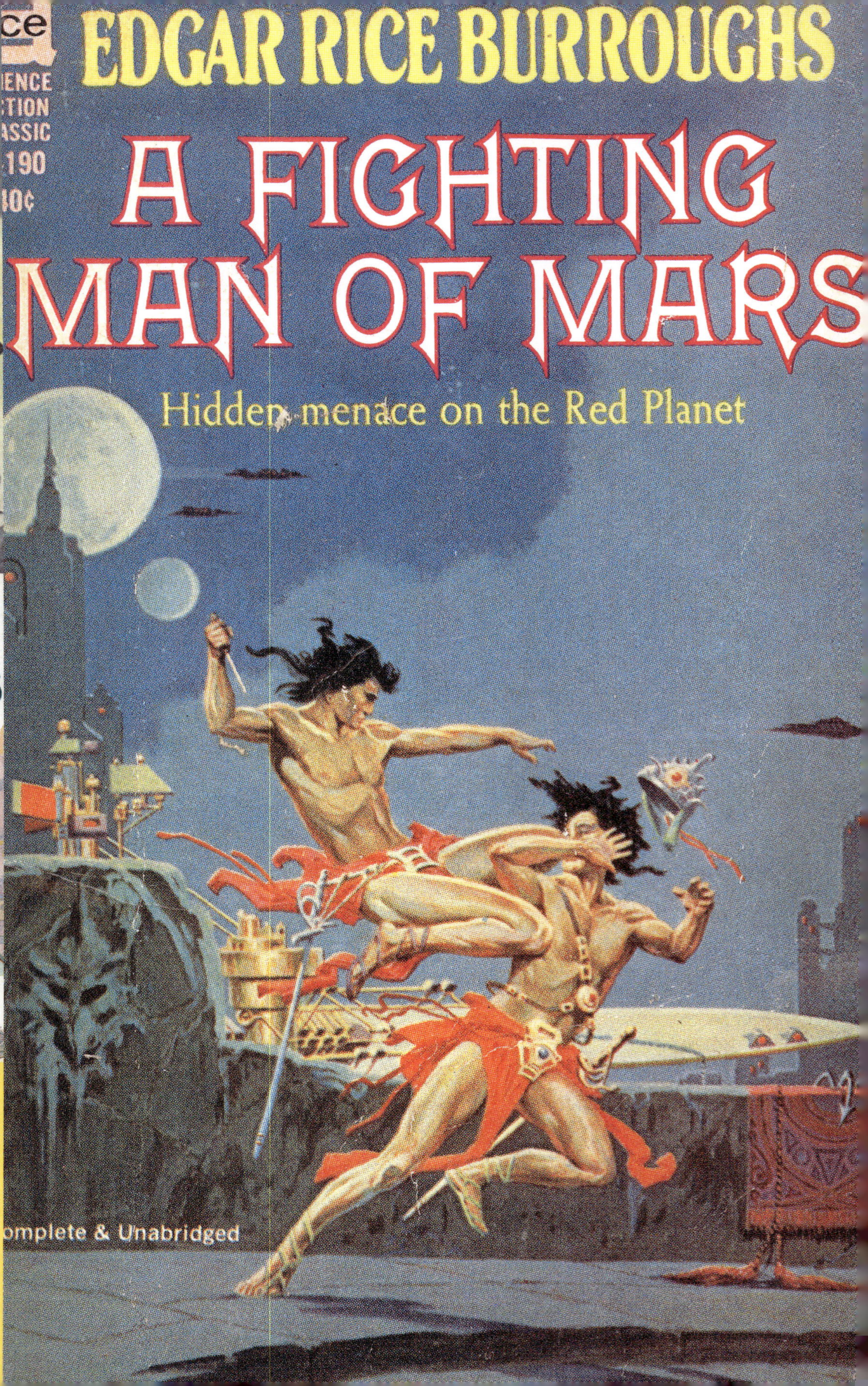

▶ ▲ ▲▲
Best known as the creator of Tarzan, Edgar Rice Burroughs also produced some of the most steadily-selling science fiction novels of all time. In the 1960s, Roy Krenkel—seen here with *Fighting Man of Mars* (1963) and *The Moon Maid* (1962)—and Frank Frazetta—*Beyond the Farthest Star*—were his main cover artists at Ace Books.

SF ARTWORK IN THE 1970s

Although the fiction magazine market in the US was beginning to falter, the long-established titles—*Amazing*, *Analog*, *F&SF*, *Galaxy*, and *If*—formed a core that seemed unassailable. Ultimately, that proved not to be the case. SF had a strong following by the 1970s, which meant hardcover publication ahead of mass marketing in paperback was becoming the norm for many of the big names; by the 1980s it was not unusual to see SF in *The New York Times* bestsellers.

However, this did not mean the end of paperback SF; indeed, specialist lists began to appear in the 1970s, spearheaded by DAW Books, set up by Donald A. Wollheim and Ballantine's Del Rey Books imprint, and named after editors Lester and Judy-Lynn del Rey. Ace Books and others still had strong lines of SF and new artists were appearing constantly. Gray Morrow (1934–) emerged in the mid-1960s, quickly establishing himself at *Galaxy*, *F&SF*, *If*, and Ace Books, although he became better known for his comic strips. Similarly, Jeffrey Jones (1944–) worked for *Amazing* and *Fantastic* and on covers (notably Fritz Leiber's *Fafhrd and Gray Mouser* titles) before he, too, departed for comics. Roy Krenkel (1918–1983) had traveled the reverse route, from EC Comics to Ace and then to DAW Books, as had Frank Frazetta (1928–). Both were masters of heroic fantasy images, best seen on their covers for Edgar Rice Burroughs' various books published by Ace, and were rewarded with Hugo Awards in 1963 and 1966 respectively.

Leo and Diane Dillon (both born in 1933) produced more abstract images, working for Gold Medal, Pyramid, and others, although it was their illustrations for Harlan Ellison's *Dangerous Visions* which brought them immediate attention, and their work for Ace Specials, which earned them a Hugo in 1971.

DAW Books engaged Jack Gaughan as art director, who used a number of talented artists, not least British-born Josh Kirby (1928–2001), now mostly associated with the covers for Terry Pratchett's hugely successful *Discworld* novels; Dutch surrealist Karel Thole (1914–2000); and Italian fantasy artist Gino D'Achille (1935–).

Two artists responsible for many of DAW's covers were George Barr (1937–) and Tim Kirk (1955–). Barr's first professional artwork had appeared in *Fantastic* in 1962 and he subsequently worked for Ballantine, Ace, Pyramid, and, especially, DAW, where his elegant, precise images in pastel watercolors were used effectively on fantasy novels. Kirk's career had gotten off to a flying start when Ian Ballantine (of Ballantine Books) purchased 26 paintings based on *Lord of the Rings* that Kirk had produced as part of his Master's degree project. His delicate fantasy images earned him five Hugo Awards as best fan artist.

DAW was also one of the launching pads in the early careers of other talented artists: Vincent Di Fate, David Mattingly, Ken Kelly, Michael Mariano, and, especially, Michael Whelan.

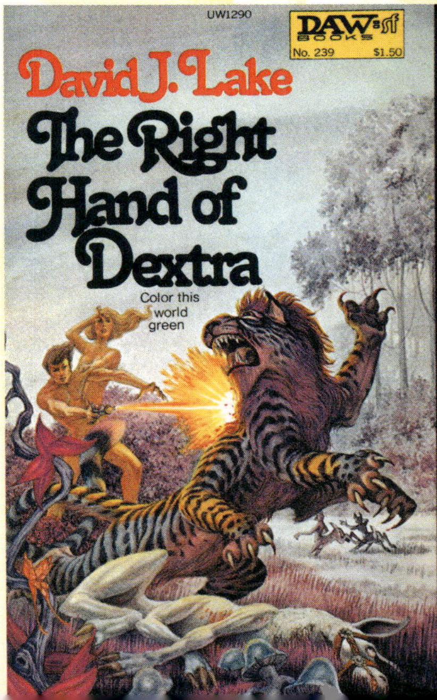

▼
George Barr was one of the main artists for Donald Wollheim's DAW Books in the 1970s. His meticulous, sometimes whimsical artwork—often (and unusually) using pastel shades—enlivened DAW's fantasy novels for many years. *The Right Hand of Dextra* by David J. Lake dates from 1977.

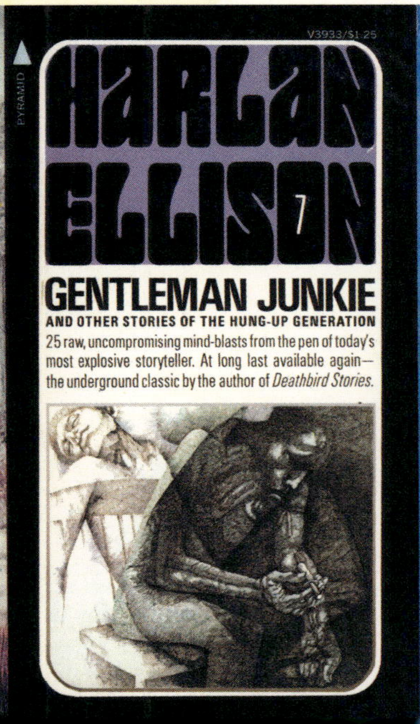

▶▼
The work of Leo and Diane Dillon was championed by Harlan Ellison, who brought it to the attention of the wider world via his groundbreaking anthology, *Dangerous Visions* (1967), and a series of reprints in the 1970s, including the very scarce collection *Gentleman Junkie* (Pyramid, 1975).

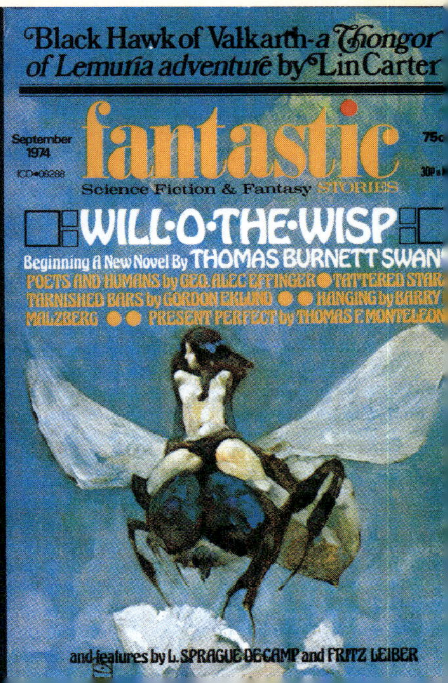

▶▶▼
Jeffrey Jones—now Jeffery Catherine Jones—is perhaps best known for her work at The Studio in the late 1970s. She was a regular cover artist for *Amazing* and *Fantastic* in the early '70s, her work informed by Renaissance paintings of old masters.

BRITISH SF ARTWORK IN THE 1960s & 1970s

As early as 1956, Ted Carnell of *New Worlds* magazine was suggesting that if fantasy art deteriorated any further, he would cease to use interior artwork in the magazine. Gerard Quinn, one of the leading British SF artists of the time, admitted that "few of our artists show the inventiveness of American artists and it can well be argued that our magazine would do better without interior illustrations."

In truth, science fiction artwork was not well served by British publishers in the 1960s. The hardcover companies rarely offered anything other than typographical covers and, where they were illustrative, they tended to be for a juvenile audience that had grown in the wake of Dan Dare's comic strip adventures. Paperback publishers such as Penguin were primarily typographical, although a single image was often incorporated into the standardized design, such as for the novels of John Wyndham. Shaking off its colored livery in the early 1960s, Penguin began to use fine art images, unrepresentative of the contents, such as the use of cubist Albert Gleizes and surrealist Max Ernst on fast-paced and satirical space operas by Eric Frank Russell.

Panther Books, home of Isaac Asimov, A. E. Van Vogt, Edmund Cooper, and others, noticeably charted the decline of painted artwork—with Josh Kirby one of the most prolific of their artists—in favor of representational and abstract art in the early 1960s; by the late 1960s, photographic covers with blobs of light or close-ups of machine parts seemed to be *de rigeur*.

Pan Books published Arthur C. Clarke, Robert A. Heinlein, and adaptations of Charles Chilton's *Journey into Space* radio series with colorful painted art by Gerard Quinn, Gordon C. Davies (1923-1994), and W. Francis Phillipps (c.1925-), but had a relatively low output. Corgi Books benefited from having an established SF artist, John Richards, as art director who was able to bring his talents to the covers of books by Ray Bradbury, Charles Eric Maine, and others.

It was left to smaller paperback companies to carry the flag of science fiction. Badger Books produced more novels than any during the 1960s, albeit of infamously low quality. Their house artist, Henry Fox (1911-1980), churned out formulaic SF and horror images enlivened with looming faces and figures. Digit Books often had colorful space scenes with torpedo-shaped rockets on their covers, but, thanks to artists like Robert A. Osborne, C. Stewart, and Brian Lewis (1929-1978), some had imagination and drama, too.

Lewis and Gerard Quinn were the star cover artists on *New Worlds* until 1962, when it switched to photographic and typographical covers to save on costs. Reduced to paperback format in 1964, only James Cawthorn (1929-) and Keith Roberts (1935-2000) really captured anything of the "new wave" style that was championed inside by editor Michael Moorcock and writers J. G. Ballard and Brian Aldiss. *New Worlds* folded in 1971 (to be continued as a paperback anthology and, sporadically, as a magazine until 1997). Another new launch, *Vision of Tomorrow* (1969-70), had lasted only 12 issues. However, as one door closed, Britain was about to go through something of a boom in SF elsewhere.

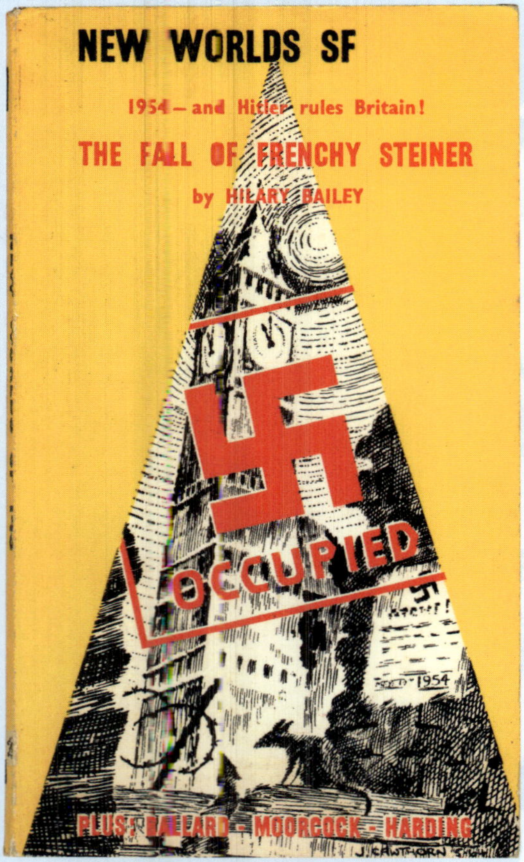

▶ ▶▶ ▶▶▶
The painted cover began to disappear during the 1960s, as seen in this trio of Asimov covers from Panther Books published in 1962, 1964, and 1965.

▶ ▶▶
Corgi and Pan Books were two of the few publishers to retain painted covers during the 1960s, from the almost abstract art of John Richards (*Silver Locusts*) to the looming hardware of Gordon Davies (*Journey into Space*).

▶▶▶
The only SF line with an illustrative "brand" was that of Badger Books, notorious for publishing some truly terrible SF novels. Elements of pre-painted covers by Henry Fox were often worked into the plots at the last minute (*Space Fury*).

◀
***New Worlds* was at the vanguard of the "new wave" of SF in the latter half of the 1960s; covers became experimental and enigmatic in the hands of Jim Cawthorn and Keith Roberts.**

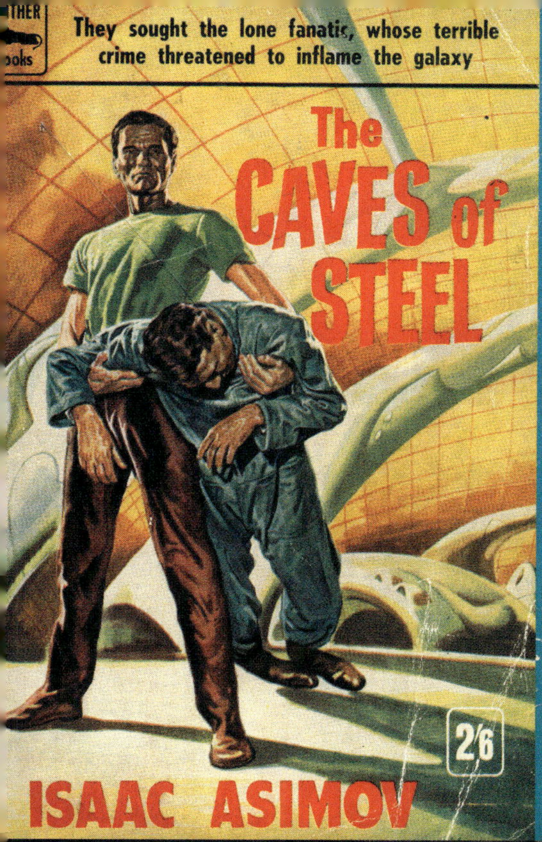
They sought the lone fanatic, whose terrible crime threatened to inflame the galaxy
The CAVES of STEEL
2'6
ISAAC ASIMOV

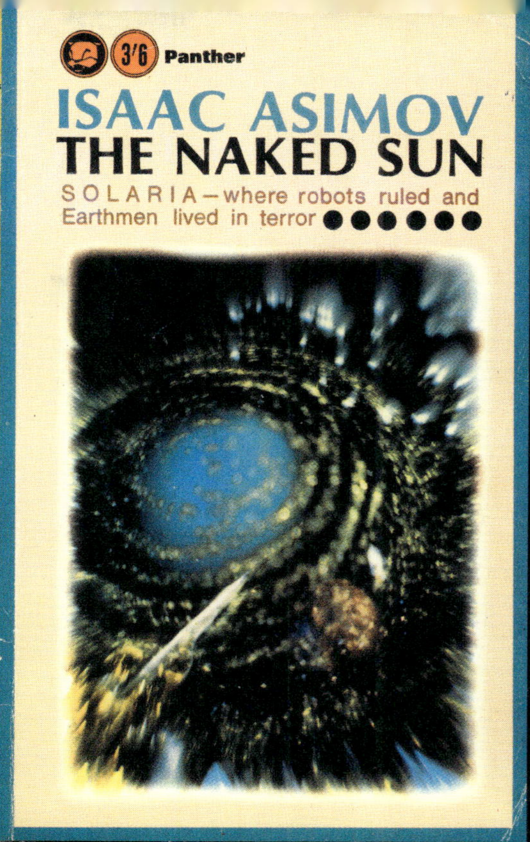
3'6 Panther
ISAAC ASIMOV
THE NAKED SUN
SOLARIA—where robots ruled and Earthmen lived in terror

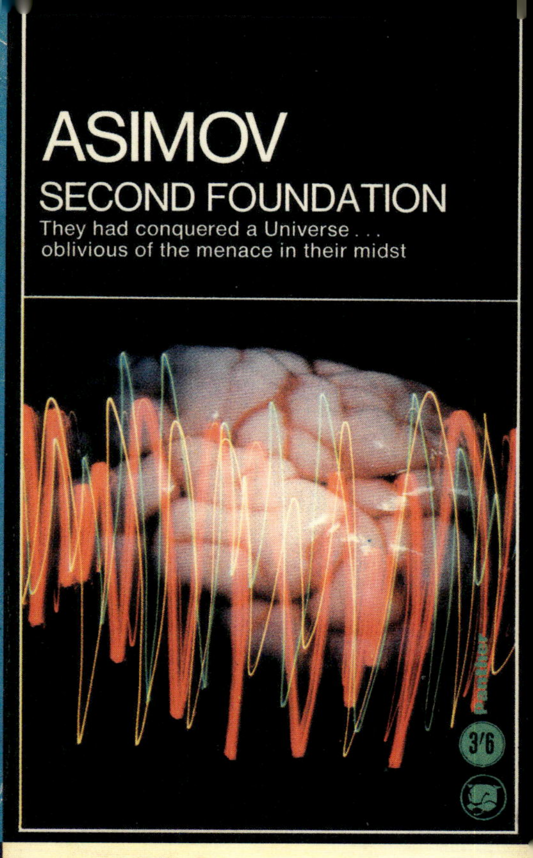
ASIMOV
SECOND FOUNDATION
They had conquered a Universe . . . oblivious of the menace in their midst
3'6

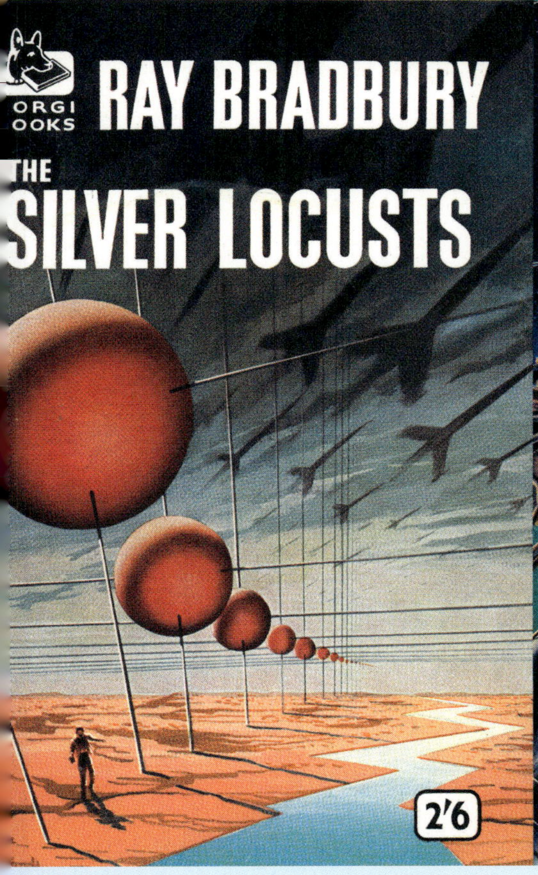
RAY BRADBURY
THE SILVER LOCUSTS
2'6

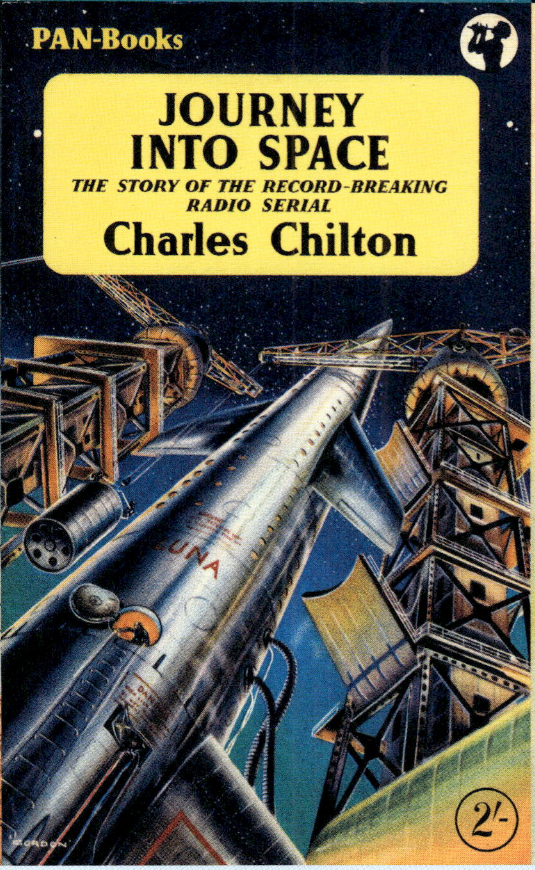
PAN-Books
JOURNEY INTO SPACE
THE STORY OF THE RECORD-BREAKING RADIO SERIAL
Charles Chilton
2/-

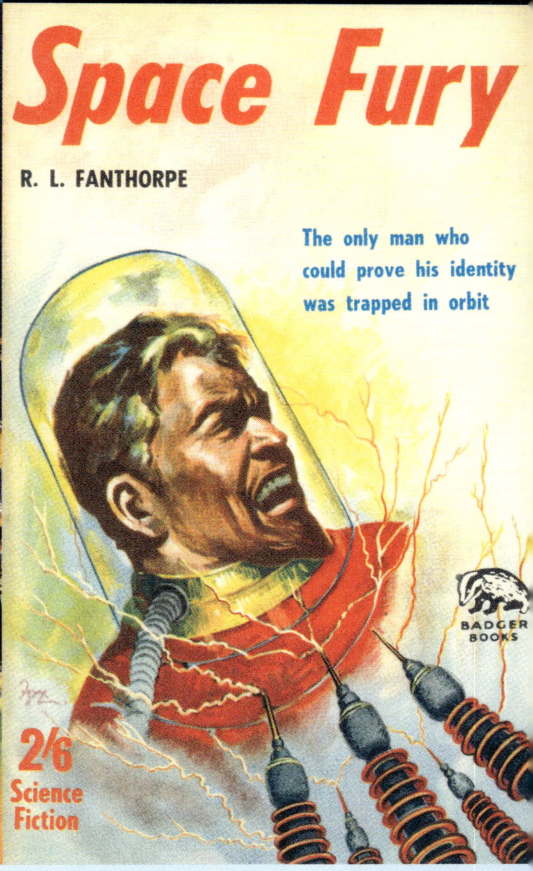
Space Fury
R. L. FANTHORPE
The only man who could prove his identity was trapped in orbit
BADGER BOOKS
2'6
Science Fiction

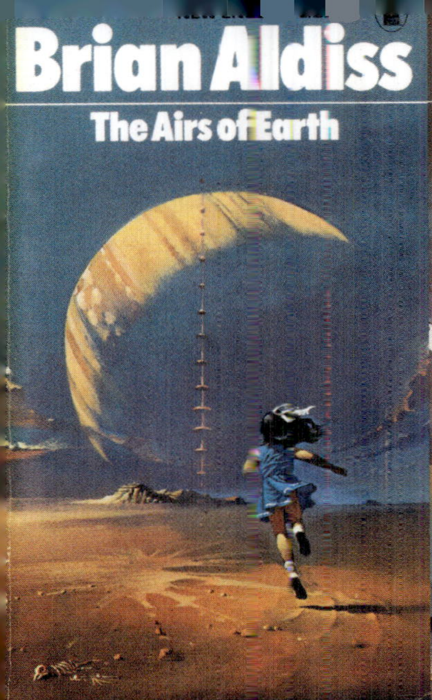
Brian Aldiss
The Airs of Earth
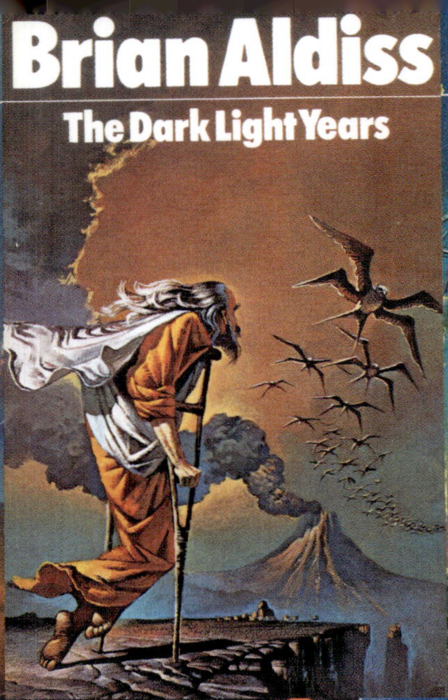
Brian Aldiss
The Dark Light Years
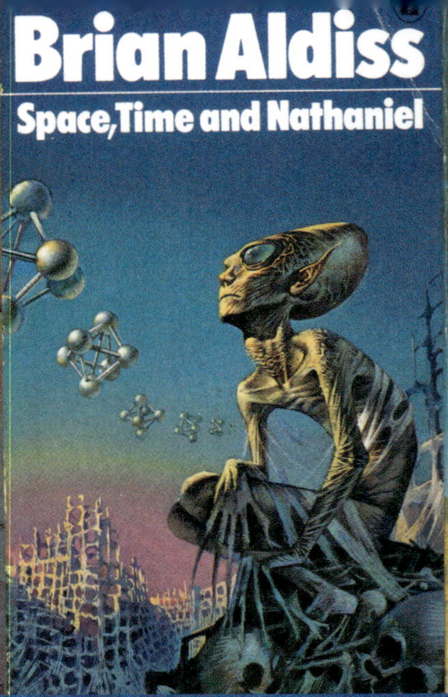
Brian Aldiss
Space, Time and Nathaniel
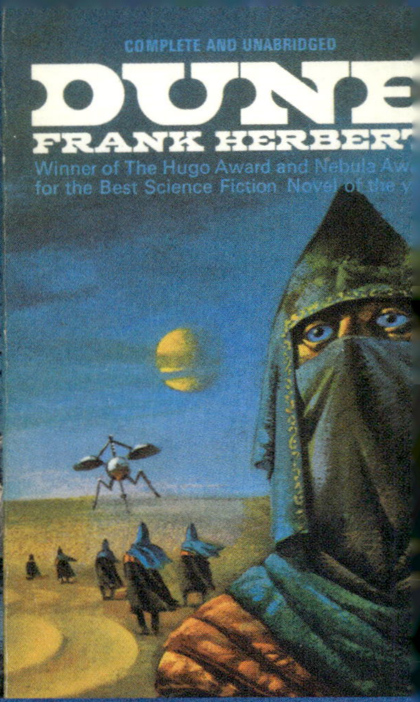
COMPLETE AND UNABRIDGED
DUNE
FRANK HERBERT
Winner of The Hugo Award and Nebula Awa
for the Best Science Fiction Novel of the y
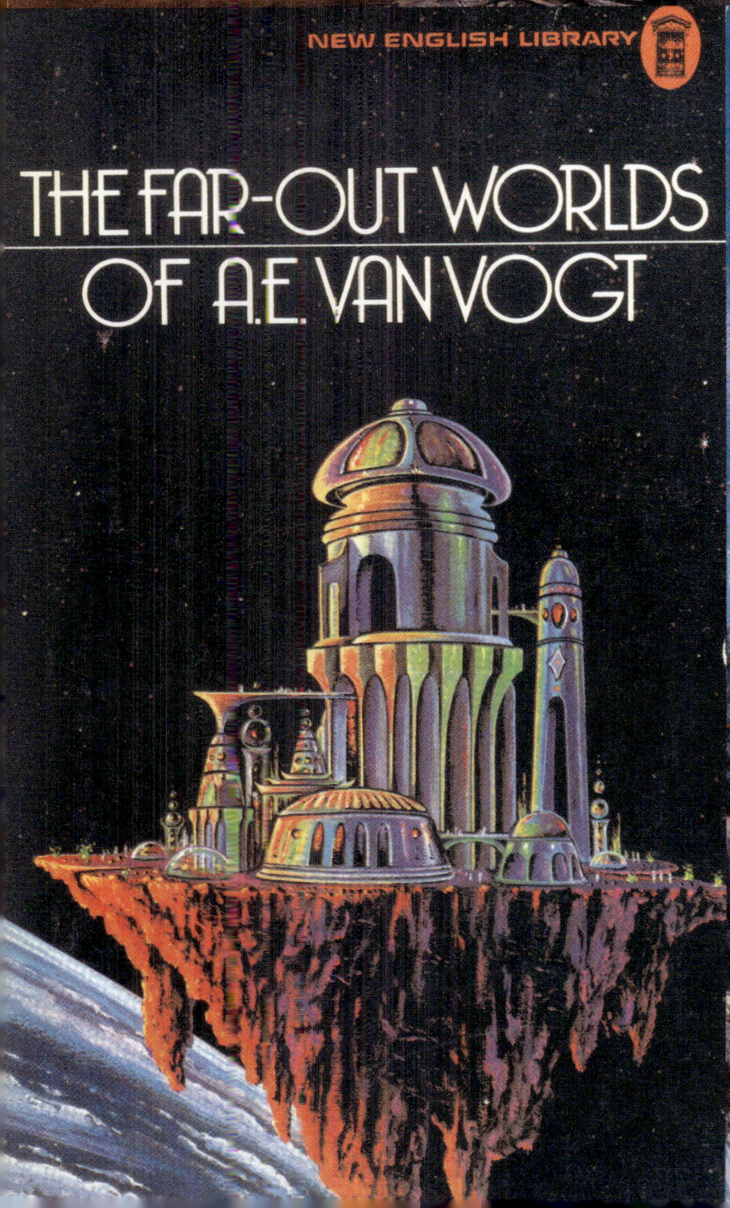
NEW ENGLISH LIBRARY
THE FAR-OUT WORLDS OF A.E. VAN VOGT
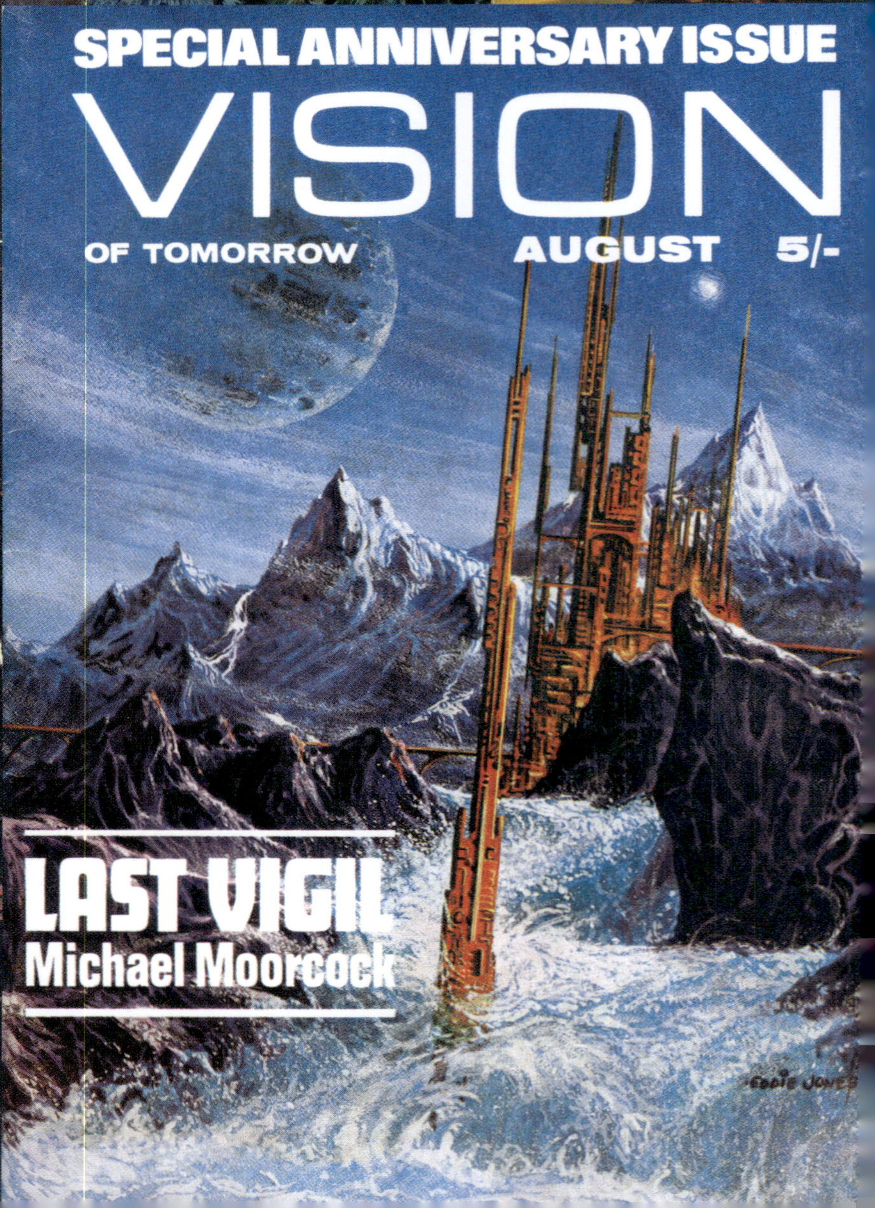
SPECIAL ANNIVERSARY ISSUE
VISION
OF TOMORROW
AUGUST
5/-
LAST VIGIL
Michael Moorcock

◀
Bruce Pennington was New English Library's chief artist for science fiction from 1971, when he illustrated three books by Brian Aldiss. One of his most enduring images is his cover art for Frank Herbert's *Dune* series.

▶
David Pelham, as well as being art director for Penguin Books, also produced some of the company's most stylish covers, including a series of stark images for J. G. Ballard's "new wave of SF" collections and novels.

◀◀
Although overshadowed by Bruce Pennington, Ray Feibush was nevertheless a versatile artist who worked for New English Library from 1973, seen here illustrating Van Vogt's *The Far-Out Worlds*.

◀
Best known as a "hardware" artist, Eddie Jones was able to produce a more diverse range of representational images while art editor of *Vision of Tomorrow*. Although active in the UK from 1958, and hugely prolific, the bulk of his work was for Germany's *Terra Astra*.

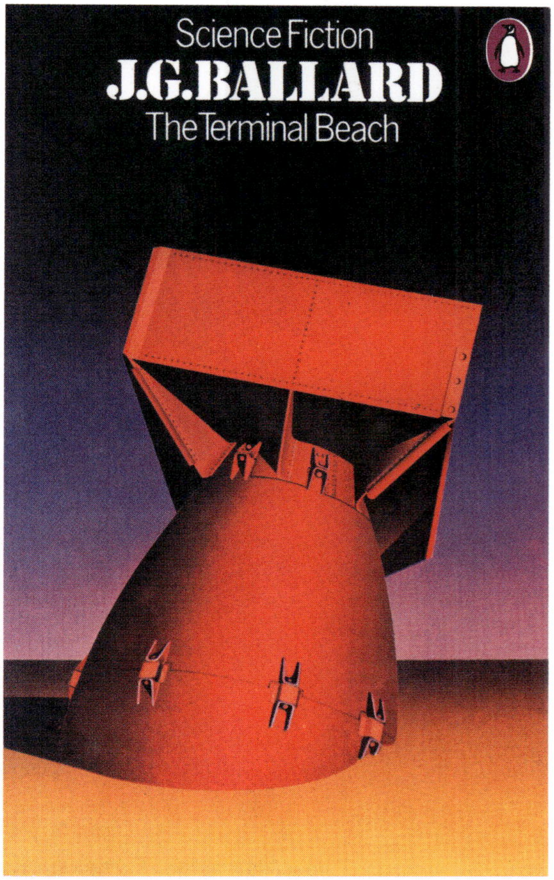

The paperback market for science fiction exploded in the UK around 1970. At the same time, fantasy and science fictional images were appearing elsewhere to great acclaim, nowhere more so than on record sleeves, where Roger Dean (1944-) began to earn a reputation with his *Osibisa* (Osibisa) and *Fragile* (Yes) sleeves in 1971. Dean's alien landscapes, often dominated by great pillars and arches of rock, or floating rocky islands, made great posters, and collections of his work (*Views*, 1975, and *The Flights of Icarus*, 1977) were bestsellers.

Bruce Pennington (1944-) was one of the new breed of SF illustrators to break through in the early 1970s at New English Library. Although his first cover (for Heinlein's *Stranger in a Strange Land*) had been published in 1967, he had spent some years illustrating horror collections; in 1970-1972 his artwork appeared on books by A. E. Van Vogt, Brian Aldiss, and Frank Herbert, notably Herbert's *Dune* and its sequels. His artwork was luminous, often featuring multiple objects or creatures against sparse skies and low horizons with a large, dominant, often alien figure in the foreground. Pennington dominated New English Library's covers for some years, winning the BSFA Award for Best Artist in 1982, before he abandoned cover illustration for more personal projects towards the end of the 1980s.

Ray Feibush (1948-1998), born in England but raised in America, had no art training but learned much from his brother Mike McInnerney, art editor of *International Times* in the late 1960s and also an SF cover artist, although best known for his sleeve art for The Who's *Tommy* album. Feibush made his SF debut in 1971 at Panther Books (*The Open Cage* by Ronald Hall) but it was with New English Library that he established himself in 1973, working on covers for Asimov, Heinlein, Van Vogt, and Moorcock, and taking over the Burroughs *Mars* series from Bruce Pennington. Feibush, although his artwork used strong, imaginative visual motifs and was picked up by DAW Books and in Europe, never established himself as a unique stylist.

The same could not be said of David Pelham (1938-), the art director of Penguin Books, who was responsible for reviving their SF line artistically after a period in the doldrums. Pelham was also the artist responsible for a series of covers for J. G. Ballard novels, a set of stark images of futuristic cars, planes, and bombs embedded in airbrushed, featureless plains published in 1974.

Other artists of note during this period include Bob Fowke (1950-), responsible for many illustrations for the Corgi SF Collector's Library series; Chris Yates (1948-), who produced photo collage covers for Arrow in the early 1970s; Bob Haberfield (1938-), whose surrealistic images appeared on Mayflower's line of Mike Moorcock titles; Eddie Jones (1935-1999), art editor of *Vision of Tomorrow* and a prolific artist for German SF publications; and Tim White (1952-), who, working for Corgi and New English Library, straddled the styles of Bruce Pennington with the airbrush artwork of a group of artists who developed a style of space art that dominated SF covers in the late 1970s.

THE CHRIS FOSS FACTOR

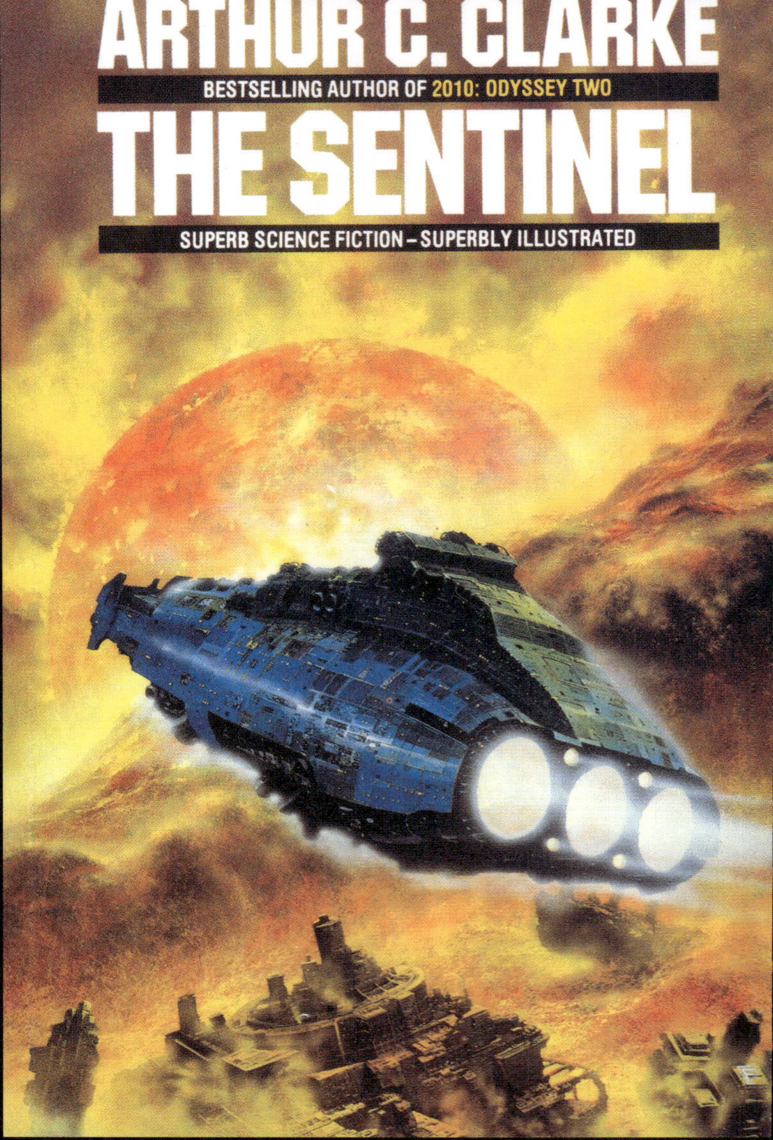

If anyone can be said to have revolutionized science fiction artwork, that person is Chris Foss (1946–). Born in Devon, England, Foss' early artwork found inspiration in the rusting railway tracks and disused mines of the West Country and semi-derelict shipyards at Poole. His fascination with the mechanical and technical led to his modeling railroads and steam engines out of scrap. This talent for modeling and sketching won him a scholarship to a public school in Dorset, and a career as an artist beckoned. He sold his first cartoons (to *Autocar*) while studying architecture at Cambridge University, although his break came with the sale of a six-page comic strip to *Penthouse*. He dropped out of University after two years and, in 1966, took a job as an architectural sculptor. Further jobs (including periods as a hire-car driver) brought in money while he worked on various projects, including an unpublished *Barbarella*-style book for *Penthouse* publisher Bob Guccione.

Commissions began to come in 1969, one an intricately drawn futuristic city for *Nova* magazine. Following the publication of a cover for *The Coming of the Space Age* by Arthur C. Clarke (Panther, 1970), Foss produced covers for thrillers and war novels. But he increasingly found himself working on science fiction novels, where his spaceships looked like vast war machines, with futuristic buildings and airbrushed starscapes replacing the towering icebergs and surging seas of his thriller covers.

Foss' space hardware became the style that dominated British paperback designs for the next decade. His spaceships were a patchwork of panels, stripes, and lettering reminiscent of Second World War aircraft. Highly detailed and bristling with antennae, rocket pods, and exhausts, many are rusting hulks, scarred and ready for the scrapheap. Lens flare dancing off the glittering stars adds to the photographic reality of the hardware. There's a real "sense of wonder" in Foss' artwork.

Working for Sphere, Panther, Coronet, Arrow, and Futura paperbacks, Foss was the artistic spearhead of a paperback boom for science fiction in Britain, and it was not long before his talent for both art and design came to the notice of the movie industry. Foss was involved in conceptual designs for Alejandro Jodorowsky's failed attempt to film *Dune* in 1975–1976 but, more successfully, on *Superman*, *Alien*, and *AI*; his influence can be seen in the opening scenes of both *Star Wars* and *Blade Runner*.

Foss' lumbering battleships and sleek fighters often had little to do with the stories they appeared on, but, illustrating Asimov, E. E. "Doc" Smith, A. E. Van Vogt, and other big names, his artwork became heavily associated with classic pulp SF. Not that all his covers are interchangeable: Foss also produced artwork for James Blish's *Cities in Flight* series and the *Demon Princes* novels by Jack Vance.

The best of Foss' early work was gathered together in the collection *21st Century Foss* (1978), while *Diary of a Spaceperson* (1990) was a more ambitious collection, linking covers with new illustrations to tell the story of a girl's adventures around the galaxy.

▲
One of Foss' earliest influences were the remnants of fortifications from the German occupation of Guernsey, an island he visited regularly through family connections. Monstrous fortified buildings that could contain lookout posts and gun emplacements litter some of the landscapes of his alien planets.

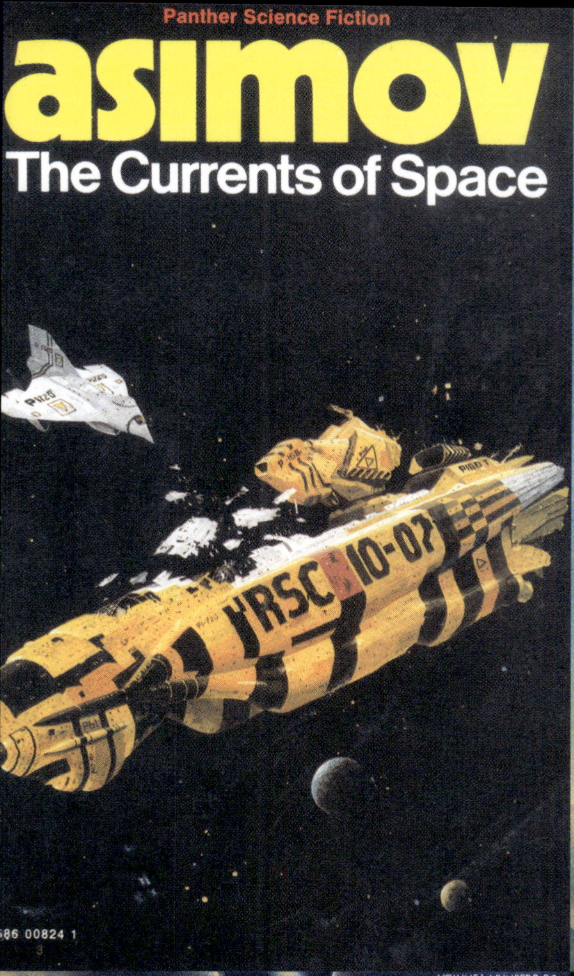

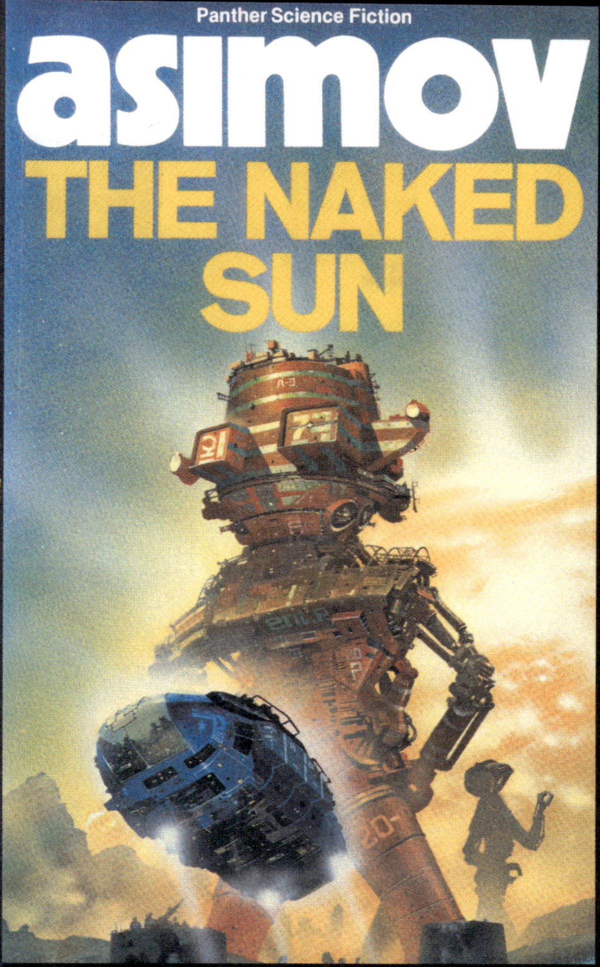

◀◀
A typical Foss leviathan from 1974. Alejandro Jodorowsky has said of Foss: "He could create battleships made thirsty dying century after century in a desert of stars waiting for the living body who would fill empty reservoirs with subtle secretions of its soul..."

◀
Foss famously illustrated *The Joy of Sex and More Joy*, but people were conspicuously absent from most of his SF paintings. Robots, on the other hand, have often appeared through Foss' cover art for Isaac Asimov's famous collections and novels. They have not always been the friendly, humanoid type—some are more akin to walking cities.

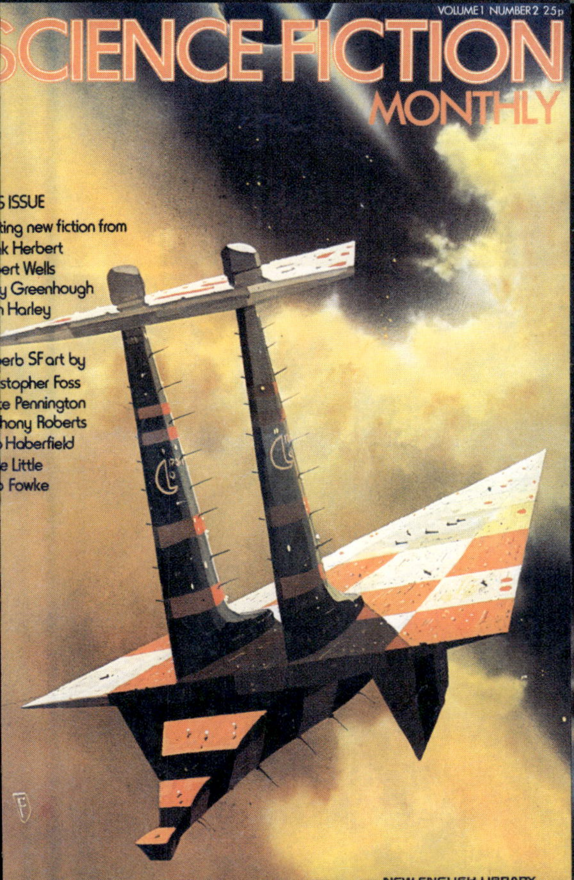

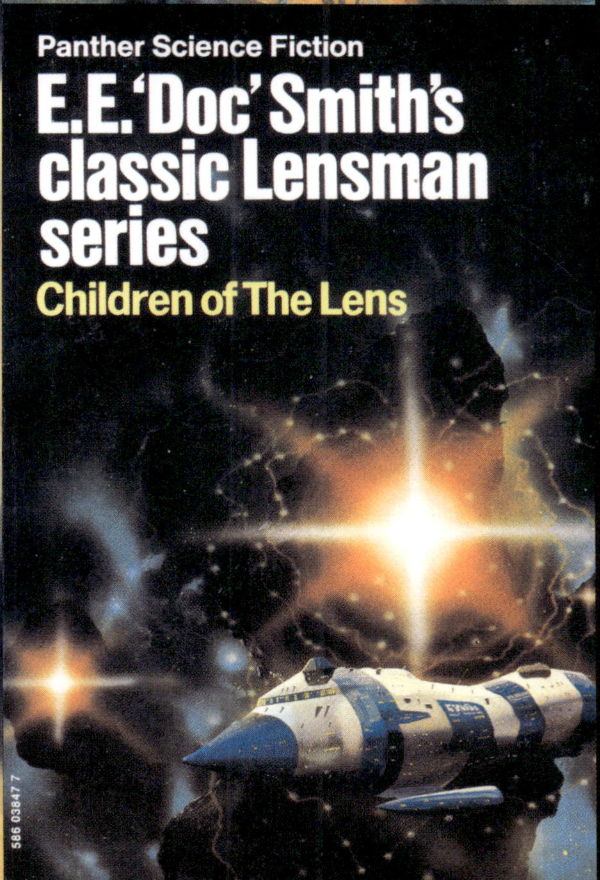

◀◀
Debuting in the mid-1970s, the poster magazine *Science Fiction Monthly* was launched as a result of the rising popularity of cover art by Foss and others. Issue 2 featured Foss' triangular spaceship from the 1975 paperback edition of *Moonbeast* by A. E. Van Vogt. An alternate version of the same ship appears in *21st Century Foss.*

◀
Perhaps it was the very title of E. E. "Doc" Smith's *Lensman* series that inspired Foss to think about lenses and light refraction. Improvements in cameras have all but eradicated lens flare nowadays, but Chris Foss put it into his artwork to add a kind of realism to the "photographs" of spaceships he was creating.

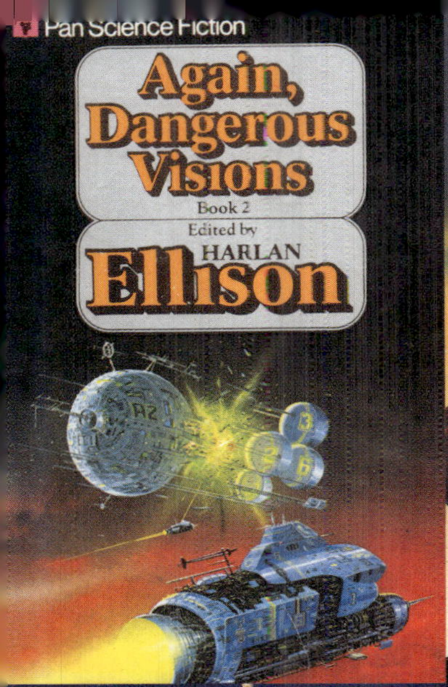

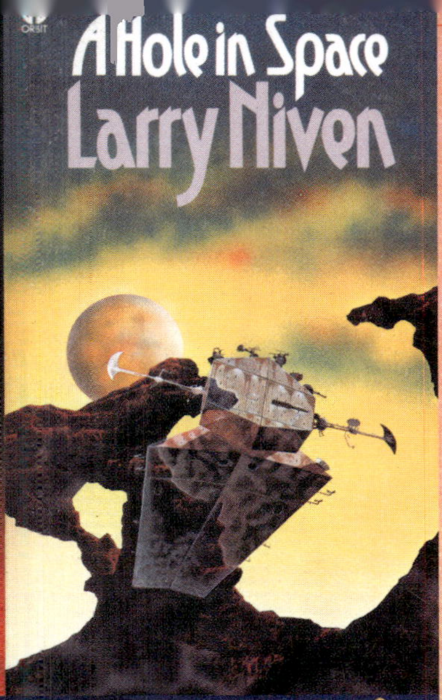

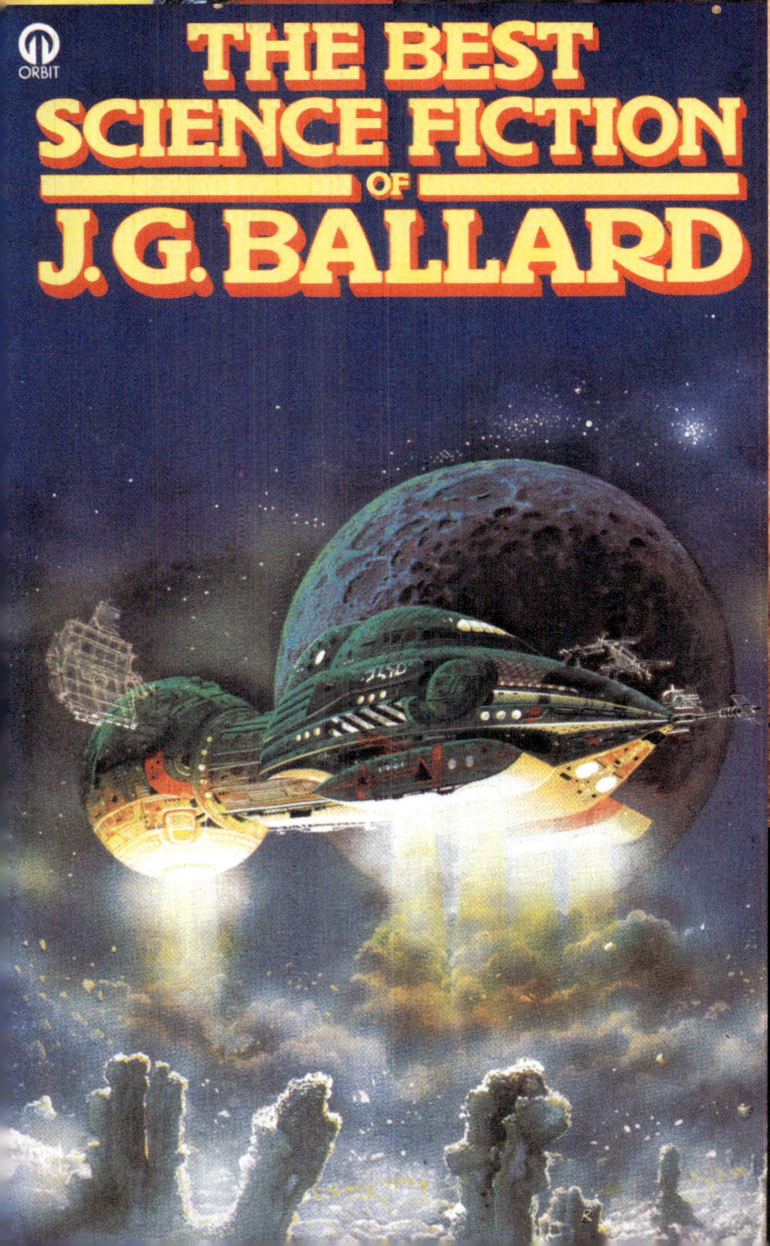

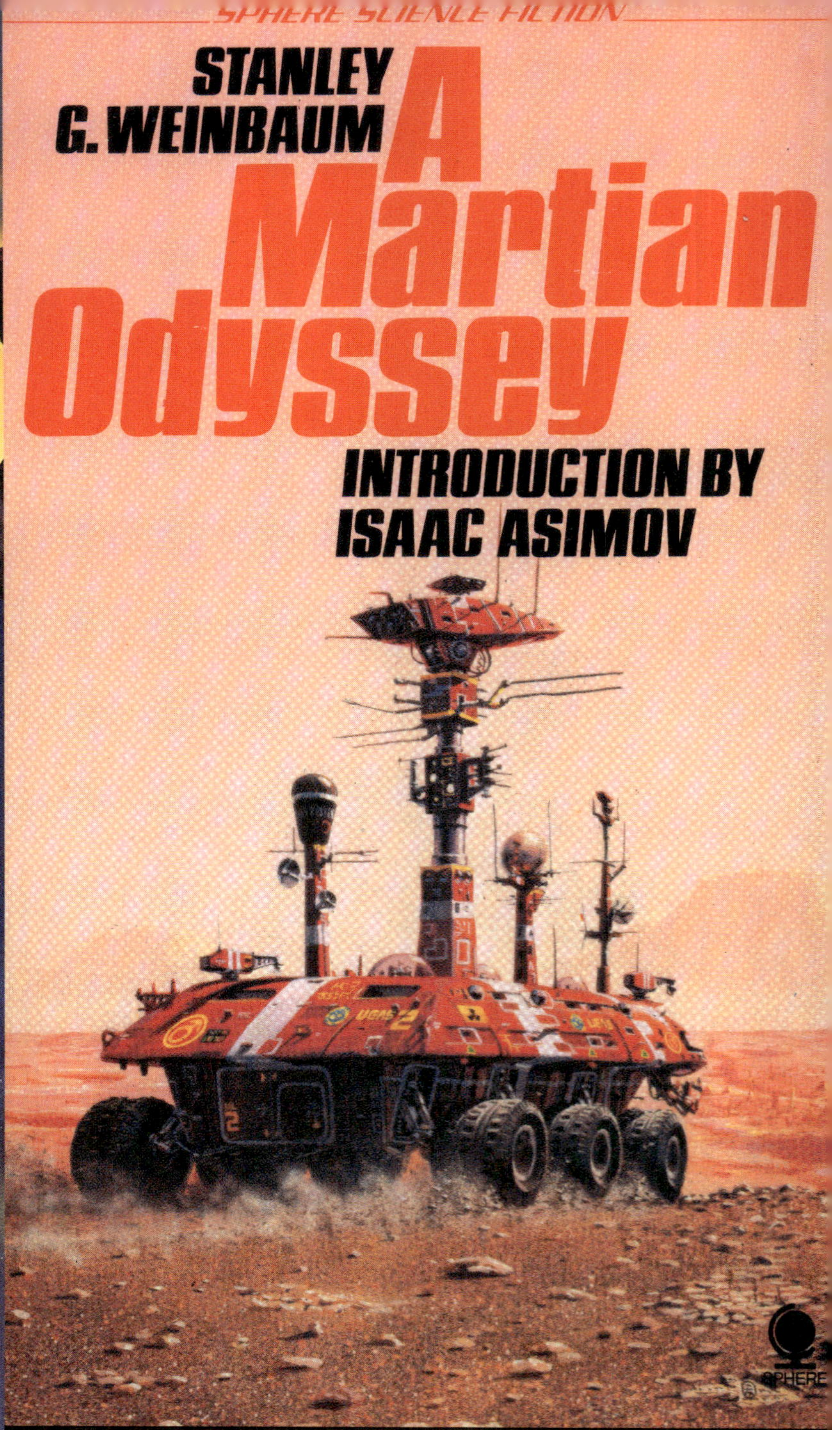

▲ Peter Elson's work was perhaps the most Foss-like of the Foss School. A fine designer of intricately detailed spacecraft and other vehicles (as can be seen on this 1977 reprint of Stanley G. Weinbaum's *A Martian Odyssey*), Elson was unable to move on when publishers began to demand more figurative images.

◀◀◀
Angus McKie's illustrations could be chunky or delicate—or both, as with Book 2 of *Again, Dangerous Visions* (Pan, 1977). McKie designed some of the best spaceships of the period, including the Hooded Swan for the Pan editions of Brian Stableford's series and numerous super-detailed designs for the *Perry Rhodan* series.

◀◀
Nobody can paint crashed space wrecks on alien planets and floating derelicts in space like Tony Roberts. But are these starships truly abandoned? And who is communicating through those aerial-decked telecommunication satellites?

◀◀
Bob Layzell's best work was a synthesis of Foss, Eddie Jones, and Bruce Pennington, although his earliest published works were whimsical fantasy images and art nouveau posters. An early criticism was that his treatment of ideas was too loose and embryonic; an airbrush and masses of detail resolved the problem for many art editors.

▶
One of Colin Hay's strengths was his depiction of architecture. A creator of leviathan-sized spaceships, he could produce superstructures and towers of equally daunting stature.

Many artists have acknowledged the influence of Foss on their work and it can still be seen in games, movie designs, and book covers. A group of artists represented by the Young Artists Agency in London were especially associated with the Foss School of spaceship cover designs—intricately detailed, sharply delineated star ships, majestic planetary backgrounds, and airbrushed spacescapes. Most publishers felt, unfairly, that the work of these artists was interchangeable and rather than establish a look for a series of books by a particular author with a single artist, the "brand" was the style of artwork. A good example of this was Futura's 39 volumes of *Perry Rhodan*, which was launched with a run of Foss covers in 1974 but would also include the work of Peter Jones, Angus McKie, Bob Layzell, Peter Elson, Colin Hay, and others.

Of these, Peter Elson and Colin Hay were closest to Foss in both his strengths and weaknesses. Hay, a Scottish artist who trained at Edinburgh College of Art, worked for Panther, Coronet, and Hamlyn, notably producing covers for a number of John Wyndham's early titles reprinted by Hodder in 1977. Both he and Elson (1947–1968) were able to mimic the intricate spaceship designs and alien landscapes but were rarely asked to develop their artwork beyond that. Hay decided to depart the SF field as demand for these kinds of covers diminished around 1980, and has since successfully transferred his attentions to 3D modeling on computers and abstract painting; Elson found himself unable to adapt and, while painting the occasional cover in the 1980s and 1990s, spent more time producing theater backdrops and murals.

Angus McKie (1951–), perhaps most recognized at the time for the run of covers he produced for the Hooded Swan series by Brian Stableford (Pan, 1977–1978), was to become more widely known when his story *So Beautiful and So Dangerous* became a segment of the *Heavy Metal* animated movie (1981). McKie has since gone on to produce many other comics (*Comic Tales*, 1982; *The Blue Lily*, 1993; *The Dome*, 1998; colors for *Martha Washington Goes to War*, *Bad Boy*, *Heart of Empire*, and more).

Tony Roberts (1950–) trained at Wolverhampton College of Art and Ravensbourne College of Art, and worked for Panther, Corgi, Futura, Pan, and others, illustrating the works of Samuel R. Delany, Larry Niven, Isaac Asimov, etc. He became one of the most famous British SF illustrators when Glenn Brown

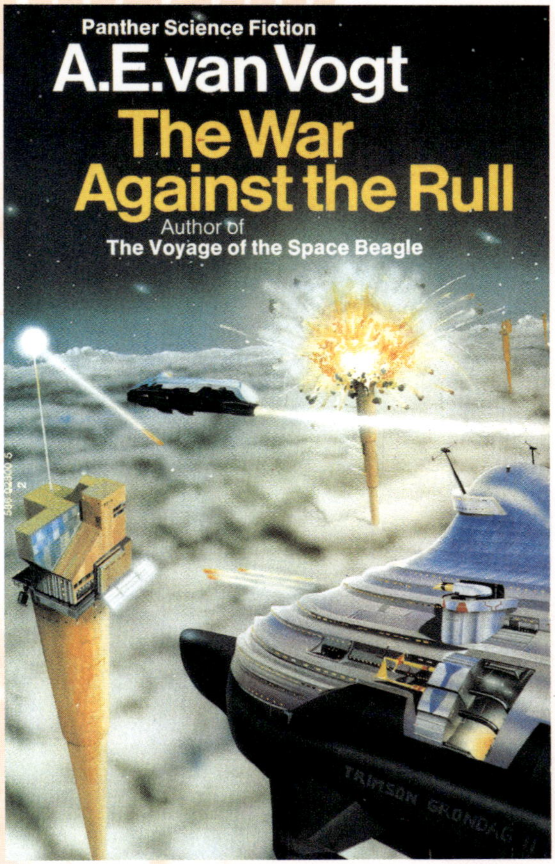

(1966–) displayed *The Loves Of Shepherds 2000* at the 2000 Turner Prize show in London, where he was one of the short-listed artists. Brown had used a spaceship design by Tony Roberts (*Double Star* by Robert A. Heinlein, Pan, 1974) and, although he filled it with detail and set it against a different planetary background, to many eyes it was a clear case of plagiarism, an accusation later settled out of court. Brown has also based other works on images from Chris Foss' *Diary of a Space Person*.

The images by these and other artists whose work was in demand in the early 1970s inspired the publication of *Science Fiction Monthly*, a magazine filled with poster-sized cover reprints. Stewart Cowley's *Spacecraft 2000–2100 A.D.* (1978) reused cover art by linking the images via a newly created future history of mankind and presenting the various craft as a kind of *Jane's Fighting Ships* of the future. Further volumes in the *Terran Trade Authority* series by Cowley and a number of similar styled books reused dozens of cover images.

AFTER THE DELUGE

In the 1980s, Britain went through one of its periodic downturns in paperback production and the call for majestic starships began to wane. Artists with a more individual style like Peter Andrew Jones (1951–) and Chris Moore (1948–) were able to survive the transition from gadget art to what publishers were now demanding of their covers.

Emerging from the St. Martin's School of Art in the early 1970s, Peter Jones produced his first covers in 1974. Although sometimes grouped with the Foss School, then in high demand, Jones' artwork saw pulp sci-fi merged with high fantasy. Richly colored and glowing with energy, Jones was at home with the buxom females of the latter as he was with the detailed gadgetry of the former, which allowed him to move into the fantasy role-playing market when SF went through a dip, although his work could still be found on books by Harry Harrison and Greg Bear in the 1990s.

Chris Moore has become one of the finest SF artists working in the UK in the '90s and the 2000s. Educated in Doncaster and Maidstone before receiving his Masters Degree from the Royal College of Art, he produced his first book cover in 1973 for Methuen. His artwork has graced the works of Clifford D. Simak, Philip K. Dick, Larry Niven, and many others, notably as one of the main artists of Orion's SF Masterworks line. A strong perspective, with spaceships in the extreme foreground, was something of a trademark of his early work, but his compositional skills work just as well with other elements, especially human figures.

Moore's work has a very finished look to it—not always airbrushed but very detailed and deliberate. John Harris (1948–) has a more painterly approach. Buildings and spaceships are often monumental in scale in his work, with indistinct edges giving the perception of distance. After graduating from a fine art course at Exeter College of Art & Design, Harris made a brief foray into SF cover art in 1970. "They were dreadful," he recalled. After five years studying and teaching transcendental meditation abroad, he returned to England where he met Philip Dunn of Pierrot Publishing. Harris' series of paintings, *Mass*, emerged, although the proposed book did not. His work has since been widely published by most major publishers in the UK and USA.

Fred Gambino (1956–) earned his first commission from Sphere (for *Beneath the Shattered Moons* by Michael Bishop) in 1978, although his real success came in the 1980s with work on novels by Frank Herbert and Isaac Asimov (including a series of six linked paintings for the *Foundation* novels). He has progressed from making models of *Thunderbirds* by hand, to modeling CGI spaceships on computer.

Lee Gibbons has been active since the late 1980s, working for Unwin, Headline, and, more recently, for Orbit, one of a number of artists who now combine the best of the starship gadgetry with lush spacescape backgrounds, as in his recent covers for Ken Macleod's *Engines of Light* trilogy. Mark Salwowski (1953–) began producing SF covers in the mid-1980s and earned an appreciative audience as the cover artist most associated with Ian M. Banks' novels, although his slightly abstract SF art is at odds with his romantic fantasy art of dragons and other winged creatures.

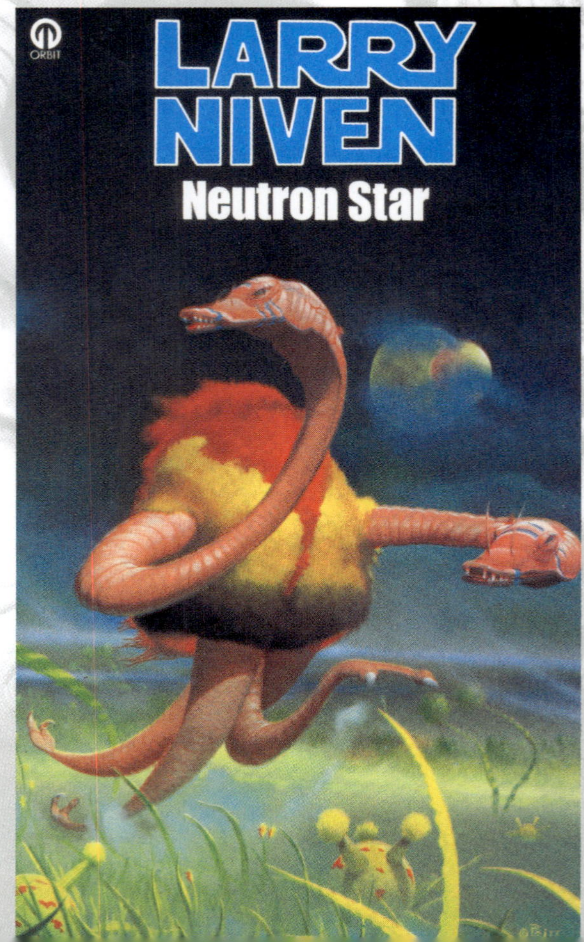

►
Against the Odds by Elizabeth Moon (Orbit, 2001) is the seventh (and last) book in the _Heris Serrano_ series of military SF to feature a cover by Fred Gambino, who has been at the forefront of the move to digital artwork. Gambino reinvented himself in the 1990s, thanks to the advent of the PowerMac, Photoshop, Bryce, and other computer wizardry, which reinvigorated his work and has kept him steadily employed this century.

◄
Peter Jones was one of the handful of Foss contemporaries whose artwork stood out as being different; his ability to create truly alien creatures and his wild use of color is unmistakable, even if the alien is as well known as Larry Niven's Pierson's Puppeteers, seen here (_Neutron Star_, Orbit, 1981).

►
Undoubtedly one of the finest SF cover artists working today in the UK, Chris Moore has survived the ups and downs of the publishing industry thanks to an extensive repertoire of styles that goes beyond the super-detailed spacecraft. An early collection, _Parallel Lines_, featured his work alongside that of Peter Elson, and he is more than able to produce that kind of Foss-esque cover as required, _Downbelow Station_ by C. J. Cherryh (Methuen, 1983) being an especially fine example.

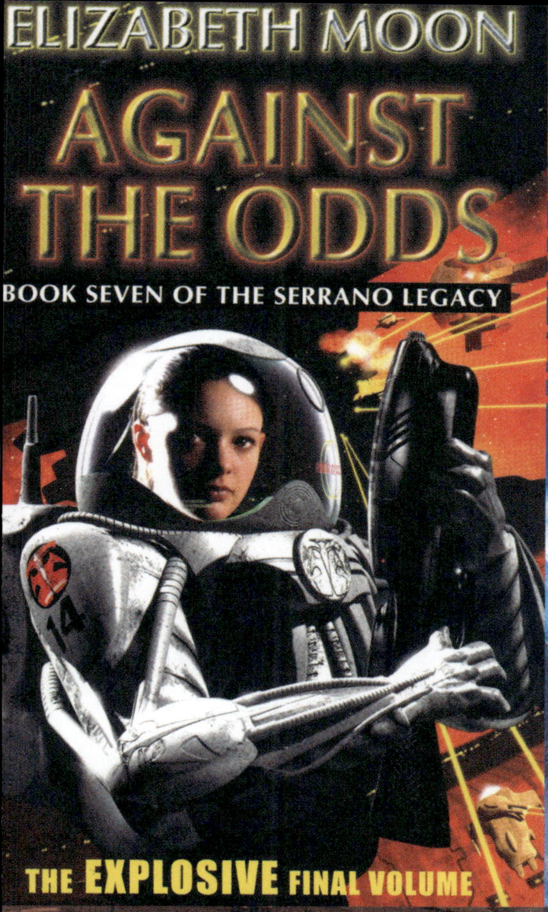

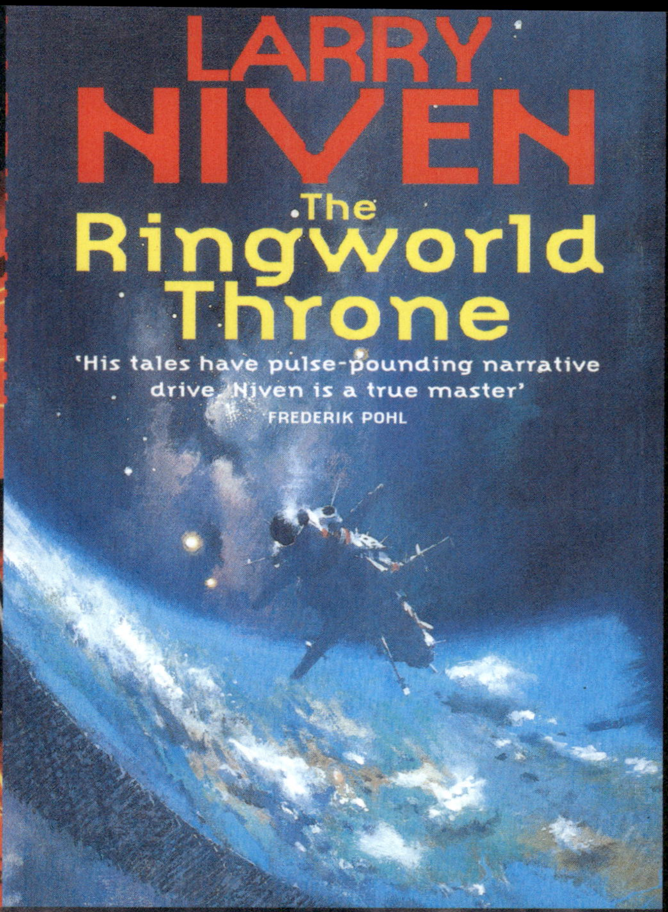

John Harris' work harks back to the art of John Martin. The power is not in the detail of his paintings but the overall way they are perceived. His work is particularly effective when dealing with such massive superstructures as Larry Niven's Ringworld, *The Ringworld Throne* (Orbit, 1996) being the third in the series.

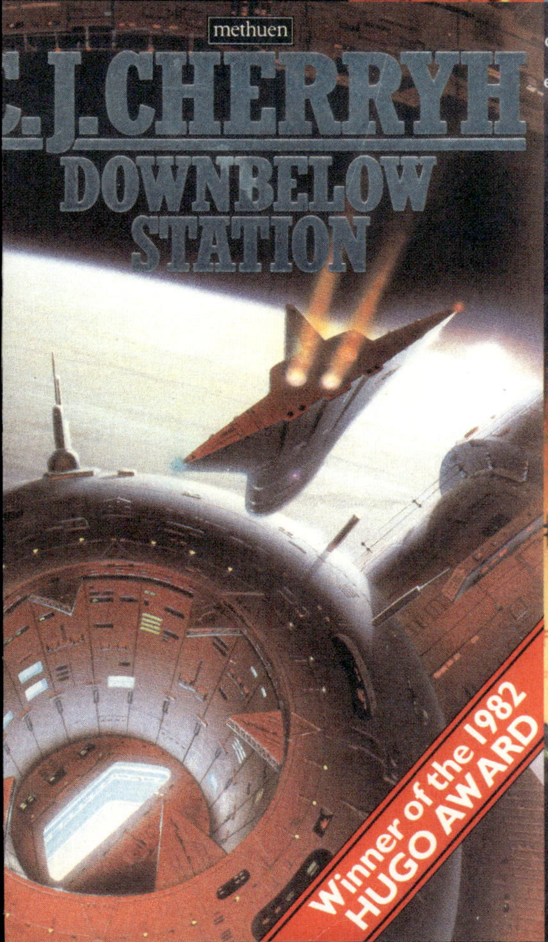

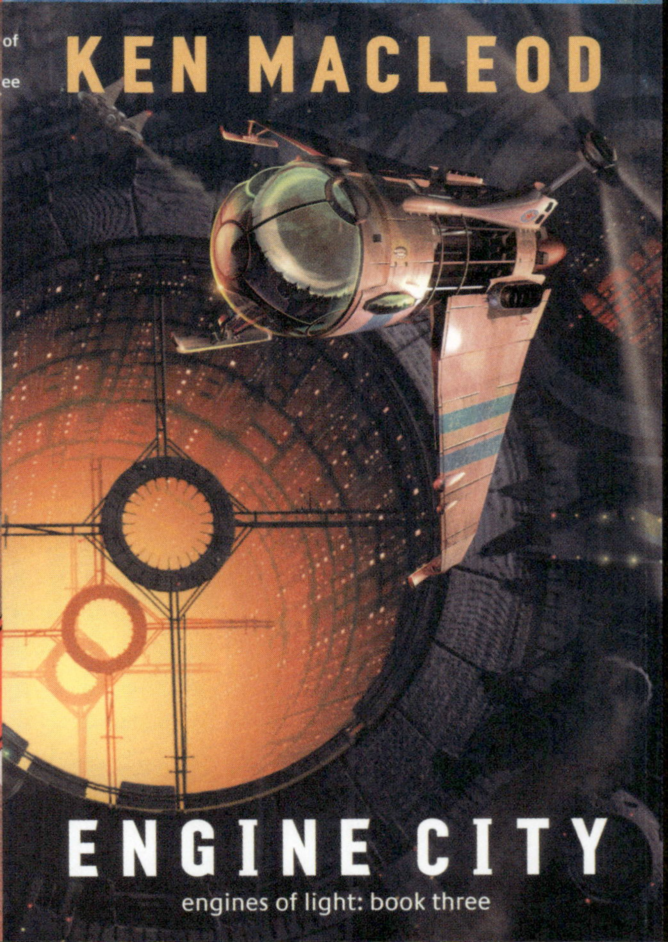

Lee Gibbons is among the new generation upholding the finest traditions of British SF illustration, his work reminiscent of a range of artists from Tim White to Chris Moore. *Engine City* by Ken Macleod (Orbit, 2002) proves that, in the right hands, a definite sense of wonder can still be wrung out of a futuristic cityscape.

THE MODERN ERA

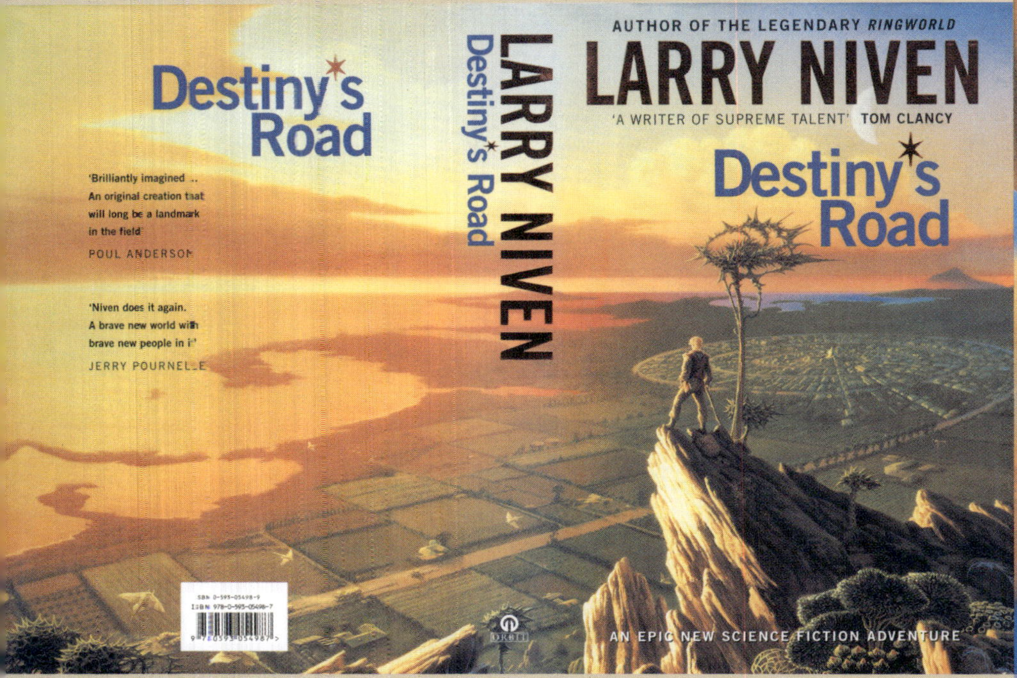

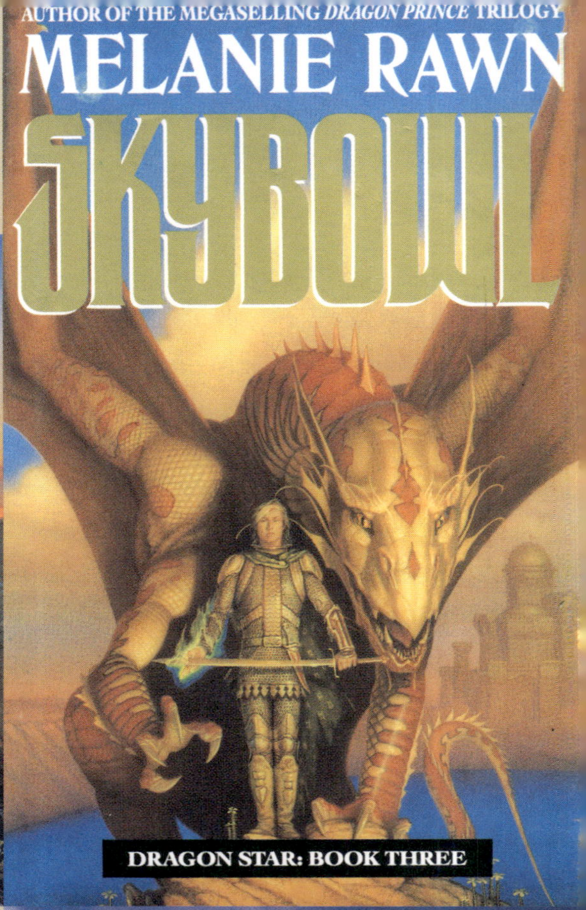

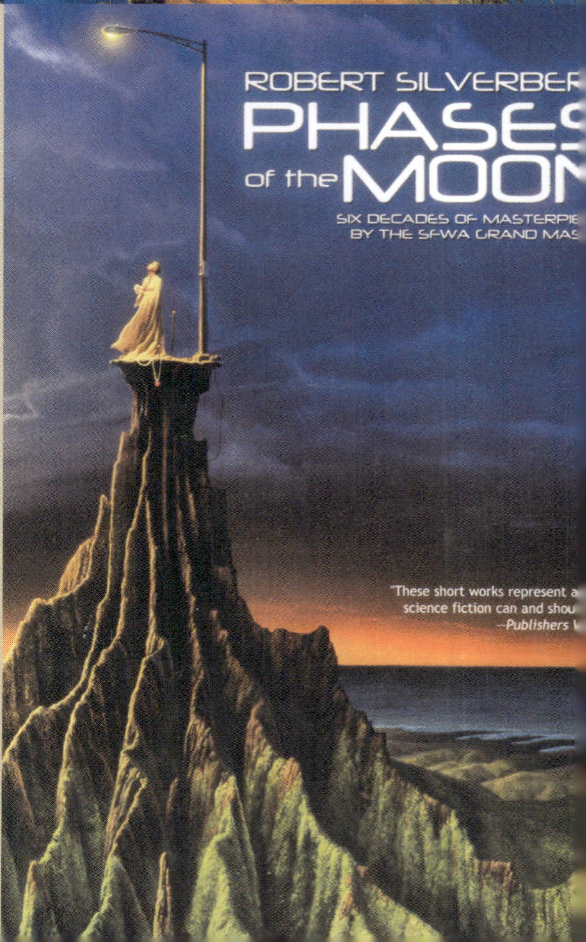

Modern science fiction cover art has been dominated by a handful of names. If measured by awards, the finest artists working in the US are Michael Whelan, Bob Eggleton, and Jim Burns, who have dominated the Hugo Award for Best Artist since 1980 with 13, eight, and three wins respectively. Whelan and Eggleton have both won a total of 12 Chesley Awards each. The latter award has been picked up 13 times by Todd Lockwood, whose work began appearing on *Asimov's* and *Analog* in the early 1990s. Lockwood (1957-), who graduated from the Colorado Institute of Arts, was on the staff of role-playing publisher TSR and has produced lush fantasy covers for *Realms of Fantasy*, *Dragon*, and other magazines, as well as design work for *Dungeons & Dragons*.

Of the three other artists named above, two are American. Michael Whelan (1950-), born in Culver City, California, but educated at different times in 11 schools in both California and Colorado, attended a summer art class in the Rocky Mountains in 1965 and, as he would later say, "fell in love with the whole thing: the smell of the turpentine, the dedication to improvement, and the devotion to the visual arts."

▲
Larry Niven, four years late with *Destiny's Road* (Tor, 1997), acknowledged Michael Whelan's artwork—which was displayed at a Chicago World SF Convention five years before the release of the book—and said, "Our landscapes no longer quite match... but the tree on the peak is his, and I snatched it up and made it the Destiny fool cage."

▶ ▲
Whelan has become increasingly associated with fantasy artwork rather than pure science fiction. *Skybowl* by Melanie Rawn (DAW Books, 1993) is a great example of Whelan's attention to detail, not just in the central figure—Whelan learned anatomy by drawing medical illustrations for the *Journal of Bone and Joint Surgery*—but in the detail of the armor and the design of the dragon.

He studied biology, physiology, and anatomy at San Jose State University but continued his art studies and subsequently enrolled at the Arts Center College of Design in Los Angeles, dropping out after nine months to pursue a full-time career. A painting exhibited at the World Science Fiction Convention was sold to European agent Thomas Schlück, and Whelan then had the confidence to approach DAW Books with his work. Sales quickly mounted to DAW, Marvel Comics, Ace Books, and privately, and he received his first award nominations.

Whelan's next major break came when he was assigned to illustrate Anne McCaffrey's *The White Dragon*, his first science fiction book to appear on the hardcover bestseller list. His debut collection of artwork, *Wonderworks*, appeared in 1979. The following year he won his first Hugo, published his first collaboration with Stephen King (a limited edition of *Firestarter*), and produced a book for National Geographic entitled *Our Universe*; by 1984, when the Jacksons' *Victory* album featured Whelan artwork, he was probably the most widely seen fantasy artist in the USA.

Further collections of Whelan's work (*Works of Wonder, The Art of Michael Whelan*, and the poster book *Something in My Eye*) have helped establish him as America's premier SF and fantasy artist. His artwork is perhaps most associated with Stephen King's *The Dark Tower* series and novels by Robert Silverberg, C. J. Cherryh, Tad Williams, and his continuing association with McCaffrey.

◀
The cover for *Phases of the Moon* by Robert Silverberg (iBooks, 2004) has the kind of evocative, inventive, and humorous image that has won Whelan more than 60 major awards in 30 years.

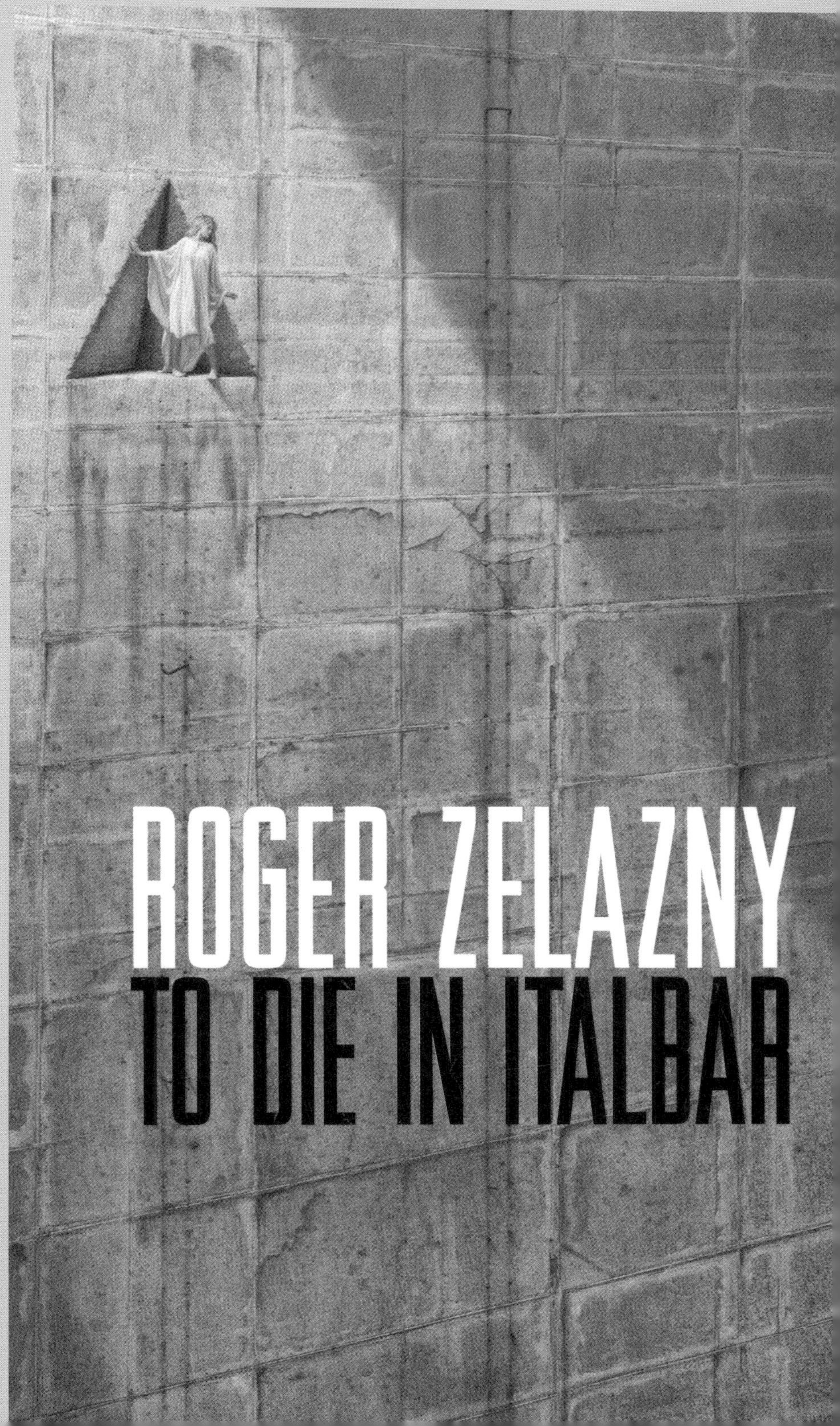

▶
A startling, vertigo-inducing image for the cover of *To Die in Italbar* by Roger Zelazny (iBooks, 2003). According to Whelan, "Very rarely will a single phrase from a book inspire a cover approach for me. Doing a cover painting usually means attempting to distil the most significant aspects of the book into a single image, trying to get the flavor of the whole experience in one picture."

▶▶
Somewhat in the tradition of Chesley Bonestell, Bob Eggleton is still able to conjure up a sense of wonder for *Farmer in the Sky* by Robert A. Heinlein (Baen, 2008), despite the slow progress of mankind's space program. Eggleton is one of the few SF artists to have had an asteroid (13562) named after him, an honor he shares with Bonestell).

▶▶
In the guise of "Edward Miller," Les Edwards has adopted a more painterly style, especially for the numerous covers he has produced for PS Publications. *The Extraordinary Voyage of Jules Verne* by Eric Brown (PS Publishing, 2005) concerns the famous French writer and a trip through time, the steampunk sensibilities of the story captured in Edwards' colorful cover.

▶
Les Edwards has been associated with Anne McCaffrey's *Dragonriders of Pern* series since the 2001 publication of *The Skies of Pern*. Edwards has said that the idea for *Dragon's Fire* (Bantam, 2005) was to give the cover the look of a Second World War dogfight, "but the dragons just wouldn't stay in formation!"

Bob Eggleton (1960–) has turned a childhood fascination with science fiction movies into a career that has now spanned 25 years. From watching *The Creature from the Black Lagoon* and *Godzilla* movies, he graduated to model making and drawing. His early ambition was to be a comic book artist but he found more success selling landscapes and portraits while still in his teens. Still interested in science fiction—especially after the arrival of *Star Wars*—he was persuaded to show some of his artwork at a science fiction convention. By coincidence, the first time he showed his artwork was at the 1980 Worldcon where Michael Whelan won his first Hugo, and Eggleton picked up an award for Best Monochrome Artwork in the Amateur categories for Popular and Artist/Peer voting.

This early promise was soon turned into a professional career and his first book cover appeared from Baen Books in 1984. He was first nominated for the Hugo Award in 1988 and won for the first time in 1994. His work ranges widely from romantic fantasy—he is particularly fond of dragons and prehistoric creatures—to SF hardware.

Never one to remain static, Eggleton has worked for comics, has been a conceptual designer for the *Star Trek—The Experience* ride and animated movies *Johnny Neutron* and *The Ant Bully*, and co-created two storybooks (*Dragonhenge* and *The Stardragons*) with John Grant.

Another popular artist who cannot be pinned down to one style is Les Edwards (1949–), who has worked in film production and gaming as well as advertising, movie poster design (*John Carpenter's The Thing*, Clive Barker's *Nightbreed*), and graphic novels. A graduate of Hornsey College of Art in the UK in 1972, and working via the infamous Young Artists agency, Edwards has had a dual career. As Les Edwards, he illustrated dozens of horror and science fiction novels for most major UK publishers; some of his gaming illustrations were collected in *Blood and Iron* (1990). Around 1998, he also began producing covers under the name Edward Miller, adopting a different approach to his artwork with this persona.

"The two approaches are quite separate and I try to keep it that way," he has said. "Different materials, different techniques, and a different outlook. Inevitably there's a certain amount of bleed from one style into the other but the two are sufficiently distinct that it doesn't matter too much… Les has learned a lot from Ed and Ed prevents Les from getting too stale."

Edwards has provided art for a number of major books, working on titles by Anne McCaffrey, C. J. Cherryh, Barbara Hambly, China Miéville, and others; as Miller, he has produced numerous covers for PS Publishing, including illustrations for the Stephen King's *The Colorado Kid*. Along the way he has won the British Fantasy Award for Best Artist seven times and has twice been nominated as both Edwards and Miller.

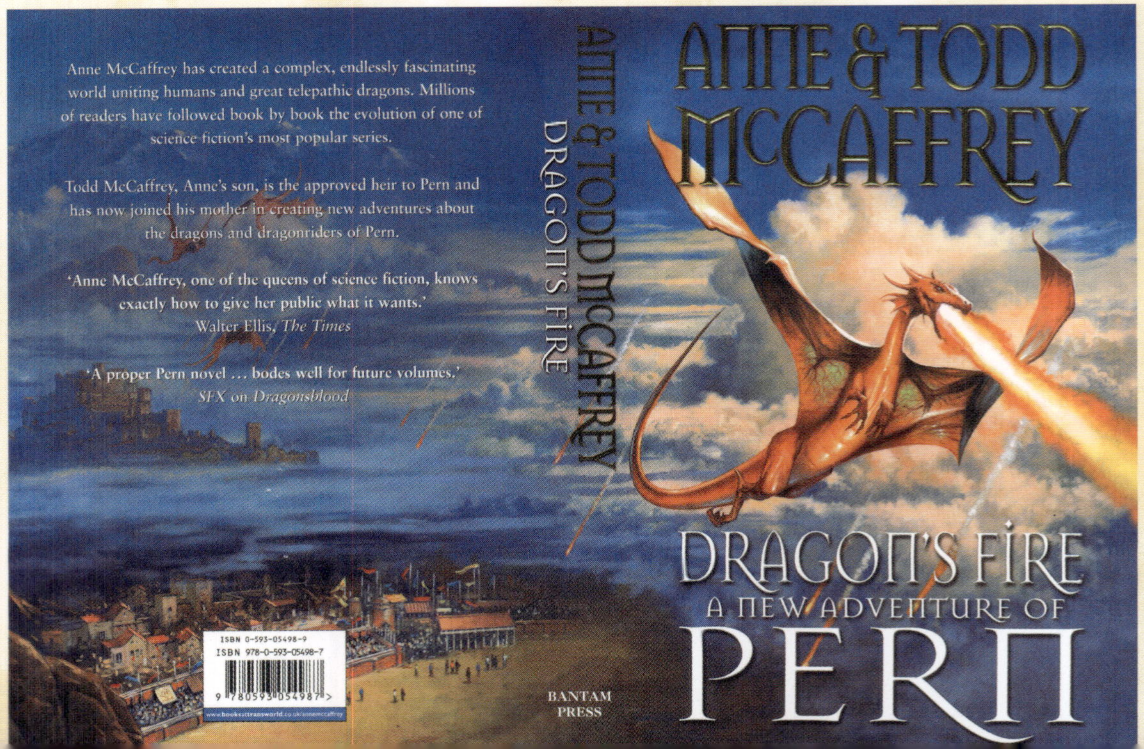

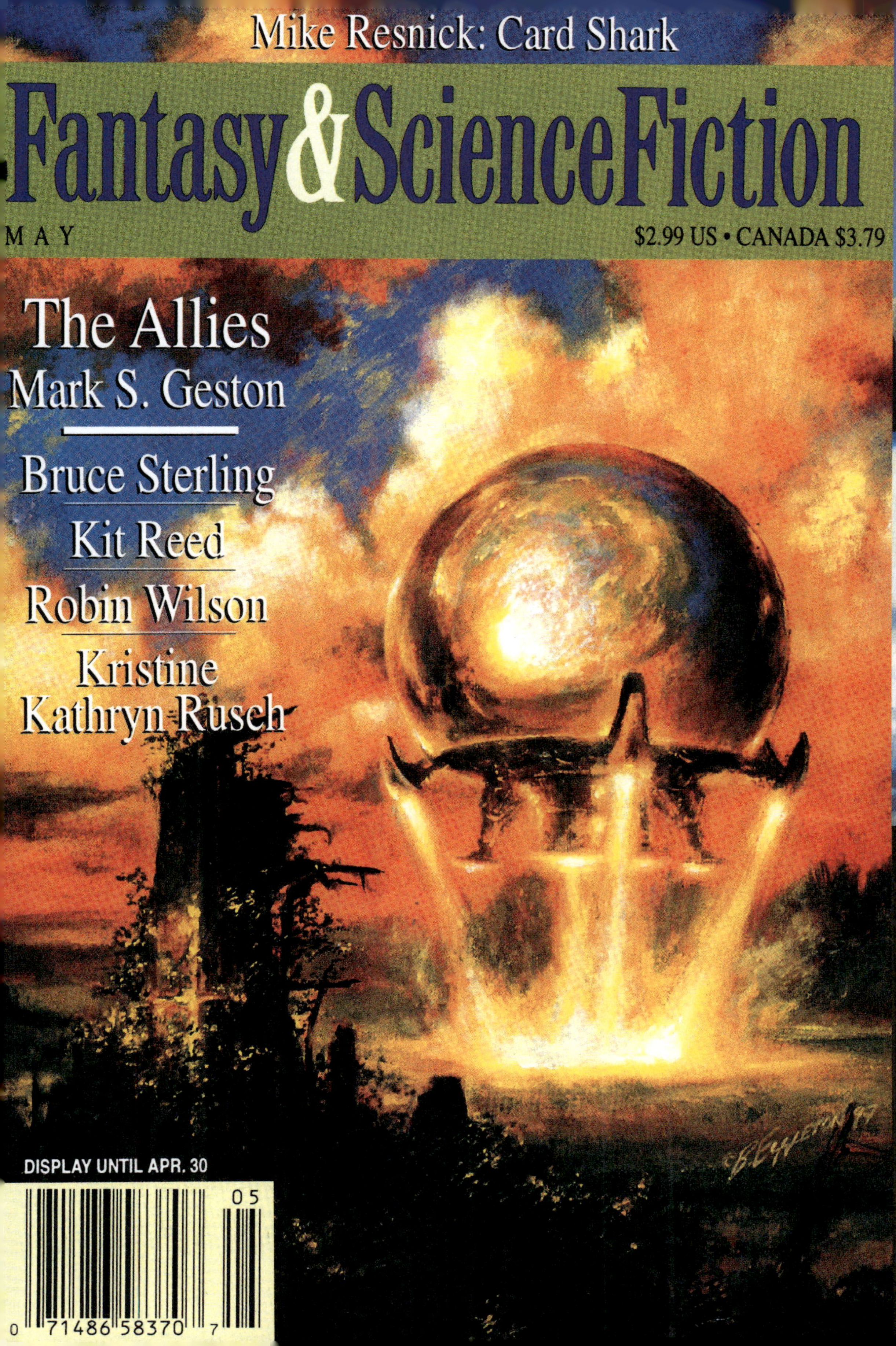

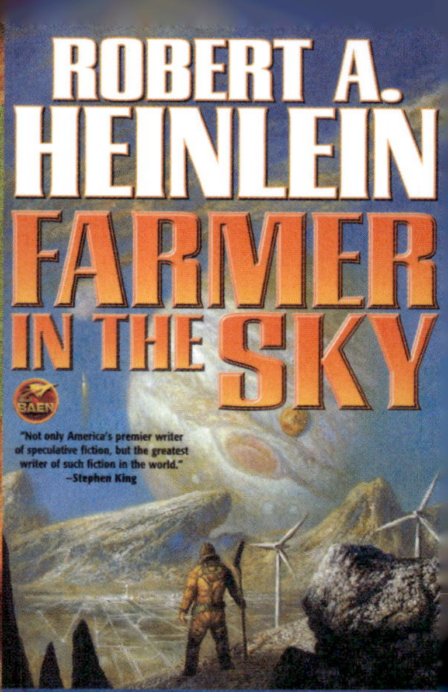

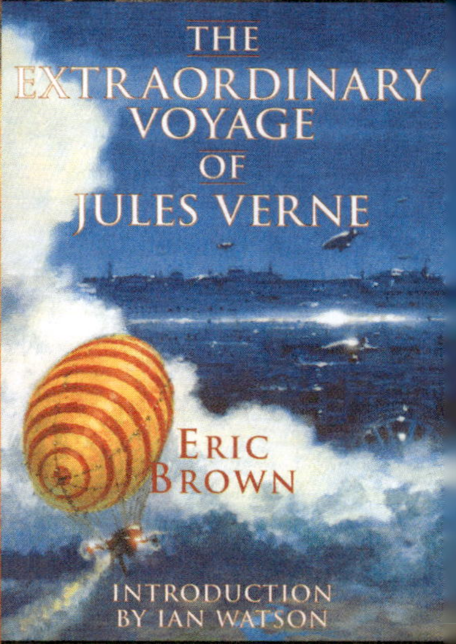

◄
Spaceships and SF hardware are a common element of Eggleton's work, both the metallic, hard-lined spacecraft of traditional SF and others that sport a more organic look. The artist has drawn a number of award-winning covers for the *Magazine of Fantasy & Science Fiction*, his illustration for *The Allies* by Mark S. Geston (May 1998) winning the Chesley Award in 1999.

JIM BURNS

Jim Burns (1948–) is the most widely respected SF and fantasy artist working in the UK. Meticulous and sophisticated, his artwork is the kind that authors aspire to have on their books. Robert Silverberg, in his foreword to Burns' *Lightship* (1985), revealed that he "spent decades searching for the right artist—the one who could lay his hands on one of my books for ten minutes and come away with such a complete understanding of the texture and imagery and *feel* of the book that he could render a perfect pictorial representation of it." Jim Burns was that artist.

A fascination with aircraft and *Dan Dare* led Burns to become a trainee pilot in the Royal Air Force, but he was not particularly suited and turned instead to his other love, drawing. A year's foundation course at Newport School of Art was followed by three years at St. Martin's School of Art and employment by Young Artists, the agency that was providing covers to most British paperback science fiction (although Burns was not limited to SF, as he also drew historical romance covers).

He worked extensively for Pierrot Publishing in the late 1970s, illustrating *Planet Story* by Harry Harrison and producing covers for *Mechanismo* and *Great Balls of Fire*. Pierrot went into liquidation in 1979 but Burns was soon in demand in America, producing dozens of covers for Bantam, Ace Books, and Avon over the next few years. He also spent some weeks doing designs for the movie *Blade Runner*.

In the late 1980s, Burns worked on *Navigators of the Empyrean* for Games Workshop, intended to be a future history of mankind told in pictures; the project was left incomplete. Five finished images appear in *Transluminal* (1999), Burns' second collection of artwork.

To create his covers, Burns reads books in manuscript, although he will not necessarily choose a specific scene to illustrate. "I let the imagination of the author create the characters and overall aspect of a scene. I apply my imagination to the detail and the ambience," Burns has said. "Ultimately one arrives at an image which has a degree of conviction about it—a potent reality emerging from a scene which has nothing at all to do with reality."

Although he has called it "the most appallingly difficult task," Burns is noted for his talent at depicting human figures in his paintings; Harry Harrison has said: "You'll find the same love of texture in the softness of a woman's skin as you will in the brittle coldness of machined metal."

Burns continues to be associated with some of the biggest names in modern science fiction, among them David Brin, Paul J. McAuley, Ian McDonald, Greg Bear, and Peter F. Hamilton.

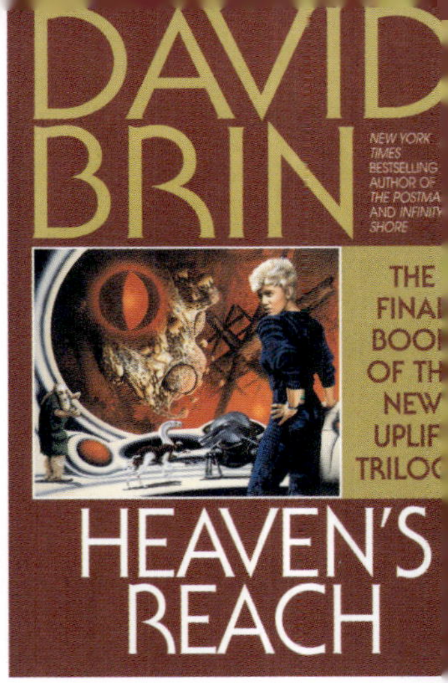

◄▼ ▲ ▼
The style of presenting cover art has changed over the years. Authors' names are now the selling point as far as publishers are concerned and illustrations have to make way for the "brand name," title, and various explanations and quotes. Burns' illustration for David Brin's *Heaven's Reach* (Bantam, 1998) is reduced to less than a quarter of the cover area, but Burns doesn't stint on the detail. Indeed, he has said that the relegation of artwork to a panel "usually means that one can ignore the design constraints of titles, author names, etc., and use the space allotted as a pure, unadulterated canvas."

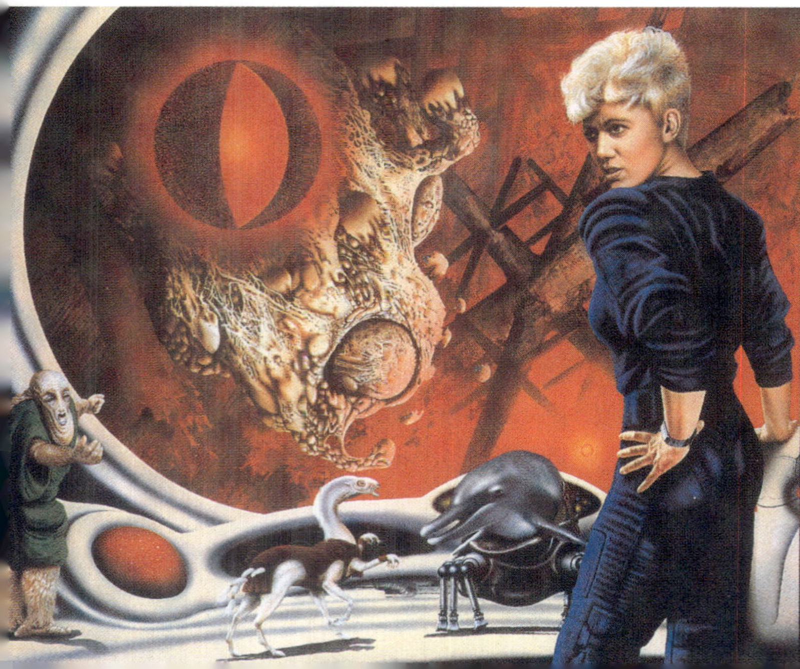

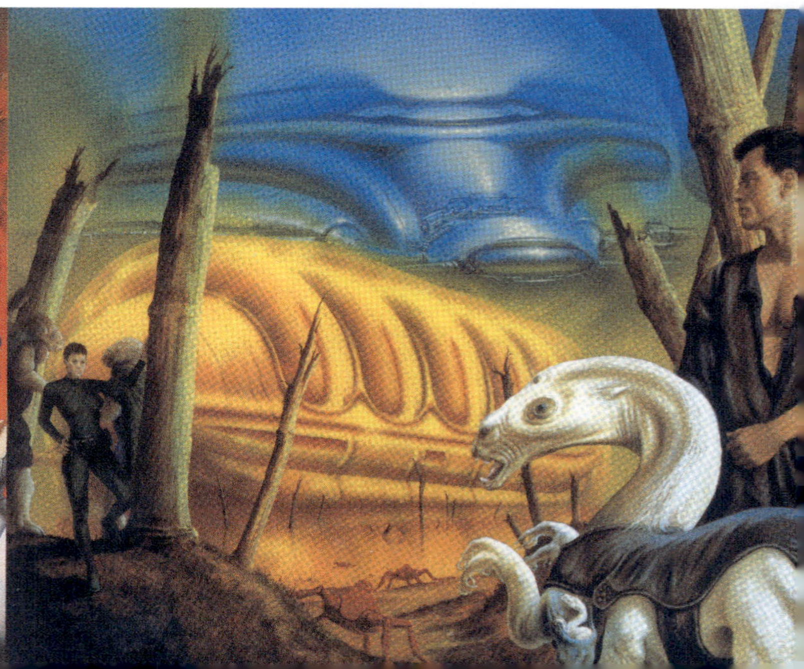

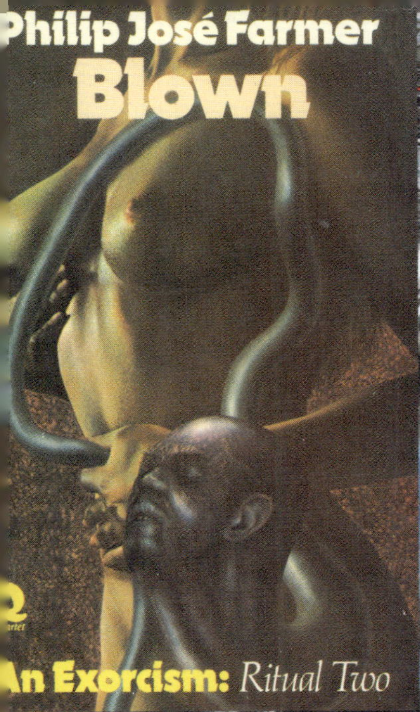

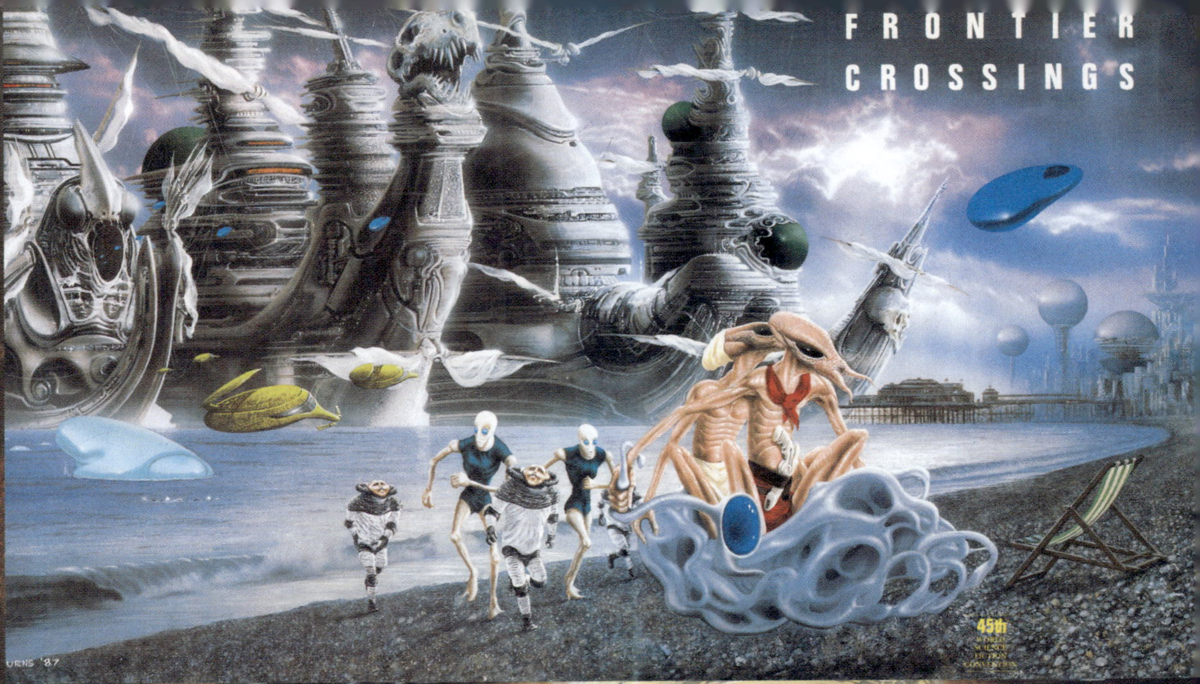

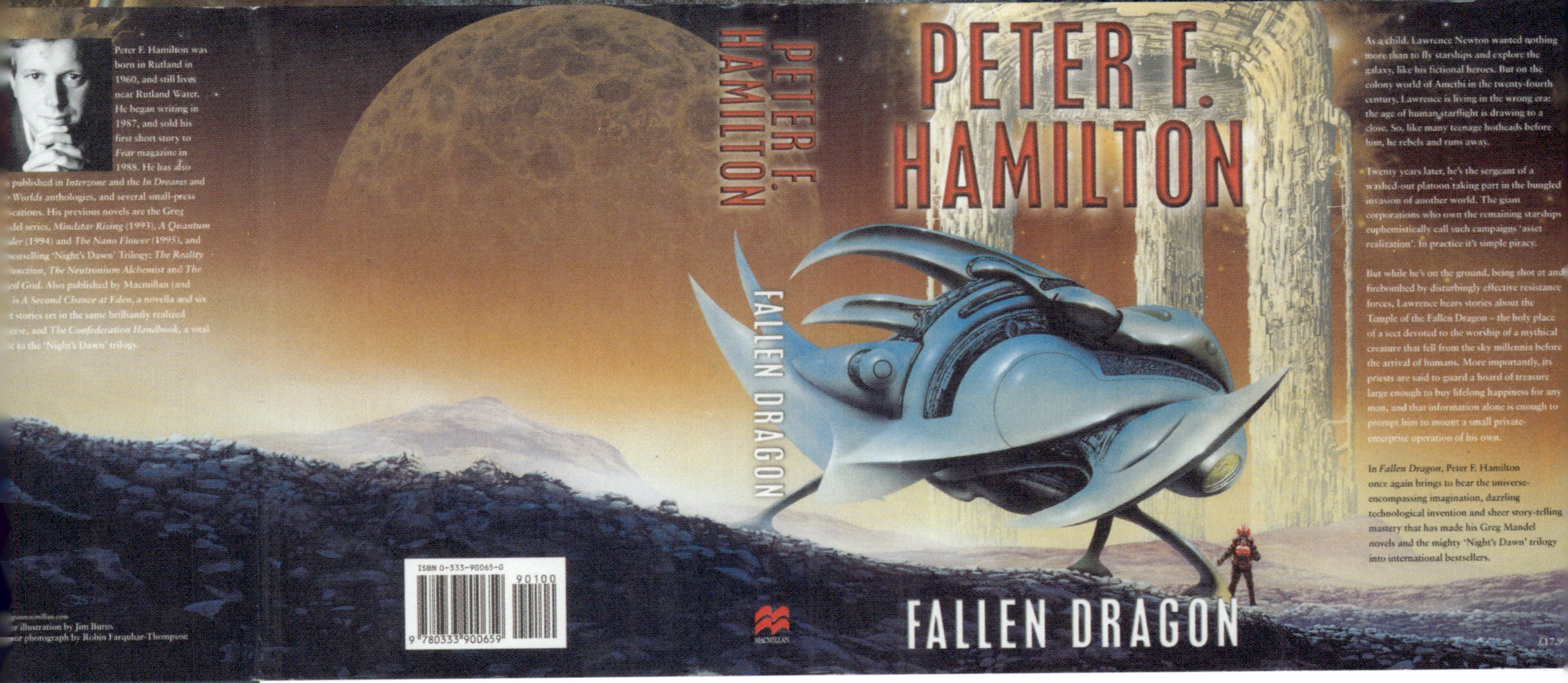

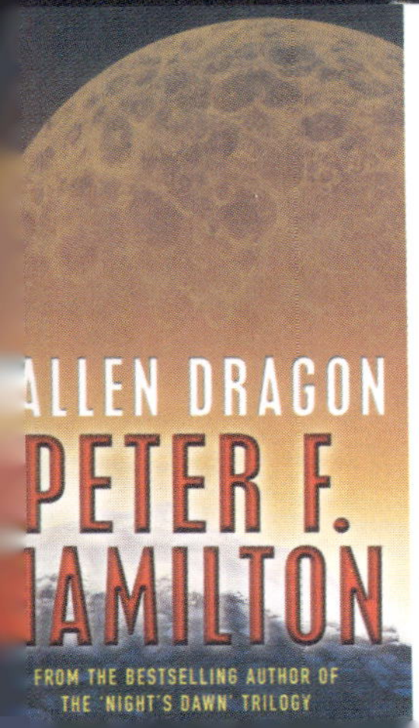

◀ ▲

Anyone buying the paperback edition of Peter F. Hamilton's *Fallen Dragon* (Pan, 2002) may wonder why Jim Burns is so highly rated as a cover artist. It's only when you witness the full widescreen splendor of the hardcover dust jacket (Macmillan, 2001) that you see Burns' work as it was intended, the original image spreading even onto the end flaps of the jacket.

◀▲▲

An early cover by Burns for *Blown* by Philip José Farmer (Quartet, 1975). Harry Harrison, who worked with Burns on *Planet Story and Mechanismo*, has commented on Burns' love of texture.

▲▲

Jim Burns' cover for the 1987 World Science Fiction Convention book, *Frontier Crossings*, shows him in more playful mood. Burns was one of the Guests of Honor at this convention and won the Hugo for Best Artist, the first of three wins. He also received the award in 1995 and 2005.

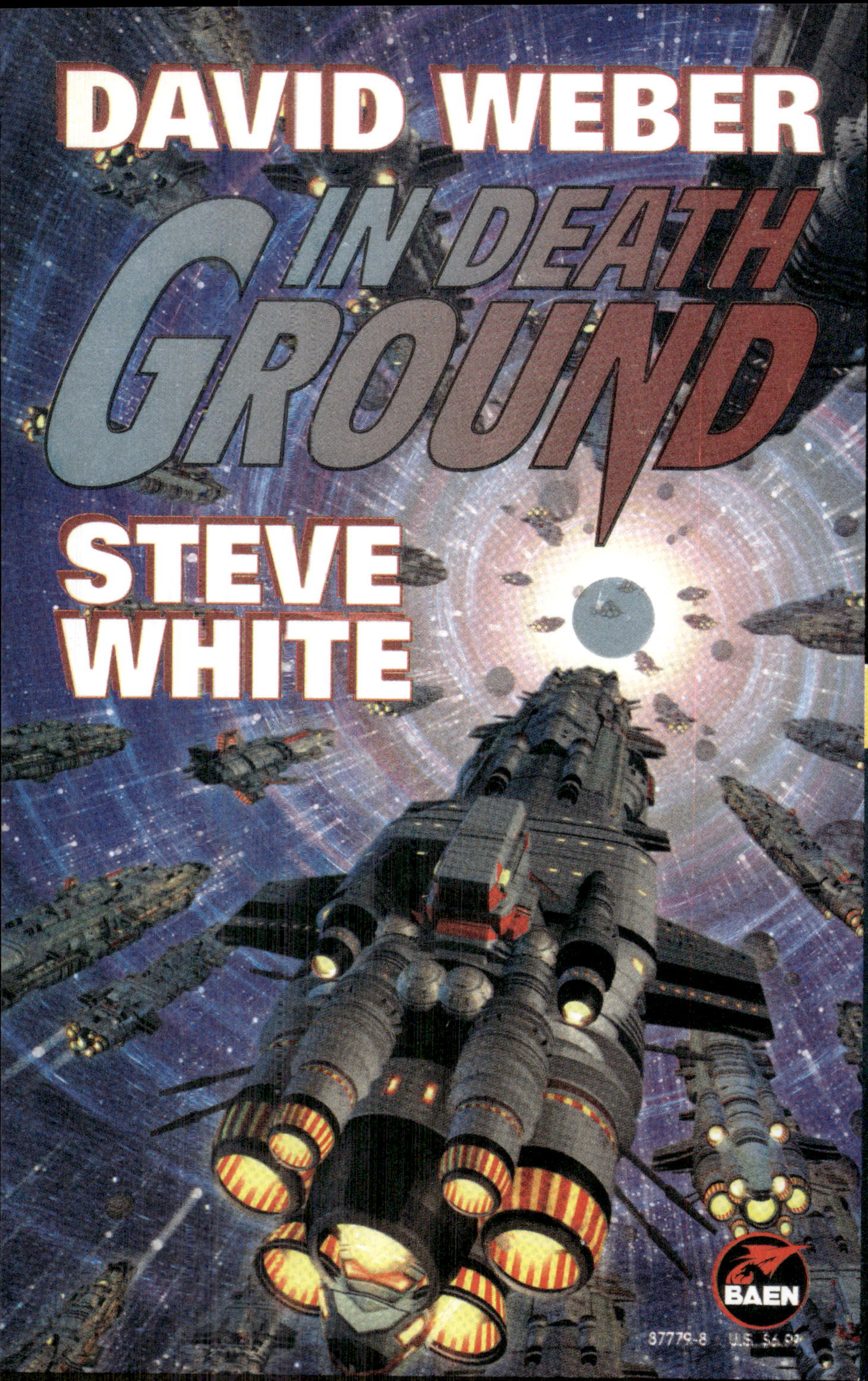

▲
In Death Ground (Baen 1997) was another military SF novel, this time set in the Starfire wargaming universe, which David Weber helped develop. Despite all the technology he uses to create his images, Mattingly has called science fiction "the last bastion of illustration."

DAVID MATTINGLY

David Burroughs Mattingly (1956-) was heavily influenced by comic books (especially Jim Steranko',
Edgar Rice Boroughs, and illustrators as widely ranging as N. C. Wyeth and Jackson Pollock. He trained at the Colorado Institute of Art, Colorado State University and later transferred to the Art Center College of Design in Pasadena, California.

Mattingly's trajectory was not straight into illustration. His career began at Walt Disney Studios, where he ultimately became head of the matte painting department, working on *The Black Hole*, *Tron*, and *Dick Tracy* among others.

He began freelancing while at Disney Studios, his first fantasy book cover appearing on Christopher

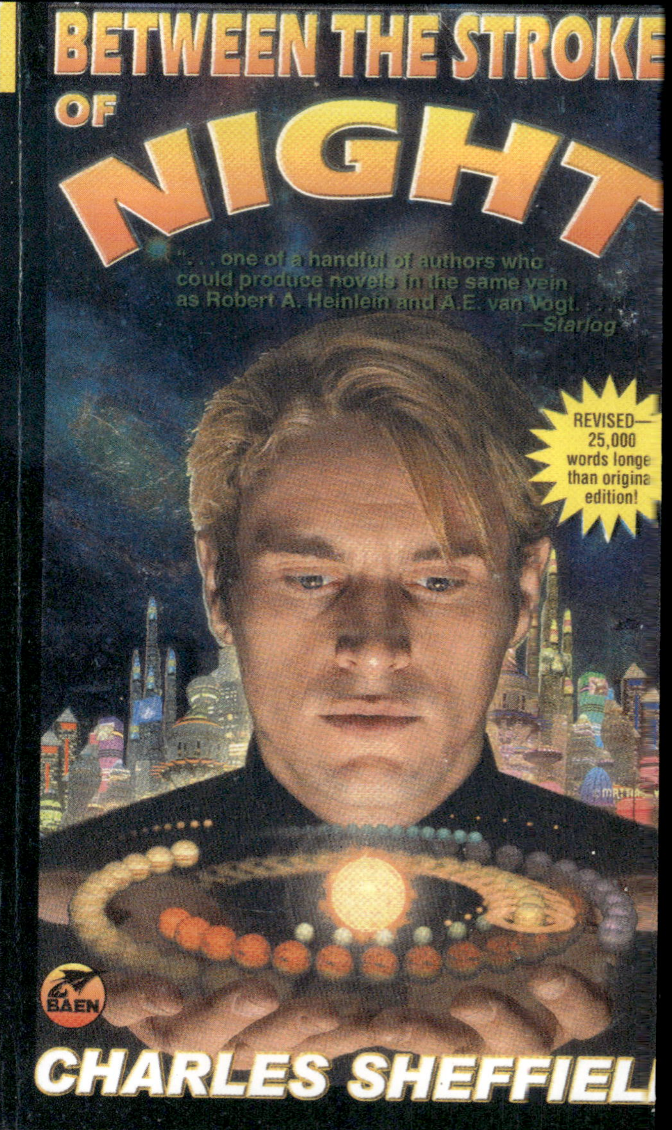

Stasheff's *A Wizard in Bedlam* (DAW Books, 1980). Departing from Disney, he moved to New York in 1983.

Over the past 25 years, Mattingly has produced more than 500 covers for science fiction and fantasy novels and magazines, twice winning the Magazine and Booksellers Best Cover of the Year Award. He has also produced artwork for album sleeves, advertising, movie studios, and computer companies.

Mattingly's career neatly summarizes the advances made in computer generated digital painting. At Walt Disney Studios, the effects for *The Black Hole* were produced using models on wires and traditional painted matte art; *Tron*, an arcade game brought to life, was the first movie to make extensive use of computer animation. More recently, Mattingly was producing digital matte paintings for New Zealand-based Weta Digital for the Will Smith-starring *I, Robot* and television commercials.

Similarly, his book and magazine cover art has developed into the digital age. Of his covers, the 50-plus he produced for K. A. Applegate's *Animorphs* series have probably had the widest circulation. His work has taken in humorous fantasy illustrations and hard science fiction and his best work has been the series of highly detailed work he has produced for the best-selling Honor Harrington books by David Weber for Baen Books.

For these, Mattingly works closely with the author to make sure the covers are accurate in every detail. Honor herself is based on a professionally photographed model, recreated digitally in Photoshop; other elements such as spaceships are designed as 3D geometry, then rendered using 3D Studio Max. His technique of mixing traditional painting and digital rendering, developed during the 1990s, has been honed over a period of years and is now used for most of his covers. While he is best known for his work for Baen, he has also produced covers for Bantam, DAW, Del Rey (including the "Pellucidar" series by Edgar Rice Burroughs), Tor, and Dell, and illustrations for *Omni* and *Playboy*. Some of his best work can be found in the collection *Alternate Views, Alternate Universes: The Art of David B. Mattingly* (1996).

His impressive body of work earned him the Chesley Award from the Association of Science Fiction and Fantasy Artists in 1992.

▼ ◄▼ ◄◄▼

The world of Honor Harrington is a gender-neutral future military, based by author David Weber in part on the British Royal Navy as depicted in Patrick O'Brian's best-selling *Master and Commander* series and the classic *Horatio Hornblower* series by C. S. Forester (it is no coincidence that Honor Harrington shares the same initials as Hornblower). The first book in the series was illustrated by Laurence Schwinger and Gary Ruddell. From the sixth novel, *Honor Among Enemies* (Baen Books, 1996), the series has been illustrated by David Mattingly.

◄

Although he uses professional photographs of models for his characters, Mattingly does not simply Photoshop them into a painting. The photographs are digitally painted over and many elements in the backgrounds are painted in the traditional way, scanned in, and worked up digitally.

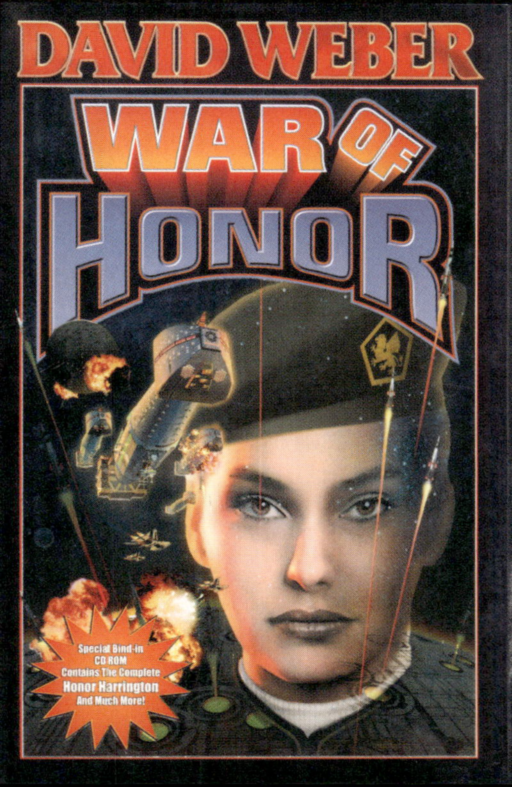

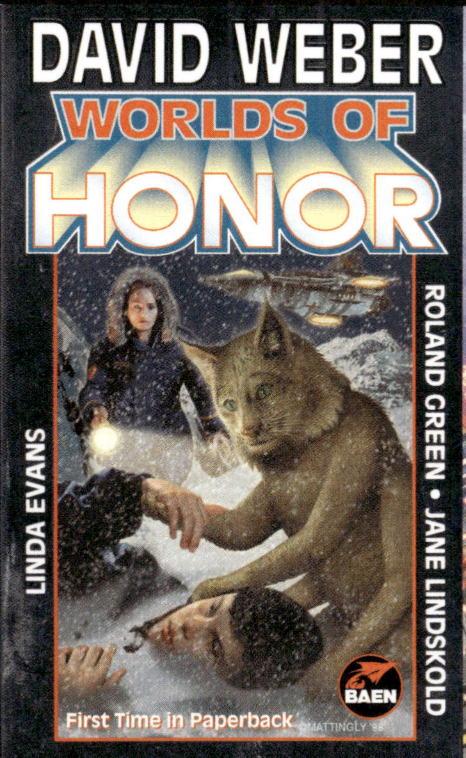

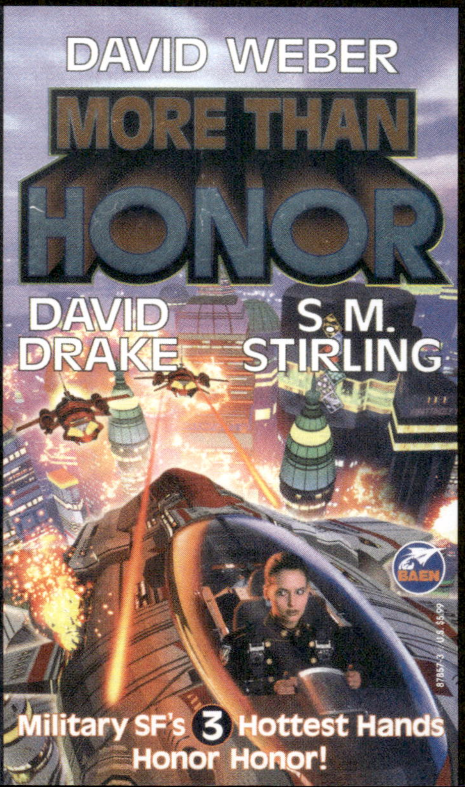

John Berkey was one of the few artists who could capture the real majesty of a spaceship. "It seemed logical that [spacecraft] would have to look like they could fly and go fast," he once said. "A triangle looks more like speed than a rectangle. Familiar elements like windows can give the illusion of size. For some reason, the more successful paintings always seemed to have the viewer looking up at the craft. We will always think of space as *up* until the day it becomes *out*."

Born in North Dakota, Berkey (1932-2008) grew up in Aberdeen, South Dakota, and St. Joseph, Montana. While at high school he made himself useful as an errand boy at a local art studio in Minneapolis. After attending Minneapolis School of Art, he began his professional career working on advertising illustrations for studios in Minneapolis for six years before joining Brown & Bigelow, the world's largest commercial calendar publisher, for eight years. He became a freelance illustrator in the late 1960s, working for diverse magazines, including *Sports Afield*, *Argosy*, *National Geographic*, and *TV Guide*.

This broad background in illustration meant that Berkey was often drawing romantic, pastoral, and historical images with a realism that required much research into the subject matter. He lost none of the realism when it came to painting technology, and some of the rustic spills over into his science fiction covers. Author Jane Frank has remarked that "John's Impressionistic renderings seemed more real than any photograph, and more romantic and mysterious than any airbrush could make them."

Berkey's science fiction covers began appearing in 1968, primarily from Dell and Ballantine. For the latter he produced artwork for the *Star Science Fiction* series edited by Frederik Pohl, an author whose work he became associated with in the early 1970s; for Fawcett and Dell he produced a number of covers for Isaac Asimov in the 1970s and a diverse range of titles throughout the 1980s and 1990s, including nautical adventures by Brian Callison and other work outside of SF.

In the 1970s he produced posters for a number of movies, including *The Towering Inferno* and the remake of *King Kong*, as well as pre-production art for *Star Wars* and *Star Trek: The Motion Picture*. His work appeared on 16 different stamps issued by the US Postal Service.

From the early 1980s, Berkey's broad brushstrokes began to break up the form of his spaceships. No longer quite so sharply rendered, they became vast space artifacts floating against planetary backgrounds. It was for these that he was best known in the 1990s when he was working for *Science Fiction Age*, although Berkey was not limited to starships; covers ranged from vistas of futuristic transport against towering cityscapes to more abstract designs and fantastic elements in the artwork he produced for his own pleasure.

The best of Berkey's paintings were gathered in *The Art of John Berkey* (2003); in 1999 he received the Spectrum Grand Master Award and, in 2004, he was inducted into the Society of Illustrators Hall of Fame.

▶
John Berkey was a regular cover artist for *Science Fiction Age* in the 1990s. Editor Scott Edelman has said of his work, "His impressionistic paintings had a dreamlike quality which made them a welcome change from the photo-realistic images that many other artists seemed to be aiming for then."

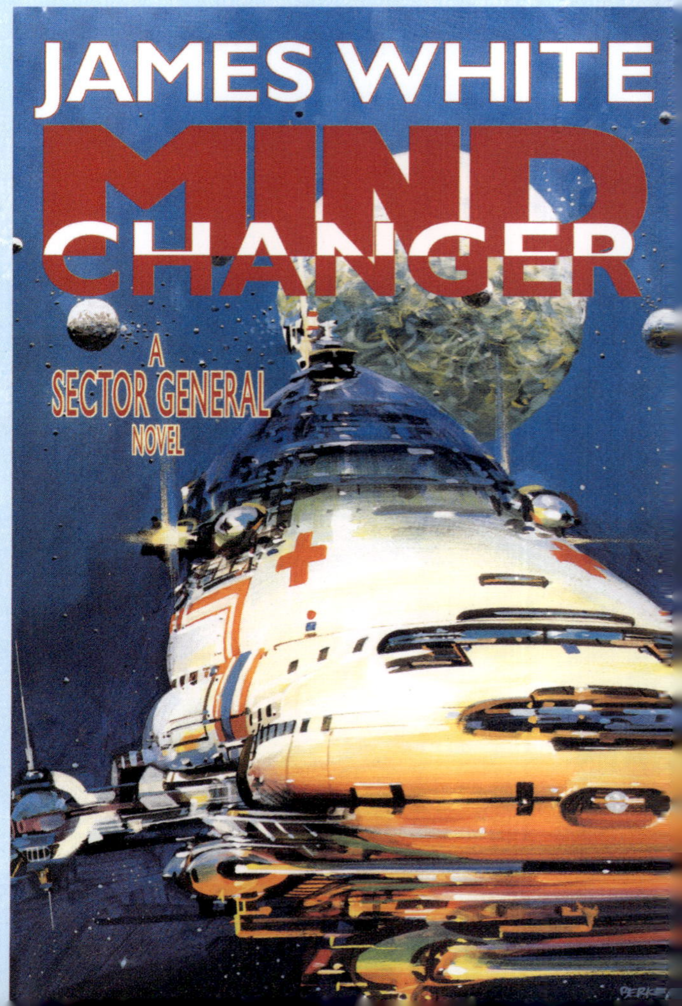

▶
Author James White was not a doctor as many thought, but worked as an assistant in a tailoring firm before joining an aircraft company as publicity officer. His 384-story Sector General hospital ship was a vast space station out on the galactic rim, catering for patients of every xenobiological type. Who better to envisage the enormous, and, in this case, colorful, space edifice than Berkey?

▶▶
Berkey's spaceships and starscapes have a majestic quality to them. His craft are not always sharply delineated; some blend into the background through which they soar, as in this illustration for *Sigmund in Space* by Barry N. Malzberg (*Omni*, July 1980).

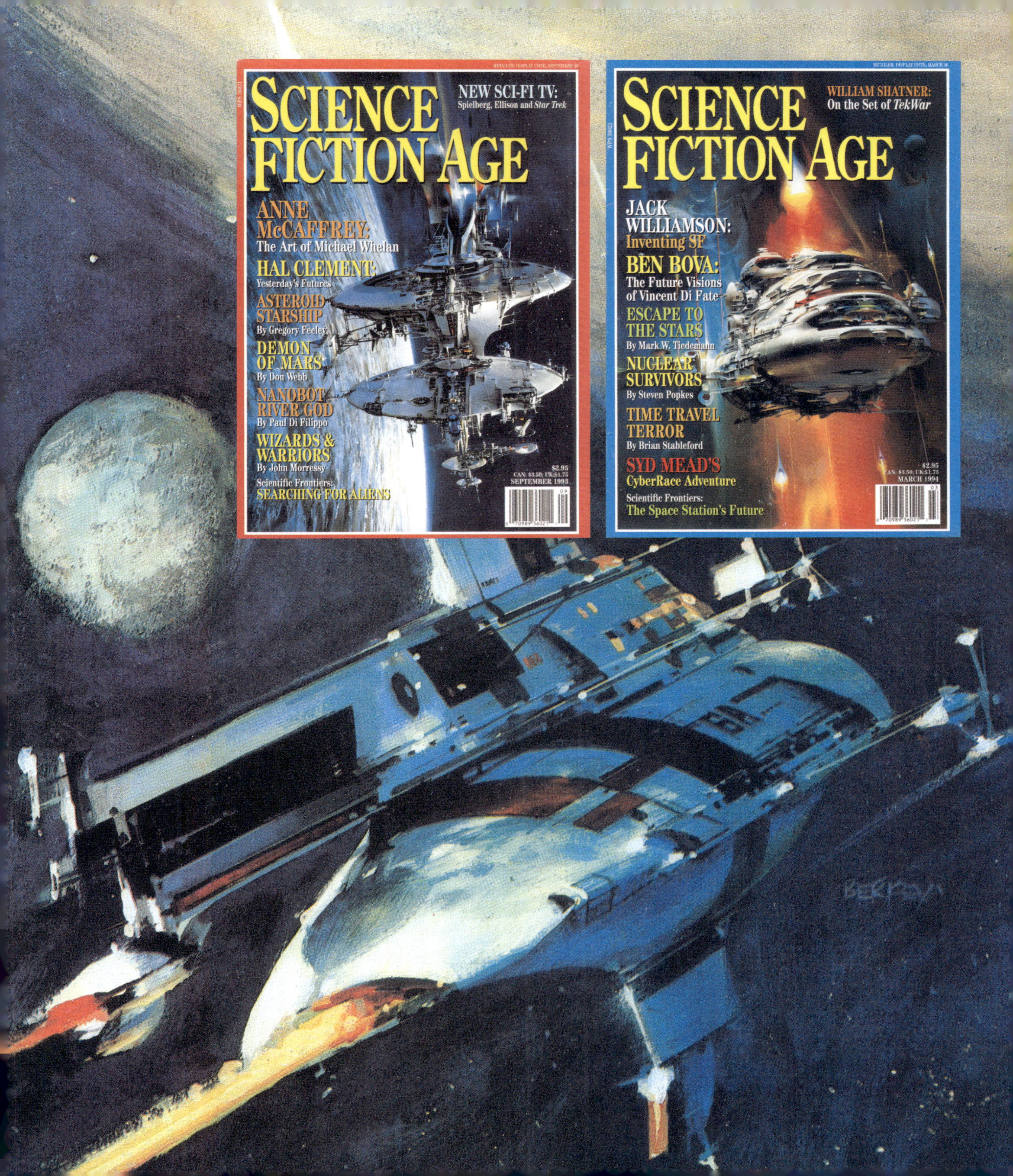
SCIENCE FICTION AGE
NEW SCI-FI TV:
Spielberg, Ellison and Star Trek
ANNE McCAFFREY:
The Art of Michael Whelan
HAL CLEMENT:
Yesterday's Futures
ASTEROID STARSHIP
By Gregory Feeley
DEMON OF MARS
By Don Webb
NANOBOT RIVER GOD
By Paul Di Filippo
WIZARDS & WARRIORS
By John Morressy
Scientific Frontiers:
SEARCHING FOR ALIENS
$2.95
SEPTEMBER 1993
SCIENCE FICTION AGE
WILLIAM SHATNER:
On the Set of TekWar
JACK WILLIAMSON:
Inventing SF
BEN BOVA:
The Future Visions of Vincent Di Fate
ESCAPE TO THE STARS
By Mark W. Tiedemann
NUCLEAR SURVIVORS
By Steven Popkes
TIME TRAVEL TERROR
By Brian Stableford
SYD MEAD'S
CyberRace Adventure
Scientific Frontiers:
The Space Station's Future
$2.95
MARCH 1994

OMNI MAGAZINE

▶
Bob Venosa's powerful vision of a Knights Inquisitor from George R. R. Martin's *The Way of Cross and Dragon*, which explores alien religion and the concept of faith; it won a Hugo Award, as did Martin's *Sandkings*, which also appeared in *Omni*.

Created by Bob Guccione, the publisher of *Penthouse* magazine, *Omni* was a glossy mixture of science fact and science fiction launched a year after the release of *Star Wars*. Conceived under the title *Nova*, the magazine went through a last minute change to avoid litigation from WGHB (a Boston-based PBS television station), who had a popular science show of the same name. "Omni" fitted perfectly in the planned cover layout.

Although Guccione had a firm hand in the magazine's conception, editorial direction, and design, staff changes behind the scenes meant that the magazine did not find its own voice for some time. Post-*Star Wars*, newcomers looking for the science facts behind the fiction—how fast *is* a parsec?—would have found the magazine's articles on future biology, radio telescopes, the Nobel Prize, and the Turin shroud a little too esoteric; there were no space battles in the fiction or the illustrations. Not to belittle *Omni*, but it was not the magazine most newcomers would gravitate toward when what they really wanted to know was how close mankind was to attaining At-At Walkers and Power Loaders.

In fact, *Omni* had put together a first-class package for its debut issue—including fiction by Isaac Asimov and Theodore Sturgeon—and had taken a confident step on the path it wanted to tread: "an original if not controversial mixture of science fact, fiction, fantasy, and the paranormal," as Guccione claimed in his first editorial.

From the point of view of visual design, *Omni* was unique; no other magazine could boast full color throughout, and few dedicated full pages and spreads to illustrations. The tone was for abstraction and symbolism rather than illustrating a passage from the story or feature. The first issue drew many of its illustrators from the school of "fantastic realists"—Austrian Ernst Fuchs (1930-), German (although living in New York) Mati Klarwein (1932-2002), and American Robert Venosa (1936-)—alongside surrealist painter Cliff McReynolds (1933-) and "psychic realist" Rudolf Hausner (1914-1995). Among Hausner's students in Vienna were Friedrich Hechelmann (1948-) and Gottfried Helnwein (1948-), who also contributed to *Omni*.

Much of the artwork was inspired by surrealism, via the Vienna School of Fantastic Realism group, with artwork by Salvador Dali, René Magritte (1898-1967), Erich Brauer (1929-), Michel Henricot (1941-), and other surrealists dominating—some of it quite playful, as in the work of Donald Roller Wilson (1938-) and Eric Paetz (1945-). The magazine brought a number of artists to the attention of a wider audience, including H. R. Giger (1940-) and De Es Schwertberger (Dieter Schwertberger, 1942-).

Perhaps more in most SF fans' comfort zone were the pictorial features, which often concentrated on space artists from around the world, including Don Dixon (1951-), Andrei Sokolov (1931-), Ludek Pesek (1919-), and David Egge (1958-).

Omni never achieved its full potential; it ran many fine stories (notably the early work of William Gibson and Ted Chiang) and saw off a number of rival publications but folded in 1995, although maintained a web presence until 1998.

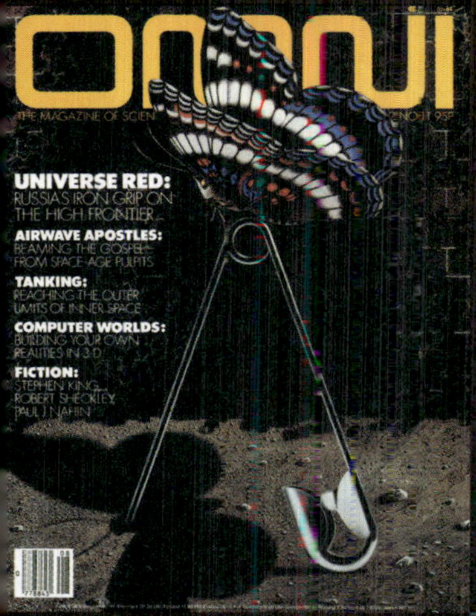

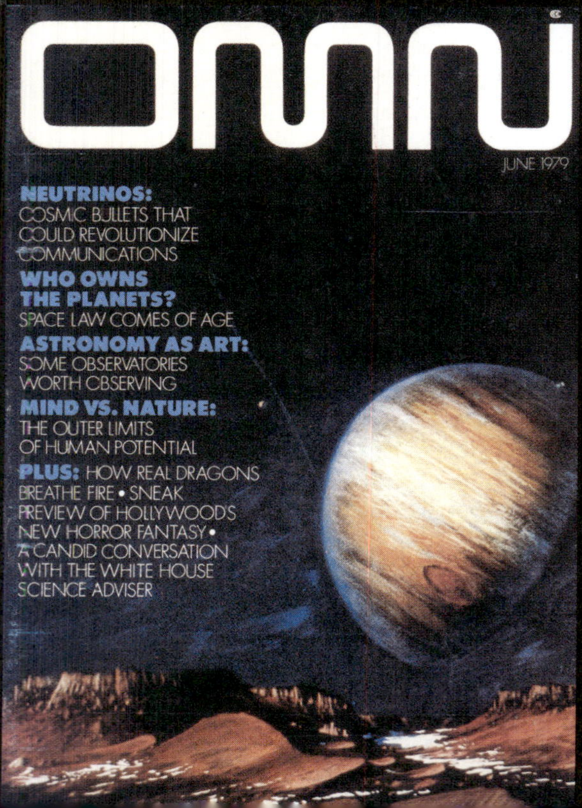

▲ ▶
Many of the artists found in early issues of *Omni* were from the Vienna School of Ernst Fuchs, who also contributed artwork; other covers were a mix of the surreal, as with Gervasio Gallardo's butterfly, or the imagined real, as with Don Dixon's view of Jupiter from one of its moons.

▶▶
Austrian-born Dieter Schwertberger, who works as De Es, was an assistant to painter Ernst Fuchs in the early 1970s. This image comes from what De Es has called his "stone period" of objects and people made from cracked rock and stone. From *Omni*, April 1979.

▶▶
H. R. Giger exploded into the consciousness of the world via Ridley Scott's *Alien* but was already making waves in the art world with his biomechanical artwork, such as this piece, used as an illustration in *Omni* in February 1979.

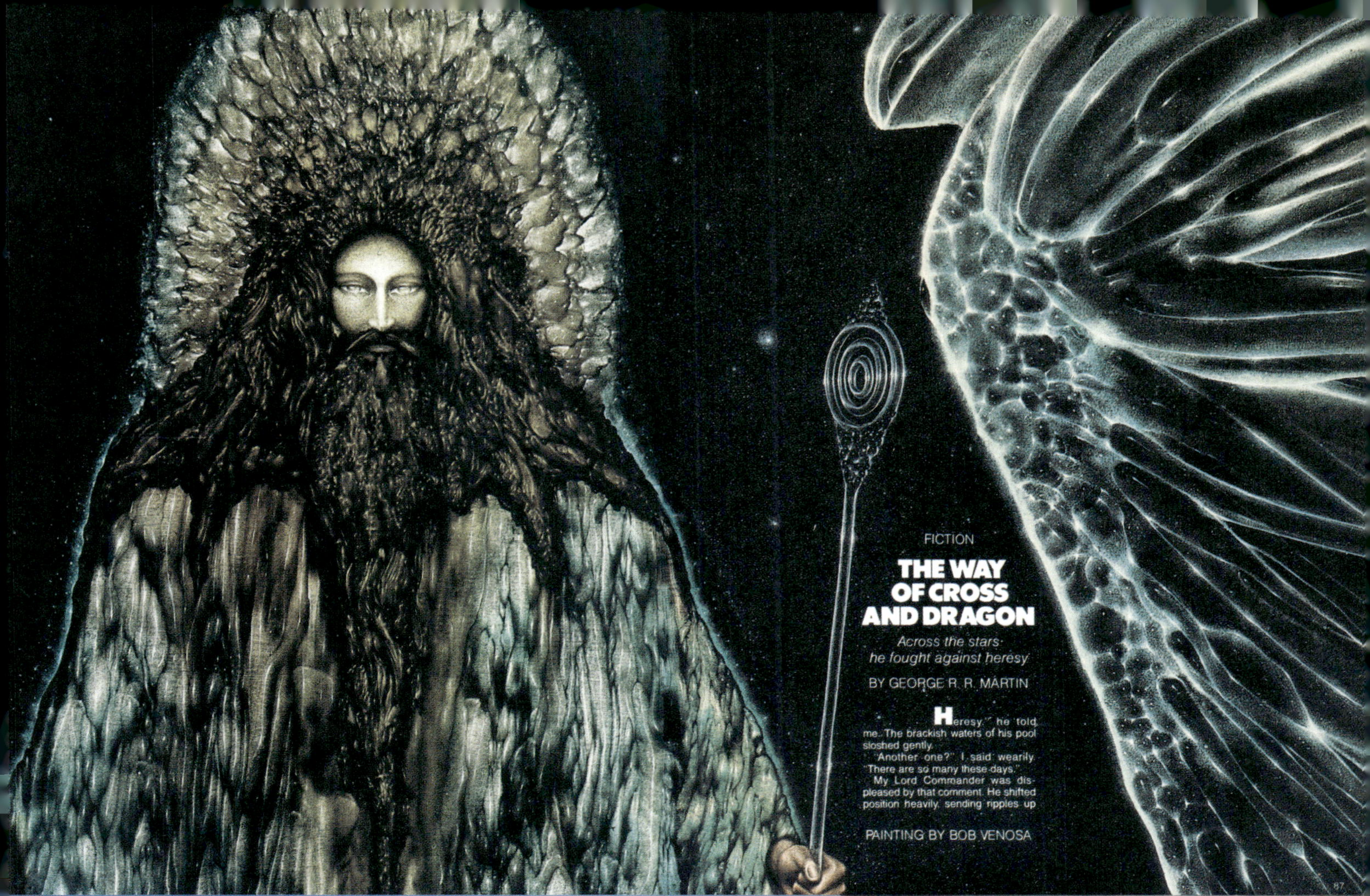

FICTION

THE WAY OF CROSS AND DRAGON

Across the stars he fought against heresy

BY GEORGE R. R. MARTIN

"Heresy," he told me. The brackish waters of his pool sloshed gently.

"Another one?" I said wearily. "There are so many these days."

My Lord Commander was displeased by that comment. He shifted position heavily, sending ripples up

PAINTING BY BOB VENOSA

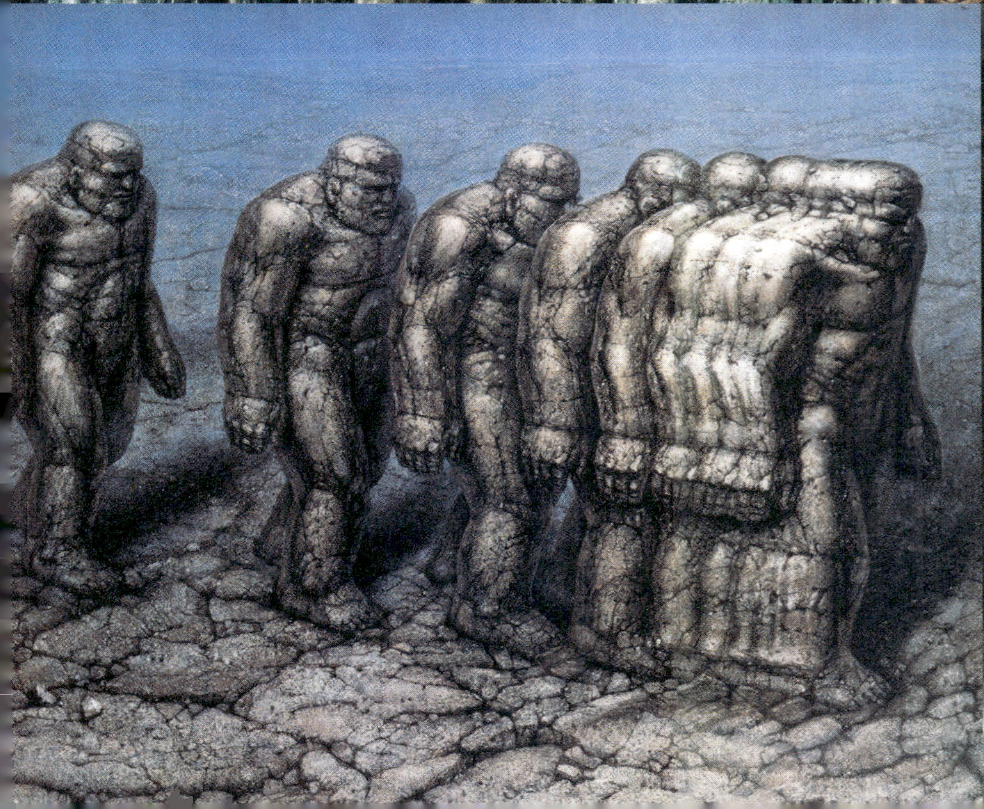

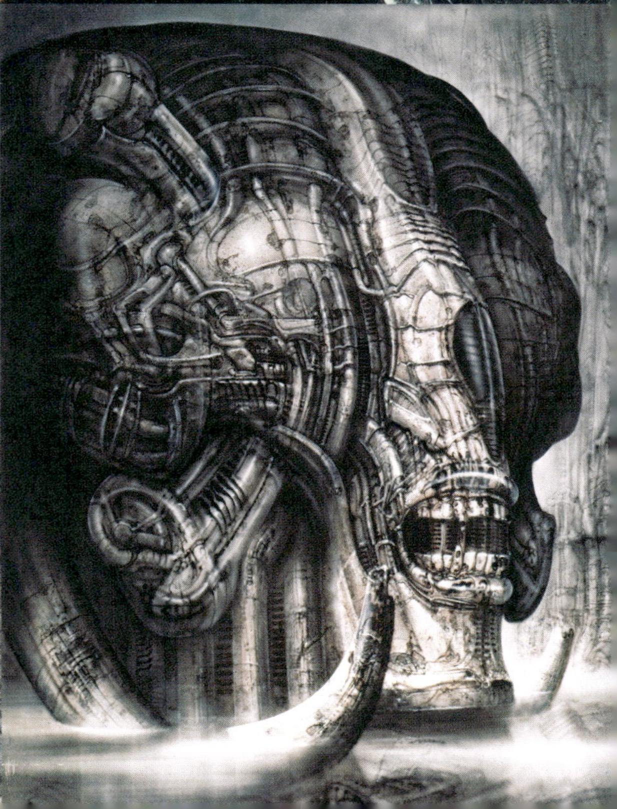

STEPHEN HICKMAN

Although born in Washington, DC, Stephen Hickman (1949–) was widely traveled before his family eventually settled in Virginia. His interest in literature was inspired by his father, employed in the foreign service, who would tell his son ghost stories and tales of his childhood in the Philippines; his mother, meanwhile, encouraged his early artistic endeavors. Educated at Francis Hammond High School and Richmond Professional Institute, Hickman's greatest influence was seeing original cover artwork at science fiction conventions and the opportunity he had to meet some of his heroes. Hickman, who had begun reading SF at around the age of 12, was particularly fond of the covers Frank Frazetta and Roy Krenkel produced for novels by Edgar Rice Burroughs.

Hickman began painting while working at Shirt Explosion in Lanham, Maryland, as a T-shirt designer. He showed these portfolio pieces to comic book artist Neal Adams, who introduced him to Charles Volpe, art editor of Ace Books. Volpe bought two of his portfolio paintings, used as covers for *Lady of the Bees* by Thomas Burnett Swann and *The Green Millennium* by Fritz Leiber (both 1976). His first commissioned cover was for *The Brain Stealers* by Murray Leinster (1974) and others for the Ace Science Fiction Specials series quickly followed.

Hickman has since gone on to illustrate some 350-400 covers for Ace, Ballantine, Del Rey, Tor, and others. Initially he was considered a fantasy artist—a gathering of his work was entitled *The Fantasy Art of Stephen Hickman* (1989)—but his covers have appeared on everything from Harlan Ellison (a painting by Hickman inspired the story *Midnight in the Sunken Cathedral*) to the future war novels of David Drake, who said of the cover for *Lacey and His Friends* (1986) "I've had a lot of good book covers. I've never had a cover better than Steve Hickman's for this volume."

A writer himself, Hickman penned *The Lemurian Stone* (1988), which has formed the basis for a series of paintings known as the Pharazar Mythos, notably

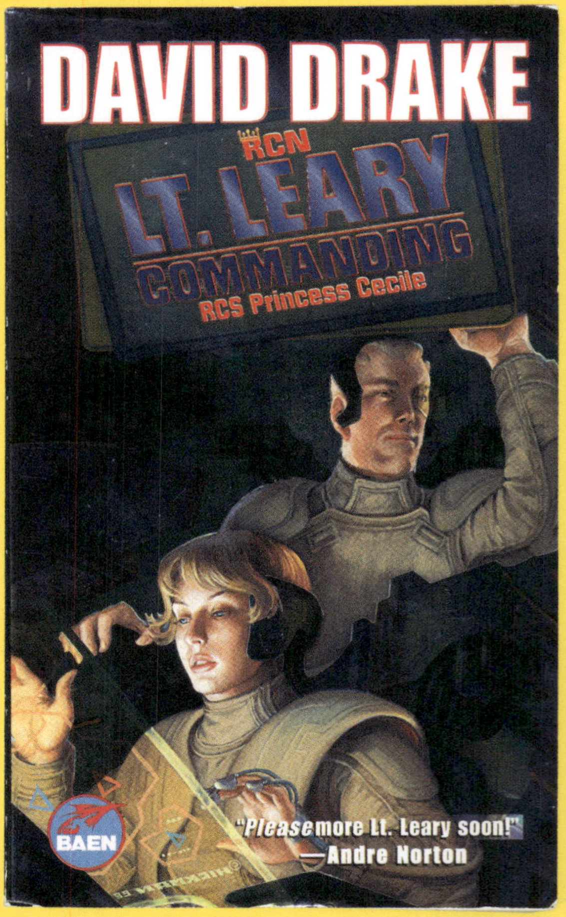

The Lion Pavilion and *The Astronomer Prince*, the latter a Chesley Award-winning image.

Hickman's talents have been widely recognized by his peers, winning him the Chesley Award from the Association of Science Fiction & Fantasy Artists five times—one Best Cover, three Best Color Work (Unpublished), and, in 2000, the Award for Artistic Achievement. To this can be added two gold awards from the *Spectrum Anthology* and a Hugo Award in 1993, prompted by the release of the Space Fantasy commemorative booklet of stamps issued by the US Postal Service.

◀ ▶▶
David Drake's take on Patrick O'Brian's Jack Aubrey/ Stephen Maturin naval history novels, transferred from O'Brian's Napoleonic Wars era to space (opera), is centered on the adventures of Lt. Daniel Leary, a rising officer in the RCN, the Republic of Cinnabar Navy. Hickman's cover also features Leary's partner-in-action, librarian and spy, Adele Mundy. Not as militaristic as his *Hammer's Slammers* series, Drake's RCN novels feature plenty of political intrigue, allowing Hickman a chance at more figurative work, as with *Lt. Leary, Commanding* (Baen, 2000) and *The Far Side of the Stars* (Baen, 2003).

▶
***A State of Disobedience* by Tom Kratman (Baen, 2003) reveals Hickman's fine sense of capturing a moment of excitement that will draw in readers—in this instance hardcore military SF set during the Second American Revolution. Baen's publisher Toni Weisskopf has said: "Steve is a painter very conscious of geometry, as well as one with a firm sense of the romance and narrative strength of science fiction."**

▶
Among Hickman's own favorites, the *Man-Kzin Wars* anthology series is a spin-off from Larry Niven's *Known Space* stories. The Kzinti are a race of bloodthirsty tiger-like aliens who would eventually fight five major wars with humanity before being subdued. Hickman's ferocious depiction of the Kzin was very much a part of each new volume. "The Kzinti characters are about as appealing as mortal enemies in SF can get," says Hickman.

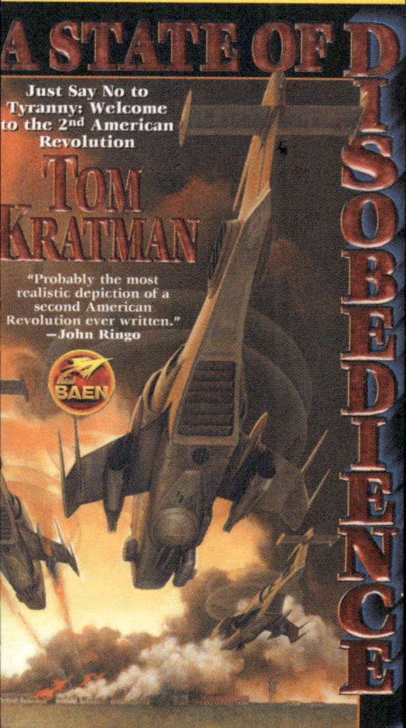
A STATE OF DISOBEDIENCE
Just Say No to Tyranny: Welcome to the 2nd American Revolution
TOM KRATMAN
"Probably the most realistic depiction of a second American Revolution ever written."
—John Ringo
BAEN

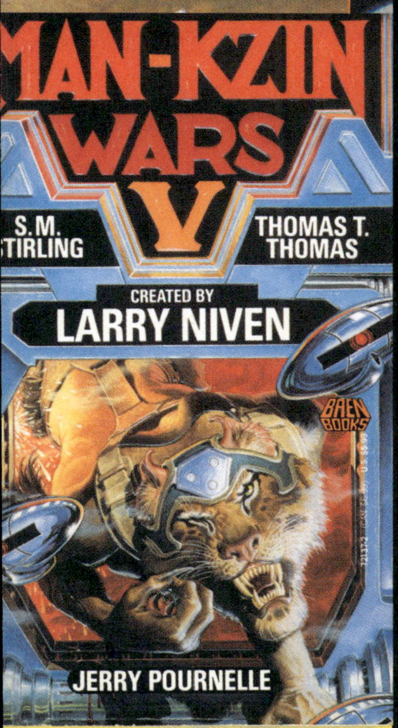
MAN-KZIN WARS V
S.M. STIRLING
THOMAS T. THOMAS
CREATED BY
LARRY NIVEN
BAEN BOOKS
JERRY POURNELLE

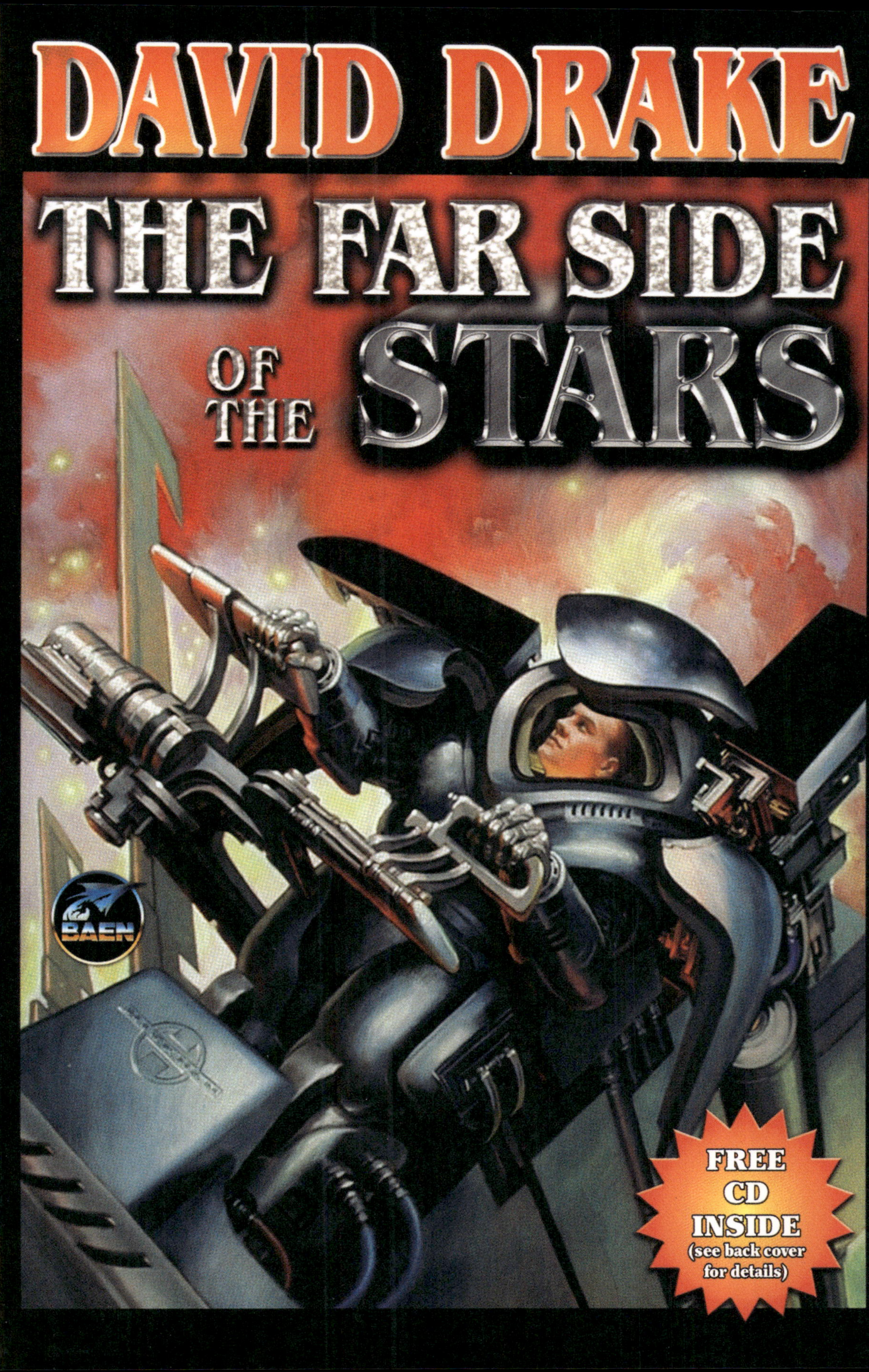
DAVID DRAKE
THE FAR SIDE OF THE STARS
BAEN
FREE CD INSIDE
(see back cover for details)

VINCENT DI FATE

Vincent Di Fate has earned a reputation as one of the finest space hardware illustrators. Still very active after a multi-award-winning career of 40 years, his importance to the field is not limited to his own artwork; he has written perceptive essays and introductions for a number of magazines and books on the history of SF illustration and compiled the monumental *Infinite Worlds* (1997), one of the most comprehensive volumes of SF artwork ever published.

Born in Yonkers, New York, Di Fate (1945–) began drawing at around the age of four and won a scholarship to the Phoenix School of Design in New York; he subsequently received his MA in Illustration at Syracuse University. He made his first professional sales in the mid-1960s while still at art school.

A longtime fan of classic SF and B-movies (still a passion of his, having illustrated *War of the Worlds* and portraits of the Creature from the Black Lagoon), Di Fate wanted to work in movies. Instead he ended up working on the animated adventures of *Spider-Man* in the late 1960s until the network broadcasting the show complained about the levels of violence and most of the staff were laid off.

Di Fate approached John Campbell at *Analog* in 1968 and left with two commissions, the first of 75 he was to receive in his first year. He has since produced some 3,500 illustrations and covers for a wide variety of clients, ranging from Reader's Digest to the National Geographic Society.

Since 1976 he has received a number of commissions from NASA; in 1987 he completed the official painting of the International Space Station, currently being assembled in orbit; the painting is on display at the Kennedy Space Center.

In science fiction, Di Fate's name has been closely associated with *Analog*, although he produced covers for most of the major magazines in the 1970s and 1980s. His first book cover, *Broken Engine* by Ron Goulart, was sold in 1969 (although not published until 1972). The best of his SF illustrations can be found in two collections: *Di Fate's Catalogue of Science Fiction Hardware* (1980) and *The Science Fiction Art of Vincent Di Fate* (2002).

Di Fate's talent has been recognized many times, his awards including the Frank R. Paul Award for Outstanding Achievement in 1978, the Hugo Award in 1979, the Skylark Award in 1987, the Lensman Award in 1990, and the Chesley Award for Artistic Achievement in 1998. Ben Bova, former editor of *Analog*, has said of him: "Great illustrators, like Vincent Di Fate, serve as guiding beacons for us; they translate ideas into pictures, they use their finely-trained talents to create images that we poor benighted mortals could never see for ourselves. They are our eyes into the future, and Di Fate is among the best of them, by any measure."

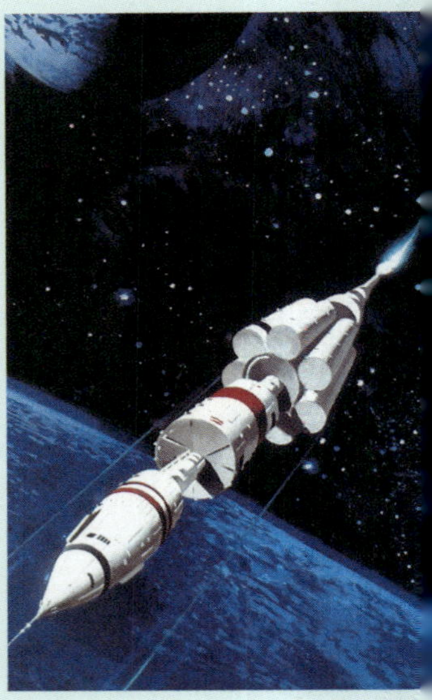

▲

The clean lines of the spaceship—for *Dark Sanctuary* by Gregory Benford (*Omni*, May 1979)—are typical of Di Fate's work, which he has called a hybrid of his influences: pulp magazines and cinema. "My first real science fiction experience was going to see *Rocketship X-M*," he has said.

▶

"Big Dumb Object" is a term of affection used to describe the impossibly large space structures that inhabit the worlds of science fiction. Di Fate's depiction of a massive space station that dwarfs shuttles and floating astronauts—for *Down and Out on Ellfive Prime* by Dean Ing (*Omni*, March 1979)—is equally affectionate, harking back to the pulp covers of yesteryear with its huge antennae array.

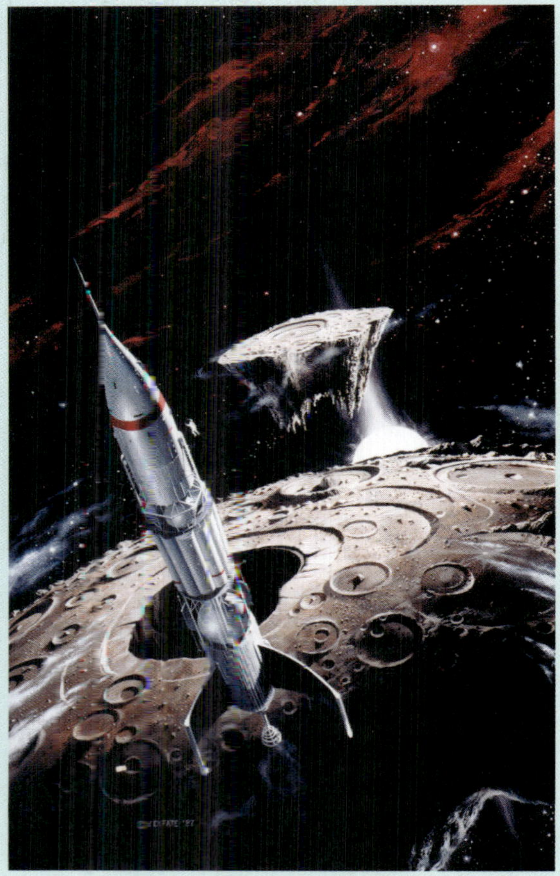

◀

Shielded by an asteroid from the intense rays of the sun, the crew of a NASA space mission work frantically to save themselves from oblivion in Paul Preuss' near-future thriller, *Starfire* (Tor, 1988). Di Fate's ability to take a relatively common science fictional image—the spaceship—and infuse it with a real sense of wonder is virtually unsurpassed.

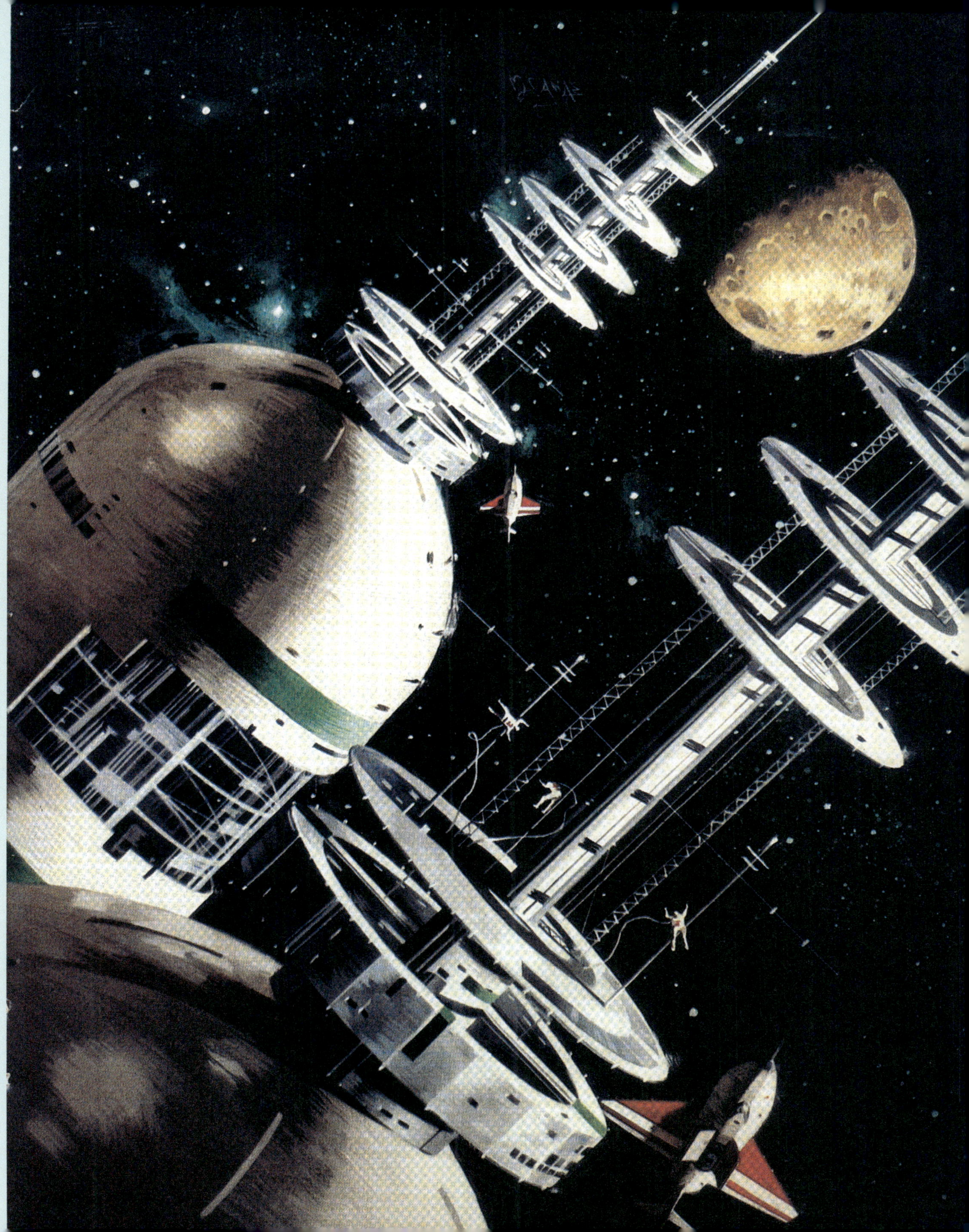

FRANK WU

Preceding a word by adding "fan" to it has usually lowered expectations. Fan equates to amateur and amateur to non-professional and, for many, unprofessional. However, as with all things, Sturgeon's Law that "90 percent of everything is crap" applies; *ergo*, ten percent of fan art ought to be good.

In science fiction, the percentage may even be higher. No other genre has so blurred the lines between fan and professional; fanzines began appearing in 1930, publishing news, fiction, and articles. Spirit duplicated and hectographic magazines with circulations from a handful to the hundreds appeared before the Second World War, but it was the mimeograph, which used wax stencils, that really brought improvements to fanzine illustrations.

Rather than being looked down upon, "fan art" has become a respectable category. The Hugos added a Best Fan Artist award in 1967 and the early winners—Jack Gaughan (1967), George Barr (1968), Vaughn Bodé (1969), Tim Kirk (1970), and Alicia Austin (1971)—have all become big names in the field.

In 2002, Frank Wu received his first Hugo nomination. He has since won the category three times, in 2004, 2006, and 2007 (in 2008 a potential fourth win was made impossible when he declined the nomination). Wu had already won the Grand Prize in the Illustrators of the Future contest in 2002.

Wu (1964–) was born in Philadelphia, grew up in Connecticut, and was educated at the University of Rochester and University of Wisconsin, where he received a Ph.D. in bacterial genetics.

Always interested in science fiction, he wrote stories without success for some years before finding a more fruitful inroad as a science fiction artist in the late 1990s. Self-taught, Wu has drawn all his life, inspired by everything from *Star Trek* to favorite book covers he remembers reading.

After joining the Association of Science Fiction and Fantasy Artists, he sold his first illustration to *Darkling Plain*. He is best known for his bold (sometimes garish) color artwork, which has appeared on small press magazines like *Fantastic Stories*, *OnSpec*, *Star*Line*, *Talebones*, books from Aardwolf Press, Wheatland Press, and various chapbooks and convention books.

Something of a magpie when it comes to inspiration, he has said, "I don't use just one style. Some pieces 'feel' like they would be better expressed by stealing from Julia Margaret Cameron, or Kinuko Craft, or Italian Futurists like Boccioni, or Richard Powers, or Frank R. Paul. I don't steal specific images, but sometimes it's fun to paint in someone else's style, but with ironic twists. For example: what would it look like if Boccioni had painted robots?"

Some of his early work can be found in the pages of *Greetings from Lake Wu* (with Jay Lake, 2003). He has also produced animated shorts, including the fan favorite *Guidolon* (2006), about a giant space chicken.

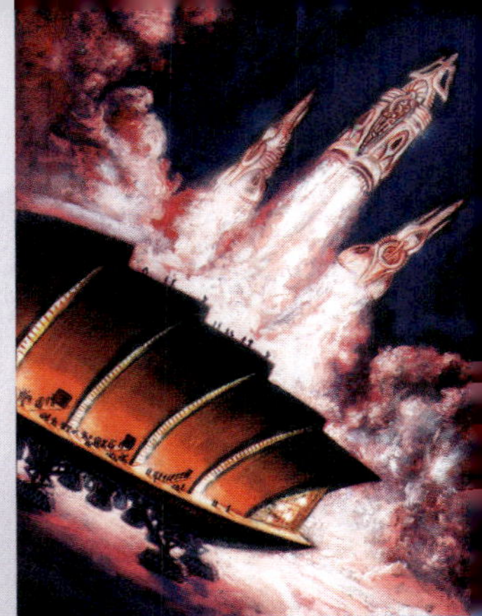

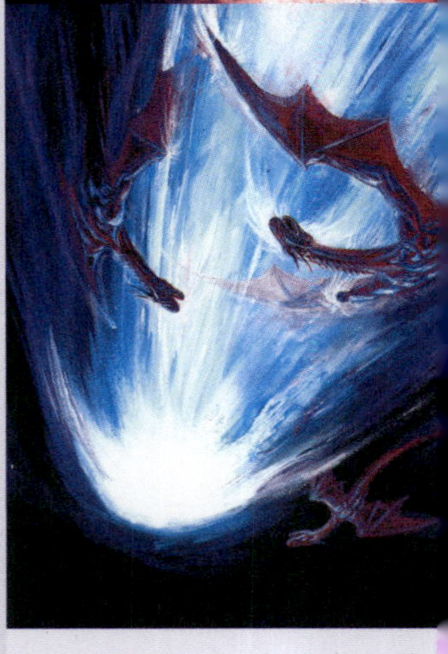

▲▲
Wu's painting *Welcome Aboard* was produced as a cover for *Ion Trails*, the "inflight magazine" inspired by the Scottish Expo Center, which, some say, looks like a spaceship. The magazine was produced for the 2005 World Science Fiction Convention, held that year in Glasgow.

▲
Dragons are a regular motif in Wu's work—as seen here in *Cometary Bliss*—but he has not succumbed to the temptation of limiting himself to that one, albeit popular, genre. As Wu has said: "I could make piles of money doing dragons and chicks in steel bikinis, but I won't do it. I really want my art to have a deeper meaning than that."

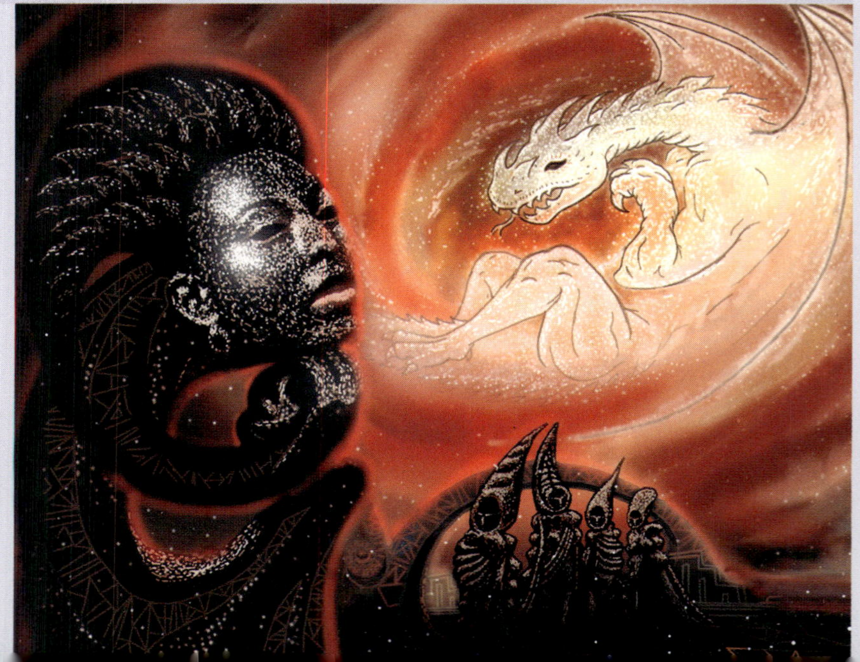

▶
In *Cloud Dragon Sky* the Earth's atmosphere has become damaged and the heroine imagines dragons in the swirling clouds. The African motif is derived from the story by N. K. Jemisin; the picture was nominated for the British Science Fiction Award for Best Artwork in 2005.

▶▶
The Wolf Paintings were Wu's illustrations for four stories appearing in *Fantastic Stories*. When joined together, they formed a larger picture of a wolf. The image illustrates the diverse styles that Wu is capable of.

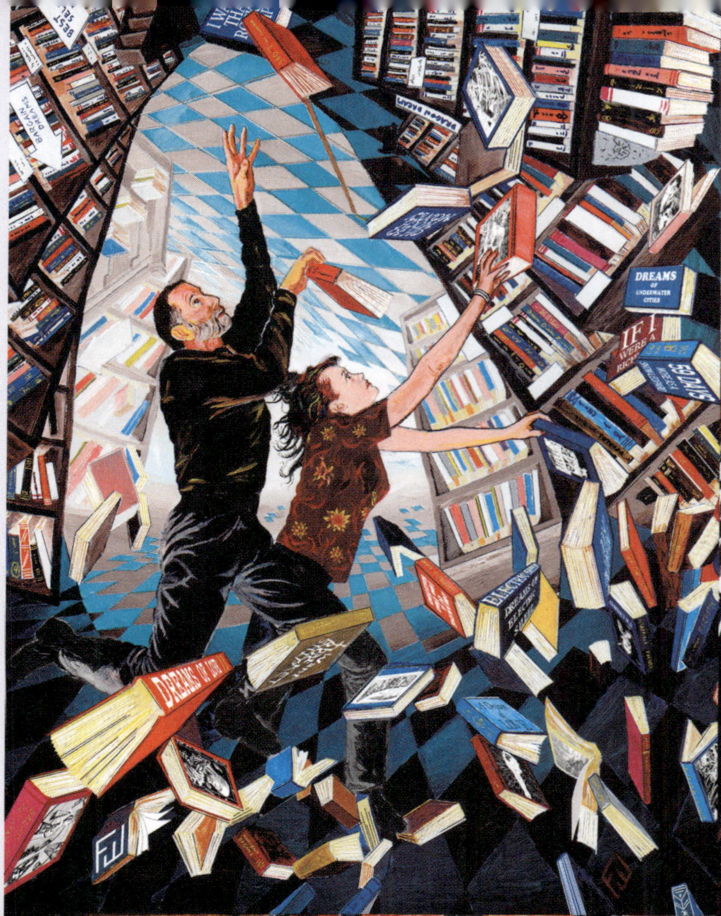
DREAMS

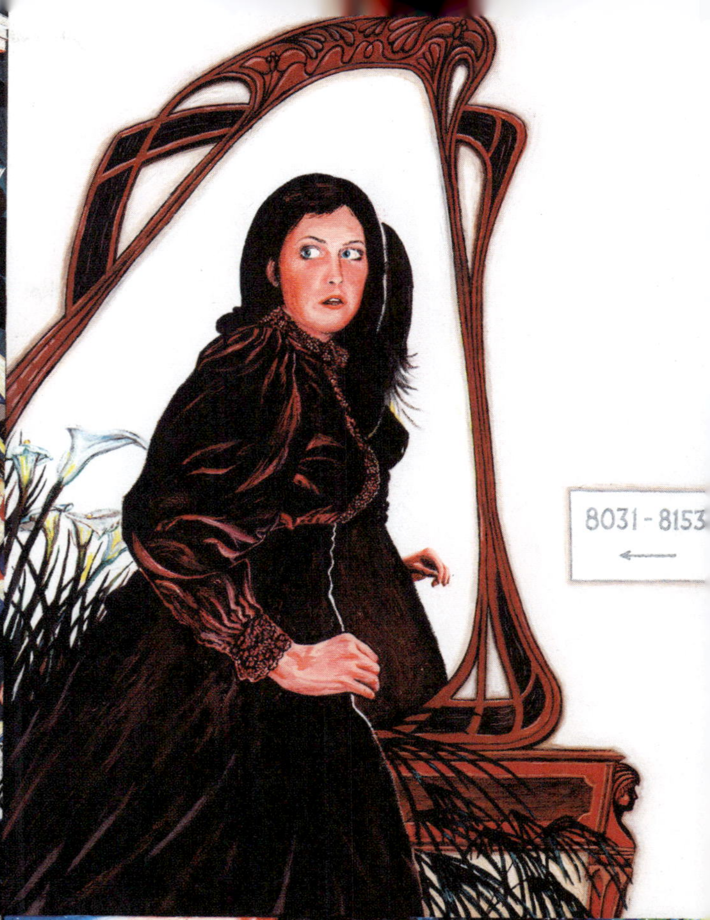
8031 - 8153

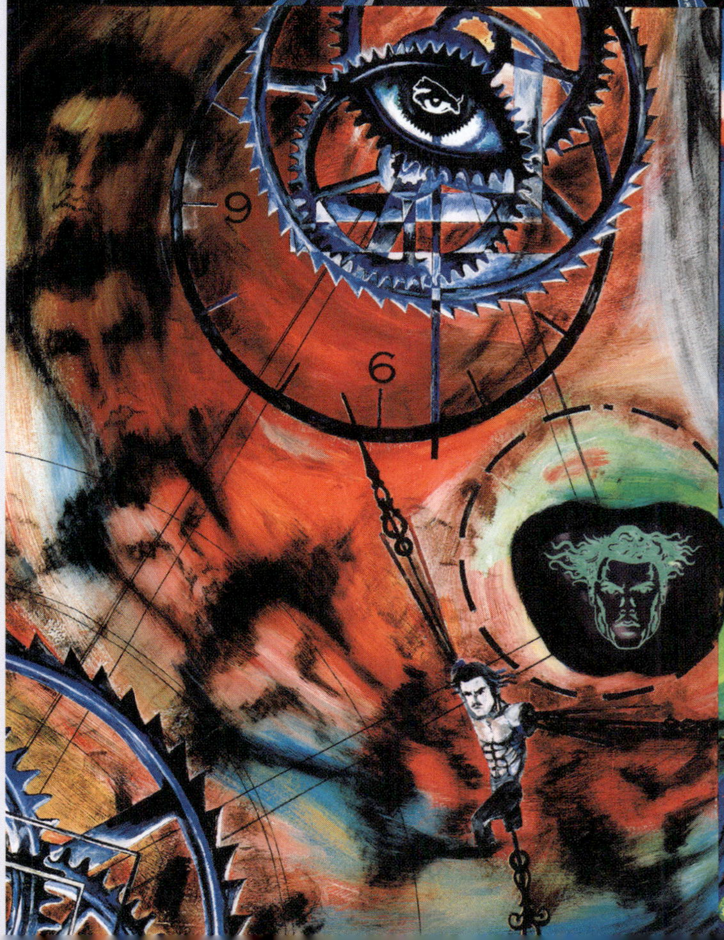
9
6

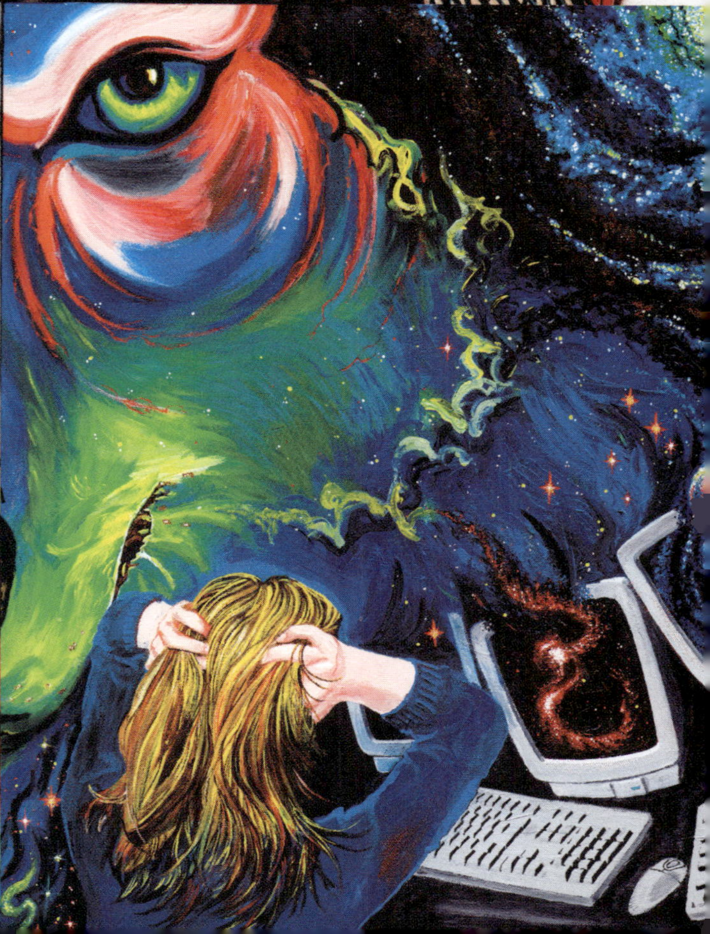

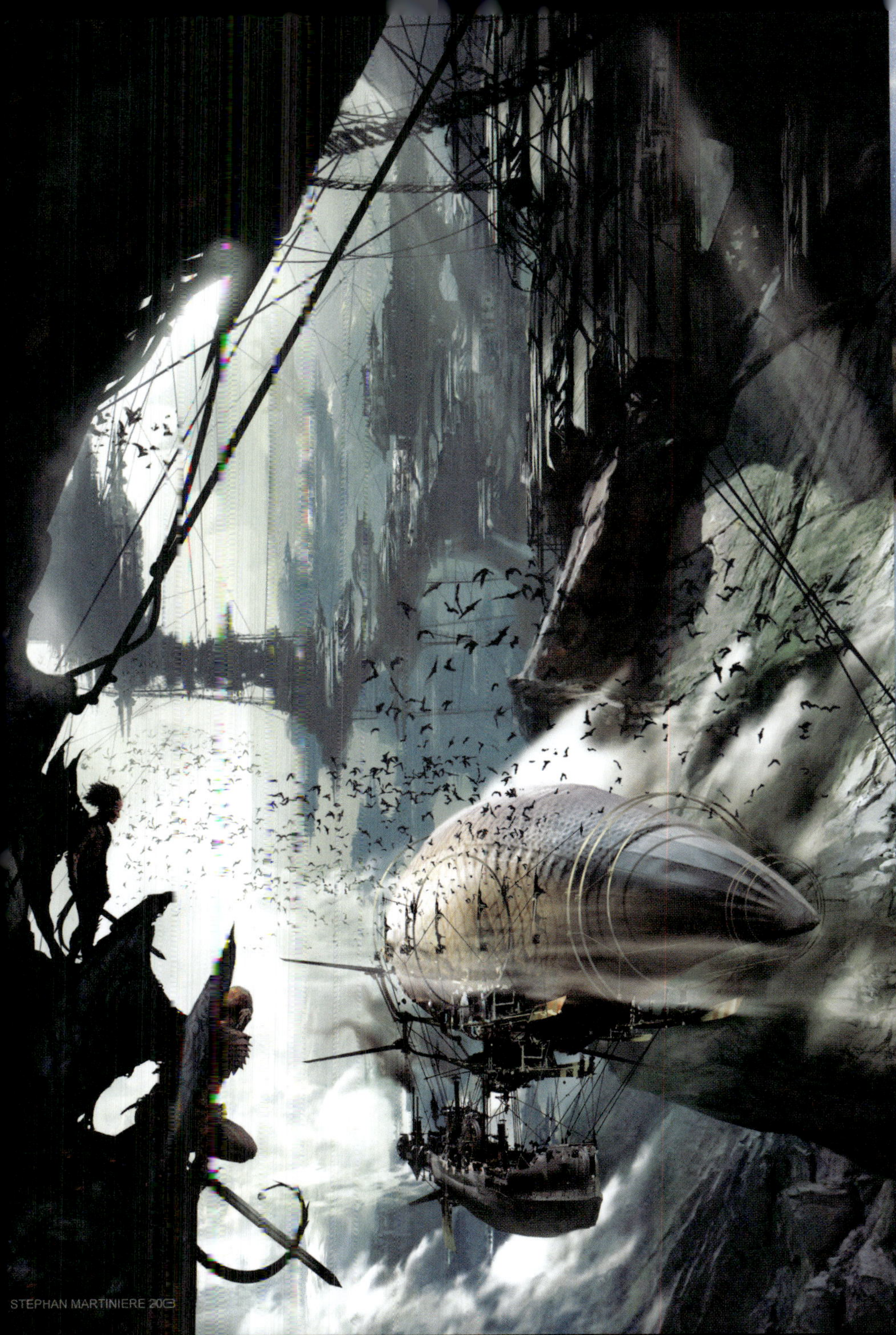

▲
SF author and editor Lou Anders has praised the work of Stephan Martinière for capturing that abstract and elusive sense of wonder, and his ability to "distill its essence into imagery that speaks directly to that sense of cosmic scope and scale. Stephan takes that breathless moment… and he freezes that moment in time." One frozen moment is captured on the cover of *Mainspring* by Jay Lake (Tor, 2007).

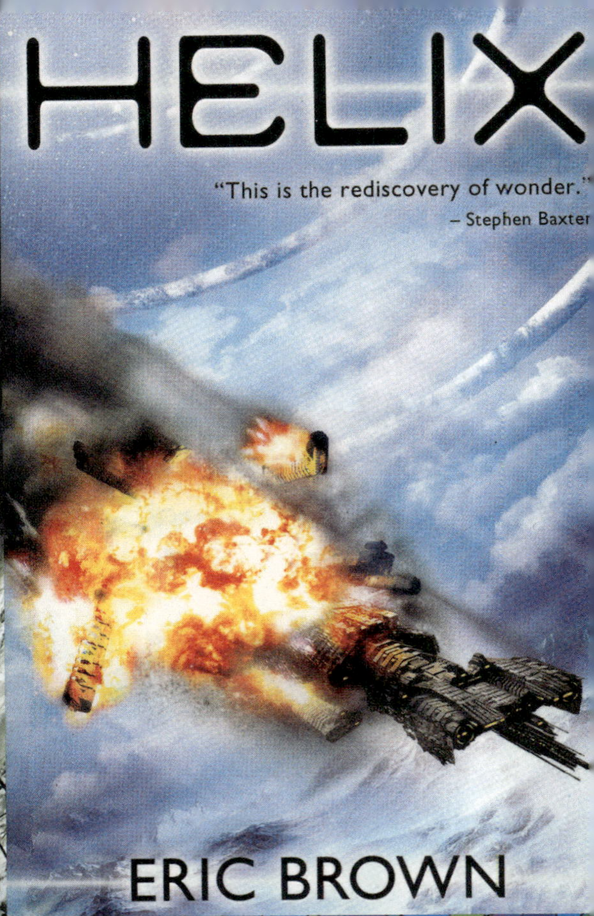

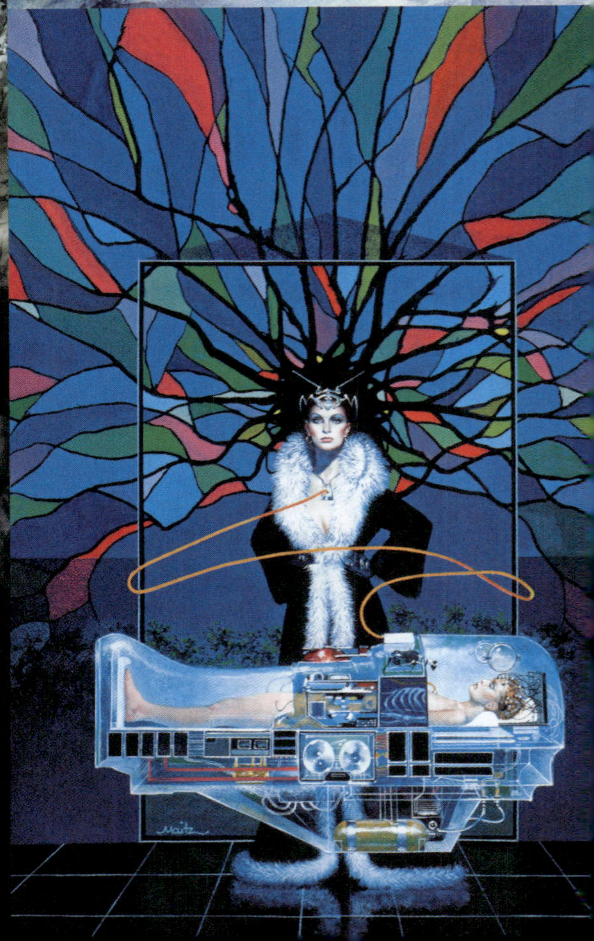

▶
Don Maitz's 1978 painting *This Year's Model* shares its title with an Elvis Costello album, also released that year. Two years later Maitz won the World Fantasy Award for Best Artist and has since collected over a dozen major awards.

LOOKING TO THE FUTURE

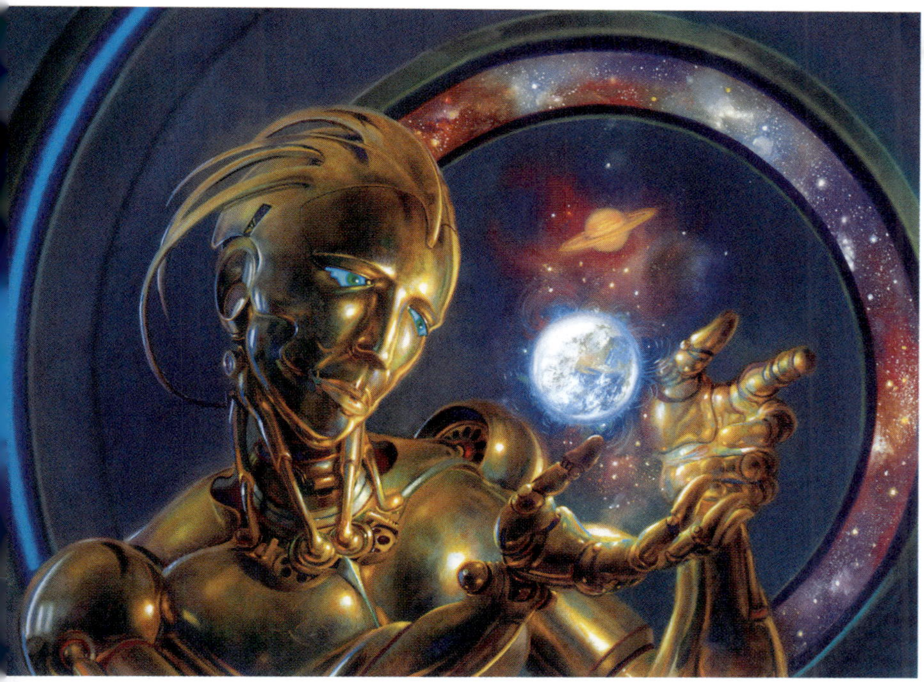

▲
Donato Giancola's painting for the Science Fiction Book Club's 2003 edition of *City* by Clifford D. Simak captures the essence of his work: beautifully delineated, colorful, inspiring. He won the Jack Gaughan Award for Best Emerging Artist in 1998, after five years selling professionally, and appreciation of his work has continued to grow with every succeeding year.

◀▲
Twice the winner of the British SF Award, Dominic Harman is rapidly making a name for himself illustrating covers for *Interzone, Isaac Asimov's Magazine, Analog,* and book covers for Macmillan and Orion's *SF Masterworks* series. *Helix* by Eric Brown (Solaris, 2007) is a throwback to the finest traditions of the 1970s.

It would be easy to believe that science fiction is something of a dying genre. We are, after all, living in the 21st century and many of the predictions of early science fiction have come true; communication has advanced in leaps and bounds since the days of wireless, man has set foot on the Moon, a permanent orbiting space station is nearing completion, and plans are advanced for manned trips to Mars. It isn't quite the future that some predicted; individual jetpacks have yet to replace the car and day-trips up the space elevator are still some years (and quite a few scientific advances) away.

The truth of the matter is that science fiction is still thriving. If it is not quite so visible these days it is due to the resurgence of fantasy as a genre, boosted by hugely successful fantasy movies (*Lord of the Rings, The Chronicles of Narnia,* etc.), crowding SF from the bookshelves. Tie-in novels, especially those relating to *Star Wars,* often make the bestsellers charts; the summer's biggest movies are often science fiction but almost as often disappoint science fiction fans. The public face of science fiction has shifted from books and magazines on newsstands to other forms of media.

New novels, collections, and anthologies appear at a steady pace. Magazine sales are down from the glory days of the pulps, but SF and fantasy can still boast five professional titles and a dozen semi-professional titles appearing regularly. Many of these smaller magazines are slickly illustrated, some in full color throughout.

Although the Hugo Awards—a useful measure of popularity among fans—have been dominated by only a handful of artists since 1980, many others have been nominated, among them Don Maitz, Donato Giancola, and David A. Cherry.

Maitz, winner of the Hugo in 1990 and 1993, has combined SF cover illustration (for such authors as Asimov, Bradbury, and Moorcock) with more commercially lucrative paintings of pirates for *National Geographic* and the Captain Morgan Spiced Rum brand, record cover sleeve art, and concept designs. Donato Giancola (1967-), winner in 2006 and 2007, has produced covers for Tor, Roc, Ace, and others, illustrations for *Playboy,* and extensive work for Wizards of the Coast since 1993. Maitz and Giancola are multiple Chesley Award Winners (over 50 nominations between them and ten and 11 wins respectively). Both Thomas Canty and David A. Cherry (c.1949-) work in a more romantic, Beardsley-esque fantasy style.

Rising stars like John Picacio (1969-) and Stephan Martinière (c.1962-) are already making names for themselves, the latter after many years' experience in animation and concept design. Upcoming names among the fan artists include Teddy Harvia (a.k.a. David Thayer), Taral Wayne, and Sue Mason. In Britain, Dominic Harman and Steve Stone are among the talented new wave of artists taking science fiction art into the 21st century.

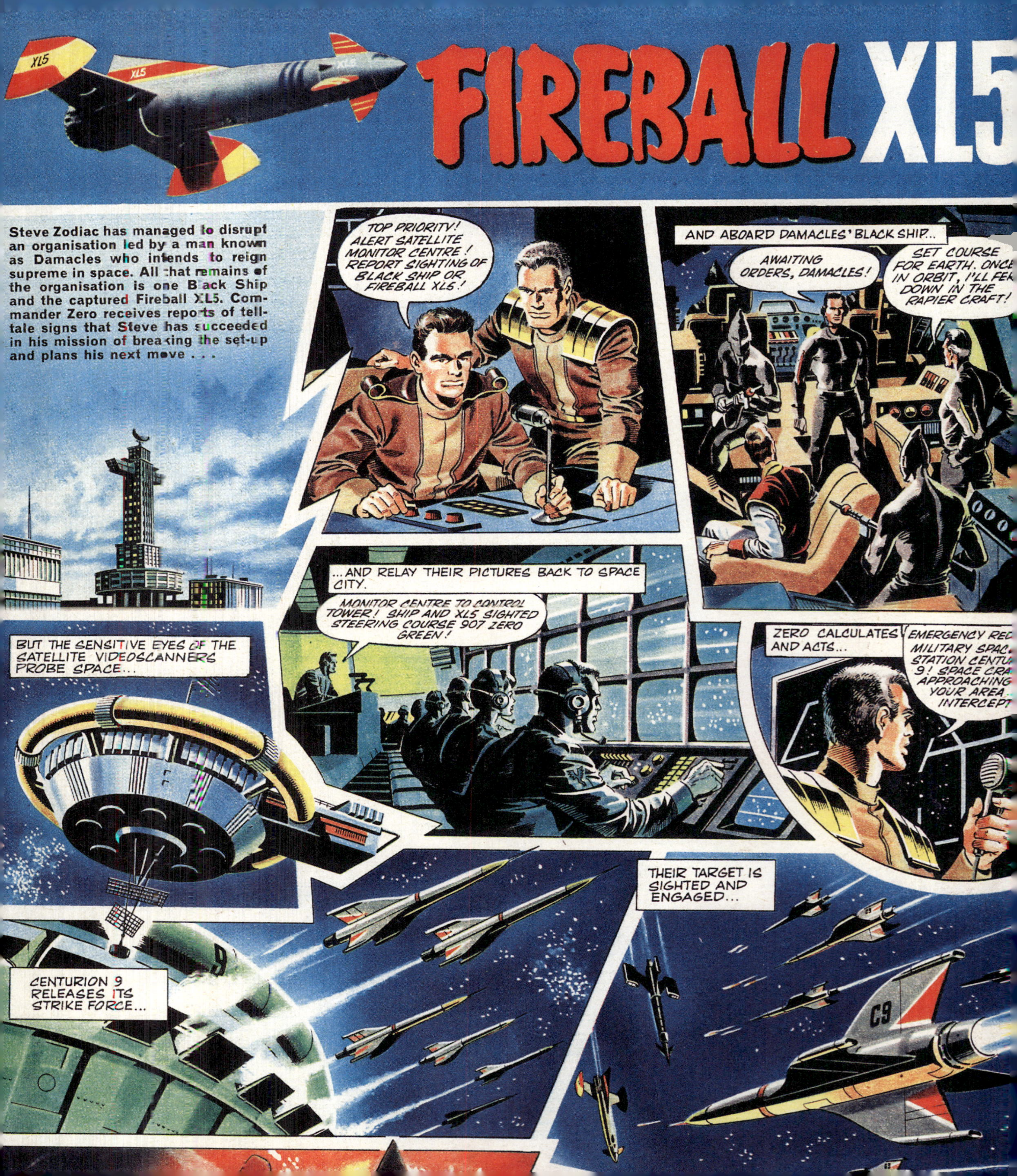
FIREBALL XL5
XL5
Steve Zodiac has managed to disrupt an organisation led by a man known as Damacles who intends to reign supreme in space. All that remains of the organisation is one Black Ship and the captured Fireball XL5. Commander Zero receives reports of telltale signs that Steve has succeeded in his mission of breaking the set-up and plans his next move . . .
TOP PRIORITY! ALERT SATELLITE MONITOR CENTRE! REPORT SIGHTING OF BLACK SHIP OR FIREBALL XL5!
AND ABOARD DAMACLES' BLACK SHIP...
AWAITING ORDERS, DAMACLES!
SET COURSE FOR EARTH. ONCE IN ORBIT, I'LL FERRY DOWN IN THE RAPIER CRAFT!
BUT THE SENSITIVE EYES OF THE SATELLITE VIDEOSCANNERS PROBE SPACE...
...AND RELAY THEIR PICTURES BACK TO SPACE CITY.
MONITOR CENTRE TO CONTROL TOWER! SHIP AND XL5 SIGHTED STEERING COURSE 907 ZERO GREEN!
ZERO CALCULATES AND ACTS...
EMERGENCY REQ MILITARY SPAC STATION CENTU 9! SPACE CRA APPROACHING YOUR AREA. INTERCEPT
CENTURION 9 RELEASES ITS STRIKE FORCE...
THEIR TARGET IS SIGHTED AND ENGAGED...
C9

3 COMIC BOOKS

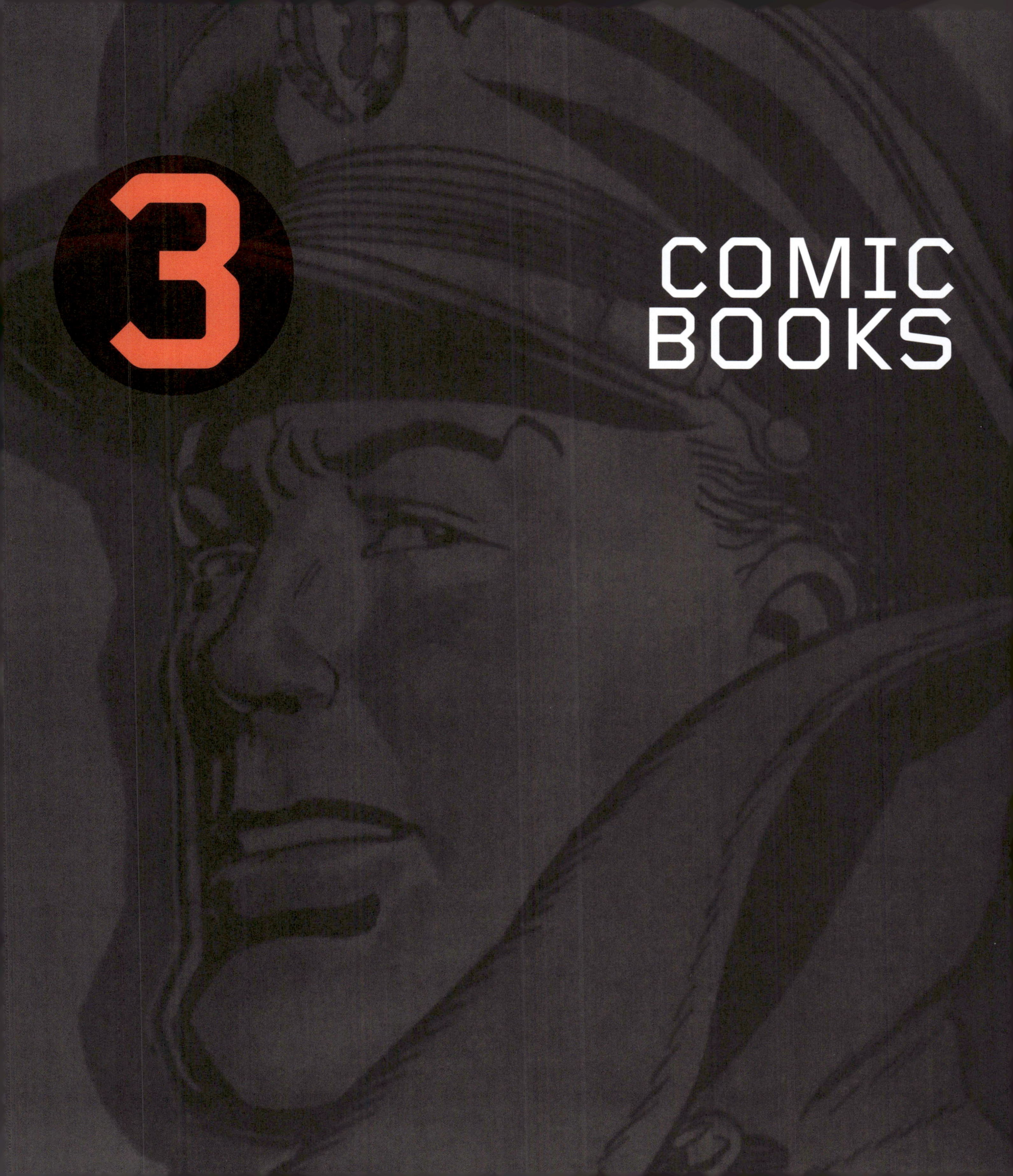

BUCK ROGERS & FLASH GORDON

When it comes to sci-fi comics, it all began with Buck.

Ever on the lookout for new features to syndicate to newspapers around the country, John F. Dille, the head of the National Newspaper Service, was struck by the potential of Philip Nowlan's *Armageddon 2419 A.D.* in the August 1928 issue of *Amazing Stories*. Dille commissioned Nowlan to adapt his story to comic strip form and assigned one of the syndicate's staff artists, Dick Calkins (1895–1962), to draw it. For good measure, Dille also changed the hero's name from plain "Anthony Rogers" to "Buck Rogers." It sounded more like a cowboy's name than a futuristic pilot's, but cowboys were a favorite with the readers of the time, and Dille was on the money.

Calkins didn't exactly take easily to drawing the future, and his *Buck Rogers* owed much to Frank R. Paul. But the technology-laden strip proved a smash hit from the moment it premiered in January 1929, and at its peak, *Buck Rogers* appeared in some 400 newspapers nationwide.

Imitators naturally sprang up, and science fiction took hold in the comics. In late 1933 a rival syndicate, King Features, decided it wanted a piece of the action and commissioned one of its artists, Alex Raymond (1909–1956), to come up with an answer to *Buck*. Raymond rose to the challenge magnificently, and *Flash Gordon* premiered in January 1934.

It's a classic example of the paradox; though explicitly conceived as a rival to *Buck Rogers*, *Flash Gordon* couldn't have been more different. Where *Buck* was heavy on the gadgetry, *Flash* was more heroic fantasy in exotic settings, and the hero was as likely to duel with swords as shoot it out with ray guns. Where Calkins' art remained naïve and his human figures awkward, *Flash Gordon* was lushly rendered and Raymond's people were sensuous and substantial—his Sunday pages in particular were dazzling displays of sumptuous forms and colors.

Buck Rogers depicted the future world of hard science (or at least credible pseudo-science); Calkins added a lot of "noodling" linework, but everything looked as if it was drawn with a technical pen, and much of the technology had the flat look of a schematic drawing. (For many readers, that was doubtless part of its appeal.) *Flash Gordon* was more fantastic. Raymond was a master of sinuous brushwork, rich texturing, and impeccably placed, "feathered" black shadows that gave everything a rounded, solid appearance. Even machinery often had an organic quality when he drew it, although his be-finned and ornately decorated rocket ships were straight out of the school of Frank R. Paul.

When comic books were invented, *Buck Rogers* and *Flash Gordon* both appeared in their own books, as well as in radio serials, then movie serials, and later in TV shows and feature films. They also inspired countless others in all these media. Some fall into the *Buck Rogers* tradition of future-science-based adventure, some into the *Flash Gordon* school of heroic fantasy with a little technology thrown in. But what's really remarkable is how they almost all had names like *Speed Lancing*, *Streak Chandler*, *Whirlwind Carter*, and *Slam Bradley*. There was *Rocket Kelly*, *Skyrocket Steele*, *Jet Powers*, and *Power Nelson*. Some might've missed the mark a tad, like *Cotton Carver*, but there wasn't an everyday first name among them. Which just goes to show, you can't Buck a trend when it's clearly more than just a Flash in the pan...

▶
The very first episode of *Flash Gordon* from January 1934. Although his line would become more polished in time, Raymond's early *Flash Gordon* work has an undeniable energy and flow.

▶▲
***Flash Gordon* Sunday page from February 1936, showing how sensuous an appearance Raymond was able to give both people and machinery. The artist also created *Jungle Jim* and *Secret Agent X-9* to order (as answers to *Tarzan* and *Dick Tracy* respectively).**

▶
An example of Calkins' elaborate machinery, heavily influenced by Frank R. Paul.

▶
Calkins' early art had a bold simplicity, while later it became significantly more ornate, although it never matched the fluidity of Alex Raymond's *Flash Gordon*.

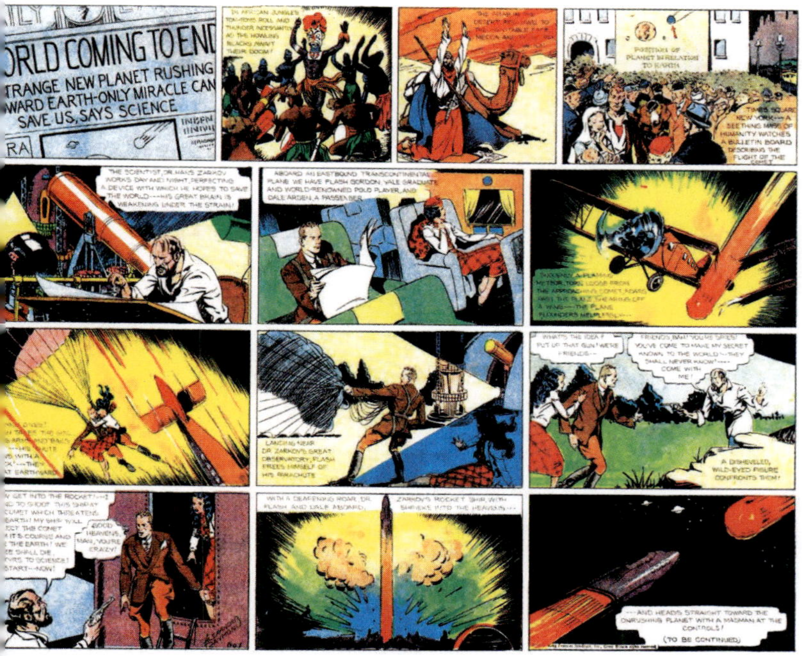
ORLD COMING TO ENI
TRANGE NEW PLANET RUSHING
WARD EARTH-ONLY MIRACLE CAN
SAVE US, SAYS SCIENCE

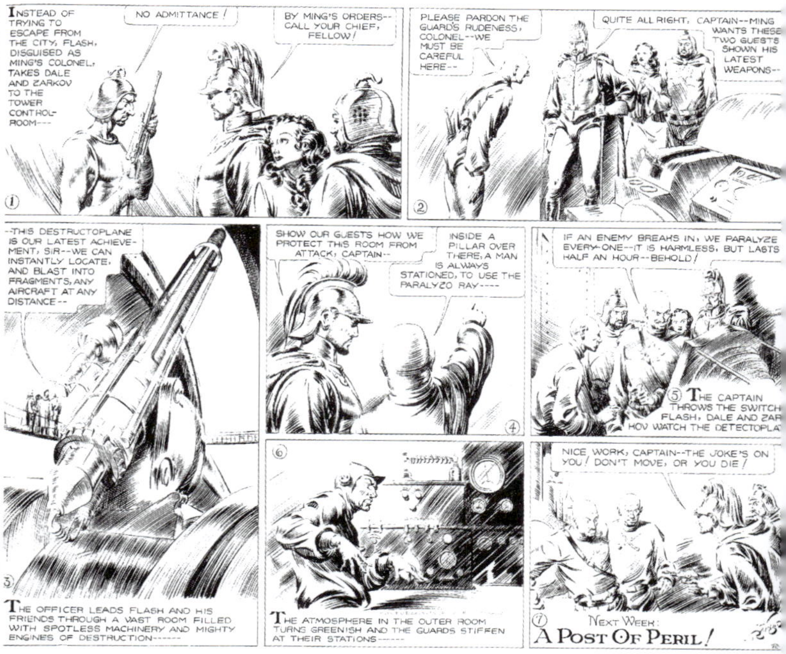
INSTEAD OF TRYING TO ESCAPE FROM THE CITY, FLASH, DISGUISED AS MING'S COLONEL, TAKES DALE AND ZARKOV TO THE TOWER CONTROL-ROOM---
NO ADMITTANCE!
BY MING'S ORDERS-- CALL YOUR CHIEF, FELLOW!
PLEASE PARDON THE GUARDS RUDENESS, COLONEL--WE MUST BE CAREFUL HERE--
QUITE ALL RIGHT, CAPTAIN--MING WANTS THESE TWO GUESTS SHOWN HIS LATEST WEAPONS--
--THIS DESTRUCTOPLANE IS OUR LATEST ACHIEVEMENT, SIR--WE CAN INSTANTLY LOCATE, AND BLAST INTO FRAGMENTS, ANY AIRCRAFT AT ANY DISTANCE--
SHOW OUR GUESTS HOW WE PROTECT THIS ROOM FROM ATTACK, CAPTAIN--
INSIDE A PILLAR OVER THERE, A MAN IS ALWAYS STATIONED, TO USE THE PARALYZO RAY----
IF AN ENEMY BREAKS IN, WE PARALYZE EVERY-ONE--IT IS HARMLESS, BUT LASTS HALF AN HOUR--BEHOLD!
THE CAPTAIN THROWS THE SWITCH. FLASH, DALE AND ZAR HOV WATCH THE DETECTOPLA
THE OFFICER LEADS FLASH AND HIS FRIENDS THROUGH A VAST ROOM FILLED WITH SPOTLESS MACHINERY AND MIGHTY ENGINES OF DESTRUCTION------
THE ATMOSPHERE IN THE OUTER ROOM TURNS GREENISH AND THE GUARDS STIFFEN AT THEIR STATIONS------
NICE WORK, CAPTAIN--THE JOKE'S ON YOU! DON'T MOVE, OR YOU DIE!
NEXT WEEK: A POST OF PERIL!

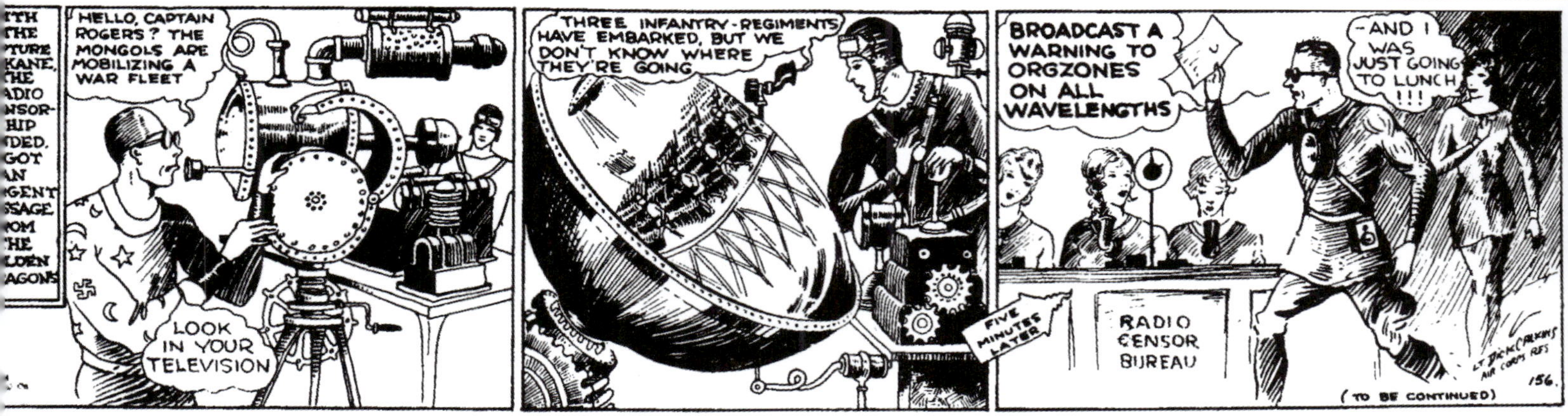
HELLO, CAPTAIN ROGERS? THE MONGOLS ARE MOBILIZING A WAR FLEET
LOOK IN YOUR TELEVISION
THREE INFANTRY-REGIMENTS HAVE EMBARKED, BUT WE DON'T KNOW WHERE THEY'RE GOING
FIVE MINUTES LATER
BROADCAST A WARNING TO ORGZONES ON ALL WAVELENGTHS
-AND I WAS JUST GOING TO LUNCH !!!
RADIO CENSOR BUREAU
LT. DICK CALKINS AIR CORPS RES.
156.
(TO BE CONTINUED)

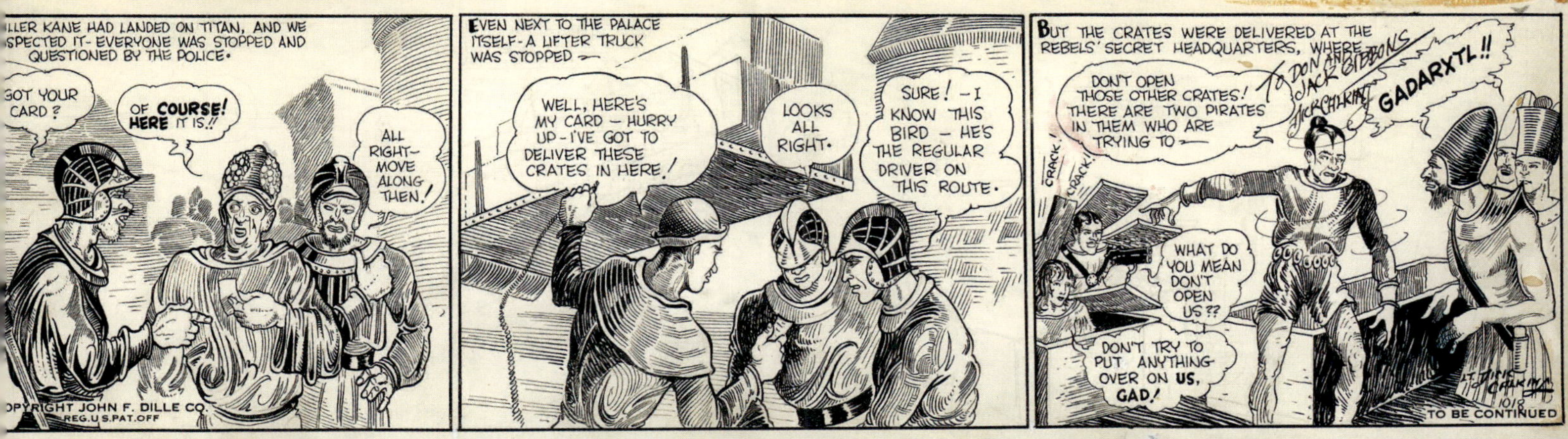
ILLER KANE HAD LANDED ON TITAN, AND WE SPECTED IT- EVERYONE WAS STOPPED AND QUESTIONED BY THE POLICE.
GOT YOUR CARD?
OF COURSE! HERE IT IS!!
ALL RIGHT- MOVE ALONG THEN!
OPYRIGHT JOHN F. DILLE CO. REG. U.S. PAT. OFF
EVEN NEXT TO THE PALACE ITSELF- A LIFTER TRUCK WAS STOPPED
WELL, HERE'S MY CARD - HURRY UP - I'VE GOT TO DELIVER THESE CRATES IN HERE!
LOOKS ALL RIGHT.
SURE! - I KNOW THIS BIRD - HE'S THE REGULAR DRIVER ON THIS ROUTE.
BUT THE CRATES WERE DELIVERED AT THE REBELS' SECRET HEADQUARTERS, WHERE
DON'T OPEN THOSE OTHER CRATES! THERE ARE TWO PIRATES IN THEM WHO ARE TRYING TO
GADARXTL!!
CRACK!
WHAT DO YOU MEAN DON'T OPEN US??
DON'T TRY TO PUT ANYTHING OVER ON US, GAD!
TO BE CONTINUED

SCI-FI COMICS IN THE 1940s & 1950s

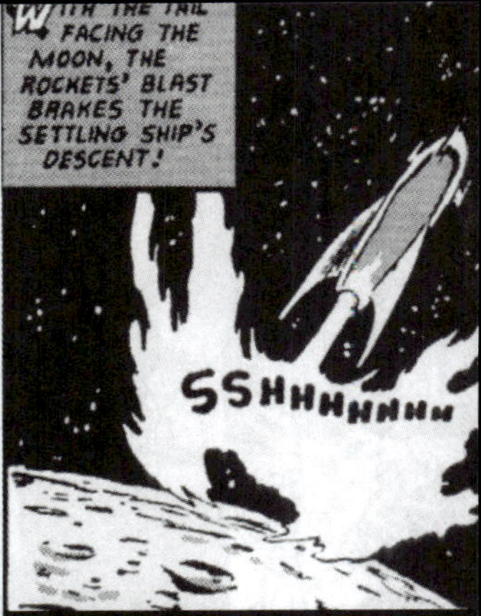

For the duration of World War II, superhero comics enjoyed a Golden Age, selling in their millions. With the end of the war, however, the comic-buying public's tastes abruptly changed, and superheroes fell out of favor. Publishers anxiously tried every other genre they could think of, hoping something would take off. Crime comics did, and westerns. Then romance comics blossomed. As if to preserve some sort of cosmic balance, so did horror. With the outbreak of the Korean conflict in 1950, war comics took off.

In the hope of expanding their market, some publishers experimented with mixing genres, giving the world such concepts as *Western Crime Busters*, *True War Romances*, and *Cowboy Love* (which of course meant something a little different 50 years before *Brokeback Mountain*).

And then there was sci-fi. SF was never the number one comics genre, but it wasn't just a fad either; its popularity grew steadily through the decade of A-bomb anxiety and flying saucer mania. A flurry of landmark sci-fi movies didn't hurt, either, starting with *Destination Moon* in 1950, then *When Worlds Collide*, *The Day the Earth Stood Still*, and other classics.

Planet Comics (1940) was the first dedicated sci-fi comic book. Its regulars included *Mysta of the Moon*, *Star Pirate*, and the bizarrely-named *Spurt Hammond*. *Startling Comics*, though not exclusively sci-fi, featured *Lance Lewis, Space Detective*, and *Captain Future*. Other sci-fi captains of the comic books included *Captain Video* (based on the network TV series), *Captain Science*, and *Captain Rocket*. Captain Comet starred in *Strange Adventures*, DC's first SF title, which launched in 1950. He was more of a superhero, however—possibly the only major superhero introduced in those post-Golden Age doldrums—but he had strong SF trappings befitting the times.

Another TV tie-in was *Tom Corbett, Space Cadet*, though DC's *Tommy Tomorrow of the Planeteers* actually preceded all the TV junior spacemen. And there were plenty more sci-fi heroes too, often with beguilingly corny names: Lars of Mars; Jim Solar, Space Sheriff; Dara Starr, Spacette…

After a high point in 1953, the comic book industry as a whole slumped amid hysteria over comics' alleged role in causing juvenile delinquency. When a revival came after a few years, sci-fi was in the vanguard. Readers were in the mood to travel *Out of This World*, visiting *Strange Planets*, and *Strange Worlds*. In the era of the space race, they were ready for *Race for the Moon* and even *Space War*.

With horror comics newly banned, some publishers steered towards "mystery" (less gory, more psychological), which blurred into sci-fi in genre-straddling titles such as *World of Fantasy*, *Mysteries of Unexplored Worlds*, DC's *Tales of the Unexpected*, and the long-running *Forbidden Worlds*. One company renowned for picking up on trends now made a name for itself with its distinctive "monster" comic books, including *Strange Tales*, *Tales of Suspense*, and *Tales to Astonish*. In a few short years, instead of following trends, it would start setting them. But that "Marvel Age" was still to come. If the '50s belonged to anyone, it was to an ambitious company that had flowered and all but disappeared by mid-decade: EC.

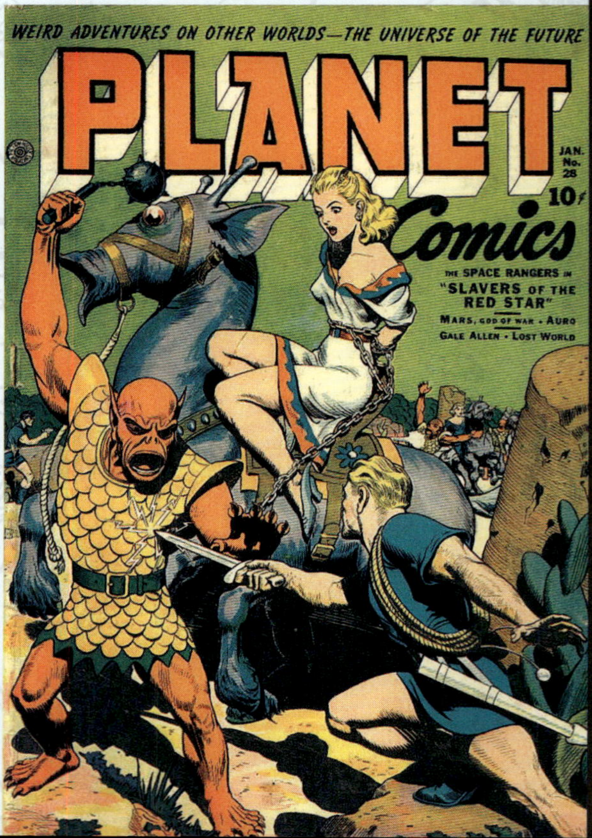

▲
Captain Video, the first SF hero on TV (1949), starred in his own comic book not long after. This page shows off the beautiful artwork by EC artist George Evans, assisted by Al Williamson.

▶
One of the most visually distinctive series of the '50s—or any era—*Spacehawk* was written and illustrated by the unique Basil Wolverton, who drew some of the most comical yet disturbing alien creatures ever seen.

▶▶
Dinosaurs and rocketships make for an irresistible combination in *Space Adventures* #25. The title began in 1952 but was suspended in the mid-'50s after 21 issues; this issue comes a few issues into its revival in 1958.

◀
The long-running *Planet Comics* stuck to a successful cover formula of hero, damsel, villain, and exotic creature. Sometimes the villain and exotic creature were one and the same; just occasionally the damsel and hero were. The art was not always as finely rendered as this example by the great Joe Doolin.

▶
A striking cover by Ogden Whitney for *Adventures into the Unknown* #67, cover-dated October 1955.

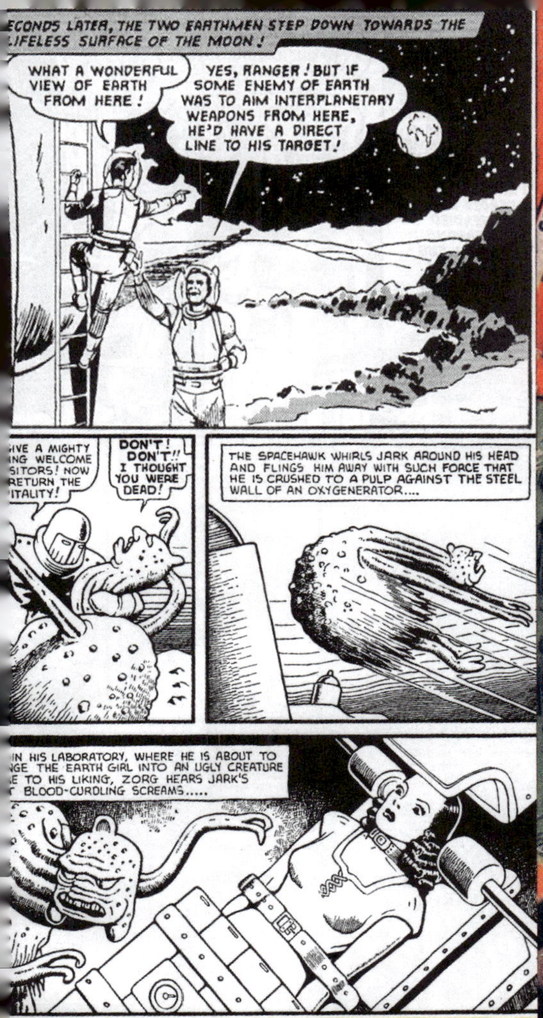
WHAT A WONDERFUL VIEW OF EARTH FROM HERE!
YES, RANGER! BUT IF SOME ENEMY OF EARTH WAS TO AIM INTERPLANETARY WEAPONS FROM HERE, HE'D HAVE A DIRECT LINE TO HIS TARGET!
DON'T! DON'T!! I THOUGHT YOU WERE DEAD!
THE SPACEHAWK WHIRLS JARK AROUND HIS HEAD AND FLINGS HIM AWAY WITH SUCH FORCE THAT HE IS CRUSHED TO A PULP AGAINST THE STEEL WALL OF AN OXYGENERATOR....
THE EARTH GIRL INTO AN UGLY CREATURE
TO HIS LIKING, ZORG HEARS JARK'S
BLOOD-CURDLING SCREAMS.....

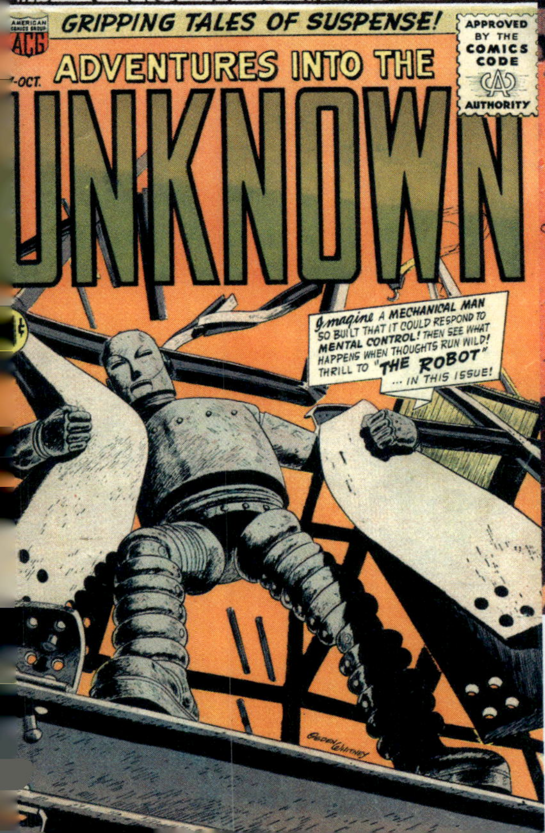
GRIPPING TALES OF SUSPENSE!
APPROVED BY THE COMICS CODE AUTHORITY
ADVENTURES INTO THE
UNKNOWN
Imagine A MECHANICAL MAN SO BUILT THAT IT COULD RESPOND TO MENTAL CONTROL! THEN SEE WHAT HAPPENS WHEN THOUGHTS RUN WILD! THRILL TO "THE ROBOT" ... IN THIS ISSUE!

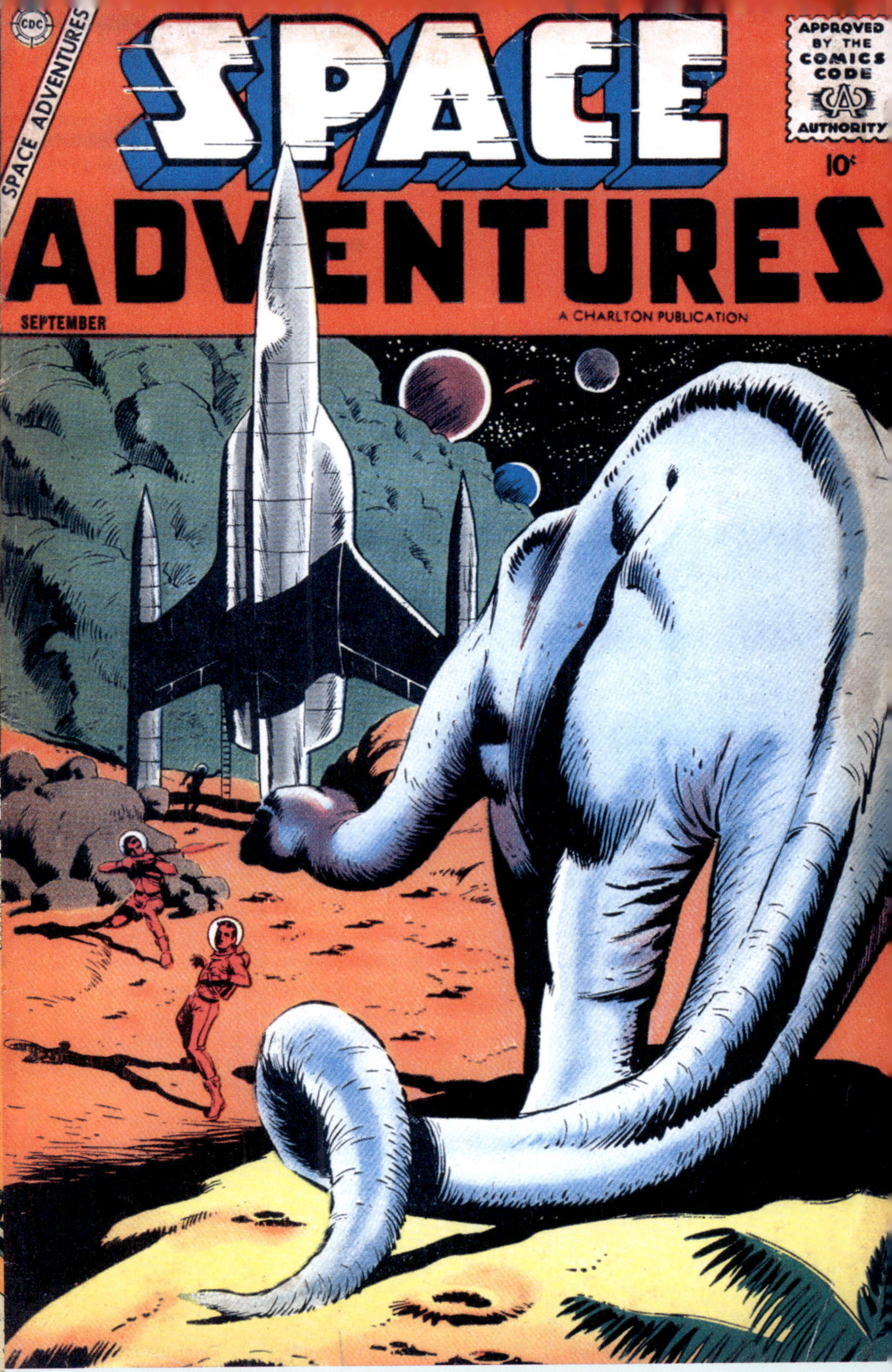
CDC
SPACE ADVENTURES
APPROVED BY THE COMICS CODE AUTHORITY
SPACE
10¢
ADVENTURES
SEPTEMBER
A CHARLTON PUBLICATION

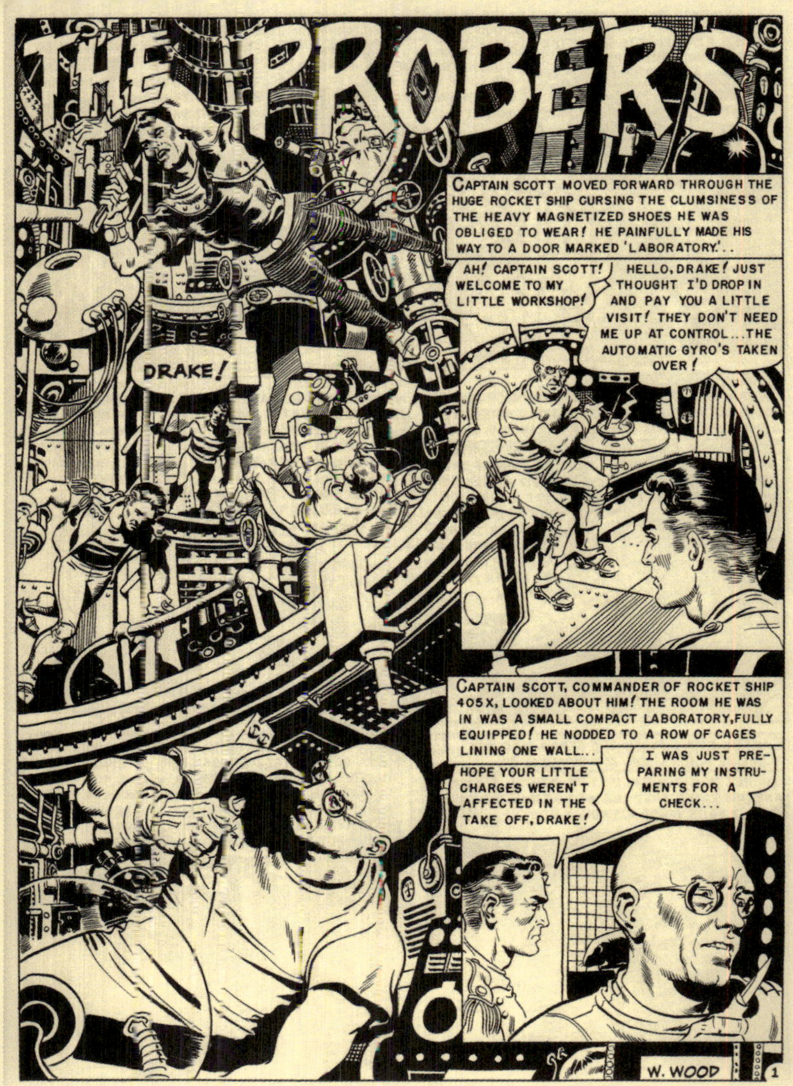
THE PROBERS
CAPTAIN SCOTT MOVED FORWARD THROUGH THE HUGE ROCKET SHIP CURSING THE CLUMSINESS OF THE HEAVY MAGNETIZED SHOES HE WAS OBLIGED TO WEAR! HE PAINFULLY MADE HIS WAY TO A DOOR MARKED 'LABORATORY'...
AH! CAPTAIN SCOTT! WELCOME TO MY LITTLE WORKSHOP!
HELLO, DRAKE! JUST THOUGHT I'D DROP IN AND PAY YOU A LITTLE VISIT! THEY DON'T NEED ME UP AT CONTROL...THE AUTOMATIC GYRO'S TAKEN OVER!
DRAKE!
CAPTAIN SCOTT, COMMANDER OF ROCKET SHIP 405X, LOOKED ABOUT HIM! THE ROOM HE WAS IN WAS A SMALL COMPACT LABORATORY, FULLY EQUIPPED! HE NODDED TO A ROW OF CAGES LINING ONE WALL...
HOPE YOUR LITTLE CHARGES WEREN'T AFFECTED IN THE TAKE OFF, DRAKE!
I WAS JUST PREPARING MY INSTRUMENTS FOR A CHECK...
W. WOOD
1

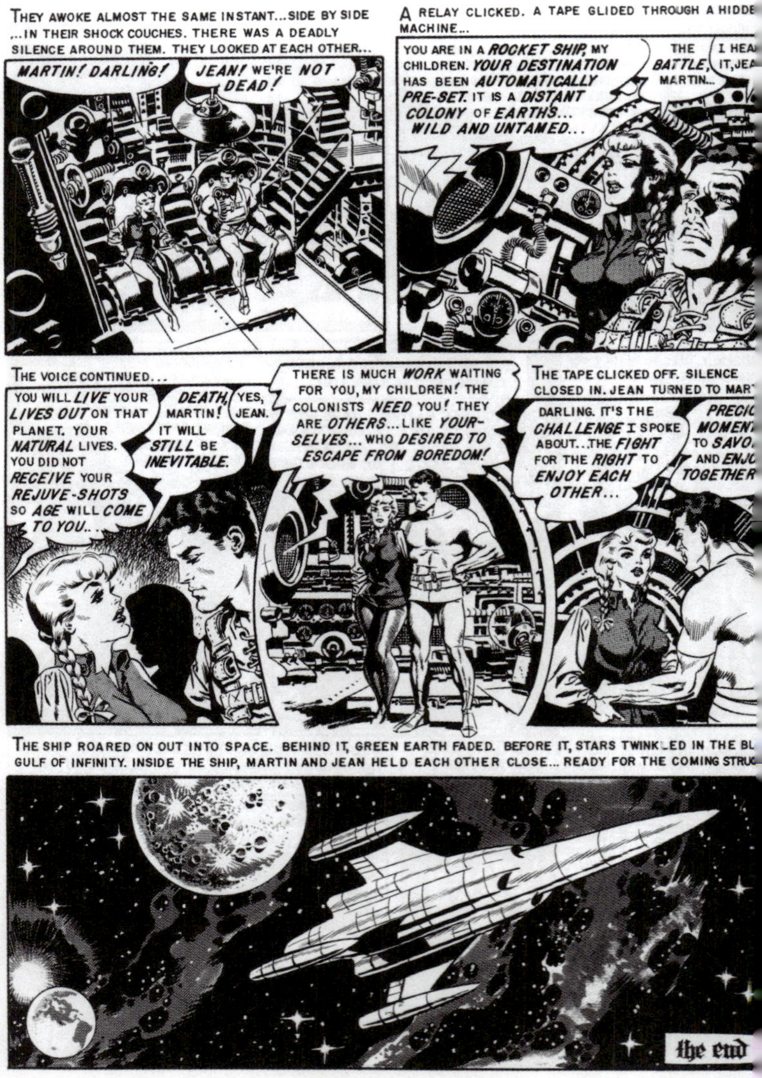
THEY AWOKE ALMOST THE SAME INSTANT...SIDE BY SIDE ...IN THEIR SHOCK COUCHES. THERE WAS A DEADLY SILENCE AROUND THEM. THEY LOOKED AT EACH OTHER...
MARTIN! DARLING!
JEAN! WE'RE NOT DEAD!
A RELAY CLICKED. A TAPE GLIDED THROUGH A HIDDE
MACHINE...
YOU ARE IN A ROCKET SHIP, MY CHILDREN. YOUR DESTINATION HAS BEEN AUTOMATICALLY PRE-SET. IT IS A DISTANT COLONY OF EARTHS... WILD AND UNTAMED...
THE BATTLE, MARTIN...
THE VOICE CONTINUED...
YOU WILL LIVE YOUR LIVES OUT ON THAT PLANET. YOUR NATURAL LIVES. YOU DID NOT RECEIVE YOUR REJUVE-SHOTS SO AGE WILL COME TO YOU...
DEATH, MARTIN! IT WILL STILL BE INEVITABLE.
YES, JEAN.
THERE IS MUCH WORK WAITING FOR YOU, MY CHILDREN! THE COLONISTS NEED YOU! THEY ARE OTHERS...LIKE YOURSELVES...WHO DESIRED TO ESCAPE FROM BOREDOM!
THE TAPE CLICKED OFF. SILENCE CLOSED IN. JEAN TURNED TO MAR
DARLING. IT'S THE CHALLENGE I SPOKE ABOUT...THE FIGHT FOR THE RIGHT TO ENJOY EACH OTHER...
THE SHIP ROARED ON OUT INTO SPACE. BEHIND IT, GREEN EARTH FADED. BEFORE IT, STARS TWINKLED IN THE BL
GULF OF INFINITY. INSIDE THE SHIP, MARTIN AND JEAN HELD EACH OTHER CLOSE... READY FOR THE COMING STRU
the end

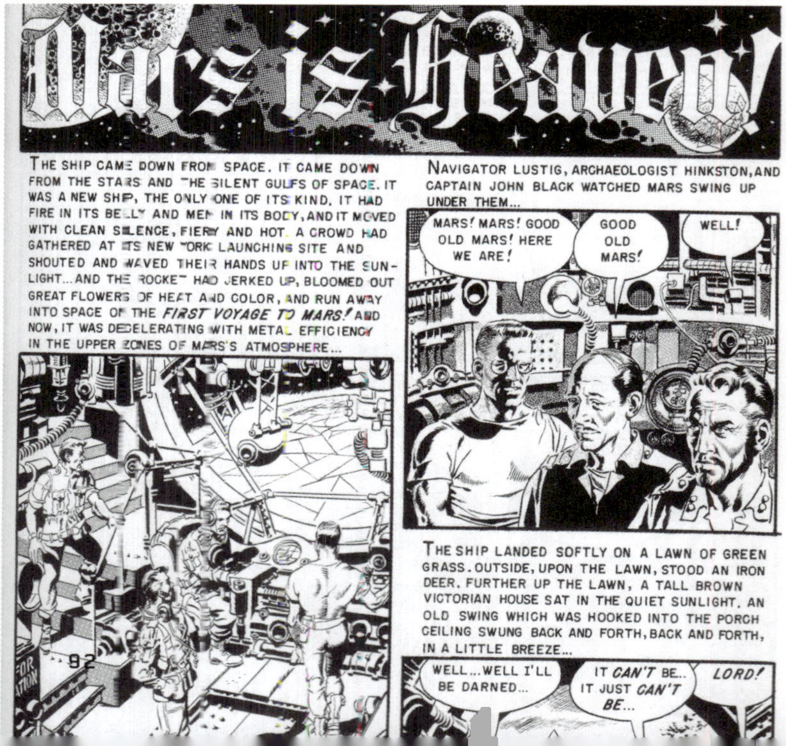
Mars is Heaven!
THE SHIP CAME DOWN FROM SPACE. IT CAME DOWN FROM THE STARS AND THE SILENT GULFS OF SPACE. IT WAS A NEW SHIP, THE ONLY ONE OF ITS KIND. IT HAD FIRE IN ITS BELLY AND MEN IN ITS BODY, AND IT MOVED WITH CLEAN SILENCE, FIERY AND HOT. A CROWD HAD GATHERED AT ITS NEW YORK LAUNCHING SITE AND SHOUTED AND WAVED THEIR HANDS UP INTO THE SUNLIGHT...AND THE ROCKET HAD JERKED UP, BLOOMED OUT GREAT FLOWERS OF HEAT AND COLOR, AND RUN AWAY INTO SPACE ON THE FIRST VOYAGE TO MARS! AND NOW, IT WAS DECELERATING WITH METAL EFFICIENCY IN THE UPPER ZONES OF MARS'S ATMOSPHERE...
NAVIGATOR LUSTIG, ARCHAEOLOGIST HINKSTON, AND CAPTAIN JOHN BLACK WATCHED MARS SWING UP UNDER THEM...
MARS! MARS! GOOD OLD MARS! HERE WE ARE!
GOOD OLD MARS!
WELL!
THE SHIP LANDED SOFTLY ON A LAWN OF GREEN GRASS. OUTSIDE, UPON THE LAWN, STOOD AN IRON DEER. FURTHER UP THE LAWN, A TALL BROWN VICTORIAN HOUSE SAT IN THE QUIET SUNLIGHT. AN OLD SWING WHICH WAS HOOKED INTO THE PORCH CEILING SWUNG BACK AND FORTH, BACK AND FORTH, IN A LITTLE BREEZE...
WELL...WELL I'LL BE DARNED...
IT CAN'T BE... IT JUST CAN'T BE...
LORD!

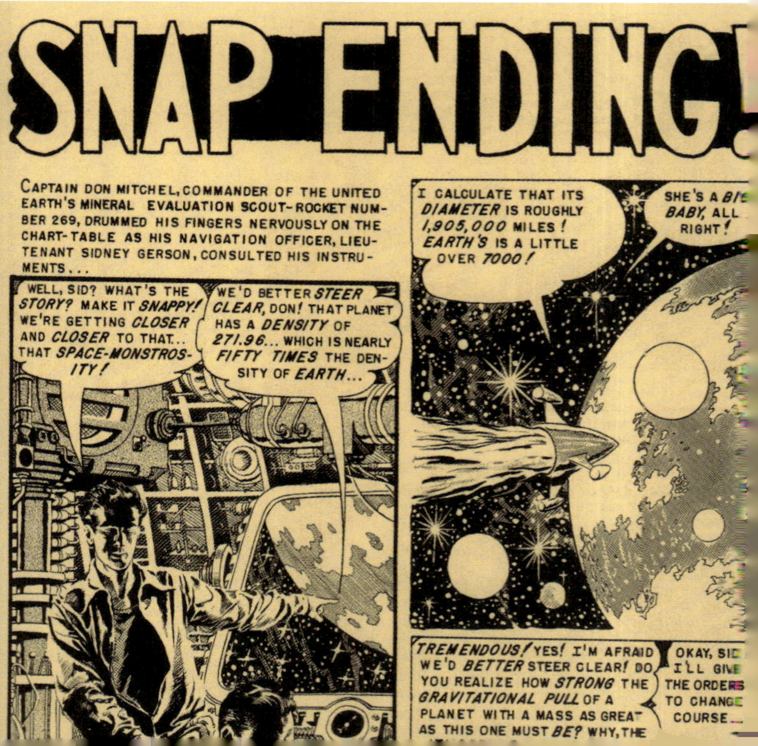
SNAP ENDING!
CAPTAIN DON MITCHEL, COMMANDER OF THE UNITED EARTH'S MINERAL EVALUATION SCOUT-ROCKET NUMBER 269, DRUMMED HIS FINGERS NERVOUSLY ON THE CHART-TABLE AS HIS NAVIGATION OFFICER, LIEUTENANT SIDNEY GERSON, CONSULTED HIS INSTRUMENTS...
I CALCULATE THAT ITS DIAMETER IS ROUGHLY 1,905,000 MILES! EARTH'S IS A LITTLE OVER 7000!
WELL, SID? WHAT'S THE STORY? MAKE IT SNAPPY! WE'RE GETTING CLOSER AND CLOSER TO THAT... THAT SPACE-MONSTROSITY!
WE'D BETTER STEER CLEAR, DON! THAT PLANET HAS A DENSITY OF 271.96... WHICH IS NEARLY FIFTY TIMES THE DENSITY OF EARTH...
TREMENDOUS! YES! I'M AFRAID WE'D BETTER STEER CLEAR! DO YOU REALIZE HOW STRONG THE GRAVITATIONAL PULL OF A PLANET WITH A MASS AS GREAT AS THIS ONE MUST BE? WHY, THE

EC COMICS: WALLY WOOD, AL WILLIAMSON & WEIRD SCIENCE

◀
Wood felt in later years that his EC work was "compulsively, neurotically overdetailed," but his settings as well as his people had an air of reality that few artists before or since have been able to match.

◀◀
The opening page of one of Wally Wood's first stories for *Weird Science*, a vertiginous view of a working spacecraft environment where "up" and "down" have no meaning. The linework is a little looser than it would soon become, but the hallmarks of his style are already there.

The world of comics owes a lot to the Gaines family. Max C. Gaines (1894–1947) invented the comic book as we know it; in 1933 he hit upon the idea that the public would pay ten cents for a half-tabloid-size booklet containing reprinted strips from the newspapers. The result was *Famous Funnies*, the first newsstand comic book. By the early 1940s, Max Gaines was a driving force in the fledgling adventure comics industry. In 1944 he set up a new company, EC (originally standing for "Educational Comics"), publishing *Picture Stories from the Bible* and a few funny-animal titles.

In summer 1947, Max Gaines was killed in a speedboat accident, and his son, William M. Gaines (1922–1992), inherited the business. Bill Gaines, then 25, was just a year short of qualifying as a chemistry teacher and at first was unhappy in his new role. By 1950, however, he'd decided he might as well make a go of it and publish comics he'd enjoy himself. EC now stood for "Entertaining Comics," and the company's "New Trend" titles caused a sensation with sharp-witted but gory horror comics including *Tales from the Crypt*, violent crime comics like *Crime SuspenStories*, and grim war titles like *Frontline Combat*.

As it happened, Bill Gaines and his editor Al Feldstein were science fiction fans, and they introduced two SF comics into their line-up. *Weird Science* and *Weird Fantasy* never sold quite as well as most of the other New Trend titles—indeed, after a while the SF titles were being subsidized by EC's far more profitable horror comics—but Gaines and Feldstein stuck to what they loved, and in doing so set the high-water mark for sci-fi comics.

Avid sci-fi readers, Gaines and Feldstein took inspiration for their plots from some of the leading SF writers of the day. The SF stories didn't always work comfortably in EC's rigid format of five or six pages plus twist ending, but the love of SF almost always came through, and the art was remarkable.

For the SF titles, Gaines and Feldstein coaxed the very best from their regular artists and newcomers such as Wally Wood and Al Williamson. Wood in particular soon dazzled with a breathtakingly detailed rendering technique. Nobody could match him for cluttered, claustrophobic spaceship interiors, lush landscapes, and convincingly slimy monsters. Indeed, for decades after EC ceased publishing comics, many fans felt he himself couldn't match his own early work.

▶▶
On the cover of the second issue of *Weird Science*, the Air Force flatly denies the existence of the flying saucer... Satiric irony was a hallmark of the entire EC line, later to find its home in the only EC title to survive the 1950s, *MAD* magazine.

▶
Wood's lovingly-rendered cover for the (real) 13th issue of *Weird Science* has everything: spaceships, undiscovered civilizations, exotic creatures...

◀◀
Wood's atmospheric opening page for EC's adaptation of a story by Ray Bradbury.

◀
Al Williamson too could draw a mean spaceship interior.

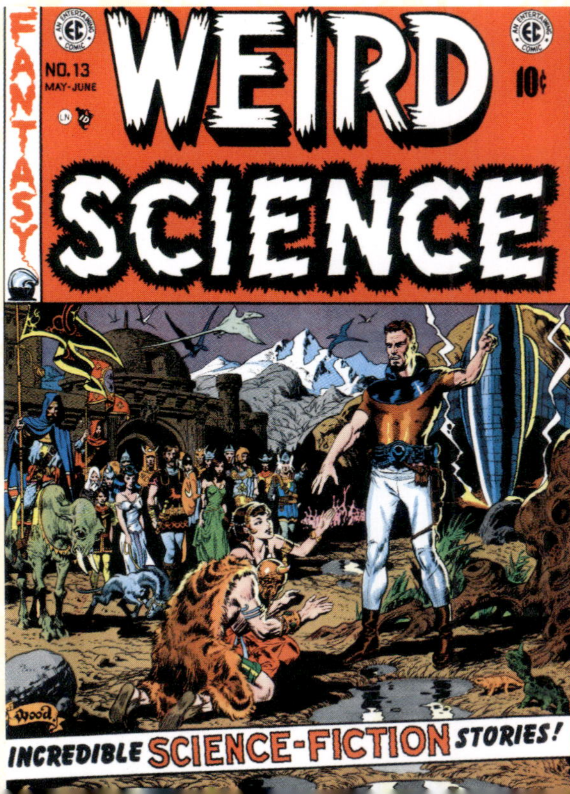

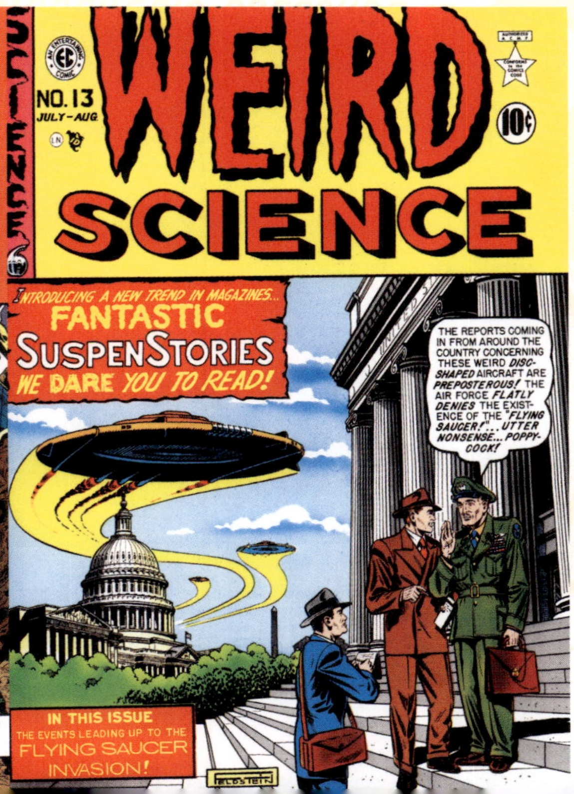

DAN DARE: FRANK HAMPSON & FRANK BELLAMY

▶
Though not an artist himself, Marcus Morris understood that he could combat the action-packed American comics of the '50s only with equally dynamic storytelling: "Technically, the *Eagle* strips marked an advance on the standards of that time (standards that had stood still for years) when most strips were not true strips but merely pictures with captions underneath. We tried to tell the stories mainly through the dramatic sequence of the pictures, with the help of not too many [word] balloons."

Britain in 1950 was a grim, gray place. World War II had devastated the economy, shortages were still common, and many basic foods were still rationed. Even worse, in some eyes, Britain's children were under threat... from American comics.

The colorful, action-packed US imports were very different from their staid, mostly black-and-white, homegrown counterparts. They were pouring into the country, partly as ballast in transatlantic shipping but lucrative thanks to a dual market; not only youngsters yearning for color and excitement in their lives, but also the large number of American servicemen still stationed in the British Isles with little to do. Maybe that's the real reason for the growing excesses of comic books into the '50s: the creators and publishers were trying to cater to the racier demands of this more adult readership worldwide and their demobbed buddies back home. One thing was for sure: voices were being raised on both sides of the Atlantic complaining that comics weren't for kids anymore.

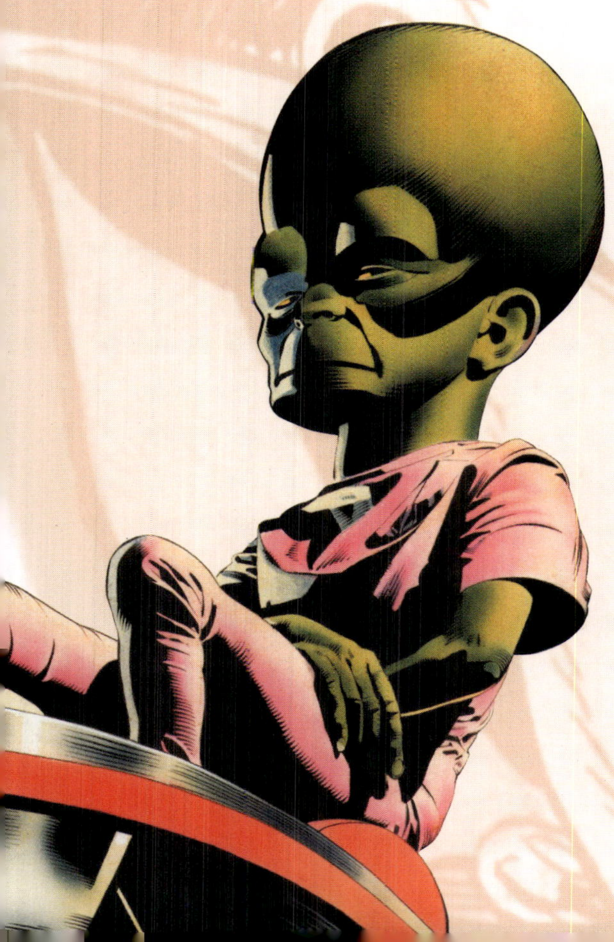

◀
Dan Dare's recurring nemesis, the Mekon, with his outsize cranium, is instantly memorable thanks to Hamson's effective character design.

One such voice was that of Reverend Marcus Morris (1915–1989), a Church of England minister with a talent for communication. He had turned his parish newsletter into a national Christian magazine, *The Anvil*, and wanted to combat what he saw as the pernicious influence of those beguiling American comics—"Comics That Bring Horror into the Nursery," as he titled one article.

His original idea was a newspaper strip starring "Lex Christian, a tough fighting parson in the slums of the East End of London." But then he thought, why settle for just a strip? Why not a whole regular comic magazine? Morris discussed the idea with his wife and the cover artist he had hired for *The Anvil*, Frank Hampson (1918–1985), and *Eagle* was born.

Eagle evolved somewhat before a publisher took it on, becoming less overtly preachy, though it preserved its core emphasis on wholesome adventure to counter the "depravities" of the US imports, and Morris was adamant that the adventure to be serialized on the back cover each week be the *Life of St. Paul*. The biggest change was to the cover feature. Lex Christian evolved first into "a flying padre, the Parson of the Fighting Seventh," and then into Dan *Dare, Pilot of the Future*.

As Morris always acknowledged, *Dan Dare* was Hampson's creation. A lifelong SF fan, Hampson brought life-affirming values like Morris' to the realm of technology. "Attitudes were so pessimistic, with The Bomb, the Cold War and rationing in the forefront of everyone's mind," Hampson explained in an interview years later. "I wanted to give hope for the future, to show that rockets and science in general could reveal new worlds, new opportunities. I was sure that space travel would be a reality. I had seen the innards of the V2 rockets while under attack in Antwerp and had been taken by the beauty and precision of the working parts. It seemed to me, somewhat ironically as we were under constant bombardment by these machines, that here was the birth of space travel."

Hampson's talent and drive matched his vision. He and Morris were determined that *Eagle* would be bigger, brighter, more colorful, better drawn, and better printed than anything else available at the time. As Hampson put it: "Into this scrap-yard of rusty old bicycles, I'm going to drive a Rolls-Royce."

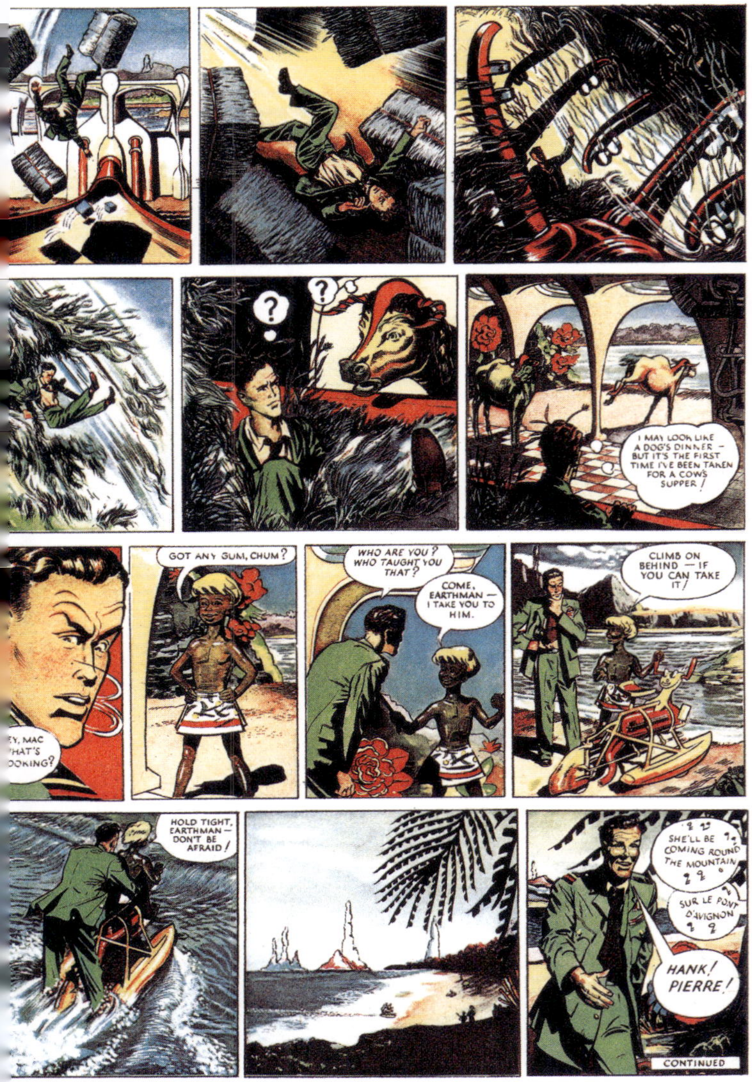

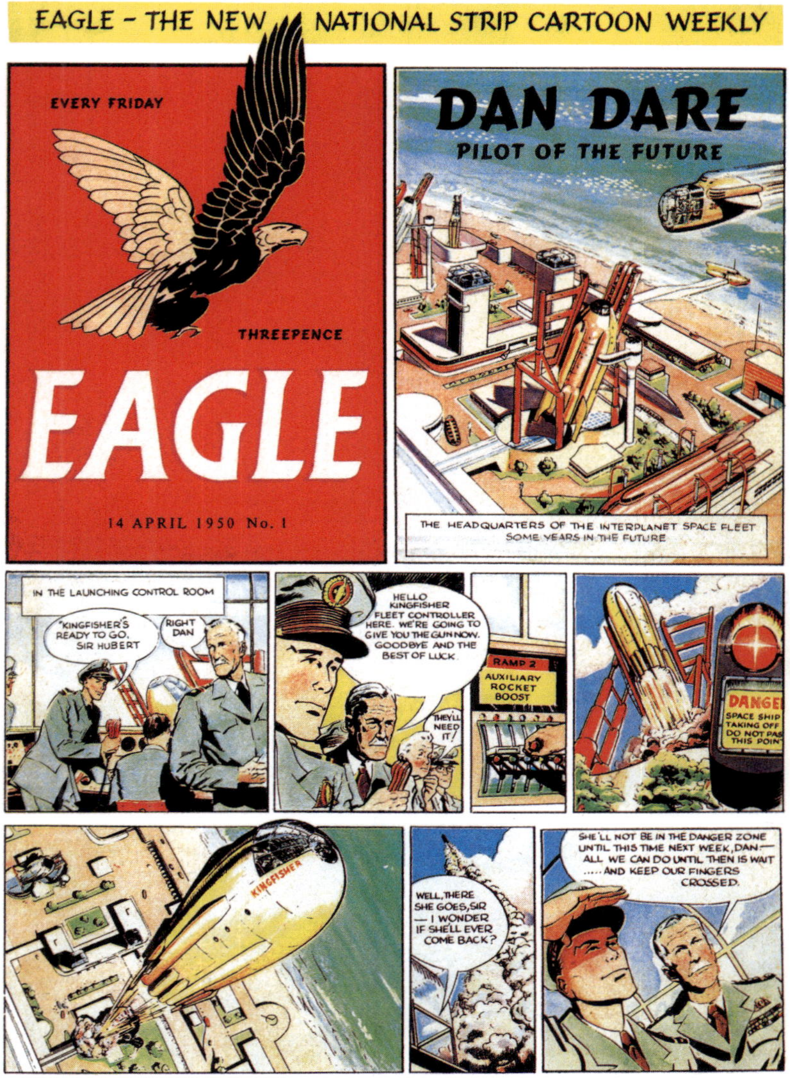

▲
Frank Hampson's father, a retired police officer, was famously the model for Sir Hubert Guest, the formidable Controller of Space Fleet, seen here in the very first episode of *Dan Dare* from *Eagle* #1, April 1950.

They delivered on all counts. As Morris noted with justifiable pride some years later, "the quality of the paper, printing, artwork, and writing set a new standard." The printers had to install new presses for the groundbreaking photogravure process that produced brighter colors and crisper linework than had ever been seen before (especially in the US comics, which were printed much more cheaply on far poorer paper). Among other editorial innovations, Morris insisted that every page of artwork was signed, so that artists felt their reputations were on the line with every page and therefore produced their best work. Morris signed his own name to the editorial every week, and so built up a personal relationship with the reader (more than a decade before Stan Lee used the same tactic in Marvel Comics).

Most colorful, most eye-catching, most brilliant of all was *Eagle*'s cover feature, *Dan Dare*. Frank Hampson plotted it, wrote it, and produced the artwork with the help of an entire studio of seven to nine people.

Hampson created initial color roughs of such quality that most publishers would have been proud to print them with little further work, but that was only the start. Reference photos were then taken of studio members (and obliging relatives) in costume; models were built of the spacecraft, alien creatures, and props; maps were drawn of the settings, and diagrams made explaining every part of every spacesuit, vehicle, and device. Only then were individual panels allocated to the artists to finish, with Hampson as principal artist and overseer.

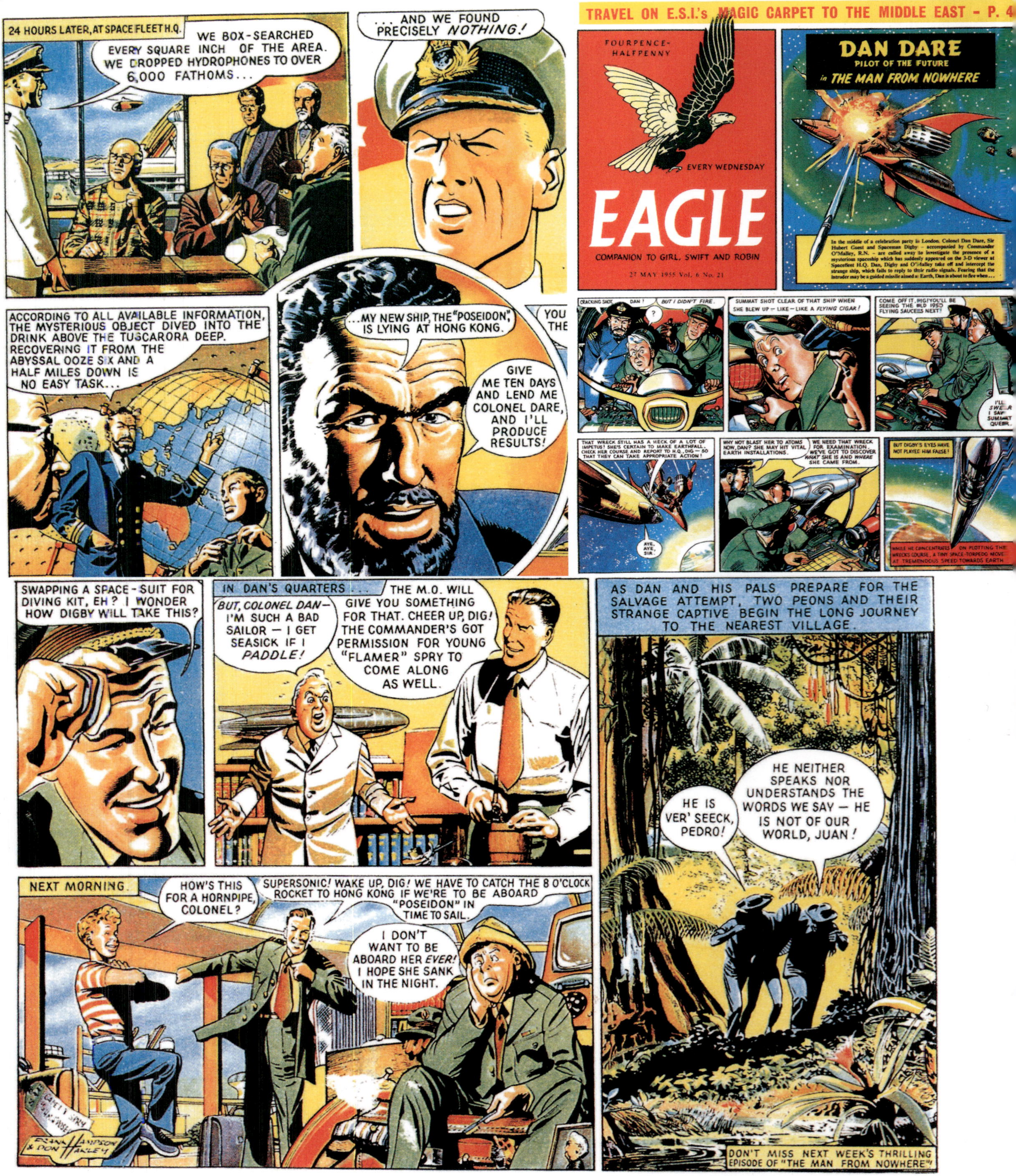

24 HOURS LATER, AT SPACE FLEET H.Q.
WE BOX-SEARCHED EVERY SQUARE INCH OF THE AREA. WE DROPPED HYDROPHONES TO OVER 6,000 FATHOMS...
... AND WE FOUND PRECISELY NOTHING!
ACCORDING TO ALL AVAILABLE INFORMATION, THE MYSTERIOUS OBJECT DIVED INTO THE DRINK ABOVE THE TUSCARORA DEEP. RECOVERING IT FROM THE ABYSSAL OOZE SIX AND A HALF MILES DOWN IS NO EASY TASK...
...MY NEW SHIP, THE "POSEIDON", IS LYING AT HONG KONG.
GIVE ME TEN DAYS AND LEND ME COLONEL DARE, AND I'LL PRODUCE RESULTS!
SWAPPING A SPACE-SUIT FOR DIVING KIT, EH? I WONDER HOW DIGBY WILL TAKE THIS?
IN DAN'S QUARTERS...
BUT, COLONEL DAN—I'M SUCH A BAD SAILOR — I GET SEASICK IF I PADDLE!
THE M.O. WILL GIVE YOU SOMETHING FOR THAT. CHEER UP, DIG! THE COMMANDER'S GOT PERMISSION FOR YOUNG "FLAMER" SPRY TO COME ALONG AS WELL.
NEXT MORNING.
HOW'S THIS FOR A HORNPIPE, COLONEL?
SUPERSONIC! WAKE UP, DIG! WE HAVE TO CATCH THE 8 O'CLOCK ROCKET TO HONG KONG IF WE'RE TO BE ABOARD "POSEIDON" IN TIME TO SAIL.
I DON'T WANT TO BE ABOARD HER EVER! I HOPE SHE SANK IN THE NIGHT.
FRANK HAMPSON & DON HARLEY
AS DAN AND HIS PALS PREPARE FOR THE SALVAGE ATTEMPT, TWO PEONS AND THEIR STRANGE CAPTIVE BEGIN THE LONG JOURNEY TO THE NEAREST VILLAGE.
HE IS VER' SEECK, PEDRO!
HE NEITHER SPEAKS NOR UNDERSTANDS THE WORDS WE SAY — HE IS NOT OF OUR WORLD, JUAN!
DON'T MISS NEXT WEEK'S THRILLING EPISODE OF "THE MAN FROM NOWHERE"!
FOURPENCE-HALFPENNY
EVERY WEDNESDAY
EAGLE
COMPANION TO GIRL, SWIFT AND ROBIN
27 MAY 1955 Vol. 6 No. 21
DAN DARE
PILOT OF THE FUTURE
in THE MAN FROM NOWHERE
In the middle of a celebration party in London, Colonel Dan Dare, Sir Hubert Guest and Spaceman Digby – accompanied by Commander O'Malley, R.N. – are called away to investigate the presence of a mysterious spaceship which has suddenly appeared on the 3-D viewer at Spacefleet H.Q. Dan, Digby and O'Malley take off and intercept the strange ship, which fails to reply to their radio signals. Fearing that the intruder may be a guided missile aimed at Earth, Dan is about to fire when...
CRACKING SHOT, DAN!
?
BUT I DIDN'T FIRE.
SUMMAT SHOT CLEAR OF THAT SHIP WHEN SHE BLEW UP — LIKE — LIKE A FLYING CIGAR!
THAT WRECK STILL HAS A HECK OF A LOT OF IMPETUS! SHE'S CERTAIN TO MAKE EARTHFALL. CHECK HER COURSE AND REPORT TO H.Q., DIG — SO THAT THEY CAN TAKE APPROPRIATE ACTION!
AYE, AYE, SIR.
WHY NOT BLAST HER TO ATOMS NOW, DAN? SHE MAY HIT VITAL EARTH INSTALLATIONS.
WE NEED THAT WRECK FOR EXAMINATION. WE'VE GOT TO DISCOVER WHAT SHE IS AND WHERE SHE CAME FROM.

The Hampson studio, reaching its peak here in 1955 with *The Man From Nowhere* storyline, produced pages on which each panel could have stood alone as a book cover, with sumptuous color and meticulous detail. The studio kept up with the latest astronomical findings and studied the work of other artists such as Chesley Bonestell in order to be sure to get the finest points right.

It's hard to imagine any artist or studio in history putting more work into two pages every week, but the final fully-painted artwork is among the finest ever produced in any comics anywhere—and it was produced week after grueling week for nine years, to a relentless schedule. It was, and remains to this day, an astonishing achievement. So meticulously detailed were the backgrounds that entire subplots unfolded purely in the pictures.

The workload was punishing, not least on Hampson himself, who had to take a few enforced vacations over the course of the decade as a result of overwork and suffered ill health for the rest of his life. His studio system was also a very expensive way to produce two pages of artwork a week, and when *Eagle*'s publisher, Hulton Press, was taken over in 1959 by a rival company, Odhams, the new owners were quick to make changes.

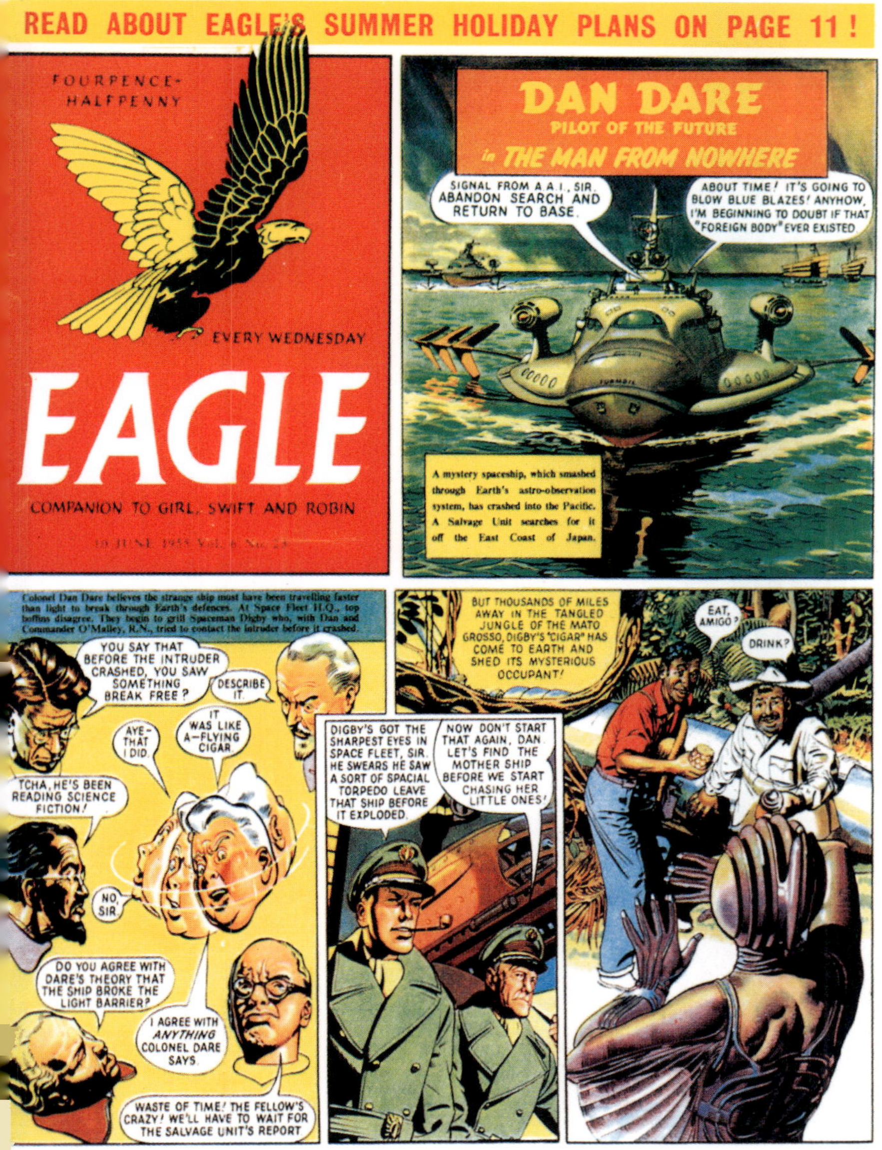

Marcus Morris, perhaps seeing what was ahead, had moved on, so there was nobody to resist when Odhams disbanded the studio. Hampson was retained to paint *Eagle*'s new back-page serial, a visually magnificent Life of Christ, but *Dan Dare* was assigned to another master stylist, Frank Bellamy (1917-1976).

Bellamy was instructed to give the strip a more dynamic look, and he redesigned everything right down to the Space Fleet insignia. His layouts were more fluid than Hampson's, and his rendering style relied less on meticulously-painted detail than on dramatic contrast, arresting textures, and sweeping action captured in mid-movement.

The workload was too great for one artist, however, so although Bellamy produced the title page alone he was assisted on the second page each week by two of Hampson's former assistants, Keith Watson and Don Harley, making for a sometimes awkward mix of the old and new styles. When his one-year contract was up, Bellamy moved on to other strips within *Eagle* and beyond, and *Dan Dare* passed first to Harley and then to Watson.

Given their history, it was perhaps inevitable that their *Dan Dare* harked back to the Hampson era—but that was also what the publisher requested, seeking to revive those early glory days. With the aid of various assistants over the years, Harley and Watson carried the torch with great distinction for almost another decade, until both *Eagle* and *Dan Dare* were discontinued in 1969.

Dogged by ill health, Frank Hampson himself worked only sporadically through the '60s and afterwards. In 1975, he fortuitously found himself at the world's premier international comics convention in Lucca, Italy, and an awards jury of his peers from around the world created a lifetime achievement award for him, naming him "prestigioso maestro"—the grandmaster artist/writer since World War II.

JEFF HAWKE: FIRST CITIZEN OF THE SPACE AGE

In the 1950s, sci-fi was in the air. In the UK, in the wake of *Dan Dare*, "pilots of the future" were all the rage: Captain Condor premiered in the first issue of *Lion Comic* in February 1952, Captain Valiant starred in *Space Comics* from 1953, and Captain Future headlined the short-lived *Spaceman: Comic of the Future* in the same year. Space Kingley featured in his own adventure annuals through the early '50s.

Sci-fi was in the air in another sense too: it was the era of the flying saucer. All this was the catalyst for a young Scottish artist named Sydney Jordan (1928-) to pitch a daily science fiction strip to London's *Daily Express* newspaper. Jordan had developed the strip, originally titled *Orion*, with ex-Royal Air Force buddies Eric Souster and Jim Gilbert, and the hero too was an RAF pilot, who in the opening storyline is abducted by a flying saucer. As Jordan later conceded, the concept was derivative of *Flash Gordon*, but fortunately the paper's manager, Max Aitken, son of newspaper tycoon Lord Beaverbrook, was himself an ex fighter pilot, and he liked the pitch—with one proviso: the hero's name had to be changed to Jeff Hawke.

Jeff Hawke premiered in the *Daily Express* in February 1954 and ran for more than 20 years. Jordan handled the art and writing chores himself, with an art assist at various times over the years, notably from Colin Andrew. Another old friend, Willie Patterson, came on board in 1956, initially to help out with the scripting, but soon became a full collaborator in the storytelling until he left because of ill health in 1969.

Jeff Hawke under Jordan and Patterson was a *tour de force* of newspaper strip art. It wasn't just slam-bang adventure or hard sci-fi, though there was plenty of both; adult newspaper readers as well as kids loved it for its whimsical humor and intelligent storylines, both often involving the complexities of society and political life in the Galactic Federation. Jeff Hawke would not only encounter imaginatively-designed, and always visually-striking, alien races, but would also have to cope with their laws and customs, their social hierarchies, and bureaucratic maneuverings. Aliens were usually inhuman in appearance but very human in their personalities, and Patterson inventively used them to present a wry perspective on the foibles and failings of human society and (especially) officialdom.

Jordan's artwork was distinguished by its sumptuous use of gray toning and magnificent detailing. Newspaper printing didn't always do it justice, and almost to this day *Jeff Hawke* has been relatively unsung in Britain compared with Europe, where readers got to see it in all its glory in well-printed compilation volumes. (UK-based publisher Titan Books has now released a couple of collections). *Jeff Hawke* is rightly hailed as a sci-fi masterpiece in France, Germany, Spain, and the Scandinavian countries, but especially in Italy,

▶
An example of Sydney Jordan's superbly detailed artwork from the 1961 story *Immortal Toys*, displaying the craftsmanship that Jordan brought to *Jeff Hawke*.

▶
Aliens in *Jeff Hawke* were not just isolated "creatures" but rounded personalities, with complex social relationships. Jordan's skill in imbuing aliens with character was matched by his virtuoso use of mechanical tints to add depth to the worlds he so convincingly depicted.

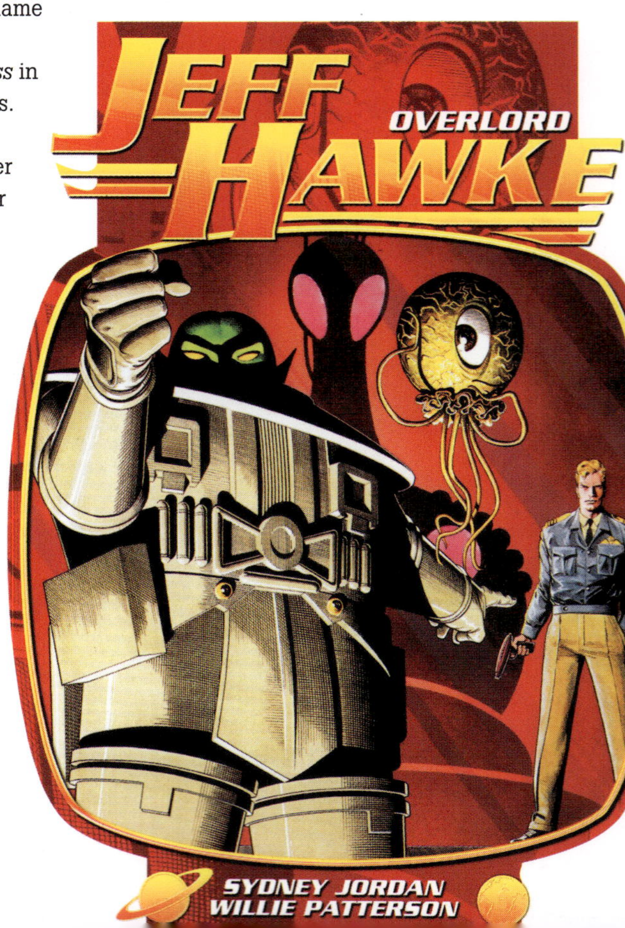

◀
British comic book artist Brian Bolland provided the cover illustration for Titan Books' first two collections of *Jeff Hawke*, capturing the feel of the strip perfectly.

▶
Jordan and Patterson's wit added an extra dimension to the most unpromising of plot devices; in one story the Earth is invaded by one million alien soldiers, but they're ant-sized, and the tide is turned by a household cat that stumbles upon them. In this example from 1962's *A Test Case*, a character is transformed into an alien form not unlike a marrow!

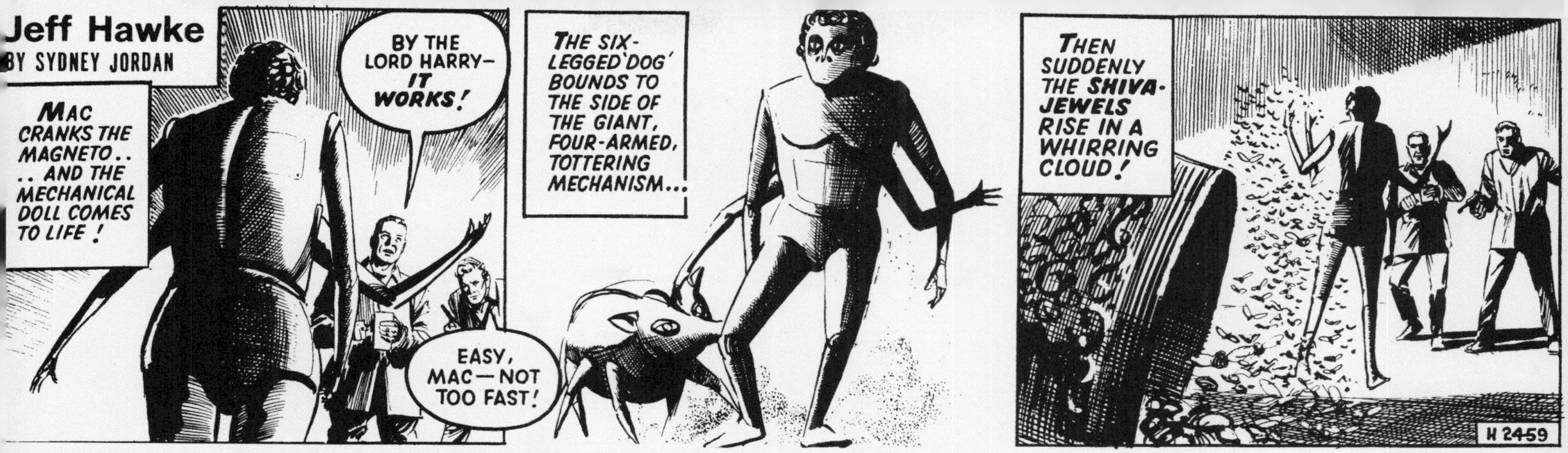
Jeff Hawke
BY SYDNEY JORDAN
MAC CRANKS THE MAGNETO.. .. AND THE MECHANICAL DOLL COMES TO LIFE!
BY THE LORD HARRY— IT WORKS!
EASY, MAC— NOT TOO FAST!
THE SIX-LEGGED 'DOG' BOUNDS TO THE SIDE OF THE GIANT, FOUR-ARMED, TOTTERING MECHANISM...
THEN SUDDENLY THE SHIVA-JEWELS RISE IN A WHIRRING CLOUD!
H 2459

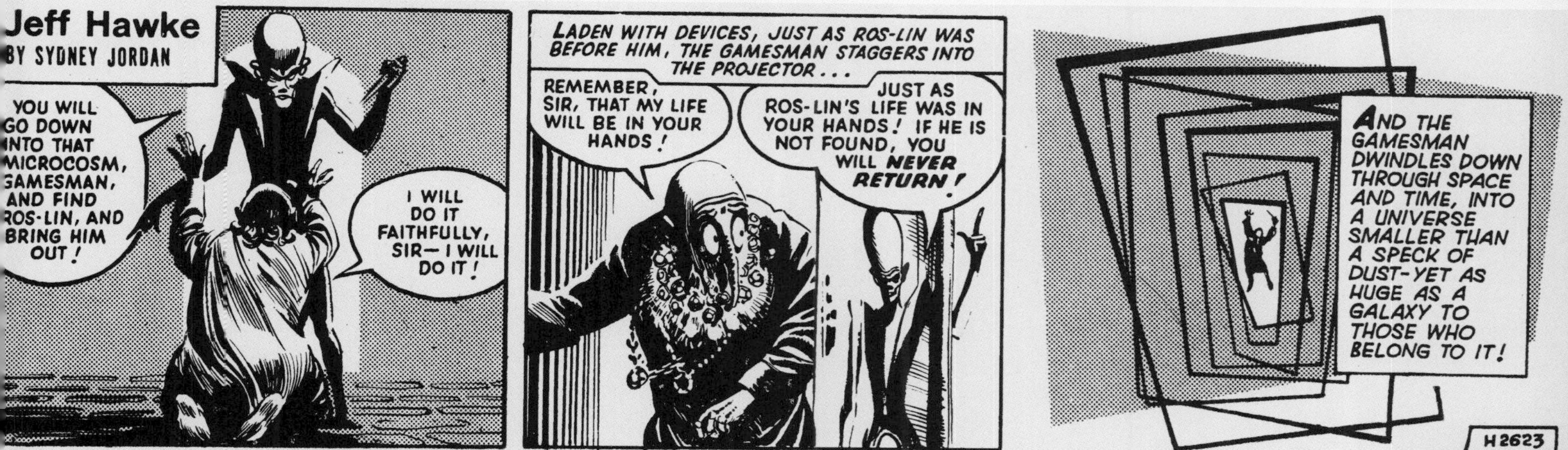
Jeff Hawke
BY SYDNEY JORDAN
YOU WILL GO DOWN NTO THAT MICROCOSM, GAMESMAN, AND FIND ROS-LIN, AND BRING HIM OUT!
I WILL DO IT FAITHFULLY, SIR— I WILL DO IT!
LADEN WITH DEVICES, JUST AS ROS-LIN WAS BEFORE HIM, THE GAMESMAN STAGGERS INTO THE PROJECTOR...
REMEMBER, SIR, THAT MY LIFE WILL BE IN YOUR HANDS!
JUST AS ROS-LIN'S LIFE WAS IN YOUR HANDS! IF HE IS NOT FOUND, YOU WILL NEVER RETURN!
AND THE GAMESMAN DWINDLES DOWN THROUGH SPACE AND TIME, INTO A UNIVERSE SMALLER THAN A SPECK OF DUST-YET AS HUGE AS A GALAXY TO THOSE WHO BELONG TO IT!
H 2623

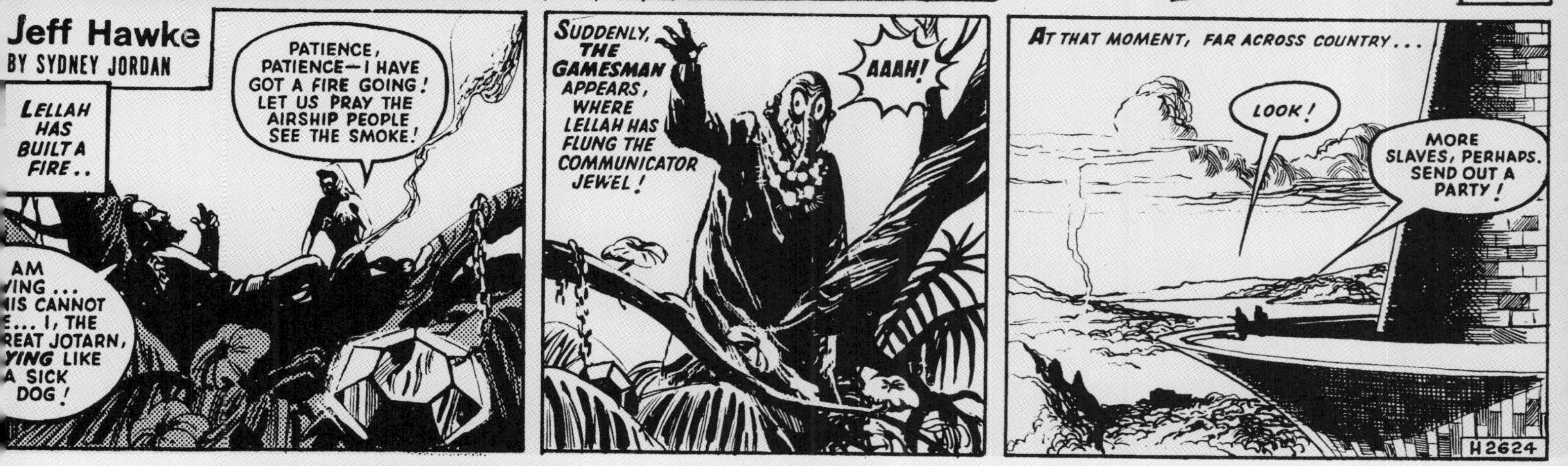
Jeff Hawke
BY SYDNEY JORDAN
LELLAH HAS BUILT A FIRE..
PATIENCE, PATIENCE—I HAVE GOT A FIRE GOING! LET US PRAY THE AIRSHIP PEOPLE SEE THE SMOKE!
AM YING ... HIS CANNOT E... I, THE REAT JOTARN, YING LIKE A SICK DOG!
SUDDENLY, THE GAMESMAN APPEARS, WHERE LELLAH HAS FLUNG THE COMMUNICATOR JEWEL!
AAAH!
AT THAT MOMENT, FAR ACROSS COUNTRY...
LOOK!
MORE SLAVES, PERHAPS. SEND OUT A PARTY!
H 2624

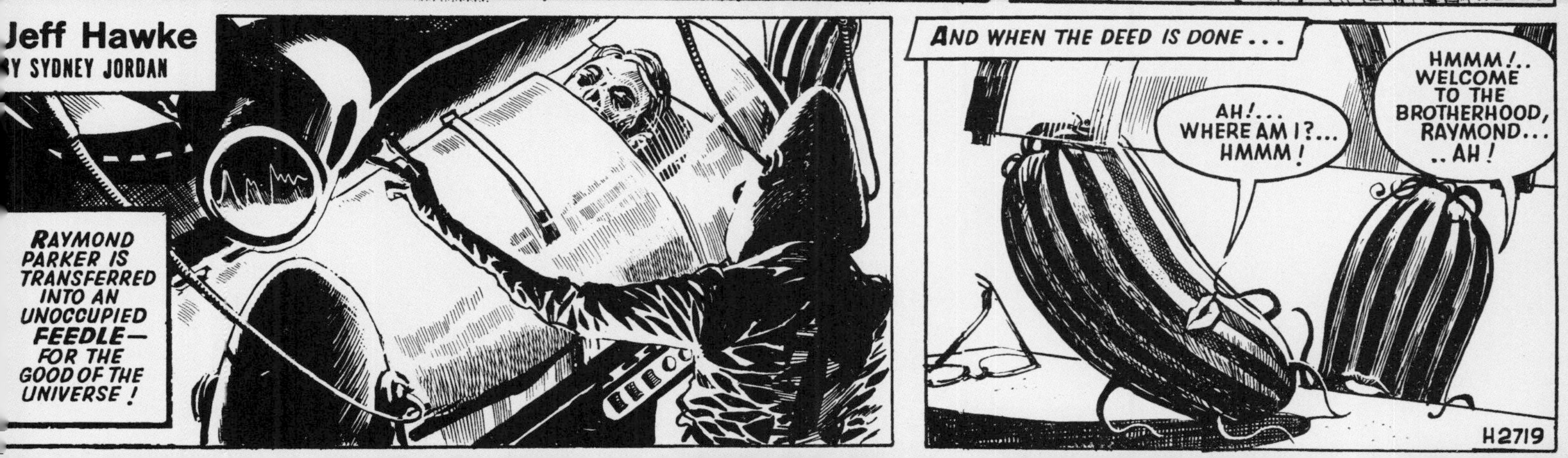
Jeff Hawke
BY SYDNEY JORDAN
RAYMOND PARKER IS TRANSFERRED INTO AN UNOCCUPIED FEEDLE— FOR THE GOOD OF THE UNIVERSE!
AND WHEN THE DEED IS DONE...
AH!... WHERE AM I?... HMMM!
HMMM!.. WELCOME TO THE BROTHERHOOD, RAYMOND... ..AH!
H2719

SCI-FI SUPERHEROES OF THE SILVER AGE

Superheroes have always had a connection with sci-fi. Indeed, the very first superhero, Superman, was a "strange visitor from another planet." But the relationship was at its closest in the late 1950s and throughout the '60s, during the revival of superhero comics known as the Silver Age.

In the Golden Age of superhero comics (1930s–1940s), Hawkman was the reincarnation of an Egyptian prince; his Silver Age namesake was a cop from another planet (though both could fly by donning wings made of "anti-gravity metal"). The Golden Age Green Lantern had a magic ring that could make anything he wished come true; the Silver Age Green Lantern received an advanced-technology weapon from an alien who crash-landed on Earth. (This weapon was a ring that could make anything he willed become actualized—clearly a completely different thing). The Golden Age Atom was a tough short guy who put on a costume and fought criminals; his Silver Age counterpart gained the power to shrink to tiny size using "white dwarf star matter."

This new sci-fi flavor was no accident. The man behind most of the Silver Age versions of these characters was long-time DC Comics editor Julius Schwartz (1915–2004), who in the '30s had been active in SF fandom and became the first literary agent specializing in representing SF authors. His interest in SF, and that of the writers he commissioned for his comics, extended to the stories too; many of the adventures of these Silver Age heroes involved aliens, or science, or alien science—plus, naturally, fighting criminals.

When it came to original characters, the SF connection was stronger still. Arguably the first completely original Silver Age character was J'onn J'onzz, the Martian Manhunter, who was trapped on Earth as the result of a teleportation experiment gone wrong. Neatly turning the tables, archeologist Adam Strange was regularly teleported to the planet Rann in the Alpha Centauri star system, where he used his ingenuity and courage (plus a nifty jetpack and raygun and other convenient gadgetry developed on Rann) to overcome the wide variety of crises that seemed to hit that planet with alarming frequency.

Other even more explicitly sci-fi-based Silver Age DC characters included Rip Hunter, Time Master; the Atomic Knights (a band of freedom fighters in the devastated world after the terrible Hydrogen War of 1986 who discover that medieval suits of armor will protect them from the rayguns of the villainous Black Baron); and Star Hawkins, a hapless future detective whose robot receptionist routinely solves his cases for him.

Over at Marvel Comics, radiation ruled. The Fantastic Four gained their powers from being bombarded by "cosmic rays" during a rash spaceflight (trying to beat the Commies to the moon). Scientist Bruce Banner was transformed into the brutish Hulk when caught in the blast of a prematurely detonated "gamma bomb" (triggered by a Commie spy). Science student Peter Parker gained spider-like abilities after being bitten by a radioactive spider (whose political leanings were never disclosed).

And so on, almost without exception. Even the Mighty Thor, the Norse god of thunder, faced sci-fi adversaries such as the Stone Men from Saturn and Zarrko the Tomorrow Man, an aspiring criminal escaping from a future world where crime had been made impossible.

▶
Marvel's creative powerhouse Jack Kirby, who in the 1950s had developed *Challengers of the Unknown* and other sci-fi titles at DC and elsewhere, took the Mighty Thor into space—but it was clearly not the same space as DC's. It was distinctively his own, and packed with his own unique style of "Kirbytech."

▶▼
Jack Kirby delighted in inventing alien cultures and filling them with exotic detail, as he did when he transported the Fantastic Four to the homeworld of the Skrulls, just one of the alien races they were to encounter.

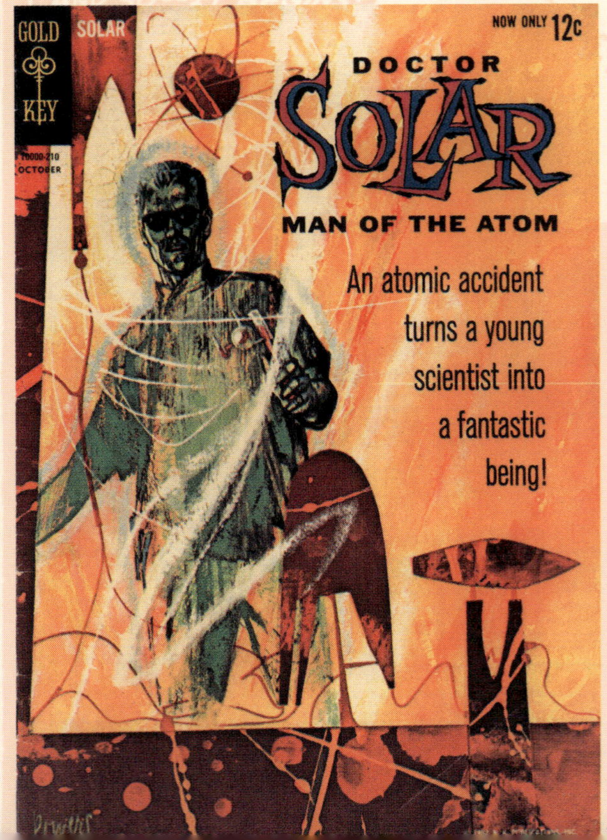

◀
When industry leader Dell had a falling out with Western Printing, who had packaged and printed their comic books for years, Western decided to go their own way and continue most of the Dell titles under their own imprint, Gold Key. They also launched new series: *Doctor Solar* #1 (dated October 1962) was the first original Gold Key title, and the covers of the first few issues were strikingly un-comic-like pieces by leading paperback artist Richard M. Powers.

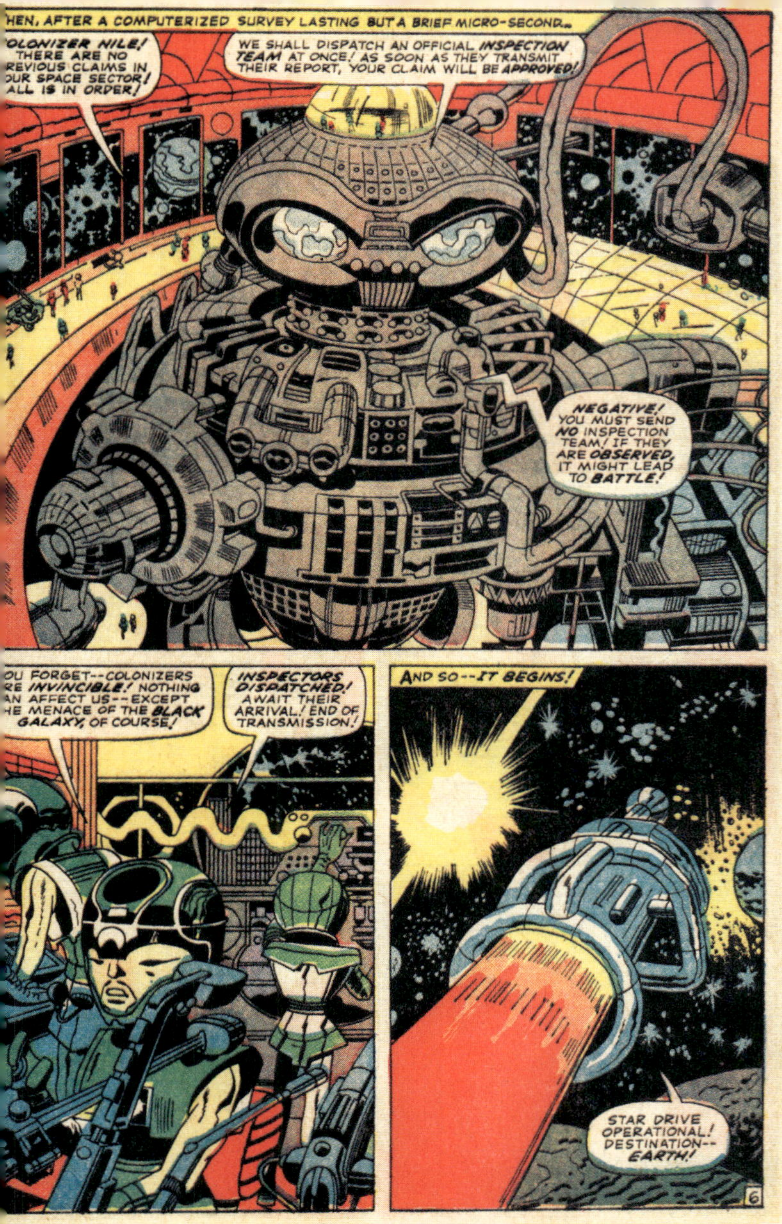
HEN, AFTER A COMPUTERIZED SURVEY LASTING BUT A BRIEF MICRO-SECOND...
OLONIZER NILE! THERE ARE NO REVIOUS CLAIMS IN OUR SPACE SECTOR! ALL IS IN ORDER!
WE SHALL DISPATCH AN OFFICIAL INSPECTION TEAM AT ONCE! AS SOON AS THEY TRANSMIT THEIR REPORT, YOUR CLAIM WILL BE APPROVED!
NEGATIVE! YOU MUST SEND NO INSPECTION TEAM! IF THEY ARE OBSERVED, IT MIGHT LEAD TO BATTLE!
OU FORGET--COLONIZERS RE INVINCIBLE! NOTHING AN AFFECT US--EXCEPT HE MENACE OF THE BLACK GALAXY, OF COURSE!
INSPECTORS DISPATCHED! AWAIT THEIR ARRIVAL! END OF TRANSMISSION!
AND SO--IT BEGINS!
STAR DRIVE OPERATIONAL! DESTINATION--EARTH!
6

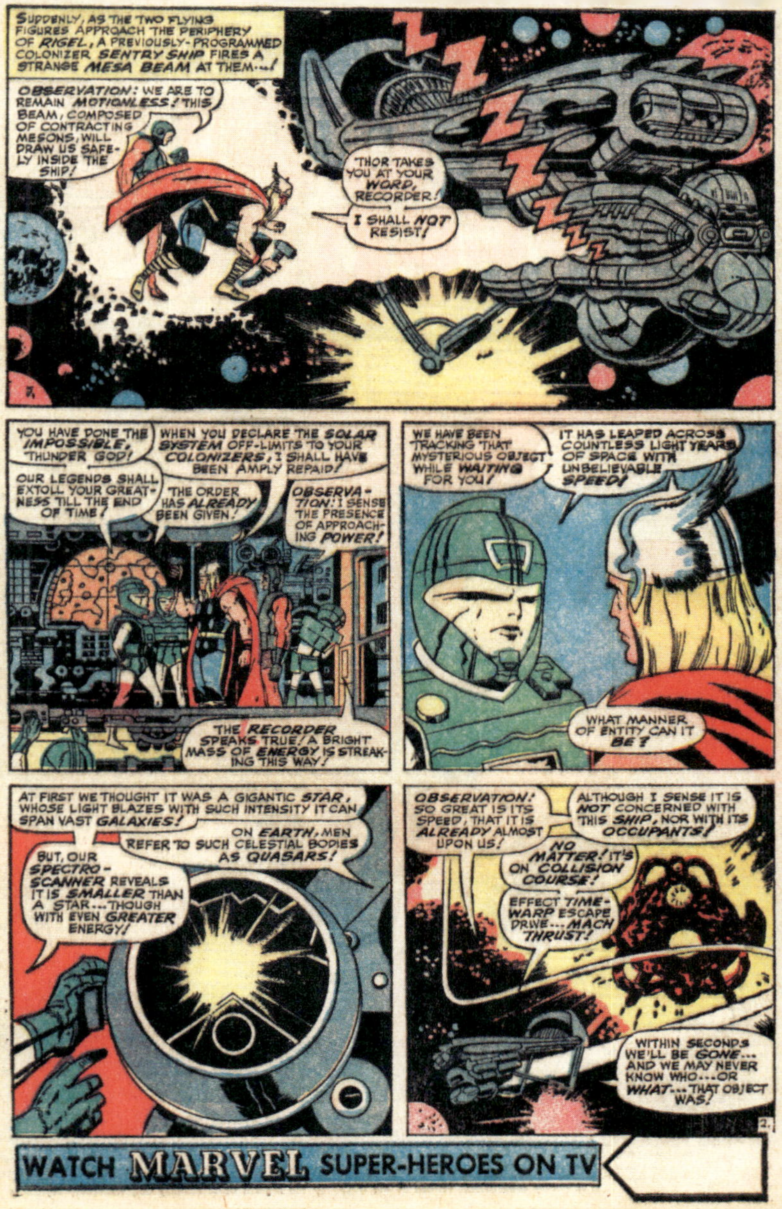
SUDDENLY, AS THE TWO FLYING FIGURES APPROACH THE PERIPHERY OF RIGEL, A PREVIOUSLY-PROGRAMMED COLONIZER SENTRY SHIP FIRES A STRANGE MESA BEAM AT THEM...!
OBSERVATION: WE ARE TO REMAIN MOTIONLESS! THIS BEAM, COMPOSED OF CONTRACTING MESONS, WILL DRAW US SAFELY INSIDE THE SHIP!
THOR TAKES YOU AT YOUR WORD, RECORDER!
I SHALL NOT RESIST!
YOU HAVE DONE THE IMPOSSIBLE, THUNDER GOD!
WHEN YOU DECLARE THE SOLAR SYSTEM OFF-LIMITS TO YOUR COLONIZERS, I SHALL HAVE BEEN AMPLY REPAID!
OUR LEGENDS SHALL EXTOLL YOUR GREATNESS TILL THE END OF TIME!
THE ORDER HAS ALREADY BEEN GIVEN!
OBSERVATION: I SENSE THE PRESENCE OF APPROACHING POWER!
THE RECORDER SPEAKS TRUE! A BRIGHT MASS OF ENERGY IS STREAKING THIS WAY!
WE HAVE BEEN TRACKING THAT MYSTERIOUS OBJECT WHILE WAITING FOR YOU!
IT HAS LEAPED ACROSS COUNTLESS LIGHT YEARS OF SPACE WITH UNBELIEVABLE SPEED!
WHAT MANNER OF ENTITY CAN IT BE?
AT FIRST WE THOUGHT IT WAS A GIGANTIC STAR, WHOSE LIGHT BLAZES WITH SUCH INTENSITY IT CAN SPAN VAST GALAXIES!
ON EARTH, MEN REFER TO SUCH CELESTIAL BODIES AS QUASARS!
BUT, OUR SPECTRO-SCANNER REVEALS IT IS SMALLER THAN A STAR... THOUGH WITH EVEN GREATER ENERGY!
OBSERVATION! SO GREAT IS ITS SPEED, THAT IT IS ALREADY ALMOST UPON US!
ALTHOUGH I SENSE IT IS NOT CONCERNED WITH THIS SHIP, NOR WITH ITS OCCUPANTS!
NO MATTER! IT'S ON COLLISION COURSE!
EFFECT TIME-WARP ESCAPE DRIVE... MACH THRUST!
WITHIN SECONDS WE'LL BE GONE... AND WE MAY NEVER KNOW WHO...OR WHAT... THAT OBJECT WAS!
2
WATCH MARVEL SUPER-HEROES ON TV

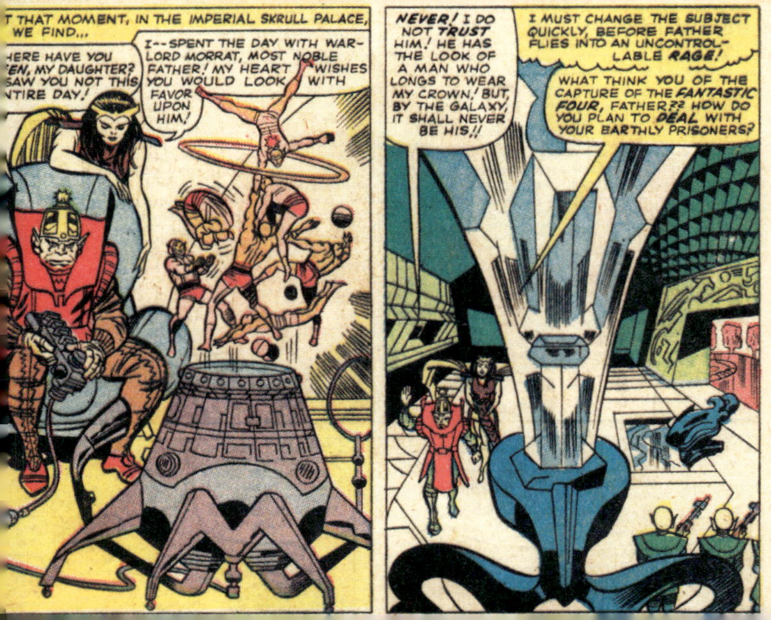
T THAT MOMENT, IN THE IMPERIAL SKRULL PALACE, WE FIND...
HERE HAVE YOU EN, MY DAUGHTER? SAW YOU NOT THIS NTIRE DAY!
I--SPENT THE DAY WITH WAR-LORD MORRAT, MOST NOBLE FATHER! MY HEART WISHES YOU WOULD LOOK WITH FAVOR UPON HIM!
NEVER! I DO NOT TRUST HIM! HE HAS THE LOOK OF A MAN WHO LONGS TO WEAR MY CROWN! BUT, BY THE GALAXY, IT SHALL NEVER BE HIS!!
I MUST CHANGE THE SUBJECT QUICKLY, BEFORE FATHER FLIES INTO AN UNCONTROLLABLE RAGE!
WHAT THINK YOU OF THE CAPTURE OF THE FANTASTIC FOUR, FATHER?? HOW DO YOU PLAN TO DEAL WITH YOUR EARTHLY PRISONERS?

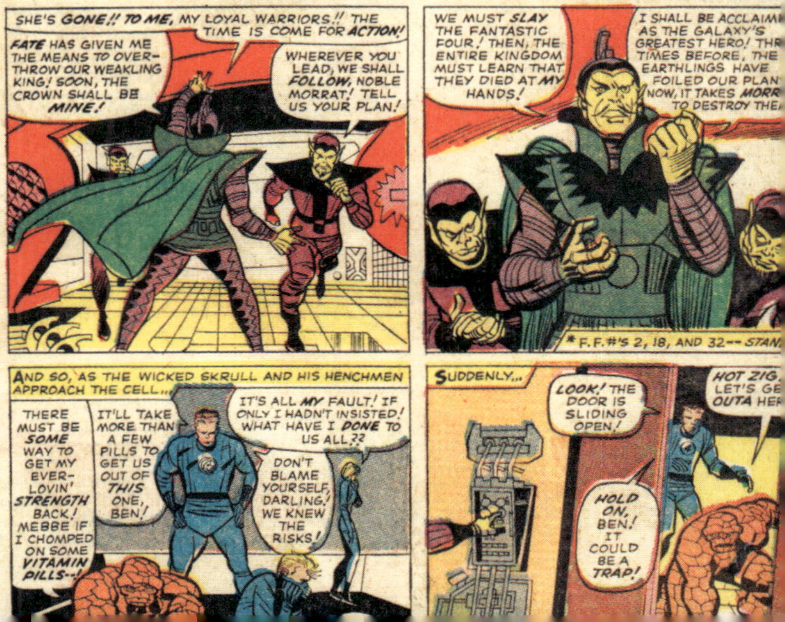
SHE'S GONE!! TO ME, MY LOYAL WARRIORS!! THE TIME IS COME FOR ACTION!
FATE HAS GIVEN ME THE MEANS TO OVERTHROW OUR WEAKLING KING! SOON, THE CROWN SHALL BE MINE!
WHEREVER YOU LEAD, WE SHALL FOLLOW, NOBLE MORRAT! TELL US YOUR PLAN!
WE MUST SLAY THE FANTASTIC FOUR! THEN, THE ENTIRE KINGDOM MUST LEARN THAT THEY DIED AT MY HANDS!
I SHALL BE ACCLAIM AS THE GALAXY'S GREATEST HERO! THR TIMES BEFORE, THE EARTHLINGS HAVE FOILED OUR PLAN NOW, IT TAKES MORR TO DESTROY THE
* F.F. #'S 2, 18, AND 32-- STAN
AND SO, AS THE WICKED SKRULL AND HIS HENCHMEN APPROACH THE CELL...
THERE MUST BE SOME WAY TO GET MY EVER-LOVIN' STRENGTH BACK! MEBBE IF I CHOMPED ON SOME VITAMIN PILLS--!
IT'LL TAKE MORE THAN A FEW PILLS TO GET US OUT OF THIS ONE, BEN!
IT'S ALL MY FAULT! IF ONLY I HADN'T INSISTED! WHAT HAVE I DONE TO US ALL??
DON'T BLAME YOURSELF, DARLING! WE KNEW THE RISKS!
SUDDENLY...
LOOK! THE DOOR IS SLIDING OPEN!
HOT ZIG, LET'S GE OUTA HE
HOLD ON, BEN! IT COULD BE A TRAP!

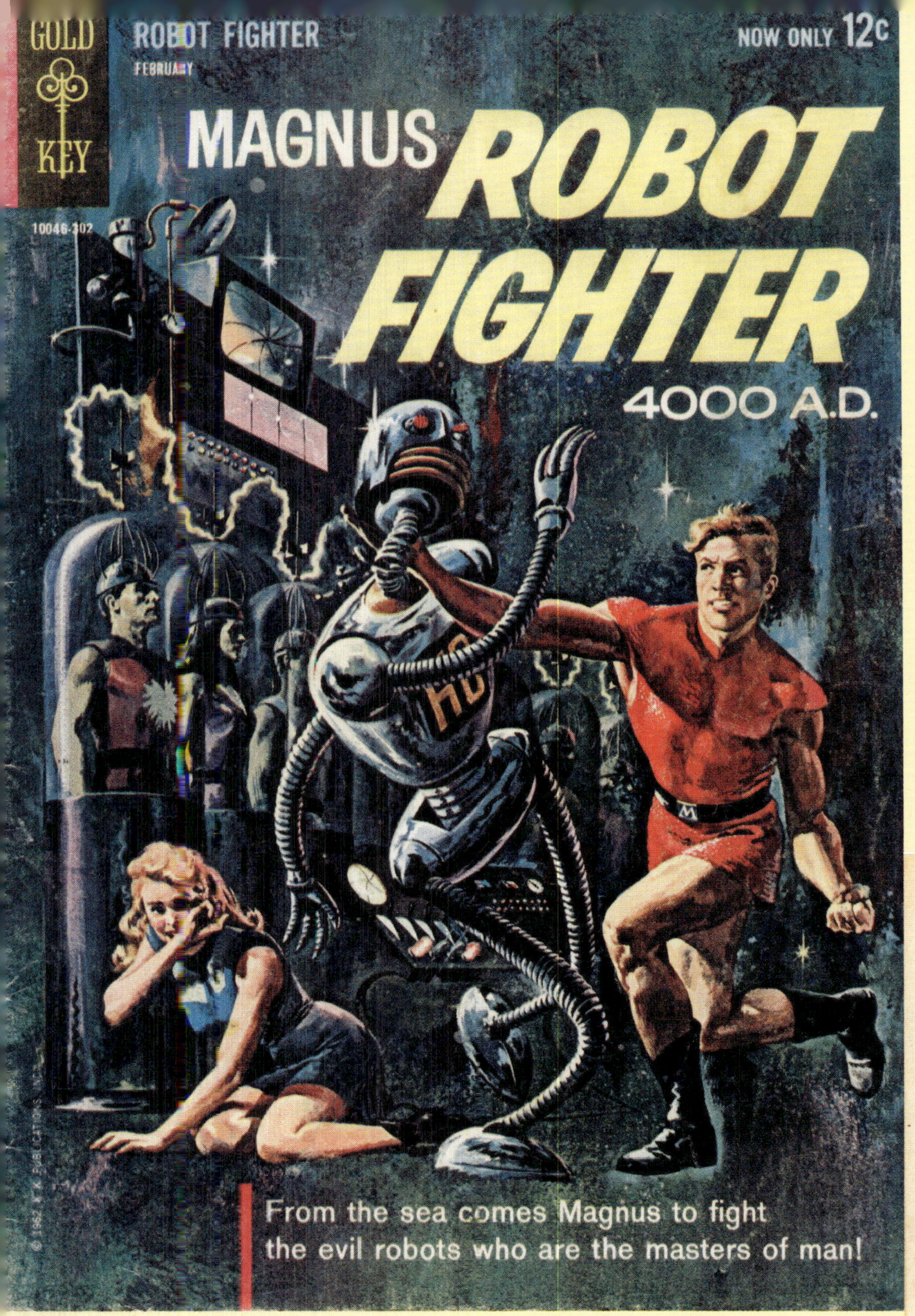

Within a few years, in addition to stirring adventures inspired by Norse mythology, Thor would go even more sci-fi. The prodigious imagination of artist Jack Kirby (1917–1994) sent him on epic quests into space, encountering the Colonizers from Rigel, the android Recorder, and Ego the Living Planet. Kirby was also the creative powerhouse behind the Fantastic Four, who would travel through time, into other dimensions, and to a sub-atomic world, confront several alien races, and battle cosmic-scale adversaries such as Galactus, the Devourer of Worlds, and his space-spanning scout, the Silver Surfer.

Outside of the big two comic book companies, King Features Syndicate dipped a toe into comic book publishing with their own *Flash Gordon* series, with sumptuous art by EC veteran Al Williamson, among others. Dell published *Turok, Son of Stone*, the adventures of two pre-Columbian natives in a time-lost valley where dinosaurs still survived. Gold Key, who specialized in TV and movie adaptations, produced a steady stream of sci-fi related titles including *Voyage to the Bottom of the Sea, The Invaders, Land of the Giants*, and the one-shot *Fantastic Voyage* (this last with art by Wally Wood).

Most fondly remembered by many Silver Age sci-fi fans, though, are Gold Key's original characters. *Mighty Samson* was set in a post-nuclear holocaust future, but was essentially "barbarian adventure" (more than six years before Marvel brought *Conan the Barbarian* to comic books). The long-running *Space Family Robinson* is widely thought to have been the inspiration for Irwin Allen's rollicking TV series *Lost*

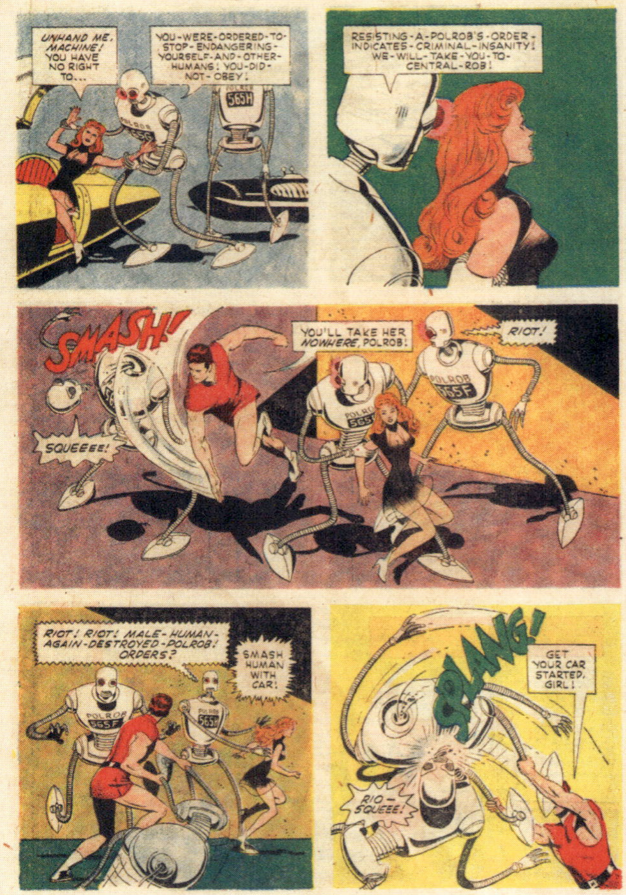

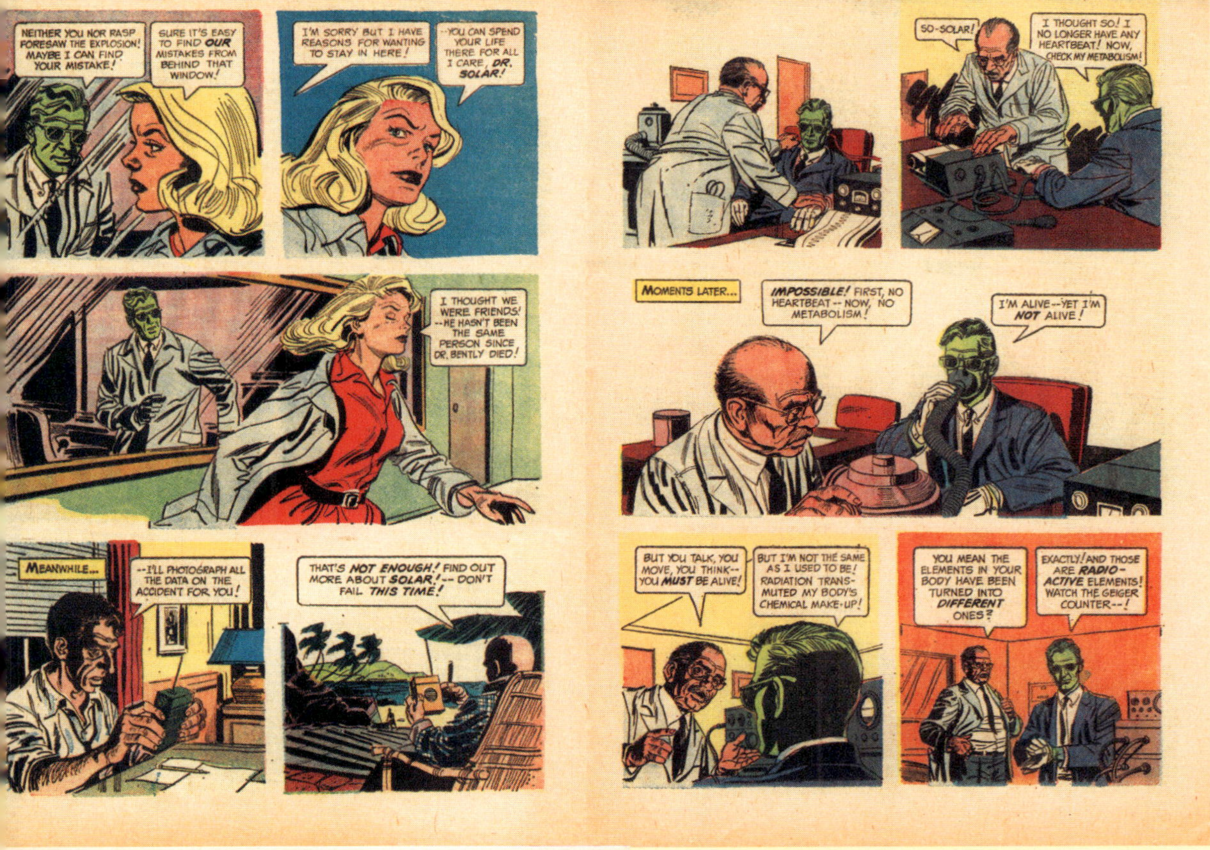

◀

Gold Key comics had a distinctive look inside, with rectangular word balloons and no black "holding line" around the panels in most books. *Doctor Solar* was further distinguished by the classic art style of illustrator Bob Fujitani, and by the fact that Solar was uncostumed; only his green coloring (strangely undetected by his colleagues) indicated he was using his nuclear powers.

◀◀

Gold Key stood out on the newsstand by virtue of their painted covers. This striking cover for *Magnus Robot Fighter 4000 A.D.*, probably by George Wilson, has all the action a comic book reader could want, and all the sci-fi elements a fan could want.

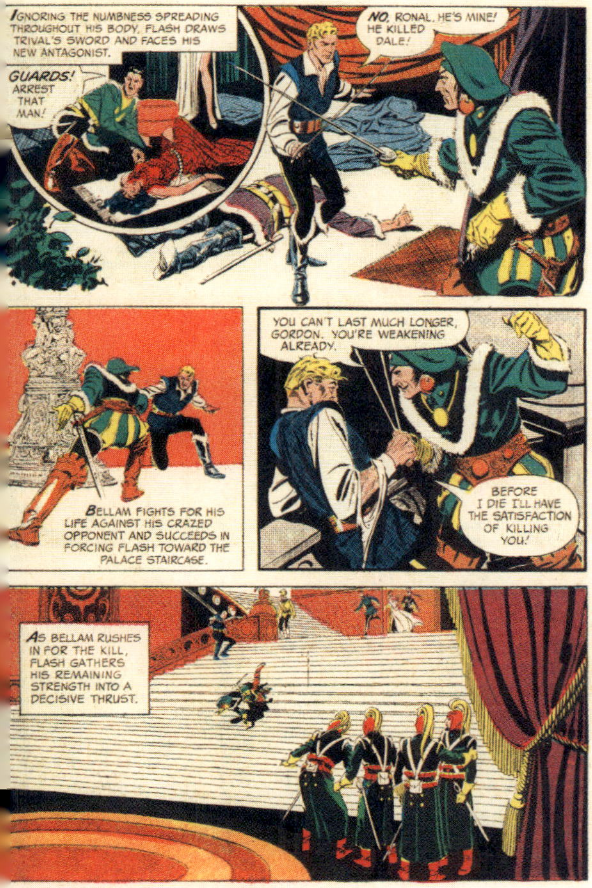

in Space; this was never explicitly acknowledged, but Gold Key were allowed to add the words "Lost in Space" to the book's title for 45 of its 59 issues...

Doctor Solar, Man of the Atom starred a scientist who was exposed to a massive overdose of radiation. But instead of dying, he gained mastery over matter and energy (much like Charlton Comics' Captain Atom a couple of years earlier). Doctor Solar was distinctive not for his powers or his origin but for his stories' unusually restrained and "mature" flavor—he didn't even gain a costume until his fifth issue.

For sci-tech fans, the pinnacle was *Magnus, Robot Fighter 4000 A.D.*, written and illustrated by Russ Manning (1929-1981). In a technology-dominated future where a soaring, multi-level city called North Am covers the entire North American continent, humanity has grown entirely dependent on robots. But not all have humanity's best interests at heart. Magnus fights for humankind with his bare hands and "steel-smashing strength." There's a political edge to the first few issues (in which Magnus smashes a lot of "pol-robs"—police robots), but even after this evaporates and Magnus faces more exotic adversaries, the series still shines for Manning's concepts and visualizations of the far future.

◀◀

The thrilling moment when Magnus rescues the rebellious Leeja Claine from overzealous police robots, who have pulled her over for speeding in *Magnus Robot Fighter* #1. Leeja's wildness, and the political edge in this depiction of the forces of law and order (and in their attitude that "resisting a pol-rob's order indicates criminal insanity") are soon softened; by the fourth issue, Magnus is sitting on the ruling council (though admittedly only as an advisor to Leeja's father).

◀

Action-packed yet delicate artwork by Al Williamson from King Features' revival of *Flash Gordon* under their own imprint in the mid-'60s.

For British kids in the 1960s, SF came with strings attached—strings that were often a little too visible…

Gerry Anderson (1929-), his then wife Sylvia (1937-), and their talented production company were responsible for a succession of internationally popular children's television series featuring adventure and derring-do in a futuristic high-tech world: *Supercar*, *Fireball XL5*, *Stingray*, and *Thunderbirds*. Many broke new ground in various ways. *Stingray* in 1964, for example, was the first British children's TV series to be filmed in color, a huge financial gamble that paid off in spades when it made possible the sale of the series into the lucrative US network market. The series were also all made with string puppets.

Gerry Anderson never really liked puppets. But they did enable him to do things he could never have raised the budget to do with live action, in particular to realize his talented designers' visions of future gadgetry and vehicles. His technical team even invented a technology they called "Supermarionation" for synchronizing the puppets' mouth movements electronically with the voice track. Anderson was never satisfied that they looked lifelike enough—and those strings, wire-thin though they were, kept showing up under the arc lights—but Supermarionation was a key factor that made it all somehow credible. It was like a world of the best toys you ever saw come to life.

Anderson's production company, APF (later renamed Century 21 Productions), was ahead of its time in other ways. They embraced merchandizing in a way that others wouldn't grasp till decades later. In addition to toys, books, games, and model kits, APF licensed comic strip versions of their characters in TV-themed weekly anthology comic books. In 1964, during filming of what was to become Anderson's biggest hit of all, *Thunderbirds*, they had the idea to produce a comic book of their own, showcasing their own stable of characters.

TV Century 21 (widely known as simply *TV21*, and later officially renamed as such) was edited by Alan Fennell (1936-2001), an experienced comics scripter, as well as a writer for Anderson's TV series. Each issue was dated exactly 100 years into the future (so that the first issue bore the dateline January 23, 2065), and each front cover was designed like a newspaper reporting the latest astonishing events in the Anderson series' (increasingly coherent) universe.

▶ **A beautiful *Stingray* installment by Ron Embleton dating from around the time the show's successor, *Thunderbirds*, premiered. With each successive series, Anderson's sculptors strove to make the puppets more lifelike, and the early *Stingray* characters would soon seem like caricatures (*Stingray*'s hero, Troy Tempest, was based on James Garner). But Embleton and the other *TV21* artists brought a vibrant air of reality to the worlds of Gerry Anderson.**

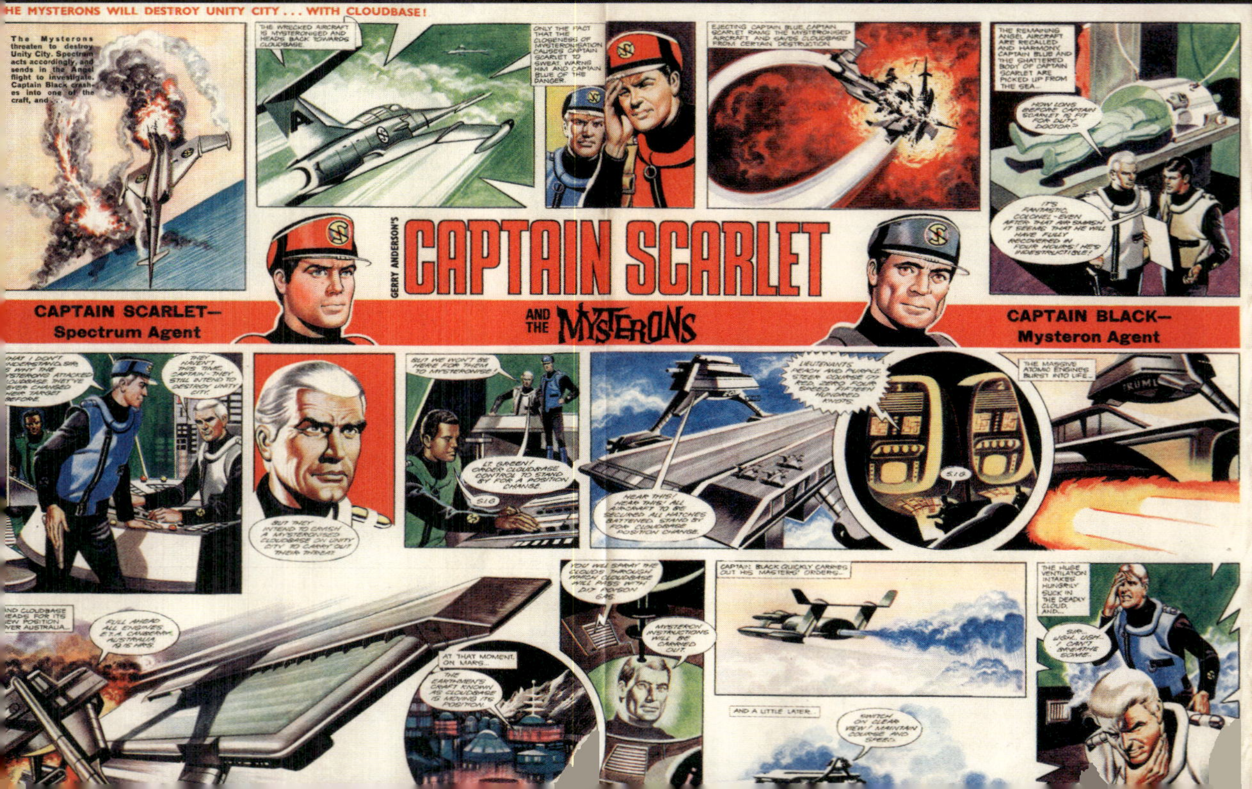

▶ The magnificent art of Mike Noble brought drama, detail, and a breathtaking sense of solidity to a succession of tales through the entire run of *TV21*, including *Zero X* and later *Captain Scarlet*. The *Fireball XL5* TV series never seemed this exciting!

◀ Gerry Anderson's most ambitious Supermarionation series, *Captain Scarlet*, was illustrated in *TV21* by Ron Embleton, who also painted the action scenes featuring the dynamic hero shown during the end credits of the TV show itself. Later *Captain Scarlet* story arcs in *TV21* were illustrated by Mike Noble, at his artistic peak.

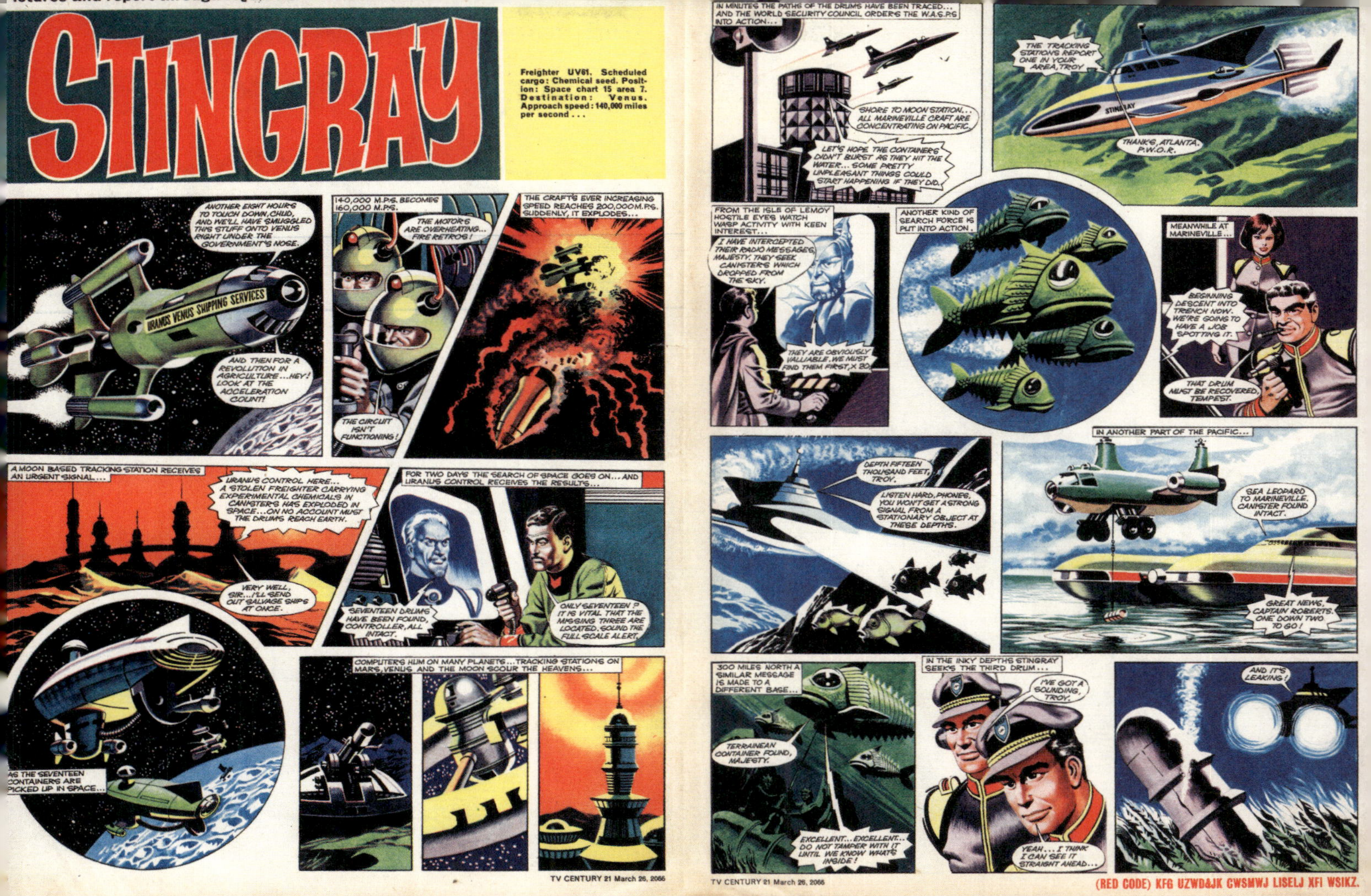

STINGRAY
Freighter UV61. Scheduled cargo: Chemical seed. Position: Space chart 15 area 7. Destination: Venus. Approach speed: 140,000 miles per second...
URANUS VENUS SHIPPING SERVICES
ANOTHER EIGHT HOURS TO TOUCH DOWN, CHUD, AND WE'LL HAVE SMUGGLED THIS STUFF ONTO VENUS RIGHT UNDER THE GOVERNMENT'S NOSE.
AND THEN FOR A REVOLUTION IN AGRICULTURE...HEY! LOOK AT THE ACCELERATION COUNT!
140,000 M.P.S. BECOMES 160,000 M.P.S.
THE MOTORS ARE OVERHEATING... FIRE RETROS!
THE CIRCUIT ISN'T FUNCTIONING!
THE CRAFT'S EVER INCREASING SPEED REACHES 200,000 M.P.S. SUDDENLY, IT EXPLODES...
A MOON BASED TRACKING STATION RECEIVES AN URGENT SIGNAL...
URANUS CONTROL HERE... A STOLEN FREIGHTER CARRYING EXPERIMENTAL CHEMICALS IN CANISTERS HAS EXPLODED IN SPACE...ON NO ACCOUNT MUST THE DRUMS REACH EARTH.
VERY WELL, SIR...I'LL SEND OUT SALVAGE SHIPS AT ONCE.
AS THE SEVENTEEN CONTAINERS ARE PICKED UP IN SPACE...
FOR TWO DAYS THE SEARCH OF SPACE GOES ON... AND URANUS CONTROL RECEIVES THE RESULTS...
SEVENTEEN DRUMS HAVE BEEN FOUND, CONTROLLER, ALL INTACT.
ONLY SEVENTEEN? IT IS VITAL THAT THE MISSING THREE ARE LOCATED. SOUND THE FULL SCALE ALERT.
COMPUTERS HUM ON MANY PLANETS...TRACKING STATIONS ON MARS, VENUS AND THE MOON SCOUR THE HEAVENS...
TV CENTURY 21 March 26, 2066
IN MINUTES THE PATHS OF THE DRUMS HAVE BEEN TRACED... AND THE WORLD SECURITY COUNCIL ORDERS THE W.A.S.P.S INTO ACTION...
SHORE TO MOON STATION... ALL MARINEVILLE CRAFT ARE CONCENTRATING ON PACIFIC.
LET'S HOPE THE CONTAINERS DIDN'T BURST AS THEY HIT THE WATER... SOME PRETTY UNPLEASANT THINGS COULD START HAPPENING IF THEY DID.
THE TRACKING STATIONS REPORT ONE IN YOUR AREA, TROY
THANKS, ATLANTA. P.W.O.R.
FROM THE ISLE OF LEMOY HOSTILE EYES WATCH WASP ACTIVITY WITH KEEN INTEREST...
I HAVE INTERCEPTED THEIR RADIO MESSAGES, MAJESTY. THEY SEEK CANISTERS WHICH DROPPED FROM THE SKY.
THEY ARE OBVIOUSLY VALUABLE. WE MUST FIND THEM FIRST, X 20.
ANOTHER KIND OF SEARCH FORCE IS PUT INTO ACTION.
MEANWHILE AT MARINEVILLE...
BEGINNING DESCENT INTO TRENCH NOW. WE'RE GOING TO HAVE A JOB SPOTTING IT.
THAT DRUM MUST BE RECOVERED, TEMPEST.
DEPTH FIFTEEN THOUSAND FEET, TROY.
LISTEN HARD, PHONES. YOU WON'T GET A STRONG SIGNAL FROM A STATIONARY OBJECT AT THESE DEPTHS.
IN ANOTHER PART OF THE PACIFIC...
SEA LEOPARD TO MARINEVILLE. CANISTER FOUND INTACT.
GREAT NEWS, CAPTAIN ROBERTS. ONE DOWN TWO TO GO!
300 MILES NORTH A SIMILAR MESSAGE IS MADE TO A DIFFERENT BASE...
TERRAINEAN CONTAINER FOUND, MAJESTY.
EXCELLENT...EXCELLENT... DO NOT TAMPER WITH IT UNTIL WE KNOW WHAT'S INSIDE!
IN THE INKY DEPTHS STINGRAY SEEKS THE THIRD DRUM...
I'VE GOT A SOUNDING, TROY.
YEAH... I THINK I CAN SEE IT STRAIGHT AHEAD...
AND IT'S LEAKING!
TV CENTURY 21 March 26, 2066
(RED CODE) KFG UZWD&JK CWSMWJ LISELJ XFI WSIKZ.

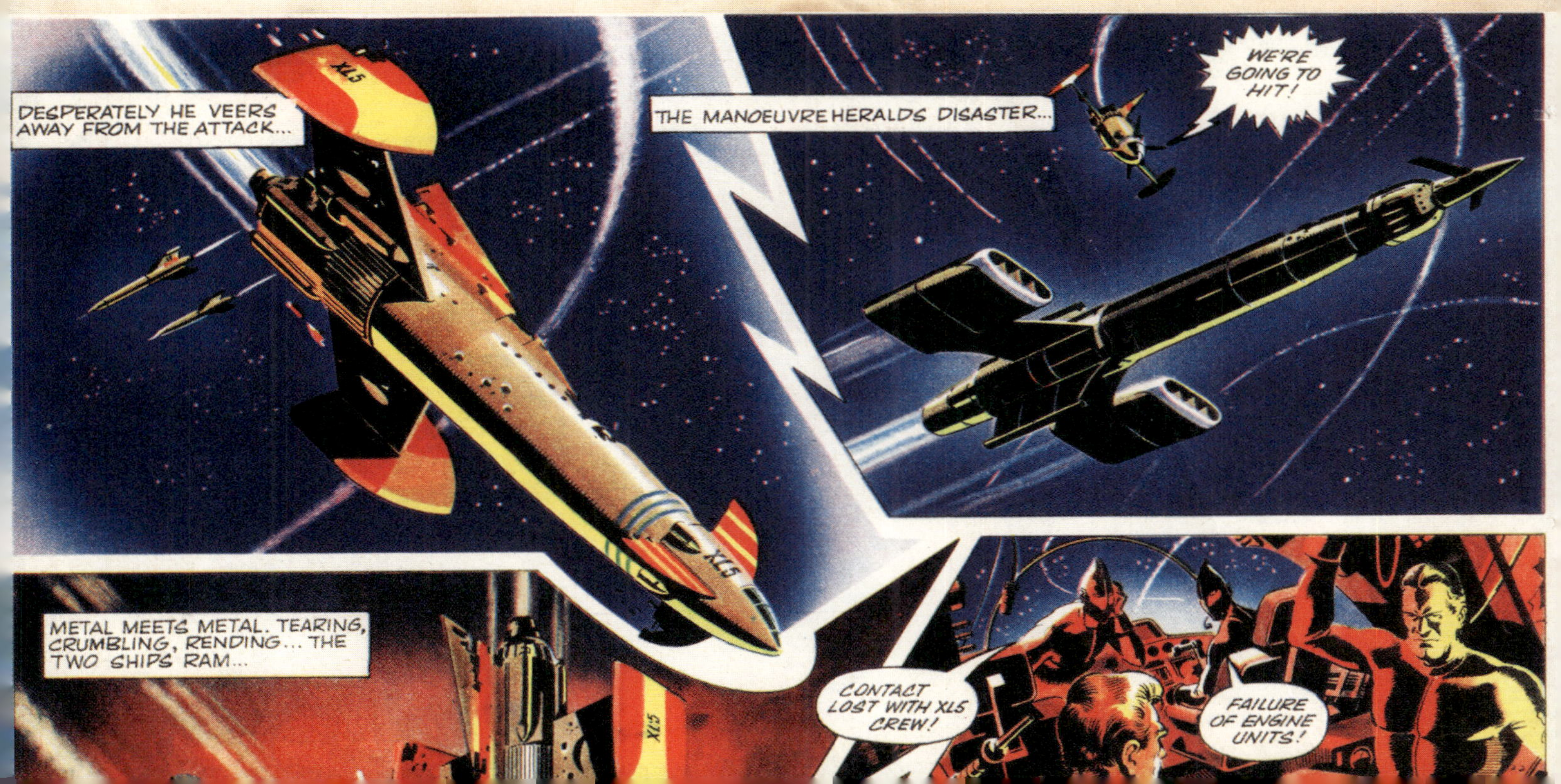

DESPERATELY HE VEERS AWAY FROM THE ATTACK...
XL5
THE MANOEUVRE HERALDS DISASTER...
WE'RE GOING TO HIT!
METAL MEETS METAL. TEARING, CRUMBLING, RENDING... THE TWO SHIPS RAM...
CONTACT LOST WITH XL5 CREW!
FAILURE OF ENGINE UNITS!

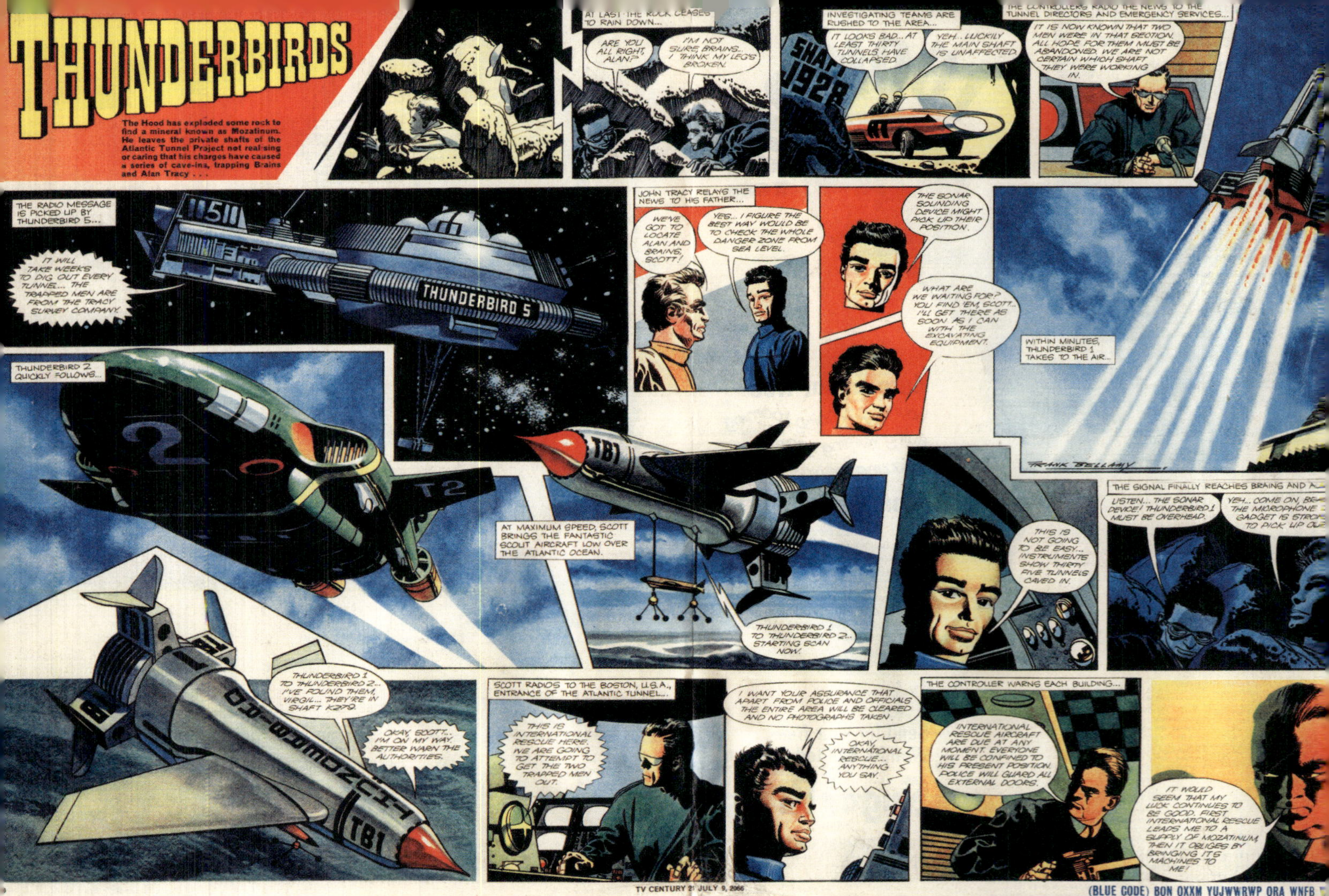

▲
When *Thunderbirds* eventually appeared in *TV21* after months of build-up, it was illustrated by the great Frank Bellamy, fresh from his triumphs on *Eagle*. He added his own sense of dynamism to the already exciting vehicles and gadgetry of International Rescue, as well as bringing the characters to life.

▶
Frank Bellamy lavished attention on his *Thunderbirds* pages, and his personal fascination with sub-Saharan Africa enriches this early story. But he could also draw a mean Thunderbird 2! Bellamy's work would continue to grace *TV21* until he left comics for other forms of commercial illustration in 1969.

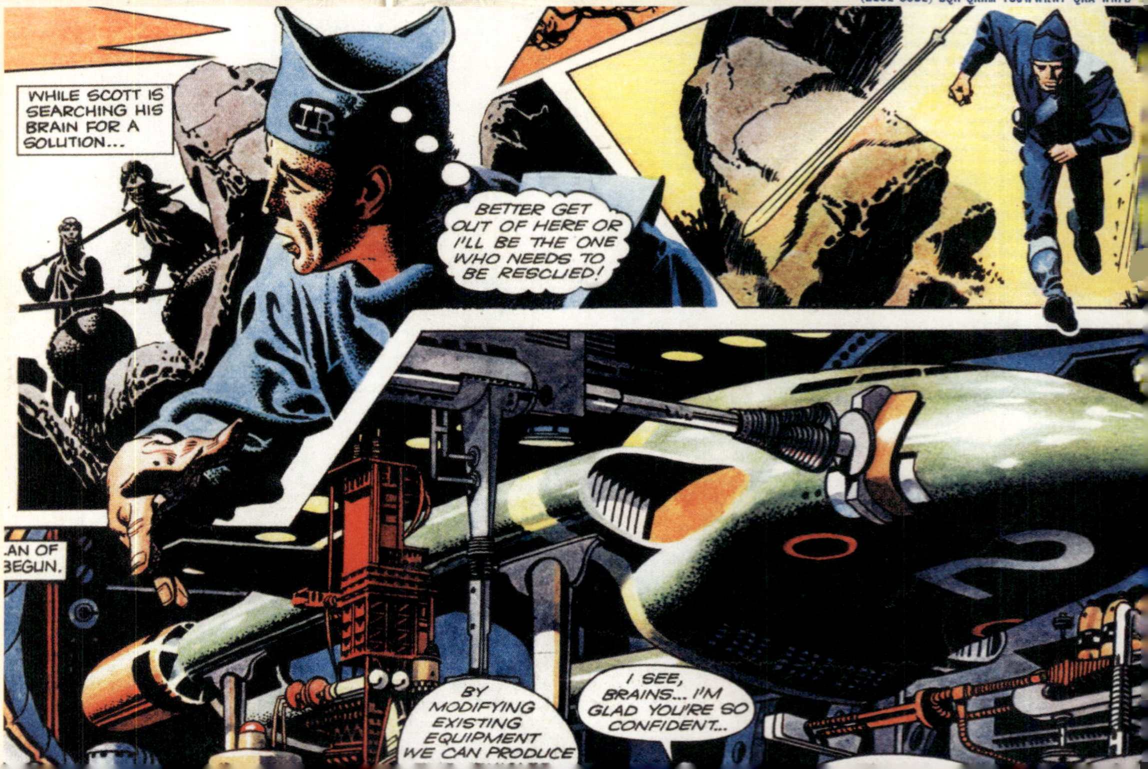

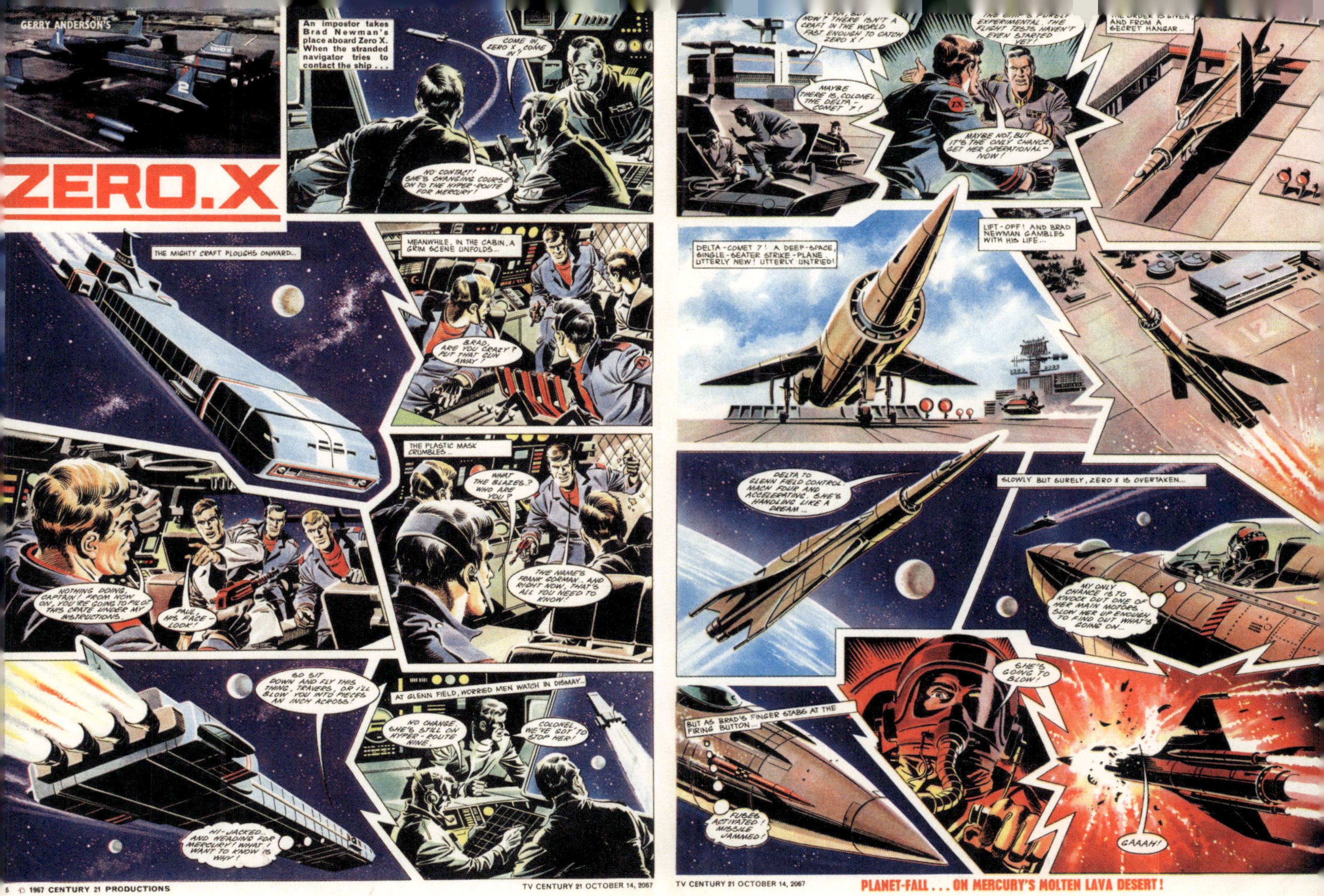

Months before *Thunderbirds* hit screens, hints and teasers began appearing in *TV21*. Lady Penelope had her own strip, filling in some of the backstory only hinted at in the series. As the TV show's premiere approached, the front-page "news reports" featured vehicles and snippets of plotlines from first series episodes, with stills actually taken on set. It was a brilliant way to build interest in the new series; *TV21* did the same to similar effect a year or so later ahead of the next Anderson series, *Captain Scarlet and the Mysterons*.

TV21 was a huge hit from day one. With its later companion titles *Lady Penelope* and *Solo*, it became the UK's top-selling comic book group ever. Its big tabloid-size pages (fourteen by ten-and-a-half inches) used the photogravure printing process that had been pioneered in comic books by *Eagle*, and like *Eagle* it was a visual treat. But where *Dan Dare* was the only sci-fi strip in *Eagle*, *TV21* was mostly sci-fi—and breathtakingly realized, fully painted sci-fi at that, by some of the finest SF artists who ever wielded a brush.

For 242 glorious weekly issues, the first series of *TV21* brought to life the adventures of the Supermarionation characters, many in sumptuous color at a time when color TV was a rarity in British homes. Piling pleasure on top of pleasure for TV sci-fi fans, the Daleks from *Doctor Who* even had their own strip on the back cover for much of that run.

As Gerry Anderson moved away from Supermarionation with *UFO* and other series at the end of the 1960s, *TV21* gradually featured less Supermarionation and less sci-fi. A second series through 1971 did include *Star Trek* and *Land of the Giants* among miscellaneous other TV-themed strips, but it was a far cry from the comic's SF heyday.

▲ **In addition to the various Supermarionation series, *TV21* included an odd mix of TV-themed strips such as *The Munsters*, *Get Smart*, *Sgt. Bilko*, and in early issues *Burke's Law*, but these gradually gave place to other strips set in the Anderson universe, though not based on an actual TV series. Among these were *Secret Agent 21* (whose cover was as a salesman for Century 21 Toys—the same merchandise that readers could buy for themselves!) and *Zero X*, recounting the adventures of a spacecraft that was introduced in the original *Thunderbirds* feature film, and would later tie into *Captain Scarlet*.**

2000 AD: THE GALAXY'S GREATEST COMIC

2000 AD is Britain's longest-running sci-fi comic book. In fact, few British comics of any genre have lasted as long—which explains the now-archaic title; when it was conceived in 1976, the year 2000 was the far future, and a British comic title could expect a life of maybe only five to ten years.

It started with a memo from SF fan Kelvin Gosnell, then a sub-editor on staff at publishing conglomerate IPC (and later himself an editor of *2000 AD*). A number of high-profile sci-fi movies were due for release in the coming year, and Gosnell suggested that IPC should launch a new anthology title to ride the expected sci-fi wave. Of course, Gosnell and IPC couldn't have foreseen just how big those movies would turn out to be: two of them were *Star Wars* and *Close Encounters of the Third Kind*.

IPC Youth Group publisher John Sanders ran with the idea and commissioned freelancer Pat Mills to develop the new sci-fi title. Mills had recently launched two mold-breaking new comics for IPC: *Battle Picture Weekly*, which attempted to tell war stories without the usual clichés and stereotypes, and *Action* (not to be confused with the American *Action Comics*, home of Superman), which applied the same approach to adventure stories. Both were more down-to-earth, and more violent, than the typical children's fare of the day—*Action* so much so, and its tone so iconoclastic, that parents and the media protested loudly, and it was axed within a couple of years. But that was in the future; at the time, it was selling well, and Sanders asked Mills to bring his magic touch to the new sci-fi proposal.

Mills acknowledged that his trick was not necessarily to innovate but to ride current trends, only with a fresh twist. One of the most controversial strips in *Action*, for example, had been *Hook Jaw*, a riff on *Jaws* told from the point of view of the shark (with plenty of added gore for good measure). So it was that when *2000 AD* launched in February 1977, its line-up included *Harlem Heroes*, a team playing a tough futuristic sport called "aeroball" (blatantly inspired by the 1975 movie *Rollerball*), and a technologically enhanced super-agent called *M.A.C.H. 1* (unashamedly based on TV's *Six Million Dollar Man*).

Also included was *Dan Dare*. Mills had come up with the idea of reviving the iconic hero as a way of attracting publicity and guaranteeing reader interest (or rather, interest from the parents of the target readership—parents who therefore might just buy their kids a copy of the new comic). But this wasn't your father's *Dan Dare*. This was an edgier, much more violent version for a new generation.

Yet it wasn't Dan Dare who became the star of *2000 AD*. It was another character—one who, as it happened, didn't appear till the second issue.

Judge Dredd was "*Dirty Harry* in the future." Originally it was conceived as the near future, like *Invasion 1988*, another serial begun in the first issue. But that changed when Mills saw the world designed for Dredd by artist Carlos Ezquerra—a world of soaring, high-tech towers as futuristic as those of *Magnus, Robot Fighter*, but grittier. Dredd himself was no Magnus, either; his look combined biker leathers, police riot gear, and elements of medieval armor.

▶▶
Judge Dredd's earliest published appearances were ironically not drawn by Carlos Ezquerra, the artist responsible for his design, but the look and tone of the strip were established very quickly by other artists such as Mike McMahon.

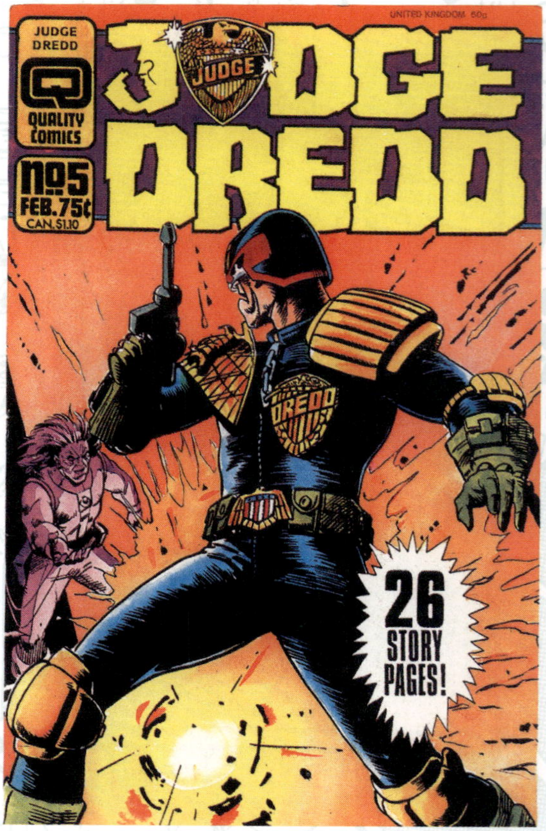

◀ ▶ ▶▶
At various times, various publishers tried to introduce Judge Dredd into the US market. Eagle Comics was an imprint of IPC; this example, with striking cover by sometime *Dredd* artist Brian Bolland, is coverdated August 1985. The Quality Comics version is from February 1987; the company was helmed by veteran UK comic book editor Dez Skinn. *The Megazine* was a 1991 version by then-publishers Fleetway for the US market of a brand extension successful for a time in the UK.

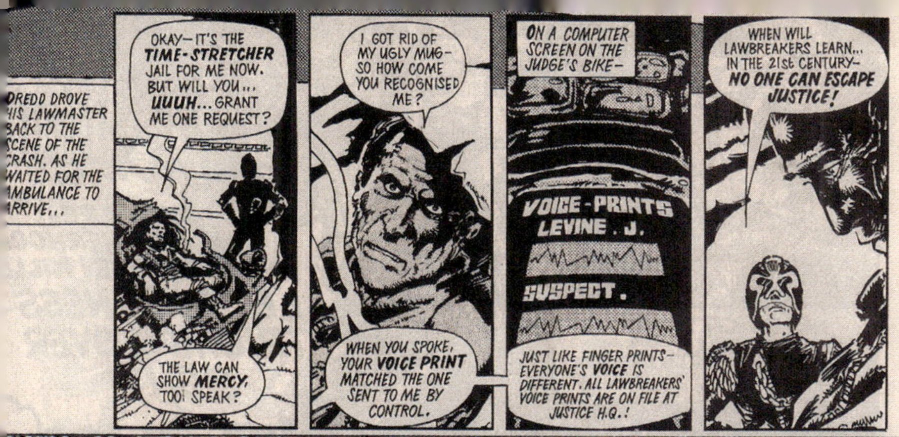
DREDD DROVE HIS LAWMASTER BACK TO THE SCENE OF THE CRASH. AS HE WAITED FOR THE AMBULANCE TO ARRIVE...
OKAY—IT'S THE TIME-STRETCHER JAIL FOR ME NOW. BUT WILL YOU... UUUH... GRANT ME ONE REQUEST?
THE LAW CAN SHOW MERCY, TOO! SPEAK?
I GOT RID OF MY UGLY MUG—SO HOW COME YOU RECOGNISED ME?
WHEN YOU SPOKE, YOUR VOICE PRINT MATCHED THE ONE SENT TO ME BY CONTROL.
ON A COMPUTER SCREEN ON THE JUDGE'S BIKE—
VOICE-PRINTS
LEVINE . J.
SUSPECT .
JUST LIKE FINGER PRINTS—EVERYONE'S VOICE IS DIFFERENT. ALL LAWBREAKERS' VOICE PRINTS ARE ON FILE AT JUSTICE H.Q.!
WHEN WILL LAWBREAKERS LEARN... IN THE 21st CENTURY—NO ONE CAN ESCAPE JUSTICE!

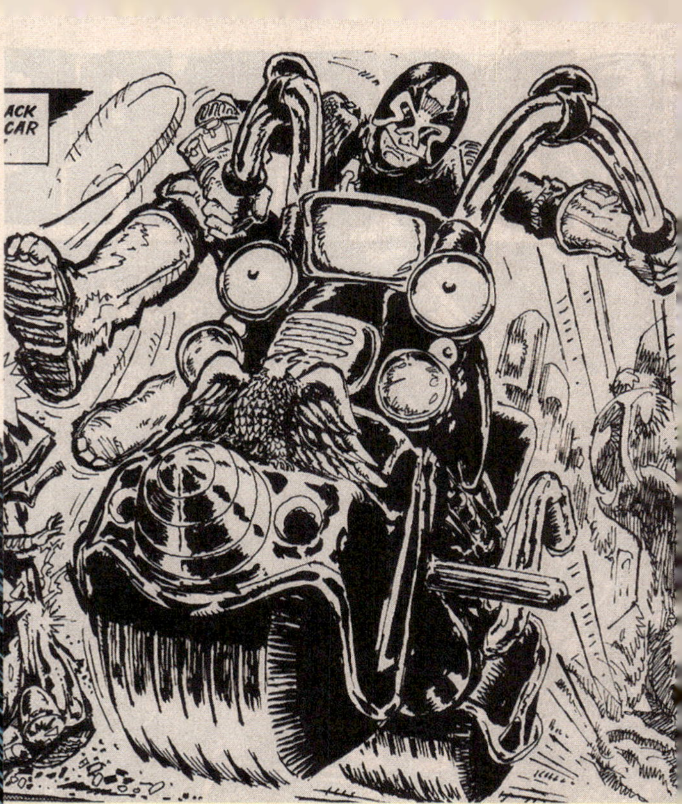

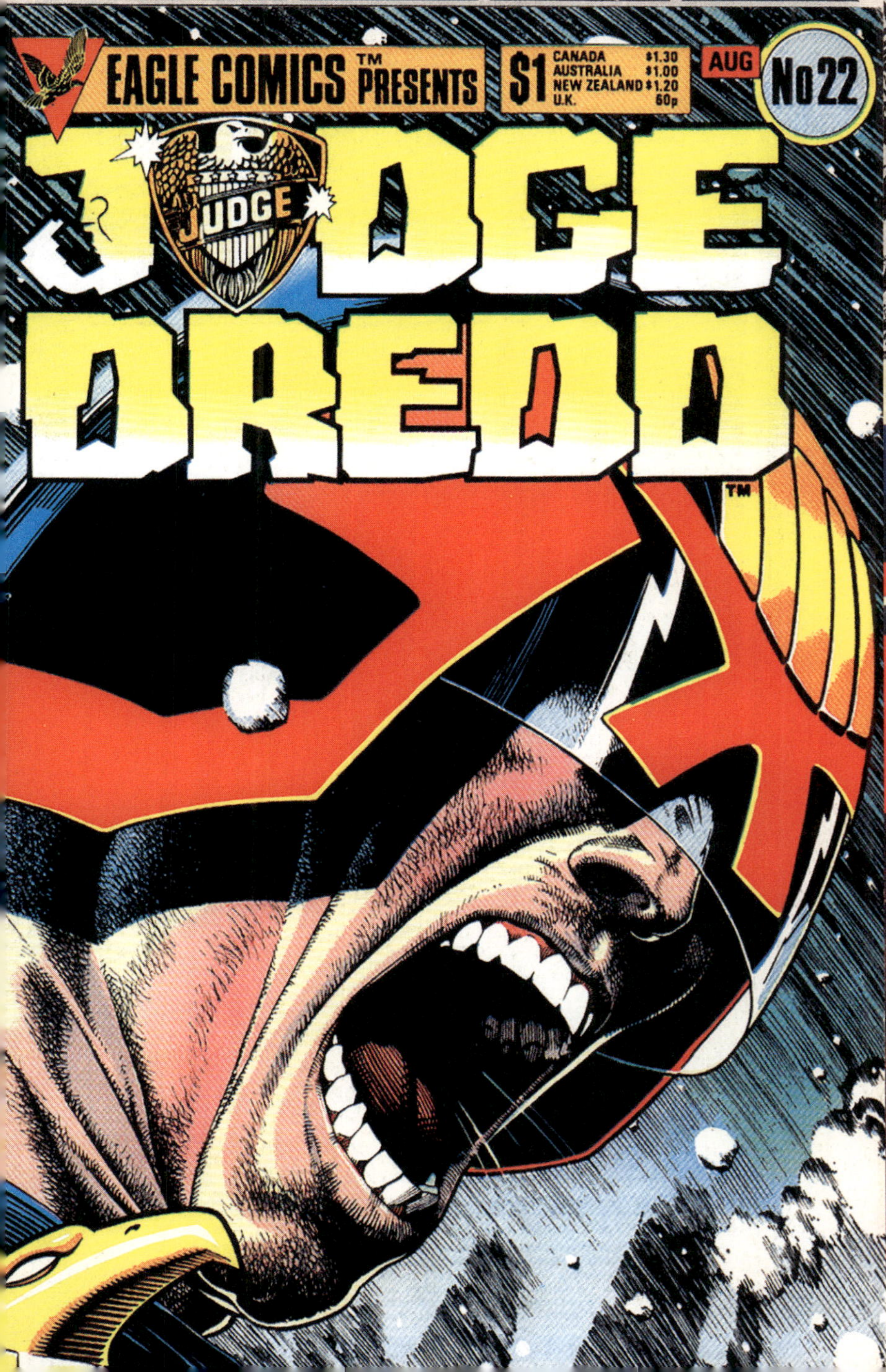
EAGLE COMICS™ PRESENTS
$1
CANADA $1.30
AUSTRALIA $1.00
NEW ZEALAND $1.20
U.K. 60p
AUG
No 22
JUDGE
JUDGE
DREDD
™

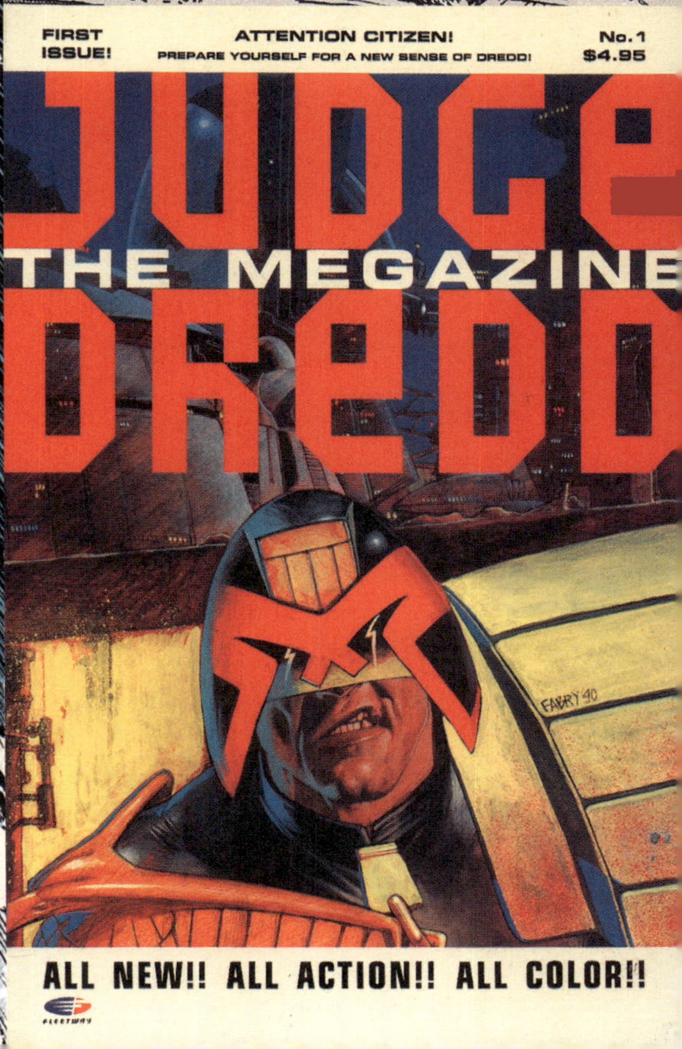
FIRST ISSUE!
ATTENTION CITIZEN!
PREPARE YOURSELF FOR A NEW SENSE OF DREDD!
No.1
$4.95
JUDGE
THE MEGAZINE
DREDD
FABRY 90
ALL NEW!! ALL ACTION!! ALL COLOR!!

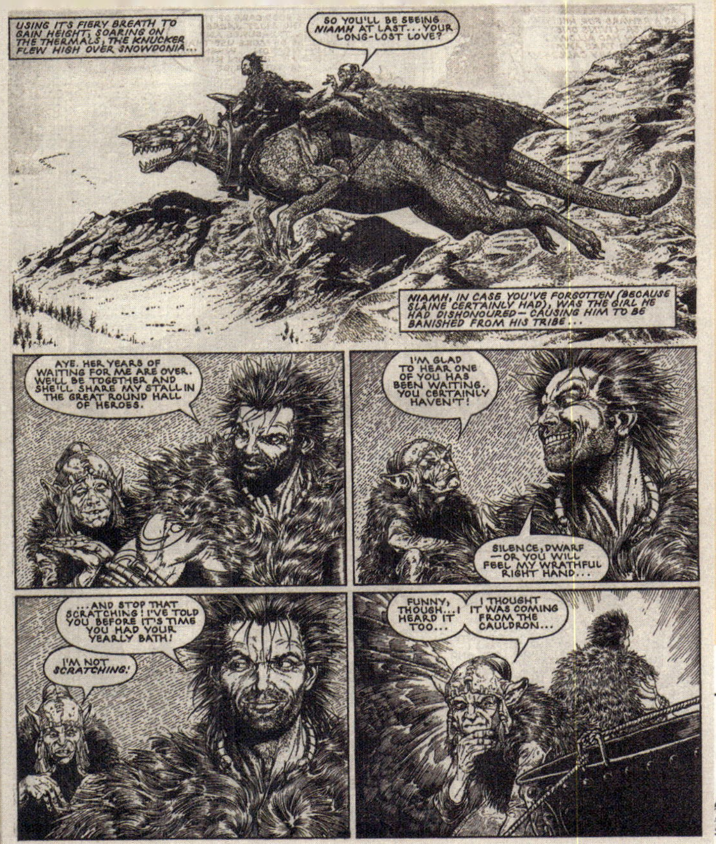
USING IT'S FIERY BREATH TO GAIN HEIGHT, SOARING ON THE THERMALS, THE KNUCKER FLEW HIGH OVER SNOWDONIA...
SO YOU'LL BE SEEING NIAMH AT LAST... YOUR LONG-LOST LOVE?
NIAMH, IN CASE YOU'VE FORGOTTEN (BECAUSE SLAINE CERTAINLY HAD), WAS THE GIRL HE HAD DISHONOURED — CAUSING HIM TO BE BANISHED FROM HIS TRIBE...
AYE. HER YEARS OF WAITING FOR ME ARE OVER. WE'LL BE TOGETHER AND SHE'LL SHARE MY STALL IN THE GREAT ROUND HALL OF HEROES.
I'M GLAD TO HEAR ONE OF YOU HAS BEEN WAITING. YOU CERTAINLY HAVEN'T!
SILENCE, DWARF — OR YOU WILL FEEL MY WRATHFUL RIGHT HAND...
...AND STOP THAT SCRATCHING! I'VE TOLD YOU BEFORE IT'S TIME YOU HAD YOUR YEARLY BATH!
I'M NOT SCRATCHING!
FUNNY, THOUGH...I HEARD IT TOO...
I THOUGHT IT WAS COMING FROM THE CAULDRON...

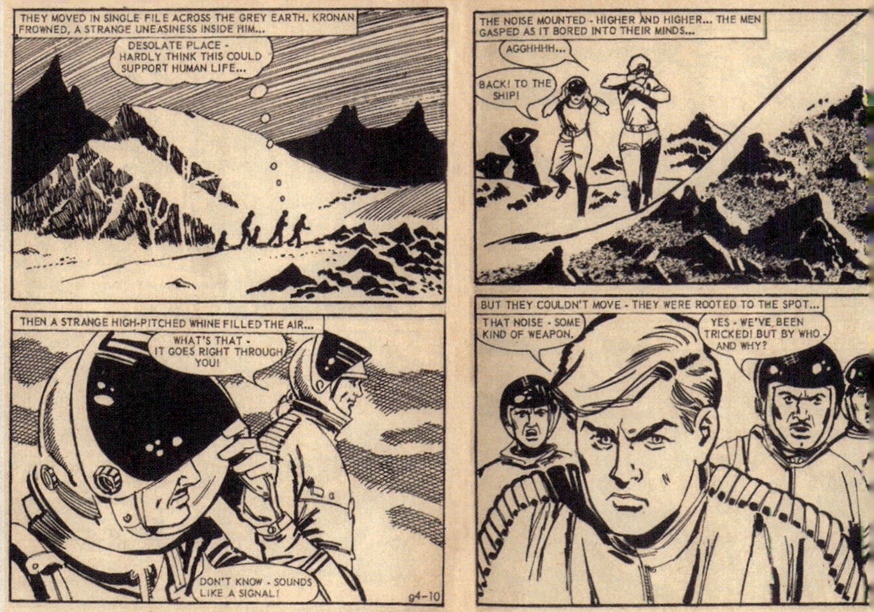
THEY MOVED IN SINGLE FILE ACROSS THE GREY EARTH. KRONAN FROWNED, A STRANGE UNEASINESS INSIDE HIM...
DESOLATE PLACE - HARDLY THINK THIS COULD SUPPORT HUMAN LIFE...
THE NOISE MOUNTED - HIGHER AND HIGHER... THE MEN GASPED AS IT BORED INTO THEIR MINDS...
AGGHHHH...
BACK! TO THE SHIP!
THEN A STRANGE HIGH-PITCHED WHINE FILLED THE AIR...
WHAT'S THAT - IT GOES RIGHT THROUGH YOU!
DON'T KNOW - SOUNDS LIKE A SIGNAL!
g4-10
BUT THEY COULDN'T MOVE - THEY WERE ROOTED TO THE SPOT...
THAT NOISE - SOME KIND OF WEAPON.
YES - WE'VE BEEN TRICKED! BUT BY WHO - AND WHY?

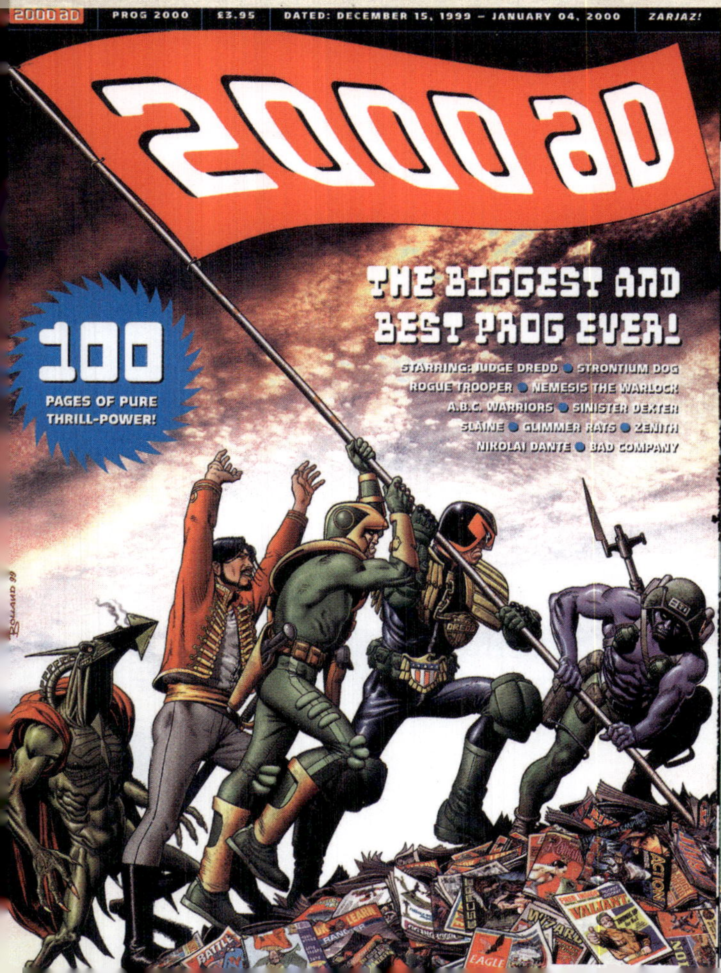
2000 AD
PROG 2000
£3.95
DATED: DECEMBER 15, 1999 – JANUARY 04, 2000
ZARJAZ!
2000 AD
100
PAGES OF PURE THRILL-POWER!
THE BIGGEST AND BEST PROG EVER!
STARRING: JUDGE DREDD ● STRONTIUM DOG
ROGUE TROOPER ● NEMESIS THE WARLOCK
A.B.C. WARRIORS ● SINISTER DEXTER
SLAINE ● GLIMMER RATS ● ZENITH
NIKOLAI DANTE ● BAD COMPANY

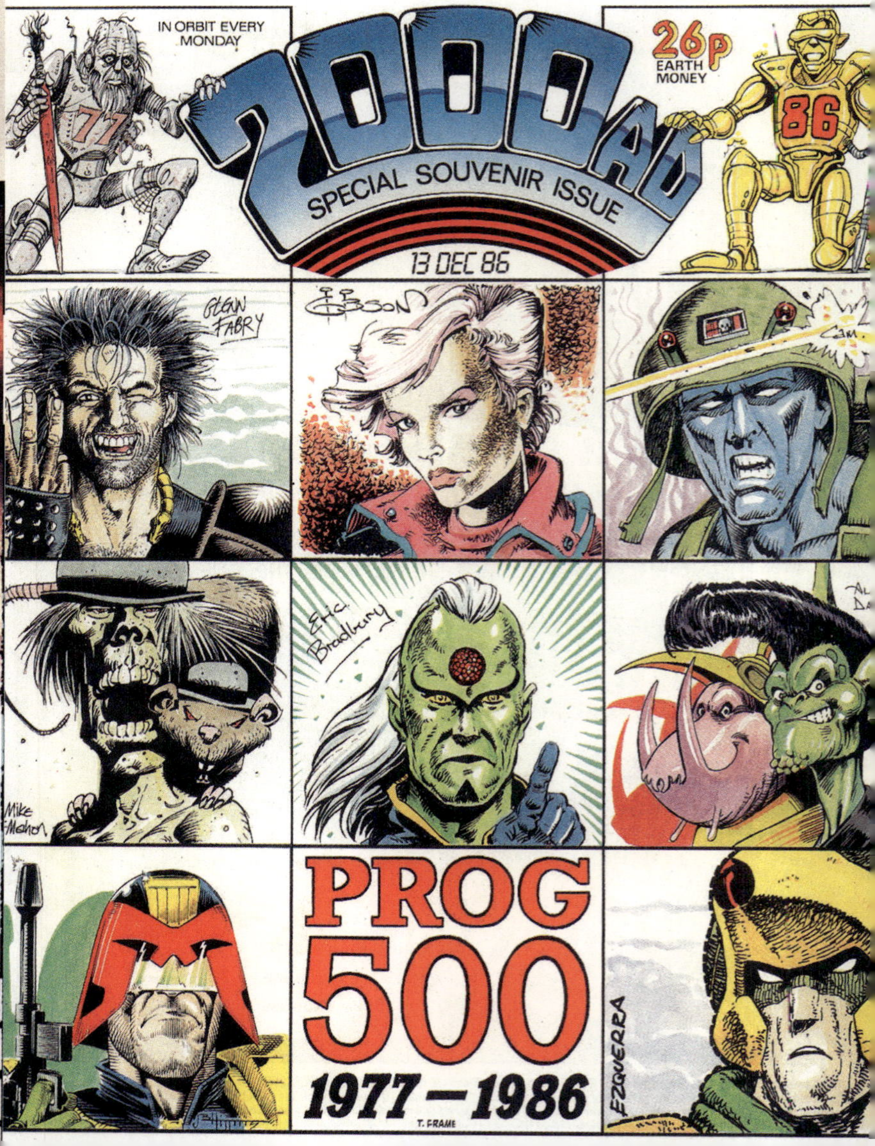
IN ORBIT EVERY MONDAY
2000 AD
SPECIAL SOUVENIR ISSUE
13 DEC 86
26p
EARTH MONEY
77
86
GLENN FABRY
Eric Bradbury
PROG 500
1977–1986
EZQUERRA

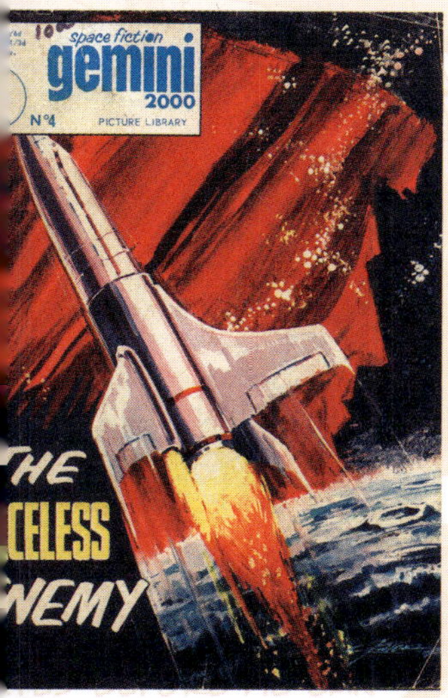

▲ ◀▲
Example of the digest-size SF comic books that familiarized British readers with the Spanish art style in the '70s.

◀◀
One of the most popular characters in *2000 AD* was Slaine, a Celtic "sword and sorcery" hero with only tenuous sci-fi credentials. Early appearances boasted densely detailed artwork by artists including Glenn Fabry; it later boasted fully-painted artwork by Simon Bisley.

◀ ◀◀
Landmark issues—or "progs"—celebrating the most popular characters in the history of *2000 AD*, among them Rogue Trooper, D.R. & Quinch, and Halo Jones. Some were introduced in a companion SF title, *Starlord*, which IPC launched in 1978. It lasted only 22 issues before being absorbed into *2000 AD*, yet the characters that the parent title inherited from it went on to become favorites, including mutant bounty hunter Strontium Dog and robot rescue squad Ro-Busters.

Mills wanted a distinctive look for *2000 AD* itself. British adventure comics, he felt, had a conservatism and stiffness about them, because so many of the artists were mainly book illustrators. He wanted something much more dynamic—as Marcus Morris and Frank Hampson had themselves wanted way back in 1950 at the launch of *Eagle*. Unlike Morris and Hampson, however, Mills also wanted something less polished, edgier. Partly for these stylistic reasons, but also because they were cheaper, Mills drafted in artists from Spain and as far afield as South America.

As it happened, other publishers had been using Spanish artists for many years, among them the publishers of various "picture library" series. These pocket-sized books, each a self-contained novella in comics form, had thrived through the 1950s and '60s; some, like the *Battle Picture Library* and *Commando* series, ran to a couple of thousand issues at the rate of two each month. A sci-fi series, *Gemini 2000 Picture Library*, appeared in the '60s and might well have familiarized hard-core sci-fi fans with the Spanish style a decade earlier than *2000 AD*.

So, the art in *2000 AD* was fresher and more exciting than its contemporaries, while at the same time for an older, hardcore sci-fi readership it looked reminiscent of the SF comics they remembered from their childhoods. The characters were edgy takes on already-popular references. The stories were gutsy, and in the early issues quite bloody. Most importantly, the tone was daring, anti-establishment, iconoclastic. (Only once did it sail too close to the wind, in a *Judge Dredd* storyline titled *Burger Wars*, which included parodies of trademarked figures such as Colonel Sanders, Ronald McDonald, and the Jolly Green Giant. Collectors still treasure these so-called "banned issues," though none was actually pulled from sale; IPC merely had to undertake never to reprint the offending stories).

Needless to say, *2000 AD* was a massive success, and is still with us today, though it has burned through several editors, spawned and then outlived several spin-off titles, and suffered a few creative slumps in the course of its long history. Like all comic books, its current sales are a fraction of the mass-market circulation it enjoyed at its peak. As an anthology title, it could often be uneven in quality, but at some time or other it has showcased or introduced most of Britain's top art and writing talent. Over the years it has broadened its content from its original focus on futuristic action, but for a generation of readers, *2000 AD*'s attitude, tone, and vision of the future defined their experience of sci-fi.

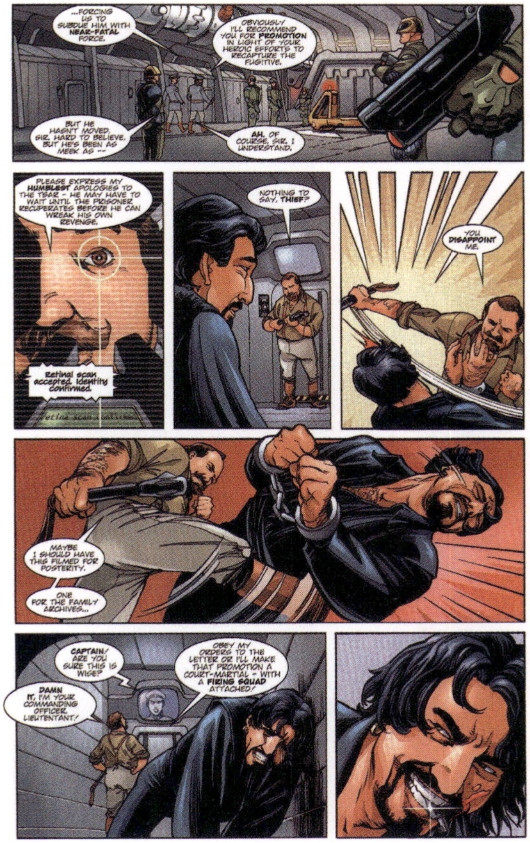

▶
A more recent hit is Nikolai Dante, a soldier-of-fortune with certain cybernetic enhancements whose adventures take place in a futuristic Russian Empire. Art chores stylishly executed by various illustrators including Simon Fraser and UK comics veteran John M. Burns.

STAR TIE-INS

TV and movie tie-in comic books have always been popular. In the days before VHS, adaptations in other media were often the only way that fans could get more of their favorites off-air. And two of the biggest TV and movie sci-fi favorites have also been phenomena in the comics.

Star Trek comic books have been published by half a dozen different companies, but the first, from mid-1967, was licensing specialist Gold Key. Evidently, though, the writers of the early issues had never actually seen the TV show, and jarring discrepancies abound: in one issue, Captain Kirk tells a crewman to "Up the infra-red periscope," and Mr. Spock orders "All rockets on full!" Dedicated fans must have wondered if this was the same show...

The art was quirky too, but then the artists were in Italy, working from reference photos. The first two issues were drawn by Nevio Zeccara (1924-2005) before Alberto Giolitti (1923-1993) took over for a long run. From #38 to the end of the 61-issue series in 1979, the art was by an American, Al McWilliams, and everything fell more neatly into line with the TV show. The covers of the first nine issues featured photo stills from the show; after this, they boasted painted covers like the rest of Gold Key's line.

Some purists still scoff at the Gold Key series, but it was very successful. The first 35 issues were reprinted in four *Enterprise Log* compilation volumes in 1976-1977 (well before the trend for trade paperbacks), and a new Checker Books reprint series, *Star Trek: The Key Collection*, began in 2004.

When the *Star Trek* franchise was revived with *Star Trek: The Motion Picture* in 1979, the comic book adaptation came from Marvel Comics, who continued the series for a total of 18 issues. A few years later, DC took over the license and produced a long, successful series featuring the original TV show characters and then the *Next Generation*. After that, publishing fell to Marvel once again for a few years, then back to DC's WildStorm imprint, and most recently IDW Publishing.

The first comic book version of the movie phenomenon *Star Wars* was from Marvel Comics, not then known for publishing licensed properties. The approach had come from George Lucas himself, who had wanted his favorite comic book company to produce the adaptation of his movie to promote it.

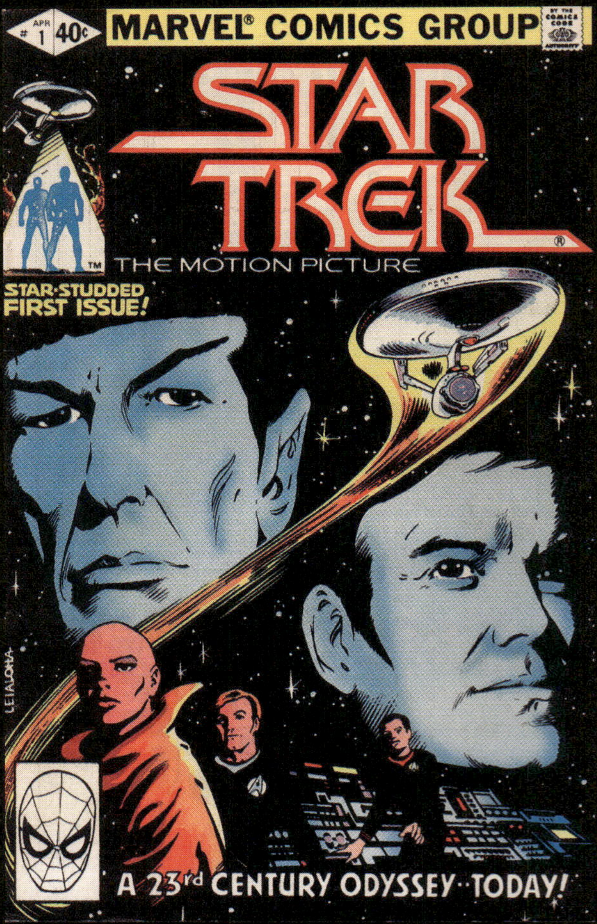

Marvel took the story "beyond the movie" after the adaptation, but the storytelling possibilities (and the characters available) were constrained by Lucasfilm, who wanted to ensure that nothing compromised the first film's sequel... which at that time hadn't even been scripted! Marvel's artists and the chief writer on the book, Archie Goodwin (1937-1988), rose magnificently to the challenge and collectively spun stories that filled out a whole *Star Wars* universe.

The Marvel series continued until 1986. After a short gap, Marvel announced a new *Star Wars* series by writer Tom Veitch and Scottish artist Cam Kennedy, but it never appeared. In late 1991 Dark Horse Comics acquired the license and began producing multiple series set after *Return of the Jedi* (including one by Veitch and Kennedy). The company continues to produce a stream of fan-favorite original stories and mini-series—all carefully slotted into the *Star Wars* universe.

◀ **Steve Leialoha's cover for Marvel's first issue of *Star Trek*, adapting the 1979 motion picture.**

▶ **Cover of the first-ever comic book adaptation of *Star Trek*, published by Gold Key.**

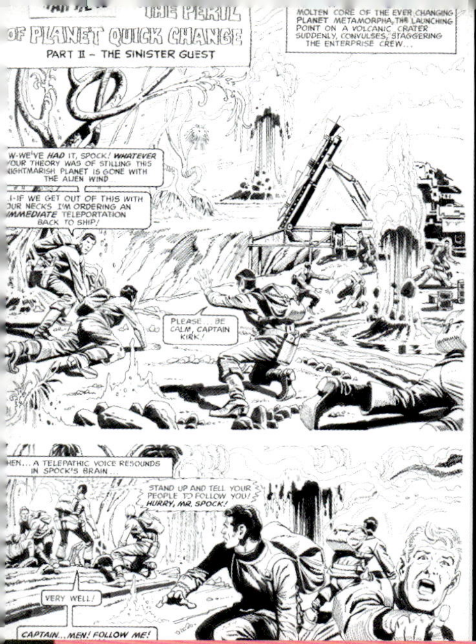

◀

Sumptuous artwork by Alberto Giolitti for the first comic book version of *Star Trek*, published by Gold Key.

▶

Beautiful *Star Wars* page by sci-fi stalwart Al Williamson, first published in #98 of Marvel's original run, August 1985, but at the time disappointingly reproduced on very poor paper stock. These classic stories are now receiving far better treatment in Dark Horse's *Classic Star Wars* reprint series.

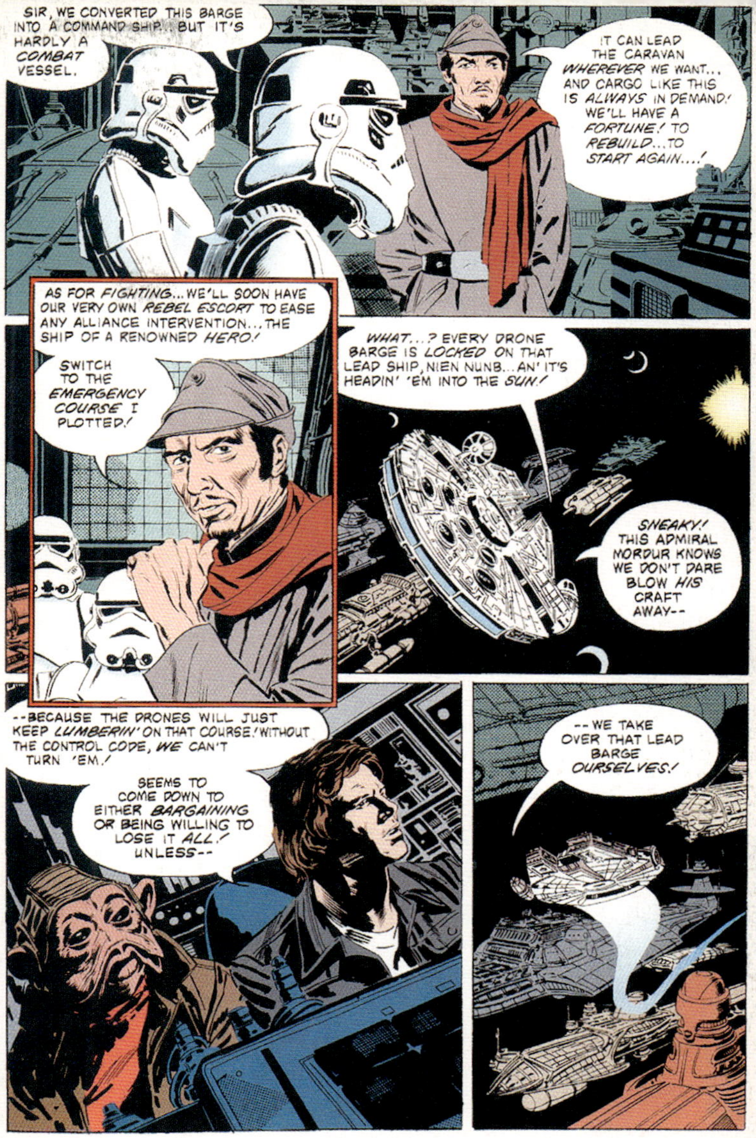

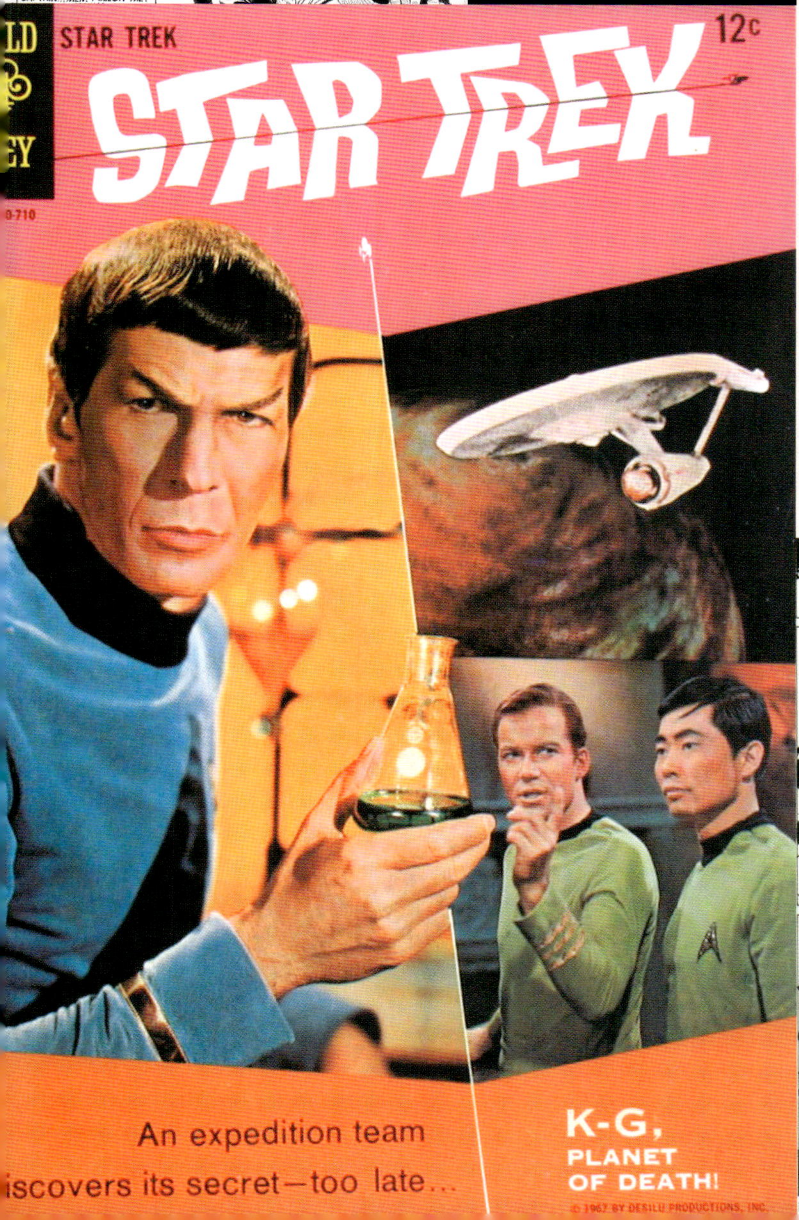

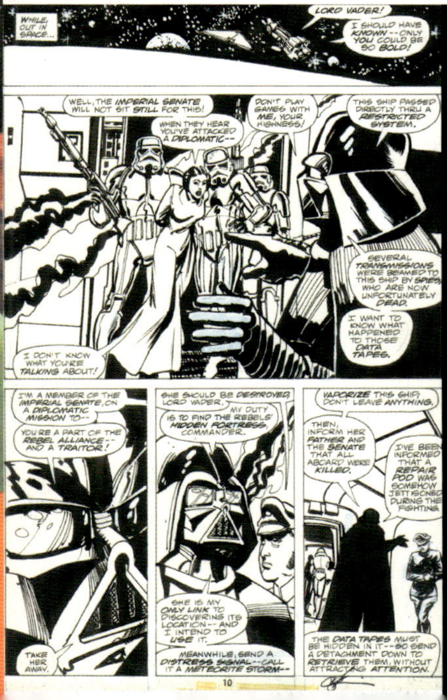

◀

The dramatic first appearance of Darth Vader, masterfully captured by Howard Chaykin and Steve Leialoha in Marvel's initial *Star Wars* series—remarkably, crafted from stills and a shooting script, without even a viewing of the movie itself.

DRUILLET, MOEBIUS & THE FRENCH CONNECTION

France has a venerable SF tradition, dating from the novels of Jules Verne and the pioneering movies of Georges Méliès. Comics, too ("bandes dessinées" in French), have always been taken much more seriously in France and Europe than in the English-speaking world. And yet it took French-language SF comics until after World War II to really take off.

One early milestone was *Futuropolis*, drawn by René Pellarin (1900–1998) in *Junior Magazine* in 1937–1938. Over in neighboring Belgium in 1943, Edgar Pierre Jacobs (1904–1987) joined the Hergé studio and became so pivotal in redrawing some of the best-known early *Tintin* stories for their album editions that he has since been given almost as much credit as Hergé himself for the development of the Belgian "clear line" style. In 1946, Jacobs created the seminal, long-running SF-adventure series *Blake et Mortimer*, in a first storyline set on the eve of WWIII.

In the 1950s, SF gathered momentum in the French-speaking countries as it did in the US and Britain. Hergé sent Tintin to the moon in *Objectif Lune* ("Destination Moon") and *On a Marché sur la Lune* ("Explorers on the Moon"), serialized in 1950–1952 and then published in book form in 1953 and 1954 respectively, though neither was exactly hard SF. In France, *Météor Comic* blossomed from 1953 to 1964, featuring *Les Conquerants de l'Espace* ("Conquerors of Space") and other space opera strips.

Throughout the '50s, Jean-Claude Forest (1930–1998) was cover artist for the then leading French-language paperback SF series. In 1962 in *V-Magazine* he created the space-age adventurer Barbarella, who was aptly described as a female James Bond cruising among the planets. Her free-spirited, free-loving ways were revolutionary for the time, and the first book collection of her adventures in 1964 was banned. But after the release of the movie starring Jane Fonda and directed by Roger Vadim in 1968, *Barbarella* became an international success, in English translation as well.

Pierre Christin and Jean-Claude Mézières (both 1938–) created *Valérian* for *Pilote* magazine in 1967. The dashing Valérian and his feisty colleague Laureline are agents of the "space-time police" of Galaxity, capital of the Terran Empire in the year 2770, and their missions take them to exotic worlds and into hair-raising dangers. In its witty depictions

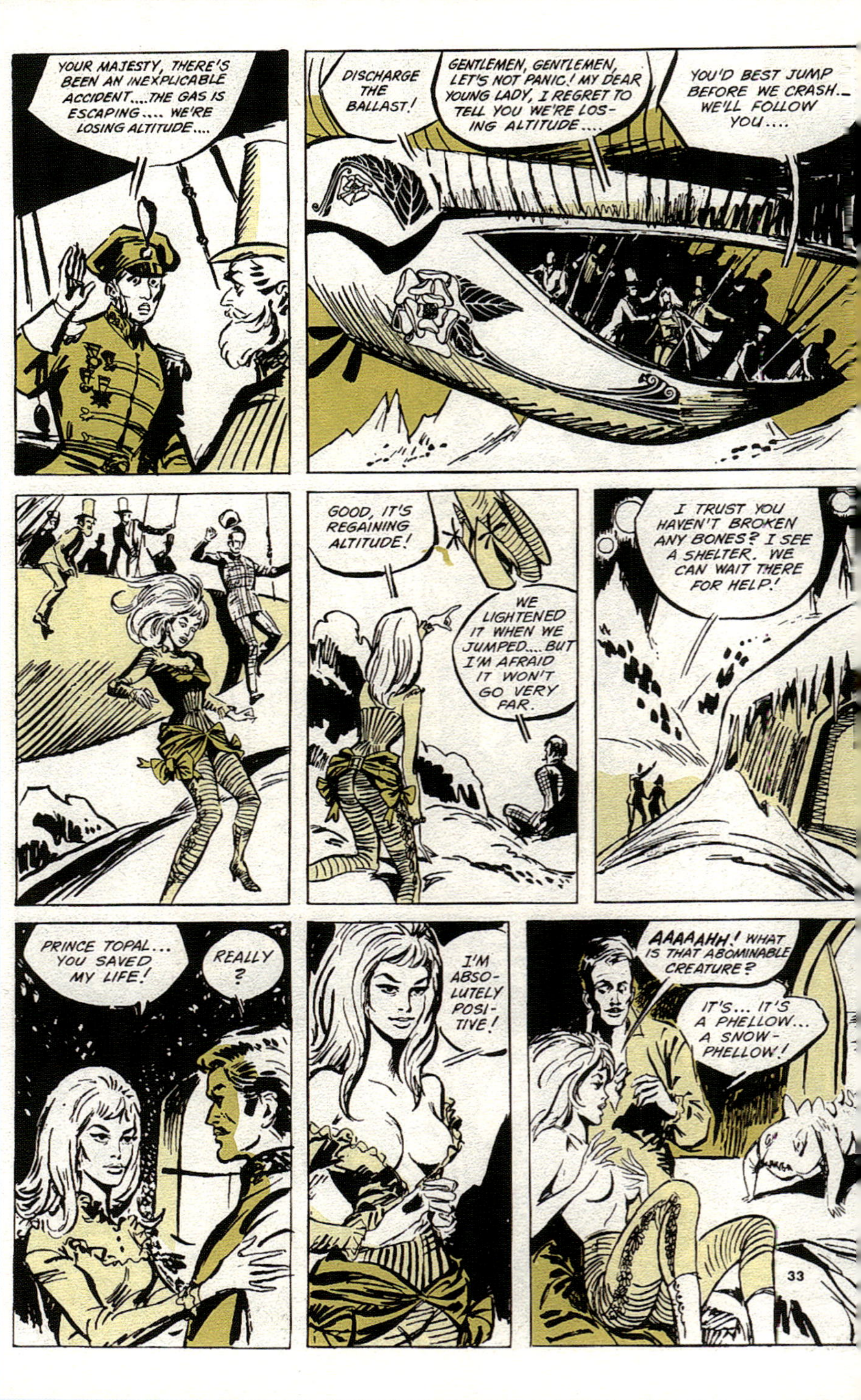

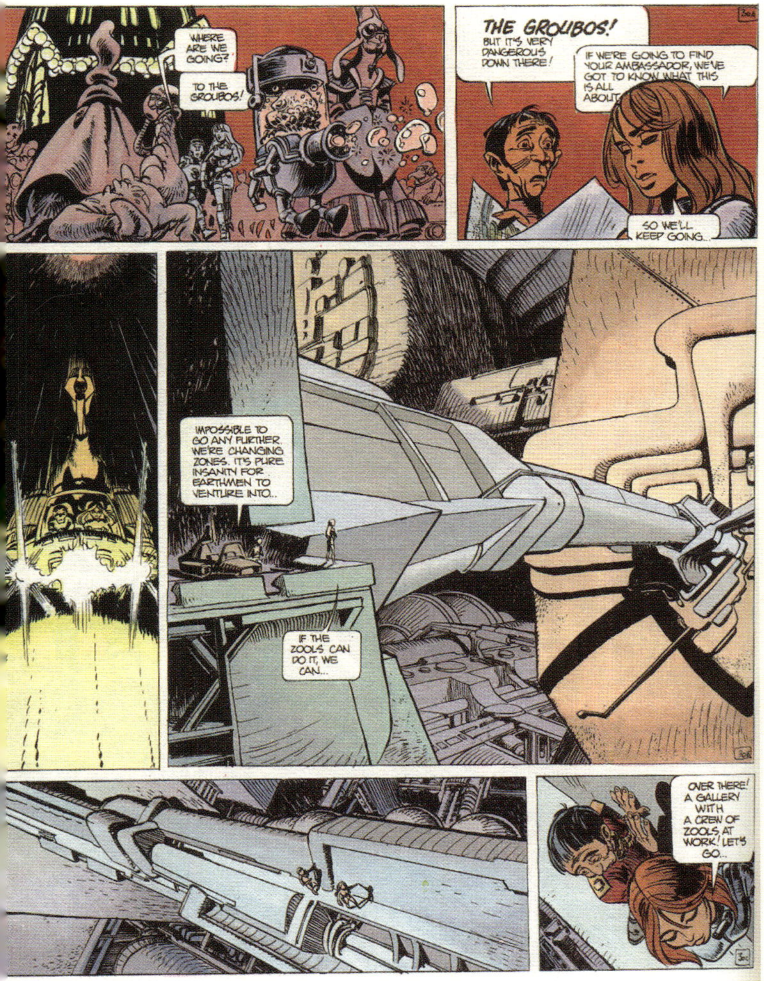

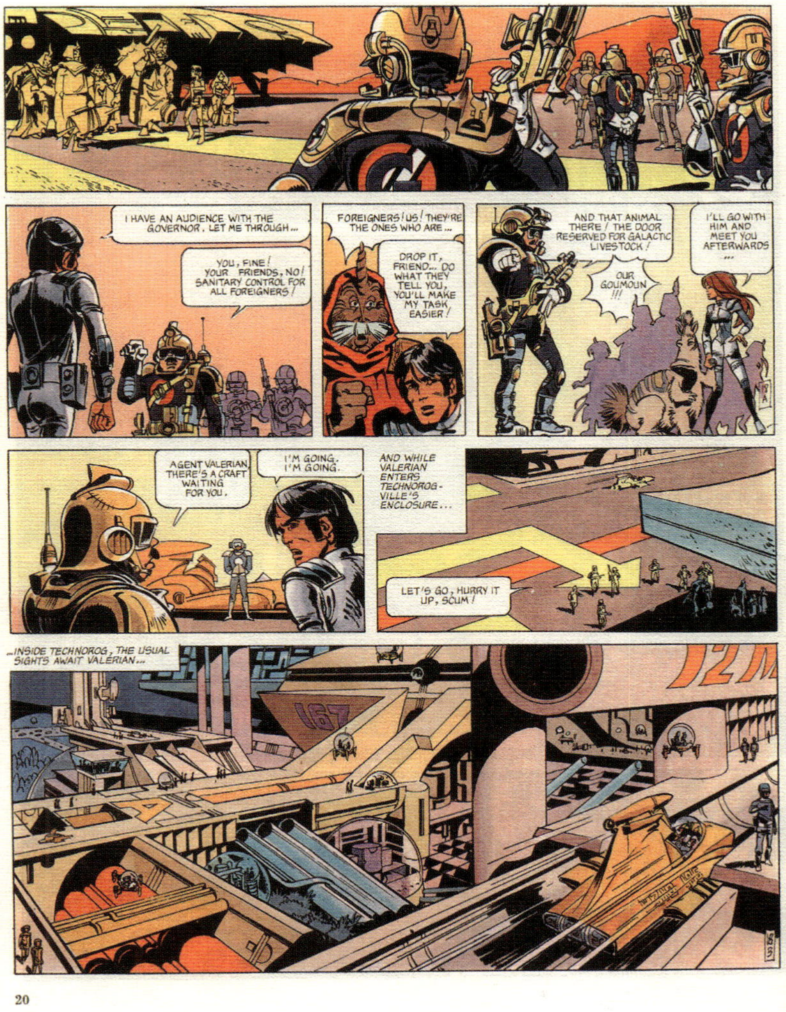

of quirky aliens, complex societies, and bureaucratic ineptitude, the series is reminiscent of *Jeff Hawke*—in fact, Valérian too increasingly doesn't just have to defeat bad guys but must solve conflicts and reconcile enemies through intelligence and ingenuity (more often than not Laureline's rather than his own!). The series is still going strong, some 40 years on, and is far and away the best-selling SF series in French-language comics.

◄▲ ▲

Christin and Mézières' *Valérian* is the best-selling French SF comic book of all, but is not widely available in English translation. Four books in English were issued by publishers Dargaud in the 1980s but are now long out of print; a new volume published by iBooks was released in 2005.

◄

After the release of the 1968 movie, *Barbarella* became one of the first French bandes dessinées to become well known in the English-speaking world, but a first English-language edition had in fact been produced for the US two years earlier. This example page includes both of the elements that *Barbarella* was famed for: whimsical adventure and a permissive attitude.

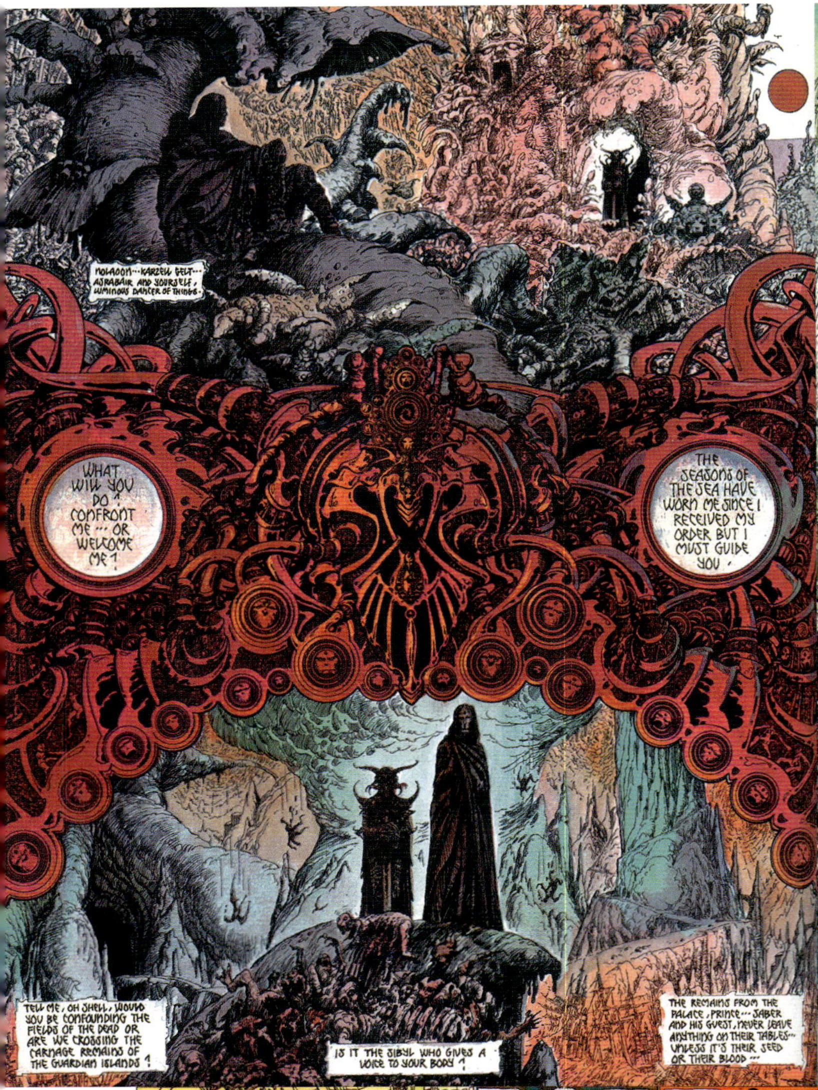
NOLAOOM... KARZELL GELT... AJRABAIR AND YOURSELF, LUMINOUS DANCER OF THINGS.
WHAT WILL YOU DO ? CONFRONT ME ... OR WELCOME ME ?
THE SEASONS OF THE SEA HAVE WORN ME SINCE I RECEIVED MY ORDER BUT I MUST GUIDE YOU.
TELL ME, OH SHELL, WOULD YOU BE CONFOUNDING THE FIELDS OF THE DEAD OR ARE WE CROSSING THE CARNAGE REMAINS OF THE GUARDIAN ISLANDS ?
IS IT THE SIBYL WHO GIVES A VOICE TO YOUR BODY ?
THE REMAINS FROM THE PALACE, PRINCE... SABER AND HIS GUEST, NEVER LEAVE ANYTHING ON THEIR TABLES... UNLESS IT'S THEIR SEED OR THEIR BLOOD...

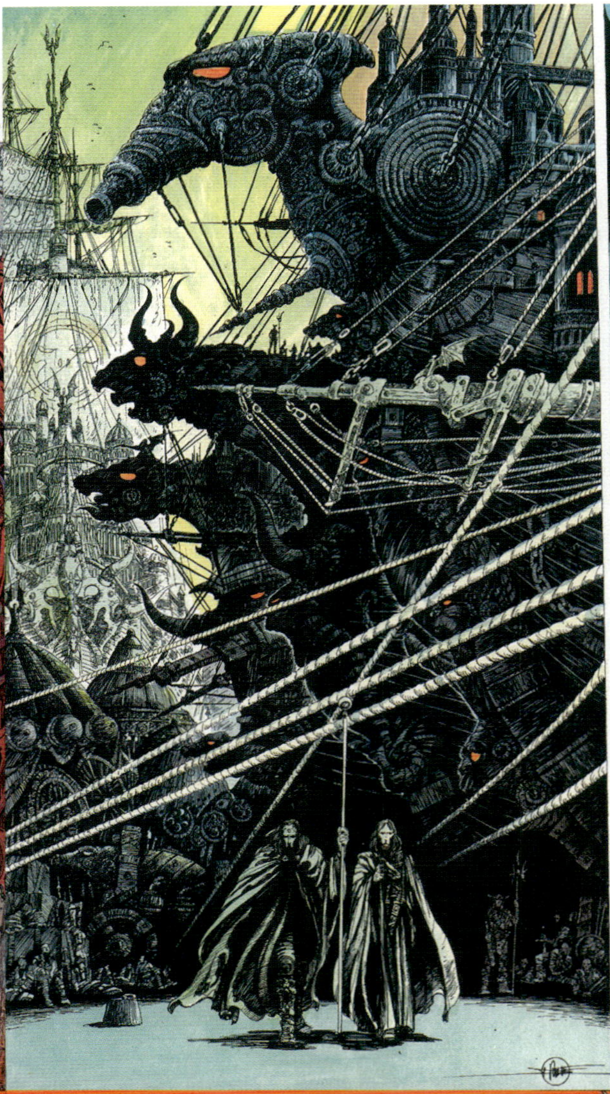

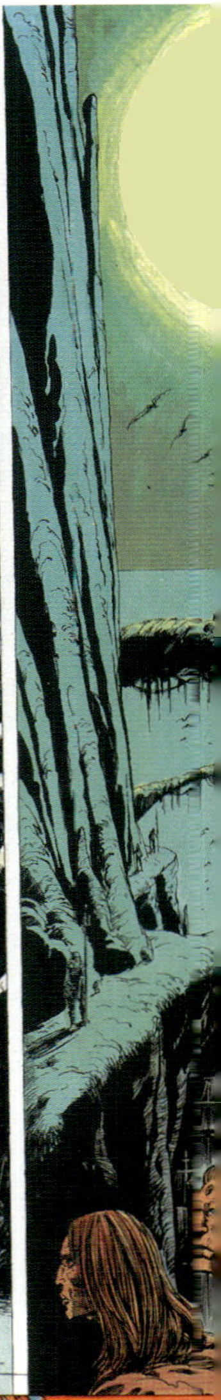

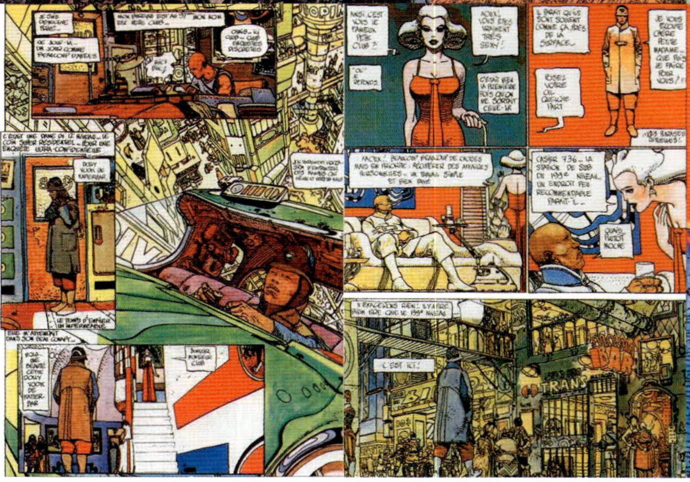

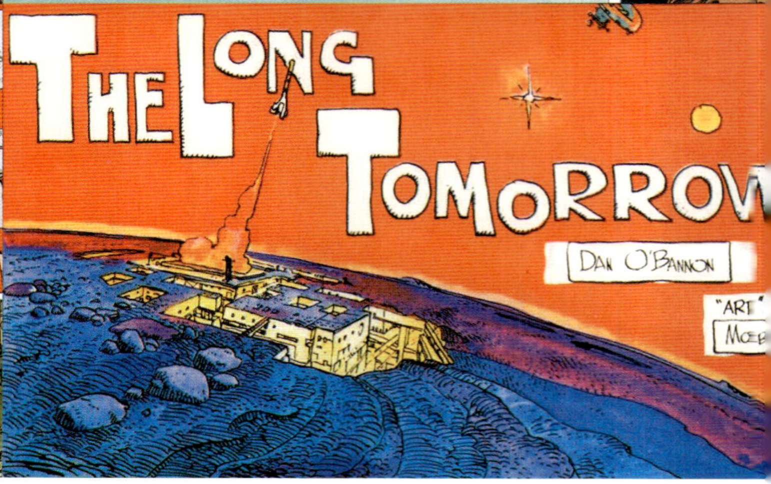
THE LONG TOMORROW
DAN O'BANNON
"ART"

◄
Philippe Druillet's *Yragaël* epitomizes his style: ornate, densely decorated, yet often wordless or without a clear narrative structure. This English translation attempted to recreate the flavor of the original lettering, which is part of the decorative effect—clarity or even legibility isn't always its prime purpose.

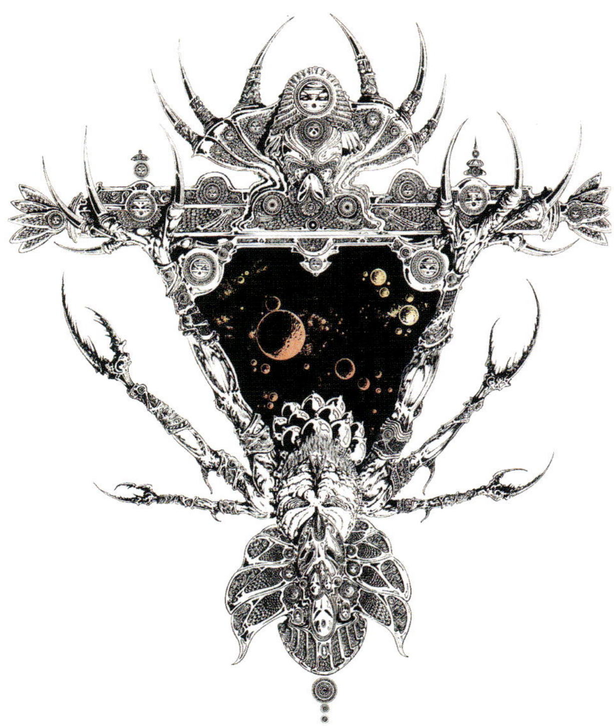

► ▼
Philippe Druillet's volumes often include non-story pages such as this.

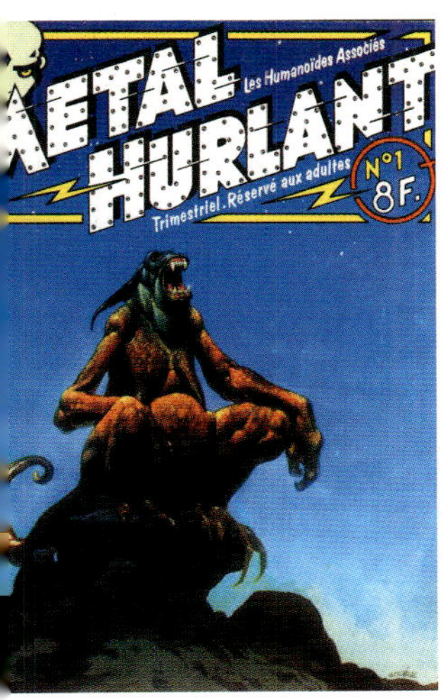

▼
Cover by Moebius for the first issue of the landmark comics magazine *Métal Hurlant*.

◄ ▼
While Moebius provided the artwork for *The Long Tomorrow*, the writer was Dan O'Bannon. O'Bannon later wrote the screenplay for *Alien*, filmed by Ridley Scott; in turn, *The Long Tomorrow* would be a visual reference for Scott's *Blade Runner*.

Also in the mid-1960s, there appeared a landmark character who in some ways was the exact opposite of Valérian. Lone Sloane is a freebooter, usually on the wrong side of the law, constantly at odds with an oppressive galactic empire not so very different from the one that Valérian serves, but also embroiled with a much darker world of malevolent ancient gods and other-dimensional forces. *Lone Sloane* premiered in 1965 and was first published in book form in 1967.

Lone Sloane was the creation of Philippe Druillet (1944-), who really hit his stride in 1970 when he revived the character in *Pilote*. A collected edition, *Les Six Voyages de Lone Sloane*, appeared in 1972, and a sequel of sorts, *Délirius*, was published the year after. Also in 1973, Druillet created the more gothic fantasy *Yragaël*, shortly followed by *Urm le Fou* ("Urm the Fool"), both scripted by SF writer Michel Demuth.

In these few short years, Druillet caused a sensation. His style was at once baroque and psychedelic, his stories complex and intense—and frequently unintelligible. His pages shattered the conventions of comics storytelling. Many readers loved their "trippy" quality; many critics (the French take these things very seriously) scorned his "lack of narrative construction" and complained that he couldn't draw the human face very well. Druillet has remained controversial, but has since pursued interests outside of comics such as photography, painting, and glass sculpture.

If Druillet seemed to come out of left field, the other superstar of the '70s came out of the West. Jean Giraud (1938-) had an early interest in Westerns; in 1963 he created *Fort Navajo* with scriptwriter Jean-Michel Charlier, which became *Lieutenant Blueberry* and began a long run in *Pilote*. But unknown to most until much later, Giraud had a double life. Under the name Moebius he was also creating sci-fi, satirical, and erotic strips for magazines including *Hara-Kiri* and *L'Echo des Savanes*, plus illustrations for SF novels and stories published by Editions Opta.

Giraud's Moebius side blossomed in the 1970s. In 1974 Giraud, Druillet, writer Jean-Pierre Dionnet, and business partner Bernard Farkas formed Les Humanoïdes Associés and launched the landmark SF comic book *Métal Hurlant* (literally "howling metal"). For the next 12 years, the magazine specialized in publishing cutting-edge, "adult," and experimental sci-fi comics by many of Europe's greatest creators. A licensed US version titled *Heavy Metal* began publication in 1977 and introduced the English-speaking world to this new, more adult, and more graphically inventive approach to comics—and of course to hit European sci-fi series, including *Valérian* in 1981.

Over the years *Métal Hurlant* (and *Heavy Metal* in turn) showcased dazzling work by Moebius including *L'Incal*—scripted by Alejandro Jodorowsky—the stream-of-consciousness *Le Garage Hermétique* ("The Airtight Garage"), and the wordless, dreamlike *Arzach*. Between 1983 and 1989, Giraud lived in the US and oversaw some English-language editions of his greatest hits, as well as creating new projects, including a *Silver Surfer* mini-series for Marvel Comics.

Moebius too has expanded beyond comics into concept art and production design work for a 1982 animated movie, *Les Maîtres du Temp* ("Masters of Time"), and many landmark SF movies, including *Alien, Tron, Star Wars: The Empire Strikes Back*, and *The Fifth Element*. Some of his comics work has been credited as one of the inspirations for the look of *Blade Runner*.

SF IN MANGA AND ANIME

Over the last ten years or so, there has been a revolution in the world of comics, and its name is manga. Comics from Japan, or in the Japanese style, have enjoyed a phenomenal worldwide boom. In the UK, an estimated 60% of graphic novel sales are manga; in the US, according to industry figures from Bookscan, it's an astonishing 75%. According to one estimate, manga now represents as much as two-thirds of comic book sales in France.

In Japan itself, according to official figures, at least one in four of all magazines sold are manga, and the diversity is mind-boggling. Here we can mention only the most prominent landmarks in the history of science fiction manga and anime (the printed and the animated media inevitably go together), particularly those known internationally.

It all began with the man universally revered as the father of manga, Osamu Tezuka (1928-1989), who established the form with his *Shintakarajima* ("New Treasure Island") in 1947. In 1951 he introduced the seminal *Tetsuwan-Atomu* ("Mighty Atom," renamed *Astro Boy* for its US TV release), who appeared in manga through to 1968 and in anime from 1963. *Astro Boy* was one of Japan's first animated TV series and an international breakthrough, although ironically, even though it was originally a comic book, Gold Key's US comic book version in 1965 was redrawn by American artists for a domestic audience not yet acquainted with the more extreme conventions of manga. The original manga series is now available in English in 23 volumes from Dark Horse Comics.

There was a lot more SF in Tezuka's prodigious output—among his very earliest hits was his so-called "science-fiction trilogy" in the late '40s and early '50s (*Metropolis*, *Lost World*, and *Next World*)—and he used science fiction motifs in too many works to list here. But the work closest to his own heart was *Phoenix*, a sweeping saga centering on an undying entity that visits the whole of space and time; overtly SF parts of this were released in 1980 as *Phoenix 2772* or *Space Firebird*.

Astro Boy was a robot boy built by a grieving scientist to replace his dead son. Artist Jiro Kuwata and SF writer Kazumasa Hirai invented a variation on the theme in *8-Man* (called *Tobor the Eighth Man* for its 1963 US TV release). Here, the mind and memories of a murdered police officer are preserved in a super-powered robot body so that he can battle cyborgs and mutants as well as criminals—and all this 25 years before *RoboCop*. (Similarly, *Cyborg 009*, in manga 1964 and anime 1968, predated *The Six Million Dollar Man* by almost ten years). One of the most popular children's TV anime series from the 1970s to date is *Doraemon*, starring a gadget-laden but bumbling robot cat from the future.

If robots are popular, giant robots, or "mecha," are even more so. Mitsuteru Yokoyama created *Tetsujin 28-go* ("Iron Man No. 28," a.k.a. *Gigantor* on US TV) in 1956, and the more obviously named *Giant Robo* in the late 1960s. In 1972 Go Nagai introduced *Mazinger Z*, notable for two things: instead of being sentient like *Astro Boy* or remote-controlled like *Gigantor*, it was the first mecha "piloted" by the young hero; and it had one of the most bizarre villains ever: half man, half woman, literally split down the middle. Later, in 1988, Nagai and artist Ken Ishikawa produced a *Mazinger* manga for First Comics, the first manga created specifically for US release.

▶ ▶▶ ▶▼
While *Tetsuwan-Atomu*, or *Astro Boy* (seen here on an original Japanese cover) is Osamu Tezuka's best-known work, his most personal is *Phoenix*, a philosophical saga that spans the distant past to the far flung future.

▼
Akira Toriyama's *Dragon Ball Z* is internationally known thanks to its anime version, but it's a curiously Japanese amalgam of martial arts and sci-fi (the hero, Goku, is martial arts champion who turns out to be an alien and battles other aliens, as well as time-travelers and weird creatures)—with a little magic thrown in (the seven Dragon Balls of the title can grant any wish).

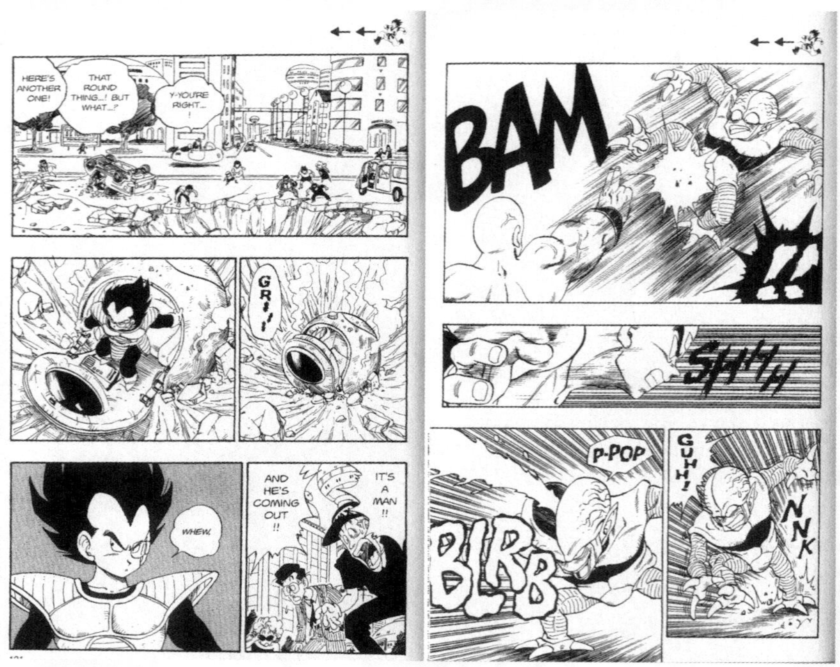

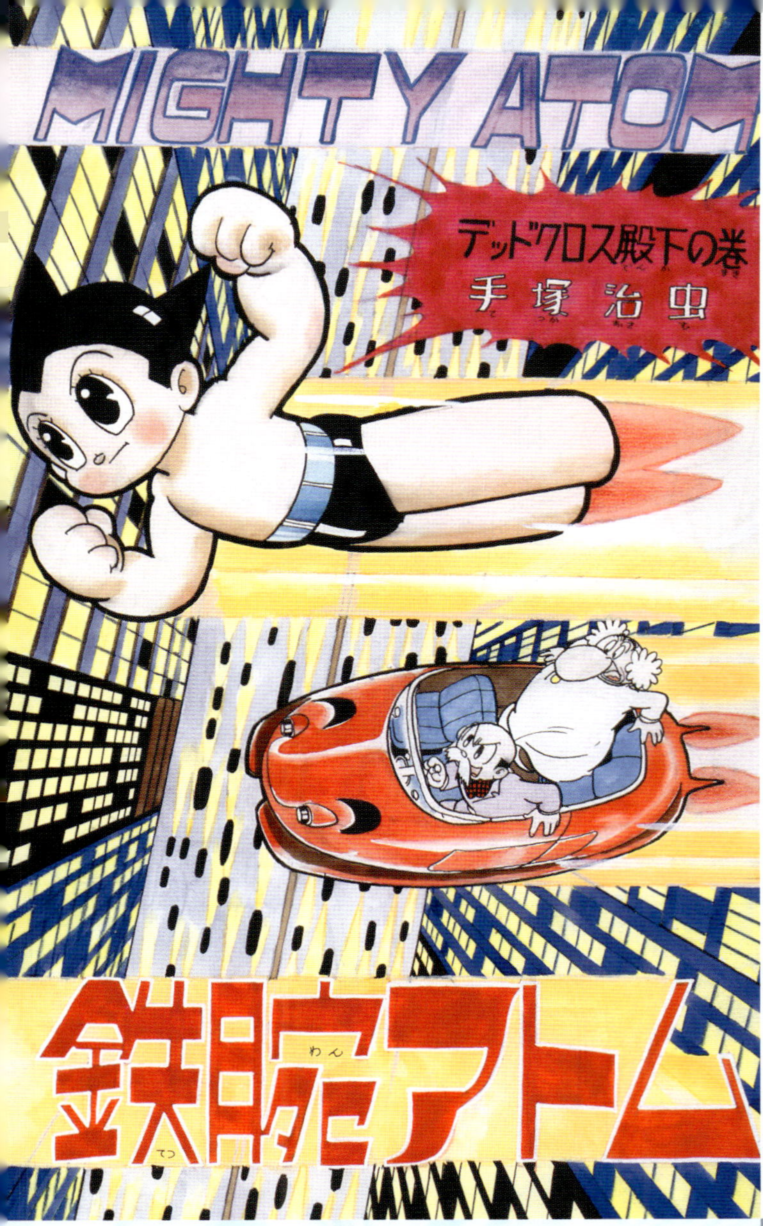

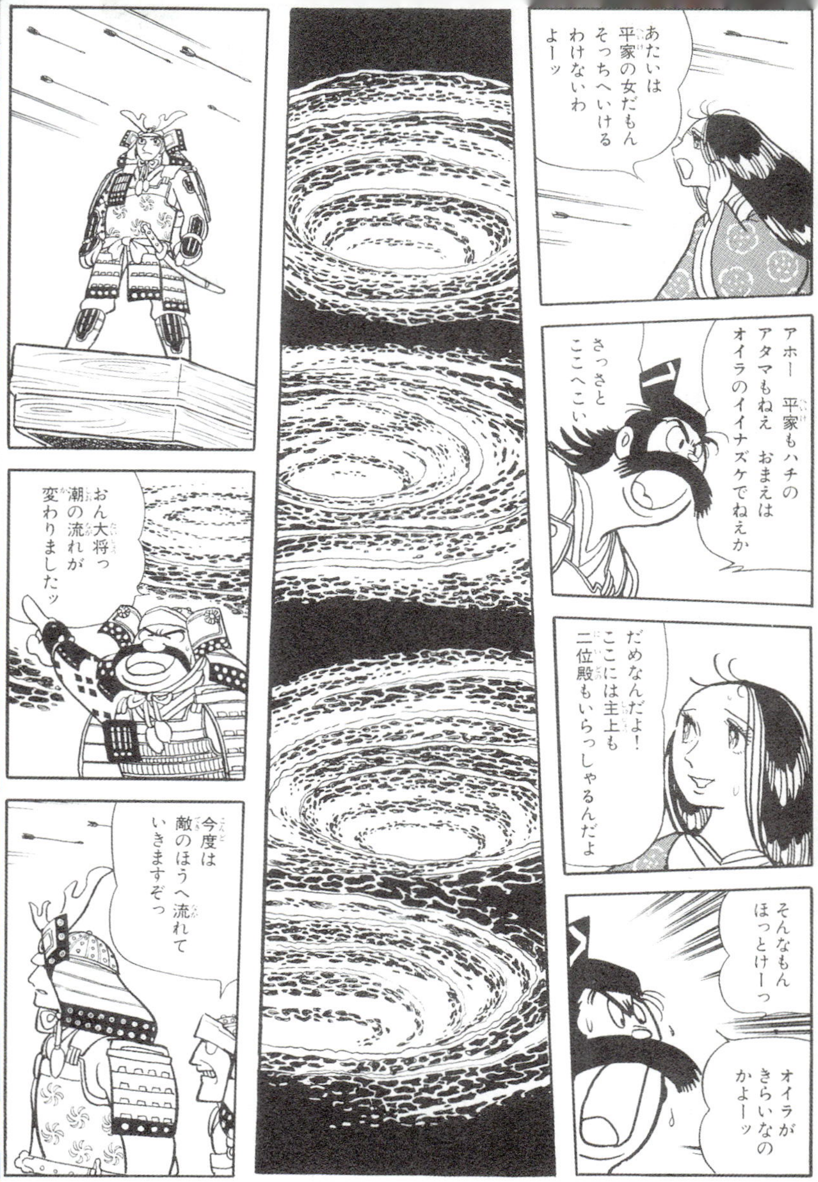

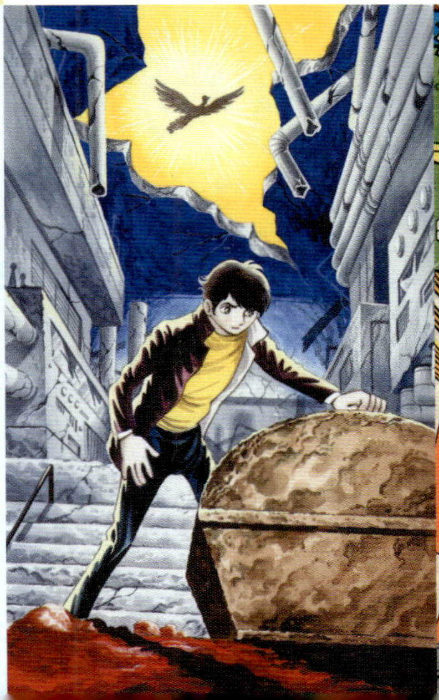

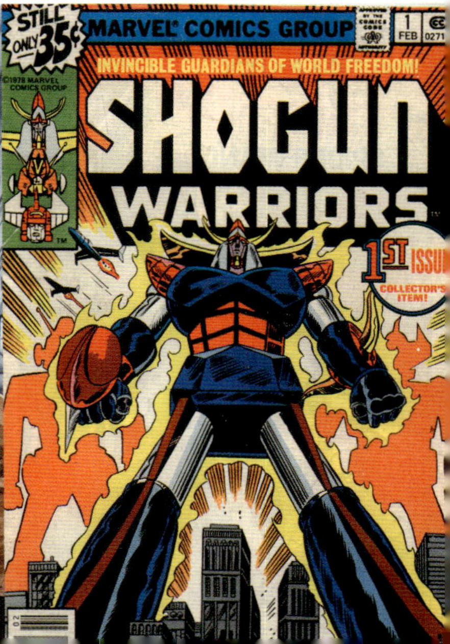

▶▶
The American audience was being introduced to mecha as long ago as 1978, in the guise of *Shogun Warriors*, but the comic book was drawn by Americans in Marvel Comics' usual style. It was not so much manga that the audience wanted but comic book tie-ins with their toys, including Americanized brands such as *Transformers* and *Robotech*.

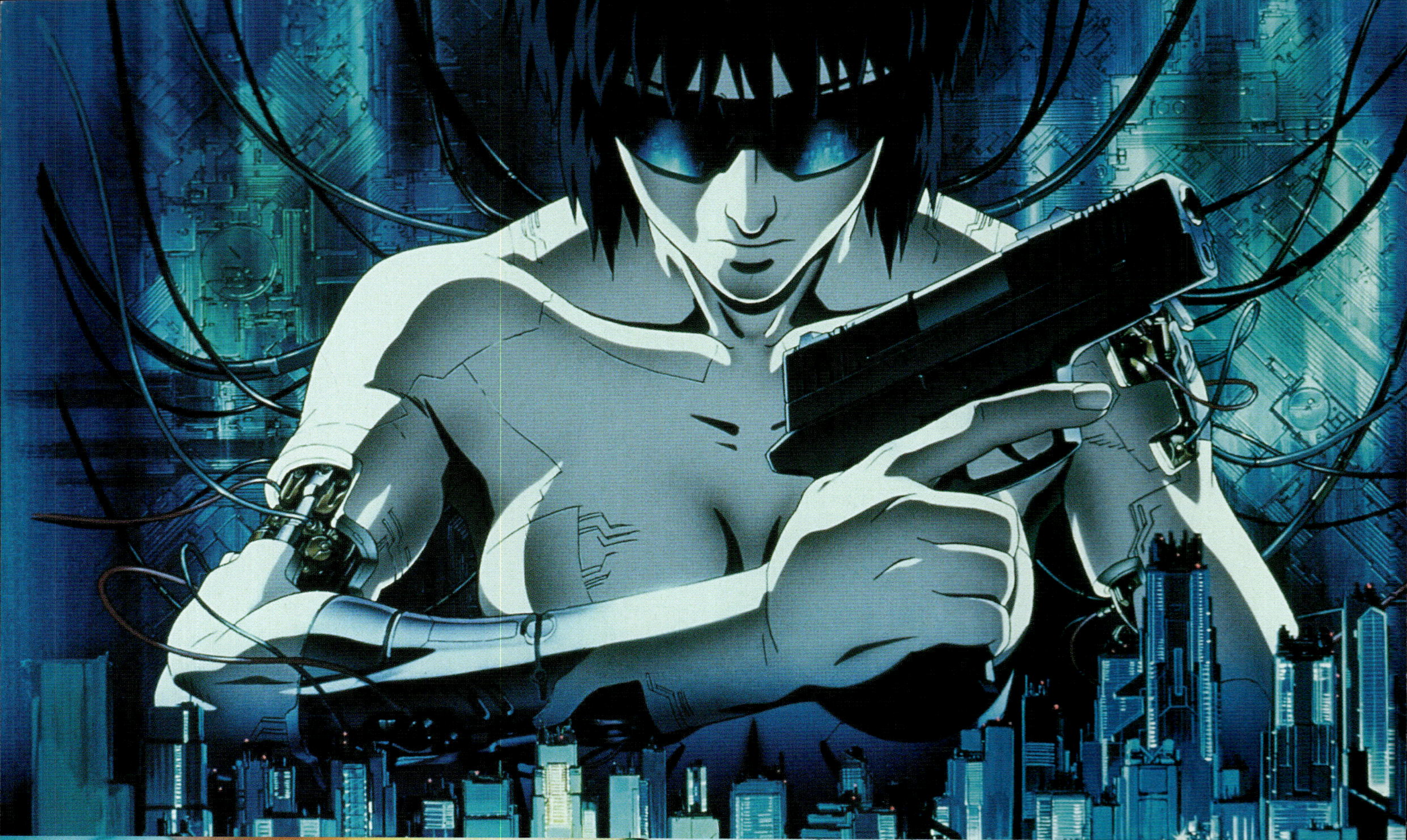

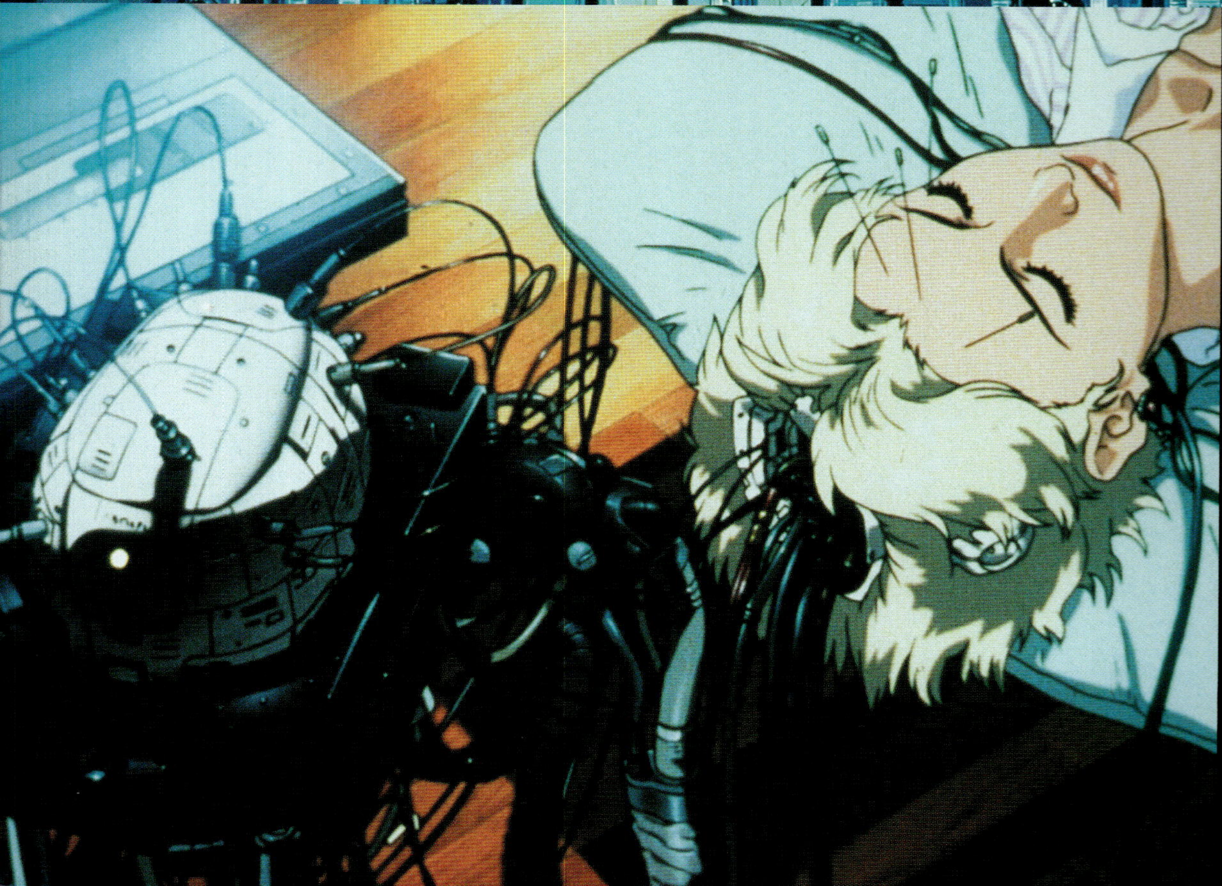

▲
The central character in *Ghost in the Shell* is a disembodied spirit who animates a mechanical body, but there's extra interest for fanboys in the fact that she (and her android "shell") are female. That said, the 1995 anime movie adaptation of the manga did attempt a more serious tone.

◀
The *Ghost in the Shell* anime adopts a much slower pace than the manga, a hallmark of director Mamoru Oshii.

Following *Mazinger*, Nagai and Ishikawa devised the *Getta Robottu* (known as *Starvengers* on US TV)—the first time three separate robots (one designed for land, one air, and the third sea) could also combine into one giant humanoid form.

Giant piloted mecha star in two of the best-known and longest-running anime series: *Mobile Suit Gundam* (and variations on the franchise, 1979 to date) and the space-war saga *Macross* (1982 to date, plus a re-edited release in the US under the name *Robotech*). The two best-received TV anime series of the '90s both center on mecha: *Neon Genesis Evangelion* adds a post-apocalyptic twist, and *Escaflowne* throws a supernatural flavor into the mix; it is also noteworthy for storylines designed to appeal to girls as well as action for the boys.

Along with *Gundam* and *Macross*, the third major international anime hit is *Uchu Senkan Yamato* ("Space Battleship Yamato," known in the US as *Space Cruiser* or *Star Blazers*), which was a modest success on its initial release in 1974 and then became a phenomenon after *Star Wars*. It has a prominent techno element (centrally the World War II battleship refitted as a spacecraft) but broke new ground with its compelling quest storyline and more adult themes.

The manga version of *Yamato* was drawn by Reiji Matsumoto (1938-), who in 1976 also created *Ginga Tetsudo 999* ("Galaxy Express 999"): atmospheric tales of a young hero traveling in a space-faring steam train and learning about life and death. Matsumoto had a third science fiction hit with *Captain Harlock* (1977 onwards), a freedom-fighter who also happens to be a space pirate.

Small teams or battle units (usually of about five people, as in the international '70s hit *Kagaku Ninjatai Gatchaman*, a.k.a. *Battle of the Planets* or *G-Force*, but sometimes fewer, as in *Dirty Pair*) are a favorite among fans. But so too are loners and marginalized characters, whether they're humans with enhanced abilities (like *Chojin Locke*, or "Locke the Superman") or cyborgs (such as *Battle Angel Alita*, or Motoko, the titular *Ghost in the Shell*).

A high point in this "individual hero"—or more usually heroine—tradition is Hayao Miyazaki's *Kaze no Tani no Naushika* (*Nausicaä of the Valley of the Wind*), a manga from 1982 and released as anime in 1984. Graphically striking, inventive, and hugely influential, it tells an eventful yet sensitive story set in a world struggling to recover from a massive ecological disaster. The anime is noteworthy also as the first project from a team that would later become Studio Ghibli, pre-eminent makers of science-fantasy anime, many directed by Miyazaki, including *Spirited Away*, the first anime ever to win an Academy Award.

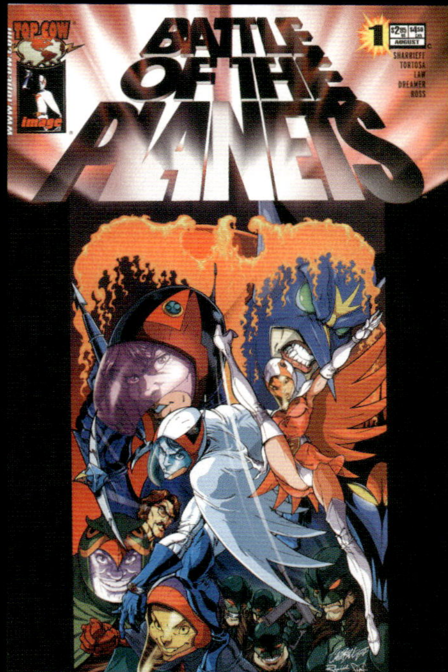

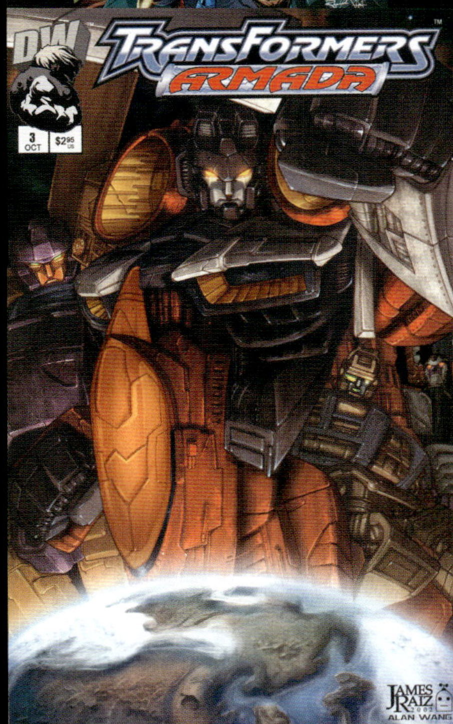

▶ **The recent popularity of manga and anime in the West has led to still more American versions of Japanese originals, most often by American creators, though sometimes in a manga style.**

AKIRA

There is a strong post-apocalyptic motif in many Japanese manga and anime—but then, as commentators point out, Japan is the only nation on Earth that has actually experienced nuclear attack followed by occupation by an "alien" power. *Akira* is a landmark manga and anime that not only uses post-apocalyptic story elements to superb dramatic effect, but also, for an adult audience, seems to consciously explore the metaphorical resonances of these elements on Japanese history and culture. It's a slam-bang cyberpunk sci-fi adventure... for grown-ups.

Akira began as a manga serial by Katsuhiro Otomo (1954–), running to more than 2,000 pages from 1982 to 1990. A colored, reworked English-language version was published over 38 issues by Marvel's "adult" Epic Comics imprint between 1988 and 1995; Dark Horse has reissued the original manga in a new English translation in six hefty volumes (2000–2002).

It was in anime form, however, that *Akira* broke through in the West in 1988. It set a new benchmark for anime, thanks to its experimental digital effects, timely visual look, and polished animation, complete with lip-sync (a painstaking rarity in anime). It struck a chord with an audience that had been introduced to cyberpunk in William Gibson's *Neuromancer* (1984), had glimpsed dystopian futures with corrupt governments or organizations in *RoboCop* and *The Running Man* (both 1987), and were getting to know an even darker vision of life to come in *Blade Runner* (not a widespread success on its theatrical release in 1982 but building a cult following on VHS as the home video phenomenon grew).

That said, it has been argued that *Akira*'s alienated biker gangs owe as much to *The Wild One* or *Easy Rider* as to cyberpunk, and that its Neo-Tokyo is reminiscent of the future-LA of *Blade Runner* only because both share the same influences. Many of *Akira*'s elements do have precedents: among other series, *Gundam* establishes the metaphor of a new generation as a "newtype" or entire new genetic breed; and *Chojin Locke* ("Locke the Superman") combines political intrigue and youngsters who possess spectacular psionic powers. But the point is that *Akira* integrates all its disparate elements into a compelling vision of a world on the edge after a third world war.

What's more, the story works both as an adventure (with plenty of shock twists, including the violent deaths of major characters) and on a deeper level. The original apocalypse that precipitates the war is triggered by a corrupt, military-dominated government. Even the violent "terrorist" group turn out to be orchestrated by a power-hungry politico for his own ends. Secret scientific experiments unleash forces that cannot be contained and destroy those who seek to exploit them. And yet, it is the efforts of rebellious youth to break free that cause a second disaster. Or is this one a cleansing fire, promising a genuine fresh start?

Even without its themes and meanings, *Akira* boasts technical brilliance, fantastic visuals, and an edge-of-your-seat story. Several critics rank it the best anime of all time... and the manga is a masterwork in its own right.

▶ ▶▼

The *Akira* anime was a breakthrough hit in the West in 1988, and marked the start of the US anime boom. Today the film is regarded as one of the greatest animated movies ever made.

▼

Cover of the first volume of the English-language edition of the original *Akira*. The manga features polished artwork, a gripping storyline, and biker gangs in a futuristic Neo-Tokyo.

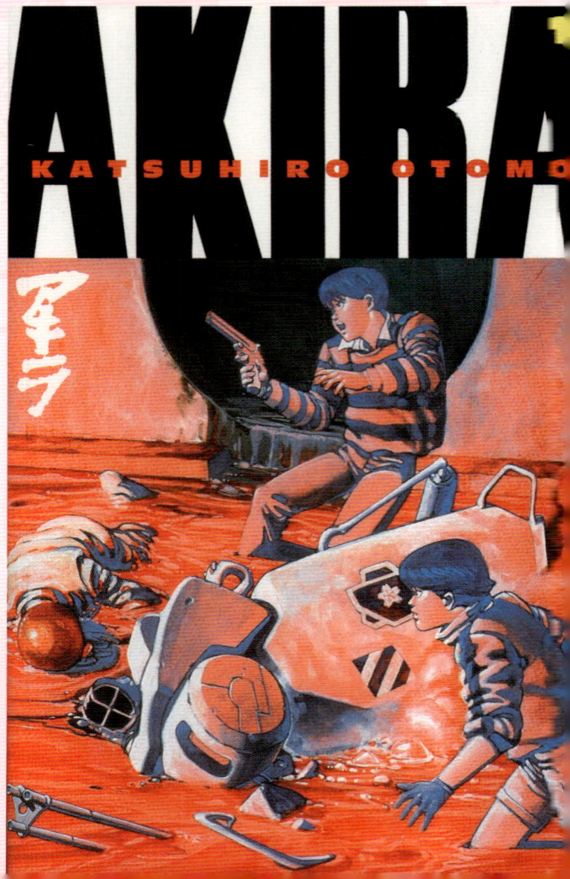

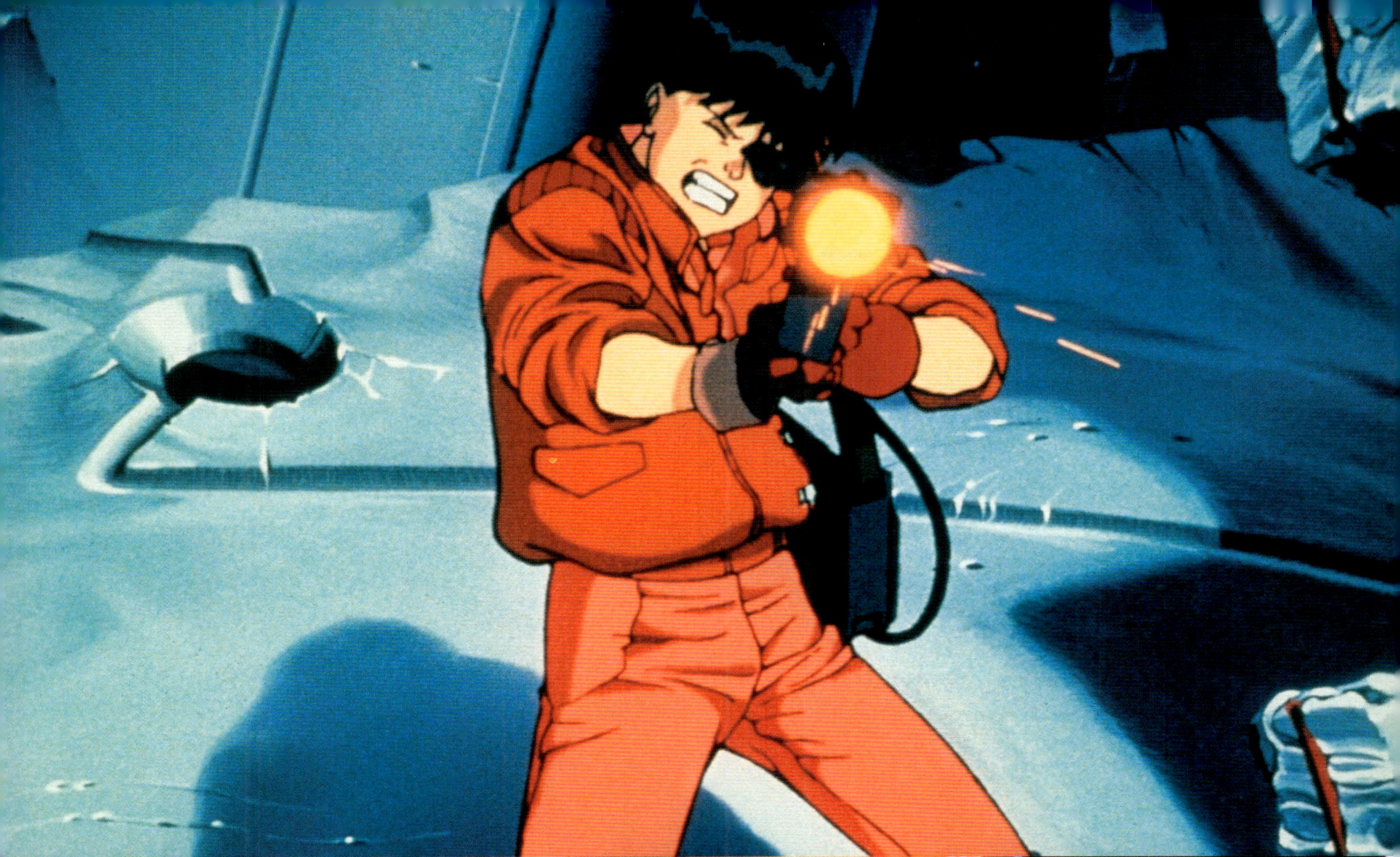

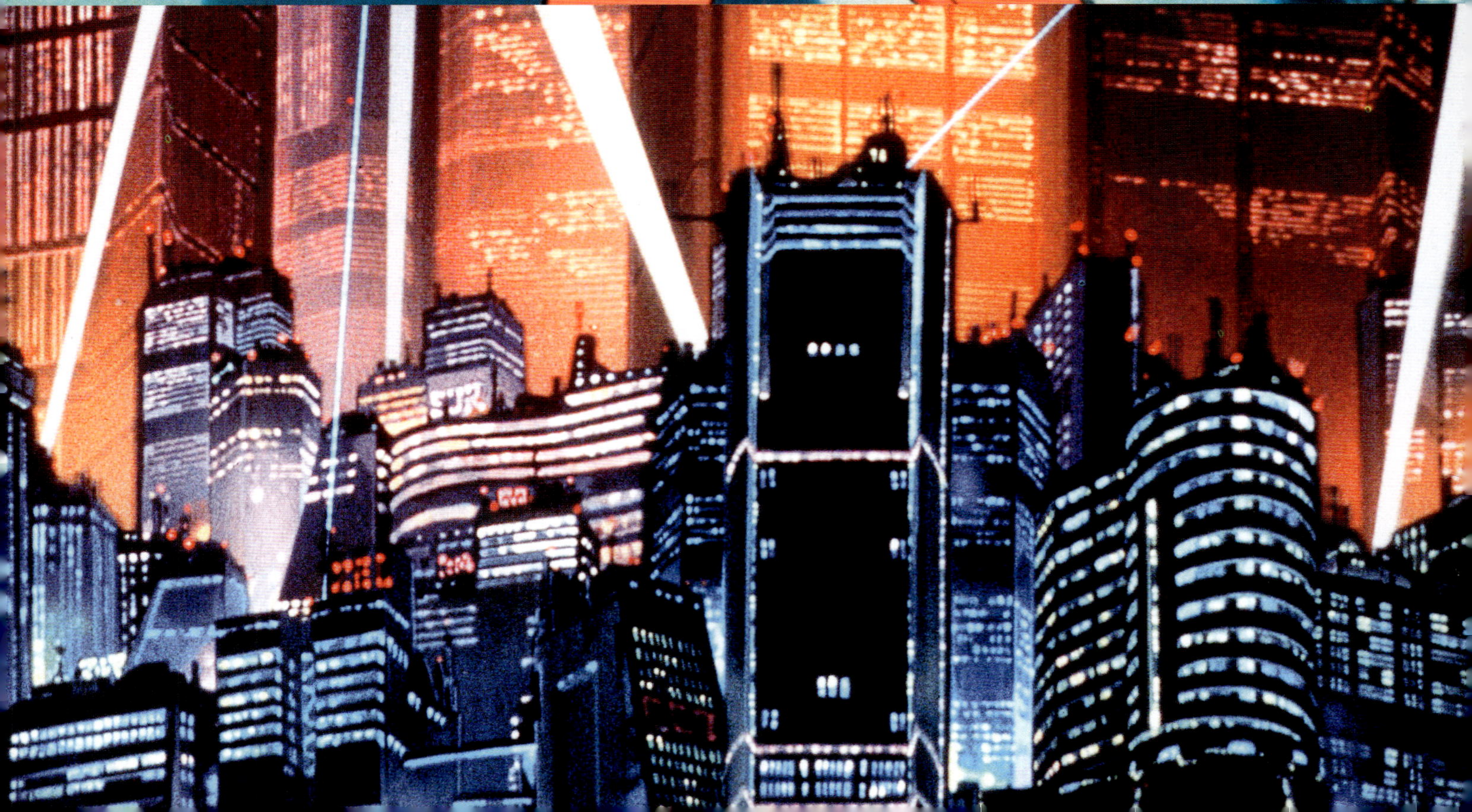

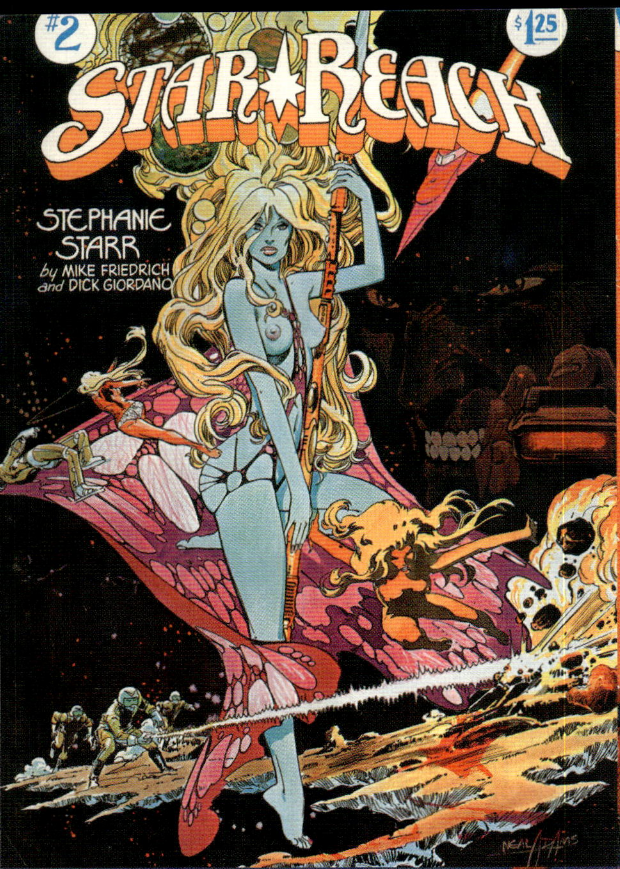

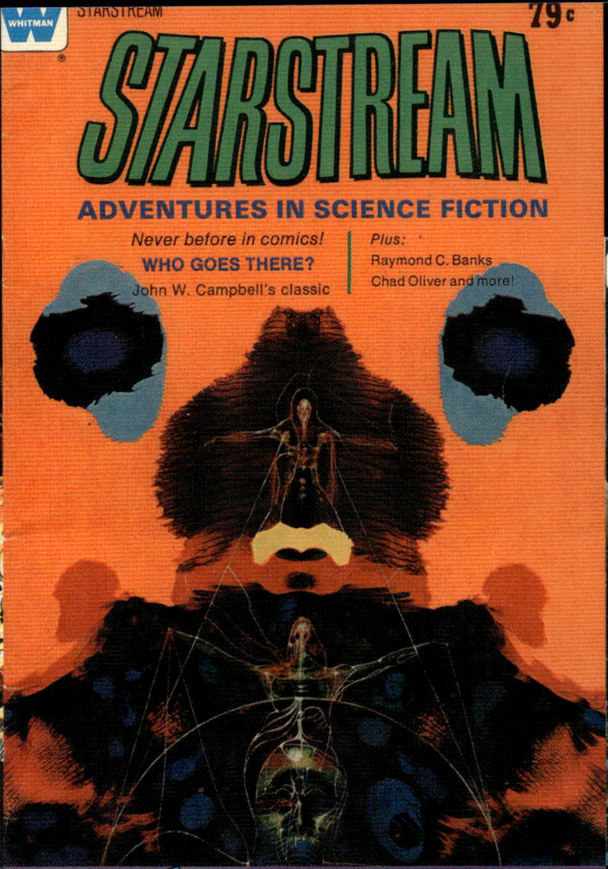

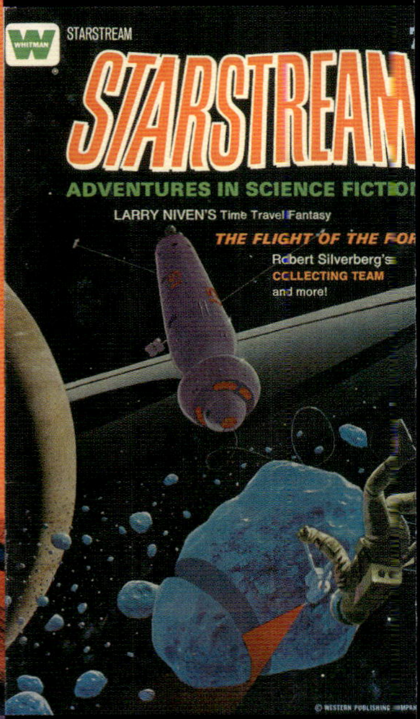

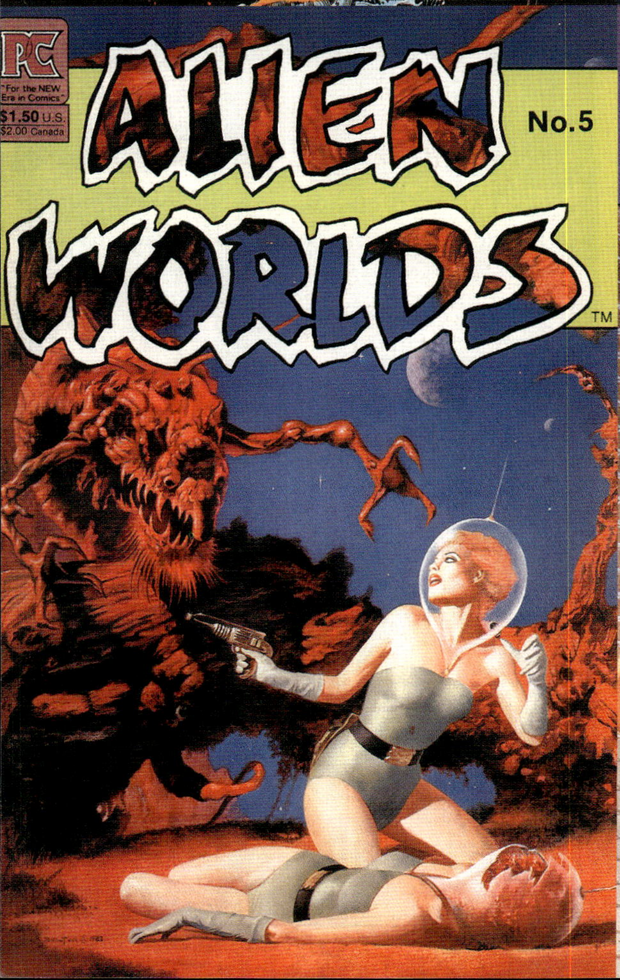

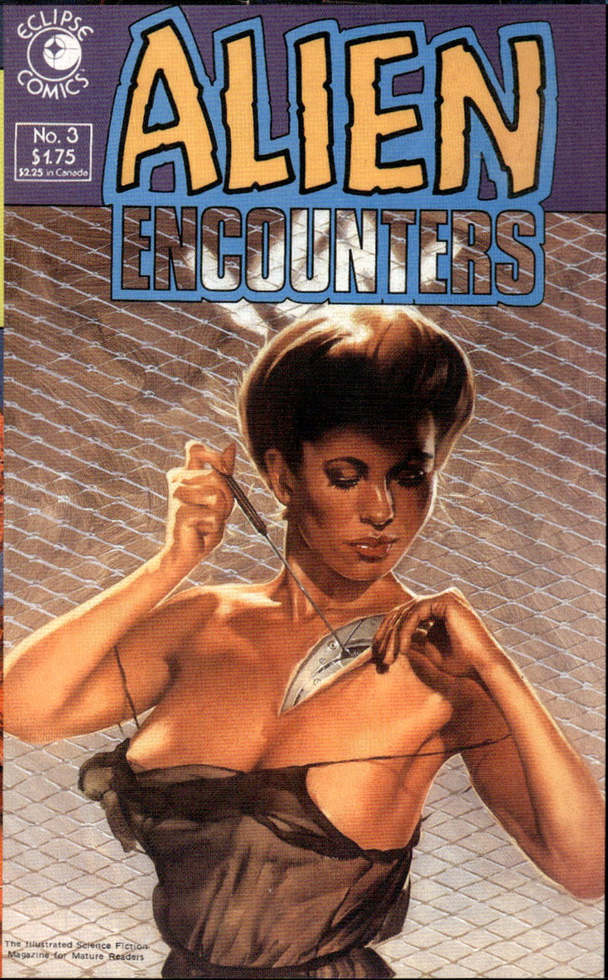

◀◀
Sumptuous, rarely-seen cover by fan favorite Neal Adams for the second issue of *Star Reach* (1975), the self-described first "ground-level" comic book (combining the freedom of the underground comix with mainstream appeal—or at least that was the aim). *Stephanie Starr* recounts the adventures of a female astronaut-cadet who, like Barbarella, can't seem to keep her clothes on.

▲
Western Publishing, publisher of Gold Key comics, produced four issues of *Starstream* in 1976, containing solid adaptations of renowned science fiction authors.

◀ ◀◀
Pacific Comics' *Alien Worlds* is well worth seeking out for its superb cover art alone. Eclipse's *Alien Encounters* from 1985 also boasted outstanding painted cover art, as well as stories with a definite "adult" edge to them.

TALES OF THE FUTURE: SF ANTHOLOGY COMICS

Manga stories tend to be very lengthy, not to say drawn-out. Storylines can stretch on and on for years, becoming more and more convoluted, while the smallest incident might take several pages to unfold. In the West, by contrast, the most common format for sci-fi comics has been the short story.

Even in the all-devouring superhero boom of the 1960s, sci-fi anthology comics hung in there. A few new ones were launched, including Dell's short-lived *Flying Saucers* in 1967, rival Gold Key's *UFO Flying Saucers* (1968-1980), and DC's *From Beyond the Unknown* (1969-1973), which reprinted sci-fi stories from their back catalog.

Following the slow-burn success of *Conan the Barbarian*, adaptations of works by major SF authors became the thing in the '70s. Marvel did it in *Worlds Unknown* (1973-1974), then in *Unknown Worlds of Science Fiction*, one of its line of black and white magazines. In 1976 Western Publishing (parent of Gold Key) launched its short-lived *Starstream*. In the mid-'80s, DC's first-ever graphic novel series was not superheroes like Marvel's graphic novels but a run of book-length adaptations of Robert Bloch, Ray Bradbury, Harlan Ellison, and others.

DC, obviously die-hard SF fans, returned to original SF time and again. In 1979 they published *Time Warp*, sci-fi tales with a "horror" twist, featuring artwork from Gil Kane, Howard Chaykin, and even Spider-Man co-creator Steve Ditko; in 1980 they briefly revived their '50s SF flagship *Mystery in Space*; and in 1996 they boldly attempted to launch a whole new SF-themed line with a dozen or so books under the Helix imprint, but it didn't last.

In 1974 comics writer Mike Friedrich launched *Star Reach*, the first creator-owned mainstream comic book, which gave creators the freedom to tell stories as personal or "adult-themed" as the undergrounds. Much of the content had a sci-fi flavor.

The 1980s saw a boom in titles from independent publishers, and many included SF in their line-ups, often with an "adult" edge, like Pacific Comics' *Alien Worlds* or Eclipse Comics' *Alien Encounters*. First Comics' line included Howard Chaykin's futuristic, satirical *American Flagg!*, Mike Baron and Steve Rude's space-faring *Nexus*, Jim Starlin's space opera *Dreadstar*, and First's longest-running title, John Ostrander's *GrimJack*. First also published the "first computerized comic," *Shatter*, a *Blade Runner* wannabe which lasted 15 issues but whose crude Mac-generated artwork is almost completely lacking in atmosphere.

In 1986 Dark Horse premiered more modestly with *Dark Horse Presents*, an anthology strong on sci-fi characters such as Chris Warner's *Black Cross*, Ron Randall's futuristic bounty hunter *Trekker*, and Paul Chadwick's thoughtful *Concrete*, a man trapped in a huge stone-like body as the result of an alien mind-transplant experiment. Many won their own books, and Dark Horse thrived with a breathtaking stream of broadly sci-fi properties that became hits in multiple media, including *Barb Wire*, *Hellboy*, *The Mask*, and *Timecop*.

Big-name adaptations made a comeback in the 1990s with *Harlan Ellison's Dream Corridor* from Dark Horse, several Bradbury titles from Topps Comics, plus Asimov and others in Eclipse Books' *Orbit*. More recently, SF comics made the leap to the web; *The Matrix Comics*, short stories by biog name creators set in the fictional universe of the *Matrix* films, debuted on the Internet before being collected in two printed volumes.

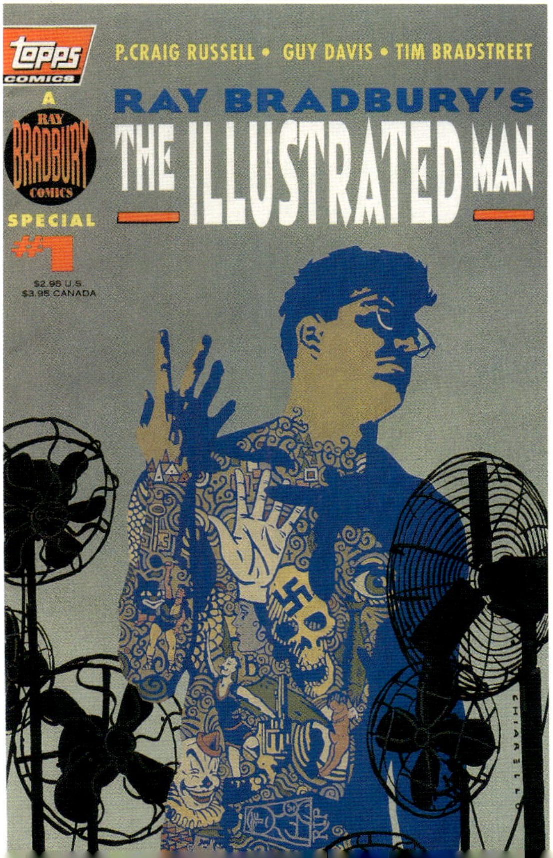

◀ **Cover of one of a series of Ray Bradbury titles from Topps in the 1990s. The contents included not only gorgeous new comics from contemporary illustrators but in most issues a reprinted story from EC, who had been the first to adapt Bradbury into comics form.**

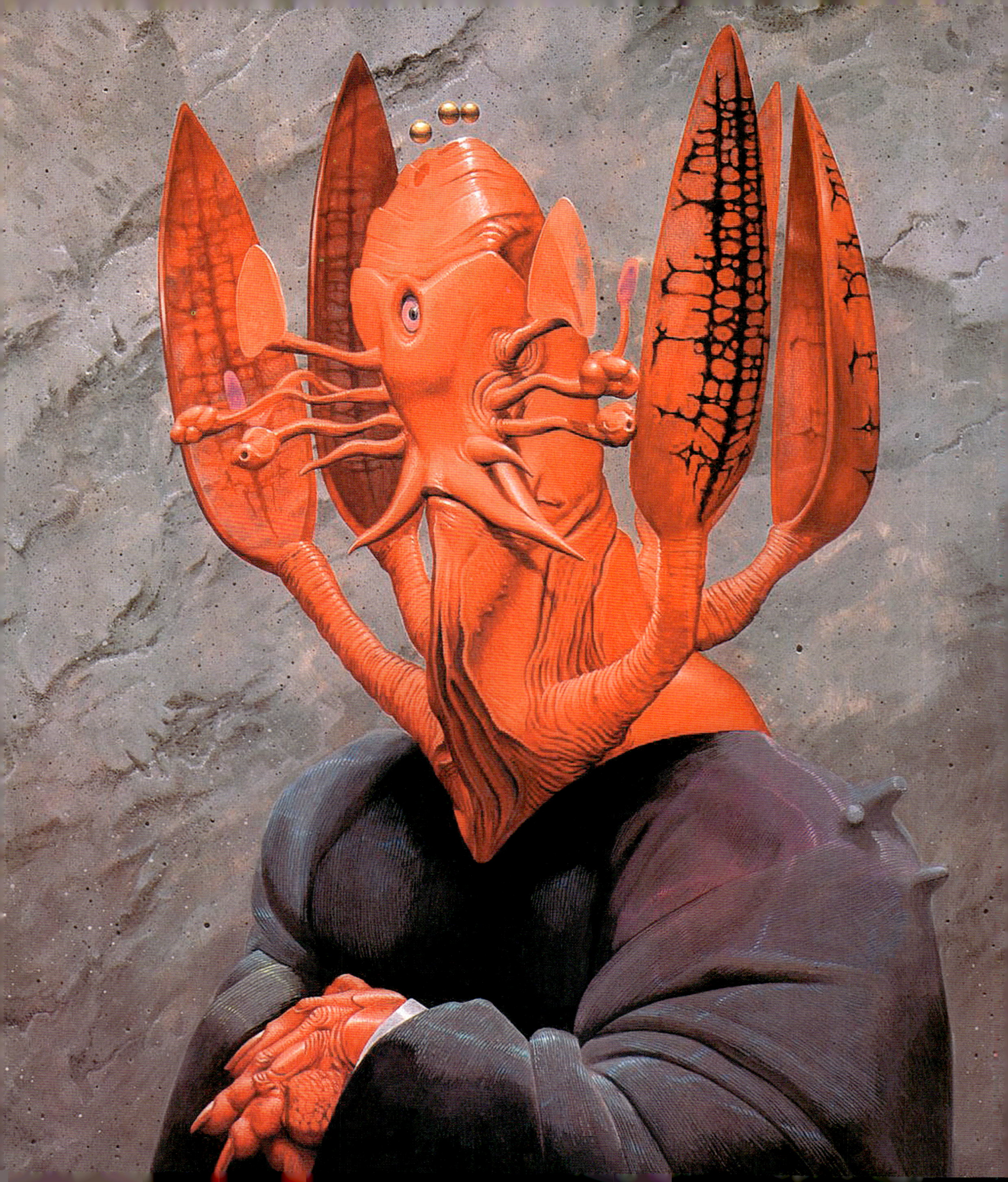

4 CONCEPT ART

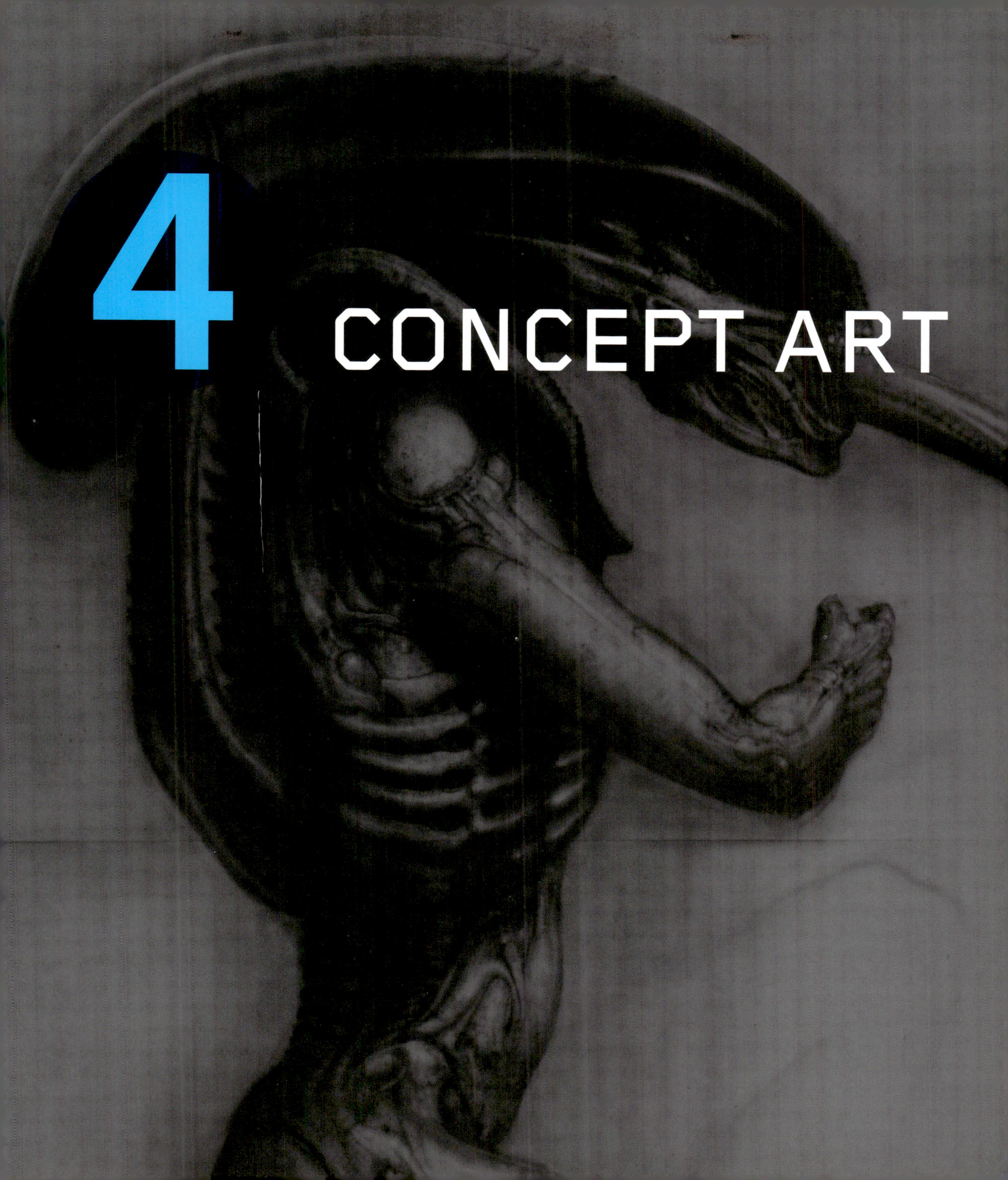

CHESLEY BONESTELL

Born on New Year's Day, Chesley Bonestell (1888–1987, pronounced Bonn-e-stell) is considered the Godfather of astronomical illustration. Bonestell's interest in astronomy took flight during a visit to the Mount Wilson Observatory in southern California, although he actually trained as an architect at Columbia University in New York City. He never completed his degree, however, dropping out in his third year, but this did not stop him from securing work as a renderer and designer for a number of top architects. His work included designing the art deco façade of the Chrysler Tower—including the iconic gargoyles—and drafting plans for San Francisco's Golden Gate Bridge.

The Depression saw his prospects collapse and he sought better fortunes in the UK, where he found work on the *London Illustrated News*, specializing, naturally, in architectural studies. However, the magazine also ran a series of astronomical illustrations during Bonestell's tenure, which rekindled his boyhood fascination. In the late '30s, he returned to the USA—specifically Hollywood. Here his skills were put to work on matte paintings, his credits including classics such as *Citizen Kane*, *The Hunchback of Notre Dame*, and *How Green Was My Valley*.

His time as a special effects artist proved formative for Bonestell, who combined his architectural skills with an understanding of perspective and lighting in setting up camera shots, and with miniature modeling. He took his new skill sets and applied them to his unique astronomical vision—depicting the planets of the Solar System from their satellites. The result was a series of paintings of a trip to Saturn that was seized upon by *Life* magazine, who, in 1944, paid Bonestell the princely sum of $30,000.

The stunning success of the series led to more magazine work, eventually resulting in a book. Published in 1949, and titled *The Conquest of Space*, the 58 collected paintings were hailed by Arthur C. Clarke as "...an outstanding example of cooperation between art and technology..." The impact on the imagination of the post-WWII generation cannot be overestimated. Countless astronomical luminaries—including Carl Sagan—numerous NASA pioneers, and far too many artists to mention cite *The Conquest of Space* as an influence.

The book became a bestseller and stimulated further movie work for Bonestell. He was hired to provide background and technical advice for several science fiction classics, including *Destination Moon*, *When Worlds Collide*, and 1953's *War of the Worlds*. *Destination Moon* saw Bonestell collaborate with writer Robert A. Heinlein in making the film as technically accurate as possible, even computing the correct phases of the Earth as seen from the Moon. The results of their efforts led to an Academy Award for the movie's special effects.

By now Bonestell's star was in the ascendant and he was invited to a Symposium on Spaceflight organized by the USAF. Present was Wernher von Braun, the inventor of Hitler's terror weapons, the V1 and V2 rockets, but now the driving force behind the USA's space program. Von Braun was deeply impressed by Bonestell's work and his vast knowledge of his subject, but found himself rebuked by the artist when he did some sketches of spaceships for Bonestell, "...only to have them returned to me with penetrating, detailed questions or blistering criticism of some inconsistency or oversight."

Between 1952 and 1954, the pair collaborated on a series of articles for *Colliers Magazine* titled *Man Will Conquer Space Soon*. They proved that the concepts needed to get humanity (particularly the USA) into space were not the realm of science ficion but entirely plausible in the 1950s. The articles lit a fire under the burgeoning US space program, supported by public enthusiasm and the emerging space race with the USSR.

Bonestell produced a 40-foot-long mural of the Moon's surface—seen by many as his crowning glory, and now residing in the National Air and Space Museum of the Smithsonian Institution in Washington, D.C.—as well as books, until his death. But his place in the annals of space exploration had been secured long before then.

▶
Bonestell didn't just depict planets and starships. This 1951 cover imagines a post-apocalyptic New York, flooded and ablaze.

▶▶
While the hardware may look a little dated today, Bonestell's attention to detail and cinematic lighting give covers like this one for *Galaxy* a real plausibility.

▶▶
A cover for *Fantasy and Science Fiction* not dissimilar to the picture that propelled Bonestell's career into the stratosphere: *Saturn As Seen from Titan*. This picture, however, has not stood up in the face of science's inexorable onward march: it is now known that Titan is enclosed in a gaseous atmosphere that would obscure the view of Saturn from Titan's surface.

▶▶
Another beautifully portrayed planet surface, this one rent by geological upheaval and irradiated by the nearby star.

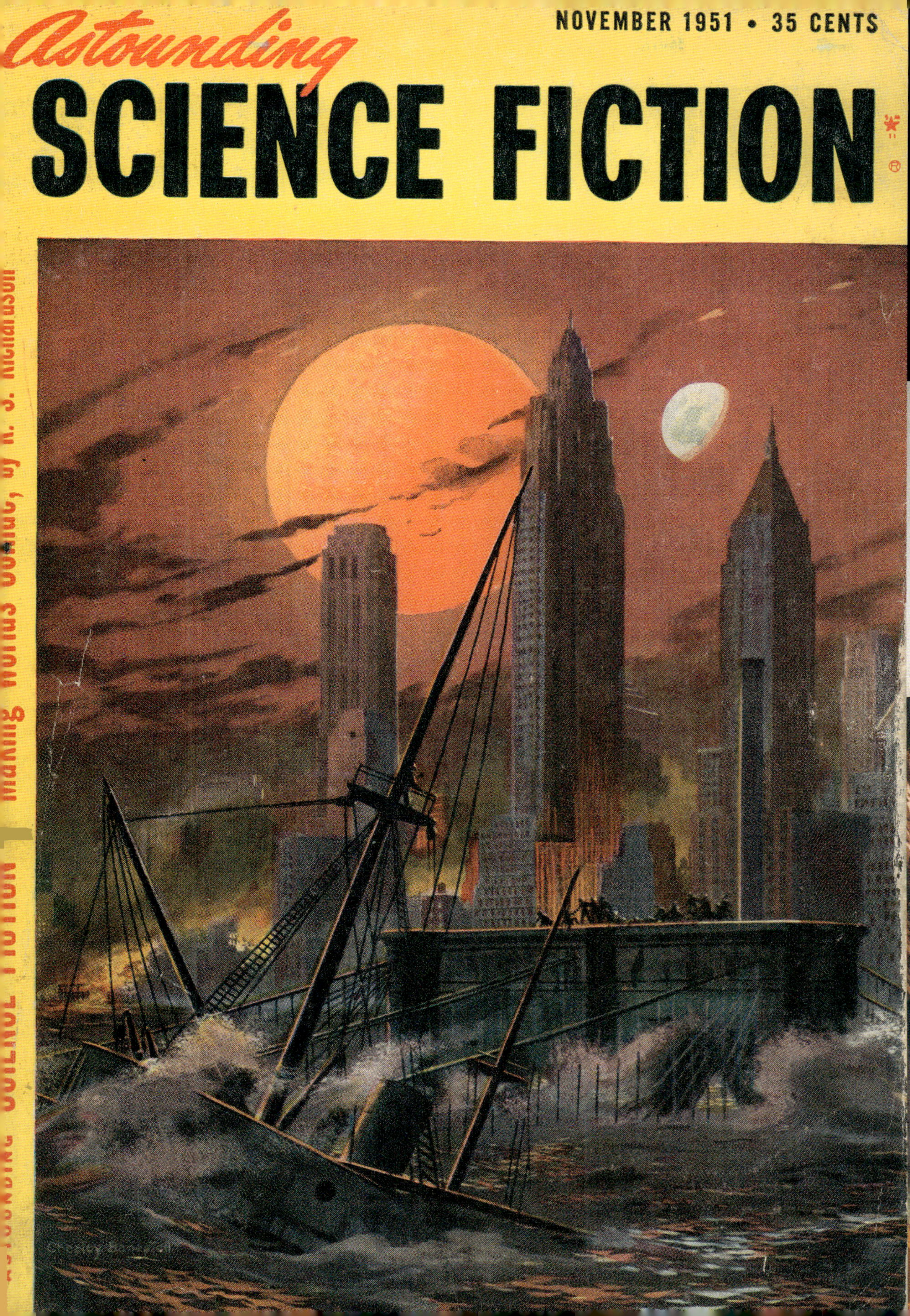

NOVEMBER 1951 • 35 CENTS
Astounding
SCIENCE FICTION

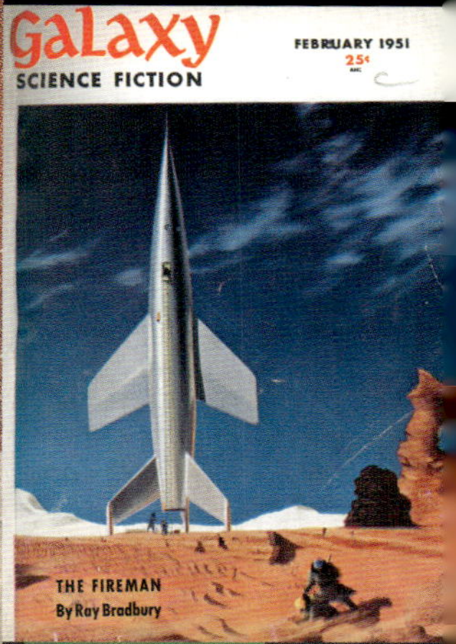

Galaxy
SCIENCE FICTION
FEBRUARY 1951
25¢
THE FIREMAN
By Ray Bradbury

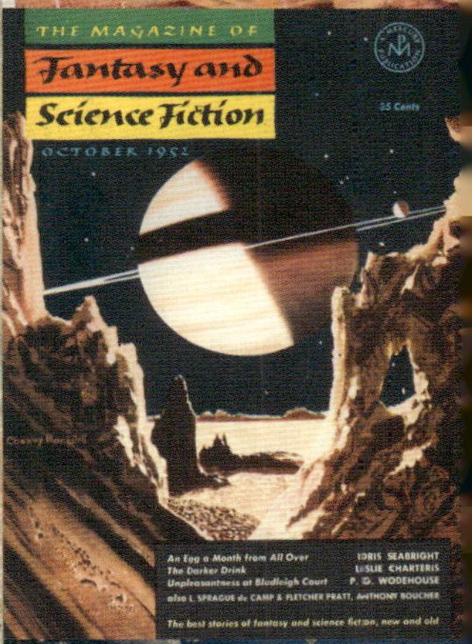

THE MAGAZINE OF
Fantasy and
Science Fiction
35 Cents
OCTOBER 1952
An Egg a Month from All Over IDRIS SEABRIGHT
The Darker Drink LESLIE CHARTERIS
Unpleasantness at Bludleigh Court P. G. WODEHOUSE
also L. SPRAGUE de CAMP & FLETCHER PRATT, ANTHONY BOUCHER
The best stories of fantasy and science fiction, new and old

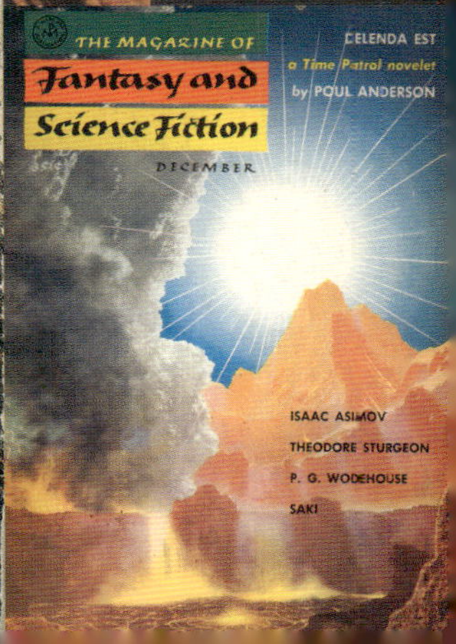

THE MAGAZINE OF
Fantasy and
Science Fiction
DECEMBER
DELENDA EST
a Time Patrol novelet
by POUL ANDERSON
ISAAC ASIMOV
THEODORE STURGEON
P. G. WODEHOUSE
SAKI

DAVID A. HARDY

David Hardy's introduction to astronomical illustration was a somewhat rushed affair. In 1954, as a mere 18-year-old, he was commissioned to produce eight black and white illustrations for a book by legendary UK astronomer Patrick Moore: *Suns, Myths, and Men*. He had just five days to create them before British national service—conscription—required him to join the Royal Air Force. The commission was all the more remarkable as Hardy had only painted his first piece of astronomical art four years previously, inspired by the work of Chesley Bonestell.

Since those early days, Hardy (1936-) has garnered numerous awards for artwork that spans the science fiction/hard science divide. Born in Bournville, Birmingham, in the UK, he honed his talents painting chocolate boxes for Cadbury's. By 1965 he had become a freelance illustrator, beginning a career that resulted in covers for dozens of books and magazines, both factual, such as *New Scientist*, *Focus*, and various astronomical publications, for which he also writes; and SF, including *Analog* and *Fantasy & Science Fiction*. 1972 saw the publication of *Challenge of the Stars*, which Hardy not only illustrated but co-wrote with Patrick Moore (the book was updated in 1978 as *New Challenge of the Stars*). A bestseller, it joined the select pantheon of book that influenced a new generation of up-and-coming astronomical artists.

By now, Hardy's work was receiving international recognition, and in 1979 he was nominated for the Hugo Award for Best Professional Artist. Two years later, another book followed: *Galactic Tours*, which as the name suggests is a "factitous" guidebook for the interstellar tourist. As a result of the book, travel company Thomas Cook approached Hardy about becoming a consultant on the future of tourism in space—long before Richard Branson had planned Virgin's conquest of the stars.

Hardy has written an SF novel, *Aurora: A Child of Two Worlds*; worked on the movie *The Neverending Story*, and on TV (*Cosmos, Horizon, The Sky at Night, Blake's Seven*); and produced record covers for—unsurprisingly—Holst's *The Planets* and for bands such as Hawkwind, the Moody Blues, and Pink Floyd.

In 2004, Hardy's long-standing partnership with Patrick Moore culminated in the award-winning *Futures*, in which the two explored the changing perceptions of space exploration since they first collaborated in the '50s, the '70s (the era of *Challenge of the Stars*), and into the 21st century. Artistically, Hardy has also embraced the growing digital trend that started in the approach to the new millennium. While still painting in acrylic and oil, he now uses Photoshop as a matter of course.

In March 2003, Hardy was paid perhaps the ultimate accolade an astronomical artist can receive: he had an asteroid (13329) named after him. Discovered in September 1998, it was christened Davidhardy=1998 SB32—high praise indeed!

◄▼
The NASA space probe Galileo depicted by Hardy as it burns up in the thick gaseous atmosphere of Jupiter, ending its 14-year mission on September 21, 2003. The painting is titled *Phoenix*, "because of its (deliberate) birdlike appearance," according to Hardy.

►
Artwork produced for *Nature* of the spacecraft Ulysses´ encounter with the tail of comet Hyakutake on May 1, 1996—the longest comet tail so far recorded.

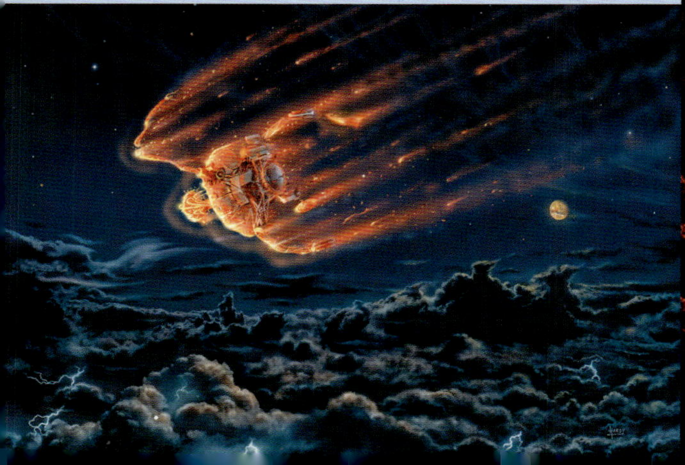

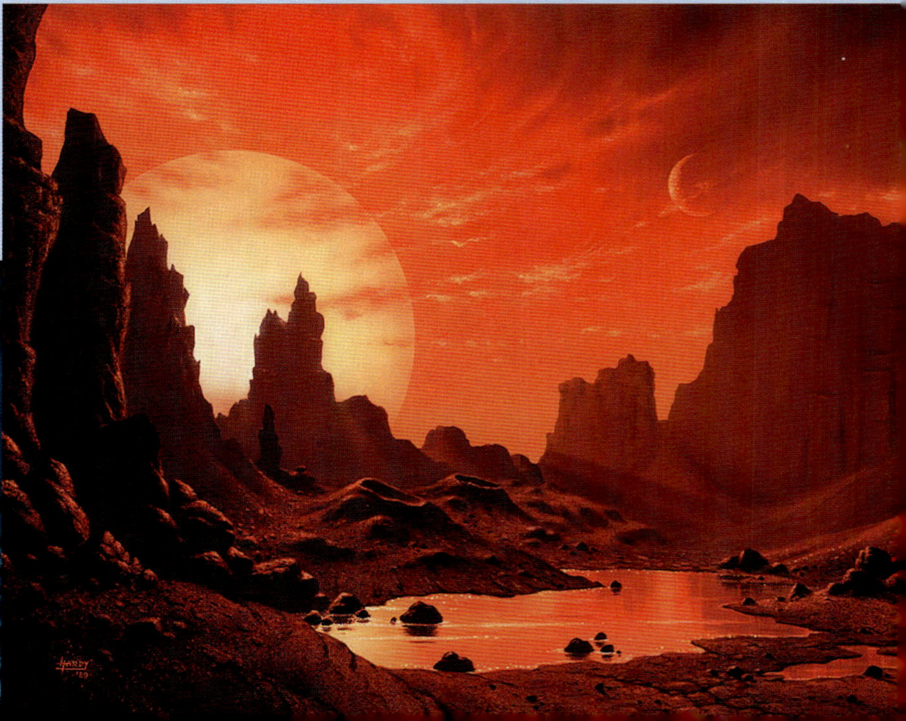

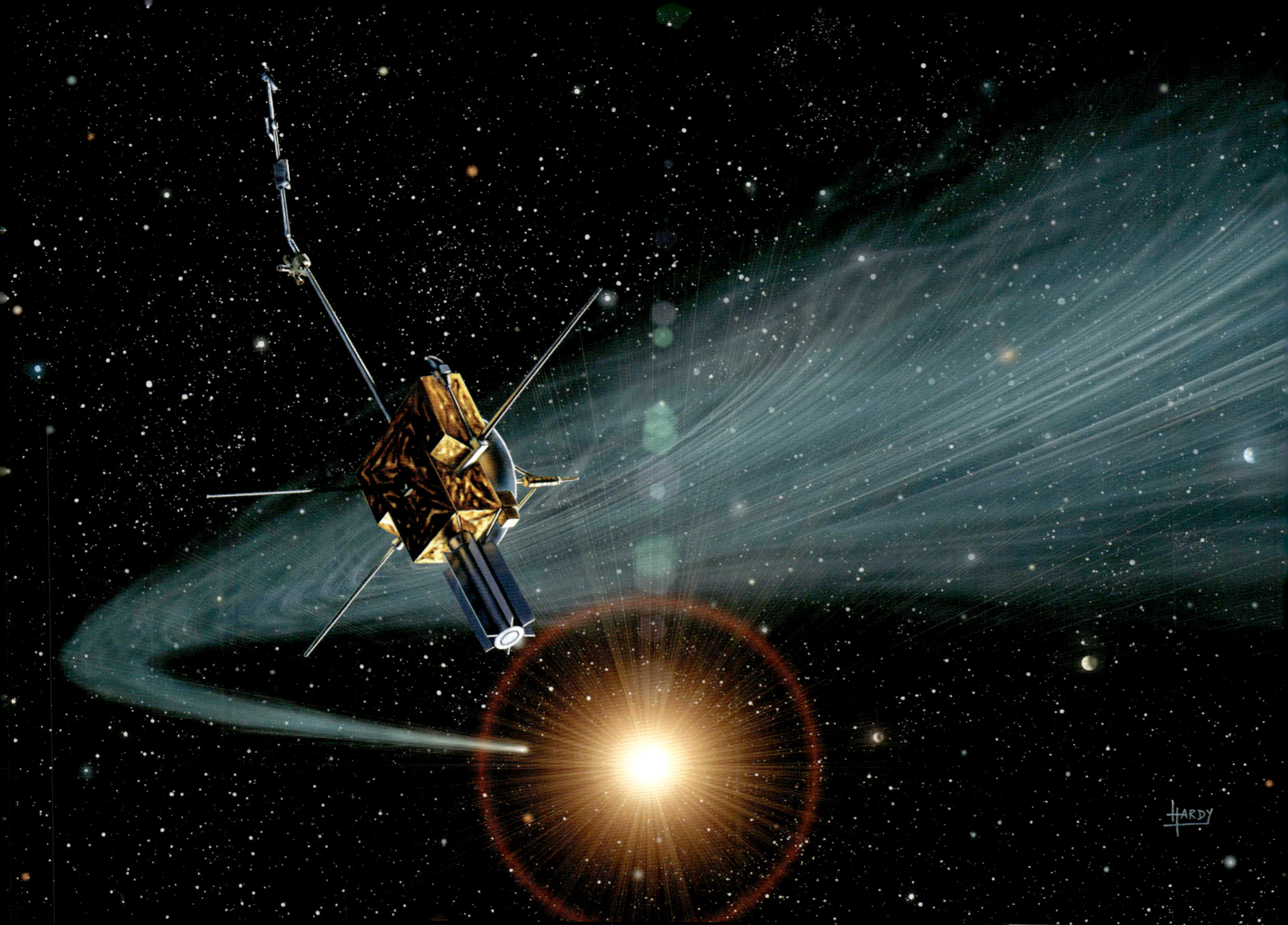

◀
Hardy, like his major influence, Chesley Bonestell, has a detailed understanding of his subject. This painting is of our Solar System's nearest neighbor, Proxima Centauri, a red dwarf star. In this artwork, Hardy hypothesized how a planet close to the star would be affected by the powerful gravitation forces Proxima would exert, which would lead to geological upheavals and a landscape of volcanic cones and lava flows.

▶
This Bonestell-esque image shows a gas giant orbiting the star HD70642, a sun in the southern constellation of Puppis very similar to our own. The presence of planets and moons are entirely hypothetical, but based on our understanding of planetary formation. It was produced for the Particle Physics and Astronomy Research Council.

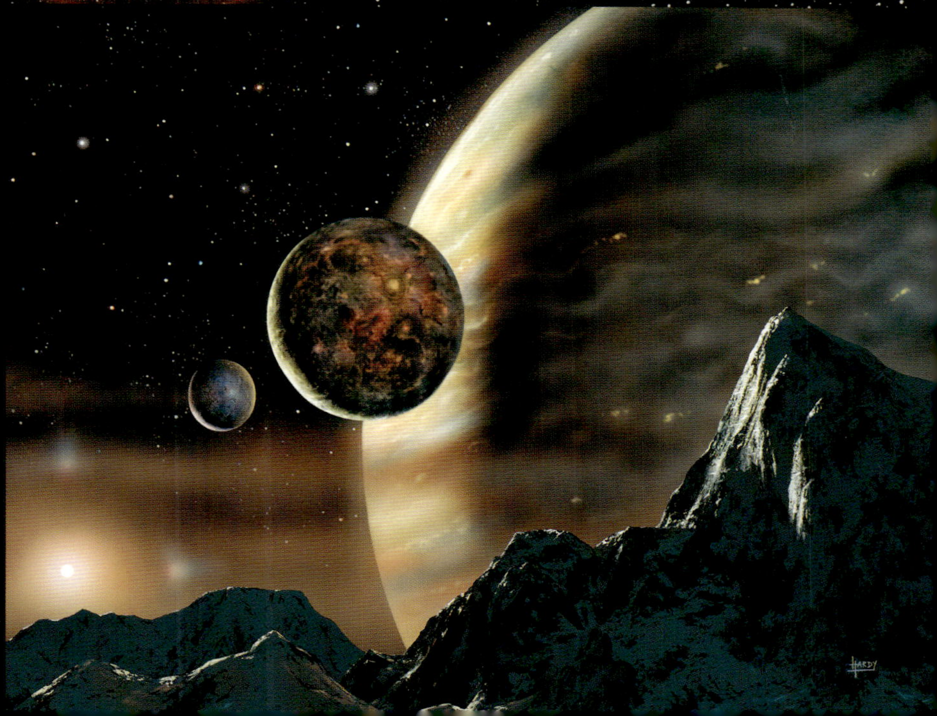

Now well over 40 years old, the *Star Trek* franchise, from the original series to J. J. Abrams' much anticipated feature, has left an indelible footprint across the wide expanses of pop culture.

But when Gene Roddenberry began creating his "totally new universe," as *Star Trek* producer Gene Coon called it, the question was where to start? Two artists, Pato Guzman and his assistant, Walter "Matt" Jefferies, were given the task of getting the ball rolling, balancing the extent of their imaginations with such practical necessities as technical limitations (in 1964, there were many), a plausibility that would allow the audience to willingly suspend its disbelief, and, of course, money.

Guzman busied himself with the interiors while ex-bomber pilot Jefferies set about applying his skills as an aeronautical designer in creating the U.S.S. Enterprise herself. Several months and hundreds of drawings, produced in concert with Roddenberry's stringent requirements, saw the ship's now world-famous shape slowly materialize.

Jefferies continued to devise other ships for the show, including Klingon battle cruisers that featured external engine nacelles like Federation vessels. Historically, this was not dissimilar to the Cold War arms race, with American and Russian hardware often bearing a certain resemblance to one another as one side seized upon a design innovation by the other.

Jefferies and his brother also had a hand in designing another series icon: the phaser—a very practical design that went against the more outlandish design philosophies prevalent in sci-fi at the time.

Many of the nuts and bolts items of the *Star Trek* universe were the brainchild of Wah Chang. Before joining the *Star Trek* production team, career highlights for Chang included designing the original 3D maquette Disney modeled the animated Pinocchio on; one of Elizabeth Taylor's headdresses for *Cleopatra*; and extensive work on classic sci-fi series *The Outer Limits*. For *Star Trek*, he got down to brass tacks, bringing to life the tricorder and communicator. He also designed the Gorn, one of the original series' more outlandish aliens—although, the dinosaurian head aside, it was still a man in a suit.

The original series also reflected 1960s cultural mores. While the worst excesses of the time were considered unsuitable for typical family viewing, the sexual revolution did show in *Trek*'s costume design, especially (and unsurprisingly) in those worn by the *Star Trek* women. With miniskirts all the rage, hemlines were high, and costume designer William Ware Theiss developed the "Theiss Titillation Theory." This stated that a costume's sexiness is directly proportional to how likely it looks like it will fall off—when in reality very little of significance is actually on show!

▶ **The Enterprise's bridge layout reflects Matt Jefferies' experiences in B-17s during WWII. Used to the "spit and bubblegum" approach to military design, he came up with a pilot's dream instead: a clean, modular look with everything at arm's length.**

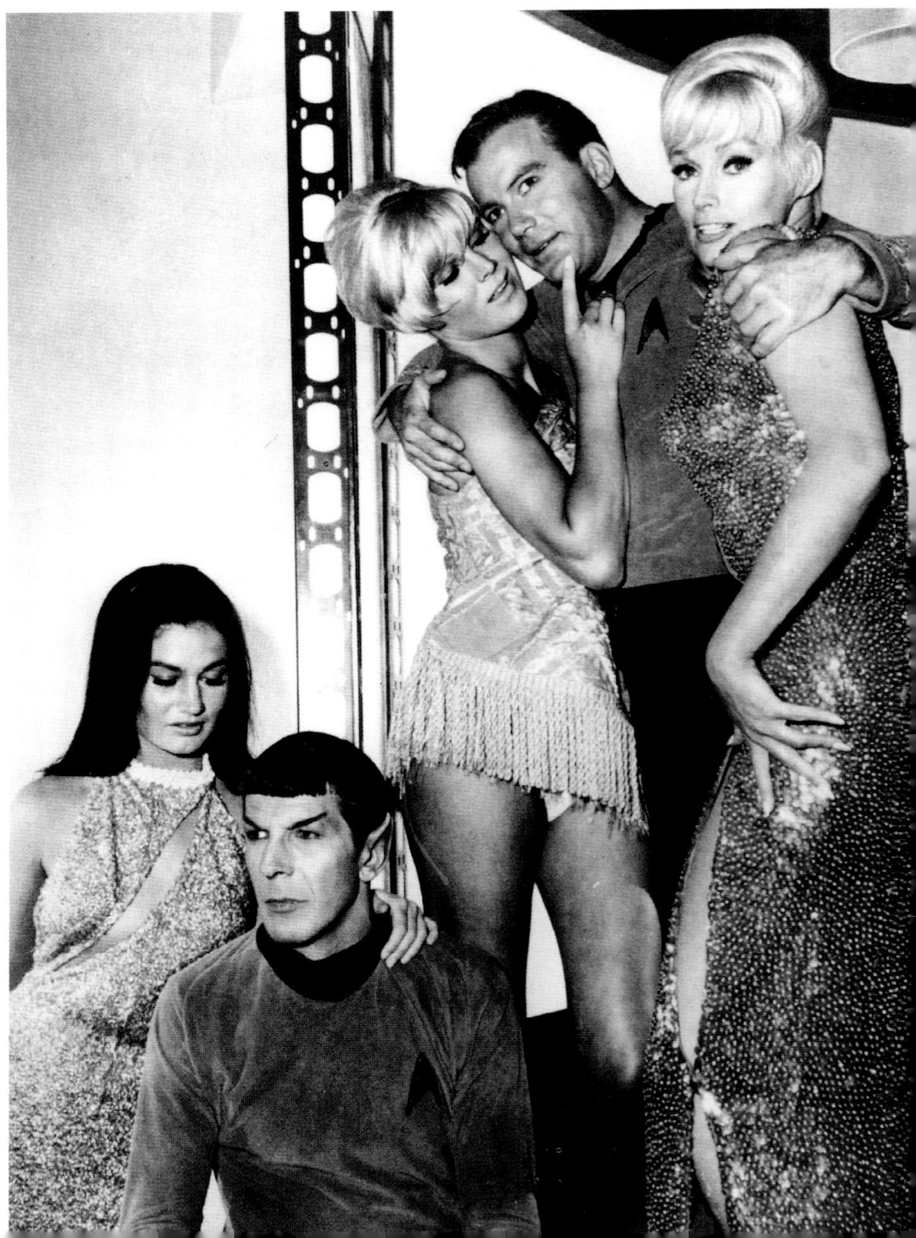

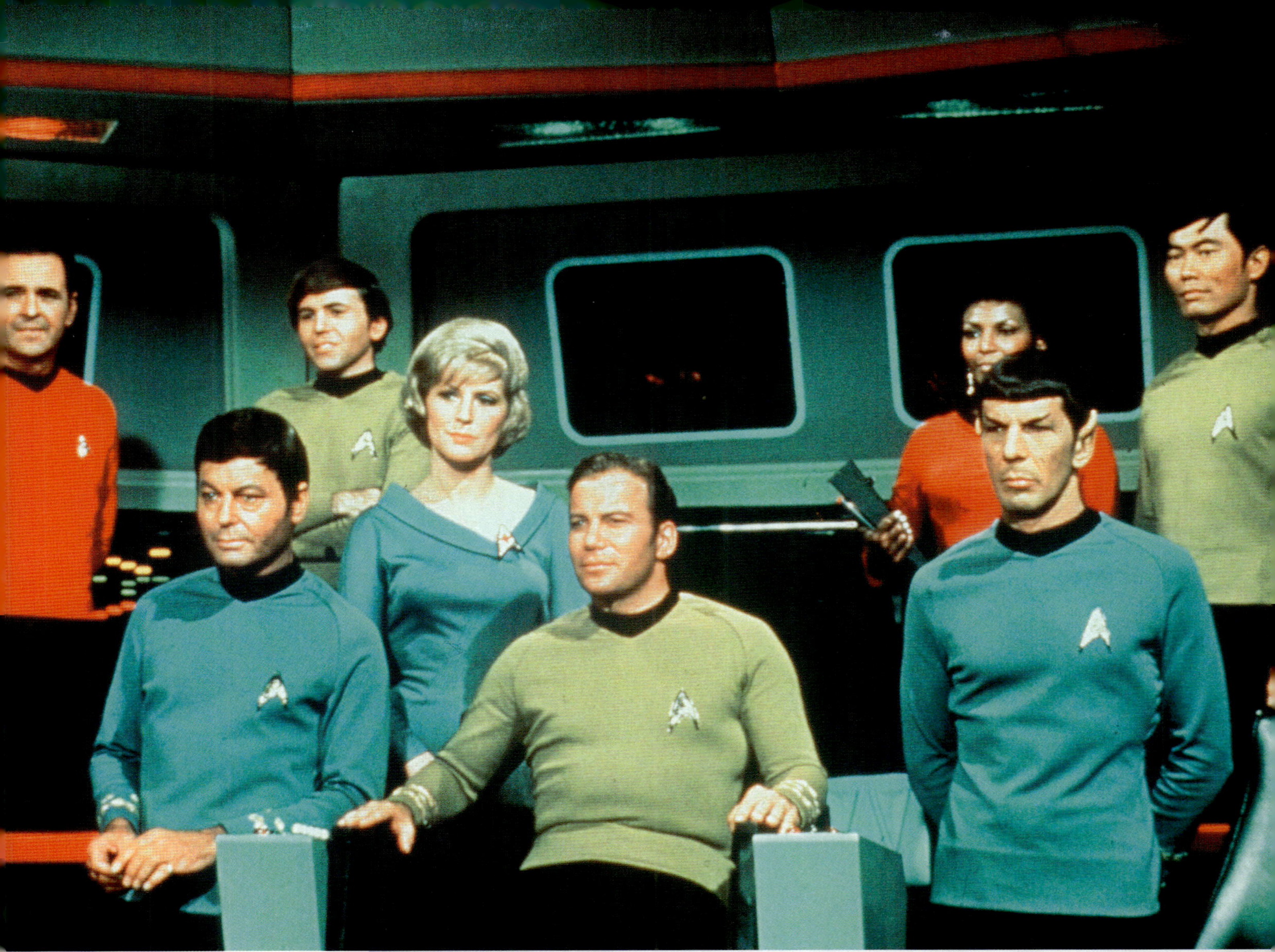

▶
External engine nacelles were early innovations in Matt Jefferies' concepts for the Enterprise, but the saucer section was initially a sphere. Four nacelles were superseded by two and the addition of the engineering hull, and various configurations toyed with until the final incarnation was sent to model builders to be rendered in 3D.

◀
A bevy of beauties sporting William Ware Theiss designs—with surprisingly little flesh on show…

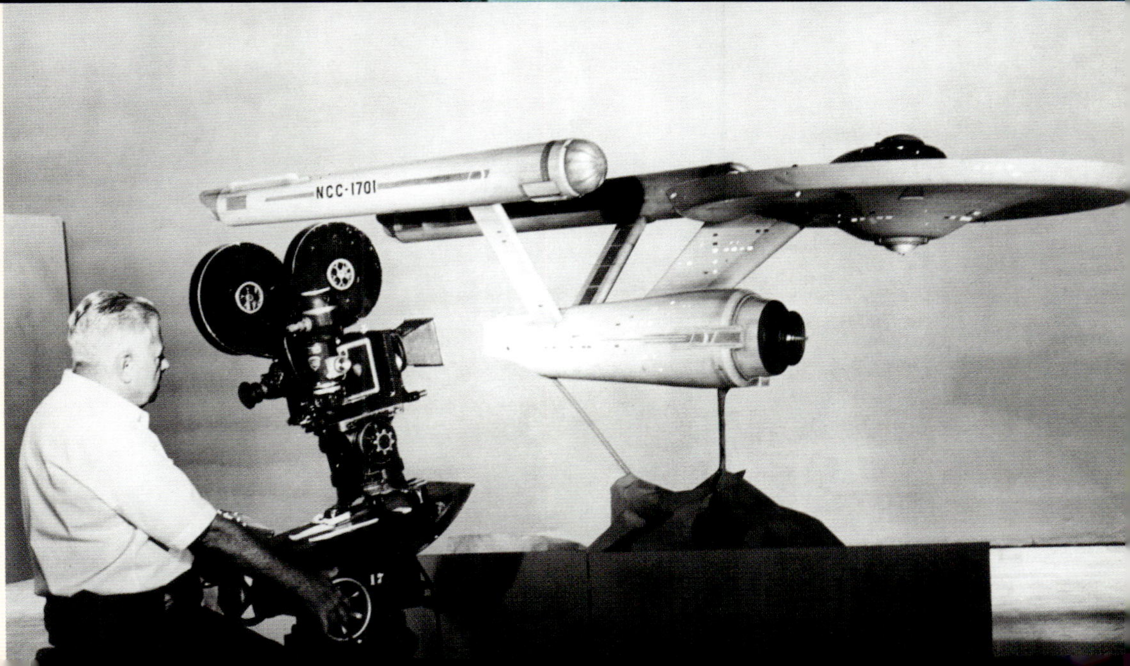

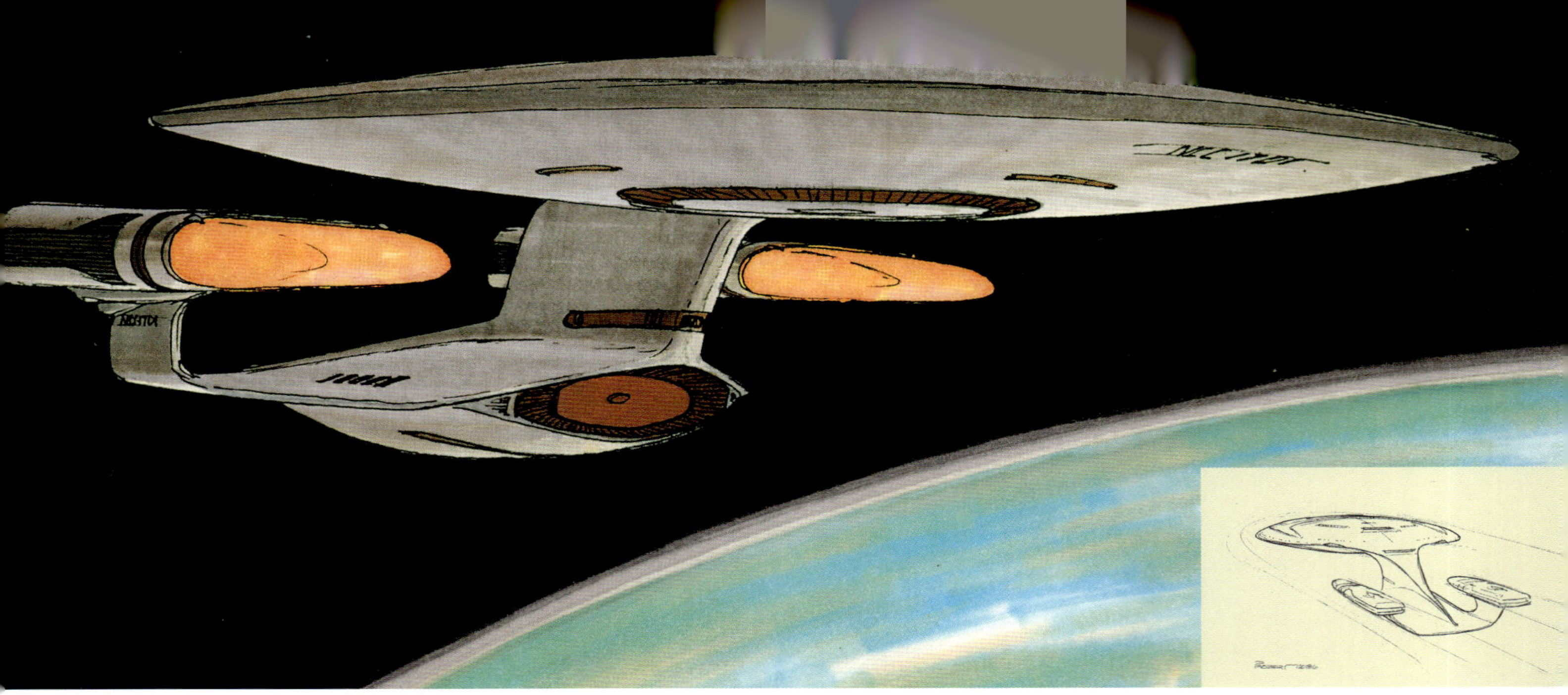

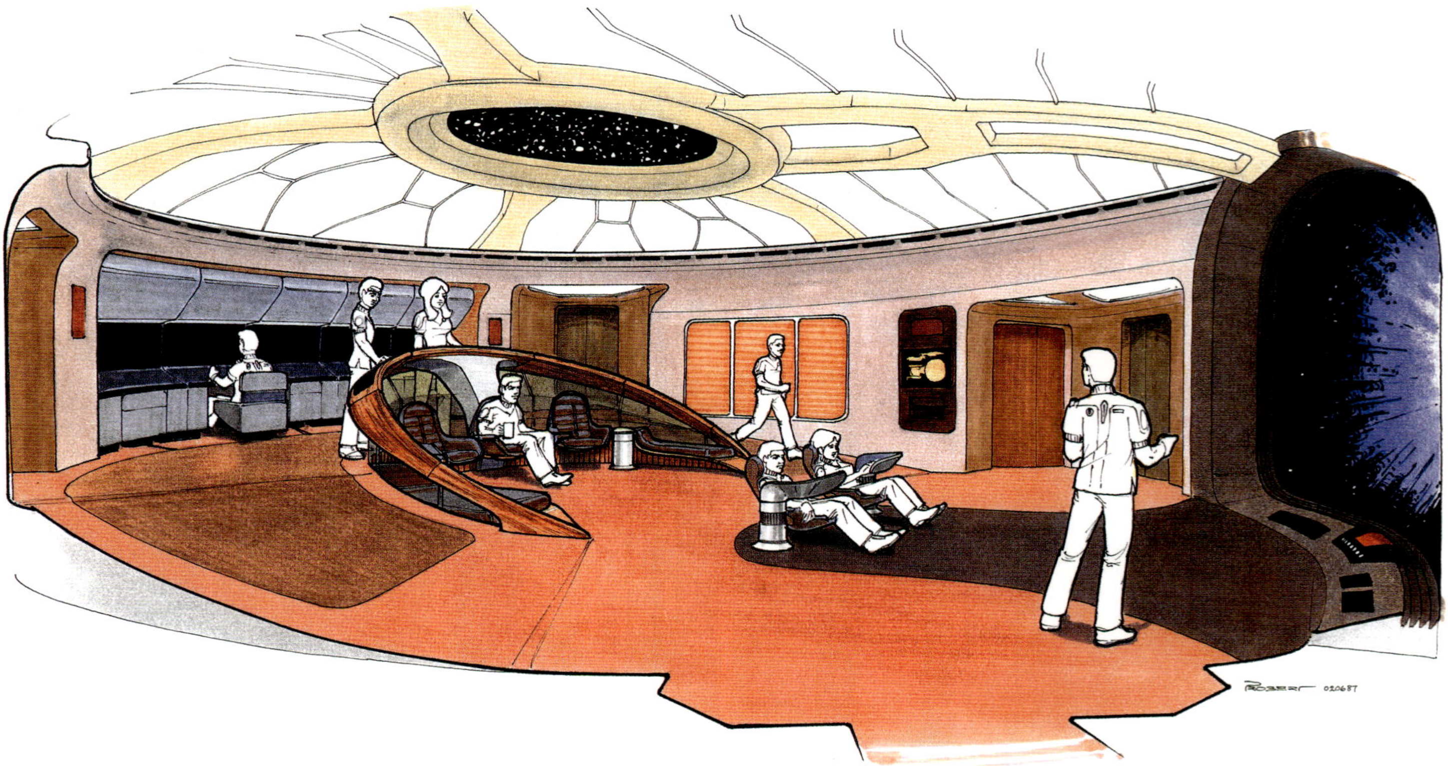

The continued cult and syndicated success of the original *Star Trek* encouraged Paramount to re-launch the series as *Star Trek: Phase II.* Some mighty names in production design were hired, including Ken Adam, the visual genius behind *Dr. Strangelove*'s war room and many a James Bond set; and Ralph McQuarrie, fresh from his success on *Star Wars.*

But it was Matt Jefferies who once again provided the backbone of the Enterprise's redesign—the cornerstone of the new show—flattening out the engine nacelles and adding distinctive torpedo launchers. The basic proportions of the redesign survived the cancellation of *Star Trek: Phase II* and became the basis for the Enterprise in *Star Trek: The Motion Picture*, which was finally released in 1979. Jefferies was joined by Andrew Probert and Richard Taylor, both fans of the original show. Love of the subject matter made it easy for them to "evolve" the look and technology of *Star Trek* while remaining true to the philosophy behind the show. As such, many items display a clear lineage back to "classic" *Trek.*

By *Star Trek II: The Wrath of Kahn*, a major revamp in design was called for. While the Enterprise remained on an even keel—so to speak—virtually every other aspect was reworked, following concerns that the interiors looked like a hotel lobby. As production designer Joe Jennings remarked, "Visually, it had no heart. It was stiff." Instead, the sets were given a more workmanlike, almost military, feel, more starkly lit, which set the tone for the series of movies that followed.

Meanwhile, back on television, stirrings were afoot. 1986 finally saw the announcement of *Star Trek: The Next Generation*, as Gene Roddenberry assembled a team of veteran designers from the previous series and the movies, starting with Andrew Probert. Both inside and out, the Enterprise was given a complete overhaul. Out went the utilitarian, militaristic design philosophy; instead the new bridge looked more like a cruise ship, with comfy sofas, wood paneling, carpets, and curved lines—much more in line with deep space exploration than a warship.

Other new additions included the rugose-headed Klingon developed for *The Motion Picture*; and a new threat to the Federation—perhaps its greatest and certainly one of its most interesting, philosophically. The Borg blended the worst aspects of social insects with a race of terminators who cannot be reasoned with and will not stop until everyone and everything is assimilated.

The Next Generation's success galvanized Paramount into gambling on a new spin-off series—*Deep Space 9.* Devised commercially as a possible replacement for *Next Generation*, it soon took on a life of its own. A variety of new races, cultures, and vessels—the U.S.S. Defiant, the Dominion, the Bajorans—gave the design team a whole host of new directions to follow, while, on the station itself, a more down-to-earth approach was taken; the uniforms of Starfleet became the workers' overall—more engineer than fleet officer.

Finally—leaving aside the "retcon" series, *Star Trek: Enterprise*—the TV pantheon was completed with *Star Trek: Voyager*, which ran with the visual and technical success of the previous shows, but took them to the far-flung Delta Quadrant. The basics laid down by Matt Jefferies more than 40 years back were still the blueprint for the new vessel, as epitomized by the bridge: wall screen before the helm and the captain; work stations arranged around the "big chair." If nothing else, it proved that the more things change, the more they stay the same...

◄ ◄▼
The design of the new Enterprise for *The Next Generation* was more quirk of fate than a product of protracted development. While designer Andrew Probert was working on Enterprise bridge designs, he was also imagining, through sketches, what the new starship might look like. When writer David Gerrold showed the design to Gene Roddenberry, he signed it off immediately. With very few refinements, the new ship was built.

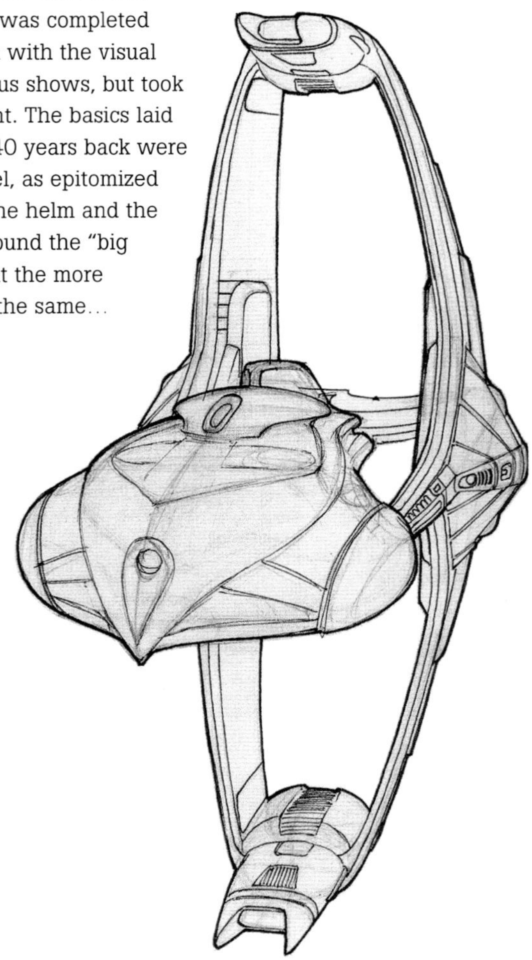

►
A radical redesign of the Romulan Bird of Prey by Andrew Probert—a valiant attempt at opening up the fairly bog-standard design of *Star Trek*'s ships. Probert's "tall" design—seen here—was later rotated 90 degrees to the far-more-familiar final "wide," or landscape, version.

SYD MEAD

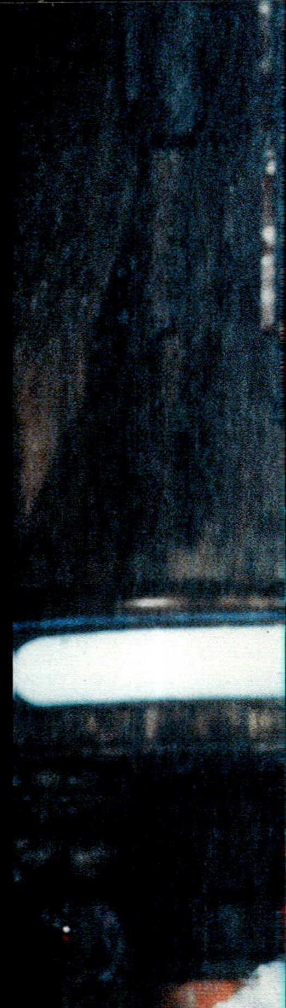

In 1982, Syd Mead was credited as the "Visual Futurist" on *Blade Runner*. That remains a startlingly accurate description of his work.

Born in St. Paul, Minnesota, Mead (1933-) was employed from 1959 as an industrial designer for the Ford Motor Company, visualizing future car concepts. His clean, beautiful style—combined with his ability to make even the most grandiose science concepts seem mundane and pedestrian, and therefore plausible—soon brought him to the attention of filmmakers.

His earliest work remains his most significant and influential, especially 1982's *Blade Runner*. Director Ridley Scott initially employed Mead to design vehicles for the movie. Not content with mere design, Mead began giving them context, setting them in his vision of Scott's chaotic cityscape. The film's Los Angeles metropolis would not be shining towers and dreaming spires; it was to be, in Scott's words, "…rich, colorful, noisy, gritty, full of textures, and teeming with life… This is a tangible future, not too exotic to be believed."

Mead's influence soon extended beyond cars, as he became involved in not just expanding Scott's concept of the city as a whole, but with the minutiae—the nuts and bolts that held 2019 LA together. From guns to tea-makers to orgasmatrons, Mead did it all. He also influenced the simmering multiculturalism of the film, folding in Oriental graphics as a visual flourish "…without being as distracting as English language signs would be for an American audience. This gives you the visual crowd and the add-on visual jumble without too much distraction."

While *Blade Runner* was not a big commercial success, stylistically it joined the select band of movies that redefined and revolutionized the approach to science fiction filmmaking, remaining hugely influential 25 years on. *Blade Runner* was just the first of a string of other movie commissions, notably *Tron*, another film where his pioneering designs would exert a powerful influence, and *Star Trek: The Motion Picture*. He continues to work on films, as well as video game design.

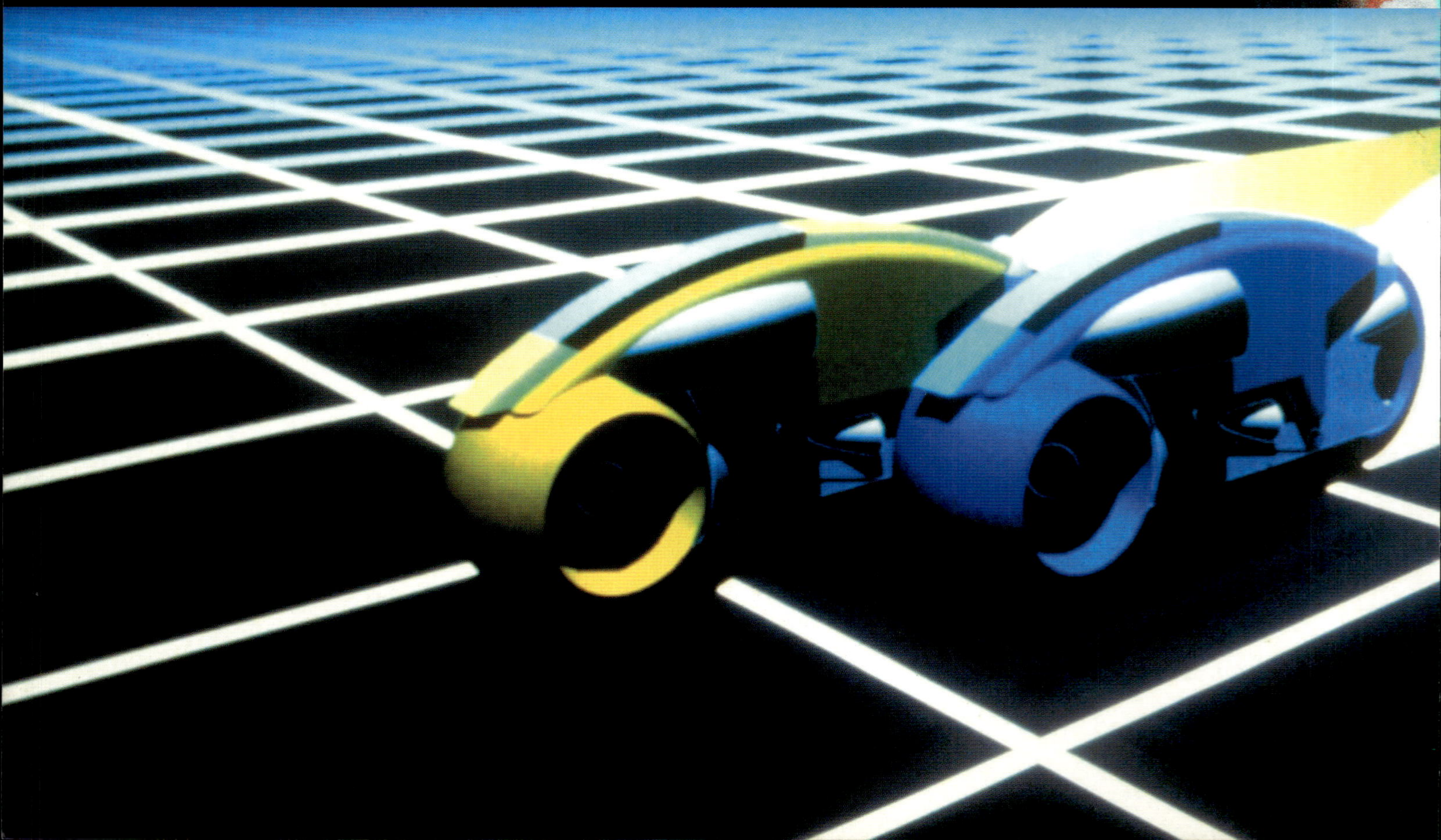

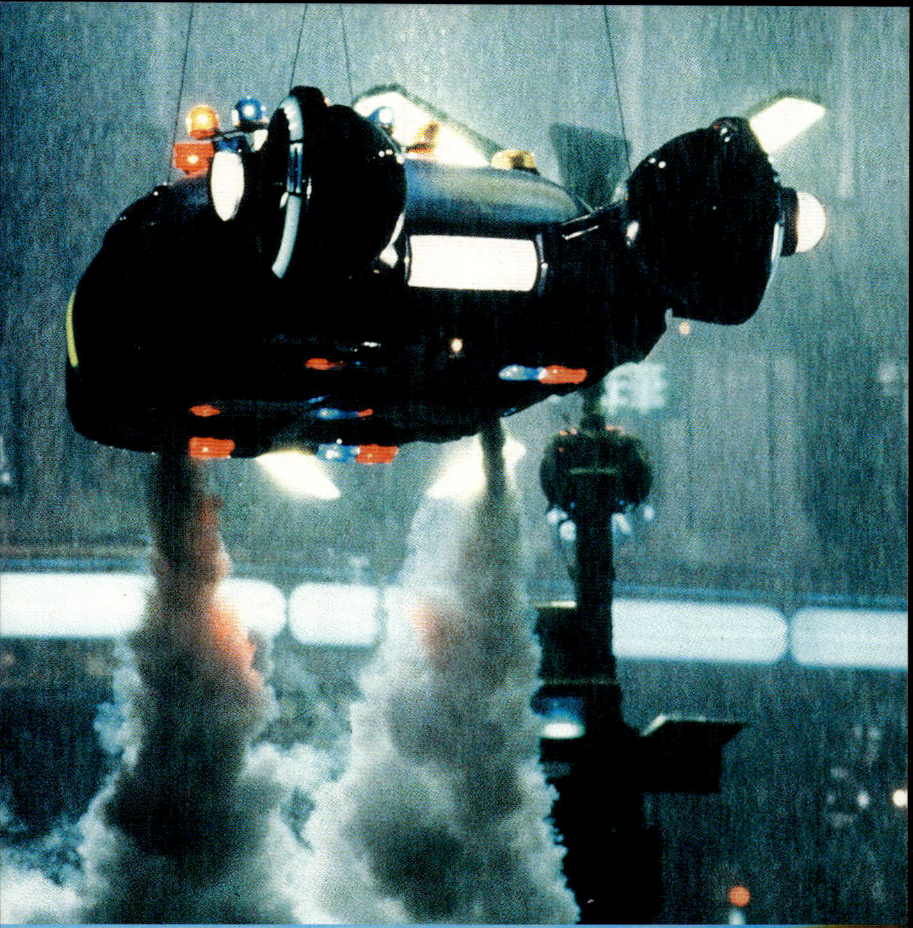

◀
A typically Meadian design was *Blade Runner*'s Spinner, a flying car featured most prominently as a police cruiser, but also, according to the film's philosophy, flown by the rich so they could keep away from the darker, danker depths of LA—high society indeed. According to Mead, "it had to be a self-contained, car-sized thing... We wanted a sort of clean shape that could roll along the ground on wheels and blend with traffic, but we also wanted a shape that looked like it would do what it was supposed to—which is fly." Mead envisaged a craft built around an engine layout known as an aerodyne. This was the same revolutionary configuration used by the Harrier VSTOL (Vertical/Short-Take Off and Landing) fighter aircraft—the "Jump Jet." Mead developed the Spinner's actual chassis configuration so that the shape and even the wheels could be used to deflect engine thrust and control vertical and horizontal motion. It was, according to Mead, "an industrial design approach to the problem."

▼
For the hardware in *Blade Runner*, Ridley Scott "...wanted things to look like they had to be jacked up a little bit to work at all." This rough-and-ready, spit-and-sawdust approach was easily transposed to Mead's work on *Aliens*, where he designed interiors and various ships and vehicles. His practical design philosophies are very much in evidence.

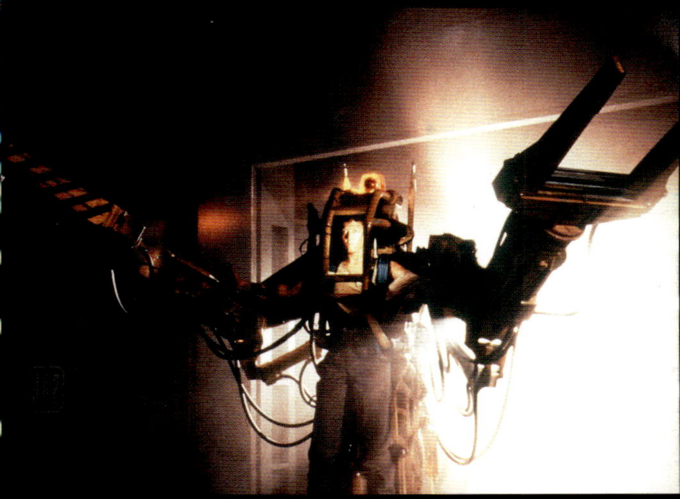

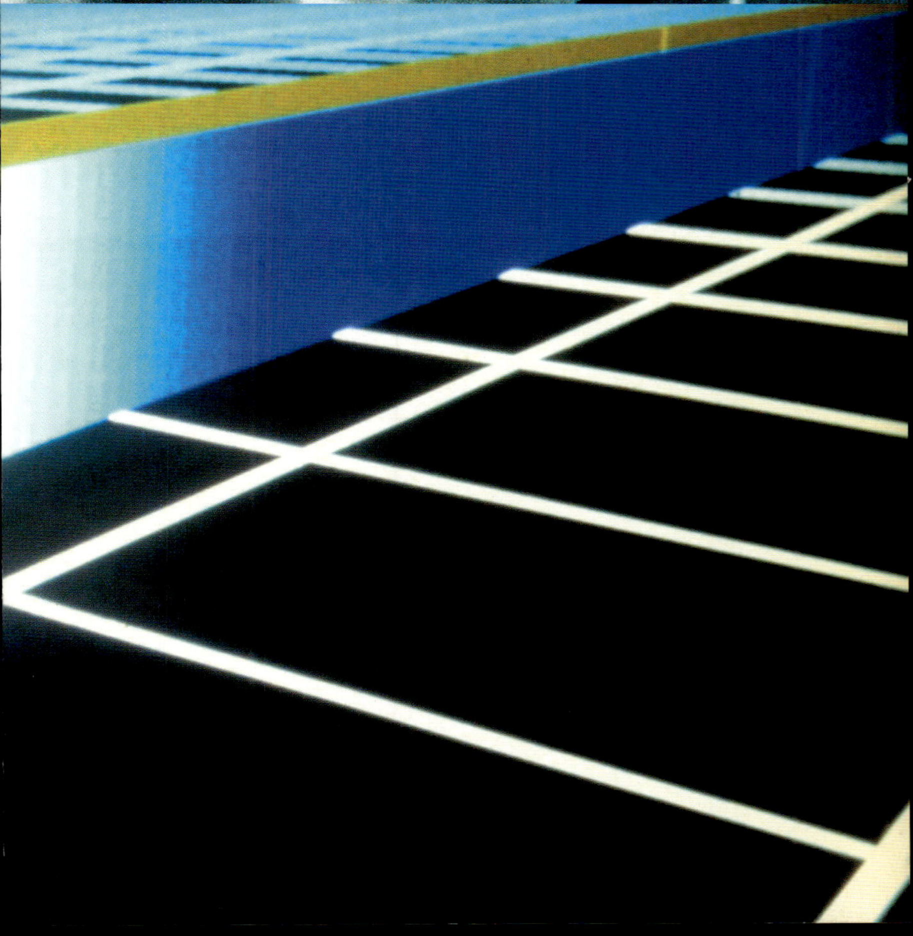

◀
The Light Cycle from the 1982 movie, *Tron*, remains one of Mead's most elegant and popular designs. Its clean, modular shape is unencumbered by the '80s computer technology that now seems downright antiquated. While Mead was involved with the production design of the entire movie, it is the Light Cycle that has become something of a pop culture icon.

H. R. GIGER

It could be said that H. R. Giger (1940-) is the Hieronymus Bosch of science fiction art, engendering the same uniquely nightmarish qualities in his provocative and deeply disturbing work.

Born in Switzerland, Hansruedi Giger's path to the dark side began with the gift of a human skull from his father, a pharmacist. Giger's nascent fascination with the strange and the unsettling was fed by his inflluences: Salvador Dalí, Ernst Fuchs, Jean Cocteau, Edgar Allan Poe, H. P. Lovecraft, and his mother, Melly, who actively encouraged his interests, even if she never understood them. However, the young artist's most profound inspiration came from within, from the night terrors he suffered: "They were horrifying but I found that when I made drawings of them, the dreams went away. I felt much better. It was a sort of self-psychiatry."

While studying architecture and industrial design at the School of Applied Arts in Zurich, Giger began drawing creatively, starting with inks before graduating to oil paints. By 1966, he was working as an interior designer, but, two years later, he became a full-time artist and occasional filmmaker, his first exhibition showing a year later.

The '70s introduced Giger to the airbrush; the rest, as they say, is history. He became an early exponent of the tool as a method for creating fine art. Strongly anatomical, psychosexual, even fetishistic, his pictures meld the beauty of the human form with slick, liquid mercury, metal constructs. The term "biomechanical"—the fusion of the organic and the artificial into a cybernetic organism—was made for Giger. His work has a jarring effect. As Harlan Ellison observed: "The man is trying to unnerve us. And that, in and of itself, is a noble, worthy artistic endeavor."

Giger himself interprets his work differently: "I always have two elements in my paintings—the horrible things and the nice things. I mean, I like elegance, I like art nouveau; a stretched line or a curve. These things are very much in the foreground of my work."

Controversy has naturally followed Giger. A piece he painted in 1973, *Work 219: Landscape XX* (unoficially known as "Penis Landscape") was used as an insert poster in the Dead Kennedys' 1985 album, *Frankenchrist*. An obscenity lawsuit was filed against lead singer Jello Biafra that almost bankrupted their record label, Tentacle Records. Blondie's Debbie Harry experienced similar problems with Giger's cover for her solo album *Koo Koo*, released in 1981, which depicted her face being skewered. As she commented, "We knew the cover would cause reaction, but maybe we were overconfident, even naïve, to believe it would simply be taken as art."

Giger's most influential work remains his designs for Ridley Scott's 1978 film, *Alien*. Scott's attention to detail in creating a plausible working atmosphere aboard a utilitarian spacecraft is outshone by Giger's designs for the Alien, its lifecycle, and the planet and craft in which it's found. As Scott noted, "The world had simply never seen anything like that before." Giger was intimately involved in the genesis of the film. Dan O'Bannon, *Alien's* screenwriter, initially asked for Giger's help in pitching the project to the studios; Giger produced three paintings that proved intstrumental in getting the movie made. Once production had commenced, Giger used "everyday" objects—wire, piping, tools, engine parts, and even bones—to create what in the end is a paradox: a style utterly unrecognizable as human. The same biomechanical logic was applied as much to the planet as to the Alien itself, resulting in a place of devastatingly desolate beauty. For his work, Giger rightly won an Academy Award, and a place in cinema history.

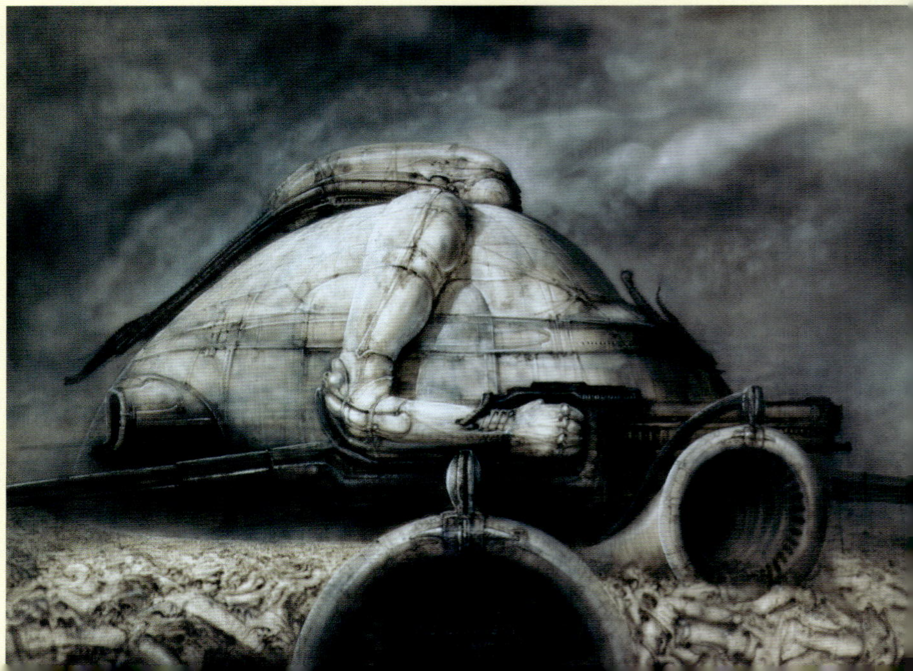

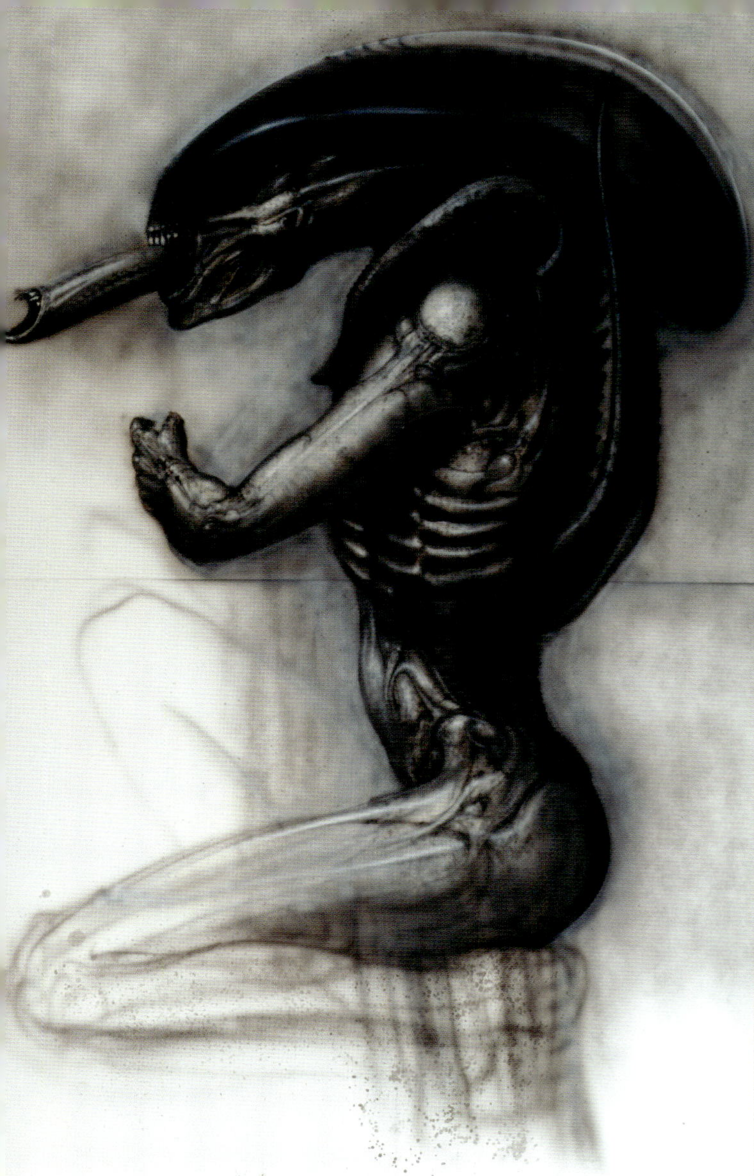

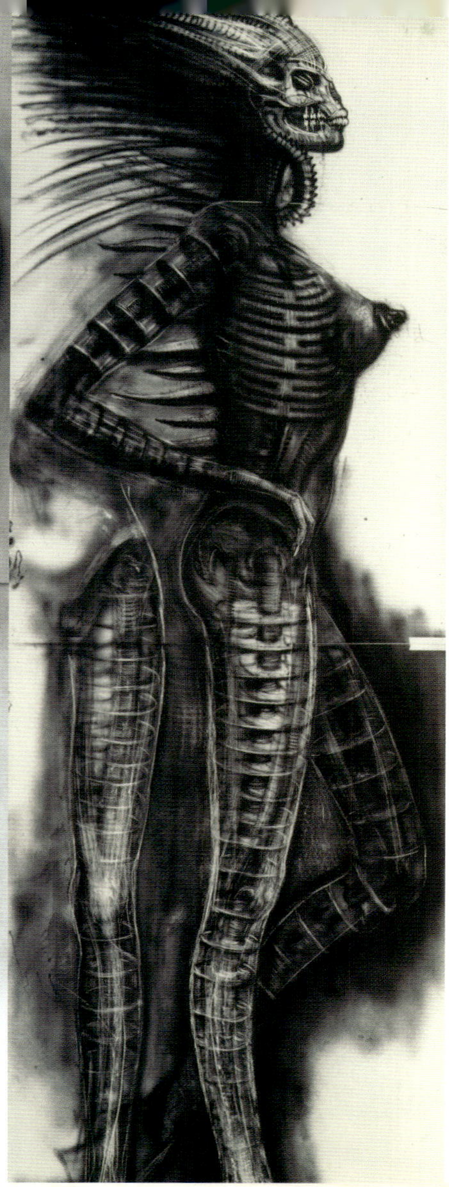

◀◀
Seeing Giger's artwork for the first time was an inspirational moment for director Ridley Scott, galvanizing his interest in *Alien*: "I realized we had the ability to create a monster that would be superior to most of those from the past."

◀ ▼
In 1994, Giger's *Alien* concepts further evolved into the alluring yet disturbing elegance of Sil, the vivacious alien of *Species*. Giger provided designs but was also on hand to render the creature in three dimensions. Giger retains ownership of nearly a third of his creations, including almost all of those produced for movies; this made possible the opening of the Museum H. R. Giger in Gruyeres, Switzerland, in 1998, which continues to attract 80,000 visitors a year.

◀
Giger was one of a cadre of artists working on production design for an abortive version of Frank Herbert's *Dune*, to be directed by Alejandro Jodorowsky. It was there that Giger first met Dan O'Bannon, future screenwriter of *Alien*; many of the artists on this un-filmed *Dune*, including Chris Foss and Moebius, would also work with Giger on *Alien*.

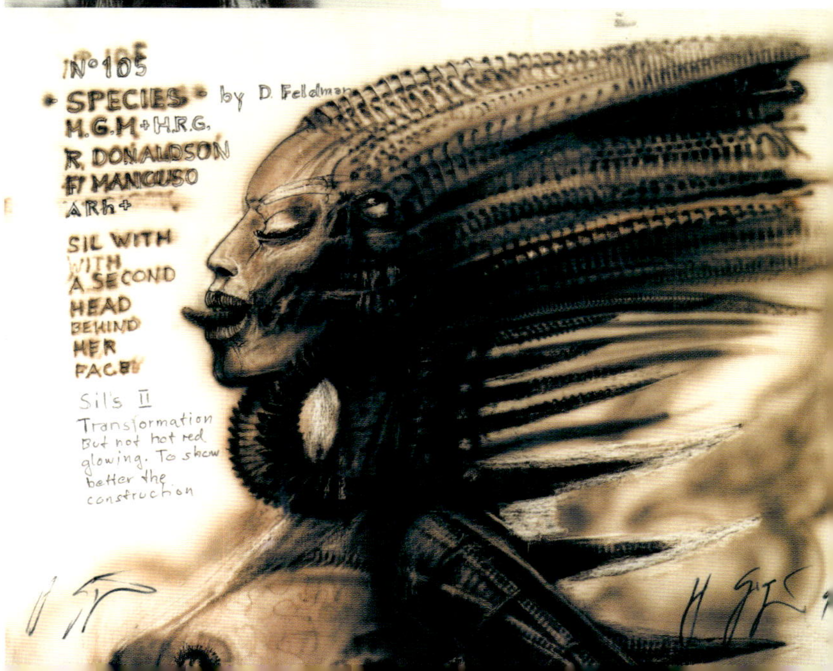

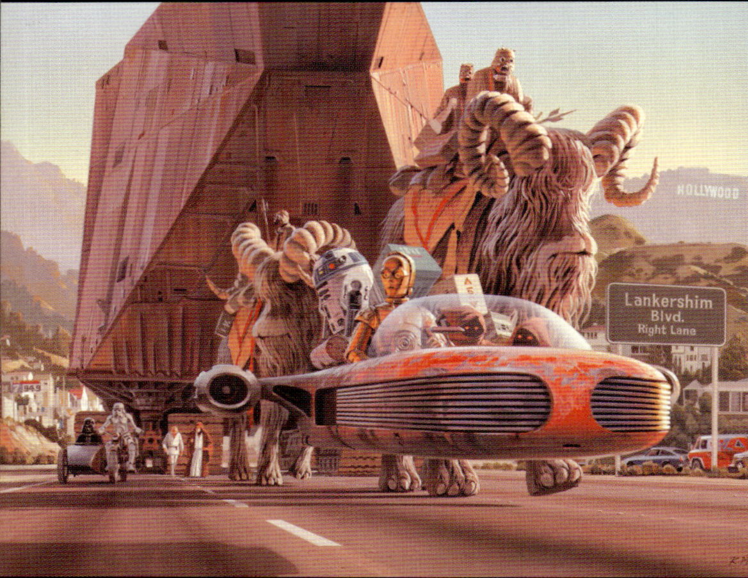

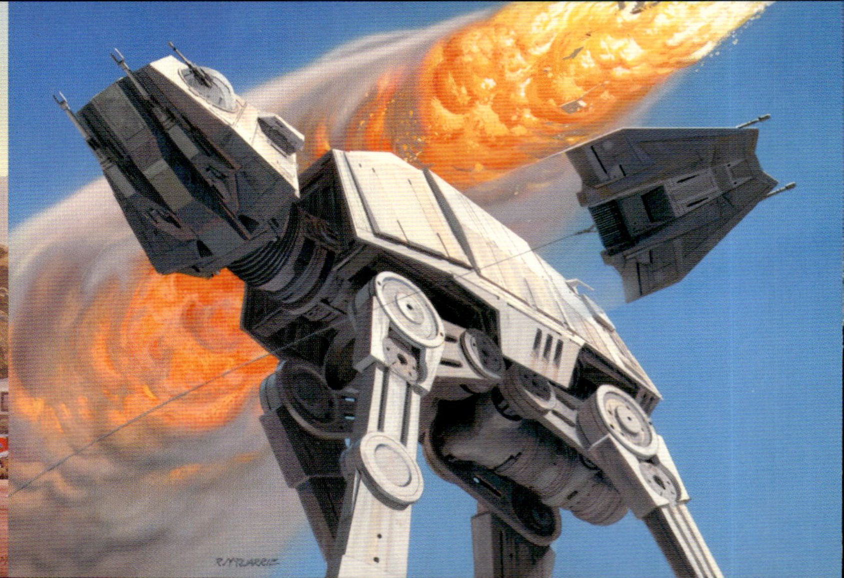

If it's said that George Lucas was the father of the *Star Wars* universe, it could equally be said that artist Ralph McQuarrie (1929-) was the midwife that brought it into the world.

Born in Gary, Indiana, to parents who were both artists, McQuarrie's own talents were obvious from an early age. Upon graduating, he went to work for the Boeing Company in Seattle, only to be drafted and sent to fight in Korea, where he sustained a head injury. McQuarrie returned to Boeing, but a freelance career as a commercial illustrator beckoned.

As luck would have it, one of his clients was NASA, for whom he put his talents to work designing realistic ships and hardware. So he was perfectly placed when, in 1974, he was introduced to George Lucas and *Star Wars* producer Gary Kurtz. The duo was in something of a bind. They had been unable to drum up studio interest in their nascent space opera—the execs just didn't get it, and it looked like the whole project would have to be abandoned.

McQuarrie was a given a script and asked to produce four or five paintings. When he later met with Lucas, he'd also sketched two of the most iconic members of Lucas' imaginary universe: R2-D2 and Darth Vader.

McQuarrie completed the five paintings, which were then shown by Lucas to 20th Century Fox. The concepts did the trick and money was released for Lucas to begin work on *Star Wars: A New Hope*. McQuarrie was the first artist to be hired on a film he believed would merely do OK; sci-fi movies were not, after all, blockbusters.

McQuarrie also began matte paintings for the production. This particular discipline, virtually as old as cinema itself, was an ideal area for McQuarrie and Lucas' growing stable of other artists to exercise their skills. Painting on glass, they used acrylic and oils. The former, while fast drying and flexible, had a tendency to dry to a different hue to the wet color. As color balance is vital in matte work, the *Star Wars* painters often used oils over an undercoat of acrylic.

Another cinematic production technique that became an art form in itself during the making of the movie was that of storyboarding. Storyboards were in essence a visual blueprint for the SFX shots that enabled Lucas and his crew to plan sequences in meticulous detail. Each drawing was done on a standardized form with a defined area for the artwork, and an area for specifications—shot number, number of elements involved, and so on—beneath.

Lucas worked closely with the storyboard artists—as he did with all of the design and production teams. Duplicates of the storyboards were placed on the walls of the production offices as instantly accessible

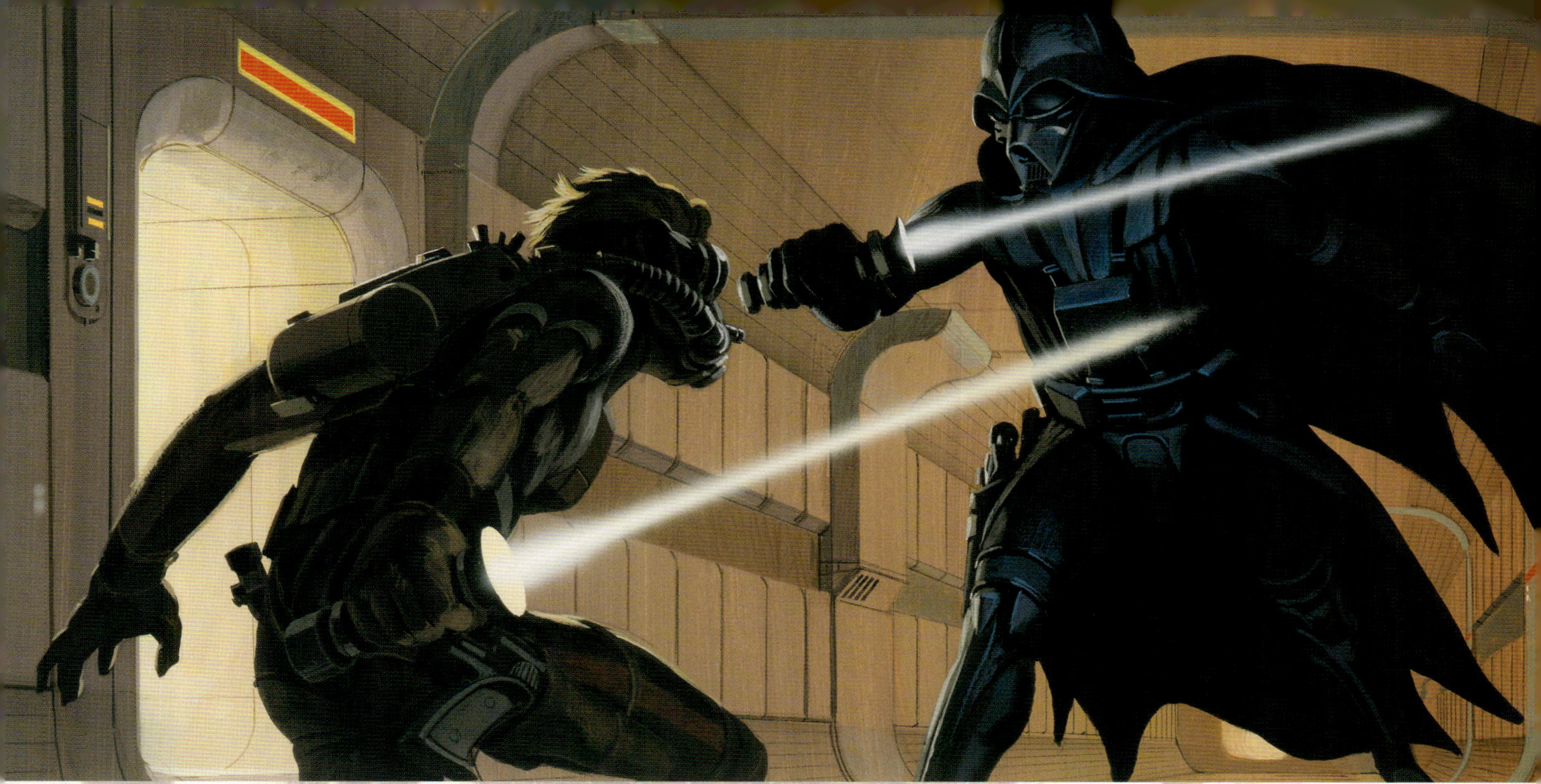

guidelines for SFX crews and directors. Miniaturized versions were carried by production VIPs as handy-sized reference devices.

Much of the success of *Star Wars* can be attributed to the artists' ability to interpret the wishes of George Lucas. Joe Johnston joined the *Star Wars* production team in 1975 and soon established himself as the pre-eminent storyboard artist, with a feel for providing camera directions that were works of art in themselves. As he noted, "It doesn't matter what it is, as long as it isn't boring. It might be a camera move or an interesting ship maneuver. Perhaps a nice sweeping turn. Everyone notices if a shot is flat and dull."

Of course, McQuarrie's belief that *Star Wars* would do mediocre business at the box office proved wildly inaccurate. The film's success was believed by many—Johnston included—to be attributable to Lucas' unique vision of a fantastic universe, realistically executed, and his instinctive feel for an interesting shot. For Johnston, this was epitomized by *Star Wars'* opening scene. "It blew people away because it was such a shock; they were forced to look at something. The lines of perspective were very strong on the Star Destroyer. It was George's idea and I'm sure that he had played it in his head a hundred times before he told me how he wanted it to look."

◀ ▲
A McQuarrie concept painting for *The Empire Strikes Back*, depicting a snowspeeder attack against an Imperial AT-AT during the spectacular Battle of Hoth.

◀◀ ▲
A Ralph McQuarrie painting, this time for Lucasfilm's change-of-address card, when they moved to Skywalker Ranch in 1979!

▲
One of McQuarrie's five concept paintings produced to dazzle possible financiers. Darth Vader was drawn with the now-familiar facemask, envisaged by McQuarrie as a necessity for Vader to move between spaceships, but seized upon by Lucas, who thought it looked sinister.

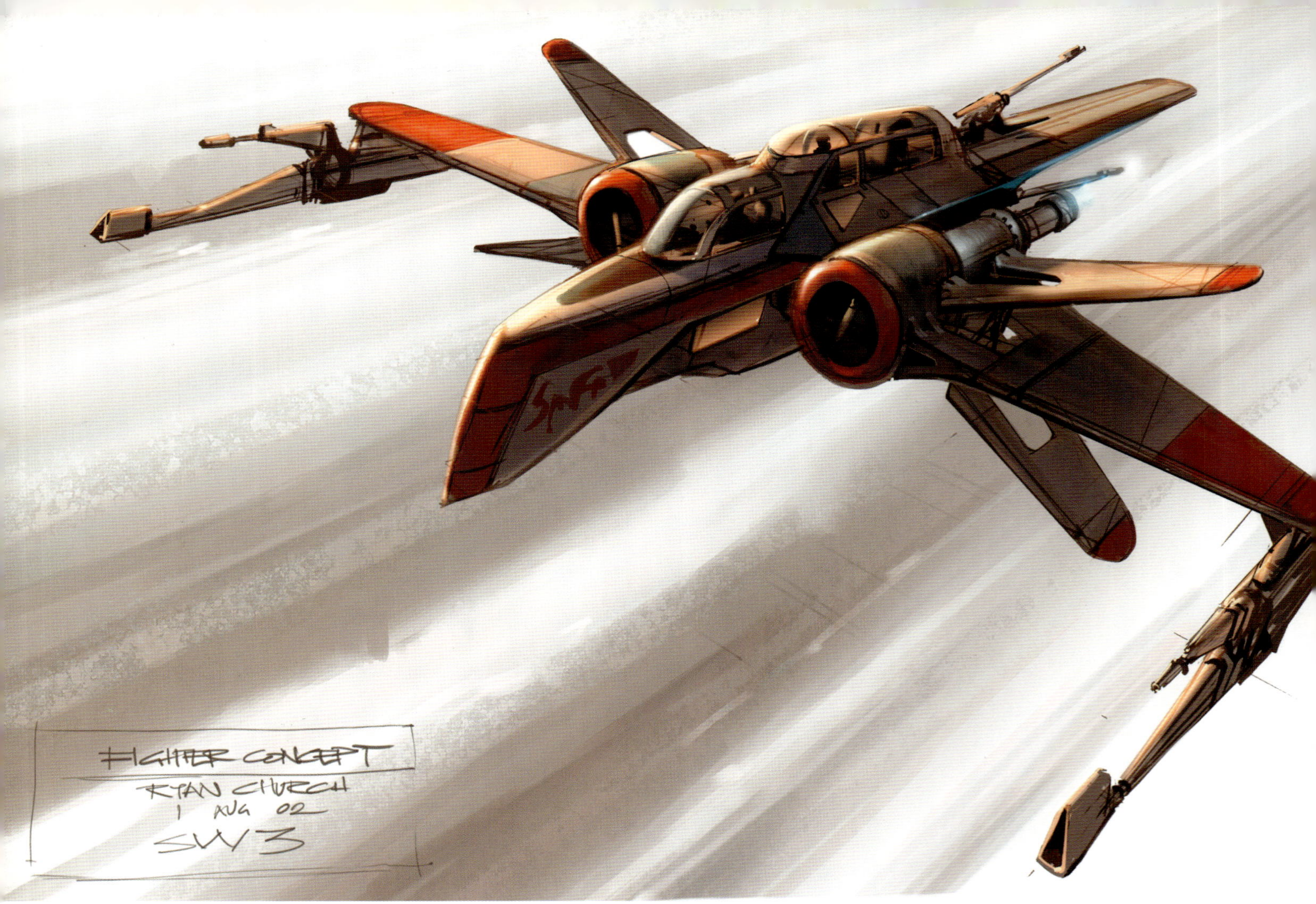

THE ART OF STAR WARS//THE PREQUELS

Autumn 1994 saw the *Star Wars* universe kick into high gear once more when George Lucas announced he was starting work on the trilogy of prequels predating *Star Wars: A New Hope*. A new team of artist and designers, many childhood fans of the original movies, were gathered at Lucasfilm's home at Skywalker Ranch in Marin County, California. There they were given a rather unique brief. While most art departments are formed after the screenplay is completed, Lucas had decided on a different tack. In his vision, art and story would develop hand in hand, feeding off each other, and providing mutual support. When work began, much of the story remained in a state of flux, but Lucas did have a hit list of various elements the team could begin work on.

The artists' usual arsenal of acrylic, inks, and pencils were augmented by a few technical innovations: markers were now very much de rigeur, favored by any commercial artist worth their salt. And, of course, the design process was well and truly based in the digital age. Photoshop was just as much a part of the designers' art box as an HB pencil.

Lucas' brief couldn't have been simpler: "Think big." What this meant in reality was more or less the opposite: the artists spent three years working on *The Phantom Menace*, producing not just warships

▲
The ARC-170 Clone Fighter gives a definite nod towards the legendary X-Wing. This concept art by Ryan Church was for

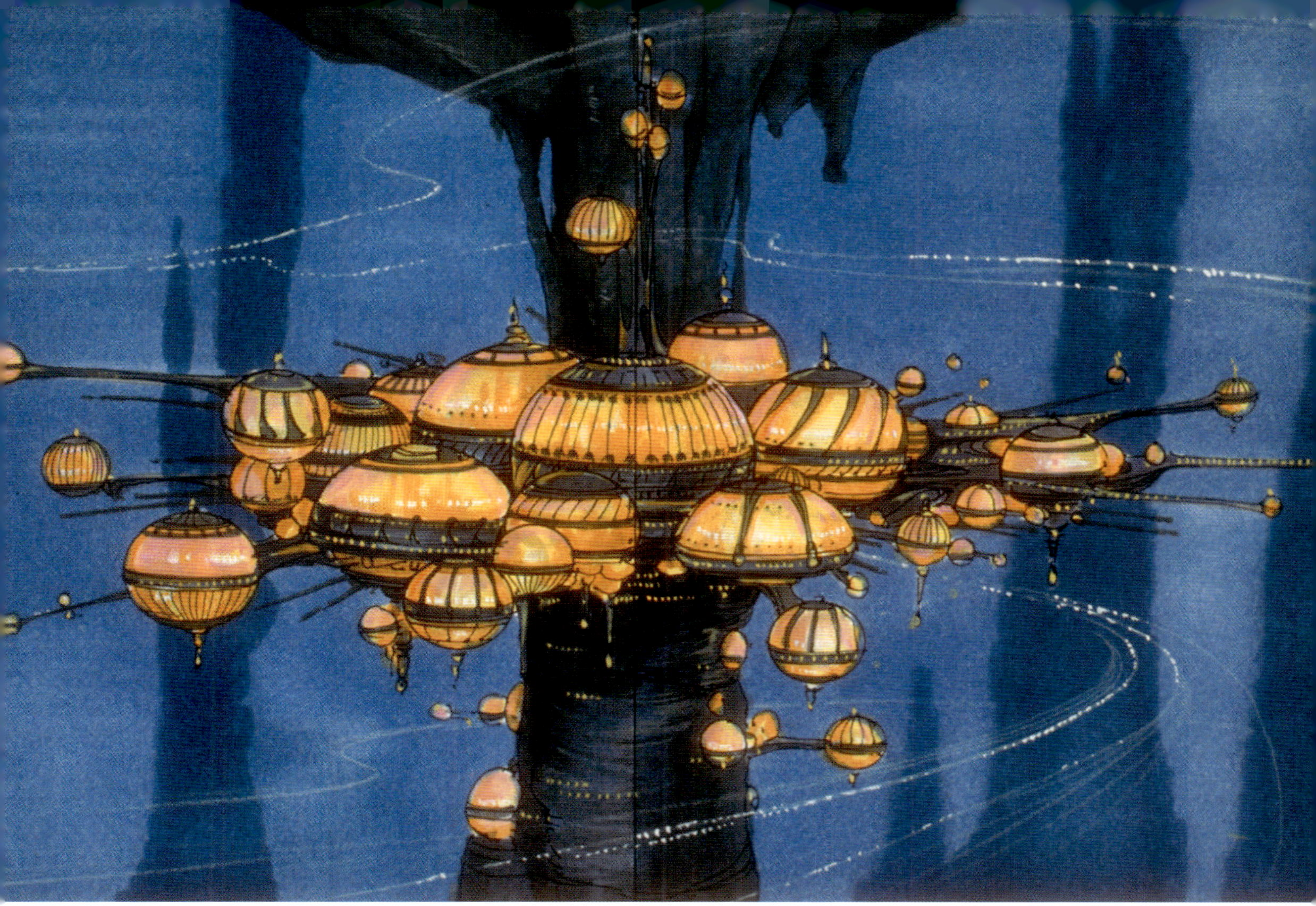

and cityscapes but the minutiae of a living, breathing civilization, and cultures of every hue—from hairstyles with symbolic significance to Renaissance-style wall panels for the city of Theed.

One interesting aspect of the prequels was the retrograde evolution needed to bring the new movies into line with the second (or original) trilogy. As such, designs were used to bridge the gap between them. Some fine examples are the clone troopers from *Attack of the Clones*. With their mythology inextricably linked to Jango and Boba Fett, the look of the troopers, designed by Doug Chiang, falls neatly between the bounty hunters and the "classic" stormtroopers. The fin on the clone trooper helmet was added by Lucas himself, perhaps reflecting his love of '50s automobiles.

Similar "de-evolutions" appear in the ships. The solar panels on Darth Maul's vessel hint at the TIE Fighters to come, while, according to designer John Duncan, the Jedi troop transport presages the Imperial Star Destroyer. Concept Design Supervisor Doug Chiang's key design philosophy was simplicity—describing a shape in just a few lines. According to Duncan, "What follows is the classic wedge-shaped starship." Which brings us neatly back to the opening shot of *Star Wars: A New Hope*, as the triangular Star Destroyer rumbles overhead.

▲
With imagination no longer fettered by the limits of SFX technology, the designers could have a ball. The various *Star Wars* cultures all carried their own unique design philosophies. The aquatic Gungans benefited from Lucas' love of art nouveau, their underwater palaces reflecting Charles Rennie Mackintosh, Aubrey Beardsley, and Gaudi, with their curves and soft, organic lines.

WAYNE DOUGLAS BARLOWE

Wayne Douglas Barlowe is a natural history illustrator—with a difference. While most artists in this field specialize in flora and fauna from known ecosystems, Barlowe's pictures are works of inspired—yet still thoroughly plausible—fantasy.

The offspring of two well-known natural history artists, Sy and Dorothea Barlowe, Wayne's first professional work appeared alongside his parents' in the *Instant Nature Guide to Insects*. But his initial solo effort was destined to become a classic in sci-fi literature. Barlowe's *Guide to Extraterrestrials* was published in 1979 to great acclaim. It was in essence a xenobiologist's manual to the aliens of various science fiction greats, ranging from Lovecraft's Cthulu old gods to the twisted humans that navigated between the stars in Frank Herbert's *Dune* series. Heaped with praise and winning numerous awards, the book spurred on a career that saw Barlowe providing countless illustrations and over 300 book and magazine covers for virtually every major sci-fi publication, not to mention *Time* and *Newsweek*.

However, it would not be until 1990 that his next major work appeared. *Expedition: Being an Account in Words and Artwork of the 2358 A. D. Voyage to Darwin IV* was a fictitious narrative of the exploration of a distant planet, and included 40 paintings and 100 black and white illustrations. Barlowe's designs were carefully rationalized and biologically credible, but his unique combination of hard science and imagination paid dividends when the Discovery Channel spun the book into a two-hour TV special, *Alien Planet*, in 2004.

By 1998, Barlow had moved into the entertainment industry, designing alien creatures and environments for the TV movie, *Babylon 5: Thirdspace*. Film work followed: more aliens for the animated movie *Titan A.E.*, and for affectionate *Star Trek* homage, *Galaxy Quest*.

1999 saw something of a departure with the publication of Barlowe's *Inferno*, his unique artistic guide to Hell, and *The Sworn Book of Honorius*, a medieval grimoire whose 93 chapters include instructions on magical lore and demonology.

The idea for *Inferno* began germinating during his college years after reading Dante and then Milton's *Paradise Lost*—a seminal experience for Barlowe, who felt Milton's depiction of Hell had "...a fullness that would shame and confound any Hollywood director." Barlow structured a narrative around the paintings, which led to a screenplay for Fox Animation. However, this fell victim to the closure of the studio following *Titan A.E.*'s terrible box office performance. *Brushfire: Illuminations From the Inferno*, a portfolio of 18 new paintings, was more successful, and a novel, *God's Demon*, followed. Although this was Barlowe's first attempt at prose literature, he saw parallels between the two disciplines of art and writing, but admitted, "It was the hardest thing I ever attempted."

The new millennium saw Barlowe's movie career kick into high gear, with work on Guillermo del Toro's *Blade 2* and *Hellboy*, followed by creature designs for two Harry Potter movies, *Prisoner of Azkaban*, and *Goblet of Fire*. He also, inevitably, moved into game design, producing preliminary work for the Xbox 360 game *Prototype*. More Barlowe monsters also appeared in the eagerly anticipated *Hellboy II: The Golden Army*. As Barlowe himself acknowledges, "The creature thing has kind of stuck with me for a bunch of years and I guess it's just because I enjoy doing them more than almost any other kind of element in films or books..."

▶
The Elytracephalid is perhaps one of Barlowe's most striking images—there is something quite clerical about the robes and the pose, as though standing for a portrait. Of course, there the similarity ends...

▶▶
The Emperor Sea Strider from *Expedition* was the result of the question, "What would something like a giant, walking mollusc look like?" Creating a viable alien ecology was something of a compromise between the truly alien and the reader's credibility; Barlowe pointed out that, "On the one hand you want your audience to relate to the creatures, on the other you don't want the fauna to be pedestrian."

▶
Another alien creature from Barlowe, the Bladderhorn was considered by the artist to be "a bit of comic relief in an otherwise savage eco-system." Envisaged as a sort of inflatable elk, the antlers are actually resonating bugles for communication.

▶▶
Barlowe's almost Dalí-esque illustration for the SF novel *Wild Seed* by Octavia Butler—a story whose African setting and psychological overtones are hinted at in the cranial menagerie costructed by Barlowe.

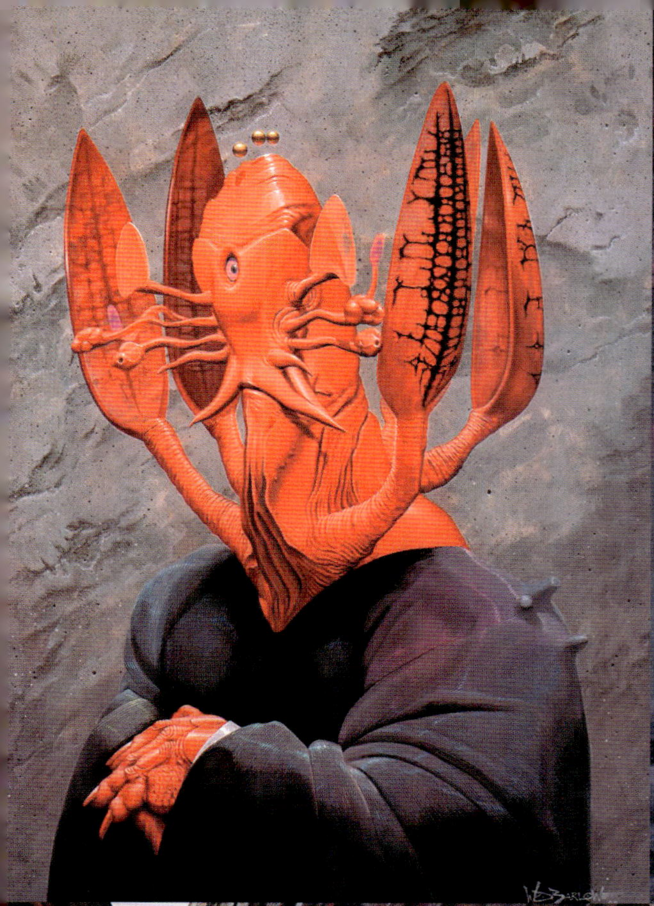

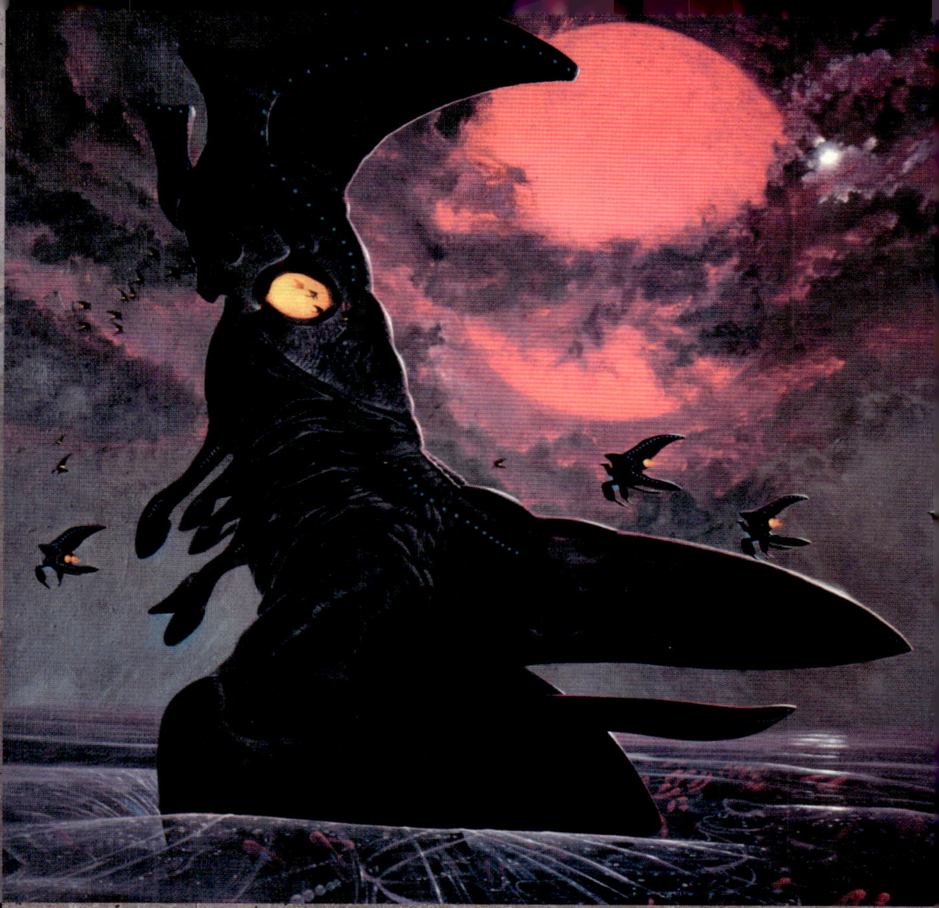

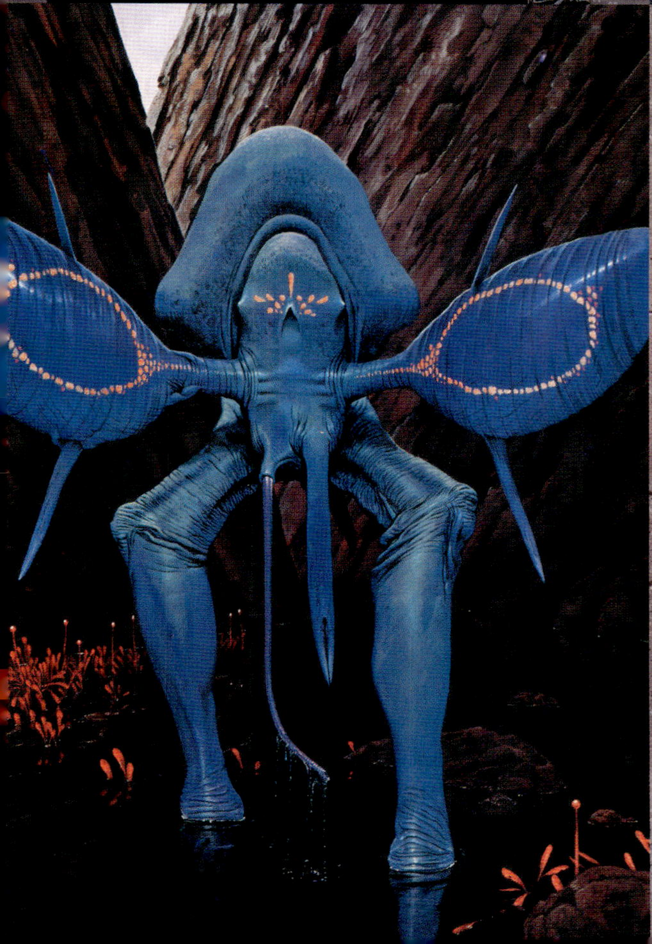

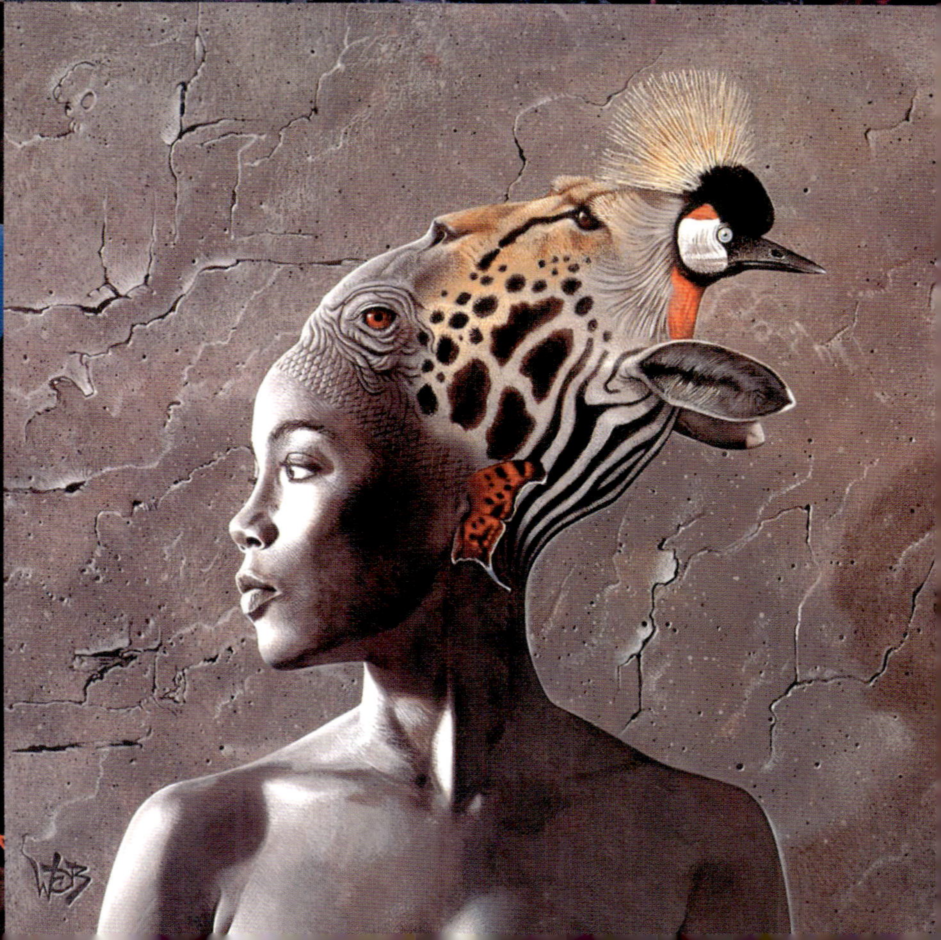
WDB

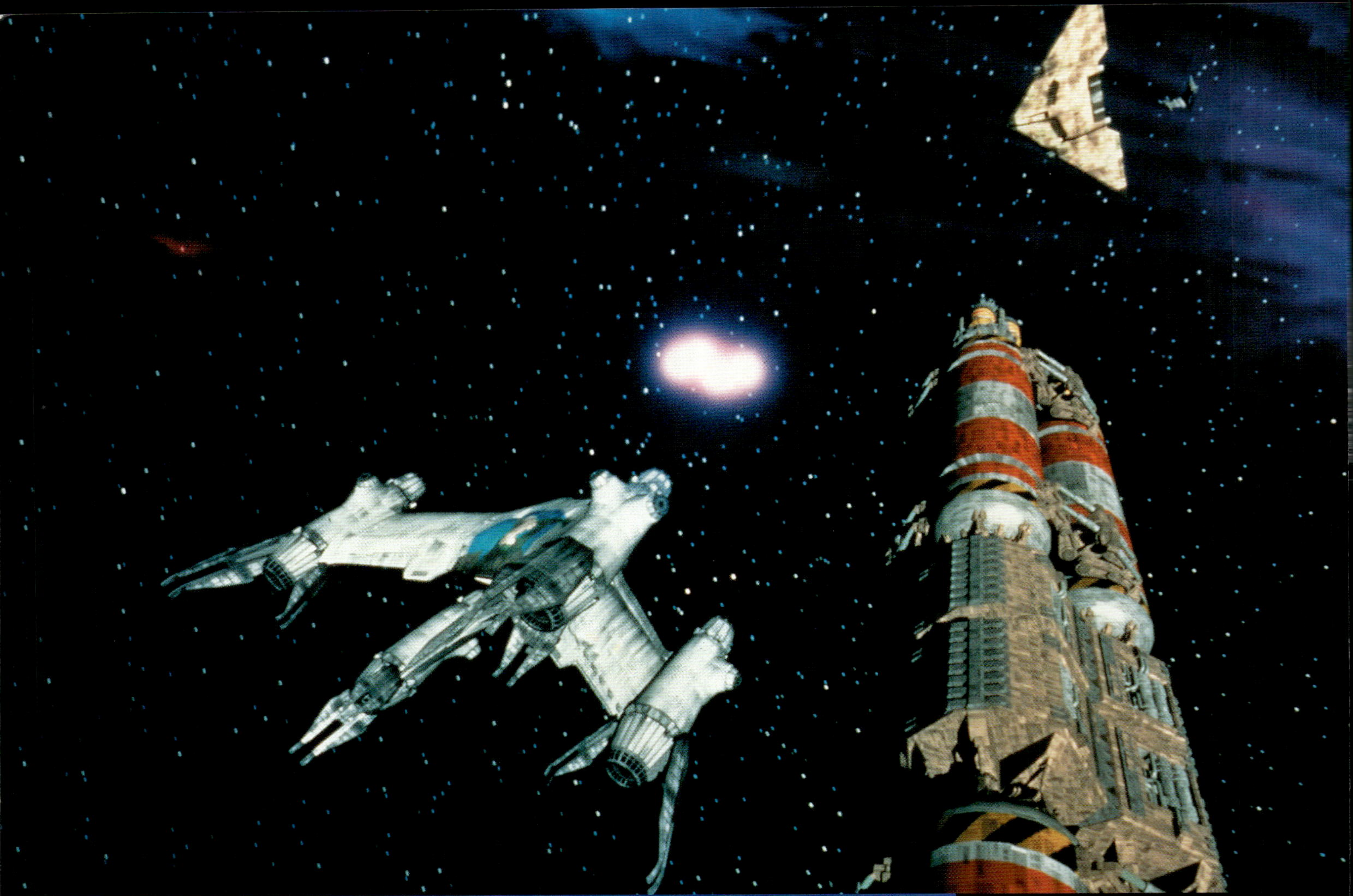

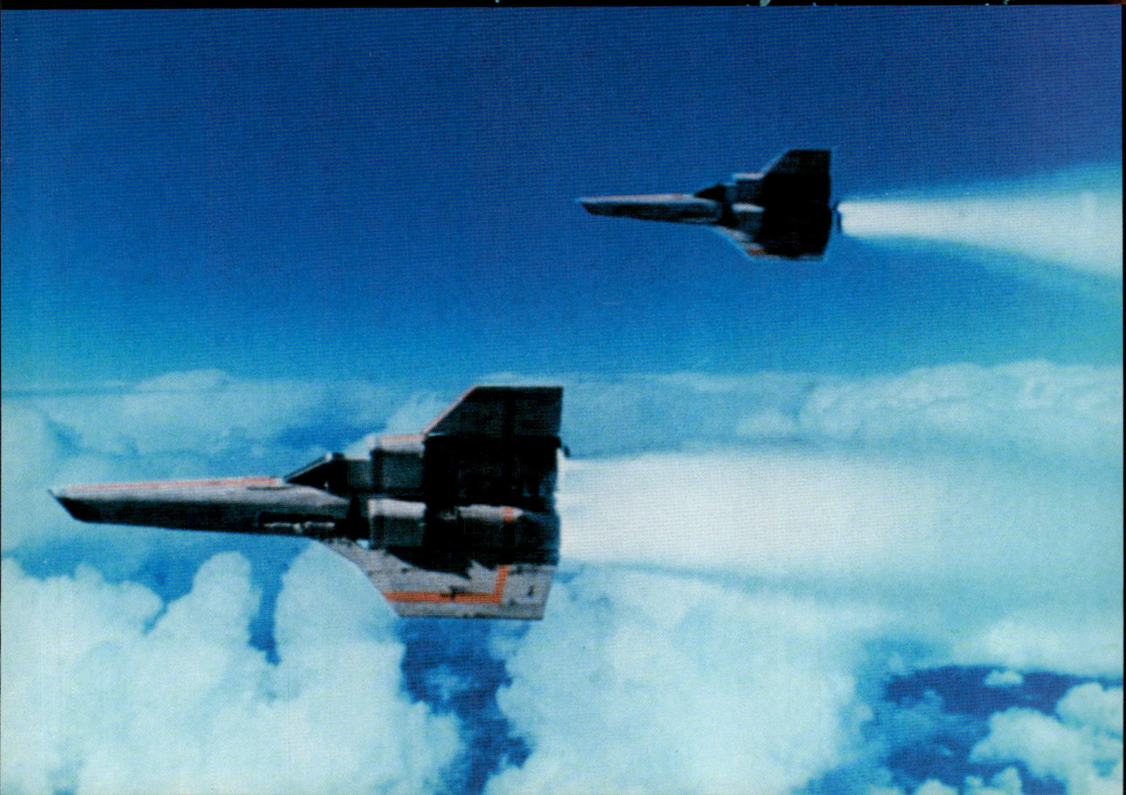

▲
The Starfury from *Babylon 5* is an extremely accomplished piece of conceptual design, using astronomical principles to create a very plausible ship that actually looks like it could be used in space warfare. Such was the authenticity of the design that NASA even considered it as the basis for a spaceborne forklift!

◀ ▶
Although not as elegant as the *Star Wars* X-Wing, the Viper from *Battlestar Galactica* still seems to show if not ancestry, then at least convergent evolution with its predecessor—no doubt due to the influence of SFX guru John Dykstra, who moved from the movie to the television show in quick succession.

SF TELEVISION

The sci-fi boom created by the arrival of *Star Wars: A New Hope* in 1977 quickly spread from the big screen to the small. While sci-fi shows had long been a staple of TV viewing (*Lost in Space, The Outer Limits, Doctor Who*, etc.), the genre was given a serious boost by the blockbuster's phenomenal success. The most obvious direct descendant was *Battlestar Galactica*. This sprawling space opera boasted *Star Wars* veterans John Dykstra on special effects and, as concept designer, Ralph McQuarrie. *Buck Rogers* was also brought out of black and white retirement and given a flash new makeover—complete with comic robot sidekick—in *Buck Rogers in the 25th Century*. And in the UK, the imaginative but budget-conscious *Blake's 7* attained cult status.

The heady days of the late '70s and early '80s never truly faded and sci-fi shows remained primetime viewing, with varying degrees of success. *Star Trek* became a billion-dollar franchise in the mid '90s, followed by movie spin-off *Stargate SG-1* and its affiliated shows, and the curious and cultish *Babylon 5*—one of the first shows to make extensive use of CGI. Although the SFX now look slightly dated, it still represented a new approach and style, and an effort to extend the boundaries of technology. And lest we forget, it introduced the world to the X-shaped Starfury—one of the great, underrated sci-fi designs.

CGI played a significant role in two cult SF shows revamped and re-launched in the recent years to great fanfare and mainstream critical praise. A "reimagined" *Battlestar Galactica* traded on post-9/11 geopolitical paranoia to take the camp '80s show and give it a much harder, tougher, more dramatic edge. Combined with a plausible approach to space warfare, tight writing, and some outstanding CGI FX, the show transcended the genre and became a massive hit, garnering serious plaudits along the way.

Similarly, in the UK the BBC finally gave the fans what they wanted after a decade of waiting, and a new incarnation of *Doctor Who* was born. Again, some excellent writing, high production values, and a grittier approach scored the BBC a massive success, and for the first time in years school playgrounds echoed to high-pitched warbling cries of "Exterminate!"

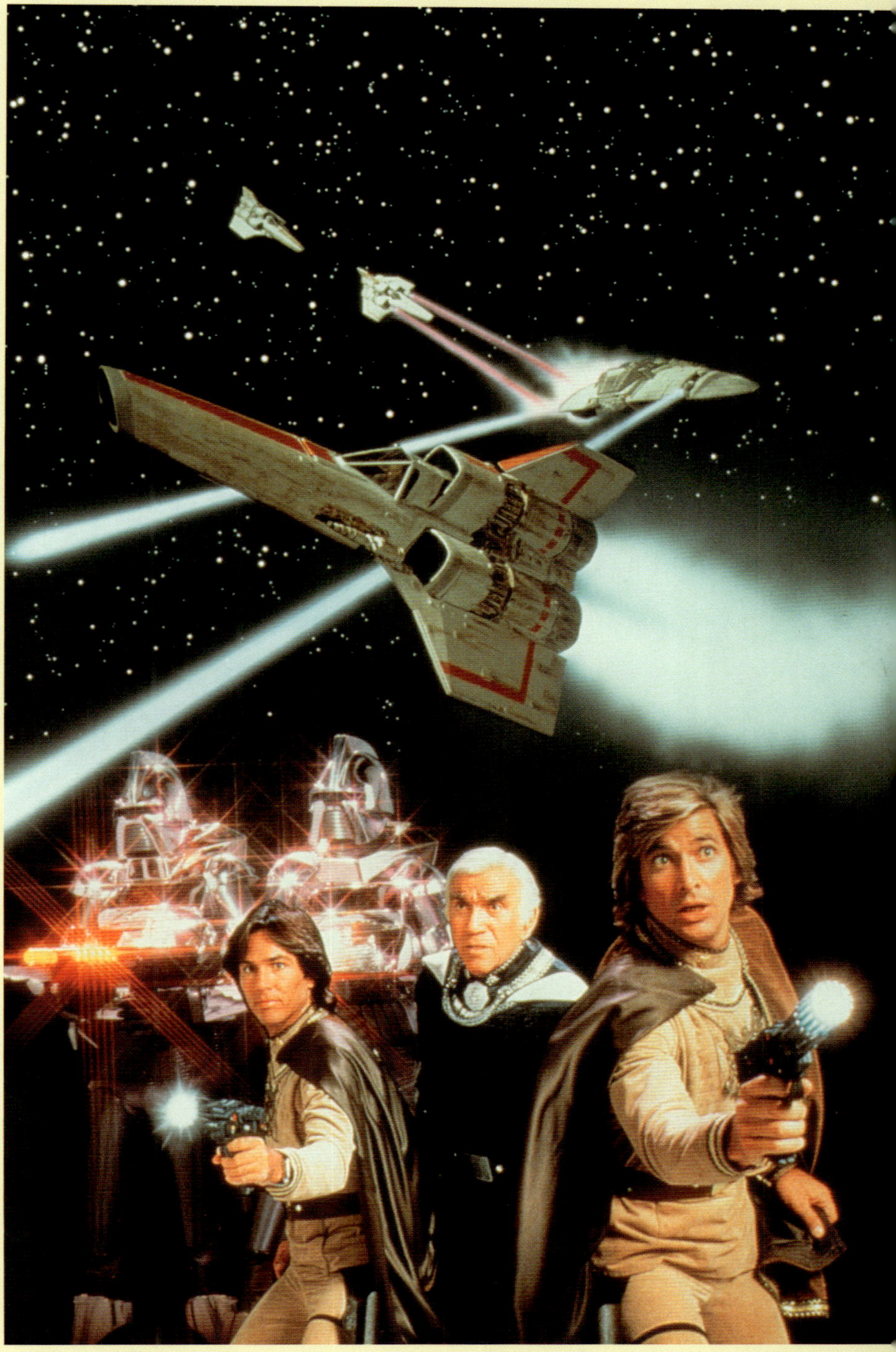

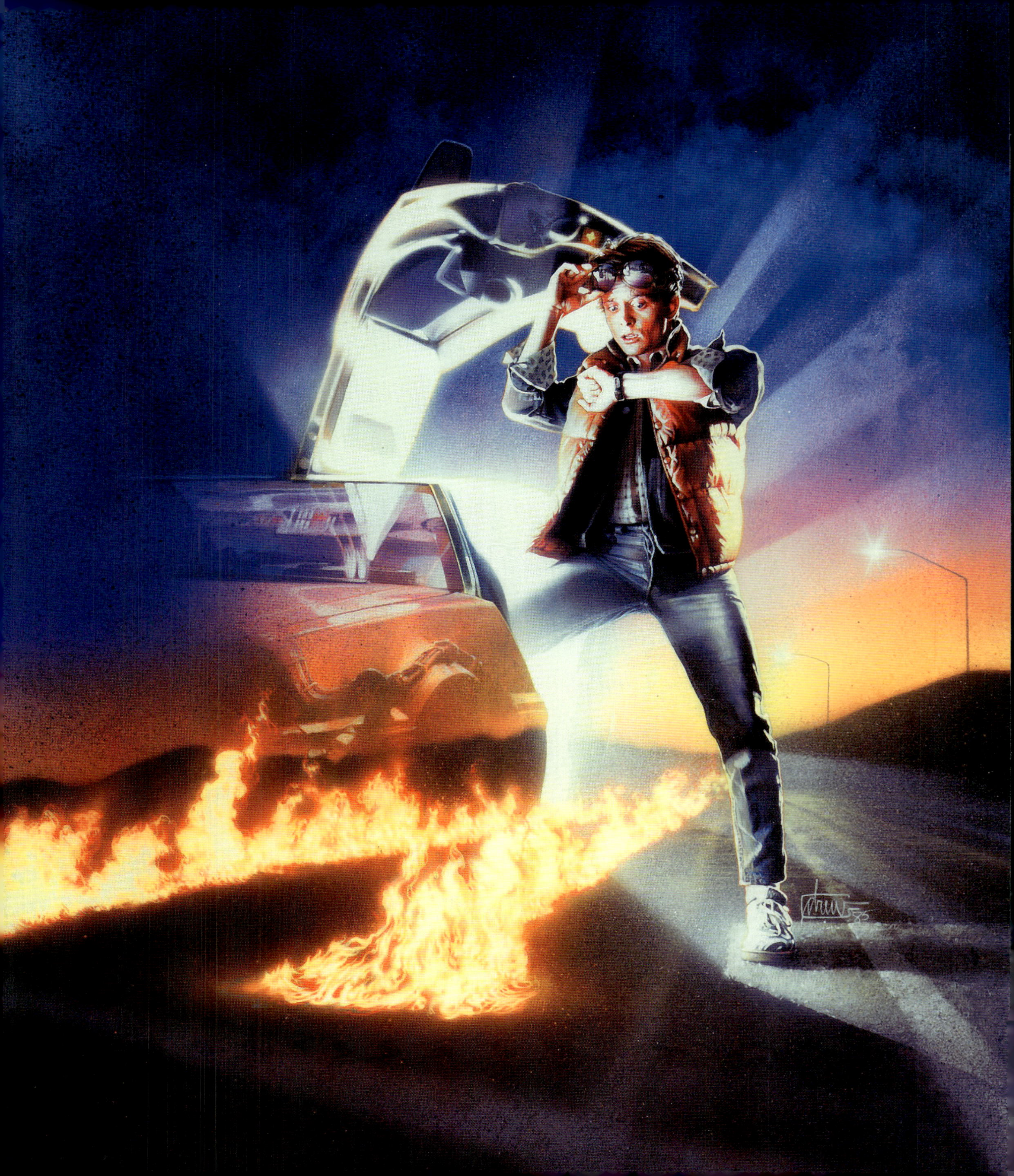

5 CINEMA ART

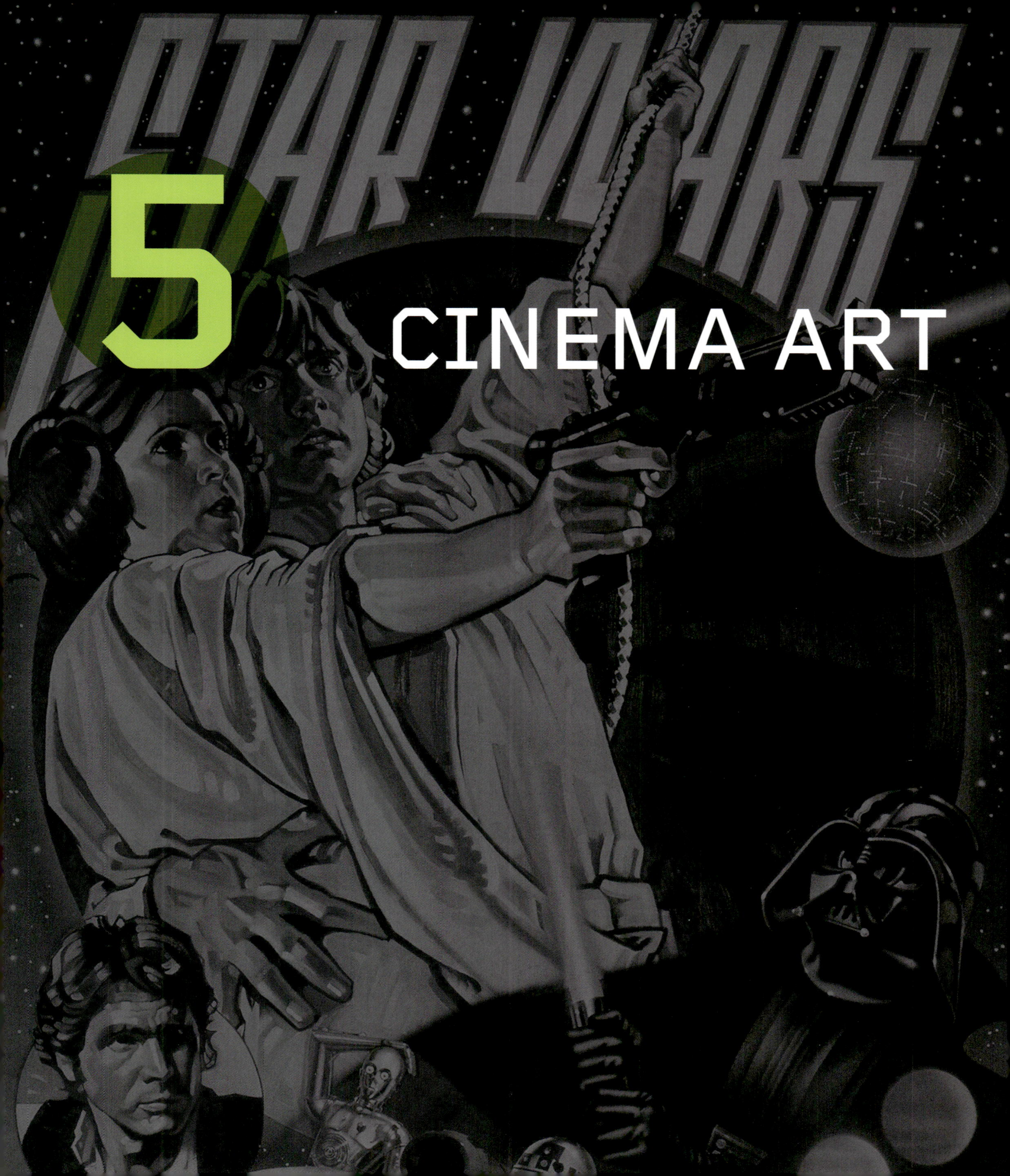

SF FILM POSTERS

Just as science fiction films have changed dramatically since the genre's first outing in 1902 with George Méliès' *Le Voyage dans la Lune* ("A Trip to the Moon"), so too have the posters that have sold them to an eager public.

Until the 1940s, posters were generally bright and jaunty, reflecting either the comedic or action packed stories of the period. The posters for *Flash Gordon*, for instance, adopted a comic book style, featuring the hero in a series of colorful derring-do action sequences. Even more serious pieces, such as H. G. Wells' *Things to Come*, used this approach to sell the movie; the Art Deco styling of the poster for *Metropolis* is the exception.

The 1950s saw SF films enjoying something of a renaissance, delivering such classics as *The Day the Earth Stood Still, Forbidden Planet, This Island Earth, Invasion of the Body Snatchers, Them!*, and many more. The posters were mostly hand-painted, with "women in peril" (particularly from alien monsters) a favorite theme, especially with B-movies.

Although light on science fiction, the 1960s produced two of the most influential films of the genre: *2001: A Space Odyssey* and *Planet of the Apes*. Their posters certainly differed from their '50s predecessors, reflecting their more serious tone: *2001* features astronauts taking readings on the moon, while the *Apes* poster depicts caged humans.

The genre boom of the 1970s was perhaps prompted by the real Moon landing in 1969. Films such as *Silent Running, A Clockwork Orange, Rollerball, Mad Max, Soylent Green*, and *Westworld* reflected the era by exploring themes of paranoia, dystopian societies, and ecological and technological threats, as did their impressive poster art. *Close Encounters of the Third Kind* was one of the few films to present a hopeful conclusion to alien contact, while *Alien* was its antithesis, a disparity captured in the pair's posters. Artists such as Tom William Chantrell, Robert E. McGinnis, Bob Peak, and Tom Jung all produced memorable poster work during this era

The '70s also spawned perhaps the most influential science fiction franchise ever: *Star Wars*. The success of George Lucas' film (which had

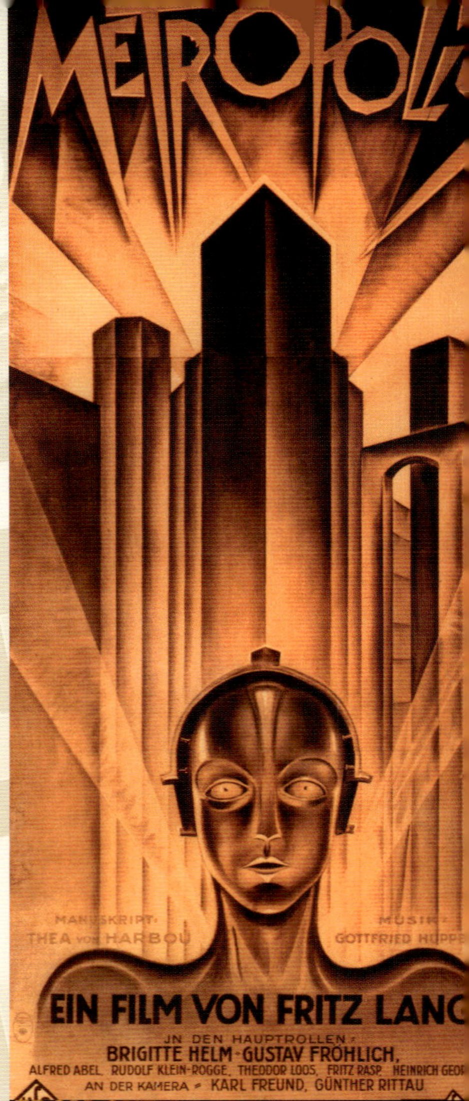

▶ **The iconic Maria from Fritz Lang's *Metropolis* influenced a generation of science fiction authors, artists, and filmmakers. The poster reflects many of the artistic influences in the film, including German expressionism and Art Deco.**

▶▶ **Artist Bob Peak, famed for his "less is more" approach, was responsible for posters for a great many science fiction films, including the first six *Star Trek* movies, *Superman*, *Rollerball*, and some James Bond pictures.**

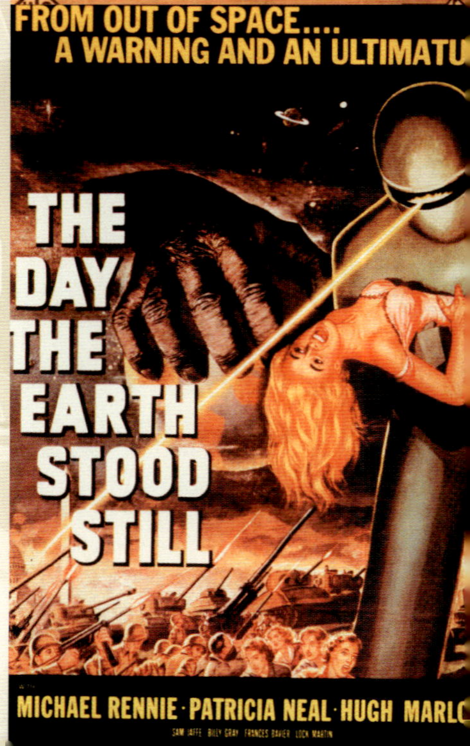

▶ **The poster artwork for *The Day the Earth Stood Still* is a good example of the popular "damsel in distress" category from the 1950s. The robot Gort grasps a woman (presumably Patricia Neal, although she is not blonde in the film) and fires death rays at the attacking soldiers.**

numerous promotional posters painted by Chantrell, Richard Amsel, and Drew Struzan, among others) with a family audience prompted the following decade's plethora of child friendly movies, including *E.T.: The Extra-Terrestrial, Tron*, and *Back to the Future*. However, the '80s and '90s would also be dominated by more adult action blockbusters, led by the films of Arnold Schwarzenegger (*The Terminator, Predator, Total Recall* etc.), the posters of which mostly focused on a big headshot of the star.

Sadly, the '80s marked the end of the painted film poster (with a few exceptions, such as *Brazil* and the new *Star Wars* movies), as distributors turned to posed photographs and digitally manipulated images. Although there is still some creativity on show today, posters of the modern era have become ever more generic as the studio marketing machines look to evoke a response to a film by aligning it with a previously popular one.

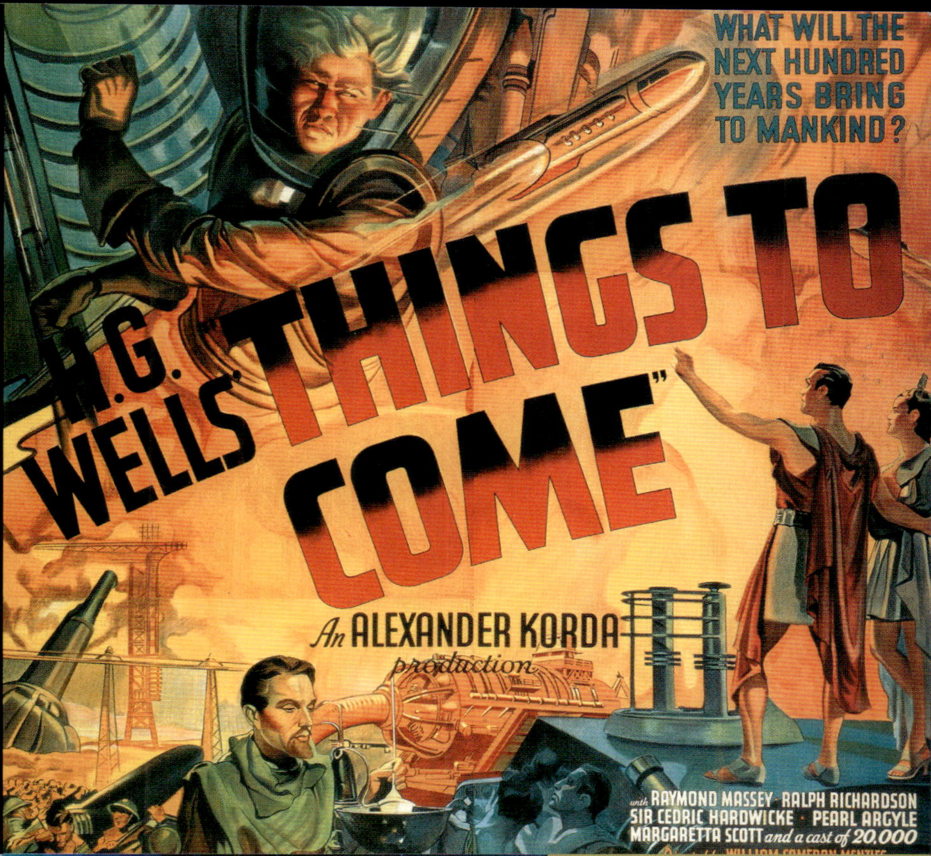

▲
***Things to Come*'s prophetic story (by H. G. Wells), pressing sociological themes, and visionary technological innovations makes it as relevant today as it was in 1936. The poster is indicative of the 1930s, with its bright color palette and scene-stealing vignettes.**

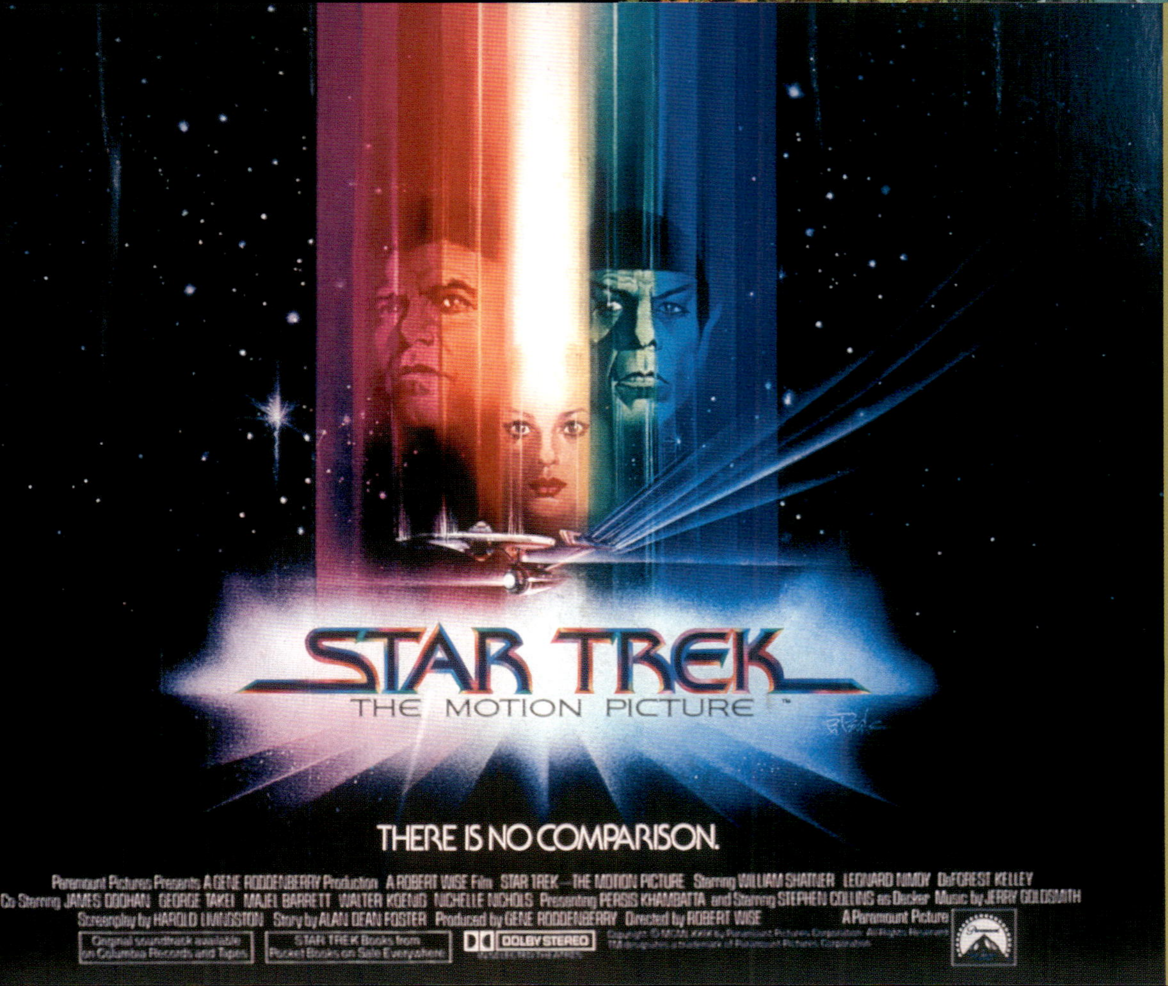

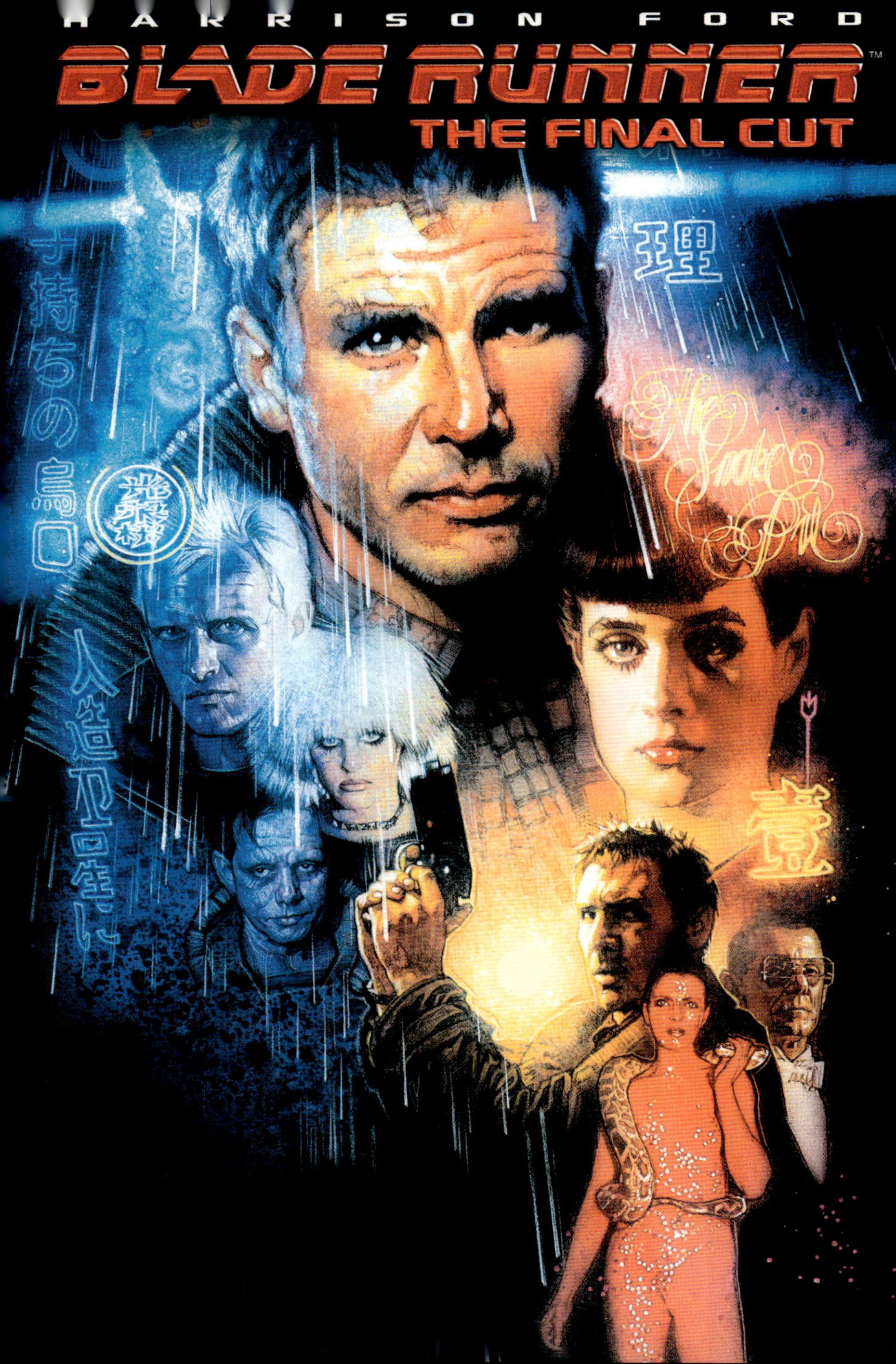

DREW STRUZAN

Drew Struzan's film posters are among the most popular—and most recognizable—ever created. From *Star Wars* to *Blade Runner*, from *Harry Potter* and back to *Star Wars* again, Struzan (1947-) has produced poster art for some of the biggest sci-fi films of recent years, and plenty more besides. George Lucas and Steven Spielberg are among his biggest fans—Spielberg insisted that he'd have no one else render *E.T.*

Struzan's life story reads like a Hollywood plot itself. As a child, he has stated bluntly, "I was poor. I didn't have anything." He struggled with dyslexia in elementary school, but his artistic talent was evident from an early age—famously, his proud parents took his drawings to be studied by researchers at Stanford. His family moved around a lot, and as he himself has put it, "I've always been introverted and intuitive," so

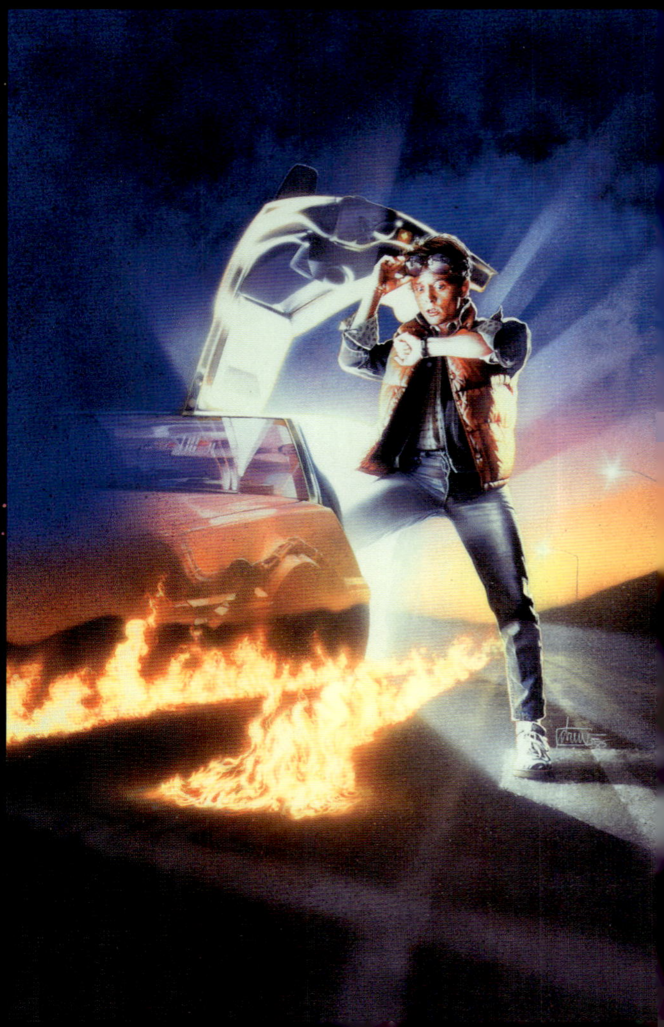

▲ **Struzan began working on this poster for *Blade Runner* in 1982, but it was never used. In 2001 he was asked if the sketch could be used for the cover of the new "Director's Cut" DVD and he revisited the painting. The result is a timeless take on an enduring SF classic.**

▶ **As well as their classic composition, Drew Struzan's posters are prized for the luminous quality of their lighting, such as this poster for *Back to the Future*.**

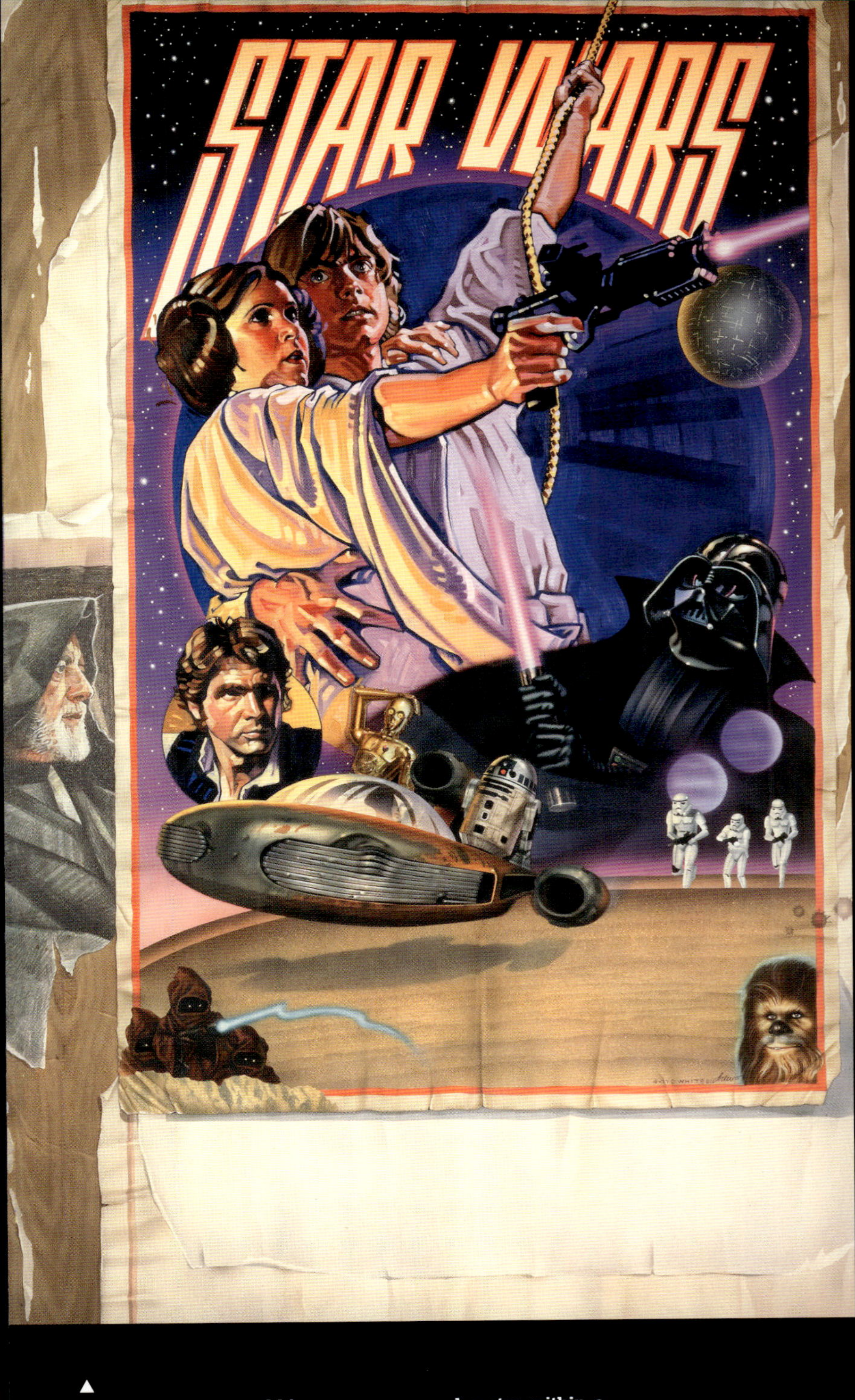

▲
When Struzan created his breakthrough *Star Wars* poster in 1977, he had few expectations. Fellow artist Charles White III asked for Struzan's help with the human figures on a poster he'd been commissioned to produce, unusual poster-within-a-poster design came about because the original needed to be extended to accommodate a bigger text block, but the poster perfectly captured the movie's revolutionary brand of space opera adventure.

his art naturally became central in his life, even when he had to draw on toilet paper because "that was the only paper around."

In 1965, having just turned 18, Struzan enrolled at art school in Los Angeles. According to Struzan, "I was the classic starving artist. I couldn't afford the tuition, so I'd go to school in the morning and they'd kick me out. Then I'd go in again through the back door." Marriage and the birth of a son meant he had to put study on hold for a year, but eventually he managed to work his way through school and even some post-graduate studies.

Faced with a choice between fine art and commercial illustration, Struzan has said, the decision was obvious: "I was poor and hungry, and illustration was the shortest path to a slice of bread." After graduation, he freelanced for the music industry in Los Angeles, then found a job in a design studio specializing in album covers. For the next five years, he turned out a wide variety of cover art—including at least one piece, for Alice Cooper's *Welcome To My Nightmare*, which has itself been acknowledged as a classic.

With his work gaining attention, Struzan started getting calls from the movie industry and decided to set up on his own with a friend who had experience of the business. For the next few years he created poster art for "a lot of monster movies and B-movies," until in 1977 a fellow artist asked for his help with the human figures on the poster for the re-release of *Star Wars*.

The poster, now widely known as the "circus" poster, was the turning point. George Lucas loved it, and Struzan's fame spread rapidly. He's been in demand ever since, at his peak in the '80s producing around ten designs a year. He's now created over 150, in all genres, but remains a favorite in sci-fi circles for his rich realism, emphasizing the human face of SF.

ANIMATED SF MOVIES

Since 1937, when Walt Disney proved with *Snow White* that cartoon characters were more than just animals you could drop a piano on; that they could act with enough pathos and conviction to bring audiences to tears, the animated feature has become a recognized movie genre.

For science fiction, animation opened up a whole host of possibilities, creating an economical method of exploring strange new worlds and meeting new life forms not limited by the model-maker's craft and actors in latex and rubber. Only once CGI began to offer almost unlimited potential at a relatively cheap price to the filmmaker was cell animation relegated to an interesting sideline.

As with so many film genres, it was European productions that pushed the envelope of traditional animation, elevating what many considered children's fare to the realm of the avant-garde.

La Planète Sauvage ("The Savage Planet"), made in 1973, was a joint French/Czech production. Director René Laloux's totalitarian themes aren't a million miles away from the more or less contemporary *Planet of the Apes*, overshadowed by the mushroom cloud of the Cold War. Czechoslovakia had, after all, been invaded by the USSR in 1968 to crush its nascent democracy. But there are also echoes of Nazi anti-Semitic persecution, proving that left, right, or Draag, a dictatorship is pretty much the same no matter its posited philosophy.

In this case, it is the maltreatment of the humans, known as Oms (the French for "man" is *homme*) by a race of blue-skinned giants called Draags. The Oms are domesticated and exterminated but are instrumental to the survival of the technologically and socially sophisticated Draags, and the two races must find a way to peacefully coexist if they are to survive.

Laloux worked alongside French graphic artist, painter, and writer Roland Topor, and composer and jazz pianist Alain Goraguer to create a unique realm of the senses, the surreal visuals accompanied by an innovative soundtrack that echoes the earlier electronic score of *Forbidden Planet*. Topor, a Polish Jew whose family spent WWII in hiding from Nazi persecution, was the artistic backbone of the film, his detailed and disturbing designs committed to celluloid in a "cut out" style not dissimilar to that employed

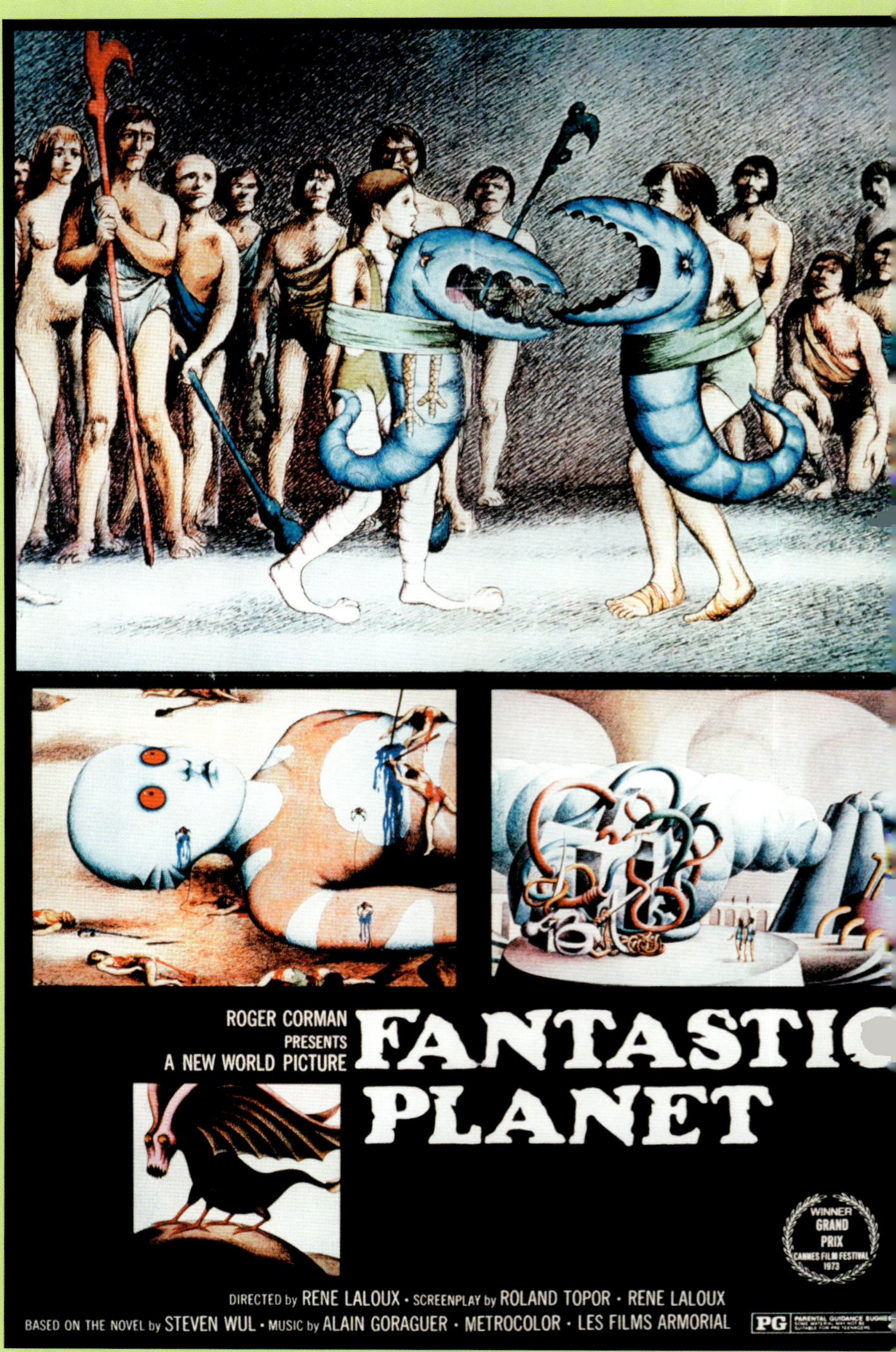

▲ ***La Planète Sauvage*—retitled *Fantastic Planet* for its US release—is now considered to be the only full-length, hand-drawn "cut out" animated movie in existence.**

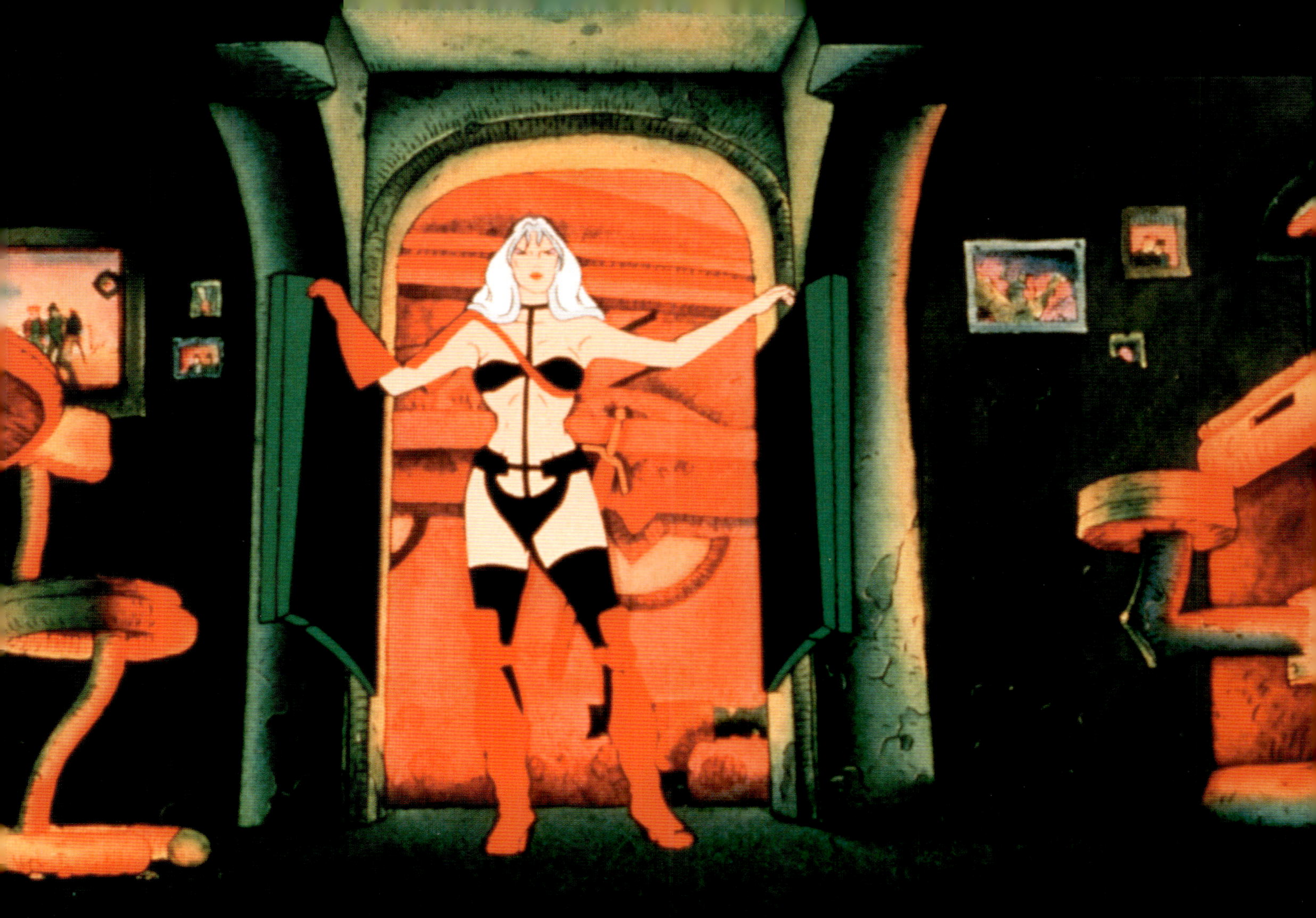

by Terry Gilliam in his animation for *Monty Python's Flying Circus*.

While the masterworks of Disney are universally recognized, *La Planète Sauvage* is not a "studio" effort but the blood, sweat, and tears of a visionary, dedicated cadre of creators and should, as such, be considered art.

The '70s also saw the first cinema incarnation of what, 30 years later, would become a groundbreaking cinema phenomenon. *The Lord of the Rings* may be classified more as fantasy than SF, but Ralph Bakshi's 1978 rotoscoped vision is notable for *Star Wars* enthusiasts: Anthony "C-3PO" Daniels voiced Legolas.

1981 saw the release of *Heavy Metal*, a cinema version of the English edition of French magazine *Métal Hurlant* (although it actually translates as "howling metal"). The anthology title had attained cult status and a solid following, largely as a result of its adult themes and generous helpings of sex and violence.

Divided, like the magazine, into several stories (although the feature did maintain a single protagonist running through its various segments), the film's credits included *Ghostbusters* director Ivan Reitman as producer; the vocal talents of future Reitman collaborators Harold Ramis, John Candy, and Eugene Levy; and *Alien* writer Dan O'Bannon. As with the comics version, the film didn't stint on the nudity and blood.

▲
Renowned French artist Moebius, a.k.a. Jean Giraud, was one of the first European comics talents to break into the US mainstream. His short story collection, *Arzach*, provided the basis for the *Heavy Metal* section, *Taarna*, and its eponymous heroine. Other well-known comics names who lent their talents to the film included horror maestros Berni Wrightson and Richard Corben.

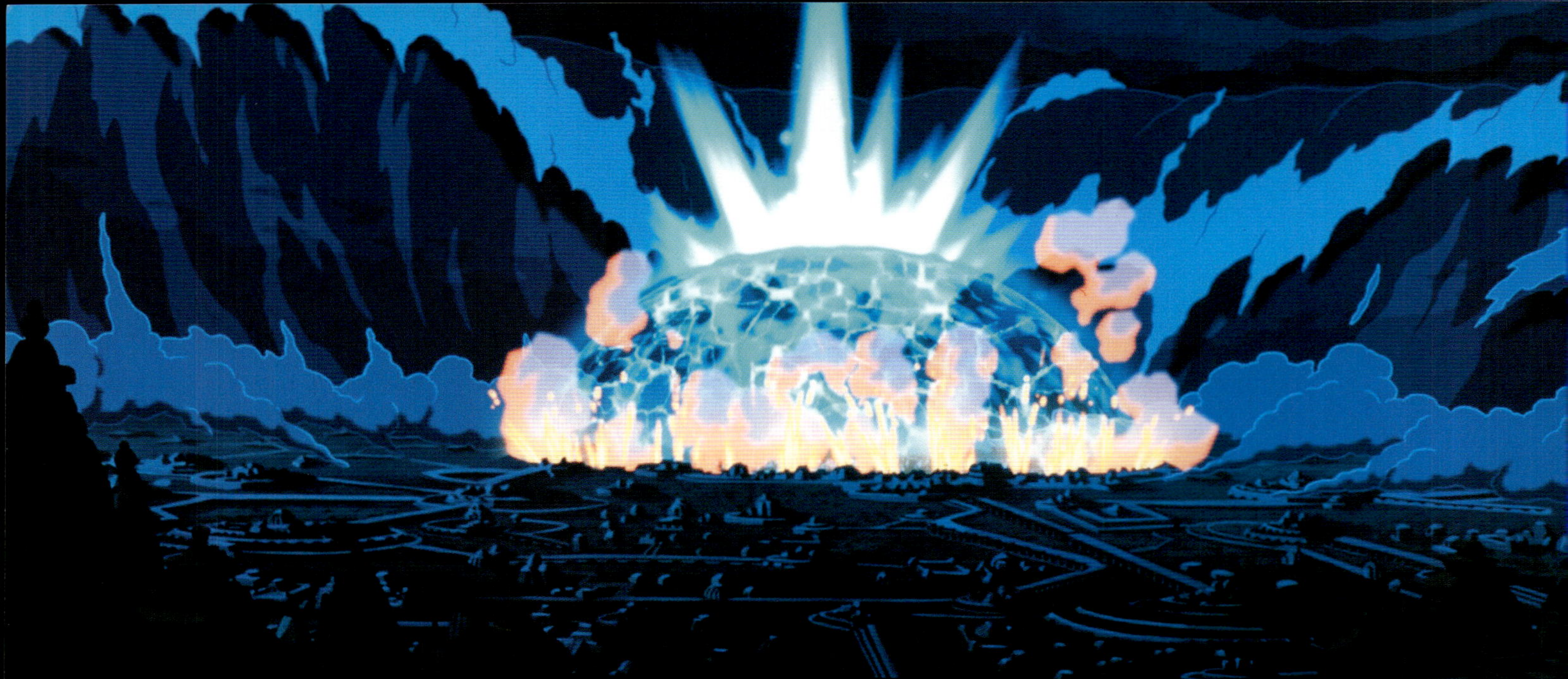

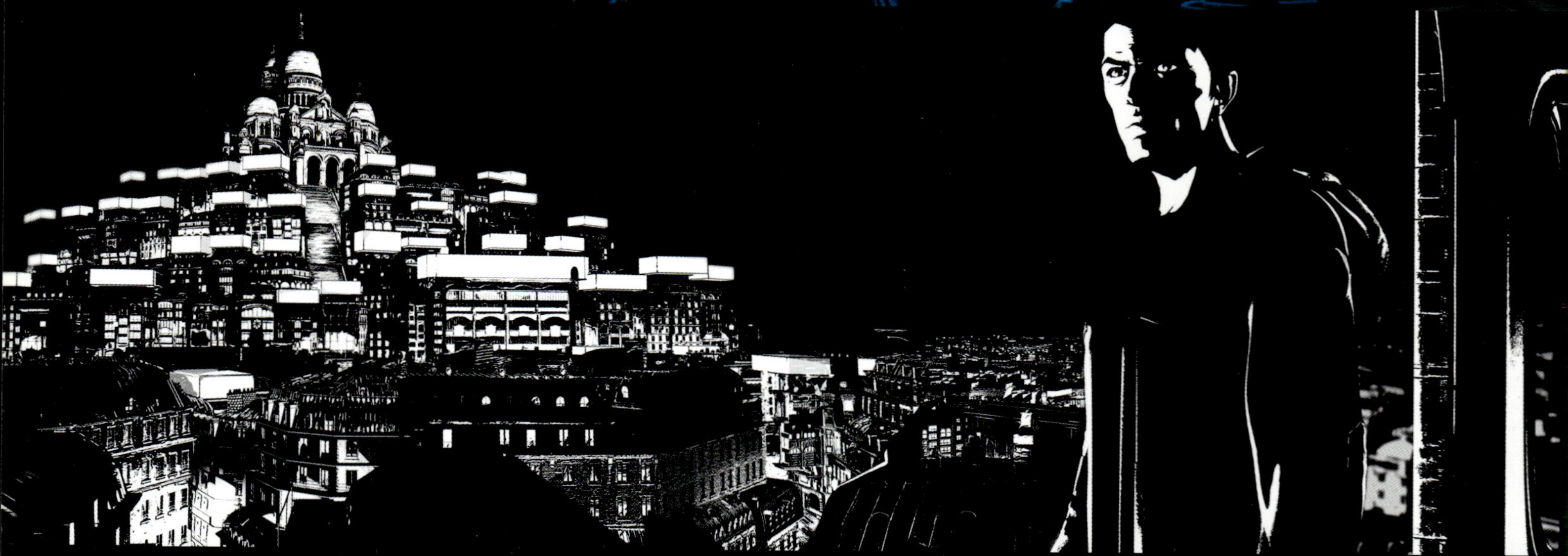

▲▲
Hellboy creator *Mike Mignola* was hired to bring his unique talents to *Atlantis: The Lost Empire*, Disney's 40th feature, released in 2001. Quasi-*Indiana Jones*/*The Mummy* in tone, it was visually stylish, but the formulaic and derivative storytelling did it no favors. It made its money back but was another distinct Disney underachiever.

▲
Renaissance employed the technique "motion-capture": a computer-literate rotoscoping that had the actors performing in sensor-equipped suits from which specially written software could then render 3D models.

▶
Aside from Orson Welles, *Transformers: The Movie* also marked the last role of Scatman Crothers—perhaps best remembered as the janitor axed to death by Jack Nicholson in *The Shining*. Vocal talents who survived the film included Leonard Nimoy, Robert Stack, Eric Idle, and Judd Nelson.

While Michael Bay's 2007 CGI techno-juggernaut version of *Transformers: The Movie* put the innovative and phenomenally successful toy range firmly back on the map, Generation 1 fans still favor the 1986 animated version. Already a successful TV series, the spin-off film took a distinctly darker tack, essentially turning it into a slaughterhouse. Losses amongst the heroic Autobots included several popular characters, including Ironhide, Prowl, and Ratchet (all of whom were, if you will, resurrected in Bay's live-action version). But most shocking of all was the death of the Autobots' iconic leader, Optimus Prime, sparking controversy among fans and leading to accusations of callous indifference on the part of the filmmakers—younger fans were said to be weeping in the aisles after their hero's death.

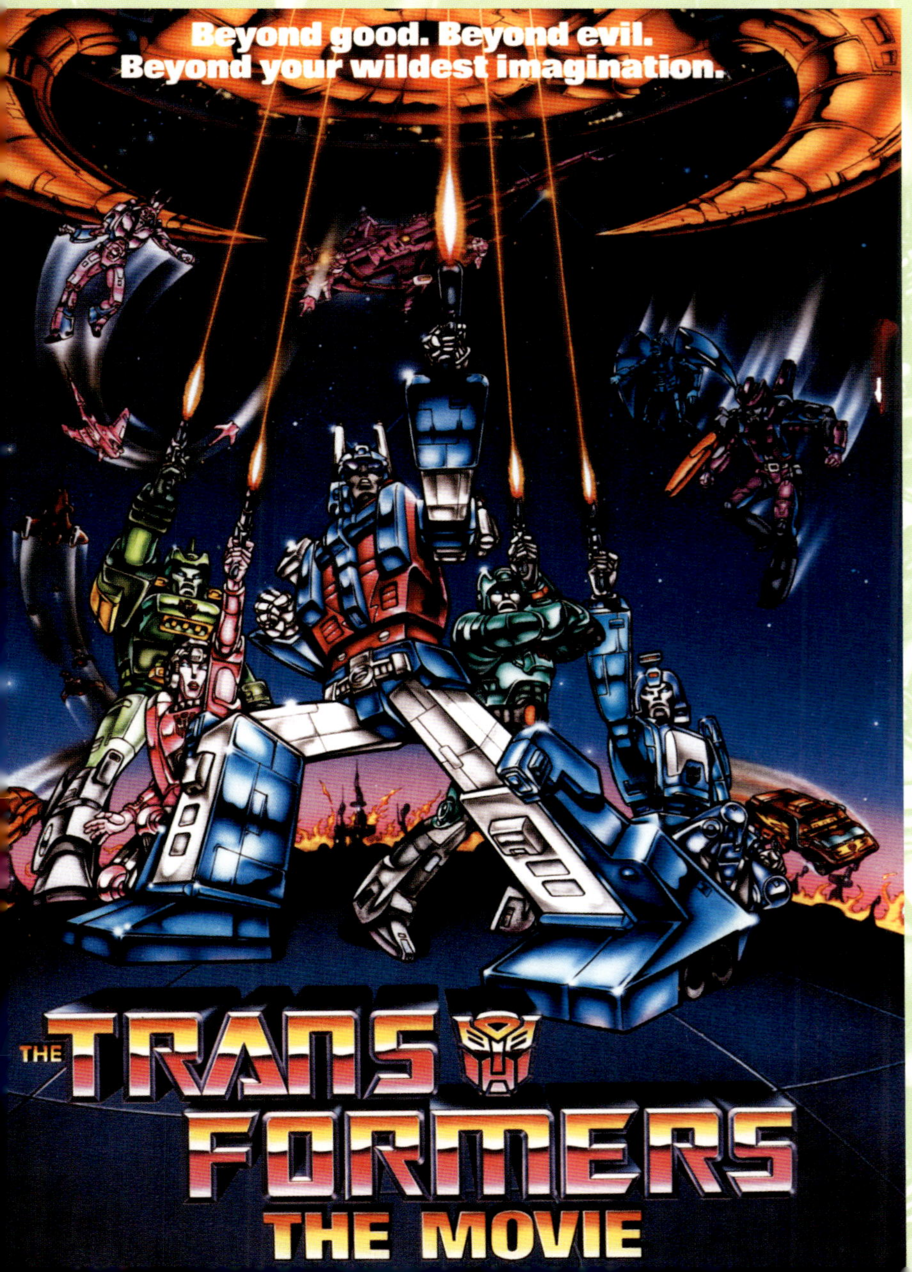

Iconic deaths on screen were matched off-screen. Orson Welles voiced Unicron, the planet-sized Transformers godhead. His voice session took place on October 5, 1985; five days later he was dead.

Perhaps too dark for younger viewers, and not engaging enough for older cinemagoers, the movie was a flop, but it has since developed a large cult following, and not just among Transformers fans.

1988 saw a major shift in movie animation with the release in the west of *Akira*. This film perhaps single-handedly broke anime in the English-speaking mainstream, opening the floodgates for a tsunami of mainly Japanese features that raised the bar for what audiences could expect from animated movies. Often these films featured cultural references and shifts in tone that left the average western child (and many adults) bamboozled. Yet nonetheless they found a receptive audience.

This did not mean there wasn't room for more traditional western animation. 1999 saw the release of *The Iron Giant*, based on Ted Hughes' novel *The Iron Man* (although with the plot relocated to the US). A critical success, it was lauded for its superior characterization, intelligent themes, and touching storytelling. Sadly this didn't translate into ticket sales and the film performed badly at the box office.

Another critically admired but underperforming film was 2000's *Titan A.E.* Although animated movies were now—largely as a result of Eastern influences—more sophisticated, this film seemed to fall foul of conflicting audience expectations. A little more advanced and less preachy than the average Disney movie, it still lacked the depth of the average anime. It was critically well received but its lack of box office success prompted distributor 20th Century Fox to close its animation studio and start out-sourcing.

Renaissance, released in 2006, saw animation adapting to new technological innovations. French director Christian Volckman combined CGI motion capture methods with a stark black and white visual style to produce a film noir/cyberpunk detective story. Despite the innovative approach the film's reception was once again rather mixed, proving that, Pixar-style CG productions aside, these remain difficult times for animated SF movies.

A SCANNER DARKLY

"What does a scanner see? Into the head? Into the heart? Does it see into me? Clearly? Or darkly?"

Such is the underlying theme of *A Scanner Darkly*, Richard Linklater's 2006 film based on the novel of the same name by famed science fiction author Philip K. Dick (the most adapted SF author in film history). While the quote paraphrases a line in the book (itself a reference to the Bible: Corinthians 1, Chapter 13, Verses 9–12), its meaning—about perception of the id and the blurring of fantasy and reality—holds true.

The story revolves around Bob Arctor (played by Keanu Reeves), a deep undercover cop known to his superiors only as Agent Fred, who is attempting to capture major drug dealers. Unfortunately, while playing the role of a user Arctor becomes addicted to Substance D, a side effect of which is to split the two hemispheres of the brain so that they are competing; Arctor and Fred do not realize they are one and the same person and he starts to unwittingly spy on himself.

Capturing the complex concepts of the book on film, particularly the paranoid delusional elements of the story, was never going to be an easy task, and director Linklater's choice to use animation was an interesting one. With the story questioning what is real and what's not, using a form of animation that delivers a hyper-real version of live action seems a natural fit. The process, known as interpolated rotoscoping, overlays animation on top of live action footage, creating a unique look. In simple terms, Linklater shot the film using real actors, edited it as he would normally and then presented it to the animation team, who then used specially created computer software to create a "painterly" version of the film.

Developed for Linklater's earlier film *Waking Life* by Bob Sabiston, the proprietary software Rotoshop allows animators to not only paint over live action footage, but also remove the need to hand draw every frame; once started, the program connects lines across several frames to create fluid animation, and can even replicate and fill in the same colors captured in the live action footage.

Even so, animating the film was not an easy process and proved to be extremely time-consuming, with the original theatrical release date moving several times. However, the finished piece offers an adult animated film with a memorable and distinct style that delivers an unsettling message that Dick would surely have most wholeheartedly approved of.

▶
The film's animation technique is called interpolated rotoscoping, and uses proprietary software called Rotoshop. This allows animators to electronically "paint" over live action footage, much as a painter applies brush strokes to a canvas. Up to 500 hours went into creating each minute of footage. Some of the simplest scenes to shoot proved to be the hardest to animate, such as this scene where all the main characters are discussing the bicycle.

▶
The role of Freck, an amalgamation of the novel's Jerry Fabin and Charles Freck, was written for Rory Cochrane by Linklater, who had worked with him previously on *Dazed and Confused*. All of the other main characters—Arctor (Keanu Reeves), Donna (Winona Ryder), Barris (Robert Downey Jr.), and Luckman (Woody Harrelson)—appear in both the novel and the film.

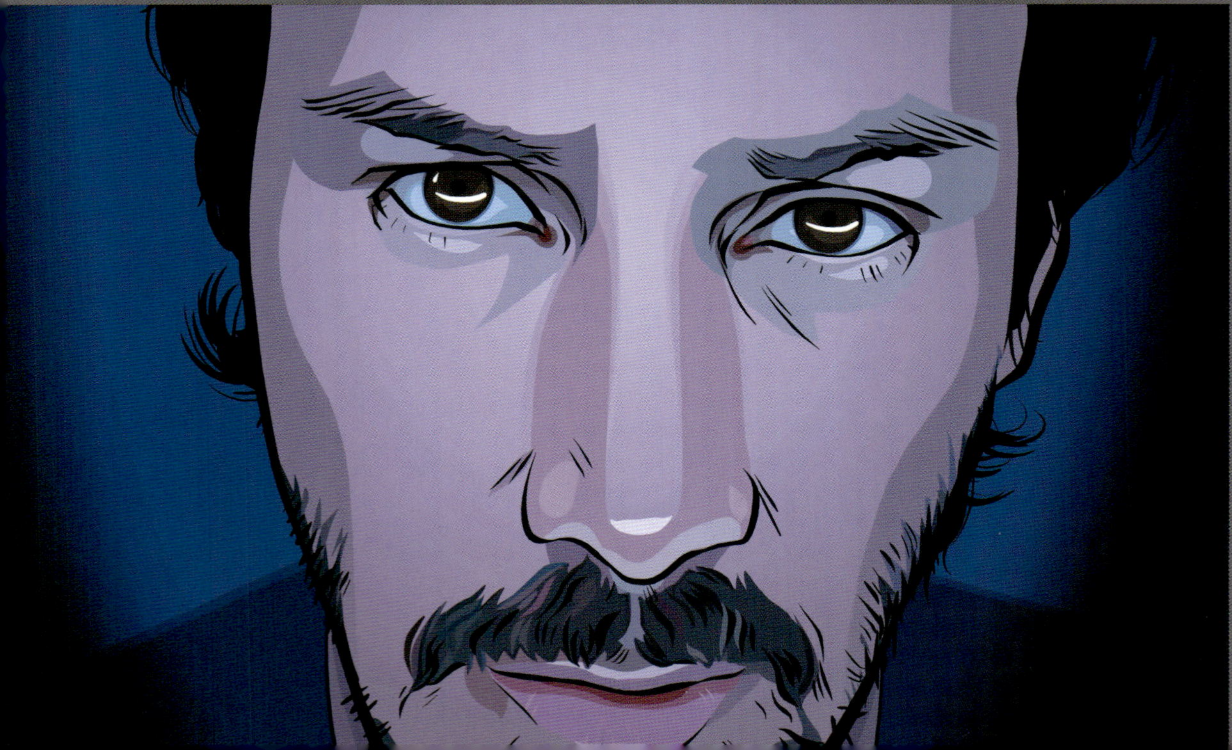

◀
Many complications arose during the animation process, which took around 15 months to complete. A style guide including details on the likes of the look of Arctor's beard, was eventually created to avoid a clash of artistic styles between different animators, which had hampered the film early on.

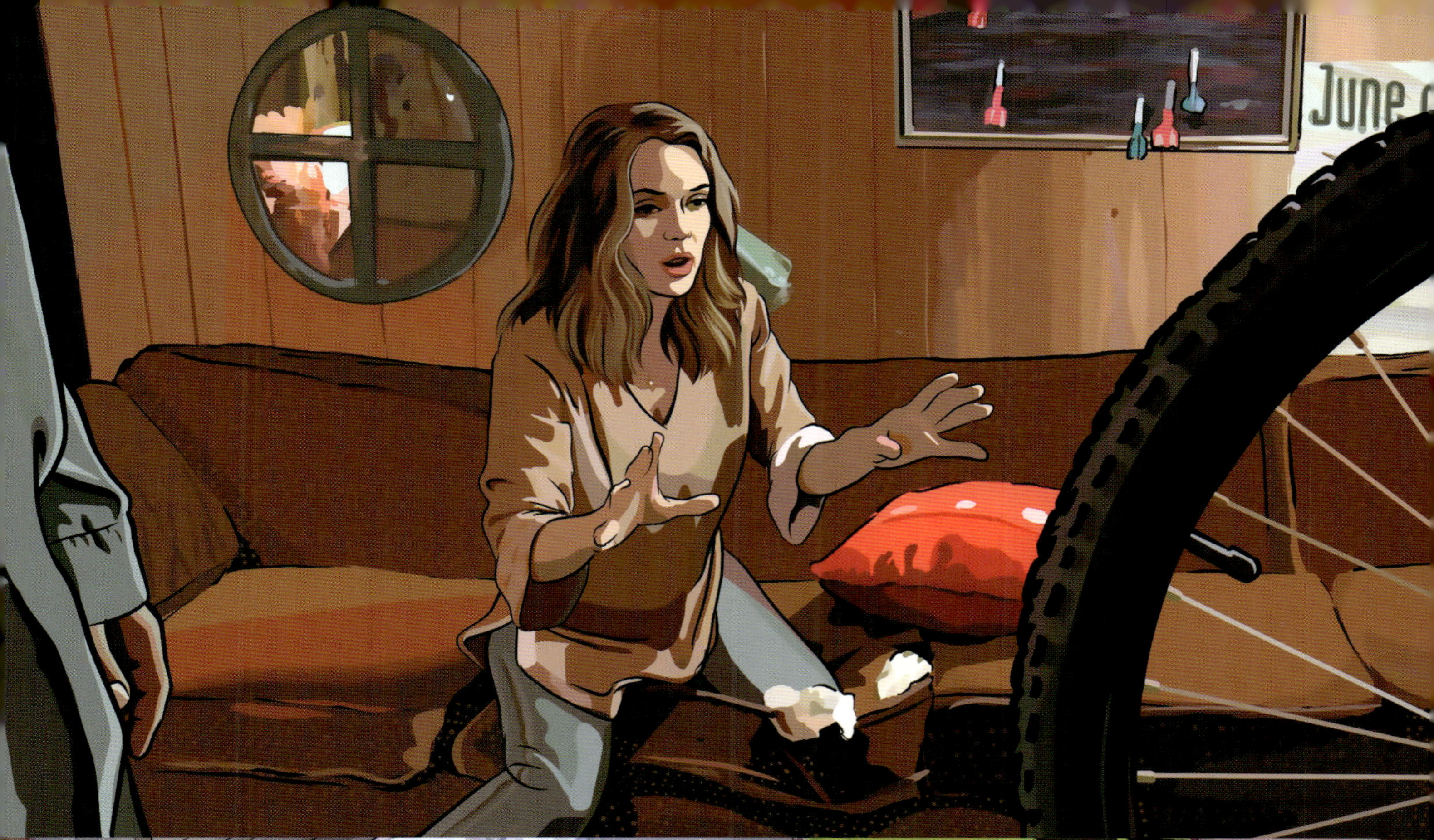
June

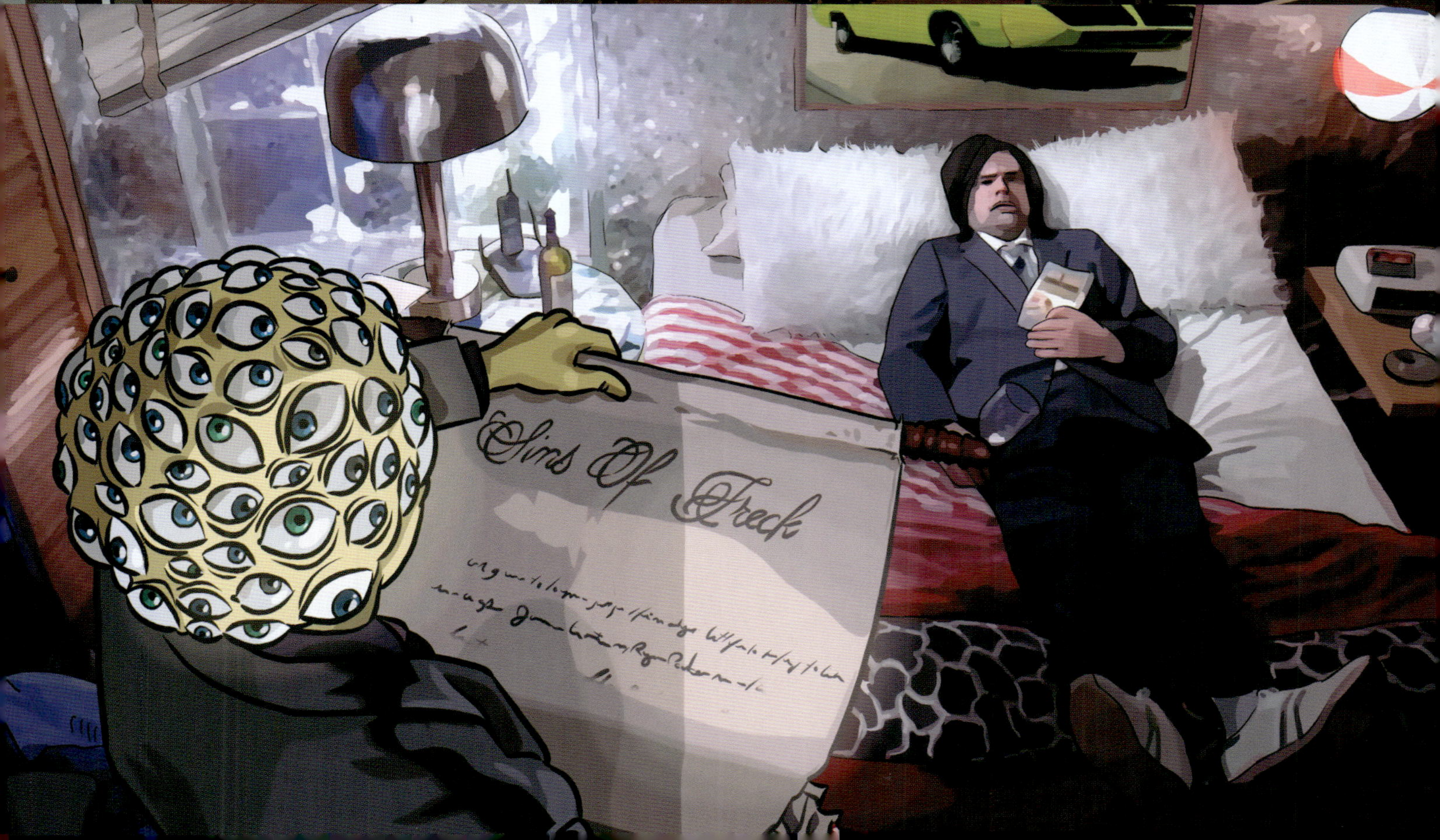
Sins Of Freck

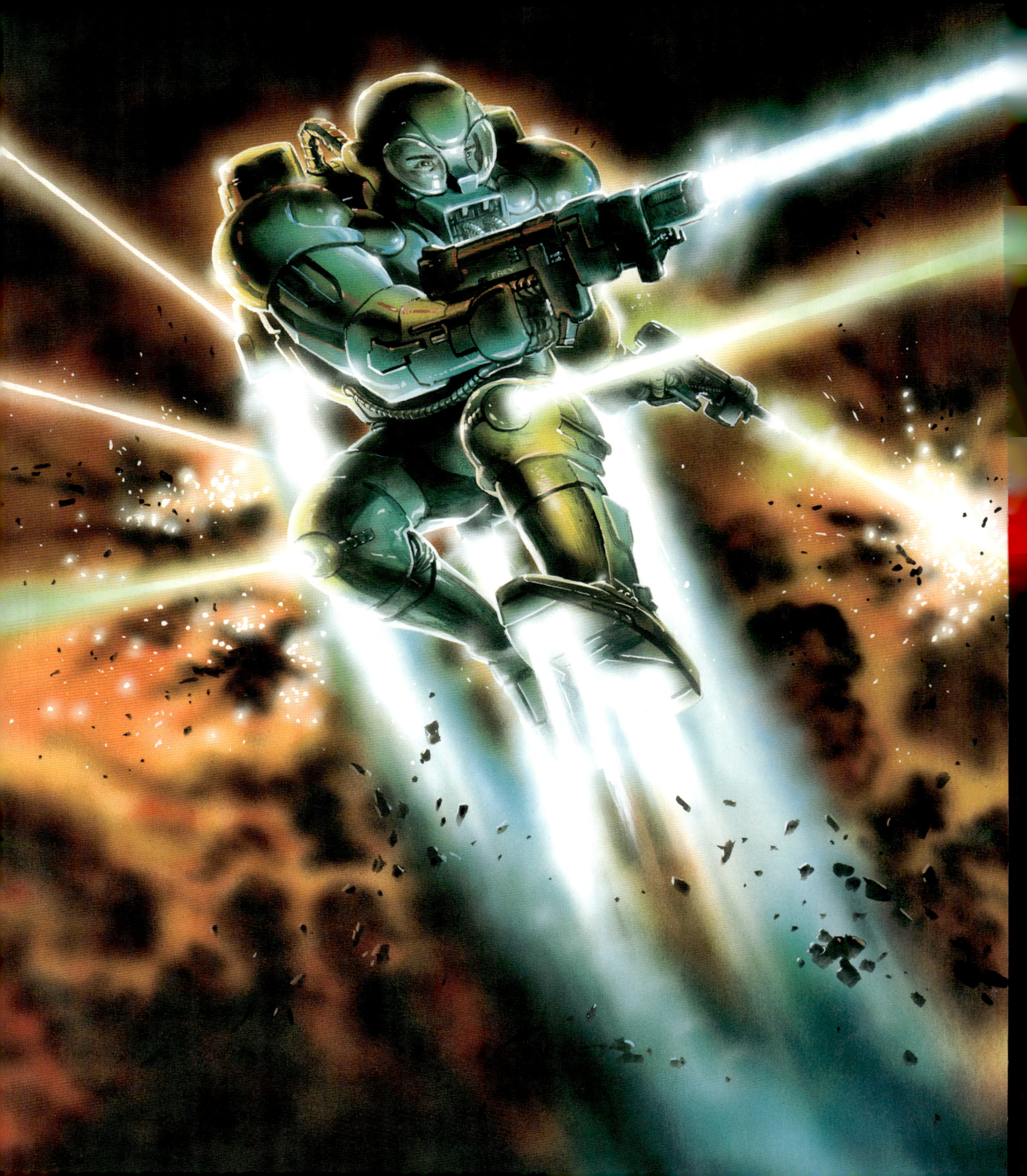

6 OTHER MEDIA

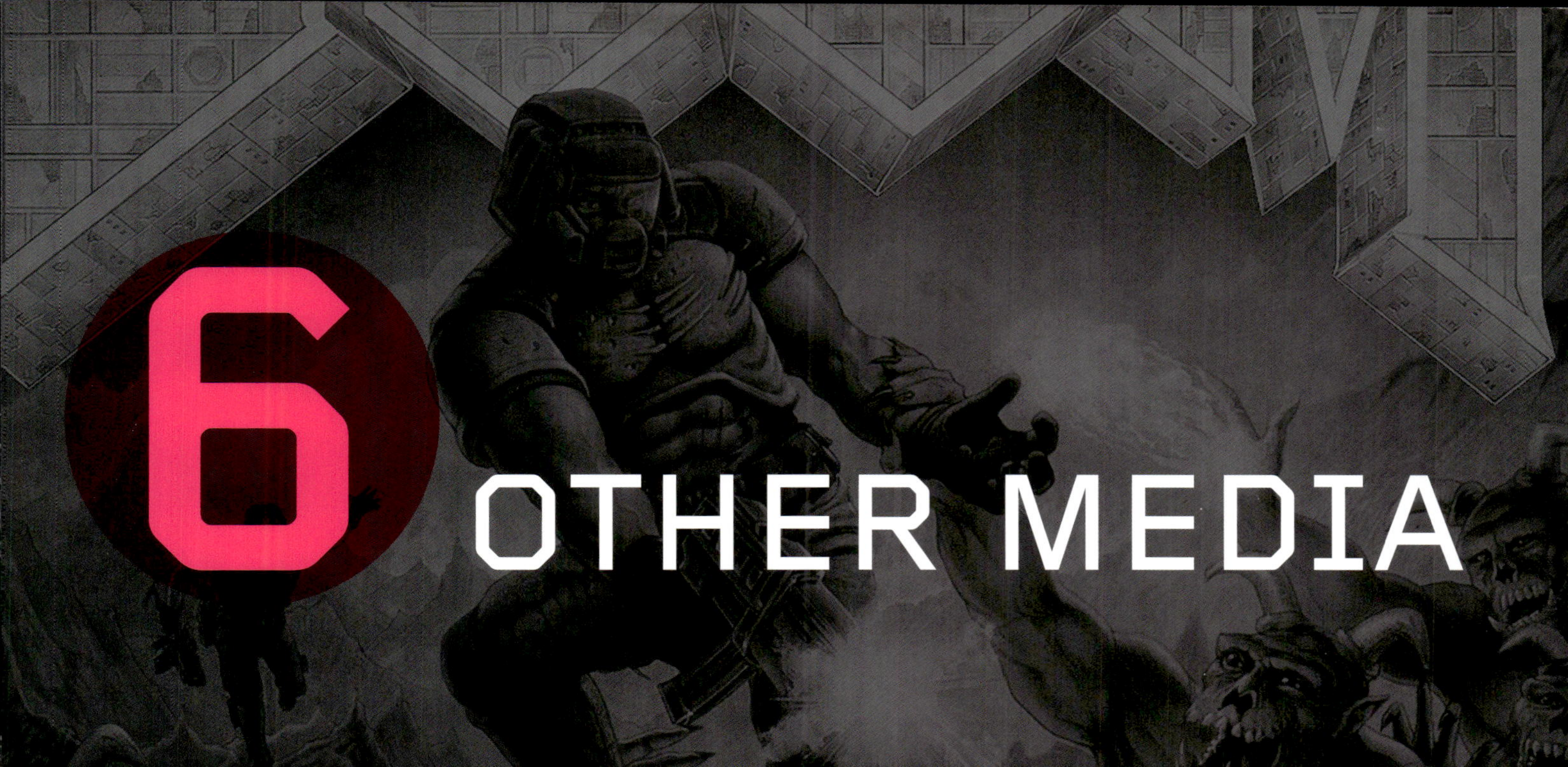

THE ART OF VIDEO GAMES

As one of the most recent entertainment formats to be created, the video game has borrowed much from its predecessors. There have been countless game adaptations of films, comics, and novels, as well as games inspired by the ideas presented in those mediums, and, somewhat unsurprisingly, some knock-off clones, too.

The science fiction genre has not escaped either, with such stirring franchises as *Star Wars, Star Trek, Spider-Man, The Hitchhiker's Guide to the Galaxy*, and many more being given life in the interactive gaming arena—some more successfully than others. But even before the advent of tie-in licensed titles, video games and SF have always gone hand in hand.

Interactivity is ultimately the main draw of video games; the ability to control what happens to the game's protagonists is what sets the medium apart from its competitors. This interactivity helps explain why games, despite their relative youth—*Pong*, released in 1972, is widely considered the first mass produced video game success story, with home computer systems not taking off until the 1980s—have become such a massive part of popular culture.

As gaming has developed, so sci-fi games have seamlessly adapted to and adopted each new format. From the early days of the coin-op arcade machine—*Space Invaders* is the best known, but there are numerous others—through the first home entertainment systems such as the Sinclair ZX80, to the more modern games consoles and handhelds like the Xbox 360 and Nintendo DS, sci-fi games have been an integral part of gaming.

There can be few gaming genres that haven't been graced with multiple SF titles. The first-person shooter is perhaps the most popular, but everything from role-playing games (RPGs) through to racing games have seen SF releases. And they encompass multiple science fiction themes: mecha; time travel; space exploration; alien invasion; apocalypse. You name it—the video game sector has likely exploited it.

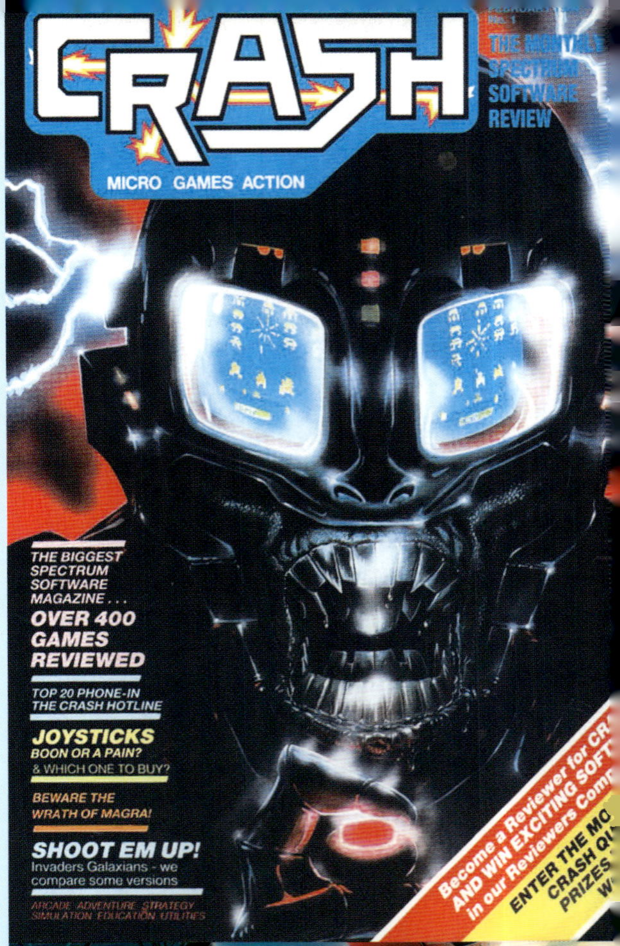

▶ **Oliver Frey is perhaps one of the forgotten heroes of early video gaming. In his capacity as illustrator on three of the UK's biggest magazines—*Crash, Zzap!64*, and *Amtix!*—his artwork caught the imagination of a generation of gamers. This cover for *Crash* #1 shows an alien playing *Space Invaders*.**

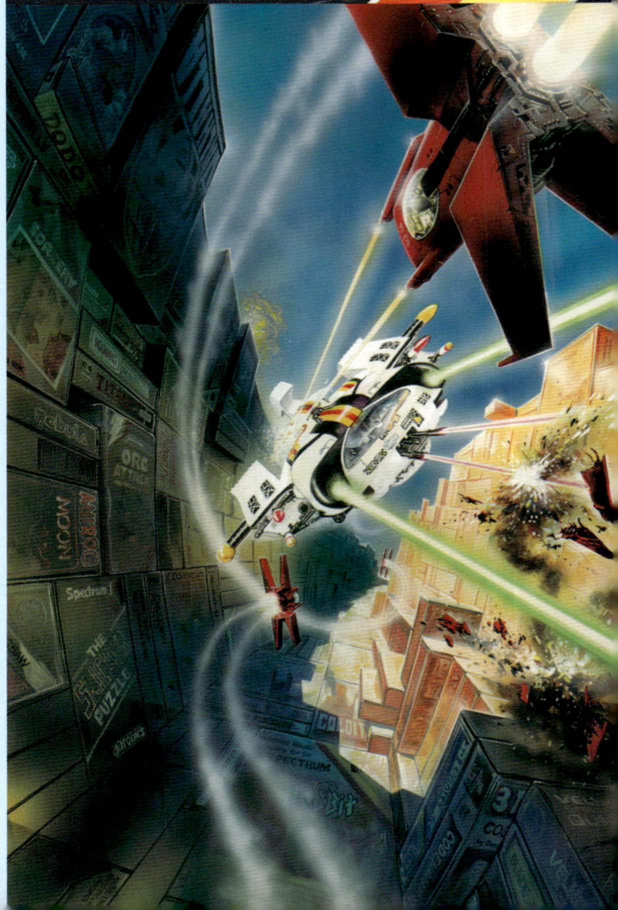

▶ **Another Oliver Frey cover, this time for *Crash* #5. With echoes of the battle in the Death Star trench in the original *Star Wars*, Frey has smartly constructed the canyon in which the ships fight out of ZX Spectrum game boxes.**

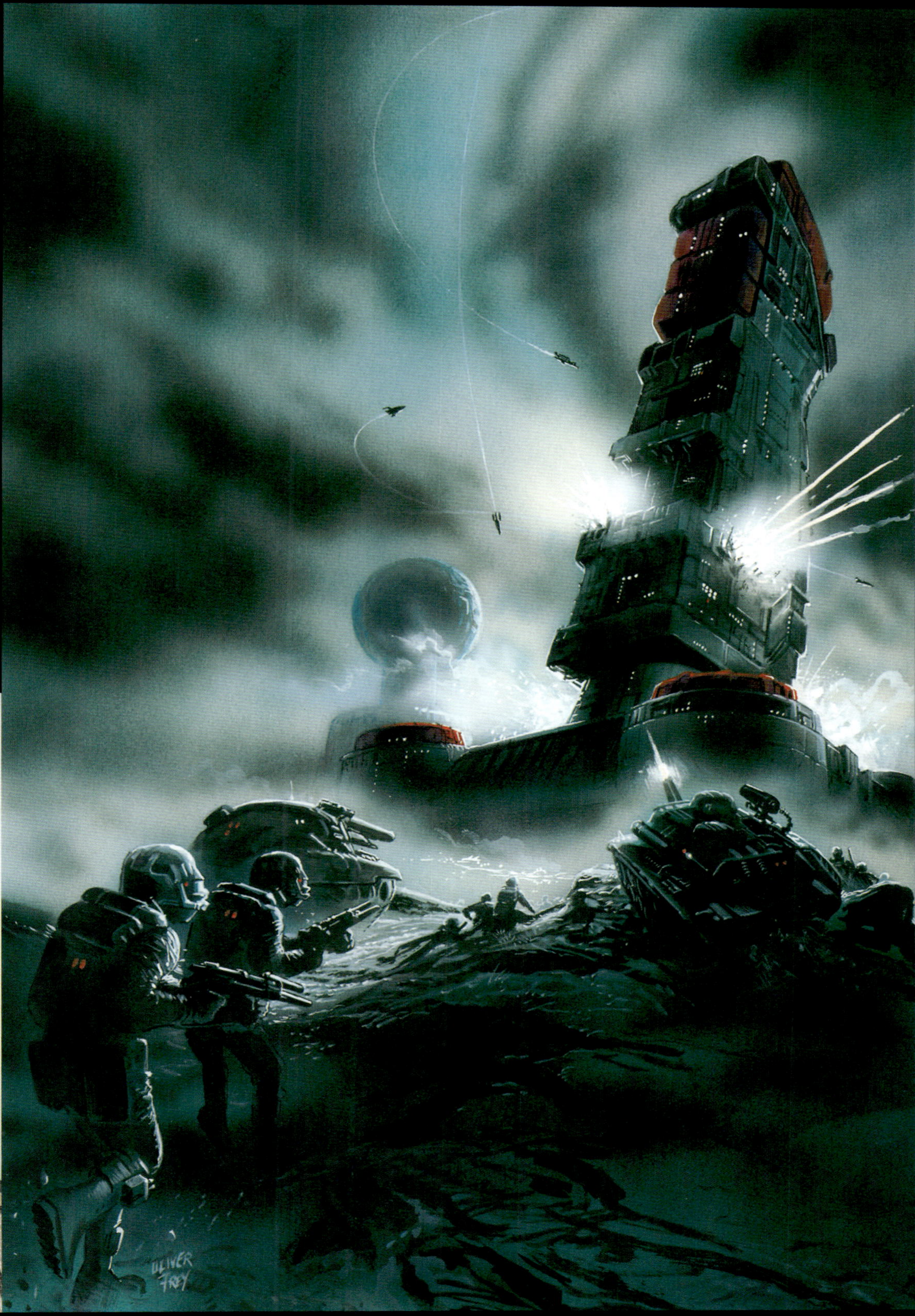

▶
Oliver Frey was often wonderfully creative in his covers, as in this rather Chris Foss-like image for *Crash* #10, depicting a monstrous grounded spaceship that is actually a joystick.

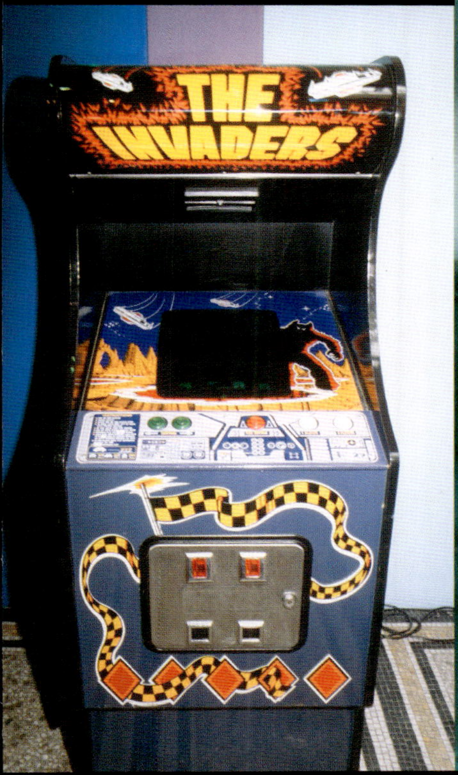

▼
Much loved by arcade junkies, *Space Invaders*, created by Tomohiro Nishikado in 1978, was one of the early success stories of gaming. It also came in iconic arcade cabinets, which couldn't help but catch the eye of the sci-fi enthusiast.

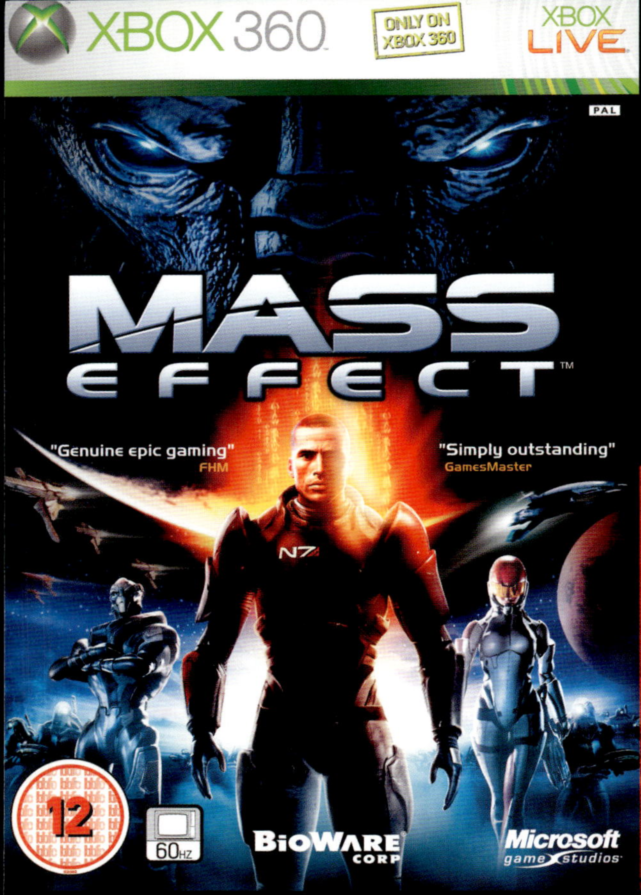

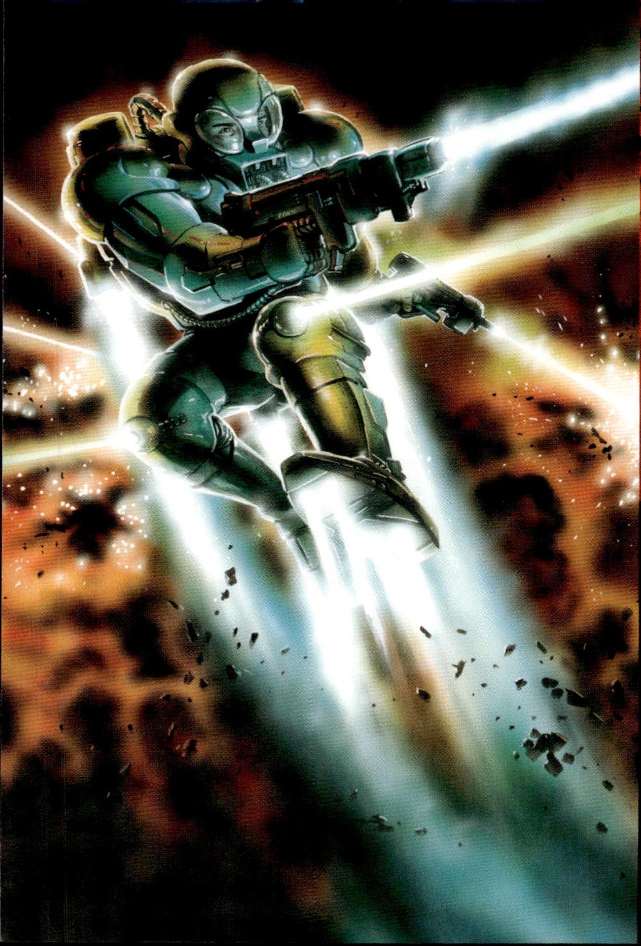

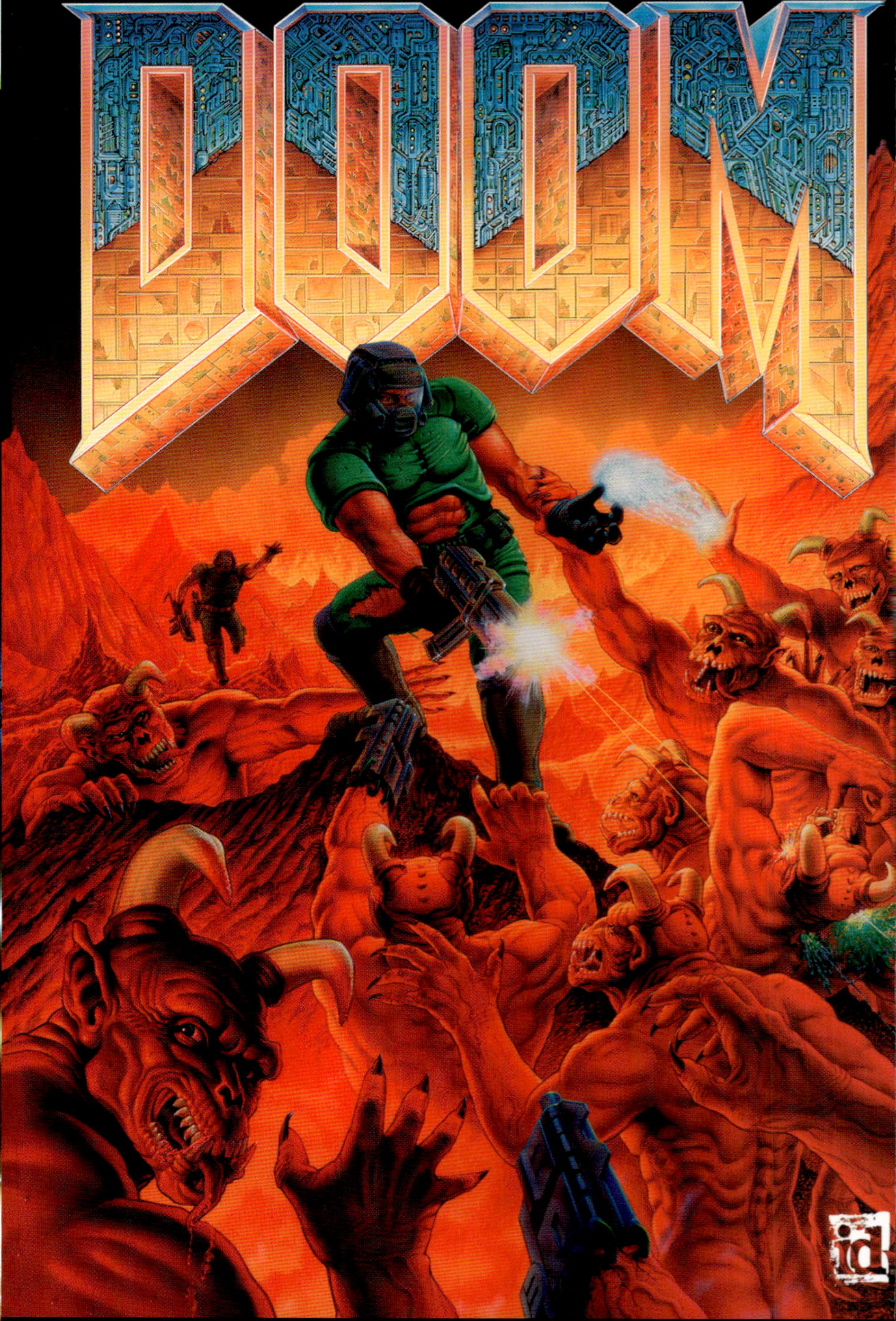

◀
As well as video game magazine covers, Oliver Frey occasionally turned his hand to box art too, including this dynamic cover for *Retrograde* on the Commodore 64.

◀▲
An example of a more contemporary piece of box art, BioWare's space-faring RPG *Mass Effect* takes its cues from numerous sci-fi film posters.

Thousands of science fiction video games have been produced in the past 40 years or so, and inspiration for both their sleeve art and their content has been wide-ranging. In the early days of video gaming and throughout much of the 1980s, sleeve art was predominantly poor and often very cartoon-like, doing little to dispel the popular thinking that video games were just for kids. However, with a canvas the size of an audiocassette, this is perhaps an unfair criticism, and there were certainly a few innovative covers during that period: *Nodes Of Yesod*, *Space Harrier*, *Alien Syndrome*, and *R-Type*, for example.

The advent of PC gaming saw the arrival of larger boxes for the games, allowing the artwork to expand and improve immeasurably. The growing popularity of gaming throughout the '80s and '90s meant an increase in investment in all aspects of the culture. In turn, this has led to the current Amaray-style plastic cases sporting some of the best art ever seen in the sector.

The influence on video game art of such legendary science fiction artists as Chesley Bonestell, Ed "Emsh" Emshwiller, Chris Foss, and Drew Struzan, among others, should certainly be acknowledged. However, certainly in the early days of home entertainment, the influence of Oliver Frey, chief illustrator for *Crash* (for the Spectrum), *Zzap!64* (Commodore 64), and *Amtix!* (Amstrad), three of the most popular magazines during the gaming boom of the 1980s, cannot be overstated. Frey's composition, style, and invention shaped many sleeves during that era and beyond.

While most covers show the influences of an artist, some publishers commissioned specially produced artwork for their video games, the most memorable relationship perhaps being the one forged between Roger Dean and Psygnosis. Dean produced several front covers for the company (including *Brattacus* and *Chrono Quest*), and even designed its famous owl logo.

Another well-known name who contributed to the video game sector was the Spanish artist Luis Royo. Famed for his *Heavy Metal* magazine work, his art featured on *Game Over* for the ZX Spectrum in the 1980s. Although widely regarded as a disappointing game, Royo's notorious cover had two outstanding points that proved irresistible to the predominantly male teen gamer demographic. Comic book artists have not been afraid to lend their talents to video games either. Another *Heavy Metal* alumnus, Simon Bisley—best known for his work on the UK's *2000 AD*—came up with the cover imagery for PC game *The Terminator: Rampage* (which was also used on a comic book), while Glenn Fabry, cover artist for edgy comic book *Preacher*, produced the image for the popular *Speedball 2*.

Several publishers proved to be more active than others in the promotion of the science fiction genre. These included previously mentioned Psygnosis, who created the popular *Wipeout* racing games (which have always had striking covers); Firebird, who produced the highly influential sci-fi game *Elite* (although its cover—essentially a logo—is not its best feature); Mastertronic Added Dimension (a.k.a. MAD), whose cover art often seemed to be inspired by the science fiction art greats; and The Bitmap Brothers, who did much to promote the use of the brawny action hero as a central image (something still aped today).

The popularity of *Space Invaders, Defender, Galaxian*, and *Asteroids* in the early days of video gaming firmly established science fiction games as a vital segment of the sector. But the more recent success of the likes of *Gears of War*, the *Halo* series, and *BioShock* are ensuring sci-fi games have a healthy future too.

◀ **Due to its high level of blood-spattered violence, *Doom* is one of video games' most notorious releases. If ever a sleeve perfectly summed up a game's content, then Don Ivan Punchatz's *Doom* cover for id Software is it.**

▶ **Legendary artist and designer Roger Dean not only created covers for game publisher Psygnosis, but also suggested the company's name and designed their famous "purple owl" logo.**

VIDEO GAME DESIGN

By their very nature, video games are a visual medium, and as such, the artistic aesthetic of a game extends well beyond the sleeve image. Video games graphically represent the world (and, in the case of sci-fi games, other worlds) around us and can be incredibly artistic. The advent of three dimensional (3D) graphics in the 1990s created a level of detail that now borders on the photo-real (see the likes of Crytek/EA's *Crysis*), while other games, such as the adventure title *Shadow Of The Colossus* and first-person shooter *BioShock*, have been described as moving works of art.

The professionalism of the modern landscape, where huge budgets are set aside to create, develop, and market a new release, has been both detrimental and beneficial to the industry. Although there's always a danger of homogeneity (and an endless sea of derivative sequels), publishers now have the financial support to really push the artistic and graphical detail of their titles—although as has been pointed out many times, stunning looks do not a good game make.

With many of the big releases, the endeavors of artists are used throughout production, from concept art and storyboard pre-production, through to the creation of the game itself, and then post-production to market the games, with inventive images used for poster art, consumer advertising, and magazine articles and front covers.

The release of concept art, often on the game disc itself (usually as unlockable extras), but also in books (whether they be official strategy guide books, art books, or novels), calendars, and on official websites, has become more commonplace too. The promotional possibilities of such art was taken to the extreme for gentlemen's magazine *Playboy* when a mock "photoshoot" of sexy female video game characters was produced, including, among others, a specially created picture of *Tabula Rasa*'s Sarah Morrison in a state of undress.

However, the fan adoration for this concept artwork—and the artists that have produced such work—particularly the likes of Konami's *Metal Gear Solid* series, Epic Games' *Gears of War*, Square Enix's *Final Fantasy* franchise, and Bungie's *Halo*, is testament to the creativity and professionalism of the modern gaming world.

▶ ▶▼

Roger Dean's designs for Psygnosis' *Shadow of the Beast* went through a number of changes between the release of the first game in 1989 and its sequel n 1990. His original cat-like designs for the Beast gave way to a much more alien and menacing look in the second game.

◀▼

It's hard to do justice to the full dazzling spectacle of such scrolling shoot-'em-ups as *Psyvariar 2* without seeing them in full motion, but they are something to behold.

▼

The creators of adventure game *Shadow of the Colossus*, Team Ico, wanted gamers to have an emotional connection to their actions, and used various graphical tricks, alongside a poignant story, to achieve that.

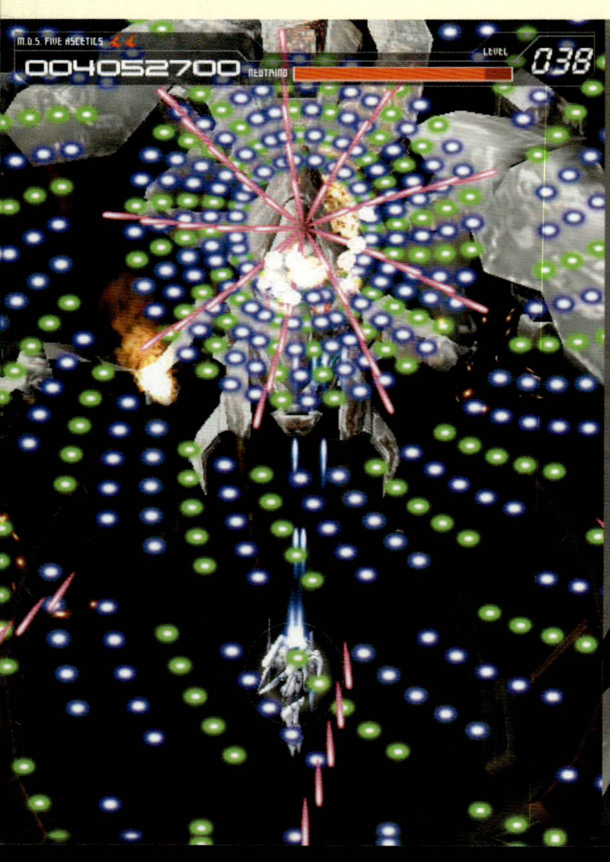

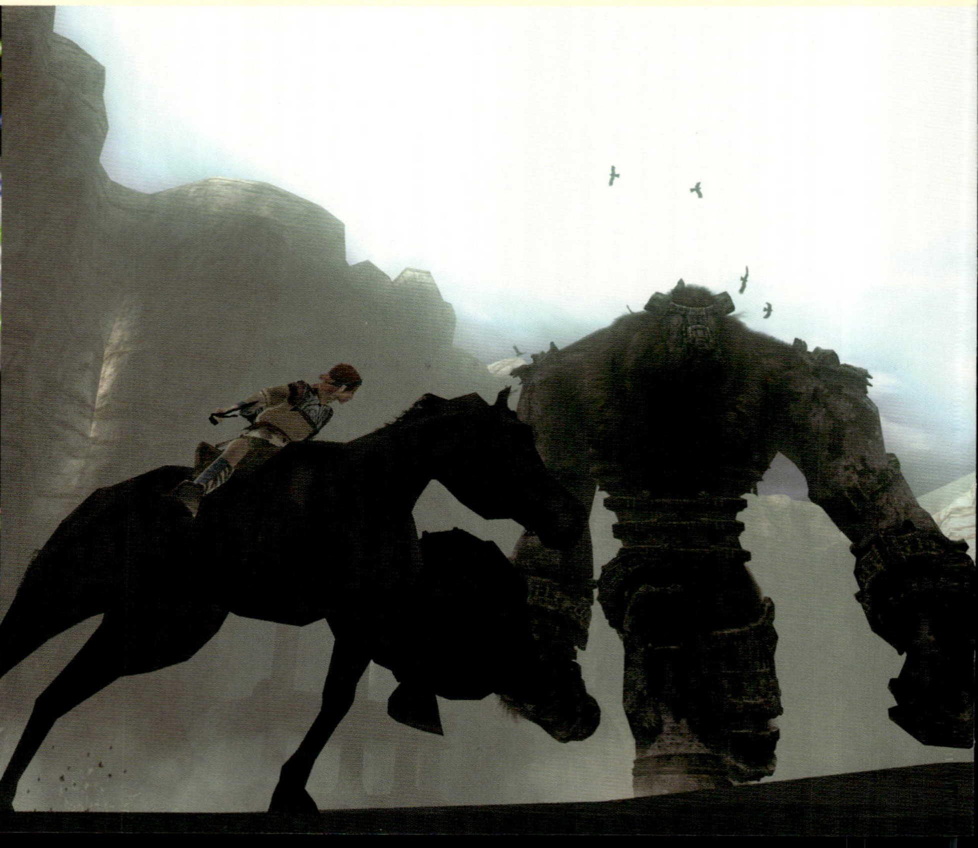

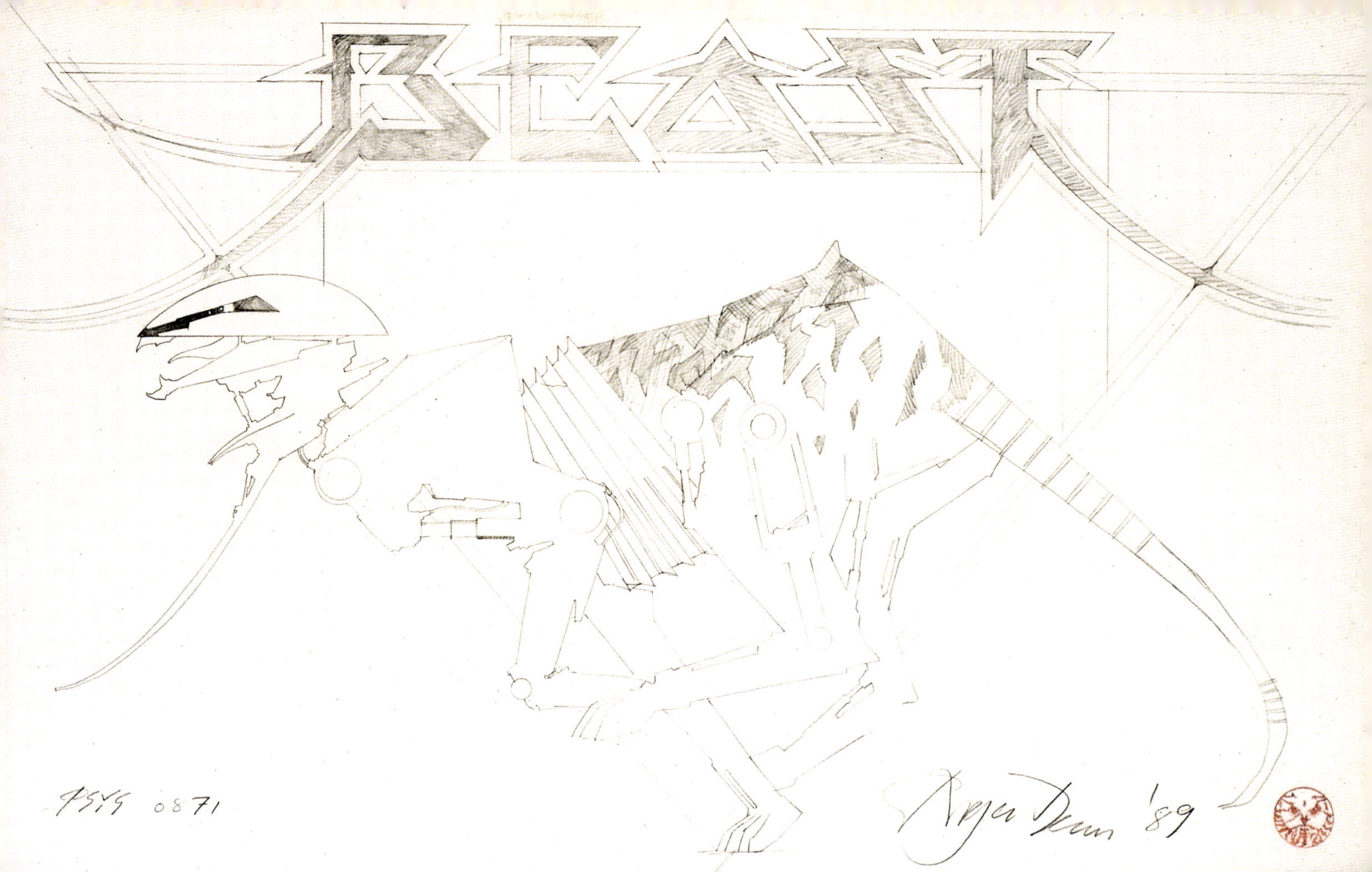
BEAST

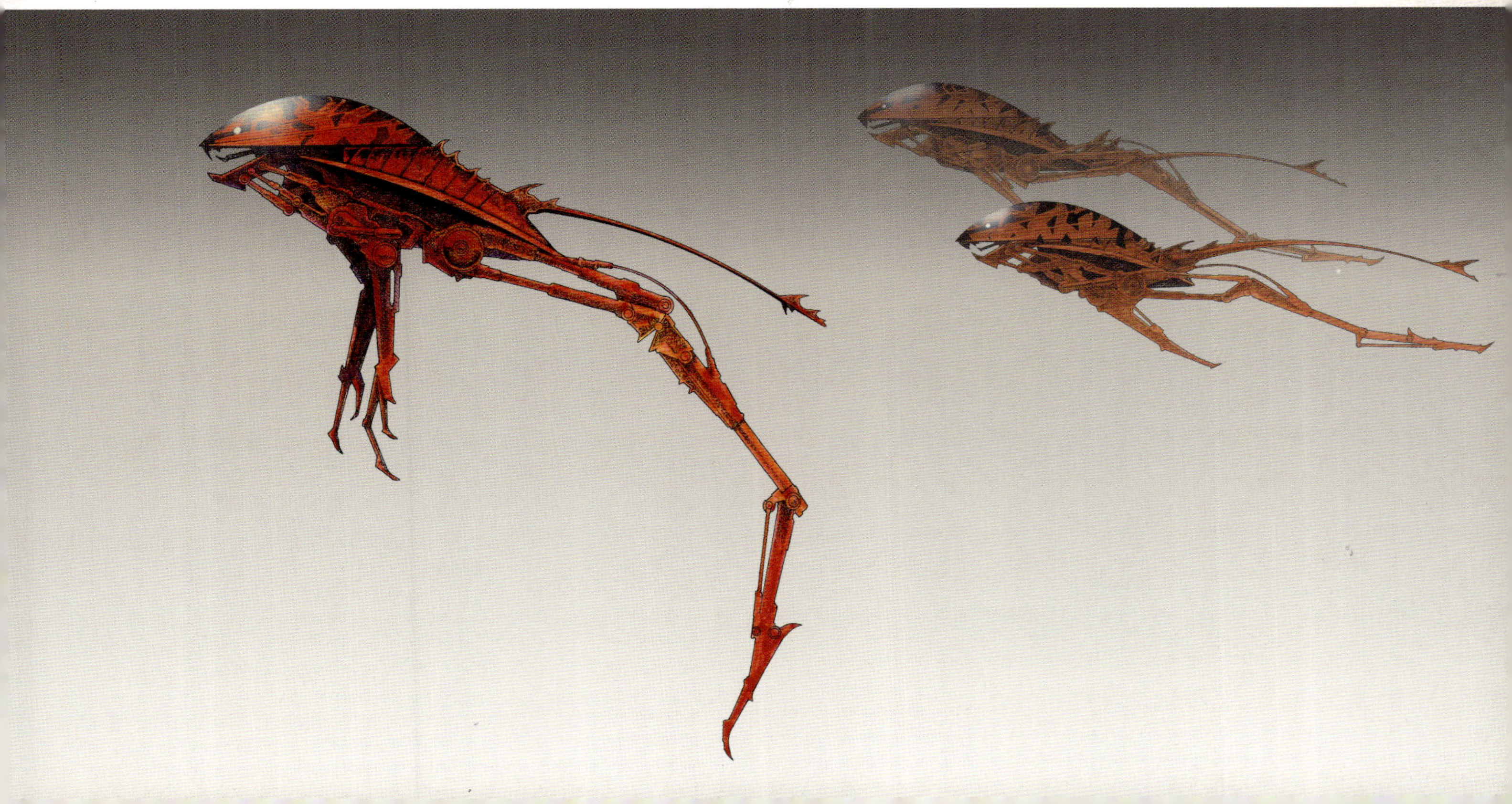

3D graphics debuted in homes in the mid 1990s with the advanced 32-bit processing power of the Sega Saturn and Sony PlayStation, which used cell-shaded polygons to create beautifully rendered 3D environments. Although the likes of *Star Fox*, released in 1993 on the Super NES, preceded the launches of both consoles, it was these two that truly delivered the first 3D experience into the home. Many gamers will never forget the first time they put futuristic racing game *WipeOut* into their PS and were blown away—not just by the speed of the races, but also the splendor of the tracks and their environs.

All of which is not to say that artistic merit did not exist in video gaming prior to 1994. While much of a game's "beauty" is dictated by the power of the engine running it, this is not always the case, and there were some key developments early on which allowed the modern game as we know it to thrive. *Defender*, released in arcades in 1980, was the first side-scrolling shooter and, alongside the vertical scrolling shooter *Xevious*, virtually created the shoot-'em-up genre that still thrives today. Special mention must also go to *Gradius*, *R-Type*, *Ikaruga*, *Psyvariar*, and, perhaps the most unique of them all, the homo-erotic *Cho Aniki*. Anyone who has seen these games running at full tilt cannot fail to be stunned by the beauty of the patterns that appear onscreen.

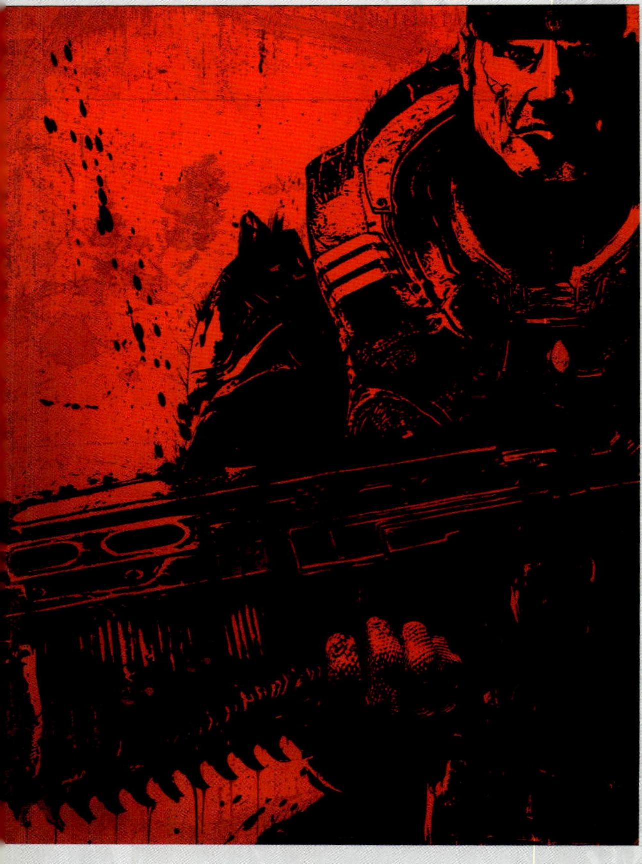

Other key developments in the artistic growth of games came via the likes of *Battlezone* (1980, arcade) and *Elite* (1984, console), which introduced wire frame vector graphics (essentially 3D worlds created using simple lines), while *Dune II: The Battle For Arakis* set the graphical standard for the real-time strategy (RTS) genre in 1992, with its detailed overhead view of the battlefield. In 1993 PC gamers were introduced to *Myst*, one of the first mass market games, in which the solution to puzzles unlocked stunning new environments on the mysterious island where the game is set.

The likes of *Starcraft* (1998) and *Eve Online* (2003) pushed the boundaries of online gaming, and the graphics therein, and remain favorites within the sci-fi genre. More recently, the Wii's 3D platformer *Super Mario Galaxy* reintroduced fun back into the SF genre, supported by mesmerizing worlds to explore.

Perhaps more than any other genre, the first-person shooter (FPS) has pushed the graphical capabilities of the video game, starting with the likes of *Quake* and *Doom* and moving through more modern contributions such as the *Metroid*, *Half-Life*, and *Halo* franchises. Unlike *Gears Of War*, for instance, where the camera is fixed behind the character, the first-person viewpoint of the FPS aims for a more realistic approach than other genres, for total immersion within the game world. *Half-Life* in particular has been influential in the modern era of gaming for its use of in-game storytelling, having ignored the usual cinematic cut scenes to further the narrative in favor of interactive sequences instead.

The growth and development of video gaming since its inception has meant the rise of a vibrant market that's very much part of the mainstream consciousness. In turn, there is a clear appetite for science fiction games within that market, not to mention all the trimmings—including some masterful art—that come with it.

▶ ▶▼
The influence of the 1920s and '30s is clear throughout 2K Games' smash hit FPS *BioShock*. Set in the city of Rapture, hidden beneath the oceans, art deco stylings appear on everything from the architecture of the buildings to the objets d'arts that are scattered throughout the levels.

▶▶
Valve Software's *Half-Life*, starring Gordon Freeman and Alyx Vance (pictured), is one of the most acclaimed games of the modern era for its approach to storytelling.

◀ ▶
In Epic Games' popular third-person shooter, *Gears of War*, players assume the role of Marcus Fenix—seen here on the right in action in a screen shot from the first game, and on the left in striking promotional art for *Gears of War 2*—battling the Locust Horde on the planet Sera.

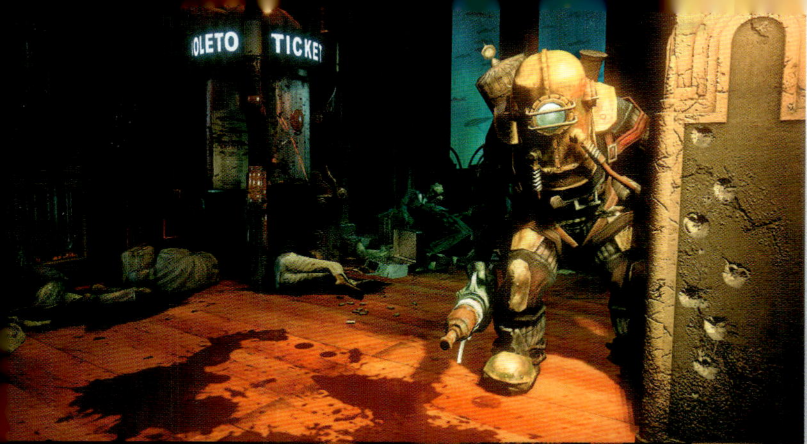
OLETO
TICKET

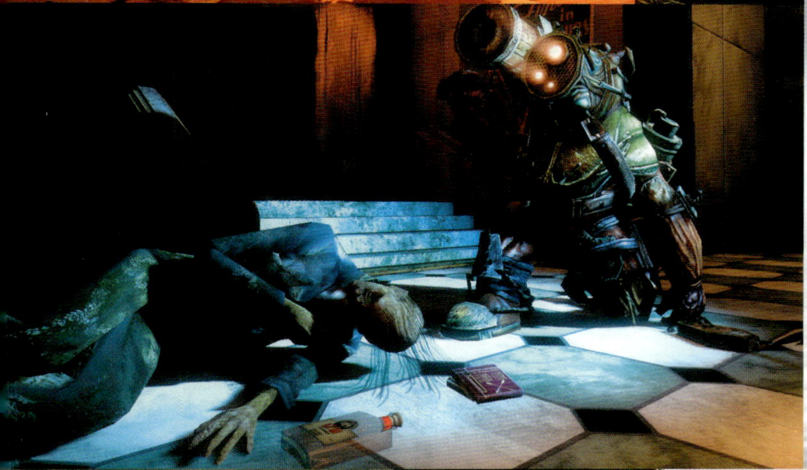

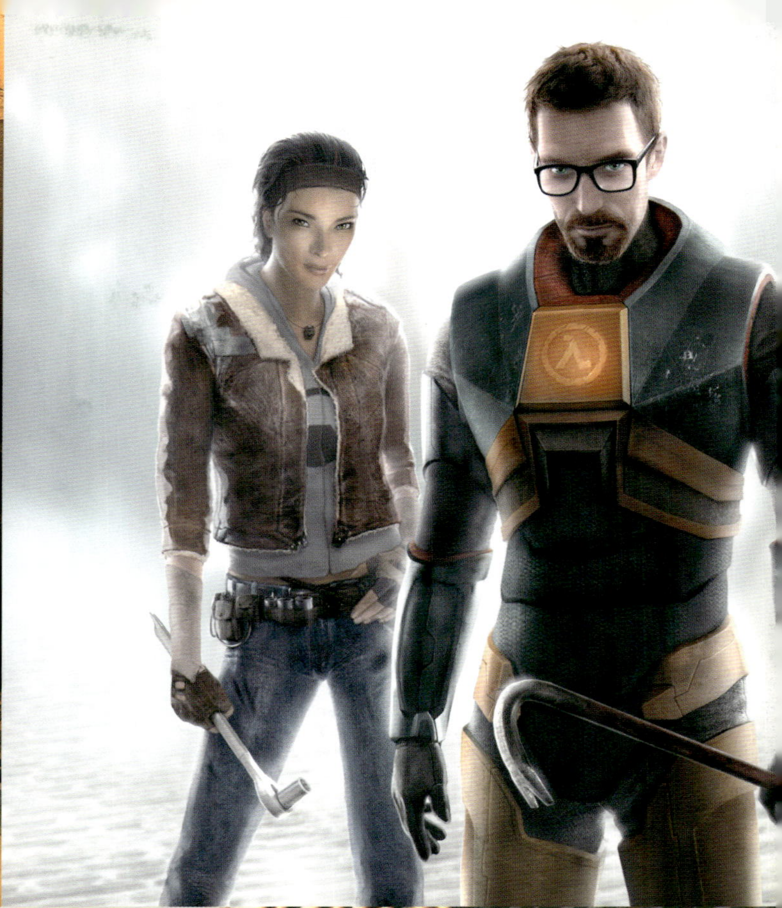

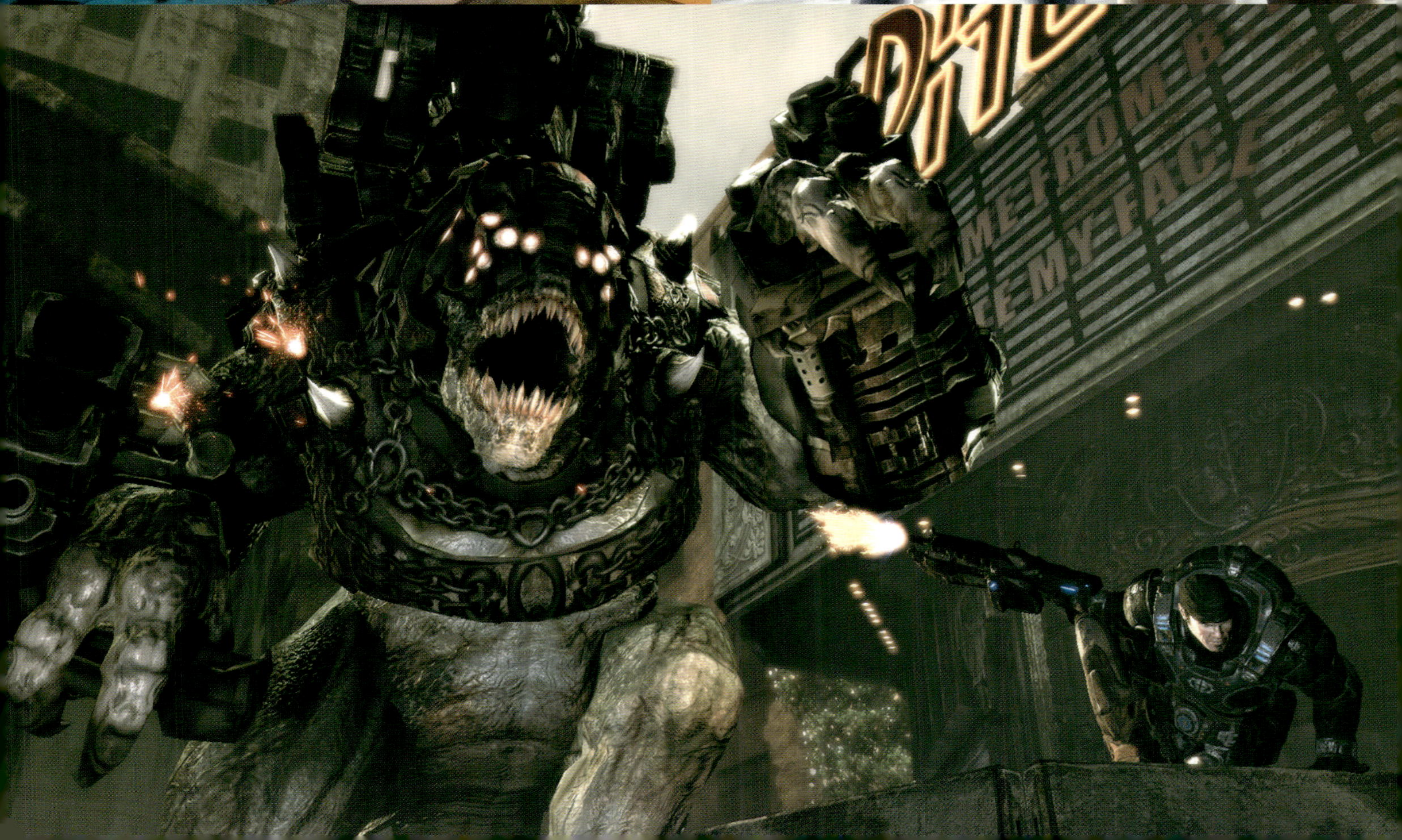
ME FROM B
E MY FACE

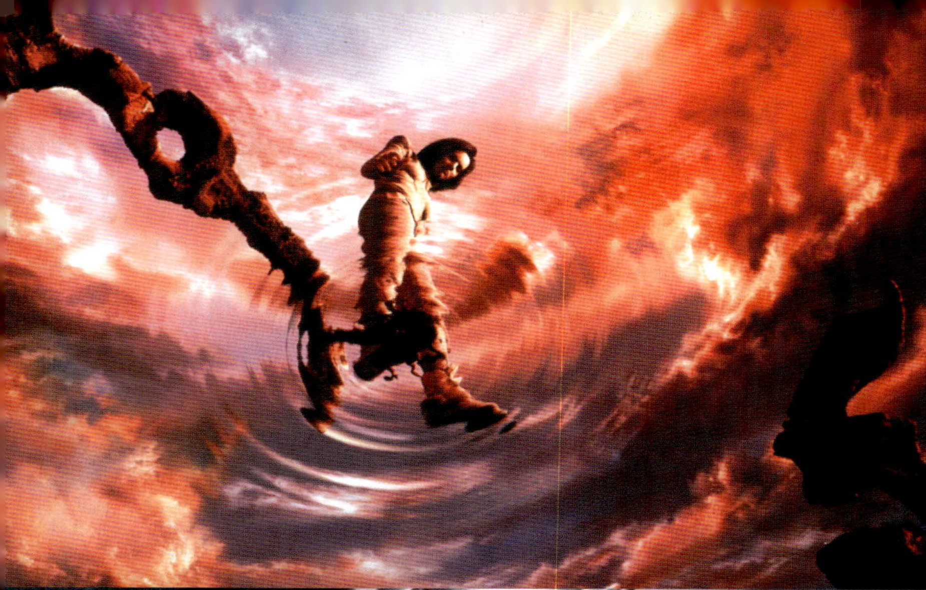

FINAL FANTASY

Few games have done more to widen the medium's appeal than *Final Fantasy*. The game was originally created as a swansong for designer Hironobu Sakaguchi at Square (later to become Square Enix). From such humble beginnings, legends are born, and the subsequent success of the game, now into its twelfth iteration (with numerous spin-offs), meant Sakaguchi's retirement was happily put on hold.

Final Fantasy is the world's most famous role-playing game (RPG), a form of adventure game that has become synonymous with the science fiction and fantasy genres, where the player controls either a single or group of characters and leads them on an action-packed quest. Created for the Nintendo Entertainment System (NES) in 1987, *Final Fantasy* was by no means the first RPG to hit consoles, but it was arguably the best. There have now been numerous volumes of the series—not all of them RPGs—covering various platforms, and the franchise has also spread out into animated series, films, novels, and toys.

Rich in detail, each volume of *Final Fantasy* features an independent story, usually with unique characters, but all share one thing in common: innovation. Under the watchful eye of Sakaguchi, who directed the first five games and produced most of the others, and Yoshitaka Amano (who was art director for *Final Fantasy* through *FFVI*, and the man responsible for the series' indelible logos) and Tetsuya Nomura (art director through *FFVII–X*), the series has become known for its deeply involving characters and stories, spellbinding visuals, and enchanting soundtracks.

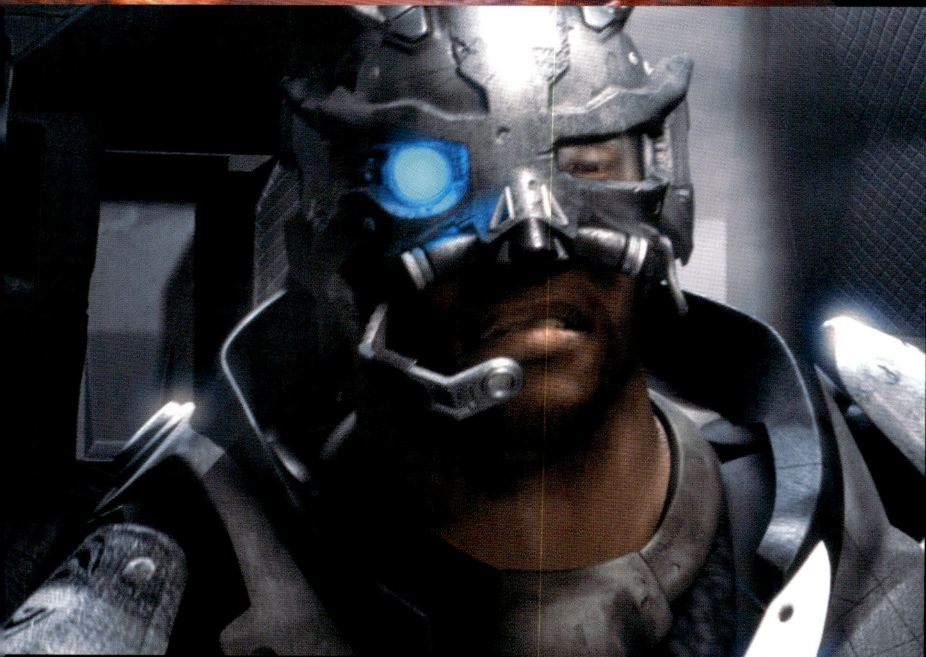

▲ ▲▲
Directed by series creator Hironobu Sakaguchi, the first full-length feature, *The Spirits Within*, was much maligned by film critics in 2001. Since then, its eco-friendly message and stunning visuals have been reappraised, and it remains a popular buy on DVD.

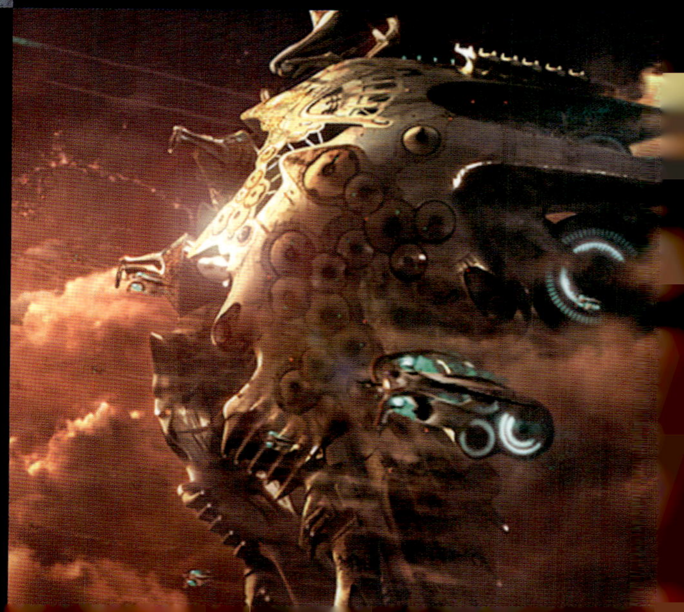

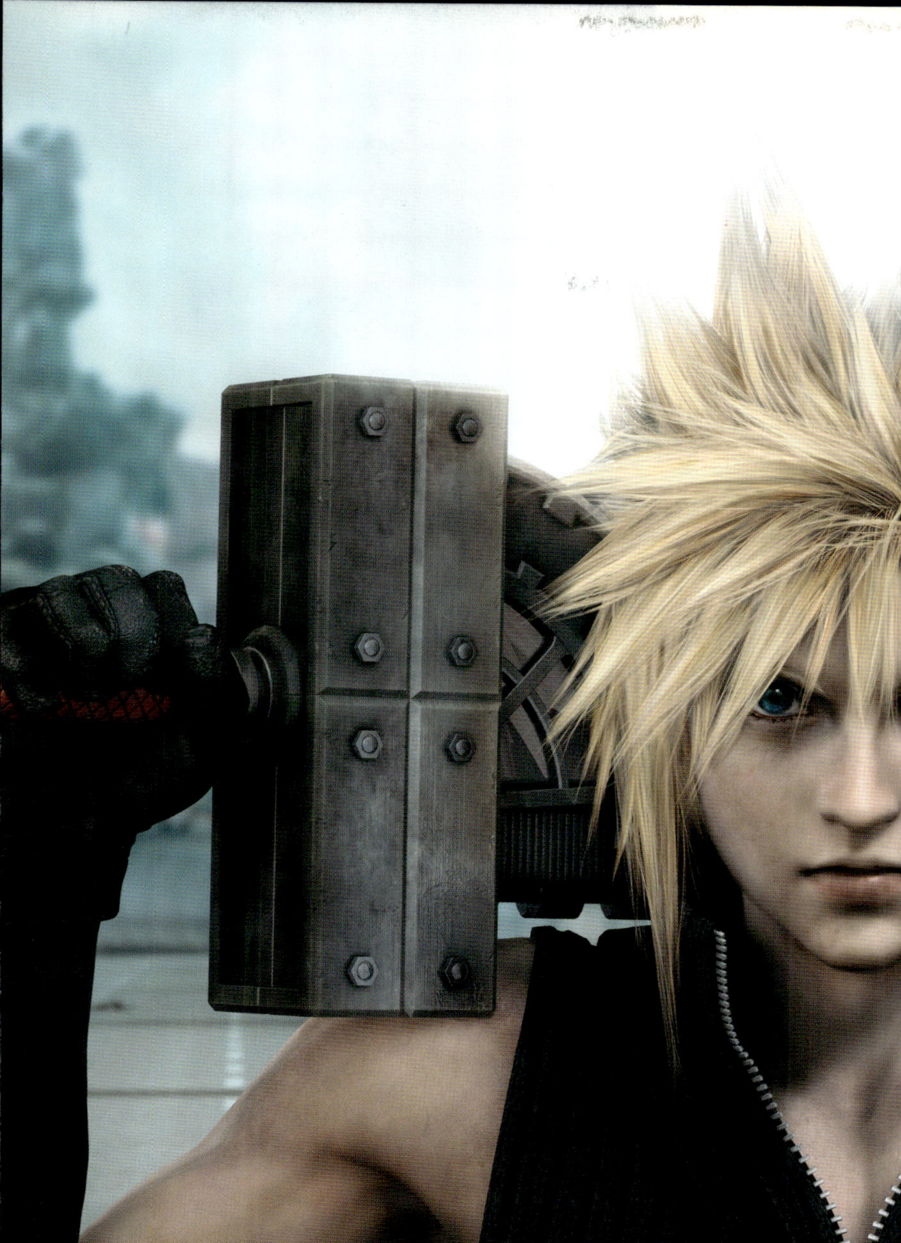

Despite their popularity in their homeland, the early games in the series had limited exposure outside of Japan, and it wasn't until the seventh edition, released on Sony's original PlayStation console in 1997, that the series garnered worldwide acclaim. The first *FF* title to use 3D graphics, and one of the first games to use artful "cut scenes" (pre-rendered video sequences) to tell a story within the gameplay, *FFVII* is the most cherished game in the series (rivalled only perhaps by *FFX*).

It's no surprise that this volume is hailed as one of the most important games in video game history, and often either tops or features in top ten polls of influential titles. It was the success of *FFVII* that prompted Sakaguchi's creation of a fully computer generated feature film, *The Spirits Within*, although it had an unrelated storyline and characters. However, a second animated film, *Advent Children*, did feature the same characters as the game, and in 2008 Square Enix returned to the *FFVII* world for a prequel game for the PlayStation Portable handheld: *Crisis Core*. Although Sakaguchi left Square Enix in 2001, his *Final Fantasy* legacy lives on.

▲
The Spirits Within **was followed in 1995 by a second** ***Final Fantasy*** **film:** ***Advent Children*****. Unlike its predecessor, this movie was much more closely linked to the games, being set two years after the events of** ***Final Fantasy VII*****.**

◀ ▶
The androgynous look of ***Final Fantasy*****'s characters was originally established by lead art director Yoshitaka Amano, but Tetsuya Nomura has been art director for more recent incarnations, including 2009's** ***Final Fantasy XIII*****.**

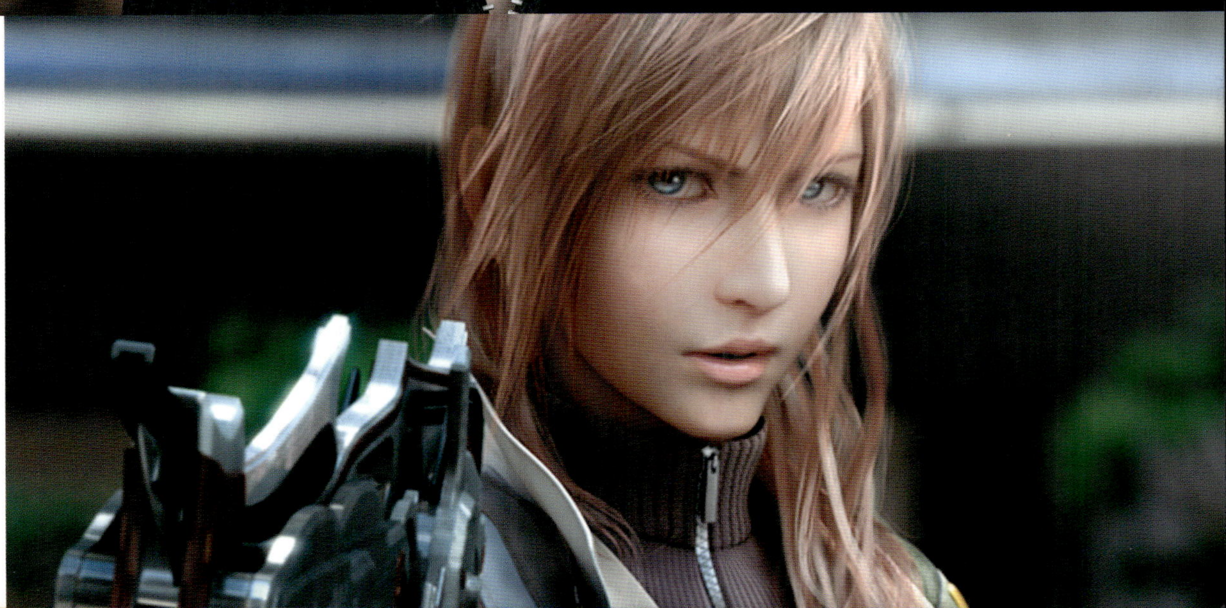

HALO

Thanks to the popularity and success of the likes of *Doom*, *Quake*, and *Unreal Tournament*, the PC has been the domain of the first-person shooter for years. Which makes it all the more surprising that probably the best example of the genre is on a console. When *Halo: Combat Evolved* was released on Microsoft's new Xbox in November 2001, it had a massive impact not just on the genre, but also on the console business and the games industry as a whole.

Developer Bungie had enjoyed success previously with its *Marathon* and *Myth* games, but nothing on the scale of *Halo* and its two sequels, *Halo 2* and *3*. Set in the 26th century, a battle rages between the Earth empire and the rebellious Covenant, who see mankind as an affront to the gods. The gamer plays as the Master Chief, an enhanced warrior who must unlock the secret of the eponymous Halo, a giant ring-shaped mega structure that is large enough to support life (shades of Larry Niven's *Ringworld*), before the alien Covenant uses it to destroy Earth's forces.

Halo's gripping narrative, impressive in-game dynamics and physics, beautiful graphics, and emotive soundtrack made the game the must-have title on Microsoft's fledgling console. Indeed, it could be argued that the console might not be here today if not for *Halo* and *Halo 2*, which was released three years later. The final entry in the *Halo* trilogy was released in 2007 for Microsoft's next gen machine, the Xbox 360, to even greater rapturous critical acclaim.

It is very easy for a developer to sit on its laurels and bring out another iteration of a bestselling franchise, albeit with slightly improved graphics, bigger levels, and so on. But the *Halo* franchise has always managed to innovate. The original was the first time a first-person shooter had worked on a console since *GoldenEye* on the Nintendo 64 in 1997, with Bungie making full use of the twin analog sticks of the controller. *Halo 2* delivered the ability to fire two weapons at the same time as well as board vehicles, and it introduced a multiplayer option that helped fashion the vibrant online gaming community of Xbox Live. *Halo 3* surprised everyone by improving the multiplayer experience immeasurably, without sacrificing subtle but equally important touches to the single player campaign.

The saying goes that success breeds success. So it has been with *Halo*, with the launch of numerous licensed products, all inspired by the game and Bungie's in-house artists. Action figures, books, comic books (with art from the likes of Moebius, Simon Bisley, Phil Hale, Alex Maleev, and a legion of others), clothing, soundtrack CDs, and other collectibles have all been produced as part of the franchise. So while the Chief's adventures on the Halo finished in the third installment of the game, *Halo 3* is unlikely to mark the end of Xbox's talisman.

▼
***Halo*'s main protagonist, Master Chief, has become something of a pop culture icon, spinning off into an array of collectibles, including action figures and statues. Shi Kai Wang, one of many artists on the first game, created the initial concept drawing of the Chief, and went on to become lead 3D artist on the sequels.**

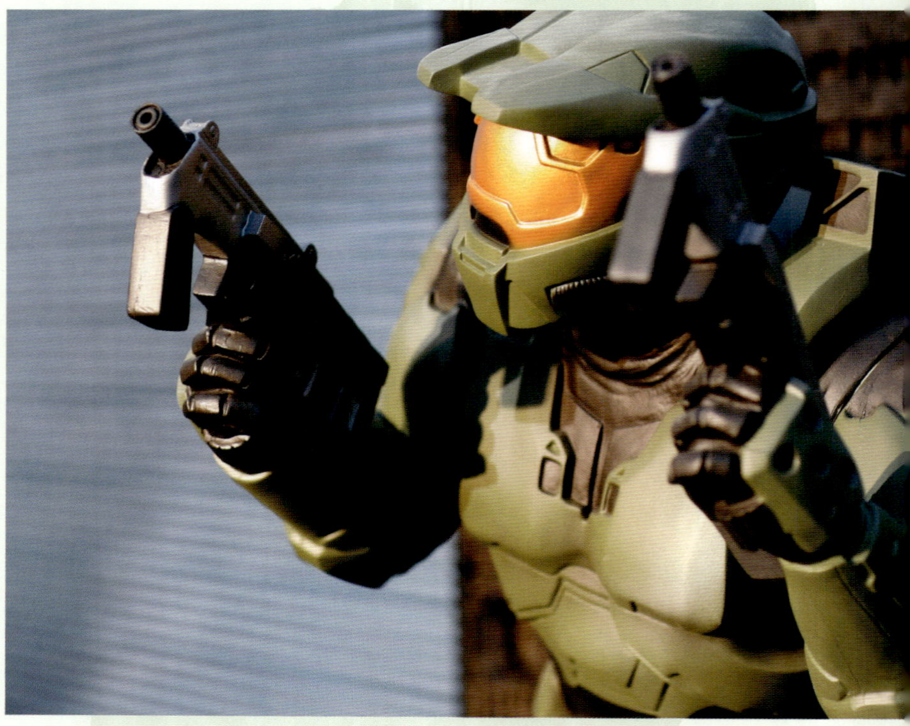

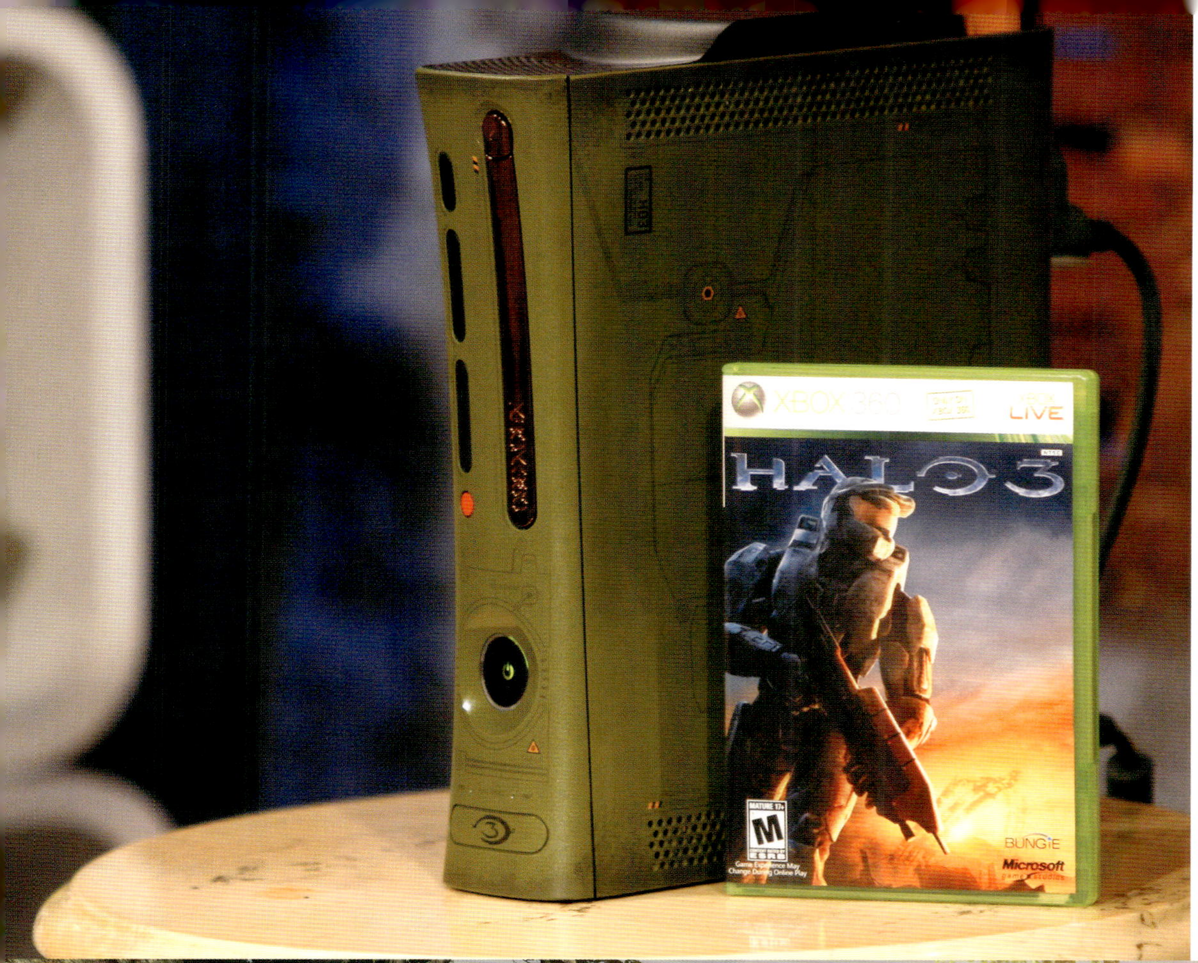

◀
When *Halo 3* was released in 2007, gamers could buy a customized Special Edition of the Xbox 360, decorated in Master Chief's distinctive military green.

▼
This screenshot from *Halo 3* shows the level of detail that goes into each game. Longtime Bungie employee Markus Lehto was art director on all three of the *Halo* games, overseeing everything from character design through to the spectacular environments.

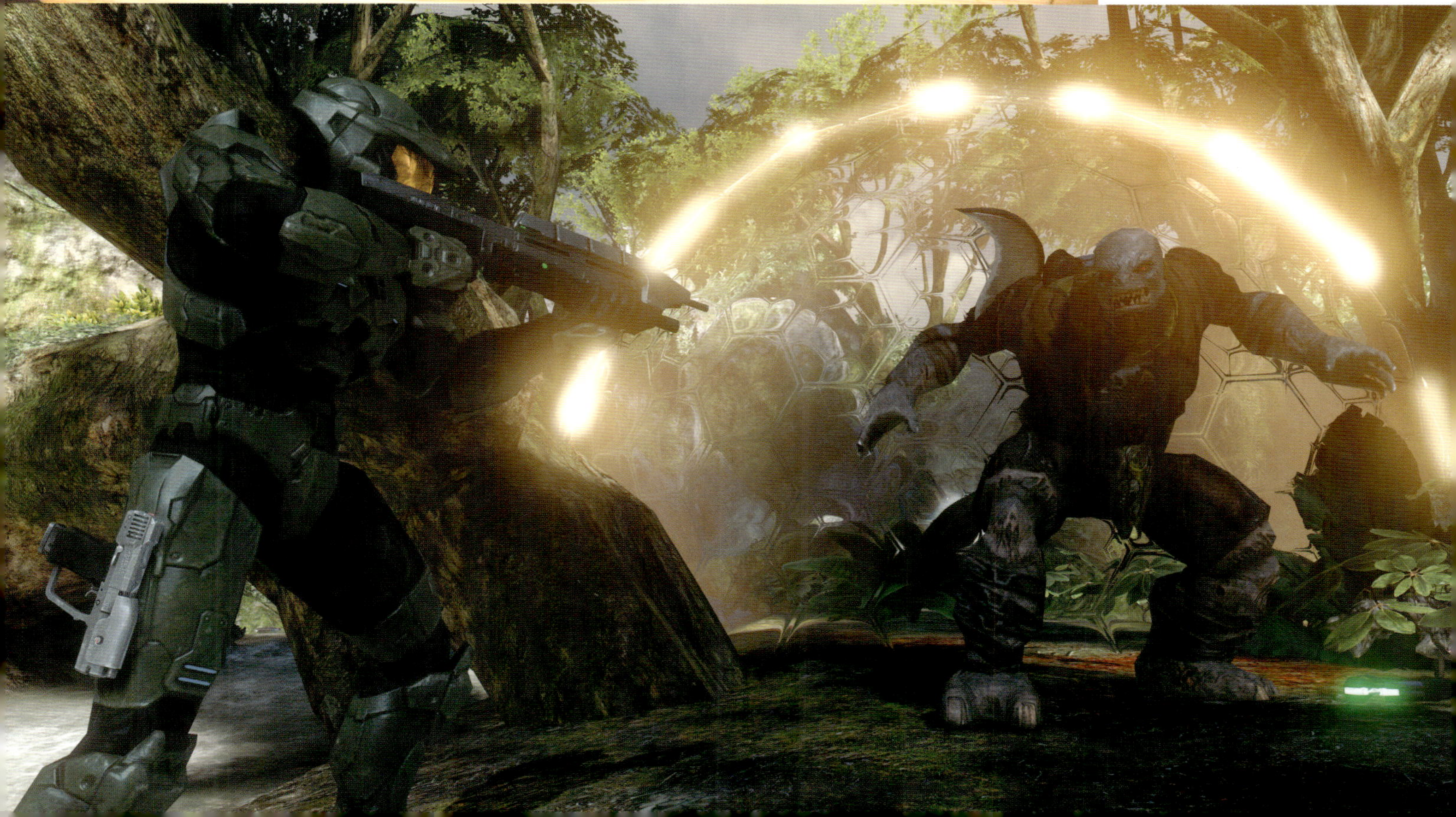

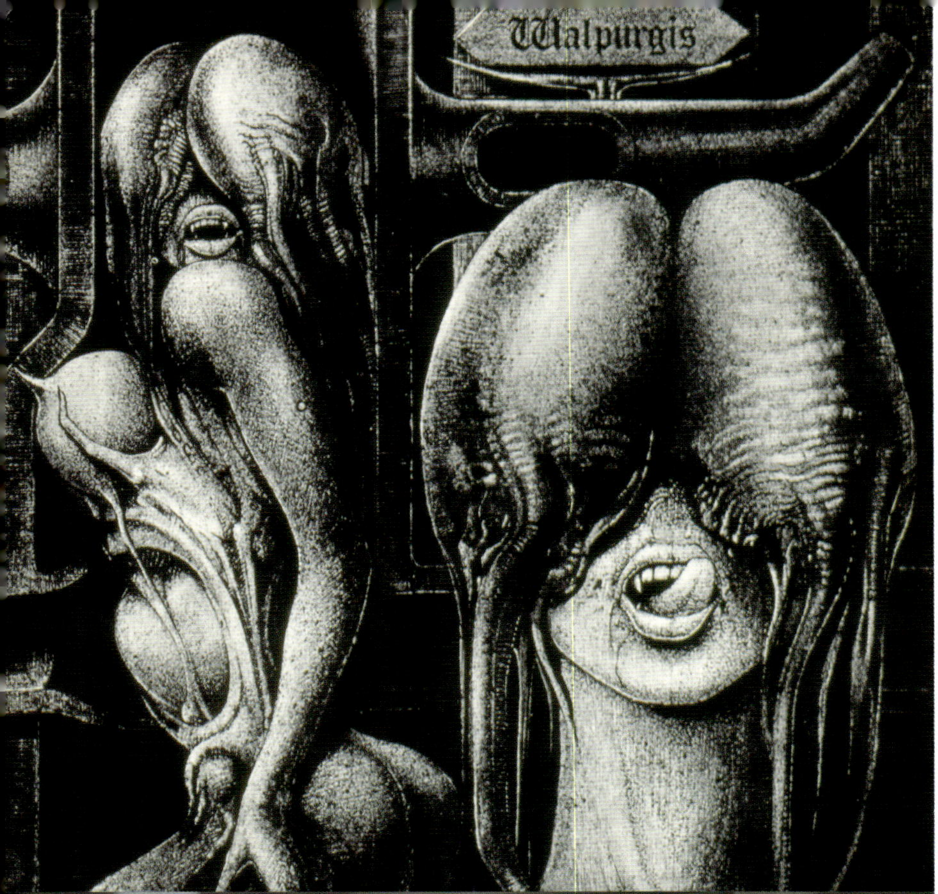

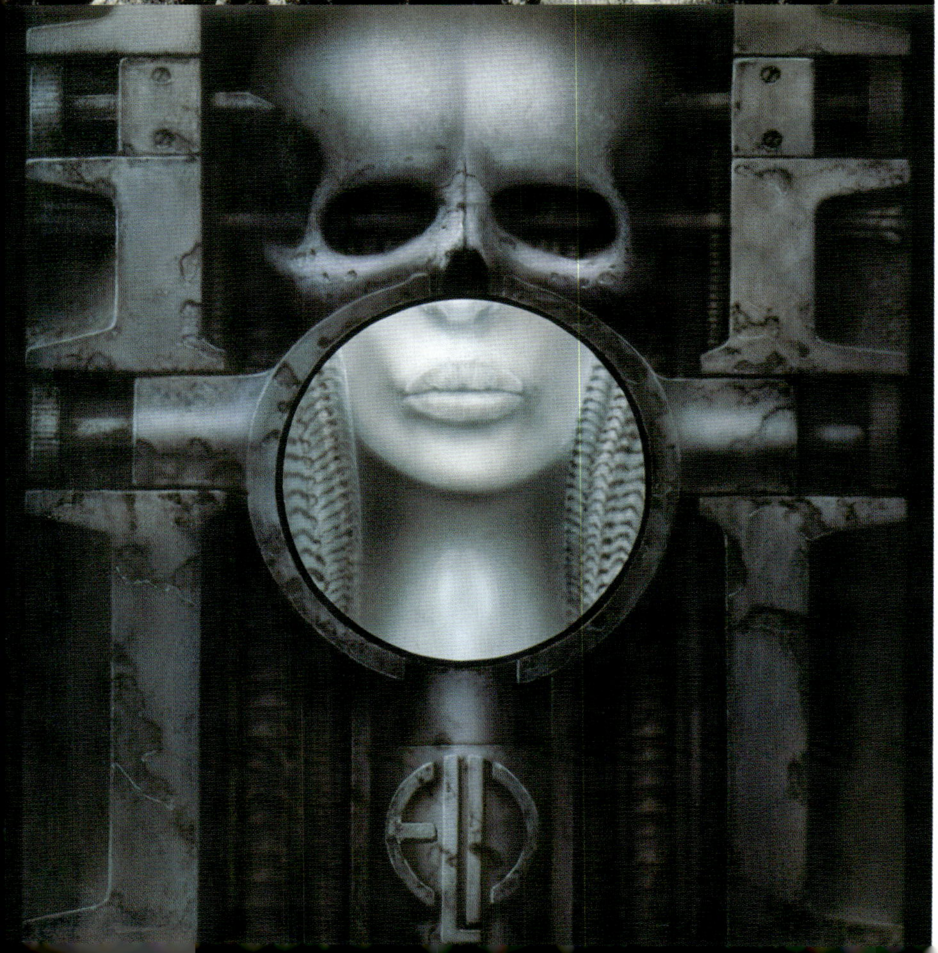

SF RECORD SLEEVES

Rock 'n' roll has always had a flirtatious relationship with science fiction. The birth of the musical genre that changed the world forever came during the middle of a great wave of interest in science fiction in films, comics, and books, as the Cold War of the 1950s gave way to a newfound fascination with watching the skies. So it was almost natural that this interest would filter through into this nascent, primitive music.

Often this was merely at the fringes of early rock 'n' roll. But there are clear reasons for this—not least the fact that sleeve art, as an idea, didn't come of age until the decade after the birth of rock 'n' roll. Artists were not yet presenting fleshed out personas and concepts; it was enough that they were merely getting on stage and singing this primitive music. And while there may have been the occasional alien invasion-themed rock tune or, as the space race arrived in the 1960s, a wave of astronaut-related songs (from Joe Meek's still impressive *Telstar* through to other less-well-known-than-The-Tornados outfits like The Spotnicks, another instrumental outfit decked out in spacesuits), it was not until the latter part of the '60s that the links between science fiction and rock music became more fully-formed.

Two factors were at the root of this: the ingestion of psychedelic drugs (in vast quantities in some cases); and the rise of the concept album (the latter probably also the result of the former and not a mere coincidence). Once The Beatles and, first, Klaus Voormann (*Revolver*) and then, more notably, Peter Blake (*Sgt. Pepper*) had created mini-masterpieces for successive albums, pushing the barrier of both sleeve art and the album as concept, the floodgates opened.

Sci-fi's influence on cover art can be deemed to roughly fall into three categories. There are the progressive, grown-up, "adult" kind of sleeves—think Roger Dean and his 1970s sleeves for rock band Yes; there is the genre's profound influence on black music, from the funky rock of George Clinton—in all his guises—through to electro and techno music; and then, of course, there's the cheap cash-in.

◀ ◀▼

H. R. Giger has made some intriguing and unusual choices when it comes to record sleeve design. His first album design, for Swiss prog rock band The Shiver's 1969 debut (and only) album, *Walpurgis*, shows all the hallmarks of his fascination with the human (and inhuman) body. But perhaps his most famous cover is Emerson Lake and Palmer's *Brain Salad Surgery*. Sadly, in 2005 the two paintings that comprised the ELP cover went missing after an exhibition in Prague; a reward for their safe return is still being offered.

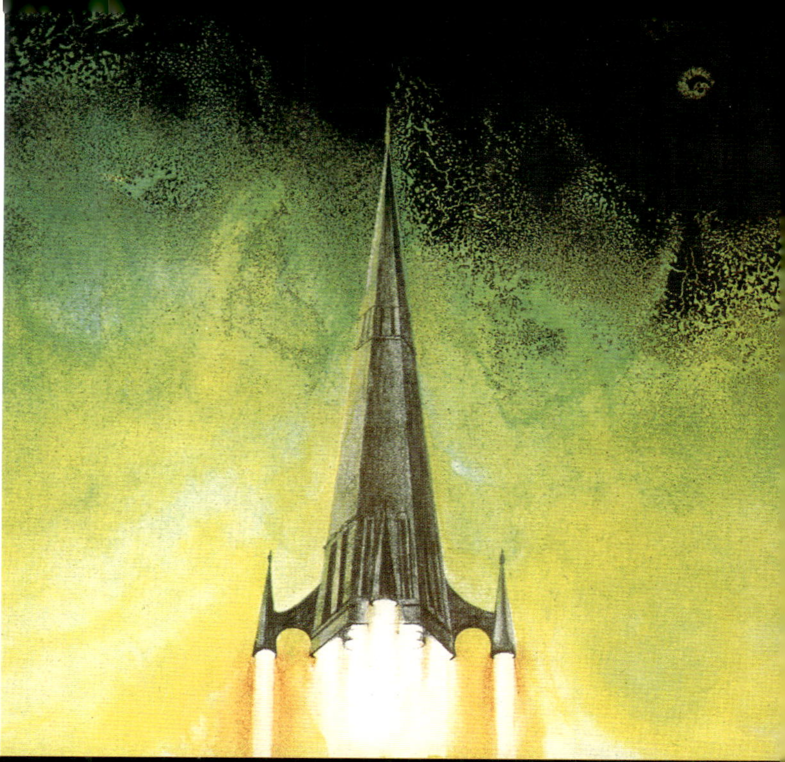

▶ ▶▼

Not necessarily Roger Dean's highest profile work, at least not compared to Yes, but one that delights record collectors. Sheffield-based central heating engineer Martin Raphael claimed to have been visited by Egyptian pharaoh Ramases (sic) and told he was his reincarnation. Thus began a recording career that included psych classic *In My Mind's Eye* and LP *Space Hymns*, released on seminal prog label Vertigo. Dean's ingenious cover, which seems to simply depict a rocket on the front, actually folded out to reveal the whole image: the rocket is in fact a church spire.

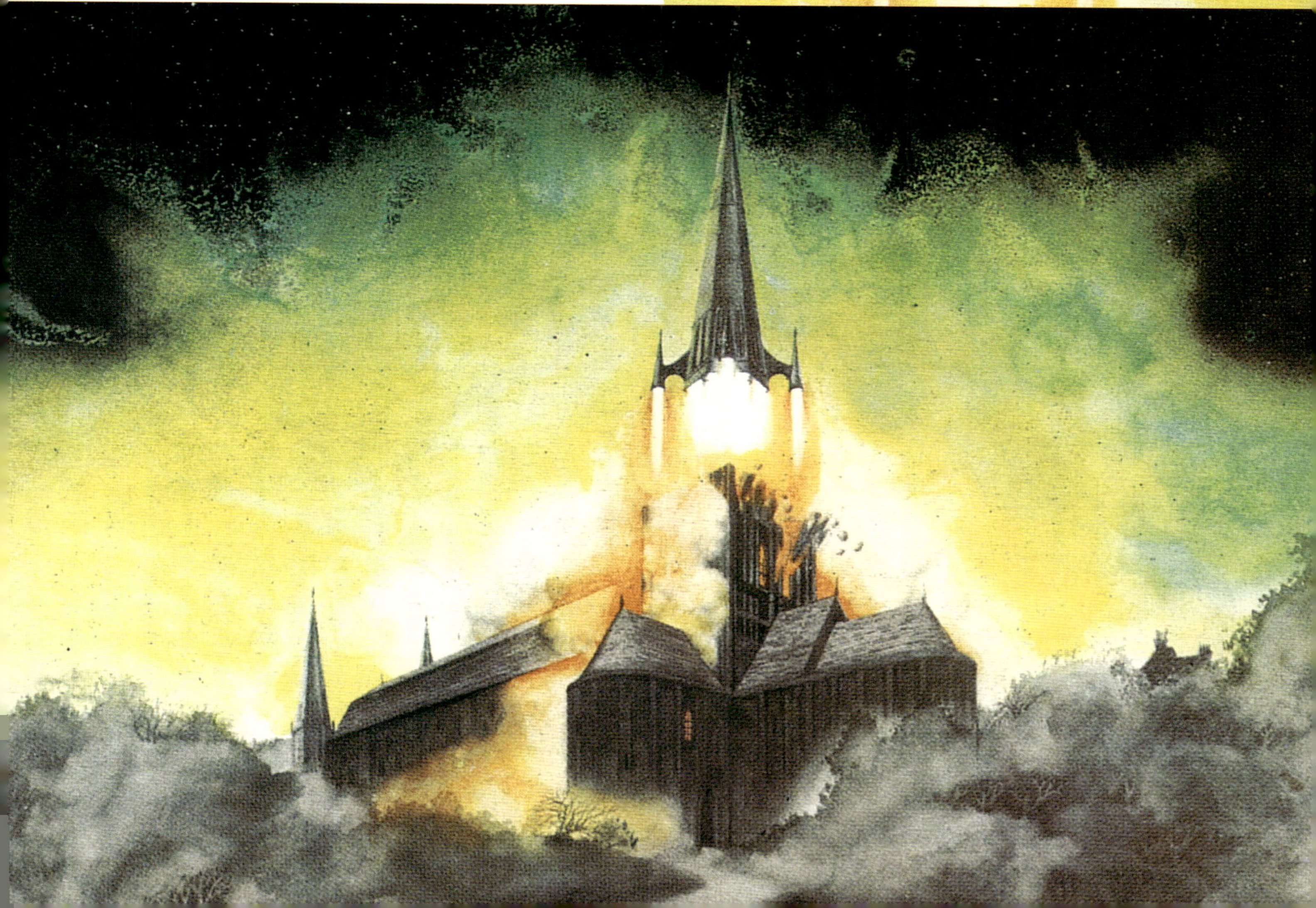

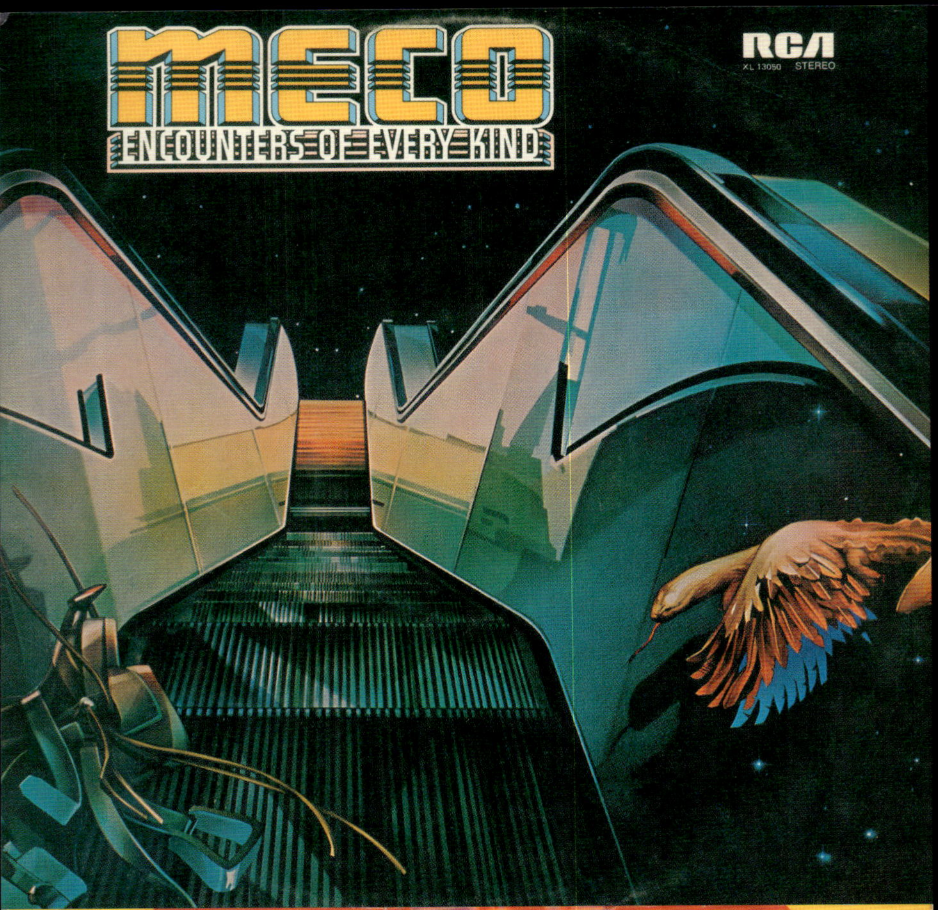

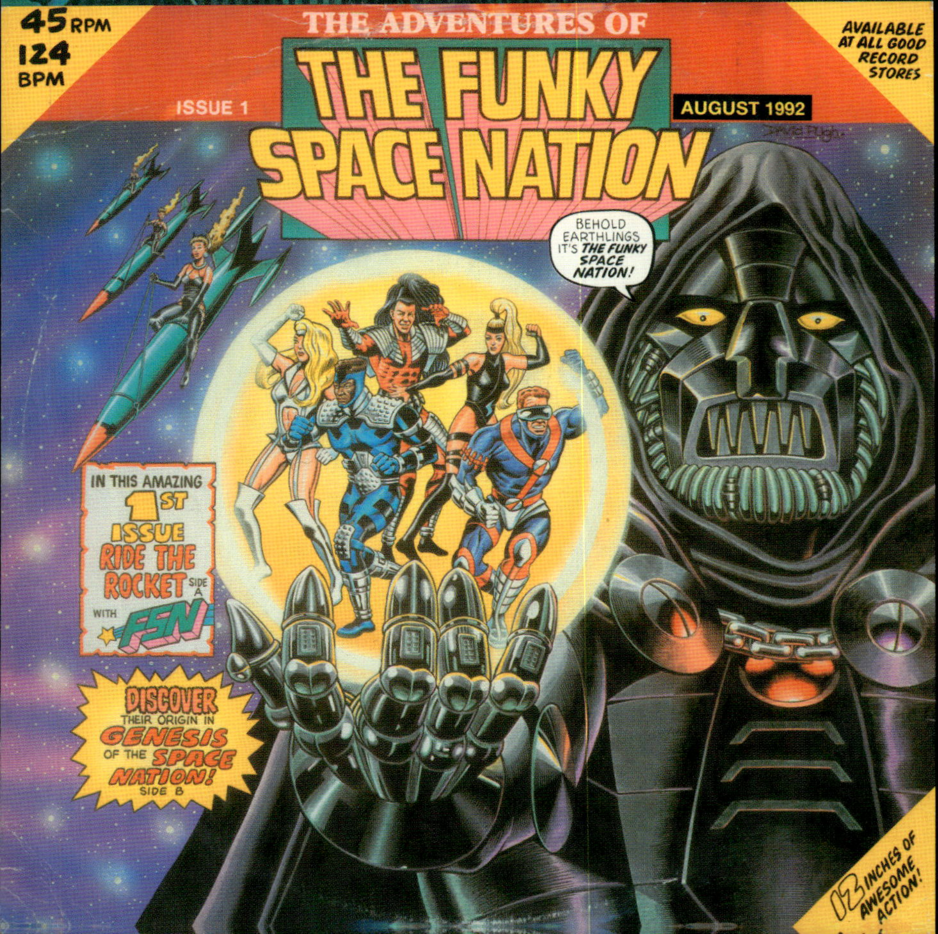

Roger Dean is the king of all prog rock SF sleeves, earning his crust working with—most notably—Yes for more than 30 years. Something of a renaissance man—as well as his distinctive, watercolor-based sleeves he is also an architect and furniture designer—Dean's work is at once a major draw for prog rock fans and the target of a certain amount of bile from non-fans. Dean's sleeves are often mentioned alongside Yes and co. as being partly responsible for punk.

While punk eschewed the fantastical, preferring instead sleeves depicting inner city wastelands, disco music was hugely influenced by sci-fi. It's no coincidence that the rise of disco—or at least its ascendancy into mainstream culture—coincided with the *Star Wars* and *Close Encounters* SF boom. The discotheque in *Saturday Night Fever*, the film that took the music and culture to the world, was even called "2001 Odyssey."

The *Star Wars* boom brought with it a number of disco cover versions, but it also helped join the dots for African American music's longstanding entanglement with science fiction. African American music's association with SF dates back to free jazz maestro Sun Ra's obsession with other worlds (as in his *Space is the Place* film, arguably one of the weirdest sci-fi flicks you're ever likely to see). From there, it took in Motown acts such as The Undisputed Truth, Mandre (who was never pictured without his robotic mask), and even, later, The Jackson Five (whose *Can You Feel It* promo recasts them as benevolent space gods), before reaching a kind of climax with the Parliament/Funkadelic axis under the tutelage of renowned space cadet George Clinton.

That lineage continued through electro and into techno, where it is still prevalent today, particularly in the radical, underground Detroit sound. Detroit-based design company Third Earth Visual Arts provide sci-fi-esque sleeve artwork for the likes of Underground Resistance and Model 500, while over in Chicago—birthplace of house music—renaissance man Alan Oldham not only DJs and makes music but creates his own SF-themed sleeves, and writes and draws his own comic books.

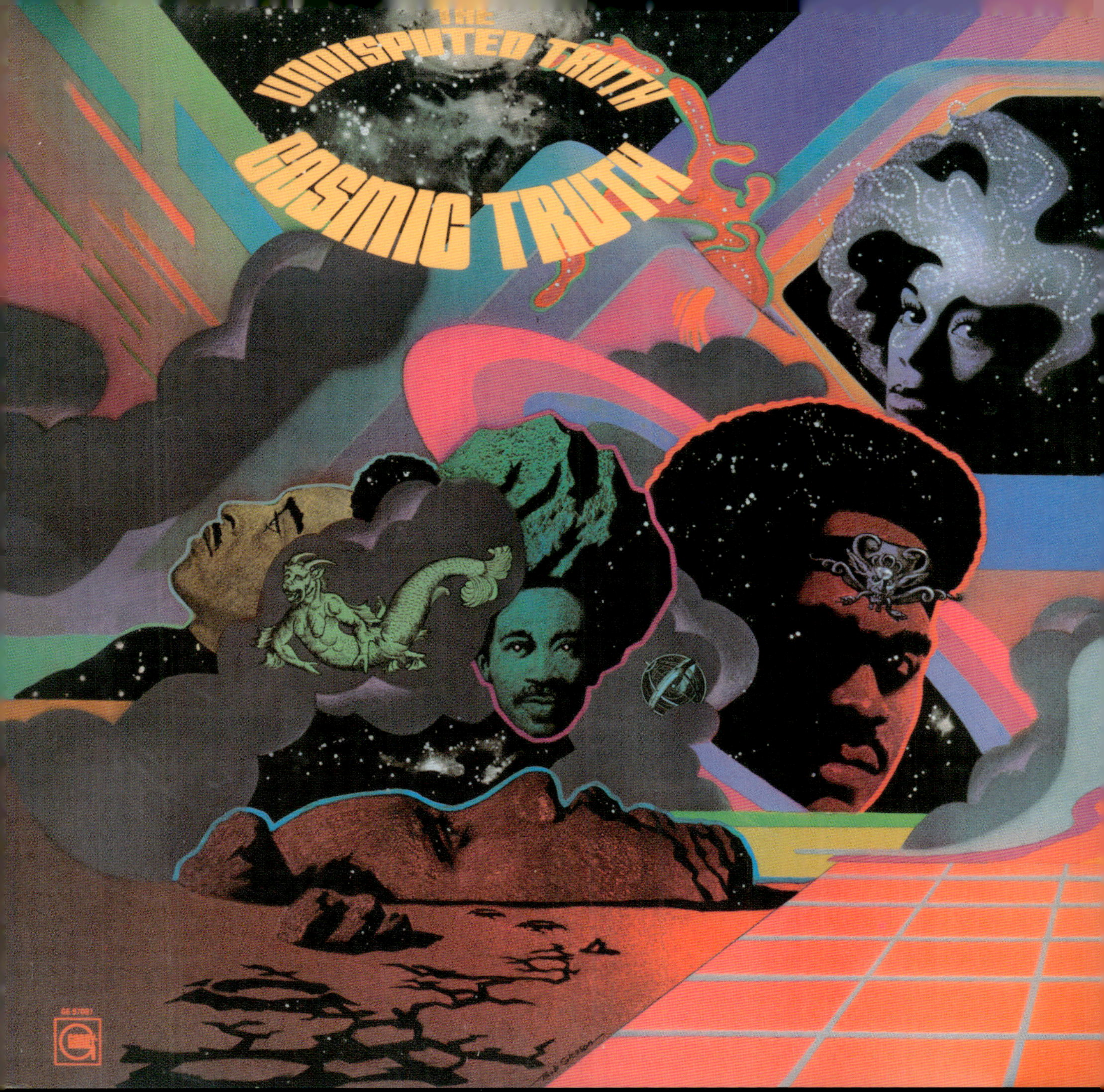

◀▲

Meco, a.k.a. Dominick, or "Meco," Monardo, was the self-styled master of the sci-fi disco sound. A session musician who had also produced Gloria Gaynor's *Never Can Say Goodbye*, his eureka moment came when he went to see *Star Wars* in 1977. Some ten or more viewings later, this had spun into an idea that involved taking John Williams' score and giving it a disco beat. Hey presto, a worldwide hit. Working on the basis that "if it ain't broke, don't fix it," he went on to build a career adapting prominent sci-fi film scores into modern pop. This sleeve is a typical example.

◀

While a number of recording artists have opted for comic book-style sleeves (notably early '80s hip hop star Afrika Bambaataa), this sleeve by Welsh artist David Pugh for a 1992 piano house single can boast a distinct sci-fi slant too.

▲

Psychedelic soulsters The Undisputed Truth—effectively producer Norman Whitfield's band—were pictured round a campfire for their first album; within a few years they were off to another galaxy, courtesy of Bob Gleason's artwork for their album *Cosmic Truth*. Gleason later came up with the seminal *Halloween* poster for the low budget horror film's first cinema release.

SF TOY DESIGN: STAR WARS

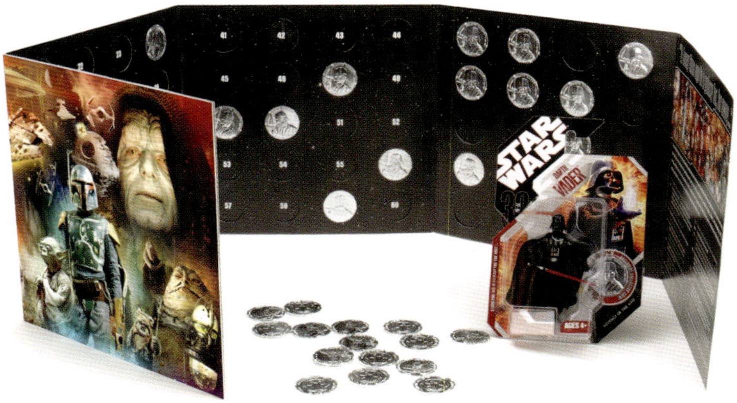

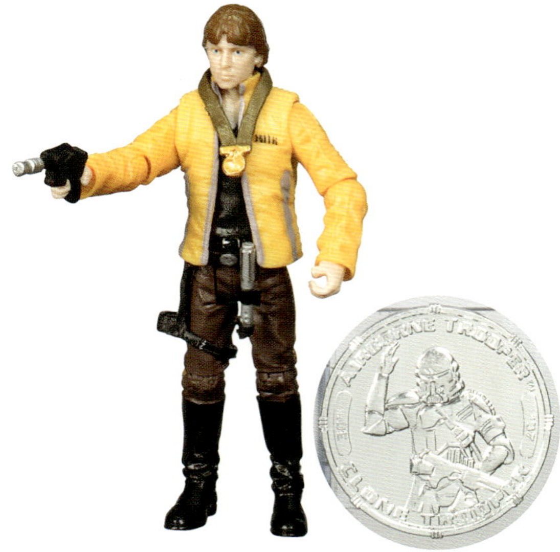

In 1976 no one would have predicted that *Star Wars* would become the cultural phenomenon it is today. So when toy company Kenner picked up the *Star Wars* toy license after others—including the Mego Corporation—had passed on it, little did they suspect they would create one of the most successful toy lines in history, and bring the art of science fiction into nearly every boy's bedroom in the late 1970s and early 1980s.

Back in the 1970s, toys based on movie licenses were rare—toy companies instead preferring original products or those based on television series, which, unlike a movie, wouldn't come and go in a space of a few weeks. Accordingly, Kenner didn't expect the market for their *Star Wars* toys to be that impressive—but they soon found demand outstripping supply.

Deciding that a driving force behind the toy line would be the ships and vehicles, Kenner opted for a smaller scale of 3.75" for their action figures. The size was a roaring success, and even today, over 30 years on, the scale is regularly used on new toy lines, becoming an industry standard.

As the launch of the line neared, it became clear that the action figures wouldn't be ready for the all-important Christmas season. Kenner offered a unique solution by selling "early bird" kits. These consisted of a cardboard stand, some stickers, and a coupon to get four figures from the action figure line mailed to you when they became available. Despite being little more than an empty box, the appeal of *Star Wars* made the kit immensely popular.

Between 1978 and 1985, Kenner produced 111 different figures for their *Star Wars* line, and sold an incredible 250 million of them. But by 1985, with no more films on the horizon, interest in *Star Wars* was waning, and a last wave of figures was released. This final wave was branded "Power of the Force," and each figure was packaged with a unique collector coin. These figures are now some of the most desirable among collectors of what is known as the vintage period (1978–1985) of *Star Wars* toys.

In 1995 the toy company Hasbro, who over the preceding years had absorbed Kenner, brought the *Star Wars* line back. Featuring a mix of new action figure sculpts and predominantly vintage vehicle re-releases, this fresh line not only appealed to a new generation of children, but also adults who had bought the original toys. Suddenly it wasn't uncommon to see both kids and adults buying *Star Wars* toys, and *Star Wars* gave birth to yet another phenomenon: the collector market.

Now action figures and toys were aimed directly at adults, as companies picked up licenses with the collectors' market in mind. *Star Wars* too begat a multitude of collectibles from a variety of companies, from collectible dolls to construction toys to busts and statues.

Buoyed by both the special editions of the original trilogy and, from 1999, the prequel movies, the *Star Wars* brand has gone from strength to strength. In 2003 Lucasfilm and Hasbro extended their licensing agreement to 2018, meaning that while the original and prequel trilogy are now complete, we will continue to see new and exciting *Star Wars* product for years to come.

▲
In 2007, to celebrate *Star Wars*' 30th Anniversary, the action figure line once again came with coins as a nod back to the 1985 Power of the Force line.

►
In 2005, Hasbro partnered up with Sideshow Collectibles to produce an ongoing line of high-end, highly detailed collectible 12" figures, featuring characters not only from the movies but from the "expanded universe" of the comics and cartoons as well.

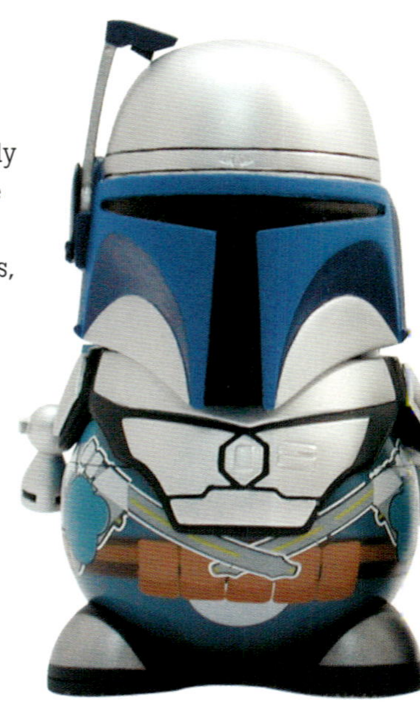

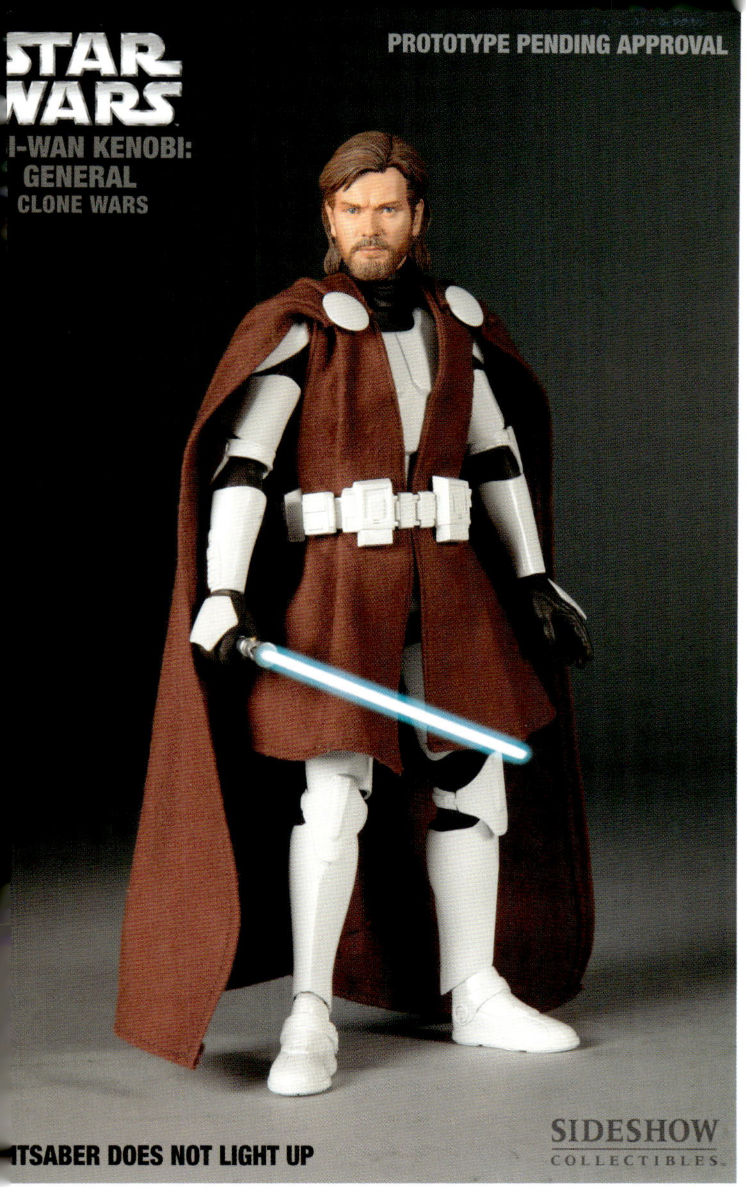

◄▼ ►
Hong Kong-based Hot Toys produce Russian doll-style *Star Wars* "Chubbies," while Kotobukiya of Japan offer a range of licensed vinyl model kits.

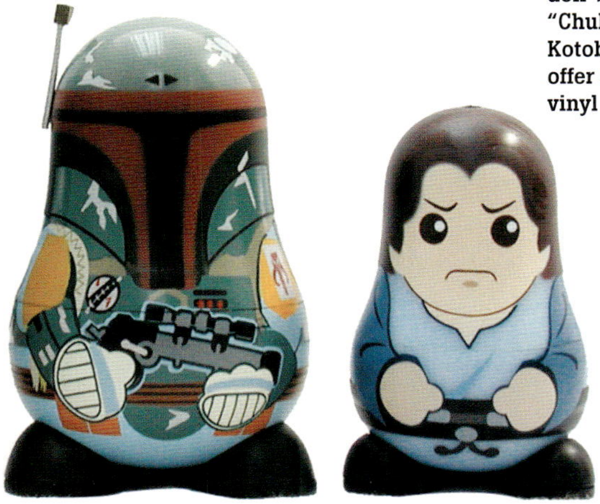

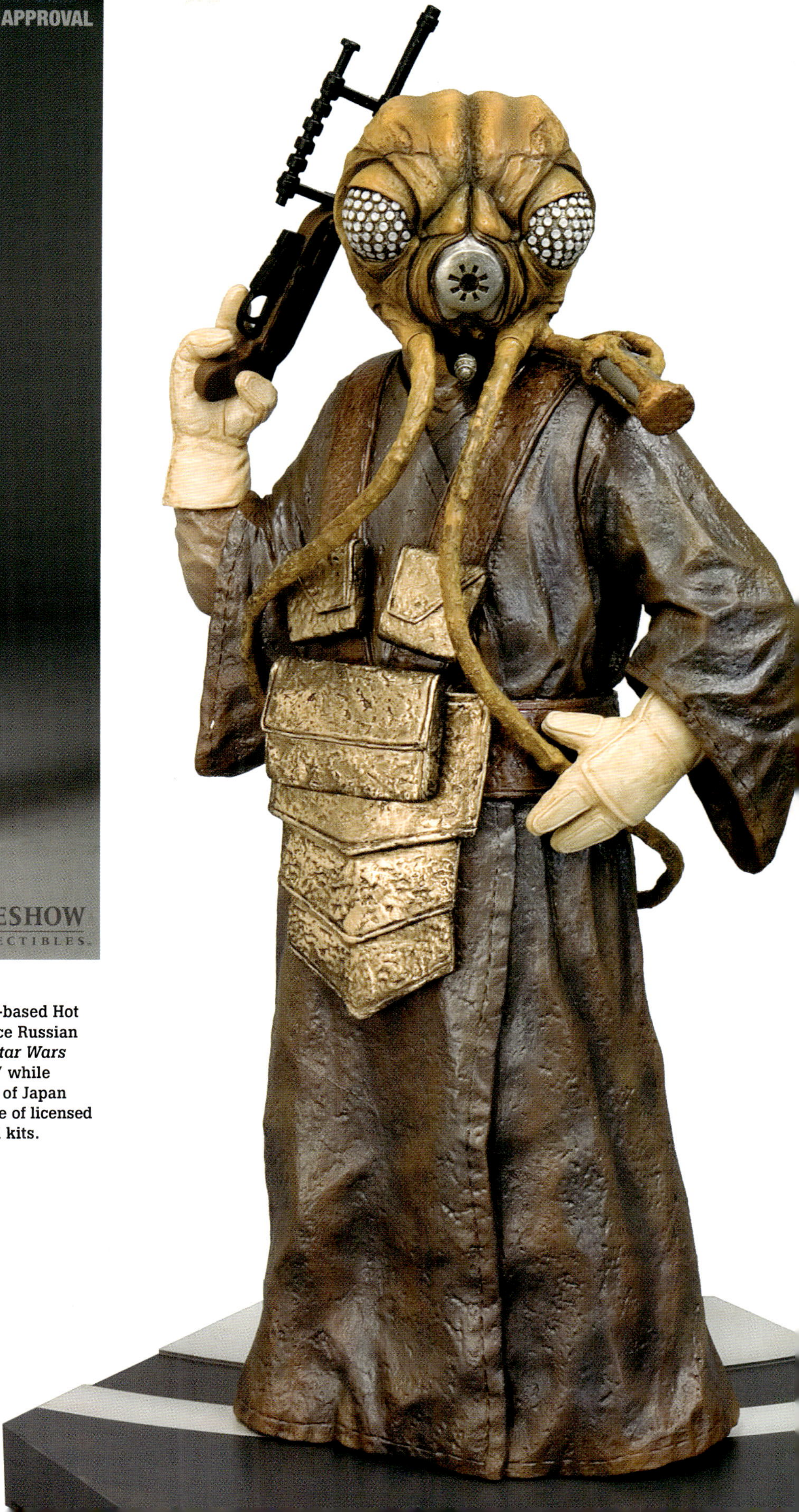

SF TOY DESIGN: JAPANESE ROBOTS

Japan's love affair with robot toys began just after the Second World War. Under General MacArthur's plans for industrial rehabilitation, Japan was given a number of low profit manufacturing industries. As part of this, the country's former weapons factories were converted into toy factories, producing friction and clockwork toys based on American designs from before the war. The Japanese manufacturers continued to improve on these schematics, adding innovations like battery power, and by the mid-'50s, Japan was the world's biggest toy manufacturer.

In 1972 toy company Takara created a revolutionary new 8" and 12" toy line called Henshin Cyborg. These dolls used molds from US company Hasbro's G. I. Joe line, but cast them in a clear plastic to show the characters' "inner workings." The translucency of the resulting figures lent them an instant sci-fi sheen.

Due to rising production costs, in 1974 Takara produced a scaled down version of the line, calling it Microman. These 4" toys were unique in that they could be disassembled and their constituent parts mixed and matched, thanks to the standard 0.2" connector used on both figures and vehicles. The first wave of figures proved so successful that Microman was spun off from Henshin Cyborg.

Microman also proved popular outside of Japan; in 1976, the Mego Corporation brought the line to the US and re-branded it Micronauts; it proved highly popular until Mego's demise in the early 1980s. Since then there have been several unsuccessful attempts by a number of US toy companies to re-launch the Micronauts toy line.

One of the most popular Japanese robots is *Gundam*. Originally an anime series from 1979, *Gundam* has since gone on to be a cultural phenomenon in Japan, with a wide range of manga, novels, collectibles, and video games. In the last 30 years there have been more than 25 *Gundam* movies and TV series, and the property shows no sign of slowing down.

The first plastic model kits from Bandai started appearing in 1980. These early models consisted of parts cut out of plastic frames that needed to be glued together. Since the early 1990s, however, most of the kits have been able to be constructed by snapping parts together. Generally, parts are pre-colored, with kits supplied with stickers or decals to give the models detail, but occasionally a kit will require painting.

As with *Gundam, Neon Genesis Evangelion* started life as an anime series, but in comparison is a relative newcomer to the market (the anime begain in 1995). The story focuses on the various teenagers who pilot the Evangelion "mecha" against the destructive Angels, and features unique designs that were initially thought far too complex to turn into toys. Over the years, however, a number of companies have managed to make collectibles of the Evas, Angels, and Pilots, bringing the appeal of the anime and manga to a much wider audience.

But arguably the greatest worldwide success in the robot genre was an American spin on a Japanese toy line. Noting the early 1980s trend in Japan for transforming robots, US toy company Hasbro decided to secure the rights to a number of Japanese brands—notably Microman and Diaclone—and release them under a single banner. Countless toys, cartoon series, and comic books—not to mention one animated and one live action movie—later, and the resulting toy line, the Transformers, reign supreme as the ultimate in robot toy design.

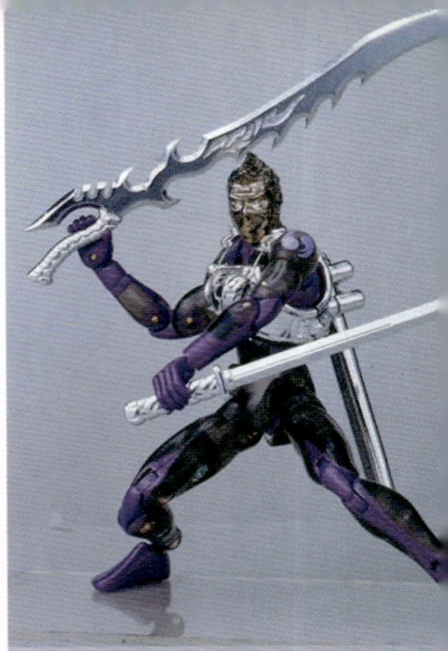

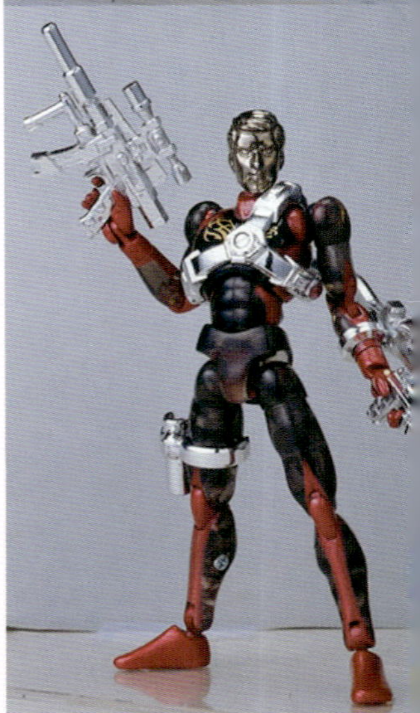

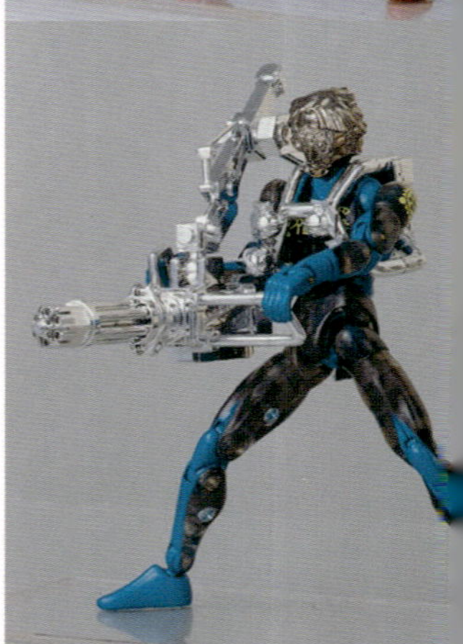

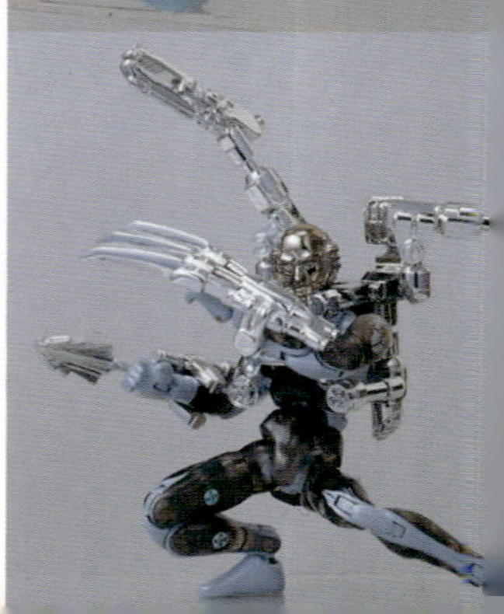

▶
Microforce was released in 2003 by Takara, each figure featuring newly designed 4" scale bodies and over 30 points of articulation Micronauts Evolution was a planned line, re-imagining the original Micronauts as 6" figures, but sadly the toys never saw release.

▶▶ ▶▲
The anime *Neon Genesis Evangelion*, with its biomechanical robots and labyrinthine mythology, has inspired a remarkable number of action figures and statues, particularly in comparsion to other mecha anime, such as *Patlabor*.

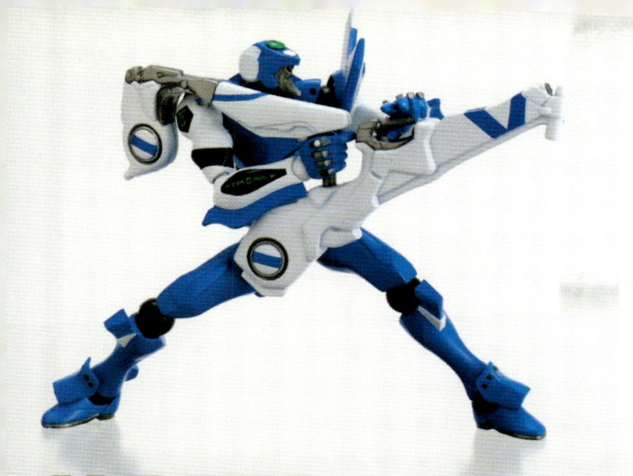

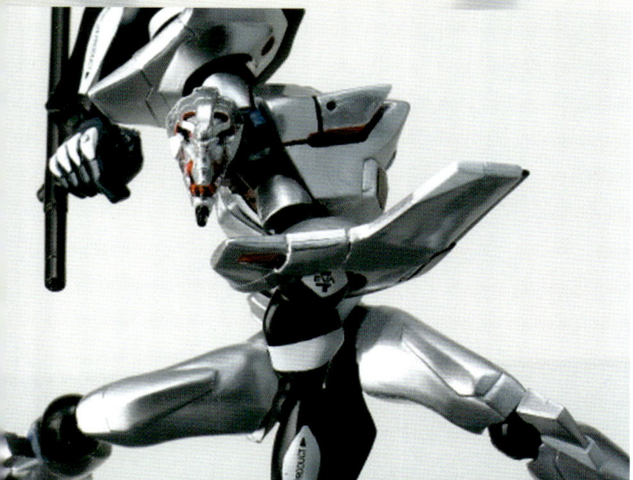

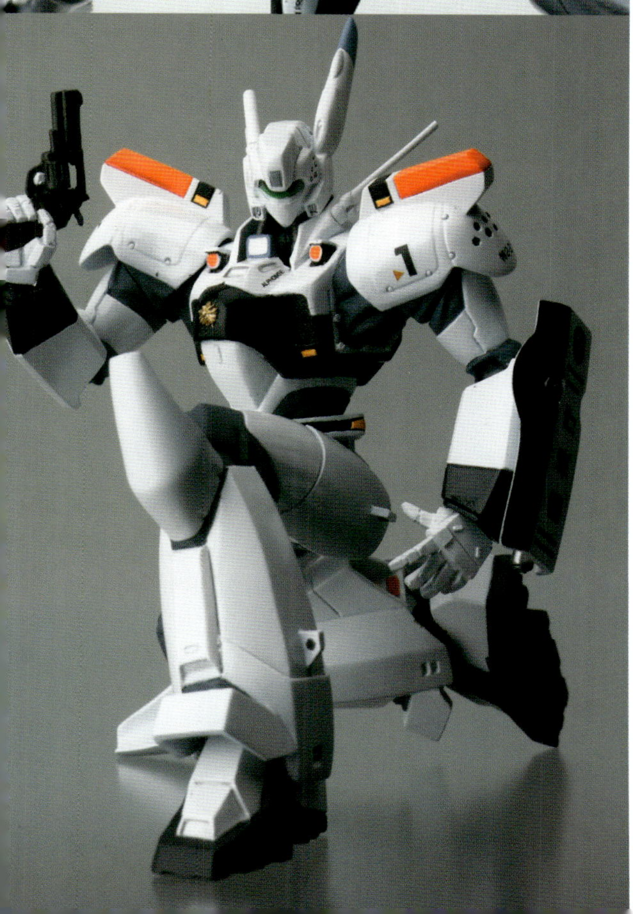

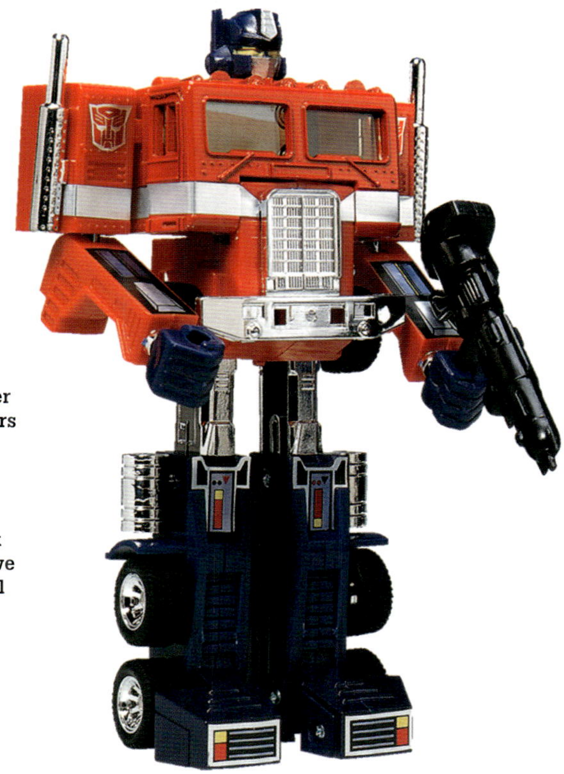

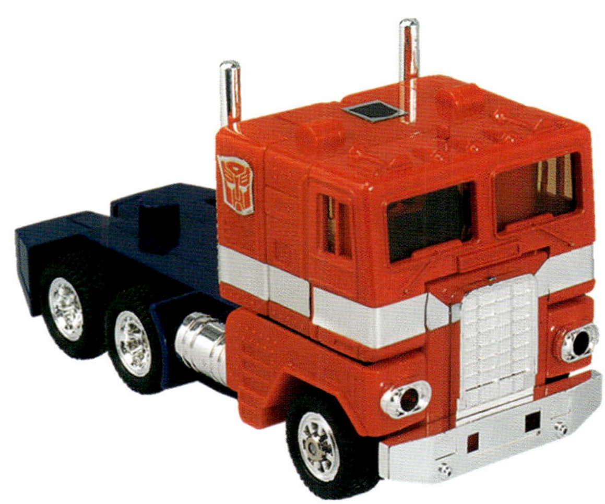

▶ ▼
Optimus Prime, the leader of the heroic Transformers the Autobots, has seen many incarnations over the years, but this Generation One design, transforming into a truck cab, remains the definitive look, and the basis for all subsequent versions.

SF TOY DESIGN: URBAN VINYL

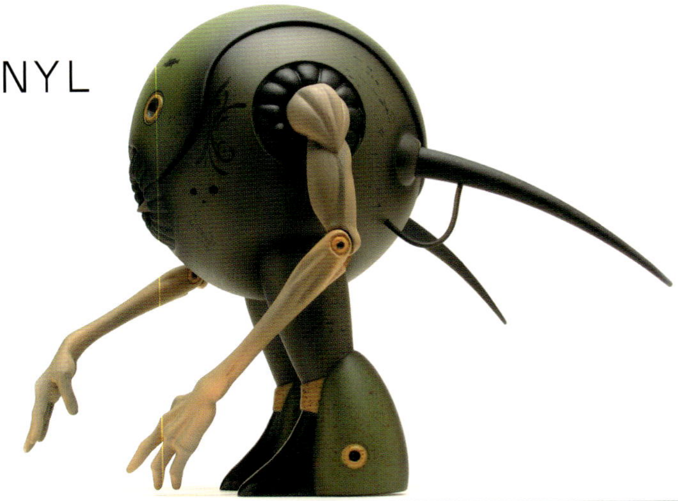

The urban vinyl—or designer toy—market is a relatively new phenomenon. The movement has its roots in the collectors' market, which in turn arose in the 1990s, when an entire generation brought up with toy properties a decade earlier—Star Wars, Transformers, Masters of the Universe, G. I. Joe—became nostalgic and started picking up secondhand toys they'd had as children. These were bought not as playthings, but as items to display or collect as a sign of fandom of the property in question.

Small, independent toy companies started springing up to cater for this emerging collector market, securing licenses to cult properties both old and current. This allowed this new kind of toy collector to acquire action figures and toys based on their favorite movies, bands, and TV shows, and display them much as they would posters or prints. A minority of collectors might buy a figure or statue based on the artist who sculpted it, but for the majority it was all about the original show or movie.

Urban vinyl is different, however. There are very few licenses, and any properties that are licensed are more often than not subjected to extreme stylization. This mini-art movement instead comprises of mostly original pieces. Urban vinyl is all about the design and the sculpt.

Its origins stretch back to 1996, and a Hong Kong artist named Michael Lau. Lau had received some recognition for his album covers, but it was an exhibition titled "Watergarden" that started to bring him to the world's

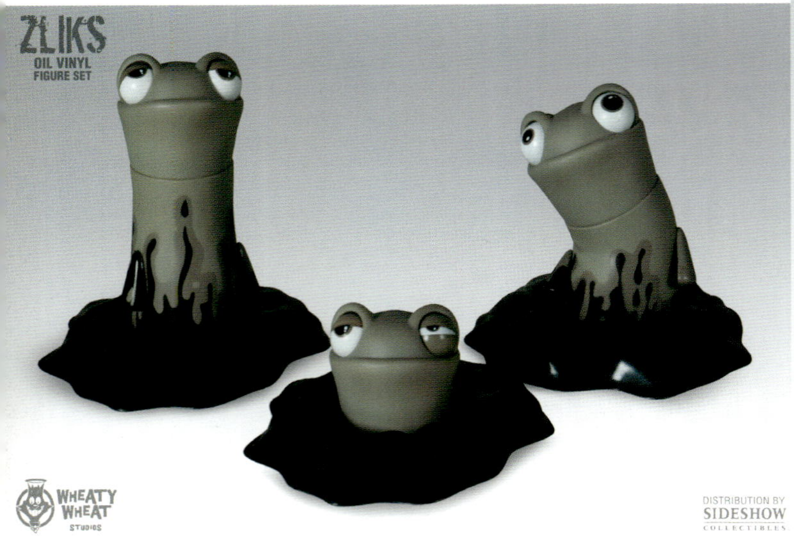

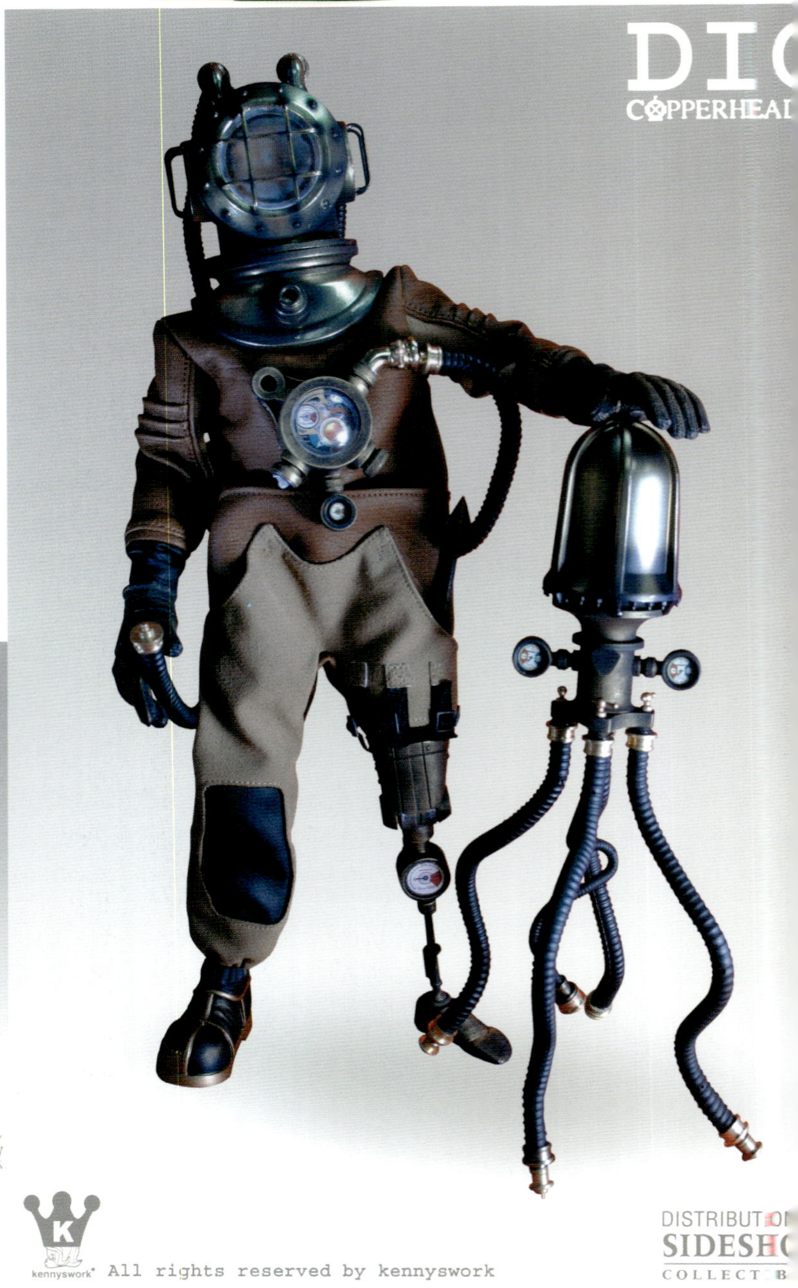

kennyswork All rights reserved by kennyswork

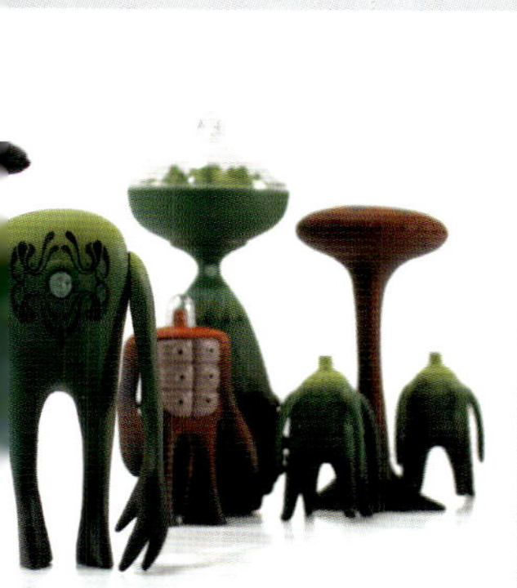

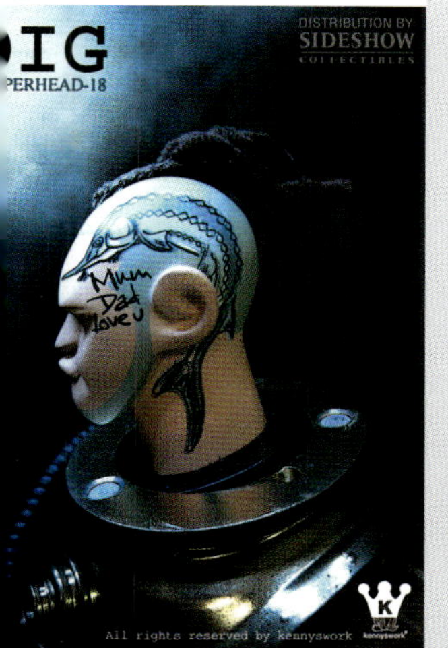

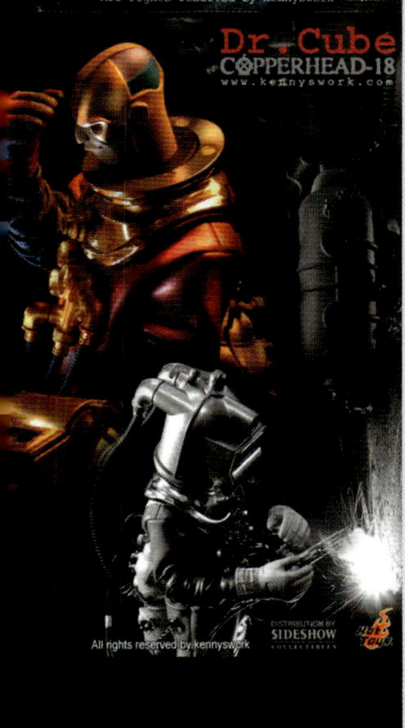

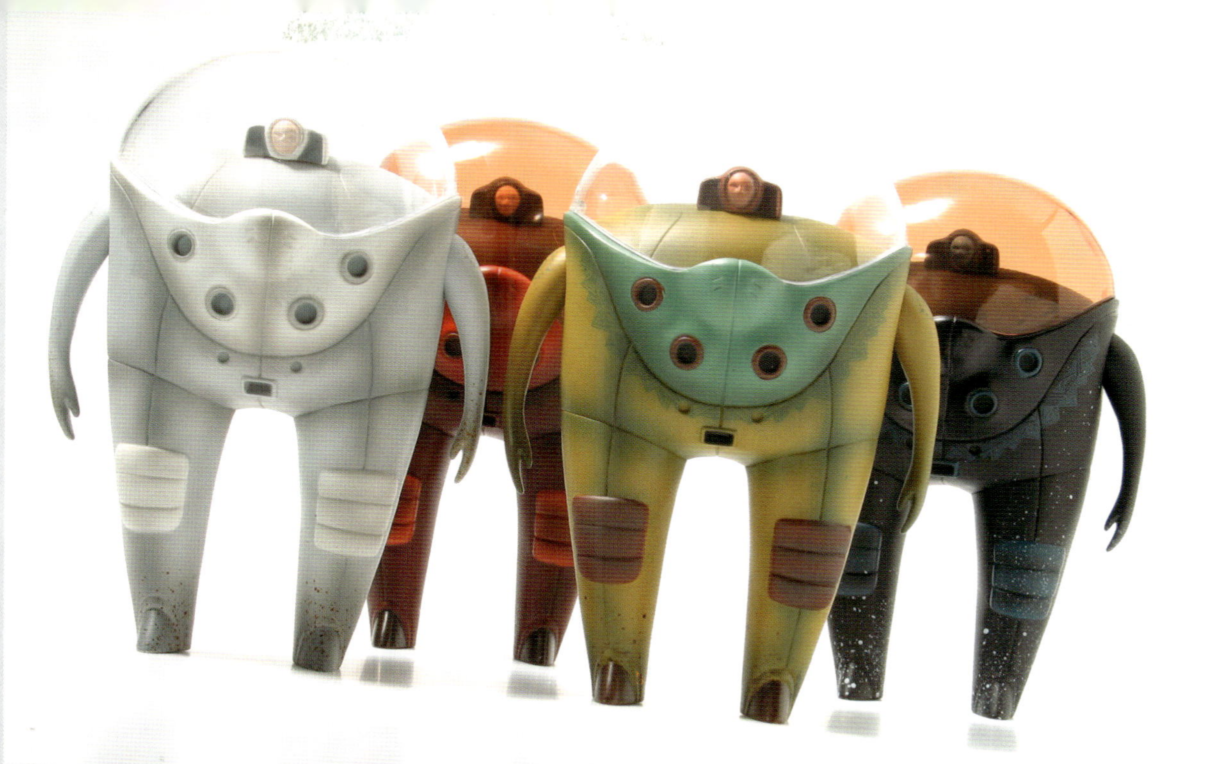

◄◄◄▼
Zliks are the creation of New York illustrator Andrew Bell, based on characters from his popular *Creatures in My Head* illustrations. Zliks are apparently a strange species of creature that live underground in burrows.

◄ ◄◄
The Copperhead-18 line was created by Kenny Wong, award-winning artist and partner of the renowned international toy designer group, Brothersfree. In 2006, the former advertising executive formed his own workshop, Kennyworks. Copperhead-18 was one of their first releases, a series of detailed 12" action figures with a complex backstory involving marine conservation.

▲ ◄▲
MARS-1 (a.k.a. Mario Martinez) is a San Francisco artist who works primarily on canvas. The theme of organics mixed with robotics is common throughout his work, which has been shown in many galleries across the US.

attention. It comprised of a number of paintings depicting creative people in everyday life reflected in water (the water symbolized the way creative people saw the world differently). At the same time, Lau was creating an album cover for the band Anidoze, and because of the amount of two-dimensional work he had been doing, he opted for 3D, using a customized action figure on the cover.

Lau liked the idea, and mixed it up with the theory behind his Watergarden paintings to create Gardenergala: 101 custom 12" tall action figures, each representing the same positive-living creative people he'd been portraying in Watergarden. Inspired by hip hop culture, these unique and arresting designs struck a chord with the "urban" and graffiti segment of the art world, and as a result, Gardenergala pieces became very sought after.

Their popularity caused a whole industry to spring up around these predominantly vinyl pieces—hence "urban vinyl." In the space of a few years urban vinyl radiated out from Hong Kong right across the globe, with many of the world's leading underground artists producing items. The notion of the toy as a blank canvas also took off, and toy companies began releasing standard sculpts with different artists' designs on them. Prices ranged from a few dollars into the thousands.

While the early pieces were predominantly rotocast vinyl, the movement has expanded to encompass other types of plastic, as well as plush pieces, and even some made of wood. With urban vinyl artists free to express their art any way they choose, it's no wonder this art movement has resulted in some great science fiction designs.

ILLUSTRATION CREDITS

Every effort has been made to credit the artists and/or publishers and copyright holders whose work has been reproduced in this book. We apologize for any omissions, which will be corrected in future editions, but hereby must disclaim any liability.

KEY

T—Top, B—Bottom, L—Left, R—Right, C—Center, BG—Background

6/7	David A. Hardy © David A. Hardy
8BG	Frank Hampson, *Dan Dare* © 2009 The Dan Dare Corp.
9	The Kobal Collection/MGM
10	Gerard Quinn, *New Worlds*
11	Roger Dean, *Chronoquest*, acrylic on board 30x20" © Roger Dean
12L	Vincent Di Fate © Vincent Di Fate
12R	The Kobal Collection
13	Oliver Frey, *Zzap!64* #30, © Oliver Frey

CHAPTER 1

14	Hans Wesso, *Astounding Stories*
15	Harold W. McCauley, *Amazing Stories*
16	Frederick Thomas Jane, *Hartmann the Anarchist*, out of copyright
17T	Warwick Goble, *War of the Worlds*, Alamy/out of copyright
17B	John Martin, *Satan Presiding at the Infernal Council*, Alamy/ out of copyright
18	J. J. Grandville, *Un Autre Monde*, Alamy/out of copyright
19T	J. J. Grandville, *Les Metarmorphoses du Jour*, Bibliotheque des Arts Decoratifs, Paris, France/Archives Charmet/The Bridgeman Art Library/ out of copyright
19B	J. J. Grandville, *The Steam Concert, Un Autre Monde*, Bibliotheque Nationale, Paris, France/Archives Charmet/The Bridgeman Art Library/ out of copyright
20L	Edouard Riou, *Voyage du Centre de la Terre*, Alamy/out of copyright
20TR	Émile-Antoine Bayard, Photos.com/ out of copyright
20CR	Henri de Montaut, Photos.com/ out of copyright
20BR	Henri de Montaut, Photos.com/ out of copyright
22L	Léon Benett, Mary Evans/ out of copyright
22R	Léon Benett, out of copyright
23	Alphonse Marie de Neuville, *Twenty Thousand Leagues Under the Sea*, Bibliotheque Nationale, Paris, France/Archives Charmet/ The Bridgeman Art Library/ out of copyright
25TL	Albert Robida, *Journal des Voyages*, Alamy/out of copyright
25TR	Albert Robida, *Un Quartier Embrouille*, Photos.com/out of copyright
25BL	Albert Robida, *La Vie Electrique*, Photos.com/out of copyright
25BR	Albert Robida, *La Guerre Infernal*, Alamy/out of copyright
26L	Artist unknown/Frank Tousey
26R	Artist unknown /Frank Tousey
27TL	Artist unknown/Frank Munsey
27BL	Artist unknown, out of copyright
27R	Howard V. Browne/Experimenter Publishing/Hugo Gernsback
28	Frank R. Paul/Experimenter Publishing/Hugo Gernsback
29T&C	Leo Morey/Experimenter Publishing/Hugo Gernsback
29B	Hans Wesso/ Experimenter Publishing/Hugo Gernsback
30	Frank R. Paul/Experimenter Publishing/Hugo Gernsback
31L	Frank R. Paul/Experimenter Publishing/Hugo Gernsback
31R	Frank R. Paul/Clayton Magazines
32L	Charles Schneeman/Clayton Magazines
32CL	Howard V. Browne/Clayton Magazines
32CR	Hans Wesso/Clayton Magazines
32R & 33	Howard V. Browne/Clayton Magazines
34L	Graves Gladney/Clayton Magazines
34TR & BR	William Timmins/Clayton Magazines
35	Hubert Rogers/Clayton Magazines
36BG	Virgil Finlay/*Space Stories*
37TL	Virgil Finlay/Leo Margulies/Great American Publications
37BL	Howard W. McCauley/Ziff-Davis
37TR	Earle K. Bergey/Thrilling Publications
37BR	Howard W. McCauley/Ziff-Davis
38L & C	Artist unknown/ Amalgamated Press
38CL & R	Serge Drigin/George Newnes
39TL	Brian Lewis/John Carnell
39TC	John Richards/Hamilton and Co.
39CR	Gerald Facey/John Spencer & Co.
39C	Norman Light/John Spencer & Co.
39BL	Artist unknown/Amalgamated Press
39BR	John Nicolson/Walter Gillings
39R	Ron Turner/John Spencer & Co.

CHAPTER 2

40	Frank Wu © Frank Wu
41	Vincent Di Fate © Vincent Di Fate
42	Hannes Bok/Shasta Publishers
43TL	Hannes Bok/Clark Publishing Company/Greenleaf Publishing
43BL	Mel Hunter/Mercury Press © Spilogale Inc.
43TR	George Salter/Mercury Press © Spilogale Inc.
43CB	Edd Cartier/Street & Smith
43BR	Chesley Bonestell/Mercury Press © Spilogale Inc.
44L	Frank Kelly Freas/Clayton Magazines © Dell Magazines
44R	Frank Kelly Freas/DAW
45TR	Frank Kelly Freas/Clayton Magazines © Dell Magazines
45BR	Frank Kelly Freas/Mercury Press © Spilogale Inc.
46L	Paul Lehr/Signet
46R	Charles Binger/Pennant Books
47TL	Mike Ludlow/Dell
47BL	Artist unknown/Avon
47R	Stanley Meltzoff/Gold Medal
48TL	Ed Emsh/Ace
48CL	Ed Emsh/Mercury Press © Spilogale Inc.
48BL	Jack Gaughan/Ace

48R	Ed Valigursky/Ziff-Davis
49L, C & R	Jack Gaughan/Mercury Press © Spilogale Inc.
50	Richard Powers/Bantam
51TL	Richard Powers/Dell
51BL	Richard Powers/Avon
51TR	Richard Powers/Ballantine
51BR	Richard Powers/Ballantine
52L, C & R	John Schoenherr © Dell Magazines
53T, BL, BC, BR	John Schoenherr © Dell Magazines
54R & BL	Roy Krenkel/Ace
54TL	Frank Frazetta/Ace
55L	George Barr/DAW
55C	Leo and Diane Dillon/Pyramid
55R	Jeffrey Jones/Ziff-Davis
56	James Cawthorn/Keith Roberts/ Roberts & Vinter
57TL, TC & TR	Artists unknown/Panther
57BL	John Richards/Corgi
57BC	Gordon Davies/Pan
57BR	Henry Fox/Badger
58TL to TR	Bruce Pennington/New English Library
58BL	Ray Feibush/New English Library
58BR	Eddie Jones/Transworld
59	David Pelham/Penguin
60	Chris Foss/Panther/Granada
61TL & TR	Chris Foss/Panther
61BL	Chris Foss/New English Library
61BR	Chris Foss/Panther
62R	Peter Elson/Sphere
62TL	Angus McKie/Pan
62TC	Tony Roberts/Orbit
62BL	Bob Layzell/Orbit
63	Colin Hay/Panther
64	Peter Jones/Orbit
65TL	Fred Gambino/Orbit
65BL	Chris Moore/Methuen
65TR	John Harris/Orbit
65BR	Lee Gibbons/Orbit
66L	Michael Whelan/Orbit
66TR	Michael Whelan/DAW
66BR	Michael Whelan/iBooks
67	Michael Whelan/iBooks
68	Les Edwards/Bantam
69L	Bob Eggleton © Spilogale Inc.
69TR	Bob Eggleton/Baen
69BR	Les Edwards (PS Publishing)
70TR, BL & BR	Jim Burns/Bantam
71TL	Jim Bruns/Quartet
71TR	Jim Burns/World Science Fiction Society
71C	Jim Burns/Macmillan
71BL	Jim Burns/Pan
72L	David Mattingly/Baen
72R	David Mattingly/Baen
73L to R	David Mattingly/Baen
74	John Berkey/Tor
75L, R & BG	John Berkey/Sovereign Media
76L	Gervasio Gallardo © Penthouse International, Ltd.
76R	Don Dixon © Penthouse International, Ltd.
77T	Bob Venosa © Penthouse International, Ltd.
77BL	Dieter Schwertberger © Penthouse International, Ltd.
77BR	H. R. Giger, *Necronom III* © 1976 H. R. Giger, 100x70cm, acrylic on paper on wood
78	Stephen Hickman/Baen
79TL	Stephen Hickman/Baen
79BL	Stephen Hickman/Baen
79R	Stephen Hickman/Baen
80-81	Vincent Di Fate © Vincent Di Fate, www.vincentdifate.com
82-83	Frank Wu © Frank Wu, www.frankwu.com
84L	Stephan Martinière © 2007 Stephan Martinière, www.martiniere.com
84TR	Dominic Harman/Solaris
84BR	Don Maitz © 1978 Don Maitz, www.paravia.com/DonMaitz
85	Donato Giancola © 2003 Donato Giancola, donatoart.com

CHAPTER 3

86	Mike Noble/Century 21 Productions © Granada Ventures
87	Frank Hampson © 2009 The Dan Dare Corporation. Reproduced by kind permission
89T	Alex Raymond © King Features Syndicate, Inc.
89B	Dick Calkins © Dille Family Trust
90T	George Evans/Al Williamson/Fawcett
90B	Joe Doolin/Fiction House
91TL	George Evans/Al Williamson/Fawcett
91CL	Basil Wolverton/Centaur
91BL	Ogden Whitney/B&I Publishing/ American Comics Group
91R	Artist Unknown/Charlton
92TL, BL & TR	Wally Wood/EC Comics
92 BR	Al Williamson/EC Comics
93L & R	Wally Wood/EC Comics
94	Keith Watson © 2009 The Dan Dare Corp.
95L & R	Frank Hampson © 2009 The Dan Dare Corp.
96-97	Frank Hampson © 2009 The Dan Dare Corp.
98	Brian Bolland/Titan Books © Express Newspapers
99	Sydney Jordan/Knight Features © Express Newspapers
100	Richard Powers/Gold Key/Western
101TL & TR	Jack Kirby © 2009 Marvel Comics
101BL & BR	Jack Kirby © 2009 Marvel Comics
102L	George Wilson/Gold Key/Western
102R	Russ Manning/Gold Key/Western
103T	Bob Fujitani/Gold Key/Western
103B	Al Williamson © King Features Syndicate
104	Ron Embleton/Century 21 Productions © Granada Ventures
105T	Ron Embleton/Century 21 Productions © Granada Ventures
105B	Mike Noble/Century 21 Productions © Granada Ventures

ILLUSTRATION CREDITS

106T & B Frank Bellamy/Century 21 Productions © Granada Ventures
107 Mike Noble/Century 21 Productions © Granada Ventures
108 Steve Dillon/Quality Comics. *2000 AD* and its characters © 2009 Rebellion A/S. All rights reserved. www.2000adonline.com
109T Mike McMahon © 2009 Rebellion A/S
109BL Brain Bolland/Eagle Comics © 2009 Rebellion A/S
109BR Glenn Fabry/Fleetway © 2009 Rebellion A/S
110TL Glenn Fabry/Fleetway © 2009 Rebellion A/S
110TR Artist/publisher unknown
110BL Various © 2009 Rebellion A/S
110BR Brian Bolland © 2009 Rebellion A/S
111TL Artist/publisher unknown
111BR Simon Fraser © 2009 Rebellion A/S
112 Steve Leialoha/Marvel Comics/ *Star Trek* © 2009 CBS Studios Inc.
113TL Alberto Giolitti/Gold Key/*Star Trek* © 2009 CBS Studios Inc.
113BL Gold Key/*Star Trek* © 2009 CBS Studios Inc.
113TR Al Williamson/Marvel Comics/Dark Horse © 2009 Lucasfilm Ltd.
113BR Howard Chaykin & Steve Leialoha/ Marvel Comics © 2009 Lucasfilm Ltd.
114 © Pierre Christin & Jean-Claude Mézières/Dargaud/iBooks
115 © Jean-Claude Forest/Grove Press
116T © Philippe Druillet/A&W
116B © Moebius/Heavy Metal/Kevin Eastman
117L © Moebius/*Métal Hurlant*
117R © Philippe Druillet/A&W
118 © Akira Toriyama/Viz Media/Shueisha
119L, TR & BL Osamu Tezuka © Tezuka Productions
119BR Herb Trimpe & Al Milgrom/ Marvel Comics/Mattel
120T & B The Kobal Collection/Shochiku/ Manga Entertainment
121T J. Scott Campbell/Top Cow
121B James Raiz & Rob Armstrong/ Dreamwave © 2009 Hasbro
122 © Katsuhiro Otomo/Kodansha
123T & B The Kobal Collection
124TL Neal Adams/Mike Friedrich
124TC & R Artist unknown/Western Publishing
124BL John Bolton/Pacific Comics
124BR Mick Austin/Eclipse Comics
125 Mark Chiarello/Topps Comics

CHAPTER 4

126 Wayne Barlowe, © Wayne Barlowe
127 H. R. Giger, © H. R. Giger
129L Chesley Bonestell/Clayton Magazines © Dell Magazines
129TR Chesley Bonestell/Galaxy Publishing Corporation
129CR & CB Chesley Bonestell/Mercury Press © Spilogale Inc.
130-131 © David A. Hardy, www.astroart.org
132-133 The Kobal Collection/*Star Trek* © 2009 CBS Studios Inc.
134-135 © Andrew Probert/*Star Trek* © 2009 CBS Studios Inc.
136-137B Alamy
136-137T The Kobal Collection
137B The Kobal Collection
138 H. R. Giger, *Dune II*, © 1975 H. R. Giger, 70x100cm, acrylic on paper on wood, www.HRGiger.com, www.HRGigerMuseum.com, www.LittleGiger.com, www.BaranyArtists.com
139L H. R. Giger, *Alien III*, Side View III, © 1978 H. R. Giger, 140x100cm, acrylic on paper
139TR H. R. Giger, *Sil, State II*, Side View, © 1994 H. R. Giger, 207x67.5cm, indian ink on paper
139BR H. R. Giger, *Sil, State II*, Transformation, © 1994 H. R. Giger, 56x81cm, acrylic on paper
140L Ralph McQuarrie moving postcard, courtesy of Lucasfilm Ltd., *Star Wars: Episode IV – A New Hope* ™ & © 1977 and 1997 Lucasfilm Ltd. All rights reserved. Used under authorization. Unauthorized duplication is a violation of applicable law.
140R Ralph McQuarrie AT-AT concept art, courtesy of Lucasfilm Ltd., *Star Wars: Episode V – The Empire Strikes Back* ™ & © 1980 and 1997 Lucasfilm Ltd. All rights reserved. Used under authorization. Unauthorized duplication is a violation of applicable law.
141T Ralph McQuarrie Darth Vader concept art, courtesy of Lucasfilm Ltd., *Star Wars: Episode IV – A New Hope* ™ & © 1977 and 1997 Lucasfilm Ltd. All rights reserved. Used under authorization. Unauthorized duplication is a violation of applicable law.
141BG Joe Johnston Death Star Trench concept art, courtesy of Lucasfilm Ltd., *Star Wars: Episode IV – A New Hope* ™ & © 1977 and 1997 Lucasfilm Ltd. All rights reserved. Used under authorization. Unauthorized duplication is a violation of applicable law.
142 Ryan Church Jedi Fighter concept art, courtesy of Lucasfilm Ltd., *Star Wars: Episode III – Revenge of the Sith* ™ & © 2005 Lucasfilm Ltd. All rights reserved. Used under authorization. Unauthorized duplication is a violation of applicable law.
143 Concept art for Gunga City, courtesy of Lucasfilm Ltd., *Star Wars: Episode I – The Phantom Menace* ™ & © 1999 Lucasfilm Ltd. All rights reserved. Used under authorization. Unauthorized duplication is a violation of applicable law.
145 Wayne Barlowe © 2009 Wayne Barlowe, godsdemon.com, waynebarlowe.com
146T The Kobal Collection
146B The Kobal Collection
147 The Kobal Collection

CHAPTER 5

148 The Kobal Collection
149 Charles White III & Drew Struzan 1978 style D circus poster for *Star Wars: Episode IV – A New Hope*, courtesy of Lucasfilm Ltd., *Star Wars: Episode IV –*

A New Hope ™ & © 1977 and 1997 Lucasfilm Ltd. All rights reserved. Used under authorization. Unauthorized duplication is a violation of applicable law.

150T & B The Kobal Collection

151T The Kobal Collection

151B Bob Peak/The Kobal Collection

152L & R Drew Struzan/The Kobal Collection

153 Charles White III & Drew Struzan 1978 style D circus poster for *Star Wars: Episode IV – A New Hope*, courtesy of Lucasfilm Ltd., *Star Wars:Episode IV – A New Hope* ™ & © 1977 and 1997 Lucasfilm Ltd. All rights reserved. Used under authorization. Unauthorized duplication is a violation of applicable law.

154 The Kobal Collection

155 The Kobal Collection

156T & B The Kobal Collection

157 The Kobal Collection

158 The Kobal Collection

159T & B The Kobal Collection

CHAPTER 6

160 Oliver Frey © Oliver Frey

161 Don Ivan Punchatz/*DOOM*™ cover art © 1993 Id Software, Inc. All Rights Reserved. Used by permission.

162 T © Oliver Frey/Newsfield

162B Oliver Frey © Oliver Frey

163L Peter Brooker/Rex Features

163R Oliver Frey © Oliver Frey

164TL *Mass Effect* cover art © 2003-2008 EA International (Studio and Publishing) Ltd. Microsoft, the Microsoft Game Studios logo, Xbox 360, and the Xbox 360 logos are either registered trademarks or trademarks of Microsoft Corp.

164R Don Ivan Punchatz/*DOOM*™ cover art © 1993 Id Software, Inc. All Rights Reserved. Used by permission.

165 Roger Dean/Psygnosis, © Roger Dean

166L *Psyvariar 2* screenshot © 2003 Skonec Entertainment

166R *Shadow of the Colossus* screenshot © 2005 Sony Computer Entertainment Inc.

167T Roger Dean, *The Shadow of the Beast* pencil sketches 24x16" © Roger Dean, www.rogerdean.com

167B Roger Dean, *The Shadow of the Beast II* acrylic on board 30x20" © Roger Dean, www.rogerdean.com

168 *Gears of War 2* promotional art © 2008 Epic Games, Inc.

169TL & CL *BioShock* screenshots © 2002-2008 Take-Two Interactive Software and its subsidiaries.

169B *Gears of War* screenshot © 2008 Epic Games, Inc.

169TR *Half-Life 2* promotional art © The Valve Corporation

170TL & BL The Kobal Collection

170BR *Final Fantasy XIII* screenshot © 2009 Square Enix

171T The Kobal Collection

171B *Final Fantasy XIII* screenshot © 2009 Square Enix

172 Getty Images, *Halo* © Microsoft Corp.

173T Getty Images, *Halo* © Microsoft Corp.

173B *Halo 3* screenshot © 2007 Microsoft Corp.

174T H. R. Giger, *Walpurgis*, © 1969 H. R. Giger, 31x62cm, indian ink on paper

174B H. R. Giger, *ELP II (Brain Salad Surgery)*, © 1973 H.R. Giger, 34x34 cm, acrylic on paper

175T & B Roger Dean, *Space Hymns*, © Roger Dean, www.rogerdean.com

176T Meco/RCA

176B David Pugh, © David Pugh/Warner Music UK Ltd.

177 Bob Gleason © Motown Record Corporation

178T Hasbro/*Star Wars* ™ & © 2009 Lucasfilm Ltd. All rights reserved.

178B & 179BL Hot Toys/*Star Wars* ™ & © 2009 Lucasfilm Ltd. All rights reserved.

179TL Sideshow Collectibles/*Star Wars* ™ & © 2009 Lucasfilm Ltd. All rights reserved.

179R Kotobukiya/*Star Wars* ™ & © 2009 Lucasfilm Ltd. All rights reserved.

180T to B © 2003 Takara Co. Ltd.

181TL & CL © Gainax Company, Limited

181BL Kaiyodo, © Headgear

181R © 2009 Hasbro. All rights reserved.

182L © Andrew Bell/Wheaty Wheat Studios/Sideshow Collectibles, www.creaturesinmyhead.com, www.wheatywheat.com

182TR & 183TL & R © 2009 MARS-1, www.mars-1.com

182BR & 183CL & BL Kennyswork/Sideshow Collectibles, © 2009 Kennyswork. All rights reserved, ww.kennyswork.com

191 Frank Wu © Frank Wu

192 Vincent Di Fate © Vincent Di Fate

INDEX

INDEX

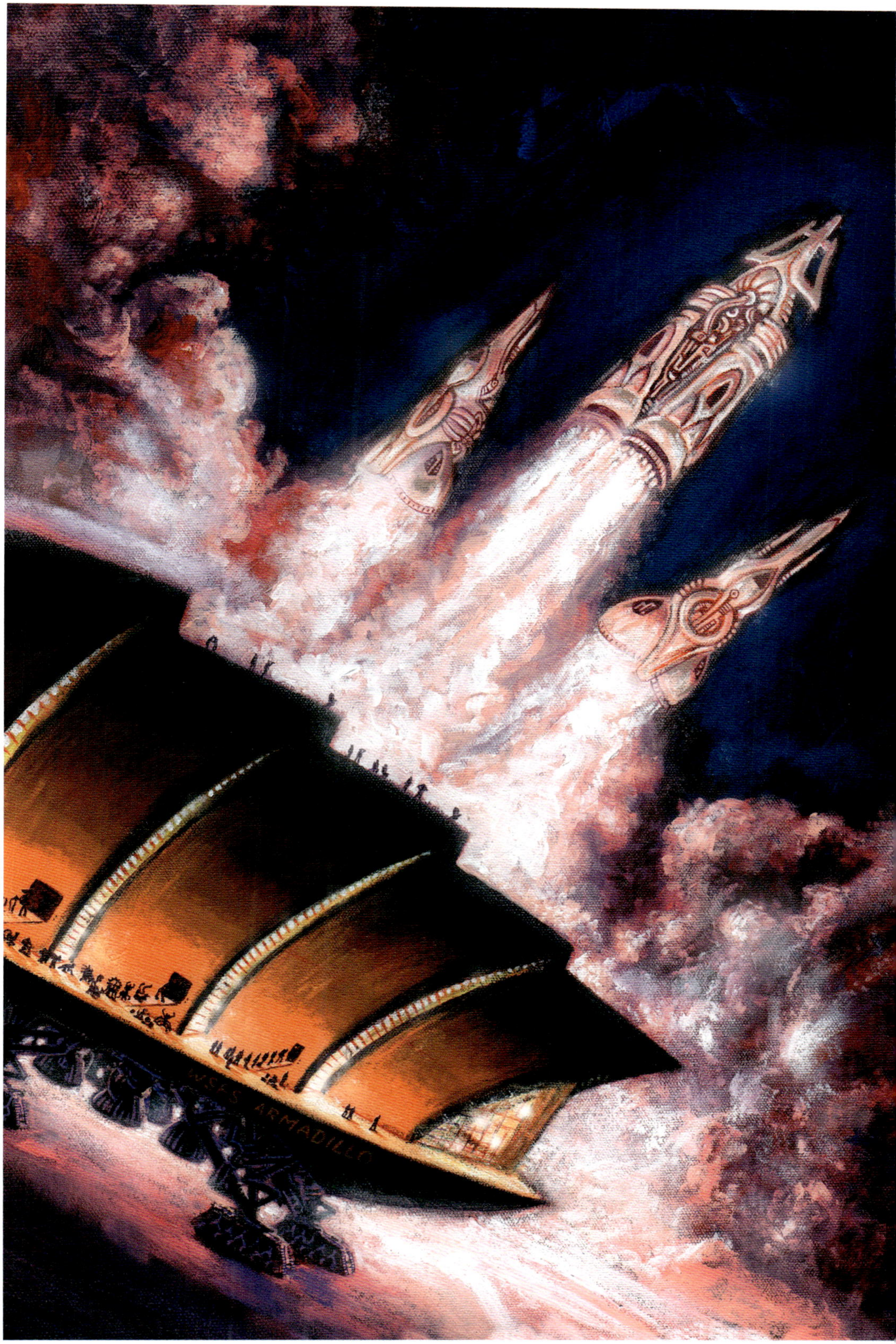

ACKNOWLEDGMENTS

Thanks first to each of the writers for all their efforts: to Steve Holland for the Introduction, Chapters 1 and 2, and for his tireless help and assistance elsewhere in the book; to Alex Summersby for Chapter 3; to Steve White for Chapter 4 and the animated movies in Chapter 5; to Toby Weidmann for the rest of Chapter 5 and video games in Chapter 6; to Adrian Faulkner for action figures in Chapter 6; and to Tim Murray for record sleeves in Chapter 6.

A big thanks to Andy Sawyer and all at the Science Fiction Foundation, Liverpool University, who provided invaluable assistance sourcing pulp and paperback cover imagery.

Huge thanks to Tamsan Barratt for her diligent picture research and patience.

Thanks to all of the artists, creators, and companies who provided artwork and were so generous with their time. Special thanks in particular (but in no particular order) to: Vincent Di Fate; H. R. Giger, Les Barany, and Matthias Belz; David Hardy; Andrew Probert; Oliver Frey and Roger Kean; Wayne Barlowe; Roger Dean; Frank Wu; Don Maitz; Donato Giancola; Drew Struzan; Stephan Martinière; Andrew Bell; Mario Martinez; and Kenny Wong.

Further thanks to Colin Frewin and Lisa Frewin at The Dan Dare Corporation Limited; Fiona Tucker at Express Newspapers; Sarah Garcia at Lucasfilm; and Matt Smith at 2000 AD/Rebellion.

And finally, many thanks to Brian Aldiss for his foreword, and for his inspiration.

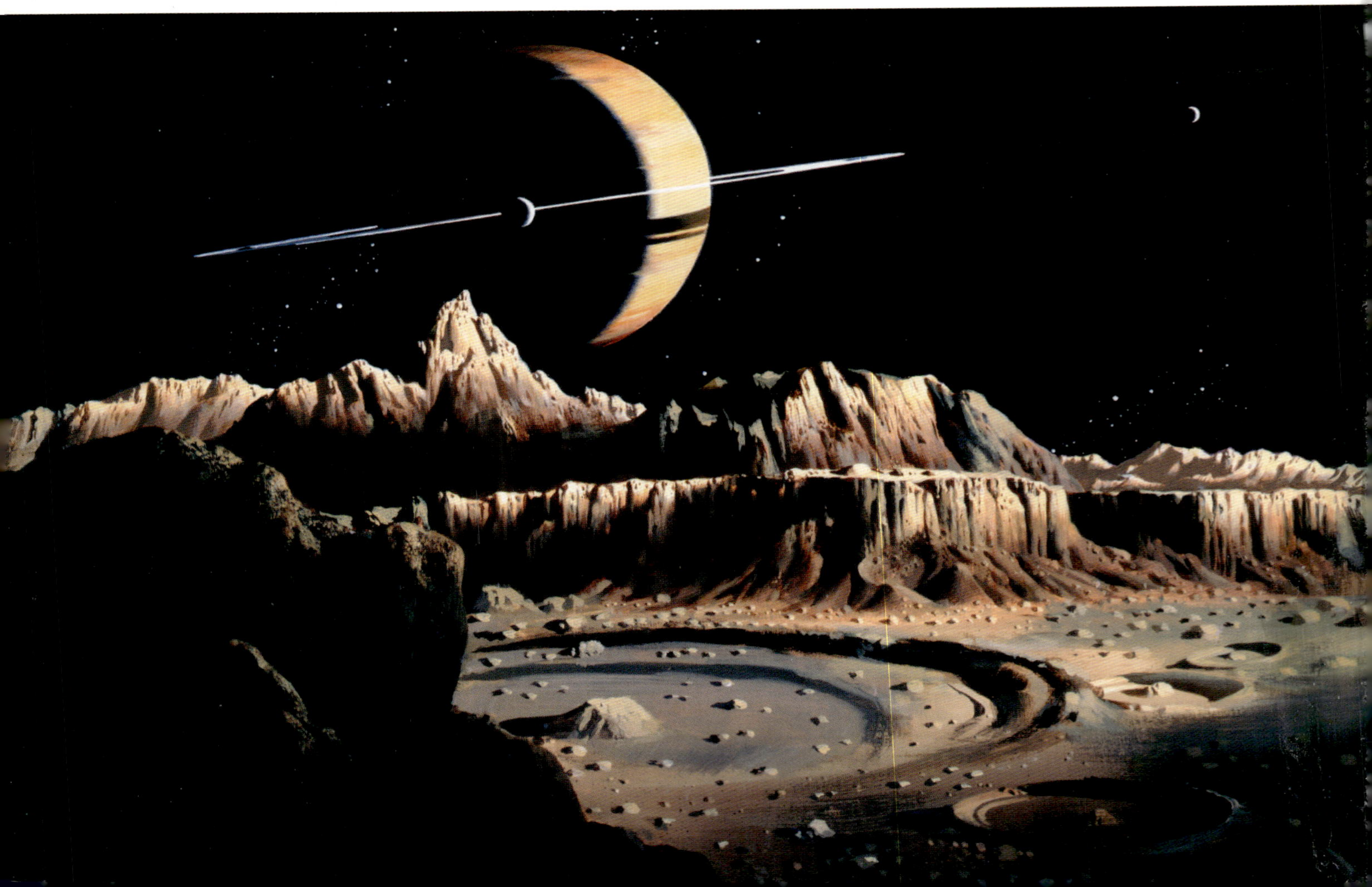